God's Gifts for the Christian Life – Part 1:
The Gift of Knowledge

Volume 1: The Gift of Knowing:
   A Biblical Perspective on Knowing and Truth

Volume 2a: The Gift of Reading – Part 1:
   Reading the Bible in Submission to God

Volume 2b: The Gift of Reading – Part 2:
   A Biblical Perspective on Hermeneutics

Volume 3 – The Gift of Seeing:
   A Biblical Perspective on Ontology

J. Alexander Rutherford

Unless otherwise indicated, all Scripture quotations are from The Holy Bible, English Standard Version® (ESV®), copyright © 2001 by Crossway Bibles, a publishing ministry of Good News Publishers. Used by permission. All rights reserved.

Unless otherwise indicated, all Scripture quotations from the book of Habakkuk or those marked Teleioteti are my own translations. Translations from Habakkuk are taken from the translation published in my commentary on Habakkuk (Vancouver, Teleioteti 2020).

ISBN-13: 978-1-989560-21-1

Cover Design: Stephen Josh Arriola, James Rutherford, and Matt Goodman

Copyright © 2021 J. Alexander Rutherford
Teleioteti publishing, Airdrie AB
All rights reserved.

The Gift of Knowing: © 1st Printing, 2019; 2nd Printing, 2020
ISBN-13: Paperback 978-1-999017200; eBook 978-1-9990172-3-1.

The Gift of Knowing – 2nd Edition: © 2021
ISBN: Paperback 978-1-989560-23-5; eBook 978-1-989560-24-2

The Gift of Reading – Part 1: © 1st Printing, 2019; 2nd Printing, 2021
ISBN-13: Paperback 978-1-9990172-7-9; eBook 978-1-9990172-9-3.

The Gift of Reading – Part 2: © 1st Printing, 2019; 2nd Printing, 2021
ISBN-13: Paperback 978-1-9990172-8-6; eBook 978-1-9990172-5-5.

The Gift of Seeing: © 2021
ISBN-13: Paperback 978-1-989560-19-8; eBook 978-1-989560-20-4.

To contact Teleioteti publishing for information or to provide feedback, please visit us at **https://teleioteti.ca** or email us at **info@teleioteti.ca**.

DEDICATION

This book is dedicated to my Lord and Saviour Jesus Christ; it is my prayer that this little book would magnify your holy name.

It is also dedicated to my children. To Asher, I wish I could see you grow in your knowledge of God your Father and Jesus your saviour, but I am thankful that you are resting with them now. Of God's many gifts, I am thankful for the hope of the resurrection, when I am confident I will see your face again. To Aliyah, I pray continually that you would commit yourselves to him and find all your hope and joy in the one who gave his life for you.

> The secret things belong to the LORD our God, but the things that are revealed belong to us and to our children forever, that we may do all the words of this law. – Deut 29:29

CONTENTS

Dedication iii

Contents v

Analytical Outline ix

Acknowledgments xxi

Introduction 1

VOLUME 1: THE GIFT OF KNOWING 5

Introduction 7

Chapter 1 – Diagnosing the Disease 11

—Part 1— Our Epistemological Situation 25

Chapter 2 – Worldview Thinking: Appropriate Subjectivity 27

Chapter 3 – The Truth is Out There: Appropriate Objectivity 35

—Part 2— The Standard of Epistemology 47

Chapter 4 – Word from Beyond: Appropriate Authority 49

Chapter 5 – The Covenantal Revelation of Creation 53

Chapter 6 – The Covenantal Revelation of God's Speech 63

Chapter 7 – The Ethics of Knowing 77

—Part 3— The Practice of Epistemology 85

    Chapter 8 – Created in the Image of God: Thinking as a Creature 87

    Chapter 9 – Created with Senses: Empirical Knowledge 93

    Chapter 10 – Created with a Mind: Rational Thought and Logic 99

    Conclusion 113

VOLUME 2A: THE GIFT OF READING – PART 1 117

    Introduction 119

—Part 1— We Need Eyes to See 125

    Chapter 1 – The Bible is the Document of God's Covenant 127

    Chapter 2 – The Bible's Worldview - Theology 145

    Chapter 3 – The Bible's Worldview - Story 163

    Chapter 4 – The People(s) of the Bible 179

—Part 2— We Need Ears to Hear 193

    Chapter 5 – Knowing When We Have Read Well 195

    Chapter 6 – Knowing How to Read Well 215

    Chapter 7 – Knowing the Styles of Biblical Writing 237

    Chapter 8 – Knowing Bible Translations 275

    Chapter 9 – Knowing Biblical Languages 289

    Chapter 10 – Knowing Tools for Reading Better 307

    Chapter 11 – Evaluating Exegesis and Application 321

—Part 3— We Need Hearts to Understand 327

    Chapter 12 – Beginning with Faith in God 329

    Chapter 13 – We Submit Ourselves before Him 335

CONTENTS

Dedication iii

Contents v

Analytical Outline ix

Acknowledgments xxi

Introduction 1

VOLUME 1: THE GIFT OF KNOWING 5

Introduction 7

Chapter 1 – Diagnosing the Disease 11

—Part 1— Our Epistemological Situation 25

Chapter 2 – Worldview Thinking: Appropriate Subjectivity 27

Chapter 3 – The Truth is Out There: Appropriate Objectivity 35

—Part 2— The Standard of Epistemology 47

Chapter 4 – Word from Beyond: Appropriate Authority 49

Chapter 5 – The Covenantal Revelation of Creation 53

Chapter 6 – The Covenantal Revelation of God's Speech 63

Chapter 7 – The Ethics of Knowing 77

—Part 3— The Practice of Epistemology..85

    Chapter 8 – Created in the Image of God: Thinking as a Creature 87

    Chapter 9 – Created with Senses: Empirical Knowledge......................93

    Chapter 10 – Created with a Mind: Rational Thought and Logic 99

    Conclusion...113

VOLUME 2A: THE GIFT OF READING – PART 1..............................117

    Introduction...119

—Part 1— We Need Eyes to See 125

    Chapter 1 – The Bible is the Document of God's Covenant.............127

    Chapter 2 – The Bible's Worldview - Theology....................................145

    Chapter 3 – The Bible's Worldview - Story 163

    Chapter 4 – The People(s) of the Bible 179

—Part 2— We Need Ears to Hear..193

    Chapter 5 – Knowing When We Have Read Well...............................195

    Chapter 6 – Knowing How to Read Well 215

    Chapter 7 – Knowing the Styles of Biblical Writing............................237

    Chapter 8 – Knowing Bible Translations 275

    Chapter 9 – Knowing Biblical Languages 289

    Chapter 10 – Knowing Tools for Reading Better................................307

    Chapter 11 – Evaluating Exegesis and Application 321

—Part 3— We Need Hearts to Understand..327

    Chapter 12 – Beginning with Faith in God..329

    Chapter 13 – We Submit Ourselves before Him 335

Chapter 14 – To Learn with Humility..339
Conclusion..343

VOLUME 2B: THE GIFT OF READING – PART 2......................347

Introduction...349
Chapter 1 – Approaches to Hermeneutics..355

—Part 1— The Role of the Bible..397

Chapter 2 – The Bible as Self-Interpreting...399
Chapter 3 – The Bible and Meaning...417
Chapter 4 – The Bible and Genre..429

—Part 2— The Role of the Reader...445

Chapter 5 – The Reader and Meaning..447
Chapter 6 – The Audience of Scripture..451

—Part 3— The Role of the Author...457

Chapter 7 – The Author and Meaning..459
Chapter 8 – The Bible in History..465
Conclusion..473

—Appendices— Theory in Application: Exegetical Essays........477

Appendix 1 – The Sovereignty of God Over the Repentance of Man: Re-Reading Deuteronomy 30:1-14...479
Appendix 2 – Will Make them like the Calf: An Examination of Jeremiah 34:17-22 in Its Literary Context...491
Appendix 3 – The Lament of the Afflicted: A Translation of Job 30 503
Appendix 4 – Do Not Say In Your Heart: An Exposition of Romans

    10:1-8 in the Context of 10:1-13 515

    Appendix 5 – 2 Thessalonians and Hell: Separation from or Wrath Coming Forth From God? 529

    Appendix 6 – Convinced of Better Things: An Exposition of Hebrews 6:1-12 535

VOLUME 3: THE GIFT OF SEEING 551

    Introduction 553

—Part 1— The Problem of Change and Identity 569

    Chapter 1 – All Is Flux 571

    Chapter 2 – History: Embracing Change 583

    Chapter 3 – Consistency: Mind and Identity 595

—Part 2— The One and the Many 601

    Chapter 4 – The Rational World 603

    Chapter 5 – The Many: The Primacy of the Particular 619

    Chapter 6 – The One: Making Sense of Abstraction 629

—Part 3— The Problem of the External World 651

    Chapter 7 – The End of Empiricism 653

    Chapter 8 – Interpretation: Bring the World into Being 661

    Chapter 9 – Truth: The First Interpreter 667

    Conclusion 683

    Works Cited 687

    Glossary 707

    About Teleioteti 719

ANALYTICAL OUTLINE

VOLUME 1: THE GIFT OF KNOWING

I. INTRODUCTION

    1. CHAPTER 1 – DIAGNOSING THE DISEASE
        A. Pre-Modernity – Autonomy in Pursuit of Universal Truth.
        B. Modernity – Autonomy in Search of Objectivity
        C. Postmodernity – Autonomy Arriving at Radical Relativity

II. PART 1: OUR EPISTEMOLOGICAL SITUATION

    2. CHAPTER 2 – WORLDVIEW THINKING: APPROPRIATE SUBJECTIVITY
        - *Excursus: Another Perspective on Subjectivity*

    3. CHAPTER 3 – THE TRUTH IS OUT THERE: APPROPRIATE OBJECTIVITY
        A. Showing a Worldview to Be True
        B. Showing a Worldview to be Self-Destructing
        C. Appealing to the Truth Suppressed in Unrighteousness
        - *Excursus: Trancendental Arguments*

III. PART 2: THE STANDARD OF EPISTEMOLOGY

    4. CHAPTER 4 – A WORD FROM BEYOND: APPROPRIATE AUTHORITY

5. CHAPTER 5 – THE COVENANTAL REVELATION OF CREATION
   A. Creation Revelation in the Testimony of the Creation
   B. Creation Revelation in the Morality of the Created Order
   C. Creation Revelation in the Human Faculties
   - *Excursus: On the Contribution of Objects*

6. CHAPTER 6 – THE COVENANTAL REVELATION OF GOD'S SPEECH
   A. The Authority and Inerrancy of Scripture
   B. The Sufficiency of Scripture
   C. The Clarity of Scripture

7. CHAPTER 7 – THE ETHICS OF KNOWING
   - *Excursus: On Reading or the Possibility Thereof*

IV. PART 3: THE PRACTICE OF EPISTEMOLOGY

8. CHAPTER 8 – CREATED IN THE IMAGE OF GOD: THINKING AS A CREATURE
   A. God is the Reference Point for Meaning
   B. We Must Pursue Knowledge in Humility

9. CHAPTER 9 – CREATED WITH SENSES: EMPIRICAL KNOWLEDGE
   A. The Biblical Affirmation of the Senses
   B. The Problem with the Senses
   C. Conclusion

10. CHAPTER 10 – CREATED WITH A MIND: RATIONAL THOUGHT AND LOGIC
    A. The Presupposition of Thought
    B. The Necessary Condition of Thought
    C. The Content of Thought
       a. Concrete Thought
       b. Abstract Thought
    D. Conclusion

V. CONCLUSION

VOLUME 2A: THE GIFT OF READING – PART 1

I. INTRODUCTION

II. PART 1: WE NEED EYES TO SEE

1. **CHAPTER 1: THE BIBLE IS THE DOCUMENT OF GOD'S COVENANT**
   A. The Bible is a Covenant Document
   B. The Nature of the Bible as a Covenant Document
      a. The Nature of the Bible
         i. *Inerrancy*
         ii. *Authority*
         iii. *Sufficiency*
         iv. *Clarity*
      b. The Structure of the Bible
   C. The Bible Guides Us in Fulfiling God's Purpose

2. **CHAPTER 2: THE BIBLE'S WORLDVIEW - THEOLOGY**
   A. Yahweh: The God who Is
      a. Yahweh is Holy
      b. The Authority, Control, and Presence of Yahweh
   B. Man: Rebellious Kings
   C. Kingdom: The Rule of God
      a. God's Heavenly Reign
      b. God's Earthly Reign
         - *Excursus: The Gospel and the Kingdom*
      c. God's Eschatological Reign

3. **CHAPTER 3: THE BIBLE'S WORLDVIEW – STORY**
   A. The Prologue: Creation and Fall
      a. Creation
      b. Fall
   B. Redemption Initiated – The Old Covenant(s)
      a. God's Covenant with Noah
      b. God's Covenant with Abraham
      c. God's Covenant with Israel
      d. God's Covenant with David
   C. Redemption Accomplished – The New Covenant
   D. Redemption Consummated – the New Creation

4. **CHAPTER 4: THE PEOPLE(S) OF THE BIBLE**
   A. The Old Covenant People of God
      a. The Establishment of Israel

- b. The Commission of Israel
- c. The Nature of Israel
- B. The New Covenant People of God
  - a. The Establishment of the Church
  - b. The Commission of the Church
    - i. Internal *Versus* External *Holiness*
    - ii. Church *Versus* National *Polity*
    - iii. Exilic *Versus* Secure *Existence*
  - c. The Nature of the Church

III. PART 2: WE NEED EARS TO HEAR

1. CHAPTER 5: KNOWING WHEN WE HAVE READ WELL
- A. Identifying the Right Responses to Scripture
  - a. Validity
  - b. Appropriateness
    - *Excursus: The Proverbs and Appropriate Application*
  - c. Fittingness
    - *Excursus: Fittingness and Typology*
  - d. Examples

2. CHAPTER 6: KNOWING HOW TO READ WELL
- A. (1) Pray
- B. (2) Identify the Passage for Study
- C. (3) Identify the Contexts
- D. (4) Identify the Translational Difficulties and Establish the Text
  - a. Translation Differences
  - b. Textual Differences
- E. (5) Observe the Text
  - a. Agassiz and the Fish
- F. (6) Identify the Passage's Relation to the Surrounding Contexts
- G. (7) Apply the Passage
- H. (8) Check Your Understanding
- I. Conclusion

3. CHAPTER 7: KNOWING THE STYLES OF BIBLICAL WRITING
- A. Narrative

a. How Narratives Communicate: Plot and Scene Arrangement
   b. How Narratives Communicate: Description
   c. Study Strategy: Storyboarding
   B. Poetry
   a. How Poetry Communicates: Terseness and Imagery
   b. How Poetry Communicates: Lines and Parallelism
   c. Study Strategy: Mapping Parallelism
   C. Didactic Prose
   a. How Prose Communicates: Grammar and Logic
   b. How Prose Communicates: Indicative and Imperative
   c. Study Strategy: Arcing and Sentence Diagramming
      - Excursus: Review of English Grammar
   D. Prophecy
   a. How Prophecy Communicates: Symbolic Imagery
      - Excursus: Apocalyptic and Prophecy
   b. Study Strategy: Intertextuality

4. CHAPTER 8: KNOWING BIBLE TRANSLATIONS
   A. Bible Translation
   B. Translation Theories
   C. Bible Translations
   a. ESV
   b. KJV
   c. NASB
   d. NET
   e. NIV
   f. NLT
   g. NRSV
   h. The Message

5. CHAPTER 9: KNOWING BIBLICAL LANGUAGES
   A. The Importance of the Biblical Languages
   B. The Appropriate Use of the Biblical Languages
   a. Ground Rules for Language Study
   b. Word Studies
   c. Grammar Studies

6. CHAPTER 10: KNOWING TOOLS FOR READING BETTER

  A. Tools for Understanding Biblical Books and Passages
    a. Introductions to the Bible
      i. *General*
      ii. *Historical*
      iii. *Theological*
    b. Bible Dictionaries
    c. Commentaries
      i. *Popular*
      ii. *Semi-Technical*
      iii. *Technical*
  B. Tools for Grasping the Unity of Scripture
  C. Tools for Original Language Study
    a. Lexicons
    b. Bible Software
7. CHAPTER 11: EVALUATING EXEGESIS AND APPLICATION
  A. Is it Valid, Appropriate, and Fitting?
  B. Can it Be Argued from the Text?
  C. Does it Illegitimately Appeal to Extra-Biblical Data?

IV. PART 3: WE NEED HEARTS TO UNDERSTAND

1. CHAPTER 12: BEGINNING WITH FAITH IN GOD

2. CHAPTER 13: WE SUBMIT OURSELVES BEFORE HIM

3. CHAPTER 14: TO LEARN WITH HUMILITY

V. CONCLUSION

VOLUME 2B: THE GIFT OF READING – PART 2

I. INTRODUCTION

1. CHAPTER 1: APPROACHES TO HERMENEUTICS
  A. Hermeneutics in Pre-Modernity
    a. Irenaeus and the Rule of Truth
    b. Allegorical Interpretation
    c. The Reformation
  B. Hermeneutics in Modernity
    a. Critical Hermeneutics
      i. *Source Criticism*

   b. Form & Tradition Criticism
   c. Grammatical–Historical Exegesis (GHE)
    i. *The Goal of Grammatical-Historical Exegesis*
    ii. *The Method of Grammatical-Historical Exegesis*
    - *Excursus: Mirror Reading*
  C. Hermeneutics in Postmodernity
   a. Structural Exegesis
   b. Feminist Interpretation
   c. Theological Interpretation
    - Excursus: The Narrative turn
  D. Conclusion

II. PART 1: THE ROLE OF THE BIBLE

 1. CHAPTER 2: THE BIBLE AS SELF-INTERPRETING
  A. Analogy of Faith
  B. Closure
  C. Linguistic Sufficiency
  D. External Sufficiency
  E. Conclusion

 2. CHAPTER 3: THE BIBLE AND MEANING
  A. The Meaning of Meaning
  B. The Text and Meaning
  C. Conclusion

 3. CHAPTER 4: THE BIBLE AND GENRE
  A. Genre and Its Problems
   a. The Issue of Genre and Audience
   b. The Issue of Composition
   c. The Issue of Identification
  B. Classification and Interpretation
  C. The Generic Categories
   a. Language Pattern
   b. Manner of Communication
   c. Form
   d. Function
  D. The Function of Generic Categories

II. PART 2: THE ROLE OF THE READER

1. CHAPTER 5: THE READER AND MEANING
2. CHAPTER 6: THE AUDIENCE OF SCRIPTURE
   A. The Audience of the Bible
   B. Our Distance from the Text

III. PART 3: THE ROLE OF THE AUTHOR
   1. CHAPTER 7: THE AUTHOR AND MEANING
      A. The Author as Originator
      B. The Authorship of Scripture
   2. CHAPTER 8: THE BIBLE IN HISTORY
      A. The Uses of Extra-Biblical Evidence
      B. The Challenge of Using Extra-Biblical Data
      C. Objections

IV. CONCLUSION

V. APPENDICES: THEORY IN APPLICATION: EXEGETICAL ESSAYS
   1. APPENDIX 1: THE SOVEREIGNTY OF GOD OVER THE REPENTANCE OF MAN: RE-READING DEUTERONOMY 30:1-14
      A. Identifying the Apodosis of The Condition in Verse 1
      B. Translating the Conjunction Ki
      C. The Time of Verses 11-14
   2. APPENDIX 2: I WILL MAKE THEM LIKE THE CALF: AN EXAMINATION OF JEREMIAH 34:17-22 IN ITS LITERARY CONTEXT
      A. Jeremiah 34:1-16
      B. Jeremiah 34:17-22
      C. Vv. 17-22 in Context
      D. Conclusion
   3. APPENDIX 3: THE LAMENT OF THE AFFLICTED: A TRANSLATION OF JOB 30
      A. JOB 30
         a. Strophe 1 – I Am Mocked by Wretches
         b. Strophe 2 – I Am a Byword to the Unrestrained
         c. Strophe 3 – I Am Afflicted by God

4. APPENDIX 4: DO NOT SAY IN YOUR HEART: AN EXPOSITION OF ROMANS 10:1-8 IN THE CONTEXT OF 10:1-13
   A. Exegesis
      a. Israel Needs Salvation, Having Rejected God's Righteousness (10:1-4)
      b. God's New Covenant Righteousness Ended the Law (10:5-8)
         - *Excursus: Deuteronomy 31:11-14 in Context*
   B. Conclusion
5. APPENDIX 5: 2 THESSALONIANS AND HELL: SEPARATION FROM OR WRATH COMING FORTH FROM GOD?
6. APPENDIX 6: CONVINCED OF BETTER THINGS: AN EXPOSITION OF HEBREWS 6:1-12
   A. Exegesis
      a. Hebrews 6:1-3
      b. Hebrews 6:4-8
      c. Hebrews 6:9-12
   B. Conclusion

VOLUME 3: THE GIFT OF SEEING

I. INTRODUCTION

   A. What Is Ontology?
   B. Why Bother with Ontology?
   C. How Will We Study Ontology?
   D. The Foundations of Ontology
      a. The Preconditions of Theology
         i. *The Surrender of Autonomy*
         ii. *The Humility of Faith*
      b. The Possibility of Ontology
         i. *The Non-Christian Dilemma*
         ii. *Biblical Ontology*

II. PART 1 - THE PROBLEM OF CHANGE AND IDENTITY

   1. CHAPTER 1 – ALL IS FLUX

A. Pre-Modernity – The World of Reason
      a. The Pre-Socratics
         i. *Heraclitus*
         ii. *Parmenides*
   B. Summary of the Problem
2. CHAPTER 2 – HISTORY: EMBRACING CHANGE
   A. History: The Medium of Change
   B. Redemption: The Mode of Change
   C. Glory: The End of Change
   D. Embracing Change
      - *Excursus: Impassibility and the First Cause*
3. CHAPTER 3 – CONSISTENCY: MIND AND IDENTITY
      - *Excursus: Mind*
   A. Subjective Stability
   B. Objective Stability

III. PART 2 - THE ONE AND THE MANY

1. CHAPTER 4 – THE RATIONAL WORLD
   A. Plato and Aristotle
      a. Plato
      b. Aristotle
   B. Patristic and Medieval Philosophy
      a. Maximus the Confessor
      b. William of Ockham
   C. The One and the Many

2. CHAPTER 5 – THE MANY: THE PRIMACY OF THE PARTICULAR
   A. Particular Individuals
   B. Particular Actions
   C. Particular Events

3. CHAPTER 6 – THE ONE: MAKING SENSE OF ABSTRACTION
   A. The Unity of God's Law
   B. The Unity of Created Likeness
   C. The Unity of Conceptual Relations

       a. Abstraction and the Greek Universals
          i. *Abstract Vs Concrete Thinking*
          ii. *Abstraction and the Possibility of Knowledge*
          iii. *The Result of Non-Christian Abstraction*
       b. Abstraction from a Different Perspective
          i. *An Abstraction is a Particular Relationship Between Objects*
       c. Problems with This View
          i. *Problem One*
          ii. *Problem Two*
          iii. *Problem Three*
   D. Conclusion

IV. Part 3 - THE PROBLEM OF THE EXTERNAL WORLD

   1. CHAPTER 7 – THE END OF EMPIRICISM
      A. Modernity – The World of the Senses
         a. George Berkeley
         b. David Hume
         c. Immanuel Kant
      B. Conclusion

   2. CHAPTER 8 - INTERPRETATION: BRING THE WORLD INTO BEING

   3. CHAPTER 9 – TRUTH: THE FIRST INTERPRETER
      A. Propositional Knowledge
      B. Person-Knowledge
      C. Conceptual Knowledge

V. CONCLUSION

ACKNOWLEDGMENTS

Countless individuals have helped me think through the issues raised in the book, too many to acknowledge. But among the many voices that have helped shape my thinking about the Scriptures and this world, Brad Copp and John Frame deserve special mention.

I had the pleasure of studying under Brad at Pacific Life Bible College. Brad was the first person who introduced me to the issues of epistemology and pointed me to Scripture as the primary authority for the Christian. It was also Brad who chose John Frame's *Theology of Lordship* as the valedictorian prize when I graduated from PLBC. It is this series that has had the most formative influence on my thinking. I am deeply indebted to the teaching of John Frame; his faithfulness to the word of God, clarity in communication, and profundity make a rare combination. Anyone familiar with his work will see its influence in what follows.

There have been too many men and women who have helped form my thinking on the matters contained in this book to acknowledge them all properly. First, without the patience of my loving wife Nicole, I would not have had the time and space (literally, my desk and bookshelves take up a massive chunk of our small home) to finish this project. She has also shown great faith in allowing me to set aside one day a week and many early morning hours for writing. I am thankful for her faith in God's continued provision and her trust that he is using my labours. Second, without the many friends who have challenged me in my thinking and raised good questions over the years, I never would have been able to complete this work. To select only a few, I am thankful for many conversations with Andre Roberge and James Hooks during my time at Regent College. My understanding of biblical narrative formed under the guidance of Phil Long has left a lasting imprint on my philosophy. I am indebted to Brad Copp and Fred Eaton for introducing me to John Frame and Cornelius Van Til, who are perhaps the most significant influence on my thinking. I am grateful for lively conversations with Craig Gay and the students in the 2017 ThM seminar at Regent College, which helped me appreciate the unique contribution of Martin Kähler to biblical epistemology. Among these friends already mentioned and many others, I am indebted to many conversations with Jonathan Hawes, Raphael Haeuser, Daniel Supimpa, Stephen Josh Arriola, Eliezer Arriola, Joel Nafziger, and undoubtedly many more. I pray that this book will profit those who helped shape it and many more.

Above all, I am entirely dependent upon the Spirit of God in all that I have done and do. Without his daily sustaining grace, I would not have pushed through the various trials that arose and continued throughout the writing process. Without his guidance, I know there would be nothing of profit found in this book. Without his action in my heart, I never would have turned to God and desired to interpret his Word rightly. For all of my life and work, I am indebted to the grace of God poured out by Christ Jesus through the Spirit.

To God be the glory, to him alone. *Soli Deo Gloria*

INTRODUCTION

His divine power has granted to us all things that pertain to life and godliness, through the knowledge of him who called us to his own glory and excellence. – 2 Peter 1:3

God has not left His people without help in the day of trouble—or in the day of prosperity, for that matter. The Bible is God's gift to His people, revealing to them Jesus Christ and the salvation he has accomplished. But the gift of Scripture does not end in revealing our need for salvation and God's provision for it; Scripture is sufficient for the entire Christian life. In his second epistle, Peter writes that God's divine power has given us everything for life and godliness (2 Pet 1:3, cf. 2 Tim 3:16-17).

Articulating just how this is the case and what this means for the Christian life is the purpose of this series, *God's Gifts for the Christian Life*. In 3 parts (divided into 9 volumes (10 books)), I hope to unpack how God has given us what we need to live faithfully in his world through the Bible. Each volume unpacks the Scriptural teaching against the background of contemporary culture and shows how the Bible provides a firm foundation for our lives. Each volume is intended to be short, 110-150 pages, and accessible to the interested reader. The primary audience is theologically interested laypeople (Christians who are not in paid ministry and have no formal theological training), students, and pastors.

This book is Part 1, *The Gift of Knowledge*. It addresses some of the questions raised by philosophy concerning truth and knowledge, articulating various facets of the Biblical teaching that give us confidence in our understanding of God, Scripture, and the world.

Part 2, *The Gift of Truth*, presents a Bible's teaching concerning itself so that the Christian would have a firm foundation for intellectual engagement from the Bible, that is, for the task of doing theology.

Part 3, *The Gift of Wisdom*, examines three facets of the Biblical teaching to equip the reader with the tools for living rightly and thinking rightly in God's world. Volume 1, *The Gift of Purpose*, articulates a framework for Christian living in the West. Volume 2, *The Gift of Family*, outlines God's purpose for the local church and its fundamental importance for God's purposes and the Christian life. Volume 3, *The Gift of Theology* (working name), articulates a vision of Christian theologising that emerges from this series.

As a whole, all three parts are intended to provide an intellectual foundation for Christian ministry in all its various facets. That is, these volumes are intended to provide a framework for faithful and thoughtful engagement with the Bible in order to apply God's Word to every facet of life. This may be the formal teaching ministry of the local church (e.g. preaching and teaching), biblical counselling, ministry to our families, or various aspects of the discipline known as "apologetics," namely, addressing intellectual challenges raised against the Christian faith in order to strengthen the faith of Christians and persuade unbelievers. More practically, I hope to equip the Christian with the tools to read the Word of God profitably and begin to shape their life in light of it. Two concerns are at the heart of these volumes.

First, I am concerned by the erosion of the doctrine of Scripture's clarity demonstrated by the modes of theology and Biblical studies taught in our Bible Colleges and filtering their way into local church ministry. I hope to set forth a vision of the Biblical interpretation, theology, and the Christian life that builds upon the best in the Christian tradition while upholding the Bible's vision of its own clarity at every point.

Second, I am concerned by the success of various philosophical challenges raised against the Bible and Christian faith, challenges that have existed throughout church history and continue to shake the faith of Christians and to shape theology and biblical studies as practised by Christian scholars and pastors. Christian theology has long engaged fruitfully with the philosophical trends of the surrounding culture. Christians have changed contemporary philosophy in line with the Bible and have refuted many challenges to the Christian faith. However, at the end of a long tradition of serious Christian engagement with the world, it appears to me that several central biblical teachings have been abandoned, especially in the contemporary discussion. I am primarily concerned with what one theologian has called "The Academic Captivity of the Theology."[1] That is, with various subtle and not-so-subtle approaches to the Bible and theology that declare the average Christian incapable of knowing God, seriously engaging His word, or living faithfully for him in the world. Consider this quote from a recent book, an explicit articulation of what is implicit throughout the academy,

> No one can be an expert in everything, but statements about God constitute theology, and theology is a single activity. Anyone who wishes to do theology of any sort—from Old Testament exegesis to systematic theology—needs basic competence in the all the following areas: the history of philosophy and theology, biblical languages, biblical hermeneutics, biblical introduction, the history of biblical interpretation, biblical theology and dogmatic theology. To ask that it be made easier is to ask the impossible; it cannot be less complicated than it is.[2]

I am convinced that Christianity is not primarily a religion for the elite (though Christ beckons men and women from all walks of life and strata of society) and that academically trained Christians are not the primary ministers of the Gospels (e.g. Eph 4:1-16). If God's true purpose is to shame the wisdom of the world by the foolishness of the Cross and the weak and nothings of this world (1 Cor 1:18-31), then we must ask, what is the vision of Christianity that best fits this purpose? Whatever value the current vision of academic Christianity has, it is not the primary purpose of God in this

---

[1] John M. Frame, "The Academic Captivity of Theology," in *John Frame's Selected Shorter Writings*, vol. 2 (Phillipsburg: P&R Pub, 2014).

[2] Craig A. Carter, *Contemplating God with the Great Tradition: Recovering Trinitarian Classical Theism* (Grand Rapids: Baker Academic, 2021). Cf. pg. 354 below and J. Alexander Rutherford, "Review of Contemplating God with the Great Tradition," *Teleioteti*, March 22, 2021, accessed August 23, 2021, https://www.teleioteti.ca/2021/03/23/review-of-contemplating-god-with-the-great-tradition/.

world, nor is its mode of discourse the primary way the Bible would Christ's people speak, live, and think. When we pay attention to the mode of life that the Bible actually articulates, I claim that the vision of theology (or intellectual engagement with God, the Bible and the world from the Bible) and Biblical studies (thinking seriously about the Bible and the practice of reading it) looks very different.

This book, *The Gift of Knowledge*, is the first part of the series. It contains the first three volumes, previously published individually: *The Gift of Knowing: A Biblical Perspective on Knowing and Truth; The Gift of Reading – Part 1: Reading the Bible in Submission to God; The Gift of Reading – Part 2: A Biblical Perspective on Hermeneutics;* and *The Gift of Seeing: A Biblical Perspective on Ontology*. Together, they provide the theoretical foundation for the next two parts. The purpose of this whole series is summarised well in Volume 1, namely, to show that God has given Christians an anchor in the world's chaos through the Bible. By tackling the key questions of authority, truth, and reading the Bible, this book hopes to give the Christian confidence that they can indeed know God, understanding his Scriptures, and engage meaningfully with his world. The following parts will flush out this framework, expanding upon the content and nature of the Bible (Part 2) and the nature of the Christian life (Part 3). I understand the last part to be the goal of the first two: we need a framework for thinking about truth, reading, and authority in order to live obediently before God. We all have such a framework; the problem is that this framework is often shaped by the trends of our culture and not by Scripture. I hope in this first part to address this head-on, to answer the question, how would the Bible confront our assumptions about such things? From that foundation, we can then begin to think constructively about the Christian life, which is the goal of Part 3. We will get nowhere in the Christian life if we do not know Scripture, and the argument of this first part is based on a big picture view of the Bible's teaching, so Part 2 provides the anchor for the whole project. In Part 2, we will explore the contours of the Bible itself to far greater depth, furnishing us with a bibliology that justifies this first part and enables the third.

Volume 1:
The Gift of Knowing
A Biblical Perspective on Knowing and Truth

INTRODUCTION

"What were we doing when we unchained this earth from its sun?" spoke the madman, "Where is it moving to now? Where are we moving to? Away from all suns? Are we not continually falling? And backwards, sidewards, forwards, in all directions? Is there still an up and a down? Aren't we straying as though through an infinite nothing?"[1] Friedrich Nietzsche, an atheist, penned these words more than a century ago, seeing better than any of his peers what atheism would do to the Western world. Does not our world feel like this some days? News story after news story evokes in us the thought that the world truly has gone mad! This madness of our world may be most evident in its rejection of the very possibility of truth

Within Christianity, the trustworthiness of the Bible is ever in question. In the culture around us, long-held moral standards have faced sustained erosion, now giving way to a tide of immorality. Without truth, anything goes; concepts of gender, religion, politics, science, and morality are all up for grabs in the Western world. The effects of the erosion of truth we now witness are not merely concerns for students and academics, philosophers and theologians. They have serious implications for every person. They have serious implications for Christians more than anyone else.

If you have picked this book up, you are probably aware of this problem. I do not hope to offer in the pages that follow anything new or an agenda for

---

[1] This is modernised from Friedrich Wilhelm Nietzsche and Walter Kaufmann, *The Portable Nietzsche* (New York, N.Y.: Penguin Books, 1982), 95.

fixing what is wrong in our society. I hope only to offer an application of the Christian Scriptures to the epistemological conundrum we now face, to the crisis of knowing we are in.[2] I hope to show how God has graciously given us what we need to persevere in and thrive while our culture continues to struggle with the noose it has tied for itself. I intend to argue that our culture has been infected with a virus; it has been afflicted with a disease that has characterised every human culture from the beginning of the creation. This disease is the belief in human autonomy; it is this belief that has eroded the concept of truth in the Western world. I will then argue that the remedy for this crisis is a Biblical epistemology, essentially that knowing is a gift from God, coming from and depending upon him.

Believing that God has given us all things we need in Scripture so that we may be equipped for every good work (2 Tim. 3:16-17), I want to show that the Bible has answers to this crisis. I have endeavoured to demonstrate that the Bible gives important insights into the subject of philosophy often called **epistemology**, a model of what it means to know and how we do so.

This volume is written for the concerned Christian, for those of us who see the problem and yet struggle with an answer. Though we will be dealing with philosophy and philosophers, I will not assume a background in philosophy. I write to those who are concerned with what they see and hear yet cannot quite diagnosis the problem or formulate a response. I will not be able to answer all of your questions. Yet by the Lord's grace, I hope to point you to the treasure trove that is Scripture so that together we can be encouraged in our faith, be driven to the worship of our heavenly Father, and be equipped to submit every thought to obey Christ (2 Cor 10:5).

To these ends, this volume's ten short chapters will diagnose the disease that has infected our culture and then point us to the Biblical remedy. First, we will begin with the diagnosis, tracing the destructive virus from its beginnings. We will then look at what we mean by "knowing," addressing the objectivity and subjectivity of knowledge and the nature of truth. With these pieces in place, we can then consider the heart of the crisis, the question of

---

[2] **Epistemology** is a 50 dollar philosophical word used to describe the study of truth and knowing, the act of attaining truth. Epistemology addresses what we think and how we think it, what truth means and how we can find it—if we can at all. This book is a study in epistemology, a study of what the Bible says about truth and the manner of attaining it.

authority. Finally, we will consider ourselves—human beings—as thinking creatures and how God has equipped us to know the world around us.

It is my earnest prayer that we would each come to see and truly believe that the fear of the Lord is the beginning of wisdom. I offer this book as an attempt to show how Scripture provides us with the anchor we need in the epistemological chaos of our time. To this end, I offer this prayer to the Lord for myself and for you, the reader,

To you, oh Lord, belong all wisdom, knowledge, and understanding,
>   to you these belong, and to those with whom you share them.
We ask that you would give us wisdom,
>   wisdom necessary to know you and your world.
Teach us what it means to know the truth and be set free,
>   to fear you and be endowed with true wisdom.
Help us take every thought captive to obey Christ
>   and to exult in the rich grace you poured out on your people,
>   in eternal life, to know Jesus Christ and you who sent him.

It is in his name that we pray these things,
amen.

1

DIAGNOSING THE DISEASE

> For the wrath of God is revealed from heaven against all ungodliness and unrighteousness of men, who by their unrighteousness suppress the truth. For what can be known about God is plain to them, because God has shown it to them. For although they knew God, they did not honor him as God or give thanks to him, but they became futile in their thinking, and their foolish hearts were darkened. Claiming to be wise, they became fools, and exchanged the glory of the immortal God for images resembling mortal man and birds and animals and creeping things. – Romans 1:18-23

In the beginning, God created, and it was good. Since then, things have gone sideways—and backwards, forwards, in all directions! The problem of truth that confronts us today is a story almost as old as time. In Romans 1:18-32, Paul describes the human condition in dark terms. The wrath of God is against all the unrighteousness of man; none of us escape his sweeping indictment (cf. Rom 3:1-23). What should strike us here is the root of the problem, that which causes all sorts of wretched actions and ideas to pour out of our minds and mouths.

My former pastor Fred Eaton once described the problem as disordered worship, disordered worship producing disordered living. Though God has made himself known clearly in the creation, humanity has exchanged the glorious truth of God's existence and character for a lie. Observe that this fundamental sin is a sin of knowledge. Setting aside the truth of God, humans have adopted a lie. Setting aside the Creator, they have made the creature the measure of truth. All human history is stained by this exchange.

Adam and Eve began this trend when they exchanged the command of God for the lie of the Devil. Did "God actually say," asked the tempter—words all too familiar to us today. In the place of the truth of God's goodness, they believed the lie that they knew what was best for themselves. Believing that lie, they fell headfirst into sin and brought all their progeny with them. Since then, all of humanity has made the same deliberate decision to exchange the truth of who God is and his commands for autonomy, the ability to choose what to believe and what to do.

The people whom God called forth from Egypt, those whom he would use to achieve redemption for the world, were not free from this. After leaving Egypt, their trials in the barren wilderness led the Israelites to forsake the promises of God, to reject his goodness and to yearn for the land from which they left:

> Now the rabble that was among them had a strong craving. And the people of Israel also wept again and said, "Oh that we had meat to eat! We remember the fish we ate in Egypt that cost nothing, the cucumbers, the melons, the leeks, the onions, and the garlic. But now our strength is dried up, and there is nothing at all but this manna to look at." (Num 11:4-6)

This was the response of those who received the oracles of God! The world outside of Israel was no different; it embraced this exchange to a much greater extent. This was seen at every level of culture and society, especially in philosophy.

A. Pre-Modernity – Autonomy in Pursuit of Universal Truth

This is no place to give an account of all Philosophy before the so-called Enlightenment and Modernity. Still, we can see the beginning of our contemporary crisis in two strands of so-called "Pre-modern" thought. Though Philosophy was not the exclusive domain of the Western world (much of the thought identified with Greece had its parallels in India), the West is what has most shaped our society. So we will focus on the philosophers and thought of the Western world.

Philosophy as we know it had its origins in Greece. From the early thinkers known as the "Pre-Socratics" to their (slightly) more famous successors Socrates, Plato, and Aristotle, Greek thought was consumed with the tension between unchanging and changing reality. The Pre-Socratics lived at a time when Greece was highly religious; the religion of the day was the worship of the Olympian gods—Zeus, Athena, Ares, etc. In the city of Miletus, around 600 BC, Western philosophy was born as an effort to explain the nature of the world by human reason without reference to the activity of gods.

Instead of explaining the course of nature (e.g. seasons and storms) with an appeal to the supposed life of the different gods and their conflicts, the first philosophers asked questions about the ultimate nature of the world and sought an explanation for their experience beyond the realm of the ancient religion. In this context, a debate emerged among the 2nd generation of these philosophers concerning whether reality was entirely changing or entirely unchanging.[1]

On the one hand, they had the experience of change: we all experience change in the passing of time, in aging, and in new experiences each day. So Heraclitus (535-475 BC), thought change was the ultimate explanation of everything—all changed! This threatened the very possibility of knowledge—for if everything changes, does "truth" change too? Others argued that if change was real, if our experience was what it seemed to be, knowledge was an illusion. Parmenides, the key thinker on this side, rejected the possibility that knowledge was an illusion and instead argued that all change was an illusion. Nothing changed; therefore, our senses could not be trusted. But our minds could come to some understanding of truth.

Philosophy did not linger here long: the next generation of philosophers—mainly Plato (5th-4th centuries BC) and Aristotle (384-322 BC)—attempted to explain change without dispensing with unchanging reality. The greatest Greek philosophers argued that neither change nor eternality (i.e. unchangingness) made sense of the world and human thoughts and experience. Heraclitus was right to observe that things change, but

---

[1] Zeno is (relatively) famous for his paradoxes concerning the impossibility of change. He was audacious enough to claim that in a race, if given a slight head start, a tortoise would beat a hare. The ridiculousness of this scenario supposedly revealed the ridiculousness of change.

Parmenides was also right when he argued that we need something unchanging if knowledge is possible. What was necessary was a combination of something changing, the stuff we experience (which they called *matter*) and that which was unchanging, the true object of knowledge. They contended that what changes is ultimately unknowable, for what it once was is no longer what it is the next moment.

Imagine yourself, they argued, in a stream. If all the water has already moved downriver after it has touched you, is the water you are currently in the same thing? On one level it is—you are still in the same "stream"—yet if the water has changed and the soil beneath your feet is being worn away, what makes this stream the same from one moment to the next? If you claim to know anything about the stream, it cannot be anything about the matter you experience; this is constantly changing. What you know is something beyond the matter that you experience. Therefore, the true object of knowledge must be unchanging, something beyond the sensible world. The sensible world, therefore, really is not knowable at all. But there is something that we do know. This knowable world must lay behind—or above—the matter we sense.

For Plato, the unchanging objects of human knowledge are the **universals**,[2] eternal ideas that exist beyond the physical world in a separate, intangible world of ideas. If you look out your window and see a tree, the true object of your knowledge, for Plato, is not that particular maple in your front yard. Instead, you know the "treeness" that the tree embodies. "Treeness" is the universal, that thing that all trees have in common. For Plato the nature of a tree, table, or human being is that unchangeable element that every tree, table, or human shares. Treeness is that thing which, if you removed it, would make that tree no longer a tree. It is not colour, for trees have different colours, nor is it size or shape. It is something intangible, inexpressible, which lays behind the variety of our experience. Every tree is merely a particular example of this universal idea, this form; it is an embodiment of an idea in matter, what some philosophers call an

---

[2] Every word in **bold-text** can be found in the glossary at the end of the book. I only bold the words the first time they occur in a chapter.

instantiation.³ At this point you may be thinking to yourself, "what does 'treeness' have to do with the modern dilemma we are in?" The answer is that the concepts with which Plato wrestled have had a profound impact on Christian and non-Christian thought since he first penned them in his dialogues. We can see the implications of his thought more clearly if we consider morality.

One of the dialogues Plato wrote is called *Euthyphro*, in which he struggled with the question of goodness. He is particularly interested in what makes a particular action good or bad. Was it the gods? We know they disagree, argued Plato, so which one do we trust? If we select the highest of them, what if he changes his mind? The Greek gods were fickle beings who did whatever they wanted for their own benefit—even the "best" of them. If morality depended on their mood and decision, could not Zeus declare rape to be right one day and wrong another? The answer to his initial question—what makes a particular action good or bad—could not be in the changing will of even the most powerful being. The answer must be in something unchanging, in the universal of goodness. The universal of goodness would be that unchanging moral standard that lies behind every declaration that something is good—whether it is a god or a human who proclaims it. If, however, this "goodness" judged even the actions of the gods, it is clear that this "goodness" is the true god—an impersonal standard existing beyond all that is sensible, unchanging and perfect. The gods, then, argued Plato, really are not gods at all.⁴ Not all Greek thinkers were so concerned about morality,

---

³ Universals can be a difficult concept to wrap our minds around. A universal, for Plato, referred not to specific examples of a tree, but the perfect "tree." By definition, such a tree could not physically exist; it could not exist in the sensible world. Therefore, it could only be an idea, a sort of template by which all other trees take their features. In one illustration, Plato pictured the relationship of universal (treeness) and particular (a tree) with an jar and its shadow. As light shines on a jar and casts a rough copy of it on the wall behind, so the idea of something creates imperfect representations of itself in the material world. In morality, there is the idea of "goodness"; every good act is an imperfect example of ideal goodness.

If you are still struggling, take comfort. I think these "universals" ultimately do not make sense and are false. You cannot imagine "goodness" apart from good acts because it does not exist apart from them; the same goes for humanness, being, etc. See chapter 10 of this volume and Volume 3, *The Gift of Seeing*.

⁴ Christianity provides an answer to this dilemma. Essentially, God's faithfulness means that He is an unchanging standard of what is good and bad. See chapter 10 and my book *Believe the Unbelievable*, 82-87.

however. For some, truth was a matter of money.

The Sophists, those who peddled wisdom and clever speech to make a wage, did not care about the truthfulness of what they taught. The Sophists cared for "truth" only as content that they were skilled enough to make money teaching or for its pragmatic value, its usefulness, for their vision of society. They were relativists. That is, truth or falsehood did not matter; only the subjective value of ideas mattered. Did it work? make them money? achieve their vision? Surely this sounds familiar. For the Sophists, only the ends they wanted to achieve and their jobs as skilled teachers mattered not the truth.

For Plato and those who followed him, we could identify their concern as the **transcendent**: they exchanged the truth of God as revealed in his creation for distant *ideas*, not tangible *things*.[5] Instead of that which they could taste or touch, they sought what could be grasped with the mind. They looked for something greater than themselves, something that explained how humans could think and know right and wrong. With transcendence came **objectivism**, the belief that truth was out there to be grasped, that truth would be the same no matter who thought about it.[6] Yet their transcendent ideas, these ideas that were so far beyond humanity and their world, were not the Biblical God. These ideas were impersonal: they explained human thinking but made no demands upon man. They never called for his submission.

---

[5] **Transcendence** is a key idea in philosophy and theology, describing that which is other than man, that which is far off or different. It is basically a spatial concept, referring to something above us, "up there." In philosophy or theology it refers to the quality of being greater than and so exercising control over. The universal ideas are greater than human thoughts, human ideas. They are the true content of human thinking and so exercise control over it.

[6] **Objectivity** is a key concept of modernity, a movement whose effects we still feel. To be objective is to be neutral, to be free from bias: if truth is objective and is attained through objective thinking, it is the exact same no matter who is thinking it. No matter who runs the test, not only should the results be the same but their interpretation as well. Is, for example, a rock red if no one observes that it is red? If so, then "the rock is red" is objective truth, but if "the rock is red" is only true when someone observes that it is red, then it is **subjective** truth.

In this, the Sophists with their self-interest and the Platonists with their rational thought shared something in common: humanity was the measure of truth or value. For the Sophists, because no transcendence imposed itself upon them, they were free to pursue whatever it was they valued most—namely, a wage attained through skill and their political ends. For the Platonists, truth was what explained human thinking. It was that which the human mind could conjure up to explain itself and its experience. Having rejected the gods, these latter philosophers sought a firm foundation for human knowledge, an objective reality beyond the mind that would be a sufficient object of human thought. They sought universal truth and thought they found it in the unchanging universals or forms.

The ideas raised by these Greek Philosophers remained influential for the next 2000 years, with many (maybe all) of the most profound philosophers of the following millennia interacting with their ideas. Though it is certainly an overstatement, philosopher Alfred North Whitehead famously wrote, "The safest general characterization of the European philosophical tradition is that it consists of a series of footnotes to Plato."[7] When Modernity emerged in the post-Reformation world, the objectivism of the Platonists won out over Sophistic subjectivism. Moderns were interested in unchanging truth. However, when Modernity was brought to its inevitable conclusions, it retained aspects of both Sophist and Platonic thought. The centrality of a person for moral judgment (as the Sophists displayed in their actions) and for thought (as the Platonists demonstrated in their reasoning) was united in radical **immanence**—or closeness, nearness.[8] In Modernity humans with their minds and their senses solidified themselves as the measure of all truth and value, they attained autonomy—or so they thought.

B. Modernity – Autonomy in Search of Objectivity

Modernity is a set of ideas that dominated the Western world from the period shortly after the Reformation into the 20th century. It is a movement of

---

[7] In *Process and Reality*, (Simon and Schuster, 2010), 39.

[8] **Immanence** is another key word in philosophy and theology. Like transcendence it is also a spatial term: it refers to something that is near at hand, close by. God's immanence is His presence with man. The radical immanence of modernity refers to the belief that all truth and standards of truth lay in human beings—not a distant idea or a supreme God.

thought that emerged out of the Enlightenment. The Enlightenment, in Philosophy, was characterized by intense wrestling with philosophical problems of knowledge.

During this time, the scientific revolution blossomed, and philosophers began to consider the relationship between the sciences—the study of that which we could sense—and ideas. On one end of the spectrum was the **empiricist** David Hume.[9] An empiricist is someone who claims that all human knowledge comes through the five senses—what we taste, touch, see, smell, and hear. David Hume (1711-1776 AD), a brilliant Scottish philosopher, was the most radical of these thinkers. For him, the human being was the centre of all knowledge. If something could not be sensed by an individual or argued from sense experience, it was not knowable. God may exist, or he may not. We have no experience of anything like "God," so his existence is a question we cannot answer. We cannot know either way. The best we can say is that maybe (just maybe) there is an explanation of the world that looks more or less (probably less) like a personal cause, to which we could give the name "God"—yet another explanation is equally likely, or better. For Hume, human experience was the final arbiter of what could be reasonably believed to be true or not.[10]

At the opposite end of the spectrum was a French Christian thinker named Rene Descartes (1596-1650 AD), who espoused a radical form of individualism. What is true is whatever humans can think of, beginning only with the assumption that they themselves exist.[11] Descartes attempted to establish all truth through deductive reasoning, through logic (e.g. If I have a generally true statement, that *lights comes from a source*; and a particular true statement, that *there is light in this room*; another statement is then true, *there is a source for the light in this room*). Descartes is famous among philosophers and theologians for the foundation of his philosophy, the claim "I think therefore

---

[9] For empiricist, see **empiricism** in the glossary.

[10] This doesn't mean "God" does not exist, only that there is no rational reason to believe that he exists, or that he has ever spoken and testified to his existence. So why believe in his existence anyway, Hume argued.

[11] This attempt to build all human knowledge on the foundation of a basic (or several basic) "axiom(s)" or self-evident truth(s) is called **Foundationalism**.

I am." Descartes found certainty in the immediate, undeniable impression of self-existence. The one thing we can be sure of is our own existence, he argued, so this is the solid point from which we can reason to other truths. He then attempted to prove from this starting point of self-existence the existence of God and, from there, everything else. For Descartes, the individual and his knowledge of himself is the foundation for all other knowledge. It is true that he went on to try and prove the existence of God, yet this proof ultimately fails: all that was certain was the self.

When Modernity emerged, it was characterized by the radical individualism of Descartes. The individual was the reference point for all knowledge. Truth was limited to what humans could grasp and defined based on their reason. However, objectivity was rooted in the objective world of the senses. Whatever one may say or not say about the world of ideas, the world of the senses was objectively available to the human mind and could be mastered, grasped, and manipulated.

In theology, this was manifest in the movement known as Liberal Protestantism, the attempt to make Christianity presentable and acceptable within Modernity. This project began with the assumption that something was wrong, that Christianity was not acceptable to Modern people and that this needed to be remedied. That is, it started from the perspective of humanity: we know certain truths about the world, and the Bible does not fit that mould, therefore it must be wrong—at least to some extent. The various answers that were produced all accepted the general contours of Modernity. They were all attempts to reimagine Christianity within this **worldview**, within this framework of interpretation.[12]

From Hume, these thinkers inherited the view of naturalism—the belief the world is a closed, autonomous system that is never interfered with. Humans have complete control over the phenomenal world, the world of our experience. We are free to imagine and understand it as we are able. This worldview had massive ramifications for Christian theology. Within this naturalistic, closed world, the options were endless. Jesus may have just been a moral man, proclaiming the closeness of God to the souls of every human

---

[12] Worldview is a key concept that we will look at in the next chapter, for now it will suffice to define it as a comprehensive framework for interpreting and making decisions: it is the sum-total of ones most basic beliefs, or presuppositions, about the nature of the world, knowledge, ethics, life's purpose, etc.

and a radical morality centred only on love, as Adolf Harnack taught.[13]

Outside of Christianity, what emerged was the radical view we could call "scientism," the belief that scientific method—formulating hypotheses and testing them by empirical (sense-based) and repeatable tests—produced truth which could be used and trusted. The scientific method was the one and only way to objective truth. This took many different forms, but these different forms of scientism shared the belief that humans could step beyond their **presuppositions**[14] to analyse the world objectively and arrive at truth on which any likewise objective observer would agree. It is obvious why religion would be such a danger: the Bible and other holy books prevented objective analysis. They ruled out certain conclusions and demanded others before testing even began.

In its time, Modernity seemed unstoppable. By exchanging the truth of God for autonomous (i.e. independent) human study of the world, significant progress was made. Modernity seemed to find objectivity not in transcendence, in gods or ideas, but in immanence, the human analysis of objective reality. Without a universal, transcendent standard of truth, Modernity sought a firm foundation for knowledge in the objective study of the world. Unfortunately, by placing such weight on the human interpreter, Modernity shot itself in the foot. As it turns out, we humans are not nearly as objective or morally unbiased as we thought!

C. Postmodernity – Autonomy Arriving at Radical Relativity

While Modernity was producing results, great technological advancement was being made; it became more and more apparent that scientists and philosophers still disagreed. If they were analysing objectively the same reality, why would they come up with differing conclusion? How could entire generations be wrong? In the philosophy of science, the idea of a paradigm and paradigm shift was formulated. It was shown that scientists did not

---

[13] It is interesting how similar ideas have reappeared in the recent work of the Canadian psychologist Jordan Peterson. See my review of his book *12 Rules for Life*, https://teleioteti.ca/2018/10/11/review-of-12-rules-for-life/.

[14] A presupposition is one of our foundational beliefs by which we automatically—without deliberate thought—interpret all our experience and form which we do all our reasoning.

analyse nature objectively but according to previous theories. They did so and even dismissed contrary evidence until enough evidence emerged and enough of a consensus was attained to topple the previous interpretive paradigm. In other words, philosophers at this time began to consider the beliefs that people used to interpret the world around them: they argued that people do not see the world objectively but through an interpretive lens. Instead of looking at the world with undistorted vision, it was argued that we look through coloured glasses.

These glasses may obscure some details while giving incredible focus to others; they might readily reveal some truths but conceal and dismiss others. These glasses were worldviews, the different interpretive frameworks every individual uses to interpret their experience. A worldview consists of all the most basic beliefs an individual has about what exists, what is truth, how truth is attained, what is right and wrong, etc. All humans have a worldview. The supposed objectivity of science was really the dominance of a single worldview. This worldview could be, and has been from time to time, overthrown (such a revolution was called a *paradigm shift*). Despite this shift in the understanding of science, from pure objectivity to the paradigm, science has continued strong. Yet other areas of thought have not been so lucky.

With the possibility of transcendence (of something beyond a person governing truth, whether a personal god or an idea) being abandoned and then the objectivity of the individual lost, the results for morality and philosophy were inevitable. If nothing greater than I tells me what is right or wrong, and my interpretation of the world around me is different from everyone else's, then the only standard for morality remaining is myself. Therefore, each individual is the standard of right and wrong, truth and falsehood. It is ultimately up to the individual to determine what is right or wrong. In the philosophy of continental Europe, this escalated quickly. Even the possibility of communication has been questioned. It is from these philosophical roots that our present situation has emerged.

This is where we find ourselves now. Morality is determined by preference and feeling, imposed on others by majority opinion. Truth is discarded in favour of one-sided tolerance—tolerance of anything that buys into the relativistic agenda. This tolerance rejects anything that suggests it is right and something else is wrong. In our schools, reading is less about understanding what a text is saying and more about analysing our response as readers to it. In Postmodernity, the autonomous search for knowledge that characterizes the history of philosophy found its end. Instead of finding a firm foundation for thought, Postmodernity found that autonomous human thinking could only result in radical relativity.

Throughout our history, humans have exchanged the truth of God for a lie, worshipping and serving the creature rather than the Creator. By pursuing this lie, we have dug ourselves an ever-deepening hole without a ladder for escape. Yet we are not without hope.

If rejecting God was what got us here in the first place, turning back to him and his revelation is undoubtedly the answer to our crisis. In our attempt to return to God, it seems wisest to begin with the questions we have just seen, namely our interaction with the world outside of us and the possibility of knowing it. That is, we will start with the questions of subjectivity and objectivity. Looking here at the fundamental problems that have shaped our contemporary crisis, we will see more clearly why rejecting God has resulted in such chaos. Concerning subjectivity, we must ask if we can interpret the world we experience without any assumptions (or presuppositions) prejudicing our results. Concerning objectivity, we must ask if objectivity is necessary for truth.

Further Reading[15]

J. P. Moreland, *Scientism & Secularism* [I-A]
John Frame, *Apologetics: A Justification of Christian Belief* [B]
* John Frame, *The Doctrine of the Knowledge of God* [I]
* John Frame, *A History of Western Philosophy and Theology* [B-I]
Ronald Nash, *Worldviews in Conflict* [B]
C.S. Lewis, *Miracles* [B]
Francis Schaeffer, *The God Who Is There* [B]

---

[15] The following resources range from (relatively) easy to quite difficult in their readability. I mark the easier reads with a **B**, those a bit more difficult with an **I**, and the most difficult with **A**. I adduce difficulty on the basis of the depth of content, knowledge presupposed by the author, and the clarity of the writing. An asterisk before a book indicates that it is especially recommended.

—Part 1—
Our Epistemological Situation

2

WORLDVIEW THINKING: APPROPRIATE SUBJECTIVITY

> For the word of the cross is folly to those who are perishing, but to us who are being saved it is the power of God. – 1 Corinthians 1:18

Why is it that some hear of Jesus's death on the cross and resurrection and reject the historicity of these events or their significance? Why do some people stubbornly maintain that resurrections are impossible or interpret Jesus's life and death as a mere tragedy that befell one of the world's greatest moral teachers? Why is it that some scoff at the thought of God becoming a man and dying for his people while others revel in the glorious truth contained therein—that they are free, free from sin, free from wrath, free to enjoy God forever! A great part of it is surely rebellion, stubborn-hearted resistance to God (e.g. Rom 8:5-8). Yet this sinful rebellion manifests in interpretive blindness, a continual misinterpretation. "How is it," we may ask, "that someone can refuse any evidence presented and maintain that resurrections cannot happen?" But if someone comes to the table already believing this to be impossible, if they evaluate the claim that a dead man is no longer dead through this lens—that God does not exist and that miracles do not happen—they will of course reject it. As far as they are concerned, it is impossible! The problem is not whether miracles can or cannot happen, but whether it is possible that they could happen in the world that someone believes to exist. Their **worldview** is governing their interpretation; their "rose-coloured glasses," as Cornelius Van Til used to say, blind them to the possibility that God could raise someone from the dead.

They are wearing glasses, but we are too. Approaching the claims of a miracle from a position of faith in Yahweh, the God of the Bible, it is obvious that he who created the world by the word of his power and called into existence all that exists from nothing could resurrect a dead man. Furthermore, nothing but the sheer incredulity of it prevents him from entering his creation! The truth is that we are all wearing coloured glasses through which we interpret the world. But, as we will see in the next chapter, this does not make truth unattainable.

If we are wearing glasses, we need to understand how they affect our experience and interpretation. We also need to know how different worldviews affect the way others think. This is the purpose of this chapter. I want us to see what a worldview is, why they matter, and—more importantly—how a Biblical worldview helps us to navigate the troubled waters of Western culture.

I have already described a worldview as a comprehensive framework for interpreting the world; this definition focuses on the practical implications of a worldview. A worldview is often considered to be the sum of a person or society's convictions about the world. There is truth to this definition, in the sense that a worldview involves all a person's beliefs as they shape their perception and interpretation of the world. However, these "beliefs" are often implicit—rarely acknowledged or observed. Moreover, in addition to "beliefs," the worldview or "tacit framework" (to use Polanyi's term) involves many non-propositional forms of knowledge. That is, our worldview involves conceptual knowledge and person-knowledge which cannot be captured by a statement such as "I believe that …." We will discuss this unseen depth of worldview in *The Gift of Seeing*. For now, we will focus on the tip of the iceberg, those conscious and unconscious beliefs that can be expressed with some ease in a statement such as, "I believe that …." This aspect of a worldview is sometimes called a philosophy or a theology, a systematic interpretation of the world.[1] Our worldviews involve our beliefs

---

[1] From a Christian perspective, the difference between "theology" and "philosophy" is not so much that one is religious and the other a-religious. The difference is that theology deals with the world from revelation and philosophy from reason. Because reason is ultimately a gift from God, an interpretive tool for interpreting his revelation in Scripture and the world, and is itself a part of natural revelation, philosophy for a Christian is properly a subset of theology—the Word of God applied to the realm of reason and logic.

about the existence or non-existence of God and what he is like, about the relationship between humanity and God, one human to another, humanity to animals, etc.[2] All our fundamental beliefs, our assumptions that lie behind all our thinking, make up our worldview. The possibility of miracles is a key belief of the Biblical worldview, an implication of the belief that God is the Lord of his creation and active (or immanent) within it.

Philosophers have generally summarized a worldview as that which we believe about what exists (metaphysics), how we know (epistemology), and what is right and wrong (ethics). This book is an effort to unpack one aspect of the Biblical worldview, its epistemology. Epistemology ultimately concerns the "how" question or method of thinking, how to engage in intellectual thought—if we can at all.

In this chapter, we will look at what worldviews *do* more than any specific worldview. We have already considered various features of the Modern and Postmodern worldview in the last chapter and will continue to do so where necessary, but our focus will not be so much on what Postmoderns believe but why it matters that they believe these things.

A worldview is all of a person's beliefs that form a comprehensive framework with which they interpret the world. "Seeing is not believing," writes C.S. Lewis, "For this reason, the question whether miracles occur can never be answered simply by experience."[3] Seeing is not believing because sight must be interpreted: if someone sees a miracle and believes with the utmost conviction that miracles are impossible, they will insist that it was an illusion—for miracles just don't happen! Our worldview factors into every decision we make, and we should be grateful that it does! When we prepare to cross a busy road, we do not have to think about whether it is wise or not to jump in front of a car: we know that to do so is foolish and deadly. But why do we know this? We know this because we believe in causality (that causes produce effects) and that the effect of being hit by a car is serious

---

[2] James N. Anderson helpfully summarizes the major beliefs of a worldview as TAKES, as in "what it TAKES to make a worldview." *Theology*, what is the absolute in your worldview? *Anthropology*, what do you believe about man? *Knowledge*, what is truth and how do we get it? *Ethics*, what is right or wrong, good or bad? And *Salvation*, what is the problem with the world and how is it fixed?

[3] C. S Lewis, *Miracles: A Preliminary Study* (New York: Harper Collins, 2011), chap. 1.

injury or death. This is a belief based on experience and the testimony of others (maybe a parent reprimanding us as a child) that we use to make basic decisions every day. For Christians, the belief that God exists and cares for his children leads us to pray in difficult circumstances. The belief that he is the source of all good gifts leads us to give thanks at meals and before bed.

The list would be endless if we attempted to analyse all the beliefs that shape our everyday actions, and we would miss many so-called "tacit" beliefs—those that we are not regularly aware of. Worldviews shape all that we do, so it matters that we get them right! What would happen if we did not believe that effects follow from causes? Would we be so hesitant about jumping in front of cars? Surely we would not live long without that belief!

If we do not believe that truth is attainable, we will not accept the truth claims of the Bible. If we do not believe that miracles happen, we will not believe the resurrection. Getting our worldview right is of vital importance, our lives in this age and the age to come rest on what we believe and do not believe. We must, then, know how we can be sure of the Christian worldview, we must refine our own worldview, and we must know how to interact with others. The remaining pages of this chapter will begin addressing these needs, looking at how worldviews are formed and how this affects the way we evaluate them. In the next chapter, we will consider how we can be sure of the Christian worldview, how we can reason with those with whom we disagree, and how we can refine our worldviews.

We have considered beliefs as the content of a worldview, but we have yet to look at how we can evaluate our own worldview and the worldviews of others. To learn this, we need to consider the beginning of a worldview, how we come to adopt the worldview we have. Someone may argue that they have done so by reason, claiming that this was the worldview that seemed most reasonable to them. Yet this is not the real explanation. Our worldviews originate a little earlier. Worldviews begin with a recipe of three ingredients, all of which rely on faith, not reason.

Our worldview begins with what we could call **innate ideas**, that is, ideas that we do not and cannot learn from experience, for experience requires them.[4] For example, we are born with knowledge of **the law of non-**

---

[4] We will consider innate ideas a little more in Chapter 10.

contradiction, the principle that no object or idea can be itself and its opposite at the same time in the same way. The letter A cannot be whatever is not-A at the same time, nor can 2 + 3 = 5 and 6 at the same time and in the same way. A computer cannot be fully black and fully white in the same way and at the same time, though it could have a fully black layer on top of a fully white one. A phone cannot be totally unbroken and totally broken simultaneously. Such examples could be multiplied endlessly. Without this law, learning is impossible. For example, though I burned my hand on the stove once, it is possible that I could not burn it in the exact same circumstances. Furthermore, without the law of non-contradiction, all thought is nonsense: I could be black and white, male and female, up and down, left and right, bee or bird, human or monkey, in space or on earth, this or that, at any time and in any way.[5] Barring disability, we are also born with the concepts necessary to interpret light as different colours and to interpret this light in order to produce a mental picture. As children, we do not wait to prove innate ideas before we use them; we trust that they are correct and employ them intuitively. Innate ideas are not enough, however, for they are only tools necessary to interpret *experience*.

We also learn our worldview from experience, especially from others telling us what to believe (e.g. that the sound "food" can be used to describe and request an edible substance required to live). For example, we learn about Jesus Christ and his saving work by hearing the word of the Gospel preached (Rom 10:14-18). According to Romans 1:18-32, we learn from experiencing every part of creation—ourselves surely included—that Yahweh exists, what his character is like, and that we should honour and thank him. This brings us to the third ingredient of our worldview: it is composed of one part innate ideas, one part experience, and one part rebellion.

That is, we all reject what we learn about God from experience and innate ideas. We reject his Lordship, his demands upon us, and replace the Creator with the creature, with ourselves—even as babies (Ps 51:5)! It is important to observe that these are not baking instructions (add innate ideas, followed by experience, then season with rebellion) but an ingredient list: all of these co-exist as we develop; none is first. With trust—apart from careful

---

[5] If the statements "J. Alexander Rutherford is floating in space, not on earth, at 10:30 am, Nov. 11, 2017" and "J. Alexander Rutherford is on earth, not in space, at 10:30 am, Nov. 11, 2017" are both true, than any contradictory state can be true (e.g. it is only snowing and only not-snowing at the same time in the same place).

reason—we accept the testimony of our minds, of our senses and others, and we trust ourselves over God. The natural worldview of humans is part truth and part lie, postured in rebellion towards God (cf. Rom 8:6-7). As we mature, we learn different things from different sources and arrive at a fuller and fuller interpretation of the world around us, eventually arriving at our present state.

You may be asking yourself at this time why you need an ingredient list. The point of looking at these ingredients is to notice that nobody forms a worldview like Descartes: none of us are born an empty hard drive to be filled by logical deduction (I exist, my existence requires God, God's existence means others exist, etc.) or experience (I experience my own existence, the existence of others, the existence of trees, of goodness, of badness, etc.). So if someone expects us to prove our worldview from one of these routes, they will be sorely disappointed! There is no objective state by which any human can step back and neutrally evaluate their own or another's worldview. All such evaluation comes from within a worldview.

A Christian needs to begin evaluating his own worldview on its terms; a Hindu must evaluate his worldview on its terms; an atheist on his; etc. This may lead us to think that we are stuck at an impasse—you have your worldview and I have mine! But this is not the conclusion we need to or should draw. This is the conclusion our culture arrives at, namely, that a lack of objectivity means there is no truth. I began this book, however, claiming that this was not the case, that the Bible provides us with a way beyond this impasse. I am not ready to give up and neither should you be. In the next chapter, we will see how we can still reason and arrive at truth despite the subjectivity our worldviews give us.

Another Perspective on Subjectivity

In this chapter, we have seen that knowing involves a subjective aspect; we all approach the world with an interpretive lens. However, another question arises when begin to think this way. Why is it that two people with the same worldview come to different interpretations of the same object or event? Consider the four Gospels: each comes from the perspective of someone who was with or learned from those who were with Jesus, yet each is distinctively different. Consider another example:

why can the act of a man walking through a doorway be alternatively interpreted as, "the man came home"; "the man went inside"; "the man walked through the door;" "the man entered the building"; or "daddy's home!!!"? All of these describe the same event from different perspectives, different ways of viewing it from different spatial viewpoints (came into the home, went inside) or understandings of its significance ("daddy's home!" and "the man entered the home" are very different in this sense).

Yet, all of these are true. God knows all possible perspectives, and so these all are part of God's multi-faceted interpretation of his universe. Each of us only has a partial perspective, for we face several limitations (e.g. I can only see something from one perspective at a time). Therefore, we possess truth but not all truth. There is, therefore, great benefit to be gained from learning with other people who share our worldview, from not limiting ourselves to only our perspective. Returning to the four Gospels, each gives us a true perspective that enriches our understanding of Jesus Christ and his work: we would be impoverished if we lost one! We can also learn from those who disagree at a worldview level, for there is truth to be found even in a rebellious worldview, something we will see further in the next chapter.

Further Reading

John Frame, *the Doctrine of the Knowledge of God* [I]
* John Frame, *Apologetics: a Justification of Christian Belief* [B]
John Frame, *Systematic Theology*, pgs. 36-50 [B-I]
John Frame, *A History of Western Philosophy and Theology*, pgs. 1-41 [B-I]
Ronald Nash, *Worldviews in Conflict* [B]
C.S. Lewis, *Miracles* [B]
Francis Schaeffer, *The God Who Is There* [B]
Vern Poythress, *Symphonic Theology* [I-A]

3

THE TRUTH IS OUT THERE: APPROPRIATE OBJECTIVITY

Sanctify them in the truth; your word is truth. – John 17:17

We left the last chapter on a cliff hanger: how can we reason with someone from another **worldview**? Can we be sure ours is true? Yet, common sense already answers this question: some worldviews simply must be wrong! Surely it cannot be as equally true that jumping in front of a car will not kill me as is my certainty that it will. It cannot be as equally true—or even as likely to be true—to claim that I am the only being in existence as to claim that my senses are trustworthy and others exist.

We are not left with common sense alone, however, for Scripture tells us clearly that truth is out there, and his name is Yahweh. According to Jesus, he is "the way, *the Truth*, and the life" (John 14:6, emphasis added) and his word is truth (John 17:17). God is true, and in him is no lie (Num 23:19, Rom 3:1-8). God cannot deceive—he does not lie—nor can he be wrong: he is Truth, and he knows all things (Job 38-41; Isa 40:28, 46:10). If God is true, if truth is his thoughts, his interpretation of his creation and himself, then truth is whatever corresponds—however partially[1]—to his thoughts. If God's thoughts are what is true, and any truth we have is an interpretation of the world and God that corresponds to his thoughts, we can define truth in

---

[1] This an important clarification: our thoughts never fully correspond to God's. His thoughts are different both in quality (He knows all things because He created them; we know what we know because we experience them) and extent (we know some things partially; He knows all things wholly).

this way: *Truth is an appropriate interpretation of reality, one that corresponds—partially yet without error—to God's interpretation.*[2] An interpretation is true not if it is complete but if it contains no error—nothing contrary to God's interpretation. Knowing what truth is and that humans can apprehend it, we need to ask, how do we go about gaining it? How do we acquire truth and be sure that it corresponds to God's thoughts?

We arrive at a right interpretation, and so truth, by perceiving the creation and God's revelation in Scripture through the senses he has given us and interpreting it through the lens of his revelation.[3] We know that our interpretations correspond to his by interacting with his world, trusting in the senses he has given us; by thinking about his world, trusting the minds he has given us; and doing all this in submission to his verbal revelation.

If truth is available to human beings, we are then left with the problem of other worldviews, how we explain their existence. The answer from Scripture is that human beings "by their unrighteousness suppress the truth" (Rom. 1:18). If all humans reject the truth as God has revealed it, the question we should ask is not why other worldviews exist but why there is any truth at all in other worldviews. There is truth in other worldviews because this unrighteous suppression of truth is not complete: God is gracious and does not allow human sin to abound to the extent that it possibly could.

This gracious act of restraint is often called common grace: this aspect of common grace is not explicitly taught in Scripture, but Romans 2 (especially verse 14) and Acts 17:28 indicate that despite their sinful suppression of truth, someone who is not a Christian maintains some truth in their worldview. This is verified by our own experience (which Scripture also affirms, see ch. 10).

We see, then, that truth exists, and it is found through God's revelation

---

[2] Defining truth in this way implicitly rejects the typical ontology of the Western tradition. Traditionally, Western philosophy has held to various forms of metaphysical realism, the belief that ideas or truths have a real existence. By identify truth as an interpretation of reality, I have inextricably linked truth to the interpreting subject, to the mind that interpret. For more on this, see Chapter 10 of this volume and Volume 3, *The Gift of Seeing* on **abstraction**.

[3] God has revealed himself in the created order, but truth implies an interpretation: "a rock" is not a truth, but "there are rocks" is. Therefore, it seems that God's revelation in nature must have two parts: the creation of *right functioning faculties* to interpret the *clear evidence of Himself within the created world*.

in Scripture and through interpreting his creation. We see also that worldviews abound and that each worldview has its own test of truth—an atheist will surely not concede that God's interpretation is the measure of truth! Therefore, we need a way to reason with someone who disagrees with us on such a fundamental level. We may do so in three ways: by showing them that our own worldview is true; by showing that their own worldview is false *according to its own criteria of truth*; and by appealing to the knowledge of the truth they have rebelliously suppressed.[4] Considering these three ways by which those of differing worldviews can interact serves our purpose by revealing a way beyond the impasse of relativism, showing us that worldviews may be right or wrong and that this can be shown.

Furthermore, understanding how to rationally defend or criticize a worldview helps us to be firm in our faith, to understand the differences we see in the views around us, and to navigate difficult **apologetic** discussions—intellectually presenting the Christian faith.[5] That being said, let us consider three ways we can interact with other worldviews.

A. Showing a Worldview to Be True

A worldview can only be proven false if it self-destructs or true if it is self-verifying. Defensively, we then need to show that our worldview is self-verifying, not self-destructing. Three tests help us here. All worldviews function to interpret their authority and the world, and so guide our actions. A worldview must therefore 1) be self-consistent on its own terms, 2) it must appropriately correspond to reality as interpreted on its own terms, and 3) it must be functional on its own terms.

First, a worldview must be self-consistent. A self-consistent worldview is not one in which there are no tensions but in which tensions are explained by that worldview. The Bible contains tensions, yet it tells us to expect them because God has all truth and has not shared it with us (e.g. Deut 29:29). If

---

[4] These three categories are roughly parallel to John Frame's three approaches to apologetic discussion: defence, offense, and proof. Cf. *Apologetics: A Justification of Christian Belief*.

[5] By apologetics, we do not imply being apologetic—sorry for our beliefs. Apologetics comes from a Greek word meaning to make a defense (cf. 1 Peter 3:15). Apologetics is sometimes defined as the rational defence of the Christian faith.

a worldview says at one point "this is true" and at another point, "this is not true," without an explanation of what has changed, this is self-destructive. For example, the Koran says that the *Injeel*, the books about Jesus, is God's word;[6] yet elsewhere it denies the crucifixion and resurrection of Jesus Christ, which the New Testament, particularly the Gospels or *Injeel*, affirms. Of course, the Muslim will claim that the New Testament has been corrupted—that it is not the true *Injeel*—yet they have no reason from history or the Koran to claim this. This is an internal contradiction. In contrast, the Bible commands food laws in one part and repudiates them in another, but it explains that this is not a contradiction. Instead, it is a change in **covenant**.

Second, a worldview must correspond to reality as it interprets it. The Bible teaches that it is God's Word and thus absolutely authoritative. Its own testimony is our primary reason for believing it to be so, but we can support its claim by showing that it claims this consistently. Subjectively, we can support the Bible's internal claim by an appeal to the Holy Spirit's attestation: the Bible claims that God's people will hear his voice, recognize him speaking in Scripture (cf. John 10:27, 2 Cor 4:1-6). I testify that I experience this when I read it. Yet this will not persuade someone who does not yet recognize God's voice. Because a worldview must correspond to reality as it interprets it, we can show how the claims the Bible makes about reality—objective morality, truth, a beginning of creation, certain historical facts, etc.—correspond to reality as we experience it. An atheist will of course object to our interpretation of reality, but we can argue that if you assume the Biblical worldview, all our experience is completely consistent with it. If a worldview says something about reality that its other claims about reality contradict, this is also a form of self-destruction. If a worldview says, "trust your senses" and then denies the existence of other people, it has denied the first claim with the second.

Third, a worldview must be liveable on its own terms: if it says you are to deny causality and so step in front of moving cars but simultaneously calls you to preserve your own life at all costs, this is a self-destruction in liveableness. That is, to follow both precepts consistently would end your life and contradict both.

---

[6] To be exact, the Muslim's claim that the *Injeel* was a book given *by* Jesus, yet it is clear that what is being referred to is what we today call the Gospels or maybe the entire New Testament, the books *about* Jesus. E.g. Sura 5:46, 47a; Sura 57:27.

As a Christian, then, we show that the Bible claims its own authority and we give examples of how it does so consistently, answering objections with Biblical answers. We also show how it gives a consistent interpretation of our world and that it is liveable (on its own terms). Doing this gives us great confidence in the Bible, in conjunction with its self-attestation, yet is rarely persuasive.

The strongest internal claim the Bible makes is that it is the only accurate, or true, interpretation of reality. That is, the Bible claims that every other worldview is wrong and therefore will fail at some point. We can thus sketch what the Biblical worldview is, answer some objections, and then focus on the next two forms of worldview evaluation. Going on the offensive, we show how all other worldviews self-destruct and we appeal to the knowledge of God that all people have. In the latter case, we make arguments from creation that presuppose the Biblical worldview but find resonance in the inconsistent remnants of this worldview others have.

B. Showing a Worldview to be Self-Destructing

If everyone has exchanged the truth for a lie, and the Bible is true, every other view must be (somewhat of) a lie. The question is, how is it a lie—how does it self-destruct? Finding the lie takes great patience and discernment. We need to listen to another person, truly understand what they believe, and see how their rejection of a Biblical truth leads them into contradiction. Now, showing someone a contradiction in their worldview takes great wisdom and gentleness, so identification is only half the battle. Consider, though, an example from a Postmodern worldview. Many who would accept the relativity of moral and religious belief hold to science and reason as valid ways of knowing, valid tools for understanding reality. However, neither reason nor empirical science is sufficient to affirm the existence of anything outside oneself—or even a definition of the "self."

Let me explain. The Bible tells us that God made the world around us and gave us trustworthy senses. The Bible teaches the existence of more than just me; it teaches the existence of God and fellow human beings. This all makes sense, and it would be ridiculous to deny it! Because the primary authority of our worldview tells us others exist and our senses, which are trustworthy, tell us others exist, we have good reason to believe this. However, if we assume a worldview where the individual and his or her mind is the final authority, the measure of truth, then it is *unreasonable* to believe in the existence of others.

Beginning with reason, as Descartes did, can you prove anything outside of your mind? What principle of reason would allow you to prove that I exist: could I not just be a figment of your imagination and this book the product of a dream? Beginning with **empiricism**, what reason do we have for believing that our senses correspond to reality? What test can we run that does not assume the existence of trustworthy senses? Assuming the authority of the self, nothing in our mind or experience justifies us in trusting our senses. If we cannot trust our senses, we have no reason to believe anything exists but the self—which we know exists only because the very act of denying our own existence proves it (remember Descartes, "I think therefore I am"). Yet, even the sort of "existence" we have is up for grabs.

Any definition of self that moves beyond "I think" relies on the senses. Do I have a body or not? How would I know if I did from my mind or unreliable senses? How, based on a worldview where the self is the ultimate authority, would someone prove that he or she is not a computer program, a brain in a jar, or even a bumblebee? If someone told us we were a human being in a physical world populated by human beings, how could we know he or she was not a figment of our imagination or a program with the very purpose of assuaging our doubts? If the self is the ultimate authority, this is where we find ourselves—yet Christians need not fear this end.

God has not left us without a testimony. He has spoken and affirmed our senses, our minds, and the existence of others. Praise our Lord that he has not left us without a witness, that he has not left us to our autonomous selves, adrift on an open sea, floating as if through an infinite nothing!

Postmodern worldviews are equally self-destructing in the area of morality. Most Postmoderns would not subscribe to purely relativistic morality—something is right because you desire it—but tend to pick and choose what aspects of morality they want to adhere to. In Canada, one's physical sex is not considered significant in identifying one's gender, and Christian sexual ethics are dismissed. Yet, those who lobby for legislation protecting the LGBTQ+ community are the same community who respond (rightfully!) with outrage to the many sexual assaults and rapes reported on university campuses. In one case, they reject one standard of morality—the Christian understanding of sexuality—and lobby for legislation that requires radical sexual tolerance. In another case, they defend a different aspect of Christian morality. What reason does their worldview give for rejecting Christian sexuality while enforcing sexual ethics regarding rape? By what standard do they do so? Their worldview provides no such standard.

This has long been recognized as the problem with naturalism, the belief that only nature exists: it gives no reason for morality, no standard by which to measure one action as wrong and another as right. These two examples reveal some ways that postmodern worldviews—the most prevalent worldviews in Western society—self-destruct. Yet these are not the only tools in our tool belt. If someone was completely consistent and reasonable, then showing such flaws would always be effective, yet this is not always the case. The reason for this is that no non-Christian worldview is completely consistent. No one is completely successful in suppressing the truth of God. This is why some truth can be found in these worldviews.

C. Appealing to the Truth Suppressed in Unrighteousness

A 20th century Christian theologian named Cornelius Van Til would illustrate this worldview-borrowing by picturing a child being held up by her father and slapping him in the face: it is only because the father holds the child up that she is able to attack him. The only reason a non-Christian worldview can disagree with and assail the Christian worldview is because they are resting on its foundation: they are living off borrowed capital. If the Christian worldview is the truth that has been exchanged for a lie, and this exchange is only partial, then what remains of the truth is a remnant of the Christian worldview. This means that there is common ground between a Christian and a Non-Christian. This common ground is not found in some neutral, objective fact on which both can agree. In fact, there are none: all facts are interpreted by a worldview. Any common ground is found in the vestiges of Christian truth, in the knowledge of God, that lays suppressed and buried within other worldviews. By drawing on this common ground, showing how all creation points to the Creator, we can—as the Holy Spirit works on their heart—bring this truth uncomfortably to the surface. This is where traditional apologetic arguments can be quite helpful.

The 18th century empiricist David Hume conclusively showed that on non-Christian assumptions—that the self was the ultimate authority—

traditional Christian apologetic arguments failed.[7] For example, we often argue that creation has an element of design in it. This makes sense when we assume as part of our worldview a designer, yet Hume pointed out that "designer" in this argument is not God but a mere human, for this is the only cause we know to produce such effects. If the design argument proves any designer, argued Hume, the designer is a finite being like humans. Furthermore, we could observe that "design" means something completely different for a non-Christian than for a Christian. For the former, it is an amazingly improbably coincidence, yet perfectly possible—for God is already ruled out as an explanation. His foot cannot be allowed to slip through the door![8] In contrast, for the Christian, design is evidence for the designer. Two different worldviews furnish the same empirical observations with different interpretations. Yet, the design argument makes intuitive sense and has convinced some people of the truth of Christianity. From what we have seen, it is evident why it sometimes succeeds. If even the most ardent atheist is suppressing the knowledge of the truth of God, then evidence of a designer corresponds to that suppressed belief. If the Holy Spirit graciously grants a repentant heart, such an argument exposes the truth being denied and reveals our rebellion.

The same can be said for the cosmological argument, which has come to the forefront in Christian apologetics through the work of William Lane Craig. Craig and others argue in this way:

---

[7] David Hume, *Dialogues Concerning Natural Religion*, Dover Philosophical Classics (Mineola, N.Y.: Dover Publications, 2006).

[8] The Atheist Richard C. Lewontin once made this startling admission in a review for *The New York Review of Books*, "Our willingness to accept scientific claims that are against common sense is the key to an understanding of the real struggle between science and the supernatural. We take the side of science *in spite* of the patent absurdity of some of its constructs, *in spite* of its failure to fulfill many of its extravagant promises of health and life, *in spite* of the tolerance of the scientific community for unsubstantiated just-so stories, because we have a prior commitment, a commitment to materialism. It is not that the methods and institutions of science somehow compel us to accept a material explanation of the phenomenal world, but, on the contrary, that we are forced by our *a priori* adherence to material causes to create an apparatus of investigation and a set of concepts that produce material explanations, no matter how counter-intuitive, no matter how mystifying to the uninitiated. Moreover, that materialism is absolute, for we cannot allow a Divine Foot in the door." (No emphasis added.)

- we know that everything that begins to exist has a cause (e.g. a car is made, a baby is conceived),
- the universe we live in began to exist,
- therefore, the universe we live in has a cause.[9]

We must then ask, what could be the cause of the world? It is then argued that only God, a being without a beginning, is the adequate cause for the world.[10] On atheistic presuppositions, Hume takes issue with this argument as well.

He wonders if the world itself could not be necessary—like the laws of mathematics—or if a chain of such causes itself needs an explanation. From experience, we know that a cause needs an explanation (if a car moves, we are right to ask why), but we have no experience of an infinite succession of causes, so experience cannot show that God is required to explain the world. Many atheists argue similarly today, suggesting that our world is one of many universes that come in and out of existence eternally.[11] Yet, as with the design

---

[9] John Frame argues that the arguments for the impossibility of an infinite universe, necessitating that the universe has a beginning, only show that the idea of a infinite series is hard to grasp, not that it is inherently impossible. If we agree with Frame, he proffers the Aquinian cosmological argument as a more persuasive alternative. Namely, even an infinite universe requires a cause: everything that exists requires an explanation for its existence, the universe exists, therefore it needs an explanation. God is not an exception to this rule because He has the property of aseity; according to His own testimony, He is the explanation of His own existence. John Frame, "'Infinite Series,'" *Frame-Poythress.Org*, last modified May 21, 2012, accessed July 28, 2021, https://frame-poythress.org/infinite-series/.

[10] Craig and others often argue from the Big Bang to show the world has a beginning. Even if we are not convinced that the Big Bang is a Biblically valid explanation of creation, we could argue from the atheist's belief in the Big Bang that the world had a beginning ("even your own belief proves my point"). Cf. William Lane Craig, *The Kalam Cosmological Argument* (Eugene, OR: Wipf and Stock Publishers, 2000); William Lane Craig, *On Guard: Defending Your Faith With Reason And Precision* (Colorado Springs, Colo.: David C. Cook, 2010).

This argument at first does not prove that the world had an uncaused cause—a Creator who is Himself not created—yet they argue that eventually you need one, so logically it is best to explain the creation of the world by God (using the philosophical principle of parsimony).

[11] We could go beyond Hume and argue that if our self is the ultimate criteria of truth, and the primary data for logic comes from senses, we have no experience of space and time coming into existence (we have only experienced the coming into existence of things existing in space and time), so "cause" in the above argument is

argument, this argument is often convincing. Though it does not make complete sense within an atheistic worldview, it does within the Christian worldview, so it may resonate with the truth that is suppressed in unrighteousness.

In this chapter we have seen that despite the subjective aspect of all knowing—even though interpretation is an inevitable and essential aspect of knowing—truth is out there; his name is Yahweh. The teaching of Scripture (what I have been calling the Christian worldview) gives us a solid foundation from which we can know truth and explains how we can interact with those who have a different worldview. We have seen three different ways that we as Christians could interact with those who have a different worldview. Yet such a discussion is most effective when all of the above are appropriately considered: when we consider how Christianity explains the world, how non-Christian views do not, and how the created world testifies to God.

In this chapter's discussion, we have seen that at the heart of the struggle between Christianity and non-Christian worldviews is the question of authority. It is here that Christianity is shown to be strongest and where its answer to the epistemological crisis of the West is found, and so it is to the question of authority that we must now turn.

Transcendental Arguments

I would be remiss if I did not mention the transcendental argument in this context. Among certain circles, the primary—sometimes the only—apologetic argument for the Christian faith is an argument which Cornelius Van Til called the transcendental argument. For our purposes, we can consider the transcendental argument as a specific way of bringing together the three methods above to interact with a non-Christian worldview.

Essentially, a transcendental argument argues for the truth of Christianity by showing that the Christian worldview is the

---

not precise enough to make a logically sound argument. The argument "equivocates," uses two different meanings for its key word.

presupposition of rational thought, so that denying the Christian worldview actually affirms it. That is, a transcendental argument for Christianity argues that to be able to deny Christianity you have to assume it is true, that the very possibility of denying or affirming anything presupposes that Christianity is right. It is not, therefore, an argument that tries to prove one piece or another of the Christian worldview, such as the resurrection or existence of God, but an argument that seeks to show that reality, knowledge, morality, etc. only make sense if the Christian worldview is true. In the words of Cornelius Van Til,

> the best and only possible proof for the existence of [the sovereign God of Christianity] is that his existence is required for the uniformity of nature and for the coherence of all things in the world. We cannot *prove* the existence of beams underneath a floor if by proof we mean that they must be ascertainable in the way that we can see the chairs and tables of the room. But the very idea of a floor as the support of tables and chairs requires the idea of beams that are underneath. But there would be no floor if no beams were underneath.... Even non-Christians presuppose [the truth of Christian theism] while they verbally reject it. They need to presuppose the truth of Christian theism in order to account for their own accomplishments.[i]

Traditionally, the transcendental argument has been presented in this *objective* sense: unless the Christian God exists, reason is impossible. Or, to deny the Christian God, someone must actually assume He exists. However, in this book I am developing a transcendental argument of a different sort, what we could call the *subjective transcendental argument*.

That is, the traditional transcendental argument considers what has to be the case, whether you acknowledge it or not. Even though an atheist denies God, their very denial presupposes that he exists. Therefore, your act of denying God demonstrates that he exists. It is an argument from any point in a worldview to the necessity of God's existence. I am arguing in this book that God's existence is not only objectively necessary for knowledge but subjectively necessary. That is, I am arguing that apart from faith in God and submission to him, there is no subjective ground for knowledge; the only option other than faith in God, if one were to be consistent, is complete scepticism. The only way to reasonably uphold reason is to submit to God as he has revealed himself in his word. The other option, which most non-Christian philosophers accept, is to build reason on an irrational basis. For example, many forms of foundationalism say that belief in the reliability of the senses is properly basic, it is "rational" for anyone to believe it. However, they are unable to give any rational reason for the belief that the reliability of the senses is rational. So instead of arguing for the existence of God, I am arguing for faith and submission to God.

[i] *The Defense of the Faith*, 2nd Edition (Presbyterian and Reformed, 1963), 103.

Further Reading

Cornelius Van Til, *Christian Theistic Evidences* [A]
Cornelius Van Til, *The Defense of the Faith* [A]
David Hume, *Dialogues Concerning Natural Religion* [A]
Francis Schaeffer, *He Is There and He is not Silent* [B]
Gregory Bahnsen, *Van Til's Apologetic: Readings and Analysis* [A][12]
John Frame, *The Doctrine of the Knowledge of God* [I]
*John Frame, *Apologetics: A Justification of Christian Belief* [B]
John Frame, "Infinite Series," https://frame-poythress.org/infinite-series/ [I]
Paul Chamberlain, *Can We Be Good Without God?* [B]
William Lane Craig, *On Guard: Defending Your Faith with Reason and Precision* [B-I]
William Lane Craig, *The Kalam Cosmological Argument* [I]

[12] Bahnsen's treatment is helpful and makes Van Til's thought more accessible. However, Bahnsen's development of Van Til moves in several rather unhelpful directions.

—Part 2—
The Standard of Epistemology

A WORD FROM BEYOND: APPROPRIATE AUTHORITY

Oh, the depth of the riches and wisdom and knowledge of God! How unsearchable are his judgments and how inscrutable his ways!

> For who has known the mind of the Lord,
>   or who has been his counselor?
> Or who has given a gift to him
>   that he might be repaid?

> For from him and through him and to him are all things.
> To him be glory forever. Amen. – Romans 11:33-36

At the heart of a **worldview**, and the centre of the conflict between Christian and non-Christian worldviews, stands the question of final authority. When all the evidence is in, who gets the final say? What is the ruler we use to measure truth?

There are ultimately only two options available to us. According to the Bible, there are two fundamental types of existence, two groups that encompass all that exists: there are the Creator and the creature. The question of authority must rest in one of these two spheres: is the standard of truth to be found in the Creator or the created order?

By exchanging the glory and truth of God for a lie, choosing to worship the creature instead of the Creator, all non-Christian worldviews find their ultimate authority in the creature. In Modernity, the standard was thought to be objective reality—just the facts. It was thought that humans could objectively interact with the world and arrive at the same conclusions, that the universe provided objective truth to those who would observe it without bias. We saw already that this authority failed: there are no uninterpreted facts! For this reason, one authority remains, the self.

Postmodernity places final authority in the self, for it is a person who provides the interpretation of reality. This is seen most clearly in morality, as legislation is based ever more on individuals' feelings and self-perception (i.e. something is wrong if it makes me feel bad). The authority of the self is also seen in learning, where personal response and creativity are emphasized over the passing on of truth. In reading, clear communication from the writer to the reader is forsaken for the reader's response. In empirical science, authority ultimately rests on the observer's interpretation. Decisions to accept or reject a hypothesis ultimately come down to subjective proof. "Does it convince me or not" is the pressing question of the Postmodern mind. It is often not the truth that is found convincing but relativism that sets aside absolute claims (e.g. Yahweh exists) for personal convictions.

Christianity, however, identifies the final authority for morality and truth in God, not humanity or creation. The creation requires interpretation—it is not objective—but man's interpretation of it is not the measure of truth. God's interpretation is. This is, in fact, where the Christian worldview stands forth most evidently as the truth. The Bible claims that God is the standard of all truth and that all things have their existence and meaning in relation to him. He is the originator and sustainer of all the creation and all of it is created for his glory. This means that in submission to him, by believing the truth about God, we can understand him and the creation he has made.

On the other hand, this also means that apart from such a posture of submission, in rebellion against him, consistent and rational thought is impossible. Any truth we retain represents our failure to abandon God consistently. We depend on his support to rebel against him. If final authority is given to the creature, then knowledge is impossible. We are left in the same place our culture is now, with no standard of truth or morality beyond the self. To regain our footing, then, we need to regain our place in the world. We need to see ourselves as creatures in the Creator's worlds, subjects of the Creator's decrees and recipients of his gracious gifts. God has not left himself without witnesses in this world, nor has he been silent. By leaving his distinct stamp on the created order, giving people the cognitive tools necessary to read it, and by revealing himself in the Word, he has made truth readily available to all who would submit themselves before him.

In the following chapters, we will look at God as the final authority for knowing, and how creation and Scripture function to present us his authoritative interpretation of reality. Beginning with creation (chapter 4), we will then consider Scripture (chapter 5), and conclude by looking at the ethical implications that result if God is our authority for knowing (chapter 6).

Further Reading

Francis Schaeffer, *The Great Evangelical Disaster* [B]
* John Frame, *The Doctrine of the Word of God* [I]
* John Frame, *The Doctrine of the Knowledge of God* [I]

5

THE COVENANTAL REVELATION OF CREATION

> For what can be known about God is plain to them, because God has shown it to them. For his invisible attributes, namely, his eternal power and divine nature, have been clearly perceived, ever since the creation of the world, in the things that have been made. So they are without excuse. – Romans 1:19-20

From the beginning of creation, God has revealed himself to his creatures through direct spoken communication, through prophets, and through the written Scriptures. God has revealed himself in this way, yet he has not done so to everyone. But we have already seen that God has not left himself without a witness, that the very creation reveals him to everyone. This creation revelation fills two important functions according to the Bible. First, God's revelation in creation is sufficient to reveal his existence and character. Creation is an abiding testimony to his glorious power and character, giving God glory through its testimony and leading those who interpret the creation into awestruck praise (Ps 19; Acts 14:17) or rebellion. For this reason, all humans are without excuse for their rebellion against God (Rom 1:18-32). Creation also testifies to the appropriate response humans should take towards it (Rom 1:20-23, 2:14-16).

The creation does this, and it does so authoritatively: humans are held accountable for their failure to respond to God as he is revealed in the creation (Rom 1:18-32) and to act appropriately within the creation (Rom 2:12-16). It is important to recognize that these functions are covenantal: the created order guides men and women in the way appropriate to the **covenant** under which they relate to the Creator.[1]

For Adam and Eve and all their descendants, this revelation would lead them in appropriate worship and service of Yahweh. Abraham and his descendants were guided by creation revelation as interpreted in light of God's verbal revelation to fulfil the purpose he had given them. With the coming of Jesus, creation—or general—revelation guides his people in the fulfilment of the great commission, guiding us in worship, evangelism, and everyday life (e.g. it gives us common ground for evangelism, leading us to glorify God for his handiwork, and guides us in applying the Word of God to everyday life in the created order).

The purpose of this chapter is to unpack and explain three interdependent ways the creation reveals God and his ways so that these functions are fulfilled. We will consider the revelation of God in the testimony of the created world, the revelation of God in human discernment, and the revelation of God in humanity's mental faculties.

Two considerations must be kept in mind if we are to properly account for God's revelation as we experience it, namely the Fall and the resulting curse. Though the world was originally created as an efficient bearer of this revelation, it has now been corrupted by the curse. Therefore, though it is a sufficient revelation to achieve its purposes, it is often misinterpreted.

A. Creation Revelation in Testimony of the Creation

According to David in Psalm 19,

> The heavens declare the glory of God,
>   and the sky above proclaims his handiwork.
> Day to day pours out speech,
>   and night to night reveals knowledge.
> There is no speech, nor are there words,
>   whose voice is not heard.

---

[1] A covenant is a formalized relationship between multiple parties. A covenant is often companied by an oath to follow written or spoken parameters that outline the covenant, but this is not always present. A Christian marriage is a contemporary example of a covenant.

> Their voice goes out through all the earth,
> and their words to the end of the world. (vv. 1-4)

Clearly there is something about the created order that testifies to God in such a way that brings him glory and leads an observer to praise him.

It is necessary for us to consider how it does this and, if it is so clear, why so many people appear to miss it, why they do not believe in God. We saw in early chapters that Modernity thought knowledge was objective, independent of the one knowing. We also saw that Modernity was wrong on this count: the world we observe does not offer us truth apart from an interpretation. Realizing that truth is the combination of the observed world interpreted by an individual through an appropriate **worldview**, leading to a true interpretation, helps us answer these questions.

Applying these observations to creation, we can say that God's revelation in nature is a combination of objects that testify to his glory and an interpretation that recognizes these objects for what they are, testimonies to his glory. It is evident that a rock does not have letters inscribed on its side reading, "GOD CREATED ME." Yet when I walk along the beach near my home in Vancouver, I can't help but praise God as I pick up rocks and admire their many colours and unique features. A rock is something beautiful, and when I interpret it for what it truly is—a product of God's ingenuity—I see that its beauty reflects the beautiful glory of Yahweh, its Creator.

Creation is glorious. It is complex and beautiful. If we see this beauty within a worldview that recognizes God as the creator of these beautiful things, we identify this created glory as a reflection of he who is truly glorious. But if our worldview deliberately suppresses this truth, the created glory is taken as an end to itself. It becomes an object of worship instead of something pointing beyond itself. It is this exchange, of the Creator for his creature, that led Carl Sagan to write,

> In its encounter with Nature, science invariably elicits a sense of reverence and awe. The very act of understanding is a celebration of joining, merging, even if on a very modest scale, with the magnificence of the Cosmos.[2]

---

[2] Carl Sagan, *The Demon-Haunted World: Science as a Candle in the Dark*, 1st Ed. (New York: Ballantine Books, 1997), 29..

When the Creator is rejected, his very attributes attested to in creation are attributed to the creature, in this case, "the Cosmos." Though it is perverted by human rebellion, creation should lead us to glorify God. God has not, however, left us only with a testimony to what is. He has also revealed in creation the appropriate way to act within and towards it.

B. Creation Revelation in the Morality of the Created Order

Creation revelation does not fulfil its function if it only shows us what is—that Yahweh exists—and not what we ought to do about this truth. Romans 1:18-32 does not just say that humans know God from the creation; it says that we are all held guilty for rebelling against God's revelation in creation. Part of this revelation, then, is the revelation of how we are to respond to the revelation of God's character in creation.

This revelation cannot stop there, however, for after listing all the sins that result from their disordered worship, Paul says that all humans have known "God's righteous decree," that these things are wrong and are deserving of condemnation (Rom 1:32). This explains why several times in this chapter Paul identifies some sinful actions as contrary to nature, contrary to the created order (e.g. v. 26, cf. 1 Cor 11:14). Paul affirms this in Romans 2:12-16 when he writes that the gentiles, who have not received the Law (the covenantal legislation in the books of Moses, Genesis-Deuteronomy), demonstrate by their works that they know the law (God's created legislation). They show that they know this law, yet he says that their discernment of it—their conscience—is confused, giving a conflicting account (Rom 2:15). What we see is that God has given to human beings revelation not only of the appropriate interpretation of the created world but also of the appropriate response they should take to God's creation.

As we noted in the last section, this created moral sense is covenantal. God has granted every human knowledge of the law governing his covenant with creation—the covenant he enacted with all humans in the first chapters of Genesis (Genesis 1-3, then Genesis 9). We have all, however, exchanged the truth of God for a lie and therefore exchanged his moral standard for our own. This moral revelation is corrupted by human rebellion, leading to even further sin. We could identify this revelation as discernment. This moral revelation is the knowledge necessary to determine the appropriate response to God's revelation in creation, to the world as rightly interpreted through the Christian worldview. It is closely tied to the objective side of revelation, the created world, and to the subjective side, the human interpretive faculties. This subjective side is what remains for us to consider.

C. Creation Revelation in Human Faculties

We saw in the first section of this book that knowledge is not purely objective, something found independently of an interpreting mind. For this reason, our account of created revelation must take both the subjective and objective sides of knowledge into account. We have already considered the objective side, those things being interpreted, so now we consider an area of created revelation not always addressed, human faculties (i.e. the senses and mind).

If created objects and the events in which they are involved testify to God's existence and character, it is because they are interpreted in a way appropriate to their actual nature: they have a quality—let's call it "createdness"—that testifies to God and need to be interpreted by a worldview that recognizes such a category. When Romans 1:25 tells us that all human beings have exchanged the truth of God for a lie, it is not telling us they have exchanged objects that testify to God for objects that do not. No, they have traded the appropriate interpretation of the created order for one that perverts its true nature. The creation was made by God, but they consider it uncreated. It points to the glory of God, but they identify this glory as a property of the creation and not its Creator.

That we can recognize God in the created order (even though we all at first reject him) reveals that we all are born with the appropriate interpretive grid for interpreting creation. This is obvious at one level, God created us with minds to understand, ears to hear, and eyes to see. He has given men and women the appropriate physical tools necessary to interpret the created order. These are necessary parts of God's created revelation, giving us the physical capacity to interact with it. But God must have granted humans something else to interpret the data received from our senses appropriately.

I do not mean the astounding ways our brain interprets light signals so that we see a picture—amazing as that is—but the mental software, the worldview, that allows us to take that picture and give it meaning. Consider a bee; it is not enough for us to see it in order to interact with it. To identify it, to know how to respond to it, we must have the appropriate pieces of data in place already. We must have something philosophers call **innate ideas**, fundamental assumptions that allow us to interpret the world but cannot be learned directly from the world. These ideas are needed before we can even begin to interpret the world.[3]

Part of created revelation, then, are important aspects of what we have been calling the Christian worldview, the interpretive beliefs necessary to look at the created world, give glory to Yahweh for it, and to then act in worshipful submission towards him. This involves the beliefs that God exists, that he is the Creator, that he is good, that he is faithful (and so **the law of non-contradiction,** see above), etc. However, if God has given humanity the necessary worldview to recognize and obey him from their birth, we must explain why many deny his existence and most do not follow him.

God has given humans the necessary interpretive framework to interpret the world and to recognize and worship him, yet humans have intentionally repudiated this gift and adopted a lie. In the words of Romans 1:18, we all "by [our] unrighteousness suppress the truth." Furthermore, according to Romans 8:6-7, the sinful mind cannot obey God. Romans 2:15 testifies to the confused conscience of human beings. We see, therefore, that the human mind has been corrupted by the Curse. Furthermore, the Curse has subjected our bodies to futility with the rest of the creation (cf. Rom 8:20), so none of our minds functions ideally. Yet this futility is not the fundamental problem that causes us to deny God and his commands.

The primary reason that humans fail to interpret creation correctly is that we are in rebellion against God. We suppress his truth and proceed to build an interpretive framework—a worldview—apart from the basic assumptions of his character and creating action. It is this denial of the right worldview that ultimately leads to the epistemological crisis we find ourselves in today. Our society's intellectual problems, then, are primarily moral problems. Therefore, salvation is as much about the salvation of our minds as it is about our souls. Because our epistemological problem is ultimately a moral problem, we need God's intervention—we need God's Word—to fix it.

---

[3] We talked a bit about innate ideas in ch. 2 and will again in ch. 10.

Further Reading

John Frame, *Systematic Theology*
John Frame, *The Doctrine of the Word of God*

On the Contribution of Objects

It may be worth nuancing the discussion thus far, for Immanuel Kant went a similar direction in his philosophy as I have in this book. However, there are many important distinctions between the approach I have taken and that of Kant.

For Kant, objects had a role to play in knowledge, yet they were ultimately unknowable. That is, at the other end of all experience was a *something*, yet this something was content-less—unknowable. Consider a tree, for example; according to Kant, everything you know about the tree is an imposition of the mind. The tree in itself is only the thing that furnishes an opportunity for knowledge. The problem is this: if knowledge is dependent on the interpreting subject, if there is no knowledge of an object apart from an interpretation, how does the object have *any* influence on knowledge. If shape, colour, smell, sound, etc. are all interpretations of the mind, how can I know what object stands behind these mental interpretations. Ultimately, this "object" is an unknowable entity, the only function of which is to provide an opportunity for experience. In fact, because the object only serves as an opportunity for knowing and contributes nothing to knowledge, it is hard to justify its existence: why should we even say that objects exist outside the mind?

This is an unacceptable conclusion for the Christian, yet it is hard to identify how exactly the object contributes to knowledge—what part it plays in our interpretation of it. On the one hand, we must say that some interpretations of an object are true or false, that the same object cannot be both a tree and a bee, yet it is hard to identify how the object itself is compatible or incompatible with either interpretation. I think, though, that we can tweak the standard illustration of Kant's thought for the role objects play in interpretation and furnish another illustration.

The epistemology of Immanuel Kant is often illustrated with a sausage machine, the machine which presses a formless mass of meat into the shape of a sausage. For Kant, the machine itself is the aspect of the human mind that brings unity to knowledge. An object sends out a signal, a packet of data, which Kant called a *percept*. This percept does not convey any information, instead it is "pressed" through the sausage machine and takes the shape of the mould. The mould of the machine is the innate categories of the human mind—shape, size, smell, taste, purpose, etc. Thus, we automatically take the formless *percept*—the mass of sausage meat—and press it through the mould of our mind, producing sense experience—a formed tube of sausage.

I have argued that our mind has a mould of sorts—it furnishes an interpretation of objects. Yet we cannot say that objects only furnish the opportunity for interpretation; we must account for their contribution to an interpretation, how they can be rightly or wrongly interpreted. Of course, the ultimate standard for interpretation is God's interpretation of the object, yet it is still an interpretation of *an object*. I suggest that we can illustrate the contribution of the object not with a sausage machine—which receives a formless mass of meat—but with two different illustrations.

First, we can illustrate it with a specific children's toy. You may remember from your childhood a toy that I have seen on many occasions, sometimes called a shape and sort. Basically, it is a box with several holes, often colour coded, with matching geometrical blocks—red and blue squares, blue rectangles, green circles, etc. The point of the toy is to match the coloured shape with the appropriate hole. In this analogy, innate ideas form the holes and colours. The data we receive from objects are the coloured shapes. The object suits some holes and not others. A large rock, for example, does not fit into the same hole as a small rock. Our mind functions to marry the proper shapes with the appropriate holes, producing knowledge. If we mismatch the shapes, we lose something in the process—forcing a cube through the circle will shave off parts and sticking the sphere through the cube will over-interpret the sphere. Knowledge only results when the data is put through a hole, yet the data is appropriate to one hole and does not suit another one. This pictures to some extent one aspect of interpretation, the recognition of empirical quantities—shape, size, colour, etc.

However, it is not appropriate for explaining non-empirical

quantities such as meaning, value, and category or relation (e.g. "dog," "cat"), each of which are furnished by an individual's interpretative framework or worldview. In these cases, the object itself does not contribute to our interpretation; our worldview is solely responsible for these values. For example, the act of punching out a co-worker is not in itself right or wrong. It only acquires rightness or wrongness when we relate this act to a network of beliefs about right and wrong and to other pieces of data about the context of the action. The standard for this aspect of interpretation is not measured by the object but by the normative worldview, God's worldview. The accuracy of our interpretation in this regard is dependent upon the accuracy of our worldview and our consistency with it. Thus, we judge interpretation in this sense by measuring our worldview against God's revelation to determine its accuracy and we rely upon reference to the interpretations of others living out this worldview (primarily those recorded in the Bible but also of our peers and those recorded in history) to determine our consistency with it.

Second, we can illustrate the relation of our interpretation to its object by considering a painting. When an artist paints a forest, for example, he does not provide an exact replica of the object. Instead, he offers a particular perspective—an interpretation—of it. He has to be selective in what he includes and excludes; he labours to present a 3D object on a 2D medium. Depending on his purpose, he will shape the painting in one way or another—presenting lighting and such to elicit a specific reaction from the viewer. The point is this: when an artist creates a painting, he interprets the object by intentionally excluding some details, including others, and presenting the whole in a specific way. The end result bears a definite resemblance to but is clearly not the object itself.[i]

In this same way, our mental interpretation of an object is like a painter's painting; it shapes the raw data into a representation of the object that resembles yet is not identical to the object of interpretation. Thus, when two people have knowledge of the same object, their interpretation should resemble one another's because they are interpreting the same object. Yet because there is a subjective element—their particular physical and mental line-of-sight—their interpretations will not be identical. Even those with the same worldview will see and so interpret objects in slightly different ways. In this case, learning the from the interpretation of others can enrich our understanding of the objects we interpret. On this point, see the excursus in Chapter 2 on multi-perspectivalism.

¹This illustration is dependent on the work of my Old Testament teacher, V. Philips Long. See especially his book *The Art of Biblical History*.

6

THE COVENANTAL REVELATION OF GOD'S SPEECH

Your word is a lamp to my feet
and a light to my path. – Psalm 119:105

Trading the truth for a lie has left humanity in a precarious place. We are continually progressing in knowledge and understanding, yet every day the assumptions that make such progress possible are being eroded. A moral standard that would lead a researcher to prioritize truth over money is no longer acknowledged. Faith in the objectivity of knowledge has been lost, and it is more clear each passing day that no real foundation remains for the sweeping truth claims of philosophy and science. In fact, in materialistic philosophy and science, it is considered legitimate to ask if we are only a computer simulation. Some philosophers and scientists answer "probably" and advise that it really may not be so bad to be someone else's computer program:

> "Maybe we're in a simulation, maybe we're not, but if we are, hey, it's not so bad," says David Chalmers.
> "My advice is to go out and do really interesting things," says Max Tegmark, "so the simulators don't shut you down."[1]

---

[1] Chalmers, a philosopher, and Tegmark, a cosmologist, are quoted in a Scientific America article on the debate over the reality of our experience. https://www.scientificamerican.com/article/are-we-living-in-a-computer-simulation/.

If we begin with ourselves as the starting point and ultimate authority for knowing, this is a legitimate, if not the most reasonable, conclusion to draw. The perverse exchange of the truth of God for the lie of human autonomy—that we do not need him and would be better off on our own—leads to these conclusions. This makes sense: if the world is created and governed by God, to think about it apart from him will have catastrophic conclusions.

This hit home for me about ten years ago, after watching the Matrix for the umpteenth time. Lying in bed long into the night, I pondered what it would be like for one of those characters living in the Matrix. How would they know their world was a lie? With a growing sense of discomfort, I could not think of a way they could. I could not figure out a way I could prove I was not in such a simulation.

Considering my senses, I pondered the possibility that they were part of a carefully written program to give the illusion of sense. Assuming that my mind was the final standard of truth and reasoning from my experience, I could not prove with logic that anything outside of myself existed—let alone that I was not a program! Would not a computer program granted self-awareness feel just like I had most of my life? Programmed to believe the experiences flitting through its brain, it would recognize its experience as normal and the truth. At the point of tears, I considered the only way to know that this was not the case, to know that my senses were trustworthy and that I was accurately interpreting my experience.

In the Matrix, it took those from outside, who knew the lie, to enter into the programmed world and offer a different perspective, a different **worldview**. Morpheus confronts Neo with a series of observations, odd things he had always noticed yet never could quite explain, and provides the interpretive key. These things did not make sense because he was not looking at them with the right interpretive lens; he was not considering his world as a computer program.

It dawned on me that night, as I opened my Bible and began to read Genesis 1, that the situation was not nearly as hopeless as I had imagined it to be. As Neo was not left on his own to figure out the lie, I was not left on my own to find confidence in the truth. I was assuming that it was my job to figure the world out, that I was the absolute authority and could trust nothing else but myself. I had bought into the lie of human autonomy. This was not the world the Bible presents, the world created by Yahweh. He created the universe and did not leave himself without a witness. He gave humanity the interpretive faculties to make sense of his world.

When we all fell into sin with Adam, our first parent, Yahweh graciously condescended to speak to his sinful creatures and reveal the truth. God spoke and corrected the lie into which we bought. Without a voice from the outside, we would truly be doomed to a hopeless scepticism. Yet we are not without such a voice. God, in a tremendous act of mercy, has spoken. He has spoken clearly and given us all we need to know him and act rightly before him. While we were lost in the darkness, blindly feeling around for some sort of guide, God provided us with a lamp for our feet. He provided for us light to make clear the path before us (Psalm 119:105).

All our knowledge problems began with rebellion against God, so the solution he provided to this rebellion will provide a solution to our knowledge problems. God has acted since the Fall to bring salvation to his people, to redeem a people for himself from among his rebellious creation. Beginning with Eve and her children, God enacted a plan to bring about the defeat of sin and death and deliver sinners from his righteous wrath against their sin. Beginning with Noah, Abraham, and then Israel, he brought this plan to climactic fruition in Jesus Christ his Son. Through his life, death, and resurrection, Jesus established a way for sinners to be made right with God. He instituted a New Covenant, a new way that humans could relate to their God.

With this **covenant** came a document, a book by which those in covenant with Jesus could know him and how to fulfil his will on earth as they await his return. His life, death and resurrection dealt with our relationship problem, reconciling us to God from whom we were estranged. What remained to be repaired was our knowledge problem. Scripture does not only tell us the good news that Salvation is available in Jesus Christ; it is a covenant document given to legislate God's covenant with us. It is given to repair our rebellious worldview so that we might properly interpret and act within God's world to achieve his purposes.[2]

The Scriptures are given as our primary interpretive key to reality. It presents the Christian worldview so that we can rightly interpret creation and act appropriately within it. God's Word not only tells us about himself and how to follow him, it also tells us everything we need to know about the world he has made so that we can function faithfully within it.

Scripture, to function in this capacity, has properties theologians call authority and inerrancy, sufficiency, and clarity. In other words, Scripture is absolutely true and our final authority. Scripture is sufficient so that we can interpret and act appropriately within God's creation. Finally, Scripture is clear so that we can use it for its intended purposes, so that we might be equipped for everything God has asked of us. For the rest of this chapter, I want to look closer at these properties, seeing how God has provided us in Scripture the answers necessary to make sense of our confused world.

A. The Authority and Inerrancy of Scripture

> But, YHWH is in his holy temple,
> be silent before him all the earth! – Habakkuk 2:20

Authority is ultimately the question of whom we trust. It is the question do we trust ourselves or God? It should be obvious that if God exists, he is the ultimate authority for his creation. As his Word, Scripture bears final authority, authority to govern our thoughts and our interpretations, to tell us how we should act and feel. Biblical authority means that Scripture's words are God's words and so our final standard for interpreting creation and acting within it. By calling the Bible authoritative, we are affirming with all the writers of Scripture that the Bible carries *God's* authority.

That the Bible is authoritative is evident from practically every page of Scripture. It is evident that God the creator and interpreter of all reality is the ultimate authority; therefore, anything He says is authoritative. 2 Timothy 3:16-17 says that all Scripture was breathed out by God, that is, it is his words. Paul here refers specifically to the Old Testament with which Timothy was

---

[2] I unpack this, that Scripture is a covenant document and how to read it as such, in the next volume of this series, *The Gift of Reading Part 1 & 2*.

raised, but Peter goes on to lump Paul's letters into this same category—*inspired* Scripture (2 Pet 3:15-16). The Scriptures are all those books God has given to govern his people in their covenant with him and so encompasses both the Old and New Testaments. All of these books are breathed out by God, his very words.

Peter also says, earlier in 2 Peter, that no prophecy found in Scripture is of the prophet's own interpretation but of the Spirit (2 Pet 1:20-21). (Prophecy refers to all of Scripture, not just texts with messages about the future.) The author of Hebrews also writes that "Long ago, at many times and in many ways, God spoke to our fathers by the prophets, [2]but in these last days he has spoken to us by his Son, whom he appointed the heir of all things, through whom also he created the world" (Heb 1:1-2). God spoke through the prophets, and now has spoken through his Son and, by extension, those whom his Son commissioned (e.g. Gal 1:12).

Some of the Old Testament records the historical speech of God, and when the prophets speak, it is difficult to distinguish between their speech and God's, so close is the connection. But the Bible repeatedly claims that *every* Biblical text, even the Psalms—not just direct speech and the prophets—are spoken by God. The authors, such as David or the prophets, are identified as his means of speaking: for example, "*saying through David* so long afterward… 'Today, if you hear his voice'….[8]For if Joshua had given them rest, *God would not have spoken* of another day" (Heb 4:7-8, emphasis added); "God spoke by the mouth of his holy prophets long ago" (Acts 3:21, cf. Luke 1:70) (cf. Mark 12:36; Acts 1:16, 4:25, 28:25).

Therefore, when we say, "the Scriptures are authoritative," we mean "The Scriptures, as the very words of God, bear his authority." The writers of Scripture are analogous—and this is a very near analogy—to the letter bearers or heralds of a great king. When heralds come to the king's subjects with a message (whether they paraphrase his words or read his words exactly), they come with his authority. Rejecting the words of the king's messengers is a rejection of the words of the king. Spurning the messengers is an insult to him. Doing so would incur the wrath of a king (cf. Matt 21:33-22:14). God is our great king, the King of kings. To reject the prophets of God and their message is to reject God himself (cf. Acts 8:51). As God's very words, the Holy Scriptures are therefore completely authoritative and demand the obedience of all of God's creation.

The authority of God, and so Scripture is ultimate: he is the creator and has unquestionable rights and authority (cf. Job 38-41; Rom 9:15, 20-21), God is also our covenant Lord. He has the authority to give commands, expect obedience, and pour out wrath upon the disobedient, as is attested throughout Scripture. The Bible, then, as God's very words, carries this same authority. This identity between God and his words is so close that David, in Psalm 56, speaks several times about praising God's word (56:4, 10-11). Because Scripture is authoritative in this ultimate sense, we must also maintain that it is inerrant, free from error. Though it may appear as though I have tried to pull a fast one, covering two points under one heading, we must see that inerrancy is not a separate issue from authority. The inerrancy of Scripture is essential to the claim that the Bible is our authority.

If Scripture is God's word, it is trustworthy and inerrant both because God is trustworthy and inerrant (cf. Ps 56, Rom 11:33-36, etc.) *and* because it is absolutely authoritative. That is, if Scripture is absolutely authoritative—bearing God's own authority—it can never be in error, for there is no authority qualified to tell us it is wrong. Think about it: if we wanted to prove God wrong, where would we go? Would we turn to science? Yahweh created the world and all that is in it. He would tell us that we are wrong, maybe tell us the reason we are wrong—perhaps not—and command us to submit (cf. Job 38-41, Hab 2:20).

Would we turn to experience? Yahweh would remind us,

> He who planted the ear, does he not hear?
> He who formed the eye, does he not see? (Ps 94:9)

Or he might say, "But who are you, O man, to answer back to God?" (Rom 9:20). Patiently, he might just lay bare our finitude. He might tell us that we cannot rightly interpret our experience unless we know ourselves perfectly. We cannot even evaluate what is going on in the deepest recesses of our heart and mind; we cannot see what biases are at play. Yet he who is completely omniscient knows the depths of our heart and everything else: how could we dare pit our finite understanding against the infinite depths of his wondrous knowledge. "Where you there," he might ask,

> when I laid the foundation of the earth?

>   Tell me, if you have understanding.
> Who determined its measurements—surely you know!
>   Or who stretched the line upon it?
> On what were its bases sunk,
>   or who laid its cornerstone,
> when the morning stars sang together
>   and all the sons of God shouted for joy?
>
> "Or who shut in the sea with doors
>   when it burst out from the womb,
> when I made clouds its garment
>   and thick darkness its swaddling band,
> and prescribed limits for it
>   and set bars and doors,
> and said, 'Thus far shall you come, and no farther,
>   and here shall your proud waves be stayed'?
>
> Have you commanded the morning since your days began,
>   and caused the dawn to know its place? (Job 38:4-12)

There is nothing in all creation that has the authority to tell the Creator that he is wrong. In the Christian worldview, only God and his creation exist; therefore, God has unquestionable authority. If Scripture is God's words, as it claims throughout, then there is nothing with the authority to show that it is wrong. It, therefore, must be inerrant—something it happily claims for itself (e.g. Isa 40:8; Ps 19:7, 8, 9; 119:43, 89-90, 127-128, 138-140, 151-152, 160, 163; Matt 5:17-18; 24:35; Luke 16:17; John 10:35; 17:17).

This question of authority is what the epistemological crisis of our age finally comes down to: do we trust in the creature or the Creator? We are born trusting ourselves, and this leads us headlong into one disaster after another. It is only by God's gracious mercy that we are not successful in our suppression of his truth. But he has not left us in this state. He has not left us with only a glimmer of light amidst endless darkness. With boundless grace he has entered his creation and made himself known, saving us first from our sinful rebellion and the wrath we deserved on account of it but also from the hopelessness of living without God in his world. Scripture, the solution to our problem of knowledge, is truly a gracious gift.

God has given us a word that we can trust, a word that tells us we can trust our senses, trust our minds, and tells us how we can know him and his world. By freeing us from the trap of human autonomy, his authoritative Word allows us to gain our footing and begin the task of knowing. But knowing that God is our authority and that he has made himself known in Scripture is only helpful in as much as what he has revealed is sufficient for the task at hand.

B. The Sufficiency of Scripture

> All Scripture is breathed out by God and profitable for teaching, for reproof, for correction, and for training in righteousness, that the man of God may be complete, equipped for every good work. – 2 Timothy 3:16-17

Many today claim that Scripture is indeed sufficient, that it is all that is necessary *to accomplish its purpose*, yet they would define that purpose very narrowly. Scripture, some claim, tells us about God and how to obey him, but it does not answer any of the sorts of questions science and philosophy answer.

If this were true, we would be in serious trouble—as I believe we have seen so far. Scripture, in contrast to this contemporary idea, does not so limit itself. The key text for our consideration here is 2 Timothy 3:16-17. Paul writes that all Scripture is spoken by God and so is useful, with the result that God's people might be "equipped for every good work." Some theologians take this narrowly, suggesting that it gives us sufficient "religious" knowledge for following God. Let us consider for a moment, however, what is necessary if we are to be ready for "every good work."

We obviously need to know what works God would have us to do, yet this is not enough. Good works in the Bible are only good in as much as they come from a heart set on God (Luke 6:43-45; Rom 8:6-8; Heb 11:6); therefore, the Bible needs also be sufficient to tell us about God, the Gospel, and the need for faith. Good works need more than this though: to be able to act towards others and the creation in a way appropriate to God's will, we need to be sure that they actually exist. We need to know that we can trust our interpretation of them, that the sense-data coming from eyes and hands is valid, and that the logic we use to apply Scriptural teachings to real-life situations is valid.

Furthermore, if we are to do good works with our eyes set on eternity, we need to know that history will progress and this creation will come to an end at Christ's return. That may not sound significant, yet many religions and philosophies teach that history is a cycle (i.e. it repeats itself for eternity). Indeed, we need to know that history is linear, that it progresses in a straightforward manner, and that the past actually happened if we are to believe that Jesus rose from the dead (cf. 1 Cor 15). These are all areas under contention in the areas of philosophy known as metaphysics, which addresses questions about reality or existence, and **epistemology**. The Bible must provide some answers to such questions, or we will not be adequately equipped for every good work.

When we look at the teaching of Scripture, it is clear that it tells us more than what to do (ethics) and whom we love and serve (the doctrine of God); it tells us how the world began, where it is going, and how we can be sure of what we know. We will consider what the Bible says about logic and our senses in the last section of this book, but observe with me that the Bible is not shy about talking of issues that philosophy and science also discuss (though it addresses them in a very different manner). Philosophy and some fields of science are very interested in the origins of the world, so is Scripture (Gen 1-3, Job 38, etc.). The Philosophy of history considers whether history began and will have an end or will continue in a cyclical fashion; these concerns are addressed by the Biblical authors for various purposes (Heb 9:25-28; 10:1-4, 11-14; 2 Pet 3:1-10). Philosophers also speculate on the different types of existence. The Bible gives us two categories: everything that exists is either the Creator or a creature. History asks many things about historical events which the Bible also discuss, e.g. the life and death of Jesus; the falls of Israel, Assyria, Judah, and Babylon; etc.[3]

Scripture speaks of all these things, and it does so with God's authority. Jesus asked Nicodemus, "If I have told you earthly things and you do not believe, how can you believe if I tell you heavenly things?" (John 3:12) The Bible is as authoritative when it tells us about history and truth as it is when it speaks of Jesus and God the Father. Scripture is authoritative in these areas and tells us about such areas so that we might be equipped for every good

---

[3] For more on how the Bible answers the questions of metaphysics, Volume 3, *The Gift of Seeing*.

work.

The Bible gives us sufficient knowledge of God and his will for us, and it repairs the worldview twisted by our rebellion. Scripture gives us sufficient knowledge of God and his created world to appropriately interpret it, glorify him in response to this interpretation, and act appropriately within it. Scripture is sufficient, yet sufficiency only helps us if Scripture is clear enough for us to understand its sufficient content.

C. The Clarity of Scripture

Your word is a lamp to my feet
and a light to my path. – Psalm 119:105

"In a word: if Scripture is obscure or [ambiguous]," wrote Martin Luther,

> why need it have been brought down to us by act of God? Surely we have enough obscurity and uncertainty within ourselves, without our obscurity and uncertainty and darkness being augmented from heaven! And how then shall the apostle's word stand: "All Scripture is given by inspiration of God, and is profitable for doctrine, for reproof, for correction?" (2 Tim 3:16).[4]

For Martin Luther, the clarity of Scripture was a doctrine essential to the Christian faith. If God intended to give us a book that would reveal himself and his will for us, why would he make sloppy work of it and leave us a book that no one could understand? If *all* Scripture is useful, does this not also mean that all Scripture is clear, that it can be understood so that it is usable? In other words, if Scripture is a flashlight to illumine our paths, God must have given clear instructions for turning it on (cf. Ps 119:105).

A favourite text of Luther's was Deuteronomy 17:8. The people were commanded to bring their disputes before the priests who would discern the appropriate solution from the Law, "But how could they be settled if the laws were not perfectly clear, and were truly as lights among the people?"[5] The issue for Luther was twofold, and he is a wise guide in this matter. First, there

---

[4] Martin Luther, *The Bondage of the Will*, ed. J. I Packer and O. R Johnston (Grand Rapids: Fleming H. Revell, 2003), 128.

[5] Ibid., 125.

is the issue of personal clarity: how can an individual Christian be sure that he or she is hearing God's voice in Scripture?

This question has been taken up by John Piper in recent years; he has done a masterful job showing how the Scriptures testify to their divine inspiration. In John 10:27, Jesus says that his sheep hear his voice, that they are his and recognize him speaking. Piper argues that through the words of Scripture, God's glory is seen—much as creation testifies to his glory—and that the knowledge God has given all of us in creation is matched to this glorious testimony. If the Holy Spirit removes the blinders of our sin, we recognize the glory of God shining forth from the words he speaks:

> there is in every human being a 'knowledge' of this God. There is a built-in template that is shaped to receive as its perfect counterpart this peculiar communication of God's glory. When God opens our eyes (2 Cor. 4:6) and grants us the knowledge of the truth (2 Tim. 2:25), through the Scriptures (1 Pet. 1:23), we know that we have met ultimate reality. And in this way, God testifies that his word is true.[6]

Every Christian needs to be able to be sure of the Divine authority of Scripture we have talked about, and not all can go through the detailed philosophical and historical arguments made for it. The personal clarity of Scripture answers this: God attests to the humble regenerate reader that this is indeed his word. His sheep hear his voice and recognize him.

Scripture cannot only possess clarity in this sense, however, for it is meant to be taught and to govern the public behaviour of Christians—not only their private thoughts. Scripture, if it is to function authoritatively as Scripture, cannot be slippery and ambiguous, unusable. Martin Luther argued vigorously that it also possesses an external, public clarity. Scripture is clear in the words with which it communicates so that Christians can settle disagreements by turning to Scripture (e.g. Deut 17:8). Scripture presupposes this sense of clarity when it commends the Bereans for "examining the Scriptures daily to see if these things were so" (Acts 17:11-12). It also assumes this in the expectation that parents will teach their children the Law (Deut

---

[6] John Piper, *A Peculiar Glory: How the Christian Scriptures Reveal Their Complete Truthfulness* (Wheaton: Crossway, 2016), 226.

6:1-9; cf. 2 Tim 3:10-17), that young men can meditate on the words of Scripture and keep themselves pure (Ps 119:9-11; cf. Josh 1:8), and that elders or pastors can hold fast and teach the word (1 Tim 4:12-16, 6:2-5; 2 Tim 4:1-2).

If Scripture is useful to equip us for every good work, then it must be understandable, clear. Yet it need not be understandable to the same degree for everyone. That is, Luther would not deny that applying Scripture to everyday life is at times difficult; Scripture does not deny this either. In fact, Peter writes of some hard to understand things in Paul's writing, "which the ignorant and unstable twist to their own destruction, as they do the other Scriptures" (2 Pet 3:16). It is clear that he does not see all of Paul's writings as equally clear, yet those who are led astray are not considered positively either. They are "lawless people" in addition to being ignorant and unstable (v. 17).

That not all Scripture is equally clear is evident to those of us who read the Biblical languages: though smoothed out by English translations, Acts 27 and the book of Hebrews are harder to read or translate than the Gospel of John or even Romans. As with our discussion of creation revelation, the clarity of the Biblical text is partly a feature of the text and partly a feature of what we bring to the text. In 1 Corinthians 2:9-16, Paul writes that those who do not have the Spirit cannot understand the Word of God, because it is folly to them (cf. Rom 8:6-8). But Christians have been given the Spirit and can properly understand the Scriptures because they have the author with them (cf. Rom 8:4-6, 9). So part of this is the proper understanding of God and the Scriptures as directed by the Spirit, yet the physical text must also be clear if this interpretive lens is to yield any fruit.[7]

We can make a further clarification, though, for it is clear that not all Christians are at the same reading level or able to understand the same types of speech (e.g. academic vs. colloquial). A child, for example, may not be able to understand a passage of Scripture that another believer is perfectly capable of understanding. Yet a child will not need to wrestle with the same depth of thought as an adult may have to, so we can affirm that the relationship

---

[7] For more on the clarity of Scripture and how we interpret it, see the second volume in this series, *The Gift of Reading*.

between Scripture's clarity and usefulness varies from person to person. I think it is reasonable to conclude that it is clear enough for all that God would have that person use it for. Furthermore, God has intended Scripture to be read and understood in Christian community, so where one person is lacking God provides another so that they might understand his will for them revealed in Scripture (cf. Rom 12:3-8, 1 Cor 12:12-31, Eph 4:11-16).

From the teachings of Scripture then, we can say that all of God's Word is clear so as to be useful for his people and so that reasonable discussion can be conducted over the meaning and application of passages (cf. Deut 17:8; Acts 17:11-12).[8] The clarity of Scripture is in large part due to its self-interpreting nature; it is sufficient in breadth to provide in some areas key ideas that are useful for interpreting more difficult texts elsewhere (e.g. interpreting Hab 2:4 in light of Gen 15:6 and Lev 18:6, with Rom 1:17, Gal 3:11, and Heb 10:38).

The clarity of Scripture, then, means that the Scriptures speak clearly with God's voice so that his sheep may recognize him speaking. The same knowledge and spiritual illumination that allows us to recognize God's glory in Scripture equips the believer to understand the Scriptures by reading all the parts of Scripture in light of other parts and the teaching of the whole. Scripture is also sufficient to equip all believers for every good work God would ask of them in this life, its clarity enabling them to understand and so use its teaching. Finally, Scripture is God's very voice and so bears his authority. It is, therefore, without error in its clear communication of all God would have us know for living before him in the world he created.

Further Reading

B. B. Warfield, "Inspiration" (in, *Selected Shorter Writings of Benjamin B. Warfield*, vol. 1). [B]
Francis Schaeffer, *The Great Evangelical Disaster*. [B]
John Calvin, *The Institutes of the Christian Religion*, Book 1, Chs 6-9. [B-I]
John Frame, *Apologetics: A Justification of Christian Belief*. [B]

---

[8] I take the clarity of Scripture to imply that God's Word is clear enough in the original languages so that one knowledgeable in them may teach from the original languages and translate the Word clearly so that it can be used by those without access to the languages.

* John Frame, *The Doctrine of the Word of God*. [I]
John Frame, *Systematic Theology*, 519-693. [B-I]
* John Piper, *A Peculiar Glory*. [B]
* Martin Luther, *The Bondage of the Will*, 124-129. [I]
Wayne Grudem, *Systematic Theology*, 47-138. [B]

7

THE ETHICS OF KNOWING

> For the wrath of God is revealed from heaven against all ungodliness and unrighteousness of men, who by their unrighteousness suppress the truth. – Romans 1:18

We have seen so far that knowledge is a right interpretation of the world and the one who created it, an interpretation that corresponds to God's interpretation of his creation and himself. Truth, then, can be defined as any knowledge that corresponds to God's knowledge and contains no error. This implies something we may not usually think about. If truth intimately involves God and the knowledge he has revealed, then knowing is not only a mental activity but also a moral activity.

Think about it for a moment; if truth is thinking God's thoughts after him, then the pursuit of truth must involve submission to and pursuit of God. Knowing is not merely thinking about something in a certain manner, but thinking about something in submission to God. To appropriately know something, we must surrender the illusion of our autonomy—the perceived right to define the world as we see fit—and accept what God says to be true. This moral aspect of knowledge is why the exchange of the truth for a lie in Romans 1:18 invites the wrath of God upon humanity and why it results in rampant depravity. Epistemological rebellion is moral rebellion. Ignorance and immorality go hand in hand.

In Romans 8, this comes out clearly: the "mind set on the flesh" does not obey God, in fact, it is unable to do so. Highlighting the thoughts of those in rebellion against God, Paul indicates that their thinking is unable to lead them to submit to God in right actions (8:6-9). Therefore, rebellious thought (having a mind of the sinful flesh) leads to rebellious action.

In John 12:40, John quotes Isaiah to explain Israel's rejection of Jesus's miracles. Why do they not believe? He identifies the root of unbelief as a hardened rebellious heart, if the Spirit changed their heart—gave them the gift of regeneration—"they [would] see with their eyes, and understand with their heart."[1] In 1 Corinthians 2, Paul writes,

> The natural person does not accept the things of the Spirit of God, for they are folly to him, and he is not able to understand them because they are spiritually discerned. The spiritual person judges all things, but is himself to be judged by no one. "For who has understood the mind of the Lord so as to instruct him?" But we have the mind of Christ. (1 Cor 2:14-16)

Therefore, humans need not only functioning brains to learn about God and his world, but they also need submissive hearts. The search for truth is as much a moral act as the question of the appropriate use of human sexuality.

This means that science, philosophy, sociology, and English—even math—are not amoral subjects in which the question of God and his existence can be shoved aside for the moment. To search for truth in these fields without consideration of the God who has revealed himself is to set oneself in opposition to God, in rebellion against him, and to doom the task to futility. No matter how many true insights are revealed, they will be shrouded in a cloud of error. Furthermore, whatever truth is found will not even be identified appropriately, for it will be considered within a **worldview** that deliberately suppresses the knowledge of God. We have seen already that there is indeed truth in non-Christian thought, yet this is not because of any great feat of understanding on their part. What truth is found is evidence of the graciousness of God in not allowing the human heart to pursue its rebellion to the fullest. This has several practical implications, but I want to bring this section of the book to a close with the consideration of two.

---

[1] "The arm of the Lord" to be revealed in context is Jesus Christ, God's power embodied in his suffering servant (Isa 53:1). The revealing of Jesus is God's regenerating act to empower sinful people to believe in him (Deut 30:6; Jer 31:30-33; Isa 54:13; John 3:1-8, 6:44-45).

First, we should not be surprised when the pursuit of knowledge without consideration of God—the pursuit of knowledge found in most North American Universities—repeatedly comes to atheistic and incoherent conclusions.

When the starting assumption is that God is inconsequential to human knowing, it is not surprising that God is irrelevant to or excluded from the so-called knowledge that results from all fields of study. Consider evolution: if someone seeks to explain the universe without the interference or revelation of God, is it surprising that the resulting picture is a world where God is uninvolved or merely relegated to the role of first cause (the one who started everything moving)?

If, however, God is the reference point for all knowledge—if his existence is essential to right knowing—then we can also expect that the results of such study will be incoherent. If someone considers the created order without a category of creation, without consideration of the one who created it and the way he did so, will not her conclusions be profoundly flawed? If someone studies human sexuality without the consideration of God who created sexuality, is it surprising that biological sex (male/female) is ignored and that all manner of human self-invention is invited?

We are not, however, without hope in this world. Accurately identifying the disease means that we can recognise and begin to administer the appropriate cure. If the problem we face is ethical rebellion, the exchange of truth for a lie resulting in all-out apostasy toward God and his wrath towards all men and women, then the answer is the Gospel.

The second practical implication of the ethical aspect of knowing is that we know the cure: the Gospel and the Bible that communicates it are the answer to our world's epistemic crisis.

The Gospel, the good news that Jesus Christ, the second person of the Trinity, entered his creation and lived the life we could not, died the death we all deserved, and was raised on the third day, is not merely about the salvation of our souls. The Gospel is what we need to hear if we are to be delivered from the wrath of God by the blood of his Son, but it is more than this. If we are to think rightly about God and his world, we need to be saved from our rebellion. If we are to act rightly before him and accomplish his purposes, we need the promise of his spirit to overcome our sin and submit ourselves to Jesus Christ. In a word, if we truly want to know God and his creation, we need to be sanctified. We need a wholesale transformation into the image of God the Son. We need to gaze upon the glory of God shining forth in the face of Jesus Christ as he is revealed in Scripture if we want truth (cf. 2 Cor 3:12-4:6).

Individually, we need to steep ourselves in God's Word and pursue him if we want truth. To know the truth and be set free, we need the Spirit and his sanctifying work (1 Cor 2:14-16); to receive the Spirit and be sanctified, we need the truth of God's Word (John 17:17, Rom 10:14-17). It is the gracious gift our Lord Jesus Christ that he began our epistemic salvation before we could even believe in him (Rom 5:6-8), that while we were still sinners, he died for us and sent his Spirit to draw us to himself (John 6:44-45). He has made known to us the truth by his grace and given us the gracious gift of his Scriptures so that we could grow in the knowledge of him and his word. To properly understand anything in this world, therefore, we need to labour in the study of God's word by the power of his Spirit (cf. Phil 2:12). The Gospel saves the souls and the minds of Christians, yet we are not the only ones in need of this salvation.

If we want to convince the world of the truth of God and his Scriptures, to see transformation in its values and beliefs, we need to preach the Gospel. The world will not know the truth unless they receive the eyes to see the world as God has created it. To do this, they need to hear the Gospel of Jesus Christ proclaimed by his people (Rom 10:14-17). The World needs the Gospel of Jesus Christ not only for their souls but also for their sciences. It is Jesus and his Word that will ultimately save us from our epistemological crisis, and God in his grace has made this salvation available to all us.

On Reading or the Possibility Thereof [i]

> How then will they call on him in whom they have not believed? And how are they to believe in him of whom they have never heard? And how are they to hear without someone preaching? And how are they to preach unless they are sent? As it is written, "How beautiful are the feet of those who preach the good news!" But they have not all obeyed the gospel. For Isaiah says, "Lord, who has believed what he has heard from us?" So faith comes from hearing, and hearing through the word of Christ. – Romans 10:14-17

In the introduction to this book, we saw Fredrich Nietzsche's striking description of the present age we are in,

> What were we doing when we unchained this earth from its sun? Where is it moving to now? Where are we moving to? Away from all suns? Are we not continually falling? And backwards, sidewards, forwards, in all directions? Is there still an up and a down? Aren't we straying as though through an infinite nothing?

Such is the state of Western society; without moorings, it is as if we are straying through an infinite void with nothing but human preference and feeling for guidance. An area where this is strongly expressed is reading and communication. In grade school and universities, television and politics, even law and Christian theology, the ability of texts (such as this book, the Bible, or the American constitution) to communicate is cast into doubt. Speech, it is claimed, is malleable or plastic from the moment it leaves the mouth or pen of the author. That is, it is open to infinite interpretation as determined by the reader and his interaction with the text.

We must ask if this is really the inevitable conclusion we must draw from reasoned thought and experience; is this the way it has to be? The stakes are not small in this, for the Gospel comes through human communication, the word of God read or proclaimed (Rom 10:14-17). If texts cannot communicate, the Gospel cannot go forth.

I want to contend briefly that the interpretive chaos in which we find ourselves does not result from unclear texts or speech (for the most part) nor an unbridgeable hermeneutical gap (there is no chasm separating our minds from the world with which we interact) but a rejection of humanity as made in the image of God and God as **covenant** Lord over man. The answer to hermeneutical chaos is the Christian worldview, in which every person is obligated to honour the communicative intent of every other person, to the extent of their abilities, and is ultimately obligated to honour God's communicative intent in creation and His written revelation.

It is true that a text is unable to force the reader to properly interpret it—to follow the natural rules of reading—but this does not mean that interpretation is open ended or subjective. This only means that the onus is on the reader to adopt the appropriate posture for right interpretation. Reading is, in fact, contractual or covenantal. For most written works or spoken communication, this covenant is non-obligatory: most of us have taken a quote out of context for comedic purposes (in jest, I often adopt Luke's tortured face from Star Wars Episode V and exclaim to my wife, "Noooooooo!!! That's impossible!!!"). We recognize such twisting of words as a comedic effort; no one confuses such a play on meaning as a valid "interpretation" of the original.

To properly read a work, we must enter into an implicit agreement with the author, an agreement that we will, if possible, honour them by seeking to interpret their work on its own terms—in its context. This applies to written and spoken communication equally, though it is more evident in the latter because of the immediate consequences. Who has not felt the hurt or awkwardness when this communicative covenant is broken? Many times, my friends have chosen to take things I have said and strip them of their context, to give them a new interpretation—much to my horror! This is so effective because everyone recognizes that there is an intentional breach of the communicative covenant. This same agreement exists in written communication, only in this case there is only the reader to ensure their own fidelity to this relationship. Reading is thus a moral act—forcing us to choose whether we will honour another person or not—but one that usually has very little consequences (e.g. to misread a novel is to do no great harm).

Yet there are communications in which such covenant breaking is a weightier matter. In legal proceedings and business, much rests on honouring the communicative covenant. To break this agreement may entail the jailing of the innocent if their testimony is twisted, the freeing of the guilty, or the defrauding of many. In academic studies (other than among postmodern deconstructionist circles) a student is expected to accurately communicate the meaning of the work being analysed. Grades, graduation, or academic probation rest on one's success or failure at such analysis. At a more significant level, communication from the government bears even greater weight. To break the communicative covenant with the law means fines or a prison sentence—even death!

However, none of these instances presents the greatest moral imperative to the reader. Our ultimate moral obligation is to God and all human beings are obligated to obey to his commands. This binds us on many levels to follow the communicative covenant. For all humanity, our first moral obligation is to uphold the communicative covenant God has established with creation. God has, according to Romans 1:18-32, revealed Himself clearly in His creation. Though they were obligated to receive this communication, this text tells us that all humanity breaks this covenant and exchanges the truth for a lie: they sin in misinterpretation. This communicative covenant exists for all God's words: all humans are morally compelled to appropriately interpret, believe and respond rightly to the Gospel proclamation. To fail in this is sin—rebellion against God.

Furthermore, The Bible is a covenant document from God and demands of its reader obedience in reading. As God's very words it demands interpretive obedience that is analogous to that of a federal constitution or royal proclamation, only to the utmost degree. If one dare not disobey and therefore misinterpret the constitution on penalty of law, or dare not misinterpret and disobey the command of one's king, how much more should one fear to do so concerning God?

The interpretive obligations imposed by God do not stop, however, with His own words: God not only binds us to communicative obedience with himself; He binds us in communicative obedience to others. That we are to submit to earthly authorities means that we are to appropriately interpret their words (cf. Rom 13, 1 Pet 2:13-17). That we are to honour others as image bearers of God and seek to uphold justice in our communication means that we are morally obligated to interpret their communication correctly. (This does not mean we cannot joke, only that such twisting of communication must be in a context where it is clear that the communicative intent is understood.) We are also obligated to interpret God's creation rightly, meaning that to ignore His revelation in creation is not ignorance but criminal negligence.

It is therefore the case that, though texts may not force us to obey their communicative intent as demonstrated by the directions they provide (context), God commands us to honour their communicative efforts. This implies, on the other hand, that authors are under obligation to ensure communicative accuracy, and are liable for breaking the communicative covenant on their end (of course, intended audience matters here).

¹This excursus is adapted from a post I wrote on Teleioteti.ca. https://teleioteti.ca/2017/11/20/the-moral-act-of-reading-a-response-to-deconstructionism/.

Further Reading

John Frame, *The Doctrine of the Knowledge of God* [I]
John Frame, *The Doctrine of the Word of God* [I]

—Part 3—
The Practice of Epistemology

8

CREATED IN THE IMAGE OF GOD: THINKING AS A CREATURE

> The secret things belong to the Lord our God, but the things that are revealed belong to us and to our children forever, that we may do all the words of this law.
> – Deuteronomy 29:29

In Part 1 of this book, we examined the nature of knowing itself, the delicate balance between the world outside of us and the interpretive software within us. In Part 2, we considered the fundamental role of authority in knowing and the role God's revelation plays in making knowing possible. In Part 3, we will consider our role as knowers. That is, we will consider how our senses, minds, and hearts work to make knowledge possible.

Having concluded the last chapter with the role of morality in knowing (with the human heart and its relation to God's authority), we will begin this part of the book with the same theme. We will answer the question "what should our attitude be as we seek to interpret God's world?" The Bible teaches that humans are creatures—the artful products of a Creator—and, therefore, that all our thinking must be done as creatures (cf. Rom 9:19-21; Eph 2:10). We have seen already that this means we must think in submission to God's revelation. In direct application to our thinking, I want to consider in this chapter how thinking as a creature means seeing God as the ultimate reference point for meaning and being aware of our finitude.

A. God is the Reference Point for Meaning

Let's begin with a question: does understanding God help us understand ourselves, or does self-understanding help us understand God? On one level, the answer is "both." John Calvin began his *Institutes of the Christian Religion* with the incredible insight that we can only know God by knowing ourselves as his creations and that we can only truly know ourselves by knowing God as our creator. If we were starting as a blank slate, this would be a hopeless circle—I could never know God or myself! Yet God has revealed himself in Scripture and given us knowledge of him from birth, so this circle of interpretation works well. Surely we have all experienced a growing understanding of God and his work as we begin to grasp more and more the depths of our sinfulness and the greatness of being made in his image! Calvin's insight is truly profound, but it is not the full story. The reason that self-knowledge helps us understand God is because he has created us in his image and created us to see him in his creation.

Unfortunately, the Fall means that this image is marred: no individual human or human relationship perfectly reflects God. If we believe that human experience is ultimate in explaining God, then we will be left with a distorted picture of the God we worship. For example, God has revealed himself as a Father. If we take the word "father" and define it from our experiences, we will horribly misunderstand God! All of us have had imperfect fathers. Some have been worse than others, but none have been a perfect father. If "father" means what I have experienced, then my view of God as Father will be impoverished. If "father" means the bigger, better version of the father figures we have experienced, then our understanding of God will still be too small. God's fatherhood embodies the best of what our earthly fathers have done, yet his fatherhood extends to so much more.

Therefore, it is crucial to recognize that our experiences of earthly fathers do not define God's fatherhood. The exact opposite is, in fact, the case. God is the perfect Father who has existed before any human counterpart. We only recognize good fathers as "good" in light of how they reflect God's perfect fatherhood. We only recognize bad fathers as "bad" in light of how they fail in comparison to the example God has given us. All of us know the invisible attributes of God from his created order (Rom 1:20), surely his fatherhood is included. We could say that God is the standard of what fatherhood should look like: we recognize as fathers those whose role corresponds to that which God has. We recognize someone as a good father when they act in their role the way God acts in that role. A bad father would be someone who does not act in his fatherhood as God does. This means that God is the reference point of meaning, the fixed standard by which we understand our experience. That God is the reference point for meaning requires a colossal paradigm shift in our thinking yet is tremendously important if we want to understand him properly.

This necessary shift in our thinking may be most evident if we consider the Biblical teaching that God does all He does for his glory. From Scripture, we learn that God created the world to display his glory (Gen 1:27-28; Isa 43:5-7; Pss 19:1, 72:19). God raises and deposes world leaders for this purpose (Isa 63:12; Hab 2:14; Rom 9:16-18), and works all things together according to a plan made before the foundations of the earth were laid to make known his character—to demonstrate his glory—to his elect creation (e.g. Isa 48:9-11; Rom 9:22-24; Eph 1:8-10). In Romans 1:18-32, the very act that brought the wrath of God against humanity is the exchange of his glory for that of the creature. If we try to understand this from the perspective of our experience, we are bound to think God is horrible!

When we think of those who pursue their own glory, the adjectives that come to mind are *proud, arrogant, selfish, sinful,* and *manipulative.* Is this how we are to think of God's actions? Are they the selfish actions of a maniacal tyrant? May it never be! If we start with the perspective of humans, we understand the pursuit of self-glory from the perspective of the perverted and vain pursuits of rebellious creatures. How, though, would God have us look at his pursuit of his own glory?

If we look to God to understand this, not our experience, it makes much more sense. The Bible teaches that God is worthy of our worship, of glory: God is infinitely beautiful and good, strong and wise, etc. Idolatry is roundly condemned as a sin because it is a horrible lie. That is, to commit idolatry is to take the good gifts of God and thank his creatures for them. Idolatry is taking the perfect character of God and attributing it to his creatures, thereby distorting and perverting his perfections to match the mangled mess of a creature we choose to worship. If it is idolatrous to attribute what is rightfully God's to his creatures, then God would be idolatrous to pursue anything other than his own glory. To do this would be to treat something that is not

God as God; this is something God cannot do. This, in fact, why the human pursuit of glory appears to us as wrong, because it involves exalting oneself to the place of God!

Another important aspect of God's pursuit of his glory taught by Scripture is that in this pursuit, humans find their greatest satisfaction. That is, God did not set out to manifest his glory in creation and create creatures who would hate this endeavour. God made humans with a desire for happiness, for fulfillment, and gave his own glory as the answer to this desire. So when God pursues his glory with his creatures, this should bring us the greatest happiness. John Piper has famously summarised this with the phrase, "God is most glorified in us when we are most satisfied in Him."[1] Our joy and God's glory are not at cross-purposes. Understood rightly, they are complementary. God would have us find our greatest joy pursuing him and his kingdom (e.g. Pss 16, 84; Matt 5:2-12).

Starting with the creature, God's pursuit of his own glory appears diabolical. Starting with God, God's pursuit of his own glory should be our greatest delight! If we are to understand God and his world, we need to begin with God and his revelation. God, not humanity, is the ultimate reference point for meaning. I suggested that for the topic of God's pursuit of his own glory, seeing God as the reference point of meaning gives us some clarity.

However, there remains much that is hidden about God's ways. Some of us may still struggle with this or another truth in God's revelation or we may encounter unanswered questions that trouble us. There comes a point in our thinking, in our pursuit of knowledge in submission to God, that we need to confess our finitude.

B. We Must Pursue Knowledge in Humility

If God is our Creator and if we are his creatures, it is obvious that he has not shared with us all of his knowledge. He knows things that we do not know. In Deuteronomy 29:29 Moses writes, "The secret things belong to the Lord our God, but the things that are revealed belong to us and to our children forever, that we may do all the words of this law." The emphasis in this passage is on God's revelation, on the Law he has revealed, yet there are

---

[1] John Piper, *Desiring God: Meditations of a Christian Hedonist*, Rev. Ed. (Colorado Springs: Multnomah, 2011), 288.

"secret things" that he has not chosen to make known. If our thinking does not have space for our finitude, we will be sorely disappointed to discover that God has not given us all his secrets.

At times we will pursue something and not find an answer. At times Biblical characters move into presumption when they reach these boundaries of human knowledge, and they dare question or challenge God. The response they receive is one we need to hear clearly today:

> But YHWH is in his holy temple;
> be silent before him all the earth! (Hab 2:20)

> Who is this that darkens counsel by words without knowledge?
> Dress for action like a man;
> I will question you, and you make it known to me.
>
> Where were you when I laid the foundation of the earth?
> Tell me, if you have understanding.
> Who determined its measurements—surely you know!
> Or who stretched the line upon it?
> On what were its bases sunk,
> or who laid its cornerstone,
> when the morning stars sang together
> and all the sons of God shouted for joy?
>
> Or who shut in the sea with doors
> when it burst out from the womb,
> when I made clouds its garment
> and thick darkness its swaddling band,
> and prescribed limits for it
> and set bars and doors,
> and said, 'Thus far shall you come, and no farther,
> and here shall your proud waves be stayed'?
>
> Have you commanded the morning since your days began,
> and caused the dawn to know its place? (Job 38:2-12)

> You will say to me then, "Why does he still find fault? For who can resist his will?" But who are you, O man, to answer back to God? Will what is molded say to its molder, "Why have you made me like this?" (Rom. 9:19-20)

By God's grace, we can know the truth! But the secret things still belong to

God. In our practical pursuit of knowing, our foundational posture must be that of humility. We must look to Yahweh to define our world, to tell us what love, righteousness, goodness, justice, peace, etc. mean. And, ultimately, we must accept—even delight in—our limitations as creatures. It is not our burden to know everything; God knows everything, and he has shared some of this with us and our children.

Further Reading

John Calvin, *The Institutes of the Christian Religion*, Book 1, Chapter 1. [B-I]
John Frame, *The Doctrine of the Knowledge of God* [I]
John Piper, *Desiring God* [B]

9

CREATED WITH SENSES: EMPIRICAL KNOWLEDGE

> That which was from the beginning, which we have heard, which we have seen with our eyes, which we looked upon and have touched with our hands, concerning the word of life—the life was made manifest, and we have seen it, and testify to it and proclaim to you the eternal life, which was with the Father and was made manifest to us—that which we have seen and heard we proclaim also to you, so that you too may have fellowship with us; and indeed our fellowship is with the Father and with his Son Jesus Christ.
> – 1 John 1:1-3

Throughout the history of Western thought, few things have been disparaged as much as sense knowledge. As we saw in the first chapter, the early philosopher quickly gave up on the world of the senses and turned to the mind for knowledge. The world of the senses simply changed too much. Even the so-called empiricist philosophers, who claimed that knowledge came through our senses, often maintained that the objects we sense do not actually matter. This was the case with Aristotle. Sense experience only helps us understand the abstract truths that are the true objects of knowledge.

In more recent times, philosophers have argued that we have no access to anything outside of our minds: we cannot be sure that our perceptions and experience have any correspondence with a world beyond our thoughts! Science relies on the data of the senses and interactions with the world outside of our selves. However, this is often done in naivete. Those who practice science often do so without a good reason to trust their senses, to believe that what they perceive is actually the way things are. But Christians do not have to give in to such scepticism! Indeed, God has revealed to us that our senses are a gift from him.

A. The Biblical Affirmation of the Senses

In the Christian **worldview**, human senses—such as sight and hearing—play an essential role in knowledge. Because the foundational authority for a Christian is God who has spoken, it is necessary to affirm that we can accurately perceive his speech. More than this, Yahweh is also a God who has acted and acts today and expects an appropriate response from his creatures (cf. Exod 9:16, 15:1-21).

For this to be the case, we need to be able to affirm that our senses, at their best, are trustworthy mediators of the outside world. The fact that God has entrusted us with the Bible, a written book and entrusted ministers of the Gospel to teach his word verbally assumes that our senses are trustworthy—that we can really read and hear. This is affirmed throughout the Bible. I opened this chapter with the opening words of 1 John because John is addressing a very similar question there. Instead of doubting the trustworthiness of the senses, John's readers apparently doubted the physicality—the sense-ability—of Jesus.

To affirm that Jesus Christ was indeed a physical human being as well as fully God, John appeals to the experience he and the other apostles had. He testifies to the Gospel encountered in and heard from Jesus Christ, a word that "we have heard, which we have seen with our eyes, which we looked upon and have touched with our hands" (1 John 1:1). Because we have a word from outside ourselves, a word from an authority—the one who formed us, breathed life into us, and orders our steps—we are able to affirm the reliability of the senses with which we were created. Surely the one who formed us knows the capacities of those he has formed! Yet, when this presupposition is abandoned—when an external authority is rejected—the historical rejection of the senses makes some sense.

B. The Problem with the Senses

Throughout this book, I have raised the problems non-Christians views have encountered with the senses. If we begin with our self as the authority, it becomes quickly apparent that it is impossible to prove the reliability of the senses. Reason alone cannot confirm the reliability of our senses and any appeal to sense data assumes **a priori**—before the fact—that they are reliable! Many assume without reason that their senses are reliable, but this is, of course, an irrational assumption: it has no foundation. Once you add in the fact that our senses are limited in what they encounter (i.e. we only experience an infinitesimally small part of the universe in our lifetime) the potential of the senses as a source of knowledge dwindles quickly.

To add salt to the wound, there is also the factor of psychological susceptibility: our senses are prone to deception! Walking down a sidewalk on a scorching day, we may just see pools of water on the path in front of us. Eat the wrong substance and we might hear voices others do not hear or see creatures that do not exist outside of our minds. There is also psychological illness, such as schizophrenia, that adds to the confusion of our senses! Taken together, the case against the senses seems firm: we cannot prove their reliability, we know they are deceivable, and—even if we could trust them—they do not experience enough of the world to ground our knowledge!

This is bad enough, but human reason does not get much farther (see Part 1). Even some who have claimed Christ have rejected the senses and have turned to their own minds to find certain knowledge. The problem here is that to trust our minds, we have to presuppose that all the knowledge we need to know is already known by us. For the non-Christian, this view is unacceptable; they must ask from where this knowledge came. For the Christian, this view is equally unacceptable. We are told in Scripture that our minds are hostile to the truth and ambiguous (cf. Rom 2:15; 8:6-8; Eph 4:18). More so, we are told that the knowledge of God comes through the created world and Scripture (e.g. Rom 1:20) and that God has given Scripture—not our minds alone—to equip us for every good work (2 Tim 3:16-17). As I have argued throughout this book, Christian knowledge is a combination of mental activity plus sense data, objects plus a subject interpreting them. And this, the subjective interpretation of objects, is accountable to an external authority, the mind of God revealed to his creatures.

We must, therefore, affirm that the human senses are trustworthy and necessary for knowledge. I have suggested in previous chapters that there is no knowledge without interpretation—that there is no perception without a mind interpreting it. The opposite also holds true; there is no interpretation without an object interpreted.[1] Against the objection that our senses are deceivable, we can respond that the evidence of some deception is not evidence that we are always and entirely deceived. Indeed, the fact that we identify some sensory experiences as "deception" indicates that we have normal experience against which we measure these anomalies. We interpret a mirage as such because we know what a real puddle of water is like, and we know the circumstances in which mirages happen, so we expect them.

This last point is an important one: our senses act according to consistent patterns that allow us or those outside of us to identify distortion or deception. For example, I know when I place a stick in water that the properties of water will distort the size, shape, and location of the stick. However, God has given our minds the capacity to compensate for this distortion; we are still able to retrieve the stick without a problem and are not shocked to discover that it does not appear exactly as it did underwater.[2] We also know to expect that imbibing alcohol to a certain degree or taking hallucinogenic drugs, or stressing our bodies to a great extent, will reduce the reliability of our senses. In each of these cases, the deception our senses face is predictable.

The cases of mental illness or unpredictable mental distortion of our senses are far more complicated, but one part of a greater answer is that this distortion is caused by the self and must be answered from outside of the self. That is, if our mind is deceiving us, others will not encounter the same delusion. On Biblical presuppositions (namely, that the senses are basically reliable, others exist, and that it is necessary to trust and rely on other people) we must rely on others to guide us through our delusions. In this case, we are relying on the reliability of others' senses and their character to correct our

---

[1] This has serious ramifications for the way we answer the question, "what is knowledge?" I explore this a bit in chapter 3, in the following chapter, and in Vol. 3, *The Gift of Seeing*.

[2] This is not only an ability of humans; fishing birds have the near miraculous ability to identify a fish from several dozen meters above the water and dive to catch it!

malfunctioning senses. The same is the case for those who are born with or who acquire later in life various impairments of the senses—such as deafness or blindness. Whether it is from the senses of others or from our own, the senses and the data they produce are essential to knowledge.

C. Conclusion

As Christians, we can and must affirm the reliability of our senses. This has significant implications. First, we cannot dispense with our senses, so being an armchair theologian or philosopher is out of the question. That is, we cannot just sit at home and think our way to answers for the world's problems. We must encounter the world and the people in it and study this world in light of the Word of God if we are going to provide true and helpful answers to the problems being raised. Furthermore, when our senses malfunction, we cannot retreat to the safety of our minds or rely on ourselves but must trust others to guide us by the hand—figuratively or literally.

Second, we can and must affirm the significance of human experience, particularly the experience of the inspired authors of Scripture, for faith and knowledge. That is, we cannot retreat to an intellectually detached view of the Christian faith but must root our faith in the historical events interpreted by and reported in the Bible—events seen, heard, and touched by our predecessors.

Third, we can use the Biblical affirmation of the senses to engage with other faiths intellectually. Daily life depends on reliable senses. The sciences that have given us the computers on which we write—on which I am writing right now—or the medicine that has saved many lives, that saved my life ten years ago, also depend on the reliability of our senses. Only the revelation of the one true God gives a firm foundation for trusting the senses.

Further Reading

John Frame, *The Doctrine of the Knowledge of God* [I]
Vern Poythress, *Redeeming Science: A God-Centered Approach* [I-A]

CREATED WITH A MIND: RATIONAL THOUGHT AND LOGIC

This Book of the Law shall not depart from your mouth, but you shall meditate on it day and night, so that you may be careful to do according to all that is written in it. For then you will make your way prosperous, and then you will have good success. – Joshua 1:8

God is not man, that he should lie,
    or a son of man, that he should change his mind.
Has he said, and will he not do it?
    Or has he spoken, and will he not fulfill it? – Numbers 23:19

Imagine a world in which our minds were not trustworthy. Imagine the paralysing fear of the illogical—what if at any moment you could be alive, dead, dismembered, transported to the centre of the sun, rich beyond earthly ambition, or racked with excruciating suffering? What if you could not trust that sitting upon your chair for work would not drop you into the depths of hell itself? What if all communication was an illusion, if these words on this page could simultaneously and irrationally communicate the essential truths of life, the recipe for my favourite pizza, or you are walking through a forest on a gloomy sunny day with a solid cheese popsicle in the hand of your favourite moose?

If you have a pulse, that was probably one of the more nonsensical paragraphs you have read. The fact that you have discerned its utter absurdity demonstrates that, to some extent, your mind is functioning. To imagine a world where our minds were utterly untrustworthy is an impossible feat; we can only do so if our minds are functioning and within the framework of a world that makes sense. This book has assumed that thinking is both possible and necessary. I have written a book, presupposing that I am capable of intelligent thought and communication and that you are capable of rational thought and interpreting my communication. The subject matter itself is thought, the foundation and nature of human knowledge and knowing. That we have made it this far is a testimony to our mental abilities, given to us by God and sustained by his Spirit.

That we are capable of thinking is hard to deny, yet it has been implicitly and explicitly rejected throughout the history of human thought (catch the irony there?). For this reason, we must affirm in closing that God has indeed made us with minds capable of intelligent thought. There is no passage in Scripture that says, "God has given you the ability to think," but it is assumed without question on every page of Scripture. For example, when God created Adam, he entrusted him with the tasks of identification (i.e. identifying what trees were to be eaten and which were not) and categorisation (i.e. naming the animals, thus identifying and differentiating them) (Gen 2:18-20). Adam was able to identify which creature would be appropriate to help him in the task he had been given, none of which were (Gen 2:20). More than this, our first parents received the commission to subdue and rule the earth as the images of God. In other words, to give God glory by imitating and acting like him in shaping and governing the created world (Gen 1:28). In all of this, thought would be required—both deliberate and automatic thought. The Bible also calls on its readers to think deeply upon its words, to discern their meaning and the appropriate response to these words (e.g. Josh 1:8). From this, I surmise that thinking is God's gift to us, created and commissioned for magnifying the glory of God through thoughtful interaction with his created world.

At times the Bible disparages forms of thinking but never thinking itself. The Bible warns throughout of thinking in a lofty manner, to think in a way that denies the creaturely status of man. To think as if one were God is sinful thinking, to which God responds,

> "Who is this that darkens counsel by words without knowledge?
> Dress for action like a man;
>   I will question you, and you make it known to me.
> "Where were you when I laid the foundation of the earth?
>   Tell me, if you have understanding.
> Who determined its measurements—surely you know!
>   Or who stretched the line upon it?
> On what were its bases sunk,
>   or who laid its cornerstone,
> when the morning stars sang together
>   and all the sons of God shouted for joy? (Job 38:2-7)

Thinking, as we have seen, is a moral act, so it must be done in a certain way. To think rationally, intelligently, we must think as God created us to think, in submission to him. To do so, we need the Spirit. That is, the presupposition of *consistent*, intelligent thought is not only adequate created minds but also regenerated, submitted hearts. Before this, our rebellion leads us into ignorance, but afterwards, we are equipped through Scripture to think rightly.

This does not mean that non-Christians do not exhibit intelligent thought or that Christians are the most intelligent people. What it does mean is that where non-Christians think well and arrive at the truth, they are inconsistent with their **worldview** and inconsistent with their posture of rebellion towards God. It also means that Christians have the potential to see the world better than their non-Christian peers, if they live out their Christian presuppositions faithfully through adequate natural gifting.

I have unpacked this idea throughout this book, showing that apart from submission to God as he has revealed himself in the Bible, human thought is subject to futility. In the rest of this chapter, I want to focus in on three facets of this truth that we have not yet considered, the specific ways that the Biblical worldview enables rational thought. What I have in mind is this: 1) the faithfulness of God is the presupposition of all rational thought, 2) the Bible hedges our thinking, and this is the essential condition of competent logic, 3) and the content of our thinking is interpreted objects.

A. The Presupposition of Thought

If you recall our discussion in chapter 1, you will remember that the early philosophers were obsessed with the idea of stability. That is, they perceived the need for a stable object of thought, something behind the fluxing world of our senses. The resolution I proposed to their struggles was to identify truth with our interpretation of objects measured against the standard of God's interpretation instead of static ideas floating out beyond our minds. There is a problem here, however, for our minds are also in flux like the world of experience; our memories fade, opinions change, and our certainty waxes and wanes.

By rejecting the stability provided by eternally unchanging ideas, it may appear that we have rejected the possibility of knowledge at all. God is a person; persons change. That is, they respond to and interact with others.[1] Someone may suggest, considering this, that God's interpretation of the world might change! From another perspective, is not God free? No human being or created thing can place constraint upon God, so could he not change the true interpretation of an object or event at any time? Could he not change the laws of interpretation—laws of logic and the so-called natural laws—at any time? To answer these questions in the affirmative would be to jettison the possibility of knowledge. But if we answer them negatively, with a firm Biblical answer, we also provide a stable foundation for human thought. The answer is no, God will not—indeed, he cannot—change his interpretation of objects or reject the laws of interpretation he has established. He will not, cannot, do so because he is faithful. Therefore, it is God's faithfulness that is the presupposition of rational thought.

When we say that God is faithful, we mean that he will always keep his word—fulfil every promise—and never act in a way contrary to his character. God's faithfulness guarantees that he will not sway or change on a whim, unlike a human: "God is not man, that he should lie, or a son of man, that he should change his mind. Has he said, and will he not do it? Or has he spoken, and he will not fulfil it?" (Num 23:19). He has pre-interpreted this entire creation, created and ordained its paths, laying out a plan for how all things will interact towards the revelation of his glory through Jesus Christ (e.g. Eph 1:7-10). God has created the natural order so that we could know it and behold him through it; this is the purpose of creation, and it depends on consistency in the way the world works. Because God is faithful to his purpose and has not seen fit to change his purpose for the world, it follows

---

[1] For the qualified sense in which God "changes," see Vol. 3 *The Gift of Seeing*.

that we can trust the rules of interpretation by which we interpret our experience—such as causality. Logic itself, the rules by which we think, is merely the outworking of the implications of God's own faithfulness. The foundational law of logic is that something cannot be one thing and another at the same time and in the same way (often phrased as "A or not-A at the same time and in the same way"). This is merely a universal application of God's faithfulness within himself and wired into the created order.

God cannot be true and false, faithful and unfaithful, good or bad in the same sense and at the same time. The consistency of our experience and the consistency of our minds depend, therefore, on the faithfulness of our God. It is his unchanging character that provides the necessary presupposition of human thinking. This is our great source of hope: "Let us hold fast the confession of our hope without wavering," writes the author of Hebrews, "for he who promised is faithful" (Heb 10:23).

A problem remains, however. Earlier, we saw that empirical knowledge (sense knowledge) is futile within the non-Christian position because it requires exhaustive knowledge to know anything. This problem remains in intellectual engagement, for reason depends on sense experience to furnish it with content.

B. The Necessary Condition of Thought

> I know that you can do all things,
> and that no purpose of yours can be thwarted.
> "Who is this that hides counsel without knowledge?"
> Therefore I have uttered what I did not understand,
> things too wonderful for me, which I did not know.
> "Hear, and I will speak;
> I will question you, and you make it known to me."
> I had heard of you by the hearing of the ear,
> but now my eye sees you;
> therefore I despise myself,
> and repent in dust and ashes." - Job 42:2-6

Think of a basic syllogism—a formal logical argument:

1) Socrates is a man
2) All men are mortal
3) Therefore, Socrates is mortal

How would you know that Socrates is a man? You might read a book, or if you were his contemporary, you would make this conclusion from your experience. However, with the limited knowledge of your senses, can you be sure that there is nothing just beyond your sensible experience that would invalidate this conclusion? The second proposition (i.e. "all men are mortal") is also tenuous on the basis of empirical knowledge: have you experienced the death of all men and women throughout history? What if one or two defied death (e.g. Enoch, Elijah, Jesus)? Can you really be so sure that Socrates is not immortal? Thinking, whether in formal arguments or informal reasoning, relies on an interaction between experience and laws of thought. If experience is befouled by the lack of exhaustive knowledge—if not knowing everything means you cannot know anything—then human knowledge, derived as it is from experience and thinking, is impossible without access to certain knowledge.

I suggested earlier that because God knows all things exhaustively and has revealed himself, we can know things certainly; we can have knowledge. This is the necessary condition of human thought, access to God's infinite knowledge. We can see how God's knowledge enables true knowledge by considering what philosophers have sometimes called **limiting concepts**.

A limiting concept, an idea that entered Christian thought through Cornelius Van Til, refers to a function that propositions (simple truth statements: e.g. the block is red) take in logic and reasoning. That is, statements are limiting concepts when they serve to prevent conclusions from being reached that would otherwise be valid. Representing propositions algebraically (**A**, **B**, **C**, etc.), we could give a formula for the function of a limiting concept like this: if it seems to be the case that "**A** therefore **B**," but we know that "**C** then **not-B**"; when C is true, "**A** therefore **B**" is false. In this logical equation, **A** is a true statement (e.g. "It is wet outside") and **B** is a statement that may be true or false (e.g. "it is raining"). **C** is another statement that excludes **B** from being true (e.g. $C =$ "it is too cold to rain") and is functioning as a limiting concept. That is, at first glance **A** "It is wet outside," therefore **B** "It is raining" seems reasonable—this makes sense! Yet the presence of **C** "it is too cold to rain" causes us to revisit our initial reasoning.

Because we cannot deduce **B** from **A**, we must consider other possibilities—of which there are many (e.g. **D** "a man is spraying the sidewalk with a hose"; **E** "there is a heater melting the snow"; etc.)! The limiting concept here reveals a problem in the initial logic itself: though **B** implies **A**, **A** does not *necessarily* imply **B**.

We could think of many Biblical examples where Scriptural truths act in this way. At first, it seems logical to conclude from the facts that God is one and the Father is God that Jesus cannot be God. However, we know from the Biblical testimony that Jesus is God, the Father is God, and the Spirit is God, so we are forced to reformulate our idea of God in trinitarian terms. Or if a scientist observes certain laws about the deposition of minerals and the rocks they form, they could reason back from the patterns they observe in rocks to determine the amount of time that it may have taken for the laws they observe to form such a formation. However, if Scripture teaches that the world is significantly younger than is posited in such a conclusion and teaches that these laws have not been consistent and universal in their application (i.e. a world-wide flood needs to be considered, Genesis 6-9), then the conclusions these scientists make must be false.

Limiting concepts encourage humility in reasoning, for they may invalidate conclusions that seem otherwise right. However, they also provide an essential condition of knowledge. Let us consider the problem once again. To properly understand any one detail in a system of truth (an interpretation of reality), one needs to have a perfect understanding of the whole. To give every true statement that could possibly be said about something—for instance, the location of my laptop—I must have access to every available perspective. It is in front of me, beside my lamp, beneath the roof, at a certain longitude and latitude, a certain distance from Alpha Centauri, etc. You may respond, "it is true that I need to know all things to describe something *exhaustively*, but practically I do not need to know every way a laptop's location could be described to know where it is!" That is true enough, but what if one of those unknown details is vital to knowing the location of and being able to use the laptop?

You cannot know if this detail is critical or not because you do not know what it is. If it turns out to be relevant—even vital—you will fail in some way when you try to locate and use the laptop.

Consider this thought experiment. Imagine if aliens visited Adam and Eve on the 7th day of creation and wanted to use their knowledge of human growth to determine when the world began. They could analyse Adam perfectly and conclude that the world began 41 years, 2 months, and 9 days ago. This would appear to be a sound conclusion, yet they would be wrong. The problem, in this case, is not that they do not properly understand human growth; their problem is ignorance of the fact that God created Adam only a day ago in a fully mature adult state. That one piece of data could ruin all their otherwise perfect calculations.

To perform proper induction (i.e. empirical science: gather a set of data and reach a conclusion from it) or deduction (concluding truths from other truths via logic), certain truths are needed from which to begin and from which to cut off the fruitless exploration of possibilities. Yet, if certainty only comes through exhaustive knowledge of everything, we need these truths revealed to us from one who knows all things. Therefore, we need God's input to begin any reasoning that hopes to describe the universe rightly.

This is where limiting concepts come in: in the Christian worldview, we trust that God has told us enough to properly understand his world (to reach appropriate inductive and deductive conclusions). Yet, he has not told us everything: he has given us a good foundation from which to reason from but also the knowledge that hedges in our reason—that constrains it—and guards us against going too far in our logic. What God has told us about himself, us, and the world serves both to guide us in interpreting and to prevent us from over-interpreting: it functions as a limiting concept.

Consider the Trinity. God has given us in Scripture adequate attestation that our reasoning is trustworthy, and the law of non-contradiction is presupposed in Scripture and human reason. Foundational to the Bible is the claim of Monotheism: Yahweh alone is God; he is numerically one (Deut 6:4-5). It is an appropriate deduction from this claim to reject every claim that there is a multiplicity of gods: if there are three "gods" ("god" describing each being in the same way) then there cannot be only one god. Yet, in the New Testament, Jesus differentiates himself from the Father and the Holy Spirit (the Helper) but claims for himself the status of the unique Deity: he is Yahweh (John 8:58). We are left with what appears to be a contradiction: God is one, yet Jesus is God, the Father is God, and the Holy Spirit is God. Because the first statement, "God is numerically one" is given to us by God, it is undoubtedly true; the same can be said for "Jesus, the Father, and Holy Spirit are differentiated; they are all God, yet there is only one God." Therefore, given that this last statement is true—it is attested by Scripture—the following argument is false:

1. There are three beings called "God"
2. If three beings are called "God," there cannot be one God alone
3. therefore, there is not one God alone.

All sorts of philosophical explanations are given for how God can be one and not-one at the same time, yet they all resolve in mystery. As Christians, our logical consistency is not grounded in an explanation of how God's oneness and his threeness are not contradictory but in the fact that God has revealed to us that these are not contradictory states. He has provided a limiting concept that prevents us from deducing contradiction from the *apparent* contradiction of the Trinity.

Ultimately, limiting concepts remind us that we are creatures and servants, not God! We do not know everything; therefore, we need God to tell us where the boundaries of our logic are. When Biblical truths function as boundaries for our logic, they are functioning as limiting concepts. Consider two other examples.

First, Arminian theologians often argue that the love of God requires him to make salvation available to all equally through prevenient grace. Yet, as I have argued in my book *Prevenient Grace*, the Bible teaches that God has not acted to save all in the same way (he has made it available to all, but has not regenerated all to receive it) and it does not teach prevenient grace.[2] The doctrines of irresistible grace and unconditional election, therefore, serve as limiting concepts, causing us to revisit our understanding of God's love and not deduce false theological conclusions from it.

Second, consider one of the arguments that could be made for the age of the universe. If light takes several billion years to travel from the edge of the universe to earth, then the universe would have to be at least that old for us to see that light, which we do. The logic is this: we know the speed of light, we can calculate the distance from the earth to the farthest point away, and

---

[2] J. Alexander Rutherford, *Prevenient Grace: An Investigation into Arminianism*, 2nd Revised Ed., Teleioeti Technical Studies 2 (Vancouver: Teleioteti, 2020).

we are receiving light from that most distant point, therefore the universe is at least old enough for light to travel from that point to earth—several billion years worth of distance. The logic follows, but if the Bible teaches that the earth and universe are relatively young (maybe 6,000-10,000 years old), then this provides a limiting concept that prevents us from drawing this conclusion—as in the case of the aliens considered above. Such a limiting concept would demand a re-evaluation of the various philosophical assumptions, pieces of data, and interpretations of that data that led to a false conclusion.

The point is this. God has given us minds that work, so we must use them; yet in doing so, we need to be aware of our limitations. Our minds are not the problem; our ignorance is the problem. We do not have exhaustive knowledge of God or the creation—we do not know all there is to know—so how can we know its parts? Praise be to God that he has given us an authoritative Word that frees us from hopeless scepticism. By building our reasoning upon the foundation of the Word of God and allowing the Word to function as a limiting concept on our thinking, we can appropriately use our minds to understand better the glorious complexity of God's creation, his Word, and God himself. By giving us insight into the created world from one who knows all things, the Bible provides us with the necessary condition for the proper use of our minds.

C. The Content of Thought

This leaves us with one last loose end I think I need to tie up. In much of Western philosophy, it has been believed that the object and content of knowledge—the things we actually know—are **abstract** ideas. Abstract ideas are categories that encompass particular objects, actions, or events. Fido is a particular object, "dog" is a category. An abstract idea would be *dogness*, the essential element possessed by Fido which qualifies him as a "dog." "Dogness" as an abstract idea could be defined as "that without which something is not a dog." That is vague, but that is about as clear as philosophy gets about abstract ideas. The abstract idea *dogness* does not refer to any physical feature of a specific dog (such as tall, short, four legs, tail, brown, spotted, etc.), for we can think of dogs with or without any of these features (e.g. my neighbour has a three-legged dog). The more abstract an idea, the less it is clear what it is; we can make some sense of *dogness*, but what about *life*? If life encompasses plants, insects, men and women, cats and dogs, what content does this idea have? Throughout Western thought, it was thought that abstract ideas—called **universals**, forms, etc.—were the true objects of knowledge. However, I have defined knowledge in such a way that rules out abstraction in this sense.

a. Concrete Thought

That is, if our knowledge is an interpretation of objects, then knowledge is not abstract: it is always involved with the particular objects of our experience. Knowledge is an interaction with the created order and the Creator (particular or concrete objects) through the interpretive framework he has given us. Therefore, our knowledge is not abstract in this non-Christian sense but, to some extent, concrete. For example, consider "dog"; we do not think of abstract "dogness" when we think of "dog," we think of particular dogs and their relationship to us. We think of the cute dog on the street, the childhood dog we grew up with, or our wife's dream dog. When we think of "love" (a different kind of abstract idea) we do not think of an abstract definition of love; instead, we think of concrete examples of love we have experienced and received. Indeed, as Christians, we think of God and the love he has shown us through Jesus Christ on the cross. Historical events, present experiences, future hopes, these are the content of "love."

Yet, it should be evident that the content of our knowledge is not concrete objects themselves. Jesus Christ, Pugimus Maximus the 3rd, Fido, or the crucifixion do not exist in our minds. Instead, as we saw earlier, what is in our minds—the content of our thoughts—is a particular interpretation of these things. So, in one sense, we can say (over against the classic Western philosophical tradition) that the content of knowledge is not abstract ideas but interpretations of concrete objects—people, events, things, etc. Yet part of thinking is still abstract in some sense. We can talk about the crucifixion but also of God's *love* shown in the crucifixion. We can think about Fido but also *dogs* in general. We use abstract categories all the time, whether they are adjectives (smallness, tallness), categories (humanity), or abstract nouns (love, goodness, evil). If abstract thought is not non-Christian abstraction, we need to offer an alternative explanation.

b. Abstract Thought

I would define abstract thought as "a relationship identified between particular objects of our experience (e.g. between specific dogs, trees, persons, events, or actions) that allows us to understand other particular objects of our experience better."[3] These relationships are not objects themselves, but bridges that allow us to move from one object of our experience to another object in order to come to an understanding of the latter and enrich our understanding of both. For example, having knowledge of several dogs—Fido the poodle, Pugimus Maximus the pug, and Wolf the husky—would allow us to identify and understand a new dog that walks by us on the street. On the other hand, encountering a Pomeranian would shed further light on the variety and features that are displayed by dogs, maybe even revealing something new about one of the original objects of our knowledge. Consider the abstract term "love":

> What is it that we think of when we think of "love" or "goodness"? As much as it is not an abstract definition we think of, we also do not think of isolated events with no relation. Instead, we think of a series of events that we deem exemplary of "love." If love is neither a floating abstract definition that lays behind these events nor a random assortment of events, what remains is that "love" is a relationship between these events. Love describes a particular feature of these events that is drawn out when they are viewed in relationship with one another. It is not a "part" of these events, as if you could take an instance of me saying "I love you" to Nicole and dissect it into parts—it is part speech, love, communication, respect, etc. Instead, love describes one way of looking at this event as it shares commonality with other similar events; it is a perspective by which all these events can be viewed.[4]

As I have argued above, such a view of knowledge means that no human can attain exhaustive knowledge of the universe, as the philosophers sought. It also implies that we cannot have knowledge of anything from reason alone. Only as we use reason to interpret our experience in submission to God do

---

[3] This section is derived from two articles I wrote on Teleioteti and my book *The Gift of Seeing*. This quote is taken from the article "What is Abstraction? – Part 2." https://teleioteti.ca/2018/09/20/what-is-abstraction-part-2/. See further, Vol. 3, *The Gift of Seeing*.

[4] ibid.

we have knowledge.

D. Conclusion

As Christians we must affirm the competence of the human mind to interpret the world. We must affirm the value of rational thinking and make an effort the think seriously and intelligently about our world. This starts with meditating on the Word of God but cannot be restricted to it; we must also reflect on how the Scriptures shape us and our response to the world in which we live. The existence of Yahweh and his revelation in the created order and Scripture is the presupposition of intelligent thought.

That we find much that is true and good in the non-Christian world is a testimony to the influence Christianity has had on the Western world and to the fact that no human being suppresses the knowledge of God perfectly—to do so would destroy all hope of knowing anything. Beginning from the Bible as the foundation of thought, we can have confidence in our capacities to think and interpret the world. But, despite this confidence, we must always bear great humility knowing that no matter how much insight we attain, this is only by the grace of God and represents only a minute fraction of his unfathomable knowledge.

Further Reading

*John Frame, *Apologetics: A Justification of Christian Belief* [B]
*John Frame, *The Doctrine of the Knowledge of God* [I]
John Frame, *Cornelius Van Til: An Analysis of His Thought* [I-A]
*John Piper, *Think* [B]
Very Poythress, *Logic: A God-Centered Approach to the Foundation of Western Thought* [I-A]
Vern Poythress, *Symphonic Theology: The Validity of Multiple Perspectives in Theology* [I-A]

CONCLUSION

For consider your calling, brothers: not many of you were wise according to worldly standards, not many were powerful, not many were of noble birth. But God chose what is foolish in the world to shame the wise; God chose what is weak in the world to shame the strong; God chose what is low and despised in the world, even things that are not, to bring to nothing things that are, so that no human being might boast in the presence of God. And because of him you are in Christ Jesus, who became to us wisdom from God, righteousness and sanctification and redemption, so that, as it is written, "Let the one who boasts, boast in the Lord." – 1 Corinthians 1:26-31

The world in which we live is in the thralls of epistemological chaos—everything is backward, sideward, forwards, up and down! There is no anchor holding us firm in the foaming waves, so we are "tossed to and fro by the waves and carried about by every wind of doctrine, by human cunning, craftiness in deceitful schemes" (Eph 4:14). We see the effects of this chaos in social media, politics, newspapers, popular books, classrooms, and universities. Yet, unlike our neighbours, Christians are not left without an anchor when the waves crash around us. We do not have to be dragged along in the stream of our culture nor surrender to the nihilism that has characterized the last two centuries.

God has not left us without a witness, he has spoken. In that act of speaking, revealing himself, he has provided us with a firm foundation to withstand all the storms the threaten to submerge our nations. Instead of leaving us in the dark, captive to Kingdom of Satan expressed through the world in rebellion against God, he has entered this created order to transfer all those who believe in his Son from the kingdom of darkness into the kingdom of his glorious light.

Initially, through the Spirit, he has shone "in our hearts to give us the light of the knowledge of the glory of God in face of Jesus Christ" (2 Cor 4:6). Through Jesus Christ, God the Father has brought to fulfillment his plan to reconcile sinners to himself through the cross. By pouring out the punishment we deserved upon Jesus in our place, he has purchased for us salvation from our sins and has enacted a new **covenant** through which we receive all of his promises, in part now but fully in the age to come. This reconciliation, this beautiful gift of salvation, is hard to believe—it is foolishness to us when we were perishing (1 Cor 1:18-31). But through the Spirit he illumines our hearts to believe in and receive the salvation provided by his Son.

When we believe in the Son, he opens our eyes to perceive his glory in Scripture and the created order. For the first time, as the veil of hard hearted rebellion is removed, we begin to see the world truly, as the theatre of the glory of God. Through those who teach us, through pastors and peers, we receive a foundation from which we are able to begin interpreting the Word of God and his world correctly—as he intends. With this firm foundation, we have the promise that we can live faithfully before God in this world, that we can see the world and learn how God would have us respond to it.

For the Christian, God's gift of knowing has endless implications. To name a few, first, we need to submit ourselves to Scripture as God's authoritative revelation. Only if God has revealed himself clearly, accurately, authoritatively do we have hope to navigate the chaos of our world. God has revealed himself in this way and it is our job to grow in our knowledge of God and his world through the Word, the means he has ordained for doing so.

Second, we need to reevaluate our assumptions. It is not safe to assume that disciplines formulated within a secular worldview will be sufficient to know and respond truly to God's world. We must ask difficult questions like, how does the truth of the Word of God change the methods and conclusions of the physical sciences? How does the revelation of God change the way we do linguistics, economics, or sociology? How does the standard of the word of God shape our political opinions? How does the Biblical revelation, especially a Biblical anthropology, shape the way we understand psychology and do counselling?

Third, we need to conduct ourselves with great humility. I think I have shown that the Bible reveals to us that we can have certainty in this life. We can have final conclusions, solid opinions, firm knowledge. Yet the cost of attaining this is total submission to God! We must submit our thinking, feeling, and acting to God if we are to attain such knowledge. This is a lifelong goal, pursuing sanctification through work of the Spirit. As we pursue conformity to Christ, we will find ourselves moving from the complete confidence in God's work for us through Christ to ever deepening confidence in our knowledge of his will and may even achieve a level of certainty about more speculative areas of Biblical application—such as philosophy. The knowledge we have, certainty we attain, is not based on our abilities or efforts but solely on the grace of God who shone light into the darkness of our hearts;

> consider your calling, brothers: not many of you were wise according to worldly standards, not many were powerful, not many were of noble birth. But God chose what is foolish in the world to shame the wise; God chose what is weak in the world to shame the strong; God chose what is low and despised in the world, even things that are not, to bring to nothing things that are, so that no human being might boast in the presence of God. And because of him you are in Christ Jesus, who became to us wisdom from God, righteousness and sanctification and redemption, so that, as it is written, "Let the one who boasts, boast in the Lord." (1 Cor 1:26-30)

For the Christian, then, the application is this: read the Scriptures and know God; read the Scriptures and believe God; read the Scripture and live for God in this world. Make known his light in the darkness through the preaching of the Gospel of his risen Son, the only message that can save sinners and the only hope for the epistemologically lost.

For the unbeliever, the gift of knowing God has given his creatures begs a response. Will you continue groping around in the dark, trusting yourself or other man-made authorities for hope? To do so will only result in hopeless nihilism now and eternal judgment when Christ returns. Yahweh is the creator of this world and apart from him, there is no hope to understand and live in it. Indeed, to seek to live apart from him is to engage in rebellion against him, to reject the Creator and worship the creature. We all worship something. The question is, will we worship the Creator or another god—sex, drugs, money, respectability, influence, power, etc. To worship another, a false god, is to invest your hope in nothing—a fleeting shadow—and invite the judgment of the one true God.

To worship the Yahweh is to cast yourself on his mercy, to repent of rebellion and trust in the life, death, and resurrection of his Son for salvation. To cast ourselves on the mercy of God costs everything—our independence, even our very life—but gains for us far more than we lost (Matt 10:39, John 12:25) . Not only are we delivered from the wrath of God against sin, but we enter his family, expressed in the local church, and inherit the purpose of magnifying his name throughout the earth. And at his return, we inherit joy everlasting in the presence of God in a new creation—a new heaven and earth free from sin, rebellion, death, and pain. This is the hope of all who believe: life and joy now through the Spirit of God among his people and life and joy forevermore in the presence of the Triune God in a new creation. This hope is life, not death; purpose, not nihilism; hope, not despair; and truth, not a lie. These are the promises of God for those who cast themselves upon his mercy and delight in the things he has revealed.

> The secret things belong to the LORD our God, but the things that are revealed belong to us and to our children forever, that we may do all the words of this law. (Deut 29:29)

Volume 2a:
The Gift of Reading – Part 1
Reading the Bible in Submission to God

INTRODUCTION

For whatever was written in former days was written for our instruction, that through endurance and through the encouragement of the Scriptures we might have hope. – Romans 15:4

There is no question more important to the Christian than this, "Can I understand the Bible?" Those who answer "yes" to this question are among the precious few who have withstood the barrage of attacks levelled against God's Word and its clarity over the last several hundred years. This book and its second part are for those who need to hear that they can understand God's Word and who are ready to learn how they might do so better.

This is a book on exegesis, the practice of reading in order to understand, specifically biblical exegesis, the practice of reading the Bible. It is the first of two parts; together, parts 1 & 2 present a biblical hermeneutic, a theory of how to interpret the Bible that is rooted in the teaching of the Bible. I hope to show in the following pages that the Bible is accessible to contemporary Christians—whether they be new Christians, mature believers, pastors, or scholars—and how we can go about reading it. Here in Part 1 I hope to give a framework with which to begin reading the Bible. I intend only to give a framework, a basic outline. Several books could be (and have been) written on the subjects raised in this book. It is not my intention to replace every other biblical study resource with this volume. Instead, I hope to lay out a methodology for reading the Bible according to its own claims. By doing so, I hope to equip the reader with a foundation for reading the Bible, a foundation that can be built upon with the many other resources available. By laying exegesis on a biblical foundation, I do not intend to nullify all other contributions to the field of biblical studies but to give the reader a way to learn from the best biblical studies has to offer without being drawn away from the biblical text by the trends within interpretation that are not founded on the Bible's own teaching. This book will be most helpful when used in conjunction with regular reading of the Bible and with supplementary aid in building exegetical skills. This could mean reading the Bible with an experienced Christian or reading some of the other books or articles mentioned in the following pages. In a teaching setting, I envision a specific role for this book; it would lay out the presuppositions for interpreting the Bible and give a method to begin such study. Class work and teaching would then focus on learning the skills outlined in the second section of this book. The second part of this series, *The Gift of Truth*, will also prove helpful in this regard.

In *The Gift of Reading – Part 2*, this book's companion, I intend to lay out at greater depth the theory of interpretation that underlies this work. That work will provide an answer to the many challenges raised against biblical clarity today and prove helpful in a more advanced hermeneutics class or for the reader who has already learned biblical interpretation from a different perspective. Therefore, the reader who has some background in biblical interpretation may desire to begin there, with *Part 2*, lest the approach of this present book deceive the reader as to its sufficiency for the task it undertakes. Indeed, I hope that this volume will show that reading the Bible is in many ways simple—hard work, yes, but not impossible work reserved for scholars and specialists alone.

The intended audience for both parts is intentionally broad. I hope to write with enough lucidity that a pastor could give this book to an interested person in his congregation and have confidence that it will be understood. I also hope to go to sufficient depth that pastors, students, and even scholars will also profit from reading it.

Before we begin, let us consider the question above; can you and I understand the Bible? First, the Bible is a book like this one, so your ability to make it this far should encourage you that you can indeed read. Yet many of us learned in high school or university that texts cannot communicate, that my communication with you through these words is an illusion. The only meaning present, some would claim, is what you bring (this is part of a literary approach known as Deconstructionism).

Others of us were taught that a massive historical-cultural gap separates the biblical writers from us so that only the scholar with knowledge of the ancient world can actually know what it says. I suspect that many of us, even though taught these things, have the nagging feeling in the back of our minds that this cannot be true: we understand Jesus most—at least some—of the time, do we not? We know we must repent and believe the good news of Jesus Christ and that murder and adultery are wrong! For those of us who feel the tension between what we have been told and what we experience, the Bible brings us great comfort.

It tells us that we can understand it. For example, young people are expected to read and meditate on the Law in order to resist sin (Ps 119:9-14). All of us are called to teach others at some point in our lives, and we are to do so in light of an understanding of God's word (Deut 6:4-9, 20; Eph 6:4; Tit 2:1-10). It is clear that the Bible was not written for the scholar but for us that we might learn and grow (Ps 102:18; Rom 4:23, 15:4; 1 Cor 9:10), and Luke considers it a Christian virtue to measure what Paul preached by the word (Acts 17:11). During the Reformation, Martin Luther saw this truth in 2 Timothy 3:16-17, writing in *The Bondage of the Will*,

> In a word: if Scripture is obscure or equivocal, why need it have been brought down to us by act of God? Surely we have enough obscurity and uncertainty within ourselves, without our obscurity and uncertainty and darkness being augmented from heaven! And how then shall the apostle's word stand: "All Scripture is given by inspiration of God, and is profitable for doctrine, for reproof, for correction?" (2 Tim. 3:16)[1]

It is true that the Bible does not ever say, "you who are reading this can understand it," yet it assumes this throughout. Therefore, our question cannot be "can we understand the Bible?" Instead, we must ask, "how has God made it possible for us to understand the Bible?" There are several different approaches to answering such a "how" question today. Though many philosophers are stuck on the "can" question, those who get to the "how" use intricate philosophical analysis to come to the answer. The

---

[1] Luther, *The Bondage*, 128.

problem with this, however, is that when they are done, reading looks nothing like our common experience of reading. Furthermore, the "meanings" they find seem to be (conveniently) the very things they have been saying the whole time. Others ask how texts were read in the past, following the church fathers and Greeks in allegorical reading (looking for a spiritual meaning behind the words) or maybe reading as the 1st-century Jews did. Still others labour hard to recreate the world in which the biblical texts were written in order to understand what the biblical authors intended to say to their audiences.

I will argue in the second volume that all these approaches fall short in one way or another. I hope to offer an alternative that is based on reading the Bible according to what it is. The Bible is, above all, a piece of writing, so there is a sense in which we need to read it like any other written document. Yet, there is a difficulty here: we recognize that there are many sorts of written documents. We read resumes differently than we do blog posts, and blog posts differently than novels—and all these differ from dictionaries! So we need to use basic skills of reading, yet we need to know what the Bible actually is if we are to interpret it. To know what the Bible is, we need to pay attention to both what it says about itself and what it shows about itself.[2] The Bible is thus our source for the knowledge of how to read it. The Bible tells us what we need to know: it is the standard by which we judge what it is and is not.

Yet the Bible is huge, too big for anyone of us to comprehend entirely. Furthermore, I have some gifts, but you have others; reading the Bible in its entirety probably requires both of us—in fact, God says it does (1 Cor 12:12-31; Eph 4:11-16). Therefore, we turn to the Bible as our standard, yet we need to read it with the help of others. We need to read it in the **context** of community.[3]

---

[2] There is a circle here, yet such a circle is inevitable when we are dealing with ultimate authorities. However, this is not a vicious circle, a self-destructing argument. It is more like a spiral, we start with an understanding and continue to refine it in interaction with our authority, God's Word. Cf. Vol. 1, *The Gift of Knowing*.

[3] "Context" is a key word that will appear throughout this book. Essentially, "context" refers to the setting in which something is found, to the environment to which it relates. Above—in this context—I am using "context" to refer to the setting in which Christians must engage with Scripture. Christians must read scripture in

This book is itself an act of reading the Bible in community. I am standing on the shoulders of many great men and women who have come before us and am attempting to lead you in reading the Word. To do this, to read the Bible, takes a lot of work—even with the help of community. Reading is itself a labour, but this is accompanied by the need to learn many new things and, as we read the Bible, the added burden of difficult truths with which we must wrestle.

These three aspects of or perspectives on our task—namely, the biblical text, Christian Community, and hard work—lay behind everything that follows. These three factors are essential at every step of interpreting Scripture.

Having addressed the necessary issues, we can begin to answer the question, "How has God made it possible for us to read the Bible?" Or rephrasing this, "what do we need to read the Bible as God intends us to?" We need three things to read the Bible: *eyes to see, ears to hear, and hearts to understand.*

First, we need eyes to see. We need to look at the Bible with the appropriate lens, with right eyes, to see it. We need to know *what the Bible is* and *what the Bible is about* in order to make sense of each of its parts. In the first section of this book, we will look at the nature of the Bible and how having the right eyes—the proper lens—lets us see correctly.

Second, we need ears to hear. The Bible is God's communication to us. Like any communication, having someone speak is not sufficient; someone needs to listen. To read the Bible, we need to know how to listen really well. Because the Bible is in some ways like every other book, everyone reading this book can, in theory, read the Bible. Yet things get complicated when we factor in bible translations, the original languages, and difficult passages. For this reason, in the second section of the book, we will look at what it means to read the Bible well and how we can do this.

Third, we need hearts to understand. The Bible is God's Word, yet

---

interaction with, for the sake of, and with the help of Christian community. In the study of literature, and so in reading the Bible, "context" refers to the words, sentences, paragraphs, chapters, books, and book in which a particular object of study (word, sentence, etc.) is embedded. It interacts with all these layers of the text, which form a literary context or setting. Context in this sense, the text in which words and sentences are embedded, is what gives parts of a text their meaning.

humans are by nature in rebellion against God, so our default disposition is hostility toward God and his word: we do not want to understand it! All acts of reading, especially reading the Bible, are moral acts. We choose to love our neighbours by listening to them; we choose to love God by listening to him. We need submission to God to follow the text where it leads, to change our views and believe what at times seems unbelievable. This is my recipe for reading the Bible well: eyes to see, ears to hear, and hearts to understand. May the Lord grant us these things:

> Let not our eyes be blinded
> > by the lord of this world,
> Let not our ears be blocked
> > by the lies of sin,
> Let not our hearts be hardened
> > to despise your Word.
>
> Give us eyes to see
> > and understand what you say.
> Give us ears to listen carefully
> > and attentively to your voice.
> Give us hearts to humbly submit
> > and bow ourselves before you.
>
> Your word is a light unto our path;
> > let us see it.
> Your word is hope for those in need;
> > let us hear it.
> Your word is a foundation for our feet;
> > let us believe it.
>
> To you be all glory and honor and praise,
> > Today and for the rest of our days,
> > Amen.

—Part 1—
We Need Eyes to See

1

THE BIBLE IS THE DOCUMENT OF GOD'S COVENANT

> But their minds were hardened. For to this day, when they read the old covenant, that same veil remains unlifted, because only through Christ is it taken away. – 2 Corinthians 3:14

The first thing we need to read the Bible is eyes; we need to look at it in the right way. Would we not read a letter very differently if we knew it was from the government rather than a spouse or a reputable account of history differently than the Lord of the Rings? In the first case, we expect the letter to be impersonal and carry the authority of those ruling over us; in the second case, we trust the words of a reputable historian to accurately describe history. In contrast, we would not use the Lord of the Rings to write a history of the Middle Ages.

There is a sense in which we need to know what a book is before we can read it. To understand any one passage, a part, we need to know something about the book, the whole. When we are confused about a detail or a scene, we know to read on or quickly skim what we have already read. We know from practice that books are self-interpreting. The Bible is more complicated than a novel or a letter from the government, yet the principle remains the same. For centuries this principle has been captured in the phrase, "Scripture interprets Scripture" or "Scripture is its best interpreter." To understand the Bible, we need to look at individual passages in light of the whole Bible. This requires great familiarity on our part; we need to be voracious readers of Scripture.

Yet we are not alone in this; God's people have been reading the Scriptures for over 3000 years and have become very good at it. At the end of each chapter of this book, I will recommend resources that can help us grow in various skills and enrich our understanding of the Bible. In this first section, we will look at what the Bible is. In this chapter, we will consider the type of document the Bible is and its features. In the next two chapters, we will look at the **worldview** the Bible teaches;[1] that is, we will look at its teaching about the universe and our place in it. First, in Chapter 2, we will look broadly at the biblical teachings about God, man, and the Gospel. Second, in Chapter 3, we will look at the **metanarrative**, or universal story, that the Bible teaches.[2] In Chapter 4, we will consider the peoples of the Bible, the differences between God's Old Covenant and New Covenant People. For now, let us consider what exactly the Bible is.

If someone were to ask you what is the Bible, how would you respond? Eventually, after explaining that it is God's very words given to man, we would describe it as a "book." Yet, what kind of book is Scripture? It is clearly not a novel nor a dictionary; is it a theological textbook or a self-help book? Having heard the acronym BIBLE, maybe you will describe it as *Basic Instructions Before Leaving Earth*. Yet does that accurately describe the Scriptures?

This question matters: we have already seen that we read books according to what they are, so a misunderstanding of what the Bible is will lead us to misread it. As we will see in *The Gift of Reading – Part 2*, this is one reason people misread the Bible: they misunderstand for one reason or another what the Bible is. I will argue in this chapter that the Bible is a covenant document: it is a written testimony to God's relationship with his

---

[1] A worldview is essentially the interpretive framework, or the glasses, through which we view the world. That is, all of us look at the world with "rose-coloured glasses": none of us see it without interpreting it. This interpretation comes from our worldview: I recognize a tree as a God's handiwork and praise him because he created it. An atheist thinks it is a testimony to evolution and wonders at the marvellous fact that something so intricate happens to exist. We considered worldviews in Vol. 1, *The Gift of Knowing*, we will talk more about what a worldview is in Chapter 2, and will revisit them in Vol.3, *The Gift of Seeing*.

[2] A metanarrative can be described as the story of history, or an interpretation of all events that have happened and will happen. We will discuss metanarratives in Chapter 3.

people designed to guide them in their relationship with him so that his purpose in the covenant might be fulfilled.

A. The Bible is a Covenant Document

To begin with, the Bible is a *covenant* document. This assumes we know what a covenant is. A covenant refers to a formal relationship enacted between two parties. In our day, a (biblical) marriage is a covenant. I pledged to my wife that I would be her husband, performing all the obligations implicit in that role, and Nicole pledged to be my wife, performing all the obligations implicit in that role. We took an oath, our vows, confirming our commitment. The Bible is full of covenants, such as Abraham's covenant with Abimelech (Gen 21:25-34), yet six are especially important. We will consider all six in Chapter 3, but it should suffice for now to consider the two major covenants discussed in the New Testament.

First is the Old Covenant, made at Sinai between Yahweh—God—and Israel. This covenant legislated Israel as a holy nation, setting them apart from the rest of the nations by their devotion and service to Yahweh: they were to live solely for him and represent him by acting in specific ways. Their relationship was consistently endangered by their sin, so this covenant also included a sacrificial system designed to (temporarily) remove the consequences of sin (cf. Heb 10:4). According to Hebrews 8, this covenant is fading away; it has become obsolete. The reason for this is the arrival of the New Covenant in Christ Jesus. The New Covenant deals once for all with human sin and legislates the Kingdom of God, Jesus's universal reign in heaven as manifest on earth through the Church (e.g. Luke 20:14-19; Acts 28:31-Rom 1:6; Rom 3:31-26; 1 Cor 15:22-28; Heb 1:1-4).[3] The Bible is a covenant document; specifically, it is the legal document governing God's New Covenant made with all who believe in Jesus Christ. The Old Testament is the covenant document governing his Old Covenant people Israel, yet it is also the foundation for the New Testament. Both Testaments together form the Bible.

There are two ways we can show that the Bible is a covenant document. The first is what it tells us about itself. The New Testament never refers to

---

[3] These are only a few examples; we will look more at the kingdom of God in following chapters.

itself as a completed unit, though we can identify it as such by its own features (such as the way the Book of Revelation closes off both the Old and New Testaments). To learn about the nature of the New Testament, and so the Bible as a whole, we need to pay attention to what it says about the Old Testament.

The New Testament authors consider each other to be in the same position as the Old Testament authors and consider each other's work to have the same character as the Old Testament; it is Scripture (cf. 2 Pet 3:15-16; 1 Tim 5:18).[4] Therefore, to learn about the New Testament, and the whole Bible, we can consider what the New Testament says about the Old. It is a curious thing that the New Testament summarizes the Old Testament as "the Law" (Matt 5:18, Luke 16:17, John 10:34, John 15:25; 1 Cor 14:21). When we hear "Law," we think of rules and regulations that must be obeyed: this is not too far off, yet the Hebrew word *Torah* and the Greek word *Nomos* (both translated Law) are being used a little more specifically. The Law often refers specifically to the legislation surrounding God's covenant with Israel, legislation found in Genesis-Deuteronomy (*the Torah*). "Law" refers specifically to a covenant document. The New Testament extends this title to refer to the entire Old Testament. Specifically, in 2 Corinthians 3:14, Paul calls the Old Testament the Old Covenant. According to the New Testament, then, every book of the Old Testament is part of the Law, the document governing the Old Covenant. By extension, we can see how the New and Old Testaments together—with their shared similarities to the Old Testament—is the document governing the New Testament believers.[5]

We can confirm this observation by paying attention to what the Bible shows us about itself, to what we see when we pay careful attention to it. Both the Old and New Testaments are clear that the first five books of the Bible, the *Torah*, are a covenant document (e.g. Judges 8:31). If we begin here, we are able to identify three functions displayed by all the passages in this document. First, there are legal texts, texts intended to legislate certain behaviours within God's covenant people (e.g. Exod 20:1-17; Lev 1:1-7:38). These texts address how the people of God were to behave towards God and

---

[4] 2 Peter refers to Paul's letters as "Scripture" and Paul refers to Luke's Gospel here as "Scripture."

[5] The names "New and Old *Testament*" is actually derived from the Latin word for covenant, *testamentum* (cf. Luke 22:20, "new covenant" is *novum testamentum*).

towards each other (e.g. Exod 20:1-17). Second, these are accompanied by case laws, narratives or scenarios that illustrate the laws (e.g. Exod 21:23-22:15). Third, there are accounts of the behaviour of the parties in the covenant: Genesis 1 – Exodus 19 gives a history of God's creation of and interaction with the world, especially with the ancestors of Israel. On the other hand, Exodus 32:1-35 recounts Israel's failure with the golden calf, and Numbers 16:1-50 gives an account of the rebellion of a man named Korah and its results.[6] These accounts are found both in narrative and poetic form (e.g. Exod 15). Thus, we find in the *Torah* (Gen-Deut) the laws governing the covenant, examples of what it looks like to live the laws, and narratives about God the covenant maker and about Israel's successes and failures in the Covenant.[7] These features of the *Torah*, of the Law as a covenant document, are displayed throughout the rest of the Bible.

As we will see below, the Old Testament was historically divided into three sections (see Luke 24:44): the Law (*Torah*), the Prophets (*Nevi'im*), and the Writings (*Ketuvim*).[8] The Law most clearly displays the legislative aspect of the *Torah*; the Prophets most clearly display the historical aspect; and the Writings most clearly display the instructive aspect, showing what Covenant life looks life. We could summarize each of these sections respectively as *The Covenant, Covenant Life,* and *Covenant Living*.[9] Extending this analysis to the New Testament, Miles Van Pelt has observed that the New Testament displays the same pattern: the Gospels give an account of the covenant institution and legislation, Acts recounts the history of the New Covenant, and the Epistles give instruction in living out the Covenant. On this analysis,

---

[6] It is interesting to observe that this feature of the Torah is unique in ancient covenant documents; we have records of similar covenant documents from peoples around Israel, yet none of these have extensive narratives woven throughout the legal texts.

[7] It may interest the reader to observe that every text in the Torah, in fact in the Bible, has these three functions. Every text is normative, telling us what we ought or ought not believe/feel/do; every text is historical, it is an expression of God's past covenant interactions with his people (e.g. the Laws are embedded in discourse, accounts of God speaking to his people); and every text is instructive, showing us not only what but also how to live out this covenant.

[8] The books of the Old Testament are ordered differently following this division, a list is provided in the following section.

[9] These titles are those of Miles Van Pelt, whose work first helped me see the significance of these sections.

the entire Old Testament has the same function as Genesis in the Torah: it shows us who God is and gives a history of his actions that lay the foundation for the New Covenant. Thus, paying attention to the biblical texts themselves confirms what the New Testament says about the Old Testament and, by implication, itself. We see, then, that the Bible is a covenant document.

B. The Nature of the Bible as a Covenant Document

We have already seen that the nature of a document determines the way we read it. That the Bible is a covenant document informs our reading in two different ways; it tells us about the nature and purpose of what is written in it. First, as a covenant document, the Bible is a Word from our covenant Lord and has the same attributes ascribed to all his actions; it reflects and communicates his character. It is also an intentionally ordered document. That is, in some writings, the order of the contents does not affect our interpretation (such as a grocery list, anthology, or resume). However, when it comes to the Bible, the order has some significance. Consider with me the characteristics or attributes of the Bible and then the order of the Bible.

a. *The Nature of the Bible*

It is beyond the scope of this book to give a detailed account of the Bible's nature (I will recommend some resources at the end of the chapter for the interested reader and will take up this topic in the second part of *God's Gifts for the Christian Life*). But we can consider four significant features of the Bible that result from its nature as a covenant document given by Yahweh, our Covenant Lord. These are *inerrancy*, *authority*, *sufficiency*, and *clarity* (traditionally, *perspicuity*).

i. Inerrancy

As God's Word, the Bible carries his exhaustive knowledge and perfection; thus, it is inerrant. That is, as God knows all truth and cannot be wrong, so the Bible as his Word—an act of his speaking (2 Tim 3:16)—has the same attribute. Accuracy is essential for a covenant document, and perfect accuracy for a document legislating a covenant with God himself, for those in covenant relationship must trust their covenant Lord. When we say the Bible is *inerrant*, we are claiming that it accurately communicates the perfect knowledge of God in every area to which it speaks. Inerrancy is a necessary result of Scripture being the speech of an inerrant God; it is also the result of Scripture being a trustworthy guide in our covenant relationship with him. But, more importantly, it is the explicit claim of the Bible. Consider that Jesus identifies Scripture as truth itself (John 17:17, cf. Ps 119:43). Additionally, the Scriptures repeatedly claim that they are unbreakable and sure (e.g. Isa 40:5-8; Ps 119:83, 89, 96; John 10:35).

Practically, if the Bible is the speech of Yahweh, who is perfect and who created and exhaustively knows all things, there is nothing in all the creation that could say it is wrong: nothing and no one has the authority to correct God (consider Isa 40; Job 38:1-42:6). Inerrancy means that we can trust everything Scripture says; the implication for our interpretation is—among other things—that we can trust what it says about itself: no passage of Scripture is ever in error. The New Testament, therefore, can help us better understand the Old. (We will see, however, that there is danger in not paying careful attention to what exactly the New Testament authors are saying about the Old.)

ii. Authority

Following naturally from inerrancy is Scripture's authority. If Scripture cannot err, then we are obligated to believe everything it says: it has authority over all our thinking. More so, as the very words of God our creator, king, and covenant Lord, Scripture carries God's own authority. Yes, Scripture has the same authority that commanded light into being (Gen 1:3) and the dead to rise from the grave (John 12:43-44), which controlled the elements (e.g. Josh 10:11-14). God has the authority to command and correct our thoughts, actions, and emotions; his Word has this same authority. Though some today attempt to separate God's authority from his Word, with a moment's thought, the foolishness of such an attempt is evident. None of us would receive a legitimate letter from our president or prime minister—or the CRA (or IRS)—and ignore it because it was only a letter! We recognize that their authority is extended to their actions and the products of their actions, such as speeches, laws, and letters. Inerrancy means that it is ignorant for us, finite human beings, to disagree with Scripture. Authority means that it is foolish, dangerous, and morally disobedient to disagree with Scripture.

iii. Sufficiency

As God's Word, the Bible is sufficient to accomplish its purpose. As God is omnipotent, able to do anything that he desires, so his Word unfailing accomplishes his purposes:

> "For as the rain and the snow come down from heaven
> and do not return there but water the earth,
> making it bring forth and sprout,
> giving seed to the sower and bread to the eater,
> so shall my word be that goes out from my mouth;
> it shall not return to me empty,
> but it shall accomplish that which I purpose,
> and shall succeed in the thing for which I sent it. (Isa 55:10-11)

Sufficiency is essential to the Bible's covenantal nature. Scripture is intended to govern our relationship with God, show us how to live before him in this world. Sufficiency means that as the product of an omnipotent God, it succeeds in this. Paul says as much in 2 Timothy 3:16-17,

> All Scripture is breathed out by God and profitable for teaching, for reproof, for correction, and for training in righteousness, that the man of God may be complete, equipped for every good work.

Scripture may not tell us every detail we would love to know about Akkadian marriage ceremonies—that is, it does not tell us everything—but it is sufficient to guide us in faithfulness to God. This does not mean, as some have claimed, that Scripture only tells us about "faith and practice," as if Scripture is only trustworthy when it speaks of God and when it gives instructions on how to act. When we consider what Scripture actually teaches us (including the nature of truth, the creation of the world, etc.), we see that Scripture is sufficient to equip us with all that we need to interpret the world correctly so that we can act for God in it. In other words, Scripture gives us a complete worldview.[10]

iv. Clarity

As God's Word, the Bible is also clear. A covenant document is not complete

---

[10] I argue this point as far as it concerns knowledge and truth in Vol. 1 & 3, *The Gift of Knowing* and *The Gift of Seeing*.

if it is only a truthful account of the covenant lord's words providing sufficient detail to govern the relationship; it also needs to be clear. A covenant document needs to communicate if it is to fulfil its purpose. Thus, clarity is also an expression of God's omnipotence or control: if God intended Scripture to govern our lives and reveal himself, he is surely capable of ensuring it does so. We have discussed clarity already in the introduction to this book, yet its importance deserves reiteration. If Scripture is not clear, then we are hopeless. If Scripture is the source of our knowledge about God, essential to worshipping him (Ps 145:18; John 4:21-25; 1 John 3:18); about the Gospel, essential to our salvation (Rom 10:5-17); about God's will, essential to the purpose for which he created us (2 Tim 3:16-17); and if Scripture is our only testimony to the truth of the resurrection and its meaning and it does not communicate these things clearly, we are above all people lost fools (cf. 1 Cor 15:12-19).

What would it say about God if he intended to communicate with us yet failed? We have already seen that this is his intention, and the Bible is clear that he is perfectly capable of accomplishing all of his will; therefore, we can be confident that he has succeeded in his purpose. Scripture is, therefore, clear: it is sufficient to communicate everything we need to do the good works for which God created us (cf. Eph 2:10). As a covenant document given to us by Yahweh, our covenant Lord, Scripture is inerrant, authoritative, sufficient, and clear. I have also claimed above that Scripture is *ordered*, that it has an intentional structure.

b. The Structure of the Bible

There are many types of literature in every language; some of these are long enough to have not only paragraphs but also sections and chapters, and maybe even books. Of these larger pieces of literature, we could identify two broad categories: there are those in which order and structure are incidental or variable, unessential to their meaning, and there are others for which structure and order are vital to their meaning. There is also a significant middle area where the order is important, yet the loss of order is not catastrophic. For example, if you were to jumble the chapters of a novel, the result would be a confusing mess: reading the chapters in order is essential to reading the novel correctly. Yet, jumbling the articles of a dictionary would only make navigation difficult; the meaning would remain the same.[11] We have received the Bible in a specific order; our question should be, does this order matter?

Is the Bible a document like a dictionary where the order is inconsequential to interpretation, or like a novel, where the order is essential? We will see that it is somewhere in between: order matters, yet ignorance of the order is not catastrophic. The latter point should not be controversial: Scripture has been interpreted for thousands of years, and many interpreters have understood it well without (intentionally) paying close attention to its order. Yet, I contend that close attention given to the Bible shows that it is indeed ordered intentionally and that this order matters. We can see this by asking three questions: what is the order of the Bible, does this order demonstrate a structure, and is there significance to this ordered structure?

First, what is the order of the Bible? In answer, you might pull out your English Bible now and look up a table of contents or recall a list of books long ago memorized, yet things at this point get a little complicated. There is some debate over the order of the New Testament, but it is clear that the Old Testament originally had an order quite different from the present order of our English Bibles. The reasons why they differ are not malicious; they are simply products of history and translation. However, it is significant that the New Testament has something to say about the order of our Old Testament, and it affirms the historical Hebrew order.[12] We can arrive at this conclusion by looking at two key texts and the supporting evidence from the rest of the New Testament. Consider, first, Jesus's words in Luke 24:44,

---

[11] Analogously, it is annoying to find radically different organizations in different grocery stores, yet the differences in organization do not hinder us from getting the supplies we need. For the student of Hebrew, compare the organizational principles of BDB and HALOT: if we set aside the differences in data gathering and interpretation, the content is largely unaffected by BDB's choice to organize by root and HALOT's choice to organize by lexical form.

[12] There are minor variations among Hebrew orders of the books, primarily they differ on the location of Ruth and Isaiah. I believe a good argument can be made, however, for the order printed in contemporary Hebrew Bibles. This order is based on the Masoretic Text, a very well-preserved tradition of copying the Hebrew Bible. However, the order of the specific books is not as important as recognizing the groups according to which the Bible is organized, so we do not need certainty on the placement of Ruth and Isaiah to affirm the argument above.

> ⁴⁴Then he said to them, "These are my words that I spoke to you while I was still with you, that everything written about me in the Law of Moses and the Prophets and the Psalms must be fulfilled."

Why does Jesus summarize the Old Testament as *Moses, the Prophets,* and *the Psalms*? In fact, the Old Testament is regularly summarized as *the Law,* or *the Law* and *the Prophets* (e.g. Luke 24:17, Acts 13:15, Rom. 3:21). Why these titles? What may not be readily apparent to us is that the Old Testament has historically been summarized with the acronym TaNaKh, the *Torah (Law), Nevi'im (Prophets),* and *Ketuvim* (the *Writings*). The first book of the Writings is the Psalms, and there is evidence that "Psalms" was sometimes used in the place of "Writings."[13] Thus, Jesus words are not arbitrary: they refer to the testimony of the three major groupings of the Old Testament. The same is true of the shorthand use of *Law* and the *Law and the Prophets*. Further confirmation can be found in Jesus's words in Luke 11:50-51,

> the blood of all the prophets, shed from the foundation of the world, may be charged against this generation, from the blood of Abel to the blood of Zechariah, who perished between the altar and the sanctuary.

I am sure we have passed by this passage before without thinking much of it, yet we may wonder why Jesus has chosen these two figures, Abel and Zechariah. His choice is not chronological: though Abel was the first martyr, Zechariah was not the last. However, it is significant that Abel is the first martyr recorded in the Old Testament (Gen. 4:8) and Zechariah the last according to the Hebrew ordering of the books (2 Chronicles 24:20-22). Thus, Jesus is saying that all the blood of the prophets as recorded in the Old Testament, from Genesis to Chronicles, is against those to whom he speaks. This saying depends on the Hebrew order of the Old Testament. Following this order, our Bible looks like this:

---

[13] This is technically called *synecdoche*, where the name of a part is used in the place of a whole (e.g. referring to the actions of Great Britain by referring to London). We see this in the writings of Philo, the Qumran community, and various later Jewish writings such as the *Tosephta* and *Talmud*.

	Old Testament	
Torah	**Prophets**	**Writings**
Genesis	Joshua	Psalms
Exodus	Judges	Job
Leviticus	Samuel[14]	Proverbs
Numbers	Kings	Ruth
Deuteronomy	Isaiah	Song of Songs
	Jeremiah	Ecclesiastes
	Ezekiel	Lamentations
	The Twelve[15]	Esther
		Daniel
		Ezra-Nehemiah
		Chronicles
	New Testament	
Matthew - John	Acts	Romans – Revelation[16]

In answer to our second question, we have seen that the New Testament affirms three groups of books in the Old Testament. Earlier, we followed Van Pelt in labelling these: the Covenant (*Torah*), Covenant History (*Prophets*), and Covenant Life (*Writings*). It is interesting that as we turn to the New Testament, it bears a similar structure: the Gospels present the founding events of the New Covenant, Acts presents its successful history, and Romans-Revelation gives various exhortations and instructions in living out this covenant.

---

[14] The Hebrew Bible recognizes 1 – 2 Samuel, 1 – 2 Kings, Ezra – Nehemiah, and 1 -2 Chronicles as single books.

[15] The Minor Prophets were historically considered one book or compilation, *The Twelve*: Hosea, Joel, Amos, Obadiah, Jonah, Micah, Nahum, Habakkuk, Zephaniah, Haggai, Zechariah, Malachi.

[16] The earliest Greek manuscripts have the Catholic Epistles (James – Jude) before the Pauline Letters (including Hebrews). Some Western manuscripts also have the Gospels in a different order, Matthew, John, Luke, and Mark.

We see, therefore, that the Bible has an order or structure (i.e. three sections). We must now ask, is this ordered structure significant? Concerning the structure, our summaries of each section indicate that they each serve a particular function. These sections are relevant to our interpretation. We see this, for example, in the narratives of each section of the Old Testament. They look dramatically different in each section. Readers have often struggled with the vast differences between the history of Israel recorded in Samuel – Kings and the same period as recorded in Chronicles. We have seen that Samuel and Kings occur in the Prophets and Chronicles in the Writings; could this be the reason for their differences? Indeed, Samuel & Kings functions much like the rest of the Prophets: they expound the themes of God's indictment of Israel's sin, his judgment against them, and his present and future salvific acts towards them. The focus is intentionally negative in order to show that despite Israel's failures, God remains faithful to his covenant. The book of Chronicles does not shy away from recording negative aspects of Israel's history but has much more to say about the positive aspects of even the wicked kings. The reason appears to be theological: the author of Chronicles intentionally demonstrates the relationship between the righteous behaviour of the kings and their successes and the consequences that follow from their unrighteous behaviour. In this way, Chronicles presents a theological interpretation of Israel's history that is very similar to the teaching of the Wisdom literature, particularly the Proverbs. By doing so, it underscores the faithfulness of God to his promises and encourages the reader to live righteously, trusting God. In this way, it is perfectly suited for its context in the Writings.

Furthermore, attention paid to the connections between books also reveals insights. For example, consider Ruth in connection with Proverbs. Is it a coincidence that Proverbs and Ruth are the only books in the Bible that contain the phrase "excellent wife" (lit. "worthy woman": Prov 12:4, 31:10; Ruth 3:11)? In fact, Ruth bears a few close parallels with Proverbs 31 (Prov 31:15, Ruth 2:6-7; Prov 31:23, Ruth 4:1-12). Side by side, Ruth appears to be an exposition of the "worthy woman" of Proverbs 31. Such parallels go on and on (consider thematic connections between Mal 4:1-6 and Ps 1-2). Because the Old Testament concludes with Chronicles, it ends on a cliff-hanger: it records the people of God still in exile, awaiting the return God promises in Deuteronomy 30:1-14. Opening with a genealogy focusing on Jesus's relationship to David, Matthew alerts the reader to the fact that Jesus will take David's throne and usher in the return from exile anticipated in the latter parts of Isaiah (chapter 40 onward) and Jeremiah 30-33. Lastly, considering the Bible as a united covenant document, we find that Genesis 1 is carefully mirrored in the account of the new creation in Revelation 21-22. The end parallels the beginning yet is shown to be better. We see, then, that the Bible has an order and structure and that this ordered structure has interpretive importance.[17]

However, the groupings of literature (Law, Prophets, and Writings) and the book ends of each Testament (Genesis/Chronicles; Matthew/Revelation), i.e. the features attested to specifically in Scripture and clearly in the manuscripts we have, remain the most significant features to which we must pay attention. Variety among the order of books in each larger grouping should not be a concern. As I mentioned above, the order is important, but its loss is not catastrophic for the Bible. Identifying the structure of the Bible helps us to better interpret it. However, following the different orders of our English Bibles (and the alternate order of the Greek Septuagint) will not lead us astray. There is some benefit in all these orders, for they draw attention to different features of the text. Nevertheless, because the Bible does speak about its own structure and we can identify the purpose for it, we should regard its structure in our reading.

The Bible is a covenant document given to us by Yahweh, our covenant Lord. It is inerrant and authoritative, clear and sufficient, with an intentional structure.[18] Knowing these features of the Bible helps us to interpret it, but

---

[17] Covenant documents in the Ancient world similarly had specific orders that were meaningful. Consider the Torah; it has the same structure as these ancient documents and the results of moving Genesis, for example, around would be significant. The Bible shows us that it is intentionally ordered, and we can confirm that this is typical for covenant documents. Cf. Meredith G. Kline, *Treaty of the Great King: The Covenant Structure of Deuteronomy; Studies and Commentary* (Grand Rapids: Eerdmans, 1963); Meredith G. Kline, *The Structure of Biblical Authority*, Rev. ed. (Grand Rapids: Eerdmans, 1975).

[18] Some readers at this point might ask where this order and structure come from. It is admittedly a lot harder to demonstrate the orderly structure of the Bible from history than it is from the features of the Bible. Yet, I do not think this should be problem for Christians. If we can affirm that God guided the writing of Scripture and the recognition of its authority among the Jewish communities and then the

we need a little bit more. The last aspect of the Bible we will consider in this chapter is its purpose.

C. The Bible Guides Us in Fulfilling God's Purpose

As a covenant document, the Bible is given to govern our relationship with God, yet it is not yet clear what that means. We could consider the purpose of the Bible in two senses: first, it is intended to do various things, such as rebuke, instruct, or encourage (see Rom. 15:4, 1 Cor. 10:11, 1 Tim. 3:16-17). We are not considering here these purposes of the Bible. Instead, I want us to consider why the Bible does these things. Ultimately, for Christians,[19] the Bible is intended to lead us from faith to faith for the glory of God.[20] That is, it is intended to lead first to initial faith, believing in Christ Jesus and having life in his name (cf. John 20:30-31), and then growing faith manifest in good works (cf. 1 Tim. 3:16-17). We can consider this purpose from three different perspectives: Scripture is meant to lead us from faith to faith, meaning that we would become Yahweh's people, know and enjoy him more, and do his

---

Christians communities who received them, why could he not also have prepared them to have a specific shape. Consider this thought experiment.

Take a group of five proficient writers. If you assigned them five distinct yet related writing projects and specified that they must follow closely the outlines you provide and include certain key words at specific junctions, what would result? If you were careful enough in your planning, you could put together a final document that bore the distinct styles of each author yet was connected by the plan you conceived (maybe having poetic texts appear at key points) and the key themes or words you prescribed. Thus, unity and meaning as found in the Bible could be achieved without the need for a final redactor uniting the work. If we could conceive of its possibility, surely the omnipotent God could execute such a feat, even over an extended period of time and multiple languages.

[19] There is also a negative purpose of Scripture: though it is primarily intended to edify and build up the believer, Scripture is also intended to harden the hearts of unbelievers as an act of judgment (e.g. Isa 6:8-13, Matt 13:10-17). We will focus on Scripture's purpose as it regards believers.

[20] John Piper's book *Reading the Bible Supernaturally* argues that the ultimate goal of reading the Bible the glory of God celebrated in the joyous worship of his people. I am considering the ways the Bible achieves that ultimate end.John Piper, *Reading the Bible Supernaturally: Seeing and Savoring the Glory of God in Scripture*, 2017.

will.[21] Let us consider each of these in turn.

First, the Bible is intended to make the reader part of Yahweh's people. In the Old Testament, the Torah laid out complex rules for the life of the Israelites, distinguishing them from their neighbours. Birth into the community made someone part of the covenant, and the Law outlined what this looked like. The Old Testament was not so much concerned with what we would call "evangelism," getting people into the community, but how to be righteous before God and so receive his blessings and not his curses (Lev 18:5; Deut 27:9-28:68). Yet, this changed with the coming of the New Covenant. The Scriptures were written not only to show God's people what it means to be a Christian but also to lead the reader or hearer into faith (John 20:30-31; Rom 10:5-17). The Bible and its teaching has as its purpose the initiation of salvation, leading the reader to confess faith in Jesus and his accomplished work in order that they might be justified, counted right before God.[22] Becoming God's people means many things, not only being declared righteous before God but also being adopted into God's family (Rom 8:12-17; Gal 4:5), being in Christ and made part of his body (Col 3:2-4; 1 Cor 12:13), and being set apart for God's purposes—made "saints," those who are holy, set apart for God's purpose (1 Cor 1:2; 6:11).

Jesus tells us that the result of belief is eternal life, knowing God and Jesus whom he sent (John 17:3). Knowing God and worshipping him as the appropriate response to that knowledge is the ultimate end of faith. The way we know God, the way we grow in relationship with him, is through his self-revelation in Scripture. God's Word is his very speech, so we encounter him

---

[21] Each of these is truly perspectival in that the whole of the Bible could be considered from any of these perspectives: everything is about knowing God, becoming his people, and following him faithfully.

[22] Though on the surface the Torah and the Gospel seems at odds, one offering justification through works and the other through Law, the contradiction is only apparent. God's people have been justified by faith throughout time (cf. Gen 15:6, Hab 2:4), yet God gave a Law that was impossible in order to imprison all under sin, to reveal human need until his answer arrived in Jesus Christ (Gal 3:15-39). Thus, the righteousness offered by the Law could never be attained, only a curse resulted. Yet this curse was removed in Christ, and we receive righteousness and the blessings of God through our Faith in Christ, who has fulfilled God's covenant on our behalf (Rom 1:16-17; Rom 3:21-31; Rom 5:12-21; Rom 10:1-5; Gal 3:10-14).

as we read. He is present, and we grow in all dimensions of knowledge (cognitive, "I know things about him;" and personal, "I know him") as we prayerfully read about God and his actions. All Scripture reveals God, not only teaching us about him but demonstrating his glory, the splendour of his majesty. As we read, we perceive his invisible attributes and character. The appropriate response to such revelation, to the glory of God, is worshipful awe and delight. As we get to know God through Scripture and encounter his glory revealed there, we will thus be led into joyous worship—the ultimate goal of creation.

Lastly, Scripture is intended to lead the Christian in the appropriate behaviour before God. By showing us God's will for our thoughts (Rom 12:2), our emotions (e.g. Deut 28:47), and our actions (1 Tim 3:16-17), Scripture transforms us into tools in his hands to do the good works he has created us for (Eph 2:10). We are equipped to love the Lord our God with all of our being (Deut 6:4-5).

We can see what these good works are by looking at Jesus' parting words to his disciples. According to Jesus, the purpose of a Christian as a part of his Church is to fulfil the great commission:

> Go therefore and make disciples of all nations, baptizing them in the name of the Father and of the Son and of the Holy Spirit, teaching them to observe all that I have commanded you. And behold, I am with you always, to the end of the age. (Matt 28:19-20)

This is not something any one person can do: this is Jesus's purpose for his people as a whole, for the Church and its local expressions. Each Christian has a role to play within this commission (1 Cor 12:1-31; Rom 12:3-8; Eph 4:11-16). Scripture thus equips each believer to be a part of the Church, using the particular gifts he has given them to build up the body and perform the work of ministry. We will consider the Church's work and so the believer's mission as part of it in the following chapters.

In this chapter, we set out to establish what sort of book the Bible is in order that we might read it accordingly. We have seen that the Bible is a covenant document possessing the attributes of the Lord who spoke it into being and an order that contributes to its interpretation. The purpose of the

Bible, as a covenant document, is to govern the New Covenant between God and his New Covenant people, all those who believe in Jesus Christ. It does this by leading the reader to faith, growing them in the knowledge of God, and guiding them in the appropriate way to follow him.

To read the Bible we need eyes to see; to this point, we have considered the Bible as a book, the broad features of which each part partakes. Now we will turn to consider the content of the Bible, namely the worldview it teaches.

Further Reading

The Bible

The Doctrine of the Word of God – John Frame [I]

Systematic Theology – Wayne Grudem, pp. 47-138 [B-I]

The Structure of Biblical Authority – Meredith G. Kline [A]

*A Biblical-Theological Introduction to the Old Testament – Miles Van Pelt, pp. [23-41] [B]

*A Peculiar Glory – John Piper [B]

Reading the Bible Supernaturally – John Piper [I]

The Gift of Revelation – J. Alexander Rutherford (expected 2021)

The Biblical Canon

The Old Testament Canon of the New Testament Church and its Background in Early Judaism – Roger T. Beckwith [A]

The Biblical Canon – David G. Dunbar, in *Hermeneutics, Authority, and Canon* eds. D. A. Carson and John D. Woodbridge [I]

*Canon Revisited – Michael J. Kruger [A]

The Question of Canon – Michael J. Kruger [A]

The Gift of Revelation – J. Alexander Rutherford (expected 2021)

2

THE BIBLE'S WORLDVIEW - THEOLOGY

> Hear Oh Israel, the Lord our God, the Lord is one; You shall love the Lord your God with all your heart and with all your soul and with all your might. – Deuteronomy 6:4-5

From the moment we wake up until we fall asleep, we are interpreters. We interpret, for example, the objects in our homes through the lens of past experience in order that we might use them. We interpret the motives and actions of others, evaluating them as good or bad, a help or a hindrance. We are constantly interpreting; a worldview describes the interlocking web of beliefs that we use to make interpretations. Our worldview functions most of the time tacitly; it is there unnoticed behind our emotions, actions, and opinions.

Consider the basic belief in the trustworthiness of our senses: we believe that what we perceive through sight and sound corresponds to reality and act as if it does. We pay the amount we read on a bill or go through a green light but stop at a red. There may be another person who does not share this basic belief about traffic lights and who acts with paralysing caution or complete disregard, believing that his perception of a green light is a lie and stopping when he sees one. We all have a worldview; it is a gift of God's grace that he has provided us with a—indeed, the only—coherent worldview in Scripture.

According to Romans 1:18-23, humanity has exchanged the proper interpretation of the creation granted to us by God for a lie, rejecting what is evident for a figment of our imagination. The Bible restores this worldview; it gives us the proper lens through which to see the world (and the Bible as a part of the world) correctly. We need to regain the biblical worldview if we are to properly interpret the Word and God's creation. There are many aspects of a worldview; one aspect is the interlocking network of beliefs concerning the objects of interpretation, the subject interpreting, and the way these interact.[1] For our purposes, we can focus on what the Bible teaches about the world we interact with—about "objects."

It will serve our purposes to consider first, in this chapter, key biblical teachings about the Creator and his creation, the objects with which we interact. Then, in the following chapter, we will consider the history and future of the Creator and his creation, the metanarrative that unites every event and object experienced in the creation. In Chapter 4, we will conclude this section by considering what the Bible teaches about humanity, specifically how God's people relate to God and his creation.

At every step, our primary authority is Scripture: as the Word of God, it is our ultimate standard of truth and the lens by which we interpret his creation. Regaining the biblical worldview lost in the fall is a progressive process; we are all growing in our knowledge of God and his world, yet we can jump-start this process by considering some of the major themes of Scripture.[2] I cannot hope to give more than a cursory summary of the doctrines of God, man, and the Kingdom of God. For those curious to go

---

[1] This book and its companions, making up the first part of the series *God's Gift's for the Christian Life*, is an effort to unpack the second aspect of a worldview, the way by which subjects come to know objects. *The Gift of Knowing* provides the framework of how humans know; *The Gift of Reading* considers how we interact with the Bible, our authority for knowing; and *The Gift of Seeing* considers the relationship between the knowing subject and the objects of knowledge.

From a different perspective, James N. Anderson helpfully summarizes the pieces of a worldview with the acronym TAKES, as in "What it TAKES to make a worldview." *T*: Theology, an absolute; *A*: anthropology, a view of man; *K*: Knowledge, a view of knowing and truth; *E*: Ethics, what is right or wrong, good or bad; and *S*: Salvation, what the problem of the world is and its answer.

[2] This process is a spiral; it begins with faith, as God renews our heart and through the teaching of the Church gives us a foundation to start with. We then bring this foundational knowledge to Scripture and find it both challenged and enriched. Our understanding grows as we reject falsehood and adopt a greater understanding of the truth.

deeper, resources for further reading are provided at the end of this chapter

A. Yahweh: the God who Is

The 66 books of the Bible and all creation testify to the God of the Bible, so I cannot hope to sufficiently introduce the reader to God their creator. The Bible teaches that we all know God, yet in our rebellion we have suppressed this truth. Consider this, then, a refresher, an account of our God as he has revealed himself to us.

To his people, God has revealed himself as Yahweh, the one who is (Exod 3:13-14). By definition, God is the one who exists, the true God over against all false gods worshipped by man. In relation to his people, Yahweh is the LORD, the gracious Lord who has entered into covenant with us, who has offered mercy and salvation to rebels deserving of judgment. Yahweh is the one true God (consider Deut 6:4, 1 Sam 2:2; Isa 40:9-31). Without losing his oneness, Yahweh is also simultaneously three: the Father is Yahweh (e.g. Ps 110:1, cf. Mark 12:35-36), Jesus is Yahweh (Acts 1:34, 2:21, 9:10; Rom 10:9, 13; 1 Cor 2:16), and the Spirit is Yahweh (2 Cor 3:17, 18).[3] Scripture is clear that the Father, the Son, and the Spirit are in perfect unity, are one; so Yahweh is three (e.g. John 17:20-26).

This is ultimately incomprehensible for finite humans: God in his grace has revealed something truly beyond our comprehension. Traditionally, this doctrine has been known as the Trinity: God is simultaneously one yet three. In God, unity and distinction—fundamental characteristics of reality—are equally ultimate: Yahweh's oneness is not more ultimate, more "real," than his threeness. There is simply too much to say about God's Trinitarian nature than we have space for. But in considering the depths of our Lord's self-revelation, we should feel in over our heads; we should feel as if we have touched upon things too great for us.

Yet, while our awe should be deep, we should also feel the joy that though limited, our knowledge is true. God is omnicompetent, competent to achieve all his purposes, so though we stand at the edge of the precipice of

---

[3] In most English translations, the divine name Yahweh is translated LORD (all capitals). In the New Testament, the Greek word *kurios* translated "lord" is used in the place of the name Yahweh.

the depths of the wonders of God, we have the certainty that all we do know is true and our source of joy—that we finite men and women are given a glimpse into the wonders and beauty of our infinite God.

Large theological treatments have the space to explore what Scripture teaches both about God's unity and threeness, giving separate consideration to God as Father, Spirit, and Son. We, however, will have to limit ourselves to God's unity. Beginning with God's Holiness, we will then consider God's relationship to us creatures in terms of his authority, control, and presence.[4]

a. Yahweh Is Holy

Throughout the Bible, the theme of holiness is repeated: Israel is a holy nation, the Temple is a holy place, and Christians like Israel are a holy people. Yet behind and above all these holy things is Yahweh, the Holy One of Israel. All holiness attributed to created things derives from God's holiness. That God is holy means that he is separated from all his creatures by his complete and consistent dedication to manifesting the fullness of his character, to display his glory, in all he does.[5] That is, we can discern from Scripture that God's ultimate purpose in creating and redeeming is to magnify his glory, that is, to make his magnificent nature clear to his creatures, to reveal himself in all his splendour (consider Hab 2:14; John 17:24; Rom 9:22-24). That God is Holy means that all his interactions are intended to share his glorious beauty and the joy he has in himself with others. This is good news for the Christian, for we learn God himself is joyful, that this sharing of himself is the ultimate source of joy for his creation (consider Ps 16:11, Ps 84, Matt 5:2-

---

[4] "Authority," "control," and "presence" are terms John Frame uses in his work on the doctrine of God. He calls them "Lordship attributes," describing God's lordship over his creation. His discussion is invaluable and rich, yet I make no attempt to follow him closely: the terms avail themselves well to our purposes. I am indebted to Frame's work, so many similarities may be discerned in what follows, yet this largely follows from the fact that we both are presenting the truths of Scripture. Cf. John M. Frame, *The Doctrine of God*, A Theology of Lordship (Phillipsburg: P&R Publishing, 2002).

[5] On the meaning of holiness as separation for a purpose, see my forthcoming book *The Gift of Seeing*.

12; 1 Tim 1:11). Out of this commitment flows all of God's actions.[6]

In contrast with this, the entire created order is twisted by sin away from this purpose for which God created the world. Man, who was supposed to worship the Creator, instead worships God's creation (cf. Rom 1:18-23). Men and women in this way are *unholy*: they are not devoted to God's purposes—indeed, they are set in complete opposition to them (cf. Rom 8:5-8). Humans, locations, and objects become Holy by consecration: God rededicates them to his purposes. Though this is the primary way the Bible speaks of holiness, theologians often use "holiness" to refer more broadly to the way God is different from his creatures.

Yahweh is different from us in his unfailing commitment to uphold his glory in all he does, but he is also profoundly different in his very nature. In this sense of the word, Yahweh's holiness encompasses all of who he is considered as different from his creation. That Yahweh is holy means that there is no one like him (1 Sam 2:2). All that God is different from his creation. God is not, like the Greek "gods," an upgraded version of creation: he is not a more powerful version of us. God is bigger and better in those ways in which he is similar to us, this is true, yet he is the source of all these similarities. God is the reference point for goodness, love, kindness, etc.: we only know what is good, what is kind, or what is love because of God. These only have meaning in reference to God, the ultimate measure of all that is good and the ultimate antithesis of all that is bad. In this way, God is different *qualitatively*, not just *quantitatively*: God is the original, we are the copy.

God's perfections are eternal; our reflections are merely derivative. That God is holy means that he is the Creator in distinction from the creation. In this way, Scripture teaches two categories of existence: there is God and all that is not God. God is distinct, separate from his creation. Visualizing this, we could follow Cornelius Van Til in picturing two circles that do not touch; one is labelled "Creator" and the other "creature." In this theological sense of the word, holiness means that the distinction between these circles, between the Creator and the creature, is never blurred. Even in the Incarnation, Christ never stopped being the infinitely Holy Creator while taking on the creation. This may be something we cannot comprehend. In

---

[6] John Piper in my estimation has done more than anyone in recent years to draw our attention to this truth. However, he uses the term "holy" in the broader theological sense noted below. See especially his book, *Desiring God*.

the Bible, holiness refers primarily to God's utter commitment to his purposes, but "holiness" is most frequently used by theologians to refer to the distinction between the creator and the creature.

b. The Authority, Control, and Presence of Yahweh

We have said that God's Holiness is all that he is in distinction from his creation and consecrated for a purpose, yet what do we mean when we say, "all that he is." Traditionally, theologians have talked about the "attributes" of God, different perspectives by which we can consider God's nature. To be clear, God's attributes are not different parts of him (he is not part omnipresent, part omniscient, etc.) but different ways we can contemplate his character as revealed in Scripture. A helpful way to talk about these attributes is to consider God's attributes in terms of authority, control, and presence. These describe the united character of God, and so equally describe the Father, Son, and Holy Spirit. Yet, we can see that in different ways, the Father is particularly associated in Scripture with authority, the Son with control, and the Spirit with presence.[7]

The authority of God describes his character as expressed in authority over his creation. God has the authority to determine what is and will be: he is sovereign. God has the authority to determine what is true: he is omniscient. And God has authority to determine what is right and wrong: he is morally pure and just. According to Joseph, God was at work even through the malicious actions of Joseph's brothers to achieve his good purpose (Gen 50:20). Similarly, Peter identifies God hand working even in the crucifixion of Jesus (Acts 2:23). God is, according to Paul, at work in both good and bad events, working all things together for the good of his people (Rom 8:28). We can summarize this in Paul's words, "[He] works all things according to the counsel of his will" (Eph 1:11). God is not a distant God; he has authority over everything that conspires in his creation. The rise and fall of great nations, even the most wicked, happens according to his will (Hab 1:5-11, 2:6-20). It is not only humans that are subject to his sovereign governance; he is the source of rain and sunshine (Matt 5:45), and even the most wicked of storms (Gen 6-8; Josh 10:10-14; Job 38:22-30). It is God who provides food for our tables, brings forth the plants in the spring, and feeds the birds

---

[7] This is also an observation made by John Frame, cf. Frame, *Doctrine of God*.

(Matt 6:25-34). God does this through means at times, such as human economies and jobs or the Church, yet all this happens only according to God's plan. God's sovereignty is the source of a Christian's hope and confidence. We can know that God will God be victorious over death and Hell in the final day, for all is happening exactly as he intends. I can have confidence that the death of my grandfather only a year ago was not a horrific accident but the perfect plan of our heavenly father who used him in the world for his good purpose and took him home at just the right time. We can have this confidence, for God works all things together according to his plan, good and bad for our good. I know that I will endure in faith only because God is in control, and nothing will catch him off-guard: nothing can separate me from the love of Christ (Rom 8:31-39). We can pursue his kingdom with selfless fervency because he has promised that he will never fail to provide for those seeking his kingdom (Matt 6:25-34).

God's authority also comprehends his knowledge and his moral purity. God, according to Isaiah and numerous Scriptures (e.g. Isa 40), is never caught off guard: he knows all things.[8] God knows the past, present, and future from all possible perspectives with perfect accuracy. That is, God does not only know about my existence, but he knows how everyone in my life interprets my existence, relates to me, views me. He even knows what a bee flying outside of the window beside which I am writing would perceive about me. God's knowledge is exhaustive: he has pre-interpreted all events and objects from all valid perspectives.[9] Not only is his knowledge exhaustively perfect, but it is also perfectly free from error. That is, God knows all true propositions (statements of truth) as true without knowing any false propositions as true. Because God knows all things perfectly, his interpretation of reality is the ultimate measure of truth: truth is that which

---

[8] This is, of course, an extension of sovereignty: if everything happens according to God's will, he knows everything that will happen. Yet there is reciprocity here: God's will is not mechanistic. He creates creatures and then plans their future and actions according to the way he has created them. He creates with consistency; his creative acts thus produce his foreknowledge by which he plans the course of his creation, and the course of his creation determines the nature of what he creates. Thus, there is a circularity here that we cannot quite comprehend: foreknowledge and predestination cohere perfectly in God in such a way that does not compromise his ultimate sovereignty.

[9] I discuss the relation between object and events and God's interpretation of them in Vol. 1, *The Gift of Knowing*.

corresponds to God's interpretation of reality. We have access to truth, therefore, through Scripture and God's creation as interpreted through the lens provided in Scripture. God's knowledge is thus the authority over our knowledge.

God is morally pure; he is good, just, free from wickedness. God's every action is good, free from imperfection: he can, in fact, do nothing wrong (1 John 1:5). God is therefore not just perfectly good; he is the standard for everything that is good. Something can only be called good if it corresponds to God's character and the revelation of that character in Scripture. Thus, God's moral purity is an attribute of authority: it is the standard by which all goodness in the world is measured. God's goodness means that we can have unfailing confidence that God will always act in ways that are ultimately good. Yet goodness is not defined as something that benefits man: goodness is defined by God's zeal for his glory. This not to say that what is good to God is not good for man. On the contrary, what God declares to be good is what is best for us, his creatures: he created us to benefit most fully from living in the world as he intended it. What is good is ultimately what brings God glory: mercy, for example, is good because it reflects God's merciful character; it is an act that glorifies God by demonstrating his character. Our actions are good only in as much as they mirror God's character on a creaturely level (that is, God can do some things that we as humans are not permitted to do).

God's authority describes God's attributes as they function as norms (or standards) for the world—for what is and will be, what is true, what is good, etc. But God does not only have authority; he is also a ruling Lord. He has control over his creation.

God's control comprehends all of his character. We will restrict our discussion of control to God's governance and omnipotence. God's governance refers to the active side of God's sovereignty: God has not only made a plan, but he is also at work in the world to accomplish it. Behind the scenes, God works through the hearts and hands of men and angels to accomplish all his will (cf. Exod 9:16, Hab 2:5-11). Furthermore, God not only actively achieves his will, but he also actively sustains his creation. According to the New Testament, all creation is held in existence by the word of Jesus Christ (Col 1:17; Heb 1:3); according to Genesis, the consistency of the natural order is because of God's oath to sustain it (Gen 9:8-17). What we call "natural laws" are, therefore, not impersonal processes but the activity of God within his creation to ensure things run as he so desires. We must then praise him each moment not only for the breath we breathe but the fact that our world remains together: we should not take for granted the stability of the chairs we sit on or the orbit of our planet—let alone the functioning of our vehicles. All this consistency owes itself to the faithfulness of God.

Governance describes God's acts of control in general; omnipotence describes his ability to control. That God is omnipotent means that his purposes will never be foiled: all that God desires he will bring about. We, as finite humans, often desire to do things we are unable to do; God does not face this struggle. Everything he desires he is able to and does accomplish. We could define omnipotence in many ways. One way is this: God is unhindered in the accomplishment of all his good purposes. Omnipotence does not mean that God can do *anything*, such as evil, but that he is unhindered. Consider whether or not God could do an evil act. In one sense, he could: most evil acts are quite simple. However, his goodness means that he never will. It would cause a contradiction in his very character, so we can be assured that this is indeed impossible for God. Yet such impossibility is not a hindrance to God, a limit to his perfection. Instead, it is the height of God's perfection that he will never desire anything contrary to himself and so will only ever desire what he can and will accomplish.

In Scripture, the primary way we see God's control revealed is his redemptive plan, which we will consider in the following chapter. Because God's control is primarily expressed in his plan to redeem a people for himself, we may consider mercy, compassion, love, and benevolence to be aspects of God's control. These are also expressions of God's presence among his creation and especially with his people.

God's presence is also known as his immanence, his nearness to the creation. God is omnipresent, meaning that there is nowhere in all creation where a creature could escape its God. In the depths of Hell, God is present; in the heights of heaven, God is there (Ps 139:8). God has probed the deepest depths of the created world and is present at the farthest reaches of the universe. God cannot be escaped: this brings great joy to God's people yet great fear to the unbeliever. God's presence for the believer is one of comfort and strength (e.g. 1 Sam 7; Phil 2:12, 1 Pet 1:5-8). God's presence with his people in the Old Testament was the greatest honour (Exod 33:15-16) but also a fearful thing (Exod 19-20); God is holy and majestic, terrifying to finite people (cf. Isa 6:1-7). For the Old Testament people of God, enjoying the presence of God required elaborate sacrifices to cover over their sin.

In the New Testament, God's presence can be a terrifying thing for the false believer (Acts 5:1-11) and is a work of judgment for the unbeliever (John 12:36-43), yet God's presence is the height of comfort for the believer (John 10:7-10, 25-29). The Spirit, God himself, is given to us as strength and comfort, and we are assured that we can safely draw near to God in our time of need through the blood of Christ (Heb 4:14-16). God's omnipresence for the believer means that God is an ever-present source of comfort, strength, and joy. Consider this: the joy which Israel sought in the courts of the Lord (cf. Ps 84) is present every day to the Christian, who is seated even now in the heavenly places with Christ (Eph 1:3), who draws near to the very throne of God—closer than any but the high priest in the Old Testament. The Christian is assured that through Christ, this presence, though at times painful (Heb 12:3-11), will never turn to white-hot wrath against our sin (Rom 5:9). The greatest implication of God's presence for interpretation is given in 1 Corinthians 2:9-16:

> as it is written,
> > What no eye has seen, nor ear heard,
> > > nor the heart of man imagined,
> > what God has prepared for those who love him—
>
> these things God has revealed to us through the Spirit. For the Spirit searches everything, even the depths of God. For who knows a person's thoughts except the spirit of that person, which is in him? So also no one comprehends the thoughts of God except the Spirit of God. Now we have received not the spirit of the world, but the Spirit who is from God, that we might understand the things freely given us by God. And we impart this in words not taught by human wisdom but taught by the Spirit, interpreting spiritual truths to those who are spiritual.
>
> The natural person does not accept the things of the Spirit of God, for they are folly to him, and he is not able to understand them because they are spiritually discerned. The spiritual person judges all things, but is himself to be judged by no one. "For who has understood the mind of the Lord so as to instruct him?" But we have the mind of Christ.

Thus, we have the Spirit with us always in order to discern the depths of the wisdom of God revealed in Scripture. The Spirit humbles us to receive what God has written and quickens our minds to better understand the meaning of what we read.

We could discuss the presence, authority, control, tri-unity, and holiness of God at endless lengths: all creation testifies to these truths! This has been my humble attempt to acquaint the reader with the contours of the doctrine of God revealed in Scripture, to complement our knowledge of God (personal, relational knowledge we have on account of our faith) with knowledge about God.[10] As we interpret Scripture, we can only hope to grow in this knowledge and delight ever more in the splendour and glory of Yahweh, our Lord.

God and his character are the main content of Scripture: it is all about him and his redemption accomplished in Jesus Christ. Yet there is more than just truths about God in Scripture. To read it well, we also need to know something about humans, the primary characters in Scripture after God.

B. Humanity: Rebellious Kings

For our purposes we can consider the doctrine of humanity, *anthropology*, in three different ways. We will consider, first, humanity in their ideal state, created in the image of God. But we obviously do not encounter humans in an ideal state. Every human we interact with is made in the image of God but does not manifest God nearly as well as he or she should. The reason for this is human depravity. We will thus consider, second, humanity's nature resulting from their rebellion against God. The image of God is the ideal of what humans could be, seen fully only in Jesus Christ; depravity is the depths to which we have dived, our dark, sinful nature that stains our actions. Yet Christians are new creations in Christ Jesus, no longer enslaved to sin and corrupted to the root of our hearts. Therefore, we must also consider, third, the state of believers, those who have been given new life through Christ.

According to Genesis 1:26-28, God created humanity in his image and commissioned them to rule the earth and multiply within it. Much has been written on what the image of God may or may not be, yet what we can say from this passage is that as God's image-bearers, we were created to represent him. This is realized partly in our physical constitution, how we are perfectly created for the ruling and representing task he has given us. This is realized partly also in the community that begins with one man and one woman in marital union, mirroring the oneness of the Trinity. It is realized thirdly in the

---

[10] See further, Vol. 3 *The Gift of Seeing*.

representing function God assigned humanity.

Humans were not created to be passive paintings representing God but active vice-regents ruling the creation under God's authority. Humanity was created, in other words, to glorify God by extending and ruling over his kingdom on earth. This was essentially the calling of each human being, to extend the kingdom of God in submission to their Lord. In other words, we were created to be kings.

However, instead of being faithful to this call, Adam followed Eve in rebellion against God. Instead of ruling the creation under God's authority, humanity became rebels attempting to exert their own authority. The result of this was catastrophic: the creation was cursed, subjected to futility (Rom 8:18-25). Marriage was cursed with conflict: wives would strive to usurp the leadership of their husbands, and husbands would tyrannize their wives (Gen 3:16). Men and women were also individually cursed in the area of God's original commission for which they were most responsible: women, primary in "multiplying" (Gen 1:28), were cursed in childbearing (Gen 3:16); men, charged with a primary role in taking "dominion" (Gen 1:28), were cursed with toil in their labours (Gen 3:17-19). Humans were thus cursed in their relations to one another (cf. Gen 4:8), in their relations to God's commission in creation, and ultimately in their relationship with God.

In his curse on Satan, God speaks of a conflict that will take place between Eve's seed and that of the serpent (Gen 3:15). This foreshadows the coming division of humanity into the people of God and the World, the rebellious human race under Satan's dominion. We learn from the New Testament that Adam's sin had a deeper consequence than this external strife: the death promised for his rebellion was transferred to his descendants (Gen 2:17). According to Romans 5:12-21 and 1 Corinthians 15:20-24, Adam's sin bound us to sin and subjected us to death. All humanity followed in his footsteps, falling short of God's glory to which they were called (Rom 3:23). Every human, as a result of Adam's sin, is dead in sin, enslaved to sin, and hardened in rebellion against God (Gen 8:21; Deut 29:4; Rom 6:17-19; Eph 2:1-5). Far from the ideal, this is the state of fallen man: we are guilty before God and incapable of obedience towards him (Rom 8:6-7).

It is in the great mercy of God that this is not all Scripture has to say about humanity. After creation, we read of people who are not quite the ideal, yet neither are they totally depraved: Noah is favoured by God and is considered righteous (Gen 6:9), Abraham is granted a covenant by God and made righteous through his faith (Gen 12:1-3, 15:6). Among the people of Israel, there were many who were unfaithful to God but also some who were faithful (Hab 2:2-4). In the New Testament, the veil is pulled back, and we see that the cause of this faithfulness in some is God's merciful gift of regeneration (cf. Deut 30:6). In Ephesians 2, Paul writes that believers were once dead in their sins as the rest of humanity, yet God in his mercy raised us to new life (2:1-5). Jesus terms it as a new birth: it is only by Spirit-wrought birth that anyone may enter into, even see, God's kingdom (John 3:5-8, 6:44-45).

The result of this new birth is new life and a recommissioning. Christians, those who believe in Jesus Christ, are made new creations by the Spirit: we are emissaries of a New Creation dwelling within the Old (2 Cor 5:17, Gal 6:15). The call to be fruitful, multiply, and have dominion is changed slightly because the concept of the kingdom has changed. Jesus issues a new commission to make disciples (multiply) under Jesus universal authority (dominion) (Matt 28:18-20). Christians are those being made anew in the image of God perfected in Christ (Rom 8:29) and expanding his kingdom through the spreading of the Church.

Much more could be said about the doctrine of man, but these points provide a good foundation for understanding humanity as found in the Bible. Created good in God's image, we fell into sin; this resulted in what we could call an "antithesis." There are two branches in humanity, representing two kingdoms: every human being is born into sin, depraved and part of Satan's kingdom. Yet through God's mercy, a new humanity has been created in Christ Jesus (Eph 2:1-5). These two humanities are in conflict (cf. Gen 3:15), with the World persecuting those who are in Christ (John 15:18-25). Yet the victory of Jesus Christ, to bring all his sheep to himself and conquer the kingdom of Satan, is assured (John 10:14-16; 1 Cor 15:20-28; Rev 19). This brings us to the last theme we will consider, the Kingdom of God.

C. Kingdom: The Rule of God

Though the phrase "the Kingdom of God" or "the Kingdom of Heaven" is not very frequent in Scripture, the concept is everywhere. "Kingdom" is rightly considered one of the key themes of Scripture. The phrase "the Kingdom of God" in the New Testament is very specific, yet Scripture makes it clear that God has a kingdom in a broader sense as well. To unpack this theme a bit, we will consider the Kingdom of God as heavenly, earthly, and eschatological.

a. God's Heavenly Reign

According to Scripture, God rules in Heaven and does all that he pleases (Psalm 115:3). Everything is under his authority (Matt 28:18). I am using the term "heavenly reign" to describe God's universal reign over creation. The world as we experience it is in conflict. We have already seen that there is a conflict between God's people and Satan's people, a conflict of two kingdoms. This is true, yet it is not the full story.

According to Jesus, he has been given all authority (Matt 28:18); having sat down at the right hand of the Majesty on high (Heb 1:3), Jesus is currently reigning over all creation (1 Cor 15:24-28; Col 2:15). In the Gospels and Revelation, Jesus's enemies are considered to be restrained while Christ reigns (Mark 3:23-27; Luke 10:18-20; John 12:30-32; Rev 12:8-9; Rev 20:1-6). There is a sense in which Christ is in complete control and Satan's "kingdom" is really rebellion kept tightly under reigns. Satan may roam about as a prowling lion (1 Pet. 5:8), but he only roams where the Lord lets him. Thus, viewing Jesus' reign from the perspective of Heaven, it is all-encompassing. Yet viewing it from the perspective of earth, it is unfolding. It is in this latter sense that "the Kingdom of God" is used in the New Testament.

b. God's Earthly Reign

When Jesus entered into his ministry, he preached that the Kingdom of God had arrived (Mark 1:15). Throughout the Gospels, the arrival of Jesus is associated with the inauguration of God's kingdom on earth. Yet, it was not the kingdom the Jews were expecting. They were looking for an earthly king to throw off the Romans and re-instate the glory of David and Solomon's kingdom. When the Jews welcomed Jesus with cries of praise as he entered Jerusalem, calling him the "son of David" (Matt 20:9), they were expecting the fulfilment of God's promises in an earthly kingdom. And they thought they had biblical warrant for believing so:

> Say to the daughter of Zion,
> 'Behold, your king is coming to you,

humble, and mounted on a donkey,
on a colt, the foal of a beast of burden.' (Matt 21:4-5, cf. Zech 9:9)

It quickly became apparent that this idea was false: Jesus had no intention of instituting a kingdom like Rome or Israel at that moment. His intent was not to institute a kingdom with an identifiable physical location in competition with other nations of the world. When Pilate asks Jesus if he is a king, Jesus does not deny it (Matt. 27:11). However, he clarifies that what he means by "king" is not what the Jews thought: "My kingdom is not of this world.... You say that I am a king. For this purpose I was born and for this purpose I have come into the world—to bear witness to the truth" (John 18:36-37). If Jesus means by the "Kingdom of God" something other than an earthly empire like Rome, what does he mean?

It becomes quickly evident that what is meant is not the "heavenly Kingdom" we have already seen, for only believers belong to the Kingdom of God (e.g. John 3:3, 5). I have labelled it "earthly" for this reason: it is Jesus's heavenly rule as it is unfolding on earth. It is his rule over and through those the Spirit grants to recognize and embrace his heavenly rule. This contrasts Jesus's kingdom considered from the perspective of heaven, which is his rule over obedient and rebellious subjects alike. From the perspective of earth, we can identify the Kingdom of God as Jesus's rule over the Church, his people. John in Revelation 5:9-10 writes as much, "for you were slain, and by your blood you ransomed people for God from every tribe and language and people and nation, and you made them a kingdom and priests to our God, and they shall reign on the earth." Though they do not yet reign on the earth, Jesus has "made them a kingdom" already. According to Graeme Goldsworthy, a kingdom implies three things: a king, a people, and sphere of rule.[11] The Kingdom of God is the present rule of *Jesus Christ* over *Christians* (those who believe in him and confess his Lordship) *in the midst of a world in rebellion against its King*. That is, the sphere of Christ's rule is all creation, but it is manifest in the Church where his Lordship is proclaimed.

---

[11] Goldsworthy outlines the Kingdom of God as involving God's people in God's place under God's rule. Graeme Goldsworthy, *Gospel and Kingdom* in *The Goldsworthy Trilogy* (Colorado Springs, Paternoster Press 2000), 53-54.

The Gospel and the Kingdom

A lot has been written in recent years on the connection between the Kingdom of God and the Gospel. Though a lot of this is very unhelpful, it is important to recognize that the idea of "kingdom" is an essential part of what we call the "Gospel." When we think of the Gospel, we usually think of historical events and their present consequences for those who believe: Jesus Christ lived a perfect life, died in our place bearing the punishment for our sins, and was resurrected to a position of authority having accomplished his work. For those who believe, this means that we receive the forgiveness of sins, the righteousness of Christ, and become his people (e.g. Rom 3:21-31; Rom 5:12-21; Gal 3:1-14; 1 Corinthians 15). This is where the emphasis in the New Testaments falls.

However, to understand how the New Testament relates to the Old Testament, we need to see that this is not the whole picture. When Jesus preached the Gospel, he declared that "The time is fulfilled, and the kingdom of God is at hand; repent and believe in the gospel" (Mark 1:15). This is also the way that Luke summarizes Paul's ministry, "He lived [in Rome] two whole years at his own expense, and welcomed all who came to him, *proclaiming the kingdom of God* and teaching about the Lord Jesus Christ with all boldness and without hindrance" (Acts 28:30-31, emphasis added). Romans begins on this note, Paul was "set apart for the gospel of God, which he promised beforehand through his prophets in the holy Scriptures, concerning his Son, who was *descended from David according to the flesh* and was declared to be the *Son of God in power* according to the Spirit of holiness by his resurrection from the dead" (Rom. 1:1-4, emphasis added). The kingdom of God is the goal of the historical events proclaimed in the Gospel and the transformation of persons achieved by the Gospel. We could, then, consider "kingdom" a third facet, or perspective, on the Gospel: the Gospel concerns historical events (Jesus's life, death, and resurrection) with present effects transforming persons (repent and believe and you will be saved) to be part of God's kingdom.

The kingdom of God in its earthly aspect thus corresponds to the second part of the great commission: Jesus says that he has all authority (Matt 28:18), which results in a commission for his people to go and to make and mature disciples (Matt 28:19-20). As there was an original commission to expand God's earthly kingdom in Genesis 1:28, believers have now inherited a command fitting Christ's present kingdom: expand the Church making disciples, baptizing them, and teaching them. Jesus died on the cross as a substitute for our sins and fulfilled God's law on our behalf in order that we might be delivered from this corrupt world (Gal 1:3-5) and be reconciled to God, having peace with him (Rom 1:16-18, Rom 5:1, 2 Cor 5:11-21). The goal of this rescue and the transformation that follows (sanctification and glorification) is that we might enjoy God forever under his benevolent rule and that we might fulfil his purpose for man as those who would rule under his authority over his creation.

This is the kingdom, but the kingdom is not passive: it is active; it is on mission. Christians are charged with extending this earthly kingdom—consisting of subjects of the King who confess his Lordship as part of the Church—in a world hostile to it. Because the success of this mission is guaranteed, there is one more aspect of the kingdom that is talked about in Scripture, its future consummation.

c. *God's Eschatological Reign*

According to 1 Corinthians 15:20-58, Christ is putting an end to the rebellion of his creatures through his people (cf. Rom 15:20). When he returns and puts an end to death and Hell, he will hand the kingdom over to the Father, and it will become the possession of all his people (1 Cor 15:24, 50). All sin and death will be crushed, and the people of God will rule over a new creation with Christ in the full enjoyment of the presence of God (Revelation 20-21). This is the hope of the Christian and all the creation (cf. Rom 8:18-25), when Christ returns, puts an end to sin and rebellion, and dwells bodily with his people. At that time, the kingdom will be fully consummated; at that time, the heavenly kingdom will be identical with the earthly kingdom of God.

In this chapter, we have considered three key teachings of the Bible, three essential pieces of the biblical worldview. We considered some of the glorious revelation of our God in Scripture, skimming quickly over the fathomless depths of his wonders. We also considered humanity as created, fallen, and redeemed. Finally, we considered the Kingdom of God in the various ways it is presented in Scripture. With this foundation in place, we will consider in the chapter that follows the **metanarrative** Scripture gives us.

Further Reading

*J. I. Packer – *Knowing God* [B]

John Frame – *Systematic Theology* [I]

*John Frame – *The Doctrine of God* [A]

Greg Gilbert – *What is the Gospel?* [B]

R. C. Sproul – *The Character of God: Discovering the God Who Is* [B]

R. C. Sproul – *The Holiness of God* [B]

Wayne Grudem – *Systematic Theology* [B-I]

Wayne Grudem – *Bible Doctrine* [B]

3

THE BIBLE'S WORLDVIEW - STORY

> Then God said, "Let us make man in our image, after our likeness. And let them have dominion over the fish of the sea and over the birds of the heavens and over the livestock and over all the earth and over every creeping thing that creeps on the earth."
>
> > So God created man in his own image,
> > in the image of God he created him;
> > male and female he created them.
>
> And God blessed them. And God said to them, "Be fruitful and multiply and fill the earth and subdue it, and have dominion over the fish of the sea and over the birds of the heavens and over every living thing that moves on the earth." – Genesis 1:26-28

So far we have considered the Bible as a united covenant document written for the New Covenant people of God, providing them with a worldview and with instruction so that they can know God, be transformed into the image of Christ, and pursue God's purpose in this creation. Historically, the Bible's teaching has often been expounded in a similar manner to the last couple of chapters, a systematic presentation of the vast teachings of Scripture. This discipline, known as systematic theology, takes the testimony of Scripture and applies it to the pressing questions and dilemmas of our age.[1] Systematic theology has a great historic pedigree and it has its uses.

In recent years, however, another aspect of the Bible has become the object of focus. It has been rightly observed that the Bible not only provides us with truths about the world but also gives a story that explains the world. The study of this story is often called biblical theology. Such a story is known as a metanarrative, an overarching story that gives meaning to everything within a worldview. Every worldview has a metanarrative; it presents an account of the beginning of time, prophecies about its end, and attempts to give a united account of all that transpires between the beginning and the end.[2] Like a novel, a worldview presupposes the there is a plot for the world: it presents a linear progression of events that move from something (the beginning) towards something else (an end). For the Christian, the comparison between a literary narrative and the biblical metanarrative is even more striking; as a novel is characterized by an author and a plot, so the biblical metanarrative is a plot authored by God—everything happens according to his preordained plan (Eph. 1:9-10). The biblical metanarrative is, therefore, the story that gives meaning to everything, that explains and gives significance to each object and action in the world.

The biblical metanarrative does not tell us anything different than a systematic account of the biblical data could but considers the Bible from a different perspective. We often talk about the features of the biblical metanarrative in non-narrative form, as we sometimes talk about systematic truths in narrative form. Yet we need both these perspectives. Systematic theology is great for bringing the whole Bible to bear on specific questions, yet in doing so, it is fragmentary. It so focuses on one aspect of the Bible's teaching that it must push aside the consideration of others. This is helpful and necessary, yet the resulting doctrines are sufficient to answer the question

---

[1] Systematic theology has been conceived in various ways, but I believe that John Frame's definition does the most justice to what we have already seen about the nature of the Bible: "theology is *the application of Scripture, by persons, to every area of life*," "*systematic* theology seeks to apply Scripture by asking what the *whole* Bible teaches about any subject." In *Systematic Theology*, pgs. 8-9.

[2] The metanarrative of many eastern worldviews is actually cyclical, where the end feedbacks into the beginning and the process is repeated endlessly. This remains a metanarrative, for it is essential to understanding how these worldviews attempt to give meaning to present events.

that raised them but not all the questions that could be answered. It is necessary to continually produce systematic theological treaties (in the form of sermons, letters, books, blog posts, etc.) as new questions arise or old answers are called into question. The result is fragmentary: it needs something to unite it. Thus we come to the narrative aspect of Scripture's teaching; the biblical metanarrative gives unity to the otherwise fragmented pieces of systematic theology. It answers "why questions"; it gives purpose to systematic theological endeavours.

The biblical story gives unity to the stories, events, truths, etc. given in Scripture. It is God's interpretation of created history, his narrative, given to us in Scripture. What, then, is this story? I think it is best summarized as *the story of God's kingdom extending throughout the creation through his covenants in order that the fullness of his glory might be displayed throughout the universe.*[3]

A. The Prologue: Creation & Fall

We can identify four major movements in the history of God's created order. The first movement is the prologue; it sets the stage for God's redemptive acts to follow. The prologue to the biblical metanarrative features both the initial creation and then the fall. After the fall, God begins to redeem his creation. The first movement of redemption is the Old Covenant (or covenants). The Old Covenant refers primarily to the relationship between God and his people legislated at Sinai, but also to the covenants which preceded this, namely the relationship God enters into with Abraham and his descendants. These covenants govern a relationship between God and his people through which he intended to redeem the world. The second movement of redemption is the New Covenant; through Jesus Christ, God acts to achieve the redemption anticipated under the Old Covenant. The third movement of redemption is the consummation, when God will complete the work promised in the Old Covenant and achieved in the New Covenant. We will consider each of these in turn.

---

[3] For this formulation, I am heavily indebted to the work of Peter J. Gentry and Stephen J. Wellum in the book *Kingdom Through Covenant*.

a. Creation

The biblical metanarrative begins with the creation. Actually, the story begins before the creation. Before the foundations of the world were laid, God the Father, Son, and Holy Spirit dwelt in perfect unity and chose to create a world in which the fullness of their glory would be displayed. A world that would display the goodness of their wisdom in creation, the severity of their justice in judgment, and the magnitude of their mercy in redemption. According to this eternal plan, Yahweh spoke the creation into existence.[4]

In the beginning, God created everything that exists. His creation was good, and its pinnacle was man, a creature made in his image. On the sixth day of Creation, God personally formed and gave life to the first man and woman, Adam and Eve. Yahweh charged them with the task of expanding his rule in the world. They were to multiply and put the creation to service under their authority, to steward and use it to image him.

b. Fall

However, trouble was brewing even as God commissioned the first humans to expand his kingdom in the creation. Behind the scenes, a rebellion was unfolding. Though the details are few, it appears that one of God's angels led a cohort of others in rebellion against their creator. This devil, Satan, then entered earth in the guise of a snake in order to bring humanity into his rebellion. He found an opportunity in God's command given to Adam that neither he nor his wife was to eat of the tree of good and evil located in their garden home. With a clever twisting of God's word, the tempter presented Eve with the opportunity to seize autonomy, to determine whom she would trust. Faced with the choice between the word of her creator God and the promise of better things if only she ate what was forbidden, she chose to believe the lies of the serpent and disobey God. Her husband, having first allowed her to enter into temptation and sin, then joined in her rebellion and sided with the serpent against God.

---

[4] On God's plan and creation, consider especially Eph 1:10-14, Eph 3:7-13, Rom 9:19-24. For specific examples that show how God's actions are intended to magnify his character—demonstrate his glory—consider Hab 2:6-20 and its central verse 2:14; also, Exod 9:16 (quoted in Rom 9:17-18).

This was the fall, the rebellion of humanity's first parents; the consequences of this one event are incalculable. Judgment came quickly, yet not without mercy. God drew forth a confession of guilt from his sinful creatures, yet instead of pronouncing judgment right then and there, he showed mercy. Spilling the first blood of the created order, he himself slew an animal to cover over their sin. The good creation now felt the stain of sin in the loss of life, yet the death promised to Adam and Eve was suspended, transferred to the first sacrifice. Death was stayed for the moment, yet their sin would not be without consequences.

No longer would they have access to eternal life in fellowship with God, the promise of the garden; now they would face physical death and one day final judgment. No longer would their task of expanding God's kingdom go forth without impediment. Instead, their task would be characterized by conflict. First, the created order would rebel against them; for the woman, her role in multiplying heirs of the kingdom would be cursed with severe pain. For the man, the ground itself would impede his task, multiplying the toil of his labour to express dominion. Second, humanity would rebel against itself; as an example of every other human relationship, the closest human relationship, marriage, would be characterized by strife. No longer would a man lead in humble submission to God; instead, he would exert his own autonomy over his wife. In turn, instead of trusting submission, his wife would seek to usurp the role given to her husband by God.[5] Third, the kingdom of God would no longer expand without opposition. As those who love God expand his kingdom, they would be opposed by another kingdom, that of the serpent. The offspring of the woman and the offspring of the serpent would be engaged in warfare: humanity would be divided between the serpent's servants and God's servants. Almost immediately the war began, with the righteous Abel slain by his brother Cain. Because they aligned

---

[5] Cf. Gen 3:16. Though the word describing the husband's rule over his wife is not necessarily negative, the word describing the wife's "desire" for her husband definitely is. It is probably the case then that both are meant to be read as negative, "desire against" and "tyrannize over." Examples of מָשַׁל (mšl, to rule) used negatively are Judg 14:4 and Isa 19:4. תְּשׁוּקָה (tᵉšûqāh, desire) occurs several verses later describing sin's desire to rule over humans (Gen 4:7), again with מָשַׁל. The New Testament calls for a reversal of this curse: husbands are still to lead, yet they are to do so in submission to God and as servants for the betterment of their wives. Wives are to submit to their husbands and give them respect as they lead according to God's word (1 Cor 11:2-16; Eph 5:22-33; Col 3:18-19; 1 Pet 3:1-7).

themselves with Satan, Adam and Eve's offspring would be born into the kingdom of Satan, not the kingdom of God. The multiplying that was to spread the kingdom of God would seem to spread the kingdom of Satan.[6] Represented by Adam in covenant before God, all mankind was condemned to death and given over to be slaves of sin (Rom. 5:15-20, 6:1-14; 1 Cor 15:20-22, cf. 42-49).

Yet, even in the midst of these curses, God's mercy shines forth in the promise of victory. From that which was cursed, the pregnancy of the woman, would come forth God's ultimate victory. An offspring would be born who would crush the serpent, though this victory would not come without a cost. Thus begins redemption, the true story of the whole world. God's kingdom would break into hostile territory and expand to encompass the creation. God's redemption of the world can be considered in terms of its beginning in the Old Covenant, accomplishment in the New Covenant, and consummation in the New Creation.[7]

B. Redemption Initiated – The Old Covenant(s)

a. *God's Covenant with Noah*

The world that came forth from the fall was not a pretty one: it was characterized by rampant sin—debauchery and idolatry of all sorts. Humanity took its great gifts, gifts intended by God for the furthering of his kingdom, and put them to work in building their own kingdom. The kingdom of humanity flourished, with God's people a mere speck in an ocean of evil. A speck though they may be, in the hands of God and in light of his promise to Eve, hope remained.

The birth of Seth evoked hope in Eve (Gen 4:25), yet he was not the offspring she had hoped for. Godly, yes, but not sufficient to overturn the enemy's kingdom. Finally, after years of sin, God acted once again in

---

[6] Cf. Eph 2:1-5

[7] This storyline has often been divided into only three or four moments: Creation, Fall, Redemption, and (sometimes) Consummation. However, my teacher Brad Copp has observed that glossing all of God's redemptive action as "redemption" fails to reckon with the significance of Jesus Christ. This formulation is my own, developed from Brad's feedback.

judgment. A flood to wipe out the inhabitants of the earth was his tool, yet again his mercy shown forth. To one man and his family, redemption was granted, deliverance from the judgment to come. With Noah, God committed to withhold such judgment again and commissioned him as he had Adam. Yet Noah was not the offspring anticipated; he sinned, and his sons were cursed. However, hope was particularly attached to the line of Shem.

b. God's Covenant with Abraham

Years passed, and humanity again multiplied, yet this multiplication was once again at the service of the kingdom of the serpent. Committed to their own glory, man sought to ascend to the heights of heaven, to be where God was. In mercy and in commitment to his covenant made with Noah, God refrained from obliterating humanity. Yet he cursed them once again. Divided by the barriers of language and location, they would not be able to work together to build their kingdom.

However, God was not without a plan. From this multitude of mankind, Yahweh chose a descendant of Shem named Abraham. From this man and his barren wife would come forth the redemption of humanity and hope for the creation. God covenanted with Abraham, promising to multiply his descendants innumerably and to give him a kingdom that would bless all the other families of the earth (cf. Gen 17:6). Yet Abraham was again not sufficient to follow his obligations; obedience escaped him.

However, the world was not doomed to a cycle of covenants and covenant breakers. As God's promises to Noah—promises which would prevent a repeat of the flood—moved forth the story of redemption, so also would his promises to Abraham. Yes, Abraham sinned, but God promised to credit his faith—as imperfect as it was—to him as *righteousness*. The very thing that the rest lacked, a right standing before God—the freedom from curse and the reception of blessing—would be Abraham's. This would not come from perfect covenant obedience, for Abraham had failed like the rest, but from God's own initiative.

In Genesis 15, we read of something unheard of in the history of Creation. Entering his world for a short time, God walked through the midst of the severed carcasses of birds and beasts that Abraham had prepared for a covenant-making ceremony. Though seemingly inconsequential, this would change the course of history: by doing this, by performing an ancient covenant ceremony in Abraham's place, God vowed to take upon himself the curses due to Abraham (cf. Jer 34:8-22). Instead of stripping Abraham of the promised blessings and replacing them with a curse, Yahweh—the Lord of all creation—promised to take the curse on himself and become Abraham's righteousness.[8] Thus, with the covenant between Yahweh and Abraham, the contours of God's plan to redeem the creation begin to appear. God would take upon himself the covenant curses and earn the covenant blessings of Abraham so that his offspring and all the nations of the earth might be blessed. What remains to be seen is how the offspring promised to Eve could possibly factor into God's plan to be the personal redeemer of Abraham and all the nations.

c. God's Covenant with Israel

Fast forward several hundred years, Abraham's descendants have multiplied greatly, yet they appear to be in no position to bless the earth. Enslaved under a wicked Egyptian king, they laboured hard while Pharaoh attempted to eradicate their children—endangering the promise of an offspring. Yet God was not silent, acting once again with salvation accompanying judgment. This time, God would judge Egypt to magnify his name across the earth and bring forth his chosen people.

The events that transpired from Moses's exile in Midian until Israel's arrival at Sinai, known as the Exodus, is one of the most significant events in Scripture. God's salvific action to deliver Israel from Egypt and bring judgment on their oppressors becomes the paradigm of all God's later salvific activities, including his climactic work through Jesus Christ. The pattern exemplified here, of salvation (for Israel) accompanying judgment (for Egypt), is repeated throughout the Bible. The goal of the Exodus was God's covenant made at Sinai. God did not redeem his people without a purpose; he did so in fulfilment of his promises to Abraham and in order to move forward his redemptive plan.

---

[8] Cf. Jer. 34. My explanation of this passage can be found in my paper, "Towards a Biblical Theology of Imputation," available at https://www.teleioteti.ca/resources/papers/.

The covenant that resulted was grand; God ordained an entire society devoted to himself. Ruled by his righteous Law, Israel was to be a beacon of his glory shining amid the surrounding nations. They were to be a kingdom of priests mediating God to all peoples. Yet a problem remained; sin was still dominant. At the centre of the Law was a way to deal with this sin, yet it fell short of the promises made to Abraham. God instituted a sacrificial system that enabled faithful Israelites to be forgiven of their sins and that would remind each generation of the consequences of sin, death.

However, God had promised Abraham that he would take his people's curse upon himself and to be their righteousness; this is conspicuously absent from the covenant at Sinai. In place of God were mere animals. Furthermore, the requirement of obedience was magnified; only perfect obedience would bring blessing, anything else would lead to horrific curses.[9] It appears that this law, which promised life, could only be a means of death. As the following accounts of the Old Testament record, Israel did not and could not obey perfectly. Their disobedience was devastating, ultimately leading to the destruction of their homes and the exile from their land. However, hope was again built directly into the covenant. In the midst of Law was the repeated call for a changed heart: this was what Israel needed. However, such a change would have to be a miracle. Yet God promised to one day work this miracle, to circumcise the hearts of his people, to put the law in their hearts so that they could obey him.[10] The Law was good yet could only enslave under sin; it could not bring the redemption God promised.[11]

d. God's Covenant with David

The inability of God's covenant with Israel to bring about redemption is clear from the accounts of Joshua and Judges. God's people only descended into deeper and deeper sin. Though commissioned to expand his kingdom over

---

[9] Cf. Lev 18:5, Deuteronomy 27-29.

[10] Cf. Deut 30:6. Deut 30:1-14 anticipates the reversal of Israel's exile by God's sovereign action. Though not commonly recognized, 30:10-14 looks to God's future action. For my translation and exegesis of this passage, see my paper "Do Not Say in Your Heart: An Exposition of Romans 10:1-8" and the first appendix of my book *Prevenient Grace: An Investigation into Arminianism*, 2nd Revised Ed (2020, Teleioteti). Both are reprinted as appendices in *The Gift of Reading – Part 2*.

[11] Cf. Galatians 3, Romans 7.

against the kingdom of Satan, they were looking more and more like their neighbours. Yet amid an ever-darkening picture (the unfolding of God's words in Deuteronomy 27-29, 32), a glimmer of hope was once more found. Throughout the Prophets and the Writings, hope was found in a glorious day of Yahweh, when he would act on behalf of his people, repeat the Exodus, and rule once again over his people through an offspring of David. The source of this hope is God's words recounted in 2 Samuel 7.

Both books of Samuel are essentially prophetic, demonstrating God's purpose to bring his kingdom to bear in the creation through a Davidic priest-king.[12] After bringing his people into the land he had promised, God eventually gave them a king in the form of David.[13] Though imperfect, David was chosen by God to be the channel through whom salvation would come.

If God's promise to Eve of an offspring leads us to anticipate a child who would destroy Satan and his kingdom, 2 Samuel 7 brings this hope to bear on a descendant of David. God would make a covenant with David's offspring, give him an eternal priesthood and kingdom, and would be to him a father and make him a son. This child would build Yahweh a temple. Though 1 Kings might lead us to think that this is fulfilled in Solomon, it is clear that Solomon and his temple were not the ultimate sources of hope.

God's action to redeem his people was still unfinished. In the years following David's reign, Israel continued its downward spiral, earning for itself destruction and exile. Though God gave great favour to his people and returned them from their physical exile, it is clear that their estrangement from him was never repaired. They remained under the law yet had sinful unchanged hearts. The temple they built failed to live up even to the glories of Solomon's. At the close of the Old Testament, God had not yet acted to bear their curse or give them the assurance of blessing. Though back in the land, God's people had not yet returned from exile.

---

[12] This is the subject of my master's thesis now printed as *God's Kingdom through his Priest-King* (Vancouver, Teleioteti 2019). This thesis is also available in its original form through the John Richard Allison Library (Regent College) and TREN, under the name James Rutherford.

[13] Saul, David's predecessor, was the king chosen by the people not by God. cf. 1 Samuel 8.

C. Redemption Accomplished – The New Covenant

Roughly 400 years after Israel returned from their physical exile in Babylon, something new began to happen. Though God seemed silent as his people languished under the rules of the Persians, the Greeks, and the Romans, change seemed to be happening. It began with a priest and his wife in their old age. Like Abraham and Sarah, God granted the gift of a child to a woman beyond the prime of her life. Elizabeth's unexpected pregnancy was accompanied by an astonishing encounter with an angel of the Lord. Zechariah's lack of faith when he heard the words of the angel resulted in a curse of silence; he was rendered mute. All wondered at the birth of their child John and the events surrounding his birth. Yet something even more amazing was happening within their family. God's plan continued to unfold through their relative Mary. God chose her to bear him a son, Immanuel, who would be conceived by the Holy Spirit, not a man. Immanuel, meaning "God with us," would be an offspring of David and God's presence with his people. Foreigners and Judeans were struck with wonder at the events unfolding in their midst.

Yet the kingdom of Satan would not stand by and be defeated without resistance. Through Herod came an attempt to wipe out the life of Mary's child. To escape his attempts, Mary and Joseph took Jesus, their child, to Egypt. For the discerning observer, how similar were these events to God's past actions! Though the enemy tried to wipe out the offspring of promise in Egypt and in Bethlehem, Israel and Jesus both survived. And as both came forth from Egypt to be God's people, so Israel and Jesus came forth to enter into God's purpose for them.[14] It seemed that God's purposes were finally coming to bear in history: God himself had entered into creation as a man to redeem his people.

In Jesus, the biblical metanarrative finds its climax. The promises made to David, that his son would sit on his throne, and the promises to Abraham, that God would bear the curse and bring the blessings of the covenant, found their fulfilment in him. In fact, all the promises of God found their fulfilment in him (2 Cor 1:20). We have already seen that his preaching ministry was focused on the proclamation of the kingdom; thus, in Jesus and his ministry,

---

[14] Matthew makes this connection in Matt 2:15.

the kingdom that had failed to expand under Noah, Abraham, Israel, and David began to expand in earnest. Beginning with twelve, it would spread in only short years to thousands and from thousands to millions. Jesus described it like a mustard seed; though beginning quite small, it would blossom into something huge. Yet if Jesus was to attain victory over the serpent, he would have to be struck; and if he was to fulfil the promises to Abraham, he would not only have to live a perfect life but die in place of Abraham and his descendants. In this way, his path to cross was laid long before his birth, and it transpired just as God's hand had ordained it to (Acts 2:23-24).

Jesus was a king, yet his path to the throne would be characterized by humble service, not violent rebellion. Eschewing every opportunity to seize his throne in other ways, Jesus intentionally set his face to Jerusalem and the cross he would bear there. His crucifixion was far from the glorious display of power Israel expected. Mocked, beaten, and spurned by the people he came to save, the Creator of the universe bore a wooden cross from Jerusalem to the hill upon which he would be slaughtered—buckling under its weight. The Lord of Glory, clothed in weakness, was nailed to a cross whose existence he planned before the foundations of the world, having brought into being the very tree from which it was hewn. Facing taunts to save himself as he had others, the eternal king hung bleeding from nails through his hands and feet. He was himself sustaining the very wood upon which he hanged as it sapped the life from him. Yet unseen to human eyes, something far more devastating was happening.

The only human who knew no sin was made sin for the sake of his people. He drank in full the cup of God's wrath they deserved. It was God's good will to strike him, and this he did (Isa 53:10). For the first time in all existence, something horrific happened between the members of the Trinity: God the Father forsake his beloved Son.

Yet that moment was not to last, having drunk fully from the cup of God's wrath, Jesus declared his task accomplished and gave up his life. The eternal God, dead at the hands of his creation. At that moment, the earth shook, the heavens darkened, and the dead were raised to walk the streets of Jerusalem.[15] Yet far more significant was an event not seen by the common

---

[15] On the rather bizarre occurrence of the dead rising, see Matt 27:52-53.

man. While the earth shook, the veil that closed the Holy God off from his people in Herod's temple was split. The heavy curtain was split from top to bottom: no more would God be separated from his people by their sin. In heaven, Jesus's work continued as he applied his own sacrifice just made to his people, cleansing them. Three days after his death, his victory was guaranteed by his resurrection. Coming forth from the dead, Jesus became the first of a new creation breaking into the old. After visiting and teaching his disciples, appearing to hundreds, he finally took his throne on High. Receiving all authority, he rules over the kingdom he created. By the blood of his sacrifice, something new began, a New Covenant to replace the Old. With this New Covenant came a new form of God's kingdom.

The New Covenant in Jesus blood brings all the promises of the Old Covenant(s) to his people; the full forgiveness of sins anticipated by the sacrificial system, new hearts enabling obedience to God, final victory over Satan, and an eternal kingdom over a new creation under the rule of a Davidic priest-king. However, though these were all bought completely through Jesus' life, death, and resurrection, they were not inaugurated fully at his ascension. Before ascending to sit at the right hand of the Father, Jesus commissioned his disciples to expand his kingdom on earth by making disciples. The New Covenant thus changed the nature of the kingdom and guaranteed the success of its expansion, but it did not yet usher in its fullness. Its promises are already here, yet they are not yet completed.[16] God's people have been given a strategic role in fulfilling this purpose, in expanding his kingdom.

After Jesus ascension, the story continued on the trajectory he set. His people went out and preached the Gospel, making disciples and expanding the kingdom in Judea, Samaria, and to the ends of the earth. At the close of the New Testament, the Gospel had spread throughout the known world, at least as far as Rome, maybe even to Spain. And wherever the Gospel spread, the Kingdom of God manifest itself in churches, in local groups of his people united in their purpose to see the great commission fulfilled. Though no single local church was or is perfect, Jesus's kingdom has progressively expanded through the preaching of the Gospel until the present age, where his name is proclaimed on every continent. Yet the biblical metanarrative

---

[16] In New Testament studies, "Already-Not-Yet" is a common way to refer to this suspension of fulfilment.

does not end with the last events of the apostles as recorded in Scripture; it also speaks of what is next.

D. Redemption Consummated – The New Creation

According to Jesus, his absence would not be long. He told the apostle John that he was coming quickly to finish what he had begun. He would come back, raising his people to new life, delivering final judgment, and beginning the new creation. From our perspective, his return has been delayed; almost 2000 years have passed, and he has not yet returned. Do not be deceived, warns Peter, though all things appear unchanged, God is not slow to fulfil his promises (2 Pet 3:1-13). God's patience is great as he gives men and women one final chance at repentance, yet we are not to count this patience as an opportunity for sin. Jesus has for 2000 years stood at the threshold: considering the plan of God in terms of major events, only one remains. All of God's promises have come to pass except the return of Christ to bring judgment and final salvation to his people, to recreate all things and dwell with his people. Therefore, history stands in tension: we are at its end, yet that end has not yet arrived. At any moment Jesus could cross that threshold and usher in glory. All creation is at the razor's edge of the passing of ages, with the consummation of all things a hairsbreadth away. And when that threshold is crossed, no word suffices to give an account of that future.

Far from a boring life sitting upon a cloud picking at harps, the consummation of Christ's kingdom will not end time but transform it. With all opposition ended, God's kingdom will extend unabated for endless ages as his people delight in him, in his glorious presence with his people. They will endeavour to bring him glory through the labour of their hands, no longer cursed to futility by sin.

This is my sketch of the story that unites all history and all the events of the Bible. It is only a sketch; much more could be said about all the events recounted, the characters that experienced them, their significance, and the God who orchestrated them. For this, we must turn to the Bible. The story just recounted will help us make sense of the events of the Bible and the purpose behind them, but one question remains before we can turn to the skills we need to read the Bible well: what is our place in all of this?

Further Reading

Graeme Goldsworthy – *According to Plan* [B]
Stephen G. Dempster – *Dominion and Dynasty* [I]
*Peter J. Gentry and Stephen J. Wellum – *Kingdom through Covenant* [A]
*Peter J. Gentry and Stephen J. Wellum – *God's Kingdom through God's Covenant* [B-I]

4

THE PEOPLE(S) OF THE BIBLE

> And I will make of you a great nation, and I will bless you and make your name great, so that you will be blessing. I will bless those who bless you, and him who dishonors you I will curse, and in you all the families of the earth shall be blessed. – Genesis 12:2-3

Considering the theology and story of the Bible as we have in the last two chapters should raise some questions. Namely, where do we fit into the biblical worldview? How does the story of the Bible and the theology recounted earlier relate to us? What is the place of those who believe in Jesus Christ, the New Covenant people of God? Such are the questions we will consider in this chapter. We are those upon whom the end of the age has come, those for whom the Bible was written (1 Cor 10:11). Living in the time between Christ's first and second coming, we are called by God to be ambassadors of a new creation, of Christ's kingdom as it breaks into this hostile World. In a word, *Christians are God's chosen and redeemed people who are called to be transformed into the image of Christ as they seek to expand God's kingdom on earth.* Our identity, our place in the world, can be considered from these three perspectives—as those redeemed, commissioned, and becoming like Christ.

Yet the unique place of Christians in this world, especially as it will impact our reading of the Bible, needs to be understood in light of the Old Testament people of God. Because God's acts to redeem Israel and then Christians, through the Exodus and then the Cross, established them as a distinct people in relationship with him, I will consider God's work to redeem

Israel and then the Church as their establishment as his people. Therefore, I intend for us in this chapter to consider first the establishment, commission, and nature of the Old Covenant people of God. Then we will, in contrast, consider our place as the New Covenant people of God.

A. The Old Covenant People of God

> You yourselves have seen what I did to the Egyptians, and how I bore you on eagles' wings and brought you to myself. Now therefore, if you will indeed obey my voice and keep my covenant, you shall be my treasured possession among all peoples, for all the earth is mine; and you shall be to me a kingdom of priests and a holy nation. – Exodus 19:4-6

As God began making covenants with those whom he chose in the Old Testament, his covenant people took on a definite shape. The Old Covenant people of God was Israel, the descendants of Abraham, Isaac, and Jacob. Made up of all those born into the community or who joined themselves to it, Israel was constituted as God's covenant community at Sinai after the Exodus. At Sinai, God entered a covenant with them (he would be their God, they would be his people) and delineates in great detail the nature of their relationship. As I suggested above, we can consider Israel from the perspective of how God prepared them as his people (establishment), what God has called them to (commission), and their particular character (nature).

a. The Establishment of Israel

Israel was at first distinguished from its neighbours by Yahweh's relation to them. Beginning with their ancestor Abraham, God chose Israel to be his people and continually acted in history on their behalf. The most significant act he performed on their behalf was the Exodus from Egypt. In fulfilment of his promises to Abraham, Yahweh performed a great act of redemption, bringing forth his people while judging Egypt. Through this act, he would establish them as his people under his covenant.

Yahweh acted towards them in a distinct manner from his interactions with nations around Israel; he made them his people. By redeeming them from Egypt and then binding himself to them in covenant, God set them apart from their neighbours and gave them a divine commission to be his people.

b. The Commission of Israel

God's people were distinguished from the rest of the nations by their unique calling. Israel was not chosen by God to be a stagnant blob on a map, to be a comfortable kingdom content with secure borders. They were redeemed for a mission. In the last chapter, we saw how the nation of Israel was part of the plan to fulfil God's promise to make Abraham a blessing to the nations. They were created to be "a kingdom of priests and a holy nation" (Exod 19:5), a nation set apart for God's purpose and mediators between God and the surrounding nations.

The first thing that may come to mind when we think of Israel's commission is the holiness aspect: we may recall seemingly endless pages of law indicating how Israel was to be distinct from its neighbours (not eating certain foods, acting in peculiar ways, avoiding certain practices). Even the most obscure of these laws functions to visually demonstrate Israel's calling to be a holy people dedicated to God. Consider, for example, the law to not wear garments made of mixed fabrics: the purity of fabric provides a visual reminder of Israel's nature as a community distinct from all others, not mixed (Lev 19:19). The same can be said of the food laws; they were to eat animals that did not mix features, again a reflection of Israel's separation from their neighbours (Lev. 11:1-8).[1] Yet what we may miss in the sea of legislation is that they were not only set apart *from* the other nations but ultimately *for* the other nations.

As God's people on earth, Israel was (intended to be) God's representatives on earth. In all their behaviour, they were to radiate his character to those around them. Sometimes this representation was fulfilling God's goals on earth, such as enacting his judgment. Examples of this may immediately leap to mind, such as Israel's commission to bring God's judgment on the Canaanites by wiping them out (cf. Gen 15:16, The Book of Joshua) or the commission God gave Saul to wipe out the Amalekites (1

---

[1] This insight is from Bruce Waltke, from a class he taught on Biblical Theology.

Sam 15:1-23).² However, the emphasis of the Law is not on such actions or on any explicit actions to reconcile the other nations with God. Instead, they were to live their lives individually and nationally as an image of God in the creation: they were to be holy as he was holy (Lev 11:44). This is why the reason frequently given for the particular laws governing Israel was "for I am YHWH" (e.g. Lev 18:4-6, 21).³ God brought them forth from Egypt to make his name known and constituted them as a nation to do the same.

If they were obedient to his commands, they would image him in his creation and receive blessings upon their land and lives, showing his power and beneficence. In this way, other nations were to be drawn to the God of Israel: this is seen at some points throughout Israel history (Josh 9:1-27; 1 Kings 10:1-13). Yet, instead of being obedient to God and remaining distinct from the nations, even from its entry into Canaan, Israel began to conform itself less to God's Law than to the surrounding nations (consider The Book of Judges). They ultimately failed to be holy as God was holy and so failed to be light to the nations.⁴ This brings us to on last important perspective by which we must view the Old Testament people of God.

c. The Nature of Israel

To this point, we have seen how Israel related to those around it, how the Exodus distinguished and established them and that their commission was to image God over against their neighbours. However, we have not said anything about Israel's "salvation." Salvation broadly conceived of in the

---

[2] I discuss accounts of God's acts of judgment recorded in the Old Testament at greater depth in my Habakkuk study guide and commentary. J. Alexander Rutherford, *Believe the Unbelievable: A Study in Habakkuk*, Teleioteti Study Guides 1 (Vancouver, BC: Teleioteti, 2018); J. Alexander Rutherford, *The Book of Habakkuk: An Exegetical-Theological Commentary on the Hebrew Text*, A Teleioteti Old Testament Commentary 1 (Vancouver, BC: Teleioteti, 2019).

[3] In Biblical quotations, I prefer to transliterate the Hebrew name of God instead of translating it LORD or Yahweh. Among many reasons for this, two are important for our purposes here. On the one hand, Yahweh is God's personal name given to his people so they might know him; on the other hand, because of the history of translations, God's name is found in the New Testament as "The Lord." By transliterating God's name, I hope to lead the reader to think of God's personal name while at the same time making the connection to the New Testament use of Lord.

[4] The Book of Jonah appears to be an indictment of the inward focus of Israel, their ignorance of God's greater purpose to make them a blessing to the nations.

Bible is a right relationship with God and the enjoyment of the blessings that follow from this relationship. Israel's experience of salvation was not completely different from ours as New Testament believers, yet it is important to observe that it was not a universal experience. In Paul's words, not all Israel was true Israel, the inheritors of God's promises (Romans 9). Israel was what is sometimes called a mixed community: the **covenant community** consisted of both those who loved and believed in God *and* those who were ambivalent or against God.[5] In the language of Habakkuk, some were righteous but others wicked (Hab 1:13, 2:4).

Salvation was available to Israel: they could be right with God, be righteous, but not all Israel had this salvation. According to Deuteronomy and Leviticus, to enjoy the blessings of God's covenant, Israel and the people within it needed to be flawlessly obedient (e.g. Lev 18:5; Deut 28:1-2). It is quickly evident that even the best of them could not do this, yet we learn throughout the Old Testament that a right relationship with God could not and so did not come from perfect obedience to the Law and through the sacrificial system (e.g. Psalm 51). At the height of Israel's sin, Habakkuk makes explicit that like Abraham before them, the righteous of Israel were not identified by their perfect obedience but by their belief in God, even when he acted in unbelievable ways (Hab 2:4, cf. 1:5). Thus, Israel was a community of believers (the righteous) and the unbelievers (the wicked) united in a relationship with God. This mixed nature ultimately led to their exile; the nation as a whole was characterized by wickedness and unbelief. Only a remnant of righteous ones remained (e.g. 1 Kgs 19:18).

Israel as a whole lacked hearts of obedience towards God. Such a heart was something only God could grant them, and he had not yet done so. Yet he promised that a day would come when he would (Deut 30:6). This became the great hope of the Prophets. Jeremiah spoke of a day when Yahweh would

> make a new covenant... not like the covenant I made with their fathers on the day when I took the by the hand to bring them out of the land of Egypt, my covenant that they broke, though I was their husband,

---

[5] **Covenant community** refers to a body of people represented together in covenant. Under the New Covenant, the covenant community consists of all those who truly have believed, believe, and will believe in Jesus Christ (past, present, and future). Under the Old Covenant, all ethnic Israel (or at least those who were circumcised or connected to a male who was circumcised) and the sojourners who attached themselves to Israel were part of the covenant community.

> declares the LORD. For this is the covenant that I will make with the house of Israel after those days, declares the LORD: I will put my law within them, and I will write it on their hearts. And I will be their God, and they shall be my people. And no longer shall each on teach his neighbor and each his brother, saying, "Know the LORD," for they shall all know me, from the least of them to the greatest, declares the LORD. For I will forgive their iniquity, and I will remember their sin no more. (Jer 31:31-34)

No longer would the people of God be mixed like Israel in the Old Testament, promised Yahweh. They would no longer be a community of the faithful and the unfaithful; no longer would anybody have to labour to get their brother to know God, for everyone in the covenant would know him.

Israel was a redeemed earthly nation called to image God among their neighbours, to be holy as he is holy, yet they failed this mission. They were not consistently a faithful people; they were perpetually marked by the presence of the faithful and the unfaithful in their midst. Though there always remained a remnant that trusted in Yahweh, their numbers were small, and they were surrounded by wickedness (cf. Hab 1:1-4), but God promised that a day would come when this would change. The Law that governed them would no longer be external; instead, it would be inside them (Jer 31:31-34; Isa 54:13; Ezek 36:25-27; cf. Deut 30:6-14 (in Hebrew)).[6] When this covenant came, a new covenant community came into existence.

B. The New Covenant People of God

> But you are a chosen race, a royal priesthood, a holy nation, a people for his own possession, that you may proclaim the excellencies of him who called you out of darkness into his marvelous light. – 1 Peter 2:9

As one reads the New Testament, it becomes evident that the Church bears some continuities with Israel: for one, we receive all the promises of God through Christ (2 Cor 1:20), and Paul places us in continuity with the true "Israel" (cf. Rom 9-11, Gal 6:16). Yet discontinuities also appear: the hope

---

[6] For Deut 30:6-14, see the first appendix of my *Prevenient Grace* and my paper "Do Not Say in Your Heart," reprinted in the appendices of *The Gift of Reading – Part 2*.

of Jeremiah is fulfilled in the Church, meaning that his picture of a believing community is realized in the Church (e.g. John 3:5-8, cf. Ezek 36:25-27; John 6:44-45, cf. Isa 54:13; Rom 10:5-17, cf. Deut 30:6-14; Heb 8, cf. Jer 31:31-34).[7] In addition, the New Testament is clear that Christians are not bound by the regulations of the Torah in the way Israel was (e.g. Acts 10:9-33; Gal 2:15-21, 3:1-6, 4:1-7, 5:1-2). This change is responsible for some of the greatest difficulties facing Christians as we seek to apply Scripture to our lives.

All Scripture was written for us, yet we are not simply Israel 2.0. We are a different community established in a different manner, with a distinct commission and nature, meaning that our obedience to God looks differently. The Old Testament was written for us, yet instructions that revealed God's character as it would be expressed through an earthly kingdom will look very different when applied to a community defined spiritually, not physically.

a. *The Establishment of Church*

Israel's Exodus was physical, from slavery to freedom in the promised land. Christians also undergo an Exodus, yet this one was spiritual: from slavery under sin to freedom in Christ Jesus (Romans 6, cf. Gal 5:1). The formative event for the Church was not the physical defeat of Egypt and the Canaanites but the crucifixion and resurrection of God on their behalf. As physical redemption established a physical nation and physical kingdom, so spiritual redemption established a spiritual nation and spiritual kingdom.

This is the first fundamental distinction between the Church and Israel: though Israel was a physical kingdom with land and distinct physical presence, the Church is the manifestation of an invisible kingdom without a land (at least not in this age) and without a distinct physical presence. That is, if one were to gather all the local churches together, this would not be the Church, nor would an earthly "Christendom," a nation-state defined by Christian values, be the Church. The Church is an exiled people sojourning in a foreign land (cf. 1 Pet 1:1; Hebrews 11).

---

[7] This is not to say, of course, that everyone in a local church really believes in Jesus. This is, unfortunately, not always the case. There are unbelievers and believers who both claim Christ as their own, yet God's covenant is only with the believers—the "invisible Church"—and thus his promises towards them and the success of his mission through them is guaranteed.

b. The Commission of Church

As exiles in a strange land, Christians also have a different commission than Israel. They are not to expand the Kingdom of God in a physical manner, radiating his image as a nation in the midst of other nations. Instead, they have been commissioned to "Go... and make disciples of all nations, baptizing them in the name of the Father and of the Son and of the Holy Spirit, teaching them to observe all that I have commanded you" (Matt 28:19-20). Thus, though both Israel and the Church were commissioned to extend God's kingdom, the way this commission manifests is different. Christians are told to "seek first the kingdom of God and his righteousness" (Matt 6:33), yet this looks dramatically different than the instructions originally given to Adam and Eve and legislated for Israel.

The great commission is a command to multiply and solidify the kingdom of God as it is expressed in the Church. That is, the Church is commissioned to make disciples and mature them. We can consider the form this takes in the New Testament in terms of three contrasts between the Old Covenant and New Covenant people of God: internal versus external holiness, church versus political polity, and exilic versus secure existence.

i. Internal Versus External Holiness

Concerning holiness, what in Israel was external holiness becomes for the Church internal holiness. Christians, like Israel, are called to be holy as God is holy (1 Peter 2), and this holiness has consequences for the relationship of Christians with those outside the Church. Yet, instead of radical physical separation (i.e. do not associate in any way), the New Testament calls for radical spiritual separation while being physically present among unbelievers.

Jesus, praying to the Father, is clear that his desire is not for Christians to separate from the world; in fact, he sent them into the world (John 17:15, 18). He stresses that Christians are foreigners in the world, sent into it from the outside: "the world has hated them because they are not of the world, just as I am not of the world" (John 17:14). Paul makes the same point,

> I wrote to you in my letter not to associate with sexually immoral people— not at all meaning the sexually immoral of this world, or the greedy and swindlers, or idolaters, since then you would need to go out of the world. But now I am writing to you not to associate with anyone who bears the name of brother if he is guilty of sexual

immorality or greed, or is an idolater, reviler, drunkard, or swindler—not even to eat with such a one. (1 Cor 5:9-11)

Christians are commissioned to exist in the world, to be present and active among those who do not believe—how else will they hear the Gospel! Yet, Christians are never to forget that their presence in the world does not mean that they are part of the world. The spiritual separation signified by the Christian's non-worldly nature manifests throughout the New Testament as a radical commitment to the Church and the kingdom at the expense of worldly pursuits.

Consider several examples. A Christian's primary relationships in the world are with the Church even over their relationship with biological family (Matt 10:34-39; 12:46-50; Luke 14:26-27). This even transforms marital commitments: Christians are to hold fast to their spouse even if they are an unbeliever, but if an unbelieving spouse leaves a believer, the latter is not bound to the usual laws concerning remarriage after divorce. And for those unmarried, Christians are only permitted to marry believers (1 Cor 7:10-16, 39-40). Not only are Christians called to separate in these ways from intimate family, but Christians are also commanded to abstain from aligning their purposes with an unbeliever:

> Do not be unequally yoked with unbelievers. For what partnership has righteousness with lawlessness? Or what fellowship has light with darkness? What accord has Christ with Belial? Or what portion does a believer share with an unbeliever? What agreement has the temple of God with idols? For we are the temple of the living God; as God said,
> > I will make my dwelling among them and walk among them,
> > > and I will be their God,
> > > and they shall be my people.
> > Therefore go out from their midst,
> > > and be separate from them, says the Lord,
> > and touch no unclean thing;
> > > then I will welcome you,
> > and I will be a father to you,
> > > and you shall be sons and daughters to me,
> > says the Lord Almighty.
> Since we have these promises, beloved, let us cleanse ourselves from every defilement of body and spirit, bringing holiness to completion in the fear of God. (2 Cor 6:14-7:1)

In this text, Old Testament holiness laws are applied to the spiritual separation to which Paul calls Christians. As the church lives out this spiritual separation, they shine for the world to see. Jesus puts it in this way,

> You are the light of the world. A city set on a hill cannot be hidden. Nor do people light a lamp and put it under a basket, but on a stand, and it gives light to all in the house. In the same way, let your light shine before others, so that they may see your good works and give glory to your Father who is in heaven. (Matt 5:14-16)

ii. Church Versus National Polity

As the change in the nature of the Church shifted the manifestation of holiness, it also changes the focus of many features of national life in the Old Testament. In the Old Testament, Israel, as a physical kingdom, had legal legislation to reflect God's character towards those in need. There were laws to regulate slavery and indicate where it was appropriate, instructions for leaving food at harvest for those who could not afford it, and instructions for carrying on the family line and inheritance in light of unexpected deaths. All of these had a function analogous to modern social welfare, only they were to be performed by individuals towards the rest of the nation of Israel and not by the state.

In the New Testament, similar provisions are made, yet their focus shifts from the national sphere to the local church. Paul leads the churches in making provision for widows (1 Tim 5:3-16), for the poor (e.g. 2 Cor 9:1-5, cf. Rom 15:25), and instructs slaves to use their slavery as a Gospel opportunity (e.g. Eph 6:5-9). Even work is encouraged towards these ends; it is encouraged so that the ministry of the Church is not burdened but supported (Eph 4:28, cf. 2 Thess 3:6-12). This church focus is summarized in Galatians 6:10 in this way, "So then, as we have opportunity, let us do good to everyone, and especially to those who are of the household of faith." The focus of allegiance and societal structures which had a national character under the Old Covenant are shifted to the Church and its local manifestations.

iii. Exilic Versus Secure Existence

Lastly, Christians are called not to the security of an earthly home like Israel had in the promised land. Instead, they are called to live as exiles within an alien land. In Hebrews 11, the author presents the heroes of the Old

Testament as examples of those who endured the hardships of life by setting their hope on a secure inheritance awaiting them in the future, a secure heavenly Jerusalem:

> By faith Abraham obeyed when he was called to go out to a place that he was to receive as an inheritance. And he went out, not knowing where he was going. By faith he went to live in the land of promise, as in a foreign land, living in tents with Isaac and Jacob, heirs with him of the same promise. For he was looking forward to the city that has foundations, whose designer and builder is God. (Heb 11:8-10)

Like Abraham, who sojourned in alien lands, and Jesus, who found no home among his people and suffered outside Jerusalem, the author of Hebrews exhorts Christians, "let us go to [Jesus] outside the camp and bear the reproach he endured. For here we have no lasting city, but we seek the city that is to come" (Heb 13:13-14). Peter uses this image to set the tone of his first epistle, writing, "To those who are elect exiles" (1 Pet 1:1). Because Christians do not find a home in this world, it frees them to become what is necessary to see the Gospel spread (1 Cor 9:19-23), to go wherever is necessary (Rom 10:14-17), and to bear the reproach that comes with proclaiming Christ (Matt 5:2-12, 1 Pet 4:12-19).

These are some of the ways that the commission of the Christians defines them in ways that differ from Israel. One last perspective remains for us with which to consider the New Covenant People of God, their nature as a people being transformed.

c. The Nature of the Church

As a covenant community, Israel was characterized by a mixture of believers and unbelievers, meaning that some of the community possessed the Holy Spirit and obedient hearts while others did not. This has changed under the New Covenant; every Christian has received the Holy Spirit empowering them for ministry (cf. Joel 2:28-29, Acts 2:14-21), and everyone who believes in Jesus does so because they have received the promised new or circumcised heart (Deut 30:6; cf. John 3:1-8, John 6:44-45).

Because the Church is a believing covenant community, its nature is not defined by a mixture of unbeliever and believer. Instead, it is composed of believers who are being progressively transformed by Holy Spirit, setting aside their old selves to don the new self in Christ. Now, though everyone who is part of the covenant community is truly a Christian, the covenant community is not identical to the local church. The covenant community is the invisible Church, the sum total of all who truly believe throughout time. The visible church is composed of all who *claim* to believe, though not all who are part of the visible church are truly saved. Though God knows the scope of the invisible Church, it is often not possible for us to identify everyone who has genuinely believed in Jesus Christ. The local church will strive to recognize only those who have truly believed as its members, yet it will not do so perfectly. Despite this qualification, this distinction is clear in Scripture and is relevant for church teachings concerning discipline and the nature of the church, among other things.

The continuing result of this transformation is the mutual ministry characterizing the Church. Israel was called to be a holy priesthood but failed in this. Christians are likewise a holy priesthood. Each Christian is enabled and equipped by Holy Spirit to walk in Spirit, performing good works towards the Church and then towards the outside world (Gal 5:1-6:10). This is especially manifest in ministry to one another as the Spirit equips (e.g. Rom 12:1-8; 1 Cor 12:1-31; Eph 4:11-16) and to the outside world so that they might hear the Gospel (Rom 10:14-17).

In a way, Christians are called to a more radical life than Israel. Israel was separate from the nations and would have enjoyed security and comfort in their own land if only they were obedient. Christians, on the other hand, are sent into a world that hates them in order to be instruments in God's hands as he saves that world. They live in a way that clearly distinguishes them but does not separate them; they are therefore open to ridicule as they live among other people in a way that is remarkably different. They exchange the allegiances of the world and its comforts for radical commitment to Christ and his Church.

The New Testament paints a picture of the Christian covenant community as one that is radically inward focused in order to be effective in reaching the world. Working together, they take care of one another's needs and see that everyone is growing up into the fullness of Christ. By doing this, they show the World their light shining like a city on a hill. The World is shown the heavenly Jerusalem imaged in the earthly church in order that they might give glory to God. This inward focus also provides the training and resources necessary to send Christians into other communities, cities, and countries in order that they might be an effective witness there. The commission to go out and make disciples, the outward focus, is thus inextricably tied to the inward focus of teaching them to obey Jesus's commandments. This is our place in the biblical story: we are God's people united in the local church on a mission to expand God's kingdom through the making and maturing of disciples.

Knowing our place, especially in contrast with God's Old Covenant people, will help us find our way as we apply Scripture, as we seek to understand how the biblical instructions direct us in living our New Covenant identity. When seeking to apply Old Covenant teaching to our New Covenant context, we must first understand what it meant for the Old Covenant people, identify the differences between the two covenants that are relevant to the application, and use the New Testament's explicit teachings as a guide to identify how this text applies to our new situation. For example, the holiness laws in Leviticus were meant to highlight the physical separation that characterized Israel. As the New Testament people of God, we are not called to be physically separate but spiritually separate. How, then, does this command to holiness apply to us today? Paul, for example, teaches that Christians should neither marry nor closely align themselves in purposes with unbelievers (1 Cor 7:39, 2 Cor 6:14-7:1), they should maintain a sort of separation; yet they are not to remove themselves entirely from these relationships (e.g. 1 Cor 5:9-13). We will consider the task of applying the Bible, including the Old Testament, further in the next part and in *The Gift of Reading – Part 2*. This should suffice for us now.

Understanding our place in Scripture is intimately connected with the metanarrative taught in Scripture; this narrative helps give us purpose and brings unity to the teachings and stories of the Bible. This narrative shows how all the events in Scripture and the lives of contemporary Christians are working together towards the fulfilment of God's purposes in the new creation. Knowing the theology of the Bible helps us begin to answer the questions raised in our reading of Scripture and to answer the questions raised as we interact with the Bible. Having these glasses, seeing the Bible as it is, will help us read the Bible profitably and not to distort it to fit any agenda other than the one for which God created it. However, having an idea of what the Bible teaches is not enough for reading it well. For this, we need to build good reading skills: we need ears to hear what the Lord is speaking.

Further Reading

John Frame – *The Doctrine of the Christian Life* [A]

Bruce Waltke – *Old Testament Theology* [A]

Peter J. Gentry and Stephen J. Wellum – *Kingdom Through Covenant* [A]

J. Alexander Rutherford – "Biblical Themes that Define Us," [https://teleioteti.ca/2017/11/01/biblical-themes-that-define-us-two-kingdoms/ [B]

J. Alexander Rutherford – "Christians and the World," https://teleioteti.ca/2017/11/29/christians-and-the-world-the-ethics-of-a-city-on-a-hill/ B]

J. Alexander Rutherford – "Is There a Cultural Mandate for Christians" https://teleioteti.ca/2018/01/31/2306/ [B-I]

—Part 2—
We Need Ears to Hear

5

KNOWING WHEN WE HAVE READ WELL

And whoever will not listen to my words that he shall speak in my name, I myself will require it of him. – Deuteronomy 18:19

When God's people Israel did not listen to him, when they did not understand and obey, God "gave them over to their stubborn hearts, to follow their own counsel" (Ps 81:12). The result of this obedience was judgment culminating in exile. The fool in the Book of Proverbs is the one who ignores the voice of God, who rejects the fear of the Lord (e.g. Prov 1:7). His end is destitution and death (e.g. Prov 10:8). In Matthew, those who called on the name of Jesus but never submitted to him, who never obeyed his Father's commands, heard the devastating words, "I never knew you; depart from me, you workers of lawlessness" (Matt 7:23). To ignore the Word of the Lord, to fail to listen, results in destruction. We who believe in Christ do not want this end; we love our Lord and want to hear from him, "Well done, good and faithful servant" (Matt 25:23). It is imperative, then, that we recognize and obey the voice of our Lord as he has spoken in Scripture. Of course, in these passages "listen" focuses primarily on our response to the words, yet such a response has several preconditions. We need the proper framework to understand the words: we need the appropriate lens to clearly see what is being said, or we need to be tuned to the right frequency to hear it. We also need an obedient, humble heart to desire to respond to what we hear. But a right response is contingent on us not only receiving the message and having willing hearts but also listening carefully so that we understand what the Lord would have us do or believe.

As we will consider in the final part of this book, having a right heart is essential to listening well, yet it is not sufficient. What good would it do if our hearts were in the right place but we were unable to understand who God is, what he has done for us, and how he has called us to live? In Deuteronomy 18, God speaks of a future prophet like Moses, a prophet God would raise up to speak his truth once more. When this prophet came, his words would be considered God's words, so obedience was essential—God would deal with disobedience (Deut 18:19)! We must, therefore, pay close attention to the words God has spoken; we must ensure that we hear appropriately so that we might obey.

In the beginning of this book, I said that to read the Bible, we need *eyes to see, ears to hear, and hearts to understand.* In the last four chapters, we considered the lens we need to read Scripture; we looked at what the Bible is and sketched its teaching. Using the analogy of sight, Part 1 has given us the right lens to bring the text of Scripture into focus. However, the right lens is useless if we have no idea how to interpret the images we see, how to string together the symbols on a page into a meaningful sentence. In this second part, I want us to consider the actual act of reading, interpreting the words we find on the pages of Scripture.

Switching analogies, Part 1 has helped us tune in to the right frequency so that we can make out the words God is saying; now we need to focus on our ability to listen to what he is saying. In this chapter, we will consider what we aim for as we read and study the Bible and how to discern when we are reading well. In the following chapter, I will outline a methodology for reading the Bible in order to understand and be changed by it. The following four chapters will then go through different challenges that arise as we read the Bible and explore tools to help us overcome these challenges. In chapter 7, we will look at the different styles of writing in the Bible and how we can adopt different approaches for reading narrative texts (e.g. Samuel and the Gospels), poetry (e.g. found in Psalms and Proverbs), prophecy (found in most prophetic books, such as Isaiah and Revelation), and didactic prose (e.g. Romans, Hebrews, 1 Peter).[1] In Chapter 8, we will consider Bible translation

---

[1] There is some overlap here with the usual discussion of genre in interpretation, but I am intentionally deviating from the standard discussions here. For a further discussion of genre, see *The Gift of Reading – Part 2*, Chapter 4.

and the uses of the different English Bible translations that are readily available to us. Chapter 9 will take us a little bit deeper, looking at the use and abuse of the biblical languages (Hebrew, Aramaic, and Greek) in studying the Bible. We will conclude in Chapter 10 with a survey of the various resources available to help us read better and in Chapter 11 with how to evaluate what we read in these resources and our own conclusions about the text.

The question of evaluation brings us back to our first purpose in this chapter: what is our aim when we read or study the Bible? We considered in Chapter 1 the grand purpose of the Bible and what we are to expect from it: the Bible is meant to lead us from faith to faith in the fulfilment of God's purposes. But this is not where our troubles lie. That is, this book is necessary because we often struggle when we read the Bible, but it may not yet be clear what we are actually struggling with. It does not seem like we struggle with accepting and responding to the Bible's general purpose: as Christians, we are progressively growing in faith in order to fulfil God's purposes. Our struggle is with understanding what we are reading, with specific texts.

Sometimes we read and do not struggle, but other times we find ourselves confused. And at other times, we understand the general meaning of the words, but we fail to connect what the text is saying with our lives. Our struggle in all these cases is moving from a general comprehension of the words on the page to *understanding*. When a passage confuses us, it is not because we cannot explain what each individual word means but because we cannot quite understand how they work together. In other words, we do not understand what we are supposed to do with what we have read. Our goal when we read the Bible must be to understand so that we can give a right response to what God is saying: we need to listen so we can obey. The response we need to give may be an emotion, to feel sadness or anger; a thought, to believe something; or an action, to do something.[2]

---

[2] In some treatments of biblical interpretation, authors divide what I am calling "understanding" into two different categories, meaning and significance. To understand is, then, to grasp the meaning and to apply is to get the significance. I am not convinced that these can be so easily separated. It seems to me that to understand a text is to grasp how it applies in one way or another. John Frame argues that we do not know what "You shall not murder" means unless we can identify circumstance that are prohibited and others that are not. Would we say someone understands what it means to say "you shall not steal" if they think it is okay to commit tax fraud? Sometimes meaning is said to be the proposition (statement of truth) made by the

Part two is about being able to listen to God's voice as he communicates to us through the Bible; in this chapter we will look at how we know we have heard God's voice, that we have read well. We can define reading well or hearing God's voice in Scripture as understanding the right responses to a text. To read well is, therefore, to know what to do with a text. What to "do" can be many different things: we understand a text if we are able to translate it into another language (e.g. לֹא תִּרְצָח, *lōʾ tirṣāḥ*: "You shall not murder", Exod 20:13)—though translations can be better or worse, reveal more or less understanding of a text. We understand a text when we can paraphrase it (e.g. You shall not murder = it is normally wrong for a person to kill another human through intentional action or negligence, except where permissible by God's law). We understand a text if we know when it applies and when it does not: "You shall not murder" means that it is a sin before God to kill another human being in cold blood (cf. Gen 9:5-6), it is a sin before God to act negligently or fail to act with the result that human life is lost (cf. Exod 21:29), but it does not mean that capital punishment or taking a life in war is sinful (e.g. Deut 7:24, 9:3, 13:6-11; cf. Rom 13:1-5).

To say that reading well is understanding the right response to a text implies that reading badly is to misunderstand or fail to understand a text and to have a wrong response to that text. It is wrong to respond to the portrayal of the utter sinfulness of Israel in The Book of Judges (e.g. Judges 19) with joy or mirth. We fail to read well when we read the 6th commandment and think that all killing in the post-fall world is sinful or think that killing is never sinful.

So if we are going to read well, we need to know how to come to a right understanding of the text (to know the proper response) and how to avoid misunderstanding the text. In the following chapters, we will look at the "*how*" of reading well. In the rest of this chapter, I want us to consider the "*what*," three perspectives by which we can identify right and wrong responses to a text.

---

text, yet this is again an instance of application or use: we are applying the text to our thinking, learning what truth we should believe from it. I discuss this issue at length in *The Gift of Reading – Part 2*. See further John M. Frame, *The Doctrine of the Knowledge of God*, A Theology of Lordship (Phillipsburg: P&R Publishing, 1987), 67, 93–98.

A. Identifying the Right Responses to Scripture

A right response to Scripture is, of course, one that is consistent with a proper understanding of the text. But this is a circle, for we only know we have properly understood the text when we have properly applied it. We must now ask the important question; how do we identify if our application of the text is right? In other words, we need at this point to know what a justified application or response to the text is. To be "justified" means that the application or response is firmly grounded, it is based on good reasons, and so is right. I think the best way to identify a justified application or use of a text is by the criteria of *validity*, *appropriateness*, and *fittingness*.[3] We could say that an application is justified when it is a *valid* use of the text that is *appropriate* for the function of the text and *fits* its field of reference. Let's look at each of these individually.[4]

a. Validity

The first criteria to determine a justified use of a text is *validity*. Validity refers to the meaning of the words we read. A use of a text is valid when it does not twist or distort the words on the page and their relationship with one another. Positively, an application is valid when it represents a right understanding of words and their relationships (phrases, sentences, and paragraphs). To know if our application is valid, we must ask questions like, "does my interpretation of the words of the text fit their context?" "Am I interpreting the relationship between these sentences appropriately?" Some examples should serve to illustrate what I mean.

---

[3] This is based on a section of my master's thesis "God's Kingdom through his Priest-King," which I expand upon in *The Gift of Reading – Part 2*. The discussion in the latter volume is supplementary to this. J. Alexander Rutherford, *The Gift of Reading - Part 2: A Biblical Perspective on Hermeneutics*, God's Gifts for the Christian Life - Part 1 2b (Vancouver: Teleioteti, 2019); J. Alexander Rutherford, *God's Kingdom through His Priest-King: An Analysis of the Book of Samuel in Light of the Davidic Covenant*, Teleioteti Technical Studies 1 (Vancouver: Teleioteti, 2019), 93–99.

[4] Though we are addressing validity, appropriateness, and fittingness as three different criteria, they are truly only three different perspectives by which we can view a text and test our application against it. If one were to fully understand a text and all its implications, as God does, every valid use would also be appropriate and fitting, and vice versa.

Consider, for example, the 6th commandment: "You shall not murder" (Exod 20:13). A valid application will be one that is consistent with the meaning of לֹא (*lōʾ*, not) and רָצַח (*rāṣaḥ*, to murder). Consider the following five examples:

1) It is sinful (a crime against God) to kill a human being without God-given authority to do so.
2) Humans are under a serious obligation to murder.
3) It is sinful to kill another human in war.
4) It is sinful for a government to kill another human in punishment for a crime.
5) It is sinful for a human to act in a negligent manner or fail to act with the result of the loss of human life.

I contend that only examples 1 and 5 are valid applications of Exodus 20:13; examples 2-4 are invalid. Example 1 is valid because the word translated "murder" doesn't merely mean "kill" but to kill in unauthorized circumstances. There are dozens of cases where killing is divinely authorized; these are not instances of "murder." However, example 1 is vague, for it does not specify under which circumstances it is appropriate to kill. Example 5 is valid because the case laws in the Torah apply the command in this way (e.g. Exod 21:29).

Example 2 is clearly invalid, for the adverb translated "no" has been interpreted as an intensive adverb, adding emphasis to the action. Instead of "shall not," it has been applied as "must do so." This is invalid because it does not fit within the range of meanings for לֹא (*lōʾ*), the Hebrew word for "no." We will explore the concept of "range of meanings" below, in Chapter 9.

Example 3 is also invalid; in this case it takes the word translated "murder" too broadly. It is clear from Deuteronomy and elsewhere in the Old and New Testaments that God permits, even commands, people to kill others in war (e.g. Deut 7:24).

Example 4 is likewise invalid; it also takes the word "murder" too broadly (cf. Deut 13:6-11, 18:20; Rom 13:1-5).

In the rest of this part, we will be looking at strategies for reading the text better, for understanding the flow of thought and interpreting the words correctly. These are the ways we determine if our application is valid or not.

Chapters 7 and 8 will deal with the issue of validity to a greater depth, looking at how Hebrew, Aramaic, and Greek words (the original languages of the Bible) are translated into English and how to determine the appropriate meaning of these words. In the above cases, the validity of these interpretations could have been tested by consulting English translations (cf. example 2), searching up the word "murder" in a concordance or רָצַח (*rāṣaḥ*, to murder) in a Hebrew-English lexicon (i.e. dictionary) (cf. examples 1, 3-5), or using cross-reference notes and bible dictionaries or topical bibles to look up the theme of killing in the Old Testament (cf. examples 3-5).

Validity deals with the meaning of the text, asking the question, "does our application respect the meaning of the words of the text in their contexts (in the paragraph, in the book, in the canon of Scripture)?" Validity is essential to any justified application of a text, but it is not by itself sufficient. We can imagine uses of the text that appear valid to us yet are not *appropriate* or *fitting*.

For example, using Exodus 20:13 to argue that a person should be joyous when they murder another human being would be inappropriate. Nothing in this statement contradicts the words on the page, it is not misusing the word "murder" or "not." However, the text is intended to discourage murder: the text gives us God's command that murder is sinful and will be punished. The appropriate response to such a command is obedience and horror when it is transgressed. It would, therefore, be inappropriate to derive an application that is valid yet does not acknowledge the purpose of the text—that twists it to its own service.

A valid use may also not be *fitting;* that is, it may misunderstand what the text refers to. For example, it would be *valid* to interpret "Seize him and lead him away under guard" (Mark 14:44) as a command; this is what the grammar indicates. However, it would not be *fitting* to take this as a command for you and your friends to arrest a stranger walking down the street. It is not fitting because "him" refers in context to Jesus, and the command is directed towards the crowd coming to arrest Jesus, not anyone else. Though these examples may seem ridiculous, illegitimate interpretations like these occur more often than we would like to think. So, in addition to being *valid*, an application must also be *appropriate* and *fitting*.

b. Appropriateness

Let's first consider what it means for a use or application of a text to be appropriate. We will then consider fittingness. "Appropriateness" refers to the goal or function of a text, what sort of behaviour, thinking, or emotions it ought to produce. Validity considers *what* the text says; appropriateness considers the sort of response we are to have to what is said. For example, a command is intended to produce an obedient response: we obey commands. A narrative, especially a parable, or poem is intended (among other things) to produce an emotional response, make us feel one way or another about a character or subject. A didactic text, a text intended to teach, is intended to make us believe something to be true or false and then to have an appropriate response in our actions and emotions. Appropriateness thus relates to the effect a text should have on our doing, feeling, and thinking and how our application successfully or unsuccessfully manifests this effect. Appropriateness also encompasses the scope of an application. If a promise is made, we ought to interpret (i.e. it is appropriate to interpret) that promise as the promiser's intent to bring about the state promised. Yet this is not the case with a proverb from the book of Proverbs. In the latter case, it would be inappropriate to read a proverb about diligence as a promise that diligent behaviour will result in wealth (e.g. Prov 12:27). A careful study of the proverbs in light of the rest of Scripture and the book itself—along with our experience—reveals that they have a different purpose, that they are not meant to be promises. Therefore, it would be inappropriate to take Proverbs 12:27 as a promise of wealth for those who are diligent.

> ### *The Proverbs and Appropriate Application*
>
> In *The Gift of Reading – Part 2*, I explain much of the approach developed in this book as an expression of the "analogy of faith," reading Scripture in light of Scripture. The Proverbs are a good example of the necessity of this approach. If we were to take a proverb such as 12:27 out of context, it would lead us to conclude that God has broken his promises or to work ourselves to death attempting to be "diligent," for obviously that will bring us wealth. However, reading the Proverbs in light of the rest of Scripture, we see that there is no simple equation such that hard work brings wealth. God does promise blessing to his Old Covenant

people if they perfectly keep his ways, but this blessing is not individual wealth and it is clear that none of his people were able to keep this law and earn this blessing perfectly. A close look at the book of Proverbs and the rest of the Wisdom literature, especially Job, yields a different picture of the function of the wisdom sayings found in these books.

The function of wisdom literature, including the Proverbs, is to instruct the People of God in the right way to live before God in his world and discourage wrong living. All life is to be lived with reference to God—in the fear of him. A proper understanding of God and his creation will result in certain behaviours, such as honesty, hard work, faithfulness, etc. The Proverbs teach this way of life by contrasting it with ungodly or foolish behaviour and juxtaposing their results: if you want blessing, you should act in one way; to do otherwise will result in horrid consequences. The blessings and consequences attached to right and wrong behaviour are a mixture of covenant blessings and the natural consequences of such behaviour—for example, hard work generally will bring success whereas idleness will lead to failure. However, it is evident from the wisdom literature and elsewhere that there are many exceptions to these general rules. They remain true enough to motivate right behaviour and so are a convenient tool for communicating God's will.

However, there is a greater perspective in the wisdom literature, one we could call "eschatological," or focusing on the end of this age. This is especially seen in Job; Job is the quintessential righteous man and initially receives the blessings of God. Yet for reasons unknown to him, God strips away all his blessings and leaves him destitute. God does restore him in the end, but The Book of Job reveals that there is no one-to-one correlation between earthly prosperity or destitution and God's blessings or curse. There is a tension in this age, we often ask "why do the wicked prosper when the righteous suffer?" The answer is found in the age to come, the new creation, when all of God's people will enjoy the fullness of life with God for ever and the wicked will reap the consequences they have sown. Reading a text in its immediate context and the analogy of faith, reading Scripture in light of Scripture, is essential to determining the appropriateness of an application.

Taking our example in Exodus, "You shall not murder," an appropriate application is one that prohibits behaviour or identifies an implication of such a prohibition: "It is wrong to murder," "I should not murder people," "I should feel bad about murder," "God does not condone murder," etc. Some applications will be appropriate but invalid, such as "it is sinful to kill in war." This application is appropriate to the nature of the command yet misunderstands the word translated "murder." Inappropriate applications of this text would be those that misidentify the intended effect of the text. "It is right to murder," "I should feel good about murdering," and "Murder is not a sin" are all inappropriate applications of the text. Each of these examples misses the proper response to a command from God. However, if the speaker was not commissioned by God, these might be appropriate applications. For example, if the speaker is Satan saying, "throw yourself down from here" (Luke 4:9), the appropriate response is not obedience, for the Bible does not expect its readers to obey such a command (this command is also directed to Jesus, so any application that applies it to us as a command is not *fitting*, which we will address below). Our applications are appropriate when they correspond to the intent of the text, discerned by paying attention to who is speaking and what they are saying. The last perspective that we need to use to determine the validity of our application is fittingness.

c. Fittingness

Fittingness ask the question, "Does my application fit with the text's referents?" A **referent** is the textual or, most often, extra-textual (i.e. in the real world) object to which a symbol such as a word may refer.[5] For example,

---

[5] Not all words have a "referent," but some do. Proper nouns, for example, refer to a person or place. The referent of a proper noun may not exist outside of the text in question—it may refer to a character earlier in the story—or it may be a person in a T.V. show, merely a product of human creative activity.

It may be helpful to observe that the *referent* is not the *meaning* of the word. For example, "Israel" has a specific function in the context—it means something specific. The nation of Israel does not *mean* anything. A word does not replace the thing it refers to but speaks about it to communicate something. In other words, words interpret reality, so a word interprets in one way or another its referent. It may speak to the referent, about the referent, or the referent may be a piece of scenery designed to evoke some response. When we consider referential words, we concern ourselves with meaning: why has the author referred to this here? What does he mean when uses this word and what does that—his use of the word—tell us about the referent?

the word Israel often—though not always—refers to the historical people of Israel; the proper name Jesus Christ refers to the Son of God, born of the Virgin Mary in the last decade BC. It is important to ask if our application or use of a text reflects a right understanding of the referents in a text.

For example, a text such as Exodus that concerns the historic nation of Israel refers to this nation and not anything else that bears the name "Israel." If we were to derive from this text a statement of historical truth, for example, "God brought Israel forth from oppressive slavery to Egypt," our application would only be fitting if the referents are those of the text. That is, if by "God" a pagan idol such as Marduk is meant, this application is not fitting. If by Israel, the spiritual people of God—including us Christians—or Jesus is intended, this application is not fitting. If "Egypt" is used to refer to the city in Arkansas, USA, instead of a historical nation in northern Africa, this application is not fitting. Fittingness is not concerned with the meaning of the words but the correspondence between the symbol and the thing it signifies.

Surprisingly, this is where most errors in application occur. The problem is usually not in the historical application but in personal application. That is, we usually do not mistake the historical nation Israel for Jesus or "Egypt" for the United States of America. We do, however, often mistake the Old Testament people of God for the New Testament people of God or specific characters in a narrative for ourselves. For example, you may have heard someone cite 2 Chronicles 7:13-14 saying that if we repent, God will deliver our nation (maybe America or Canada) from a particular crisis:

> When I shut up the heavens so that there is no rain, or command the locust to devour the land, or send pestilence among my people, if my people who are called by my name humble themselves, and pray and seek my face and turn from their wicked ways, then I will hear from heaven and will forgive their sin and heal their land.

This seems to be a *valid* application: this is what the words say. It also appears to be an *appropriate* one: this is indeed God's intent. But it is not a *fitting* application, for God is not addressing Christians in America or in any earthly empire. In this context, God is speaking to Solomon after he prayed to dedicate the newly built temple to Yahweh. God is not speaking in a vacuum; he is drawing upon the curses given in Deuteronomy that would come upon those who broke God's covenant with Israel (Deut 28:1-29:29). He is saying that he would respond graciously if his people repented and relent from calamity. Christians are not under the Old Covenant made at Sinai, so its curses and blessings do not apply to us. Also, Christians are a different sort of people than historical Israel; we do not have a "land." According to Peter and the rest of the New Testament, we are sojourners and exiles among all the nations (e.g. 1 Pet 1:1). This means that no nation on earth bears the relationship this text describes with God.[6]

Or maybe you have heard it said that as a Christian, you "Lack one thing; go, sell all that you have and give to the poor, and you will have treasure in heaven; and come, follow me" (Mark 10:21). This is again a *valid* and *appropriate* application, but it is only a *fitting* application for the rich young man in this passage. In the narrative, Jesus is addressing a specific person in specific circumstances. For this reason, the command of the text is *fitting* only for that specific person in those specific circumstances. Indeed, if this man repented of his greed, sold everything, and then read this passage 20 years later, it would not necessarily be *fitting* for him to go and sell all he had again. We saw already that all Scripture is given by God to be useful for all Christians, so this passage must have some application for us today, yet that application may not—and often will not—be identical to what the text says.

We first must understand what Jesus is saying and why he is saying it, then we can understand what Mark (who recorded Jesus words to make a point) wants us to learn and do. If I were asked to apply this text to my church and life right now, I would say something like this.

> Christians are called to be committed wholly to Jesus Christ and follow him at any cost, giving up all things that stand in the way of pure and whole-hearted devotion to God. If wealth is an idol in your life, something that causes you to worship a created thing (money, security, etc.) instead of the Creator, you must choose

---

[6] Some would argue that this text reveals a general pattern of God's faithfulness, that he is inclined to bless those who live in obedience to him—including nations. I am not convinced that this is an appropriate understanding of God's relation to the world in this age. But even if it were, this would not be an application of this text but of a general theology of God that is manifest in this text and others. So I would say that as concerns the application of *this text*, we cannot identify our nations as fitting referents. This text does however reveal the faithfulness of God to his promises, so we can derive confidence from it that God will uphold his promises to us, such as that found in Matthew 6:33.

God over your wealth. Indeed, God may be calling you to give up everything for his name's sake. Are you willing to count all as loss for the sake of Christ, to give up comfort and ease for, maybe, life as a missionary to the tribes of the Amazon rainforest?

It may not be wealth, though, that holds you back. Is it that home you just paid off? Maybe the risk of moving and taking out a new mortgage is keeping you from going where God has called you. Is it that girl or boyfriend that is drawing you away from Christ who called you? How about your image—and this one hits home for me—do you horde up the praise and adulation of others as a sort of wealth from which you derive security and peace? Does this hold you back from confessing your sin, repenting for your wrongs, and from joyfully enduring suffering with thanksgiving instead of drawing attention to yourself through it?

On Matthew's version of this passage, R.T. France writes, "The demands of discipleship will vary for different individuals and situations. But they will never be less than total availability to the claims of Jesus, however differently these apply in practice."

Let's consider one more example of "fittingness." Have you ever heard an exhortation to "Pray for the peace of Jerusalem!" That is, have you ever heard Psalm 122:6 used as a call to pray for the peace of present-day Jerusalem, located in modern-day Israel? I humbly suggest that, though *valid* and *appropriate*, this application is not *fitting*. Such an application—you ought to pray for present-day Jerusalem—confuses the present Jerusalem with the historical capital of Israel and confuses the Old Covenant people of God to whom this was first addressed with the New Covenant people of God who now sing this psalm.

Considering the identity of Jerusalem: it is true that modern-day Jerusalem sits on the site of historic Jerusalem, so there is continuity in name and location. The inhabitants then and now are also ethnic Jews, among others. However, there are important differences. Jerusalem in Psalm 122 was the capital of the Old Testament people of God; it was the centre of God's power on earth expressed through the Davidic monarchy and his presence in the tabernacle and later the temple. This Jerusalem represented all God's people at that time; its peace meant the blessings of covenant faithfulness, its demise the curses of covenant unfaithfulness. Much has changed in 3000 years. Jerusalem is no longer the home of God's people; Christians are exiles in the earth awaiting a heavenly Jerusalem (1 Pet 1:1; Heb

11:1-40; Rev 21:1-27); and the Old Covenant is no longer valid, having passed away with the coming of the New Covenant (Heb 8:1-13, Gal 3:1-21). Present-day Jerusalem is home to the State of Israel but not to the covenant people of God, which Jerusalem represents in this Psalm. Indeed, the end of that city with its role representing God's people came in AD 70, when it was utterly destroyed by the Romans (cf. Matt 24:1-2).[7] The Psalm was addressed to the covenant people at that time, for whom it would be appropriate to pray for the Jerusalem that then existed.

If it is not *fitting* to apply this Psalm in such a straightforward manner, how then shall we "Pray for the Peace of Jerusalem"? Essentially—arguing this would take some time—the role Jerusalem plays in this Psalm is replaced by the Church universal and its local expressions. I suggest, therefore, that a *fitting* application for a Christian would be to pray that the Jesus' Church would experience relief from persecution and suffering so that it can accomplish its mission. Also, Christians ought to pray for unity within the Church, that God's people would seek to emulate Christ's character in their relationships with one another—as brothers and sisters. In his commentary on the Psalms, Derek Kidner puts it this way,

> What Jerusalem was to the Israelites, the church is to the Christian. Here are his closest ties, his *brethren and companions* [v. 8], known and unknown, drawn with him to the one centre as fellow-pilgrims.... And whatever limitations of its citizens, Jerusalem was where God saw fit to build his house. The simple response to this, *I will seek your good* [v. 9], was the least that such a fact demanded; and it had no upper limit. For the Christian it has, besides, no territorial boundary. For the inspiring implications of this, see Hebrews 12:22-24; for its immediate application, Hebrews 13:1-3.

---

[7] This is not to say that God is done with ethnic Israel; this is not the case. Romans 11 indicates that God will draw to himself a large majority of Jewish people at some time in the future, before Jesus returns. Cf. Romans 11:1-36.

It is important to observe that God does not save them as Israelites, those under the Old Covenant, but through faith in Jesus Christ. Jews will be saved as Christians under the New Covenant, thus there is urgent need of evangelism to Jewish people (cf. Paul's approach in Romans 1:16).

Fittingness asks, who is this text about, who is it directed to? Once the subject of the passage is identified, we then need to ask: am I, or the one whom I am applying the text to, identical with the subject? If not—if we are not Israelites or the rich young man—how are we different, how are we similar? By looking at what was fitting for the subject and identifying how we are different and similar to the subject of the passage, we can identify what a fitting application might be for us. This takes practice, but be encouraged that for many passages, it is pretty easy: "you shall love the Lord your God with all your heart and with all your soul and with all your mind and with all your strength" (Mark 12:30; cf. Deut 6:4-5) applies to us as it did to the Israelites, only the particular ways we do this have changed. Learning what fitting applications look like in clear passages trains us to identify them in more difficult ones. This holds true for learning to identify valid and appropriate interpretations also. Knowing about the storyline and peoples of the Bible, as we discussed earlier, is also helpful.

Fittingness and Typology

There are cases where questions of fittingness are not so easy. The discussion above may appear to say that when a text has a referent, there is only one. However, there are significant instances throughout Scripture where this is clearly not the case, where two or more non-textual objects or individuals are referred to with the same symbol (word or phrase). There may be a couple of places where the author intends overlapping referents, analogous to instances where both senses of a word are clearly valid in context (cf. John 3:7, where the word translated "again" can also mean "above"). However, I know of none. There are, however, many places where multiple referents are in view through corporate solidarity or typology.

Corporate solidarity refers to the union (however the connection is conceived) between various members of a group, such as a nation, family, or covenant party. Where there is solidarity, what is true of the group is true of its members. For example, because God is the covenant Lord of Israel in the Old Testament (a corporate group), he is the covenant Lord of every Israelite, i.e. one who is part of the group "Israel." A particularly important case of corporate solidarity occurs between a group and its representative: for a covenant group, there is often a covenant head; for a nation, there is a king. In our day, analogous relationship exists between a CEO and a company or a president/prime minister and a country. In both cases, the representative (CEO or national leader) has the ability to make decision that will be binding upon the entire corporation or nation. In the Bible, corporate solidarity is found among family, between heads and children (Abraham and his descendants, cf. Heb 7:4-10); among covenant heads and the covenant people, namely Adam and the creation and Jesus and the New Covenant people of God (Rom 5:12-21; 1 Cor 15:22, 42-49); and between kings and their people (2 Sam 24:1-25). Where corporate solidarity exists, both a representative and the entire people could be referred to in the same text. For example, in Daniel 7:13-16, the son of man figure appears to refer both to Christ Jesus and the saints (cf. Matt 16:27-38, 24:30-31, 26:64). This is true because what is true of Christ in this case will be true of the saints, for they will inherit his kingdom with him. A similar relationship is found in Isaiah 40-53 concerning the servant of the Lord, who is clearly Jesus and yet also the people of God. This also probably explains how Malachi 1:2-5 can use "Esau" and "Jacob" simultaneously to refer to historical individuals and the nations that descended from them. Solidarity accounts for many instances where a text seems to have more than one referent in view; another possibility is the use of typology.

Typology has been the subject of much discussion throughout the history of interpretation, so there are many competing ideas concerning what typology is. However, for our purposes we could define typology as a divinely ordained correspondence between historical events or persons.[i] Every instance of typology is, first, divinely ordained: typology refers to a relationship God has ordained to exist between events or persons across history. It was God's intention, for example, that Melchizedek—the enigmatic figure of Genesis 14—would prefigure Christ (cf. Heb 6:2-7:28). Second, it is a correspondence between historical entities: typology refers to an intentional relationship where one item prefigures or points to another, as Melchizedek who was the priest and king of Jerusalem pointed towards Christ who was the ultimate priest-king of Jerusalem. It is similar to prophecy, for both anticipate and tell us about something ahead of themselves; yet whereas prophecy is clearly forward looking, typology is retroactive, we see and learn from the correspondence only after the type (that which points to something) and the antitype (that which is pointed to, or the fulfilment of the type) have both appeared.

It is because of such a relationship that Matthew can identify Jesus coming forth from Egypt as the fulfilment of Hosea 11:1, "out of Egypt I called my son" (Matt 2:15). In its context, "my son" clearly refers to Israel, so an application to Jesus would appear to not be fitting. However, Matthew sees Jesus as fitting into and being the fulfilment of the historical pattern of God's relationship to Israel. Jesus came out of Egypt as they did, was tested in the wilderness as they were, yet he was not disobedient like them; he fulfils this pattern by being the true and faithful son Israel was called to be. Matthew rightly sees Jesus as a referent in this text, in addition to historical Israel, because the entire pattern of Israel's history was meant to point to Jesus. It is debated whether we are able apart from Scriptural guidance to identify types, but at the very least we can say that in those cases where Scripture makes such an application, multiple referents will be "fitting."

---

i. Cf. G. K. Beale, "Positive Answer to the Question: Did Jesus and his Followers Preacher the Right Doctrine from the Wrong Texts? An Examination of the Presuppositions of Jesus' and the Apostles' Exegetical Method," in The Right Doctrine from the Wrong Texts?: Essays on the Use of the Old Testament in the New, ed. G. K. Beale (Grand Rapids: Baker Books, 1994), 394.

d. Examples

In this chapter, we have considered what makes a good application of a text. I have attempted to answer the question, "What does a justified application of Scripture look like?" My answer was threefold: we could say that an application is justified when it is a *valid* use of the text that is *appropriate* for the function of the text and *fits* its field of reference. An application is valid when it is consistent with the text interpreted in its context. An application is *appropriate* when it is consistent with the force or intent of the text. An application is fitting when it is consistent with the referents of a text. Instead of jumping immediately into the next chapter, this is a good time to put into practice what we have just learned.

Below I have provided several applications of Romans 8:28; many of them are applications I have encountered in conversations, read in books, and used in my own teaching. Considering the text and its context (pay particular attention to 8:28-39), which of the following applications of the text are justified? Ask yourself why it is justified; is it valid, appropriate, and fitting? If it is not justified, why not? In the footnotes, I have provided what I think are the appropriate evaluations of these applications. If you disagree with me, ask yourself why. Why have I evaluated them the way I have? How have you evaluated them differently?

> And we know that for those who love God all things work together for good, for those called according to his purpose (Rom 8:28)

1. Because God works all things for the good of Christians, I am free to do whatever I want—maybe get drunk and drive home—knowing that it will work out for my good.

2. As a Christian I can have the confidence that even when I sin, God will work this out for my good.

3. As a Christian, I can be confident that no matter what I do or what happens to me, I will receive wealth, peace, and prosperity in this life.

4. As a Christian, I can have the hope that every horror in my past, every present and future suffering—including those brought on by my own sin—will contribute to God's good purpose in making me more like his Son.

5. I can be confident that whatever I do will turn out for good because God is good.[8]

---

[8] **Not justified:** **#1** is not justified because it is inappropriate: it uses a text meant to give confidence in God's gracious sovereignty as an excuse for sin. **#3** is not justified because it is invalid: it misunderstands the word "good," failing to interpret good within the New Covenant context of the New Testament and v. 29 in particular. **#5** is not justified because it is neither fitting nor valid. It appears to be a non-Christian speaking, so the text does not refer to him: it is not fitting to apply the text to someone who does not love Yahweh. It is also invalid because the statement that God's goodness is the reason for this promise is not taught in this text, regardless of whether or not it is true.
Justified: **#2** is justified because the text is directed to all Christians (so it is *fitting*), "all things" encompasses sin (so it is *valid*), and it is a promise from God in which we can have confidence (so it is *appropriate*). **#4** is also justified, for much the same reasons as **#2**. Furthermore, in contrast to **#3**, **#4** is valid because it rightly identifies "good" as the conformity to Christ mentioned in v. 29.

J. Alexander Rutherford

6

KNOWING HOW TO READ WELL

This Book of the Law shall not depart from your mouth, but you shall meditate on it day and night, so that you may be careful to do according to all that is written in it. For then you will make your way prosperous, and then you will have good success. – Joshua 1:8

To this point we have mostly talked theory: we have looked at the big picture of the Bible in Part 1 and then looked at the immediate goal of reading the Bible, understanding and its application, in the last chapter. What we have yet to touch upon is the act of reading the Bible, the methods and means by which we arrive at our applications of the text. In this chapter, we will begin looking at the act of reading, often called exegesis. My main purpose in this chapter is to give an overview of the steps involved in reading the Bible. In our discussion of each step of exegesis, of interpreting the Bible, I will go over the basics of reading a text well. In the following chapters, we will take up the more technical yet sometimes necessary aspects of biblical interpretation.

Each step discussed in this chapter is essential to sound biblical interpretation, but the order in which I present them will not necessarily be helpful for every reader. If you are new to reading the Bible in a reflective and thoughtful manner, I suggest that you follow the method as I outline it and then tweak it as you become more comfortable in your study of the Bible. Some readers will find that they do these things reflexively, without deliberate thought, and others will probably find that what I identify as one step may be two or vice versa. All this to say, reading the Bible is more of an art than a science; others can share from their experience and provide time-tested tips, yet bible study will look different for every reader.

I break the method of exegesis, or Bible reading, into the following eight steps: (1) Pray, (2) identify the passage for study, (3) identify the contexts, (4) identify the translational difficulties and establish the text, (5) observe the text, (6) identify the passage's relation to its context, (7) apply the passage, and (8) check your understanding.

A. (1) Pray

> and take... the sword of the Spirit, which is the word of God, praying at all times in the Spirit, with all prayer and supplication.
> – Ephesians 6:17-18

The first thing we need to do when we begin to read the Bible is not reading. If reading is a moral act, as I have suggested in the introduction and will unpack more in the last part of this volume, we need to pray for a right heart as we read the Bible. In this sense, reading the Bible is not like reading any other book, or at least it is not like reading any other book calmly at home in peace and quiet.

Instead, it is like reading in the middle of a war zone—akin to taking a seat outside a bombed-out building and opening your favourite book while machine guns are being fired around you and bombs are exploding a few meters away! And I do not mean it is difficult to focus because of the endless distractions available to us; this is true but not the most perilous danger facing us as we read the Bible.

The picture the Bible paints of the Christian life is one of warfare; it is not by accident that Paul calls his young compatriots "fellow soldier" (Phil 2:25, Phlm 2). As Paul famously writes in Ephesians, "we do not wrestle against flesh and blood, but against the rulers, against the authorities, against the cosmic powers over this present darkness, against the spiritual forces of evil in the heavenly places" (6:12). He does not have to argue *that* we are in a war; he only seeks to identify the proper nature of this warfare. It is not flesh and blood combat but spiritual warfare waged by spiritual means. Because we are at war, writes Paul, we need to equip ourselves; one of the key pieces of equipment we need is "the sword of the Spirit, which is the word of God" (6:17). If reading the Bible arms us to do battle for the glory of God, we cannot think our enemies will let us arm ourselves without opposition.

We must be praying at all times—notice how Paul connects prayer with the whole act of equipping ourselves for battle (6:18). We pray that God would protect us from the various strategies the enemy would use to make our time in the Word of God ineffective. He may bring distraction, but his most effective tool may very well be stirring up our sinful hearts to blind us to what God wants us to hear. Indeed, before God saved us, we were in complete blindness—for "the god of this world has blinded the minds of the unbelievers, to keep them from seeing the light of the gospel of the glory of Christ" (2 Cor 4:4). Satan veiled our eyes from truly seeing what God wanted us to see. By the grace of God, this is no longer the case: God "has shone in our hearts to give the light of the knowledge of the glory of God in the face of Jesus Christ" (2 Cor 4:6). Though this total blindness is gone, it is still the case that we face times of blindness caused not by hearts totally sold out to sin but by the sin that still tempts us.

That is, Satan has an ally—an inside man—in his efforts to make our reading of the Bible ineffective. According to Paul, the Christian life from now until Christ's return is characterized not only by this external battle but also by an internal one, a battle between the vestiges of our old self and the new life we have in Christ through the Holy Spirit. In Galatians 5:16-17, Paul calls the Galatians to walk by the Spirit and not their sinful passions, "for the desires of the flesh are against the Spirit, and the desires of the Spirit are against the flesh, for these are opposed to each other, to keep you from doing the things you want to do" (5:17). If we are going to be effective in reading the Bible, we need to be doing battle on both these fronts: we need to make war internally, against sinful desires, and externally, against spiritual opposition. This begins with prayer. We pray that the Spirit would reveal our sin, lead us to repentance, and defeat the deceit of the enemy. We will consider this aspect of Bible reading further in the final part of this book. But there is one other reason we begin our reading and continue it with prayer.

To put it plainly, it would be stupid to do otherwise—and I confess I am guilty of this stupidity more often than I care to admit. Not only is the Spirit our greatest ally in defeating the deceit of the enemy and our sinful flesh, but he is also the author of the Bible. How often have you come upon an interesting or difficult part of a book and wished you had the author there beside you to help you understand. I have definitely wished this. Would it not be utterly dumbfounding to witness someone struggling with a difficult text all the while ignoring the author sitting right beside them, never once asking for a little help?

Paul argues that the natural man, someone apart from the Spirit of God, considers the Scriptures to be foolish and cannot accept them. He does so because he does not have the Spirit who reveals the Scriptures to us as the wisdom of God (2 Cor 2:6-16). In this passage, Paul argues that the Spirit, as God, has a full understanding of God's thoughts and words. This makes sense. This means, because we have the Spirit always with us, we have access always to the author of the Scriptures—the one who knows exactly what God intended to say through the human authors of Scripture and how this applies to us today. Therefore, it makes sense to ask him to help us as we read his Word. It is not as though he is going to give us a key to understanding the text that is not in the text itself; no, the Bible is sufficient and clear. However, he can call to our minds others passages that may shed light on what we are reading or help us to notice something we missed. We pray that he would quicken our minds to perceive what was there the whole time.[1] With the

---

[1] I know some authors, and maybe some of the readers of this book, have dismissed this aspect of illumination. They argue that every passage that refers to the Spirit helping us understand and obey God refer to his help overcoming our sinful blindness. I suspect this is a misunderstanding of the Spirit's work as portrayed in the Bible and a subtle—though unintentional—capitulation to the naturalism of our day. Though the Spirit's primary work in Scripture is spiritual, associated with giving us believing, obedient hearts (regeneration) and helping us live out our faith in obedience to God (sanctification), this is not the only work he does. In 1 Corinthians 12:4-11 and Romans 12, the Spirit is said to gift people with particular skills or abilities for the sake of the Church. We often focus on the so-called supernatural gifts, but several gifts in both lists are what we would usually call "natural" (e.g. wisdom, knowledge, distinguishing between spirits, teaching, serving). It is not as though the Spirit codes these things into our DNA and lets them play out in our lives; on the contrary, in Philippians 2:12-13 Paul tells us Christians "work out your own salvation with fear and trembling, for it is God who works in you, both to will and to work for his good pleasure." God accomplishes the "doing" in our lives. If we look at the Old Testament, we see that the Spirit's work was not only Spiritual: he empowered Samson with supernatural strength (Judg 14:6, 15:14) and specific Jewish individuals—especially Bezalel (Exod 31:1-5)—with artistic skills and craftmanship (Exod 28:3). In these instances, the expression of these "natural" abilities is in explicit conjunction with the filling of the Spirit (e.g. Exod 31:3, Judges 14:6). I conclude that it is wrong to restrict the Spirit's work to the spiritual realm and that it is perfectly acceptable—indeed, necessary—to ask for the Spirit to

Psalmist, we need to pray,

> Deal bountifully with your servant,
>   that I may live and keep your word.
> Open my eyes, that I may behold
>   wondrous things out of your law.
> I am a sojourner on the earth;
>   hide not your commandments from me! (Ps 119:17-19)

B. (2) Identify the Passage for Study

After praying, we need to identify the text which we will study. In many contexts, this will be given to us. However, there will be times when we want to study a passage or are given the freedom to teach or preach on a passage of our choosing. In these situations, we need to be able to identify the contours of the passage that we will study. No sentence, verse, or passage in the Bible exists in isolation; every word, sentence, paragraph, etc., is intimately related with what precedes and follows it. For this reason, we cannot arbitrarily pick a block of text to study. Instead, we need to identify the boundaries of a paragraph, verse, or scene/pericope (smallest textual unit in a narrative).

Doing so will help us to understand what the text is saying and to not artificially take a chunk of text out of context (as if you could study "blessed are those who mourn, for they shall be comforted" [Matt 5:4] apart from the speech in which it falls). It will also keep us from doing an unnecessary amount of work. This second problem arises when we realize that every word is related to every other word, every sentence to every sentence, and so on until our study of a passage encompasses the whole Bible—a task too great

---

quicken our intellect, eyesight, and memory so that we might understand the Scriptures.

I hope the emphasis on Scripture so far would caution against the movements today that would encourage seeking the Spirit's leading above and beyond Scripture. Though I would not disavow some form of prophecy continuing today, it is clear that the primary way God speaks to us is in Scripture and that whatever prophecy may look like today, it will never be contrary to Scripture. Furthermore, because Scripture is sufficient for the Christian life, prophecy and other supernatural works of the Spirit should be understood as God giving insight into our situations and circumstances in order that we might be better equipped to live obediently to his Word.

for any of us! By carefully identifying our passage for study, we keep our study to closed units of a text, such as a full paragraph, scene, or poetic verse. The passage we study may not be identical with the passage we teach, for we may be given only a single verse to teach, yet our passage of study must encompass both the text we teach and the surrounding material that makes a complete thought or textual unit.

Though it doesn't match how we write, completed texts can be visualized as a string of blocks that are put together like Lego pieces to make a whole. A clause is made up of several different types of "blocks" (verbs, adverbs, adjectives, nouns, prepositional phrases). A sentence (or line in poetry) is made up of several forms of these clauses (independent and dependent clauses). Paragraphs are made up of different sentences, sometimes connected by conjunctions (e.g. "and, or, but, for") and sometimes not (asyndeton). Paragraphs are strung together to form larger blocks of text, and these are strung together to form books. To establish the boundaries of our study, we are looking for the larger blocks made up of sentences or lines of poetry that form a unit. For example, the ESV considers Galatians 6:1-10 to be a single section, assigning it the heading "Bear One Another's Burdens," and it divides this section further into two paragraphs (6:1-5, 6-10). The whole section or either paragraph would serve well as a passage for study. In poetry, the smallest completed unit is a series of lines called a colon (e.g. Hab 3:2 is divided into one bi-colon, made of two lines, and one tri-colon, made of three lines). These groups of lines, colons, are then put divided into larger sections.

A unit of text will look different for each style of text we study—e.g. whether it is narrative or poetry. In the following chapter, we will look at the different styles of texts in the Bible and the units that make them up, with techniques to better understand how the text is shaped and how to identify and relate the units of text that make up a passage. It is important to remember that verse and chapter numbers, though helpful, are not sure guides to the divisions of a text or to identifying the units of thought that make it up. These divisions were added in the last millennia (13th-16th cent.) and represent an interpretation of the text. Many translations and original-language Bible's will provide paragraph divisions and section headings; these are helpful but not inerrant.

C. (3) Identify the contexts

Every passage we study is embedded in various levels of context. It is essential to identify these layers at the beginning of our study and consider them throughout it. Context is the literary setting, the textual environment, in which a passage resides. The immediate context is those blocks of text—sentences, paragraphs, scenes, lines, chapters, etc.—that precede and follow our text. It is most intimately related to these, yet it also has relation to the chapter, book, canonical section, and testament in which it is found.

Consider, for example, the book of Habakkuk. If our passage of study is Habakkuk 2:2-4, the immediate context will be God's response to Habakkuk given in 2:2-20. The greater context is the discourse between God and Habakkuk introduced in 1:1 and extending to 2:20. It is part of the book of Habakkuk, which is part of the Minor Prophets or the Twelve, which is part of the *Nevi'im* or The Prophets—the second division of the Hebrew Bible. It is part of the Old Testament, and it is part of the Bible.

One particular feature of the biblical context that we must observe is where our book fits in the metanarrative or story taught by the Bible (cf. Ch. 3). We must ask where in the story of God's unfolding work does this book take place: considering the big movements of this story, is this before or after Christ? It is also helpful to observe where it fits more precisely: for example, Habakkuk takes place sometime near the end of the kingdom of Judah, so it is similar in themes and addresses a similar period of time as the book of Jeremiah and the end of the books of Kings and Chronicles.

When we first consider the context of our passage, we only want to identify the broad features that will help us understand our passage. We need to understand how the Old Testament differs from the New, but also that our passage fits into the whole Bible, which testifies about Jesus. As part of the Twelve, Habakkuk serves to communicate with the rest of the Minor Prophets a picture of God's indictment of sin, judgment of sinners, and future salvation for his people. It is helpful to observe that its place in The Prophets means it is going to provide an authoritative revelation from God concerning the relation his people have to him and how he has or will deal with them.

The most important piece of context will be the book itself. At this stage of study, it is important to read the entire book—ideally in one sitting—and make observations about the book as a whole. Consider, for example, the main theme or themes of the book (e.g. Habakkuk focuses on *faith, judgement, righteousness*, and *salvation*; Romans likewise focuses on these four themes in addition to other things). Observing repeated words—especially word roots (see Ch. 9)—is helpful in identifying key themes, but at times a theme will be introduced without any specific vocabulary to identify it. It is also important to observe the contours or flow of the book; how does the author unfold his argument, lay out his narrative, or structure his poem? What parts are most closely connected to each other? This part, outlining a book, will probably require you to consult secondary resources, such as a good commentary or biblical introduction (see Chapter 10 for more on these resources).[1] As you read the book, especially an epistle, consider the purpose the author has for writing. Given what he says, what is the goal he is hoping to achieve—to correct false doctrine, provide encouragement, give specific instruction, etc.? Habakkuk, for example, appears to be written to encourage the believing community of Judah to hold fast to God in the midst of horrific conditions, to trust him for salvation even when salvation looks worse than the problem. Romans appears to be written to help reconcile Jewish and Gentile believers in the Roman church. Identifying the purpose of the book helps us to trace its argument, understand our text's role within the book, and identify its key themes.

Identifying themes and outlining the flow of a book helps us answer the key question we need answered to interpret books of the Bible: why is the author writing this? Careful attention to these features reveals, for example, that Habakkuk is writing to encourage believing Jews to trust God despite his unbelievable deeds—namely, the Babylonian invasion of Judah. Galatians is written to persuade the Galatian Christians to turn from false teaching and persevere in the true Gospel, namely that all of God's promises are given through faith in Jesus Christ and not through obedience to the Law.

At this stage of exegesis, we are merely getting a general feel for the contexts in which our text falls. After looking closer at our passage of study,

---

[1] As discussed in *The Gift of Reading – Part 2*, identifying the shape or flow of book is more important for some forms of Biblical literature, such as narratives, than for others, such as poems. With didactic prose, such as the New Testament epistles, it is less important to grasp how the author might group his thoughts (such as having a thanksgiving section and a body) than to see how his argument unfolds.

we will then revisit these contexts and ask more intentionally how our passage relates to them (see step 6).

D. (4) Identify the translational difficulties and establish the text

Having identified the passage of study and the contexts in which it is embedded, we must now turn to consider the details of the text. The first thing we need to do is identify the best text to use. That is, translations will sometimes differ from one another; we need to identify which translation best represents the original biblical text—what is often called the *autographa*.[2] This will look differently depending on whether you are reading the original language texts (Greek, Aramaic, or Hebrew) or a translation. There are two issues that need to be considered when establishing the text. There are issues, first, of translation difference and, second, of textual difference. The latter issues are relevant mostly to readers of the original text. Generally, for most readers of the Bible, it would be best to trust the translation you are using unless you are given a significant reason otherwise.

When it comes to differences in translation, there are many helpful tools that can guide readers in resolving the issue. However, when it is necessary to resolve a textual difference—even for those who have the knowledge base and skills to resolve a significant textual difference (namely, reading ability in the original languages)—we will be highly dependent on the work of scholars who specialize in the field of text criticism and who know the original languages. For these reasons, it is necessary to use secondary resources (such as commentaries or study Bibles) in this step of exegesis. Though we will discuss both types of issues here, this book will mostly address issues concerning different translations. The recommended reading in this chapter and later chapters will provide additional resources for those who want to

---

[2] The *autographa* are the original canonical texts—the texts given to us by God under the guidance of the Holy Spirit to act as a covenant document for his people—not necessarily the original text that left the named author's hand. For example, the *autographa* of the Pentateuch involve various editorial details that were added after the text was written by Moses; these editorial editions (such as the notice about Moses' death or notices about changes in place names) should be considered part of the *autographa*.

pursue text-critical issues.[3]

a. Translation Differences

When you are reading a translation—or translating the text—you must identify what the best translation of particular words or phrases is. For most of us, our concern will not be with every word in a text but only with those places where one English translation differs from another. Consider, for example, Habakkuk 3:13:

> You *went* out for the salvation of your people,
>   for the salvation *of your anointed*. (ESV, cf. NASB, emphasis added)
> You *come* forth for the salvation of your people,
>   for salvation *with your anointed*; (my translation, cf. KJV, emphasis added)[4]

I have chosen the ESV and NASB translations for comparison because, as we will see in Chapter 8, the more literal translations are the best translations to use when studying the Bible. There are two differences here that need to be considered if we are going to properly interpret this passage. First, is it "salvation *with*" or "salvation *of*" God's anointed? Second, is this text referring to Yahweh's past ("went") or present ("come") action?

If you are not familiar with the original language of the passage (Hebrew in this case), this may be a difficult difference to resolve, yet there are helpful resources that will guide you in making a decision. We need to figure out, first, why the translation is different. Namely, we must ask if there is a difference in the underlying text or if the translations are disagreeing on the translation of the same underlying text. To identify the problem, the use of a study Bible or some sort of interlinear text will most likely be necessary.[5] Again, for many readers of the Bible, this step will be unnecessary. If such a question arises, it may be wisest to seek the help of a pastor or language expert in your church.

---

[3] If you are going to be studying in the original languages, especially in Hebrew, it will be necessary to learn the basics of text criticism.

[4] My translation is taken from my Habakkuk commentary. Rutherford, *Habakkuk*.

[5] We will look at such resources and there use in Ch. 10.

Study Bible's will often have a footnote stating alternate translations and why they are different. They will often give a source, such as a different text (e.g. LXX, the Greek translation of the Old Testament) or an emendation (a deliberate correction made by the translator) for the difference between the footnote translation and the one in the text.[6] Looking at an interlinear for both translations or using Bible software (see chs. 9 and 10) will also show someone with basic knowledge of Hebrew whether translators are translating the same text or different ones.

If there is a disagreement over the underlying text (if one translation says it is word-A but the other word-B), the way to resolve this disagreement is textual criticism, which we will consider briefly below. But if translations agree that it is the same word, only differing in how to translate it, several steps can then be taken. The first is to identify the word in question (in Habakkuk 3:13 it is אֵת (*'et*)) and do a word study (see Ch. 9). A word study will, in this case, reveal two things; first, there are far too many instances of this word to study. Second, this word is actually a homonym, two different words spelt in the exact same way. One word is a preposition meaning "with"; the other is a textual marker that indicates which word receives the action of a verb (called the marker of the definite direct object; that is, it is used to indicate two grammatical categories, that a word is *definite* and the *direct object* of a verb). The question is, which word is Habakkuk using? A good commentary will discuss the pros and cons of each translation, and a Hebrew Grammar or lexicon (i.e. dictionary) will give examples of how each word is used.

In this case, a commentary may argue that the marker of the definite direct object (DDO) is not often used without a verb and that "for salvation," though resembling a verb, is clearly a noun with the preposition "for" (לְ) attached to it. Furthermore, it will be observed that Habakkuk, like most Hebrew prophecy and poetry, very rarely uses the marker of the DDO (3x, 1:4, 6; 2:14). From this evidence, we could then conclude that the most evident reading of the text is "with your anointed," unless the context

---

[6] Consider Hab 2:5, the ESV footnote on "wine" says "Masoretic Text; Dead Sea Scroll, *wealth*." That is, the standard Hebrew Text (Masoretic Text, MT) has a Hebrew word meaning "wine," but the Dead Sea Scroll has a Hebrew word meaning "wealth." By putting "wine" in the text, the translators indicate that they think this is most likely to be the original.

indicates that this is not correct. However, a close study of the context reveals that this makes great sense.

Regarding the tense of the verb, "went" or "come forth," a scan of several commentaries should reveal that the Hebrew verbs behind this whole chapter (Habakkuk 3) are ambiguous: they could refer to a past or future event. Considering the events Habakkuk is describing in Chapter 3 in light of the first part of the book (cf. 1:5 and 3:2, 3:16-19), I think that the present translation is far more likely.[7]

b. Textual Differences

In other cases, the difference between two translations may not be a question of grammar or word meaning but of which words the biblical author intended. That is, the Bibles we read today are obviously not the original pages written by the biblical authors, nor are they translations of the originals. Instead, what we have are copies and translations of copies—and we have a lot of copies (20,000+ NT manuscripts)![8] When we read the Bible, we are interested in hearing what God is saying, what he led the authors of Scripture to write. So we are interested in the original words of the authors.[9] None of these copies is perfect, so the discipline of *text criticism* was developed to recover the original text from the copies we have. None of our English Bibles represents a single manuscript. The texts usually printed as the Greek New Testament (Including the Nestle-Aland, UBS, and Tyndale Greek New Testament) are known as critical texts, produced from comparing the manuscripts we have in order to reproduce what was most likely the original text. The Hebrew Old Testament text as it is usually found (including the BHS and similar editions) is known as a diplomatic text: it presents the

---

[7] I discuss this example further in my study guide *Believe the Unbelievable* and in my commentary on Habakkuk (Teleioteti, 2019). Essentially, Habakkuk is portraying the coming Babylonian invasion—in all its horror—as a salvific act of God.

[8] This number includes Greek language manuscripts and early translations into Latin and other languages.

[9] To be specific, we are interested in the canonical *autographa*. That is, the original texts that God has ordained to govern his people. In the time between the original writing of some books, such as the Pentateuch (Genesis-Deuteronomy), and the writing of the last book by the end of the 1st century AD, some editorial comments were added but are considered authoritative—part of the *autographa* (these include, for example, updated place names in the Pentateuch).

content of a single manuscript, the Leningrad Codex, and presents the alternative evidence in the critical notes (i.e. notes that offer alternative textual readings and the evidence for them).

Sometimes translations disagree on which textual reading (which manuscript text) best represents the original. For instance, in 2 Thessalonians 2:13, the ESV translates "because God chose you as *the firstfruits* to be saved" (emphasis added) but the NASB "because God has chosen you *from the beginning* for salvation" (emphasis added). This is a textual difference; firstfruits translates the word ἀπαρχῆς (*aparchēs*) and "from the beginning" the phrase ἀπ' ἀρχῆς (*ap' archēs*). As you can see, these are very similar, only a space differentiating them. The manuscript evidence is strong for both readings. Therefore, to make a decision in such a case, text critics use what are called internal evidence. That is, they ask how the context help us identify which one of these is most appropriate. In my own study, I have concluded that Paul's intention here and use of both these words (or lack thereof) supports the manuscript evidence in favour of ἀπ' ἀρχῆς, "from the beginning."[10]

A more significant difference is found in the book of Mark. English translations make some sort of break between Mark 16:8 and 16:9-20, noting that the later verses are not found in the earlier and generally more trustworthy manuscripts. In this case, a text-critical decision is not over which word is original but over whether a section of text (cf. John 7:53-8:11) is part of the original text. In both cases, Mark 16 and John 7:53-8:11, the current consensus is that these are later additions to the text, inserted by scribes in the years after the canon was closed (i.e. after the last biblical book was written). This decision is made primarily on the basis of manuscript evidence, evaluating the testimony of the manuscripts for and against each reading, both their age and quality. But internal considerations are also made.

If you intend to read and study the Bible in its original languages or study the Bible for teaching, it would be wise to familiarize yourself with the basics of text criticism, at the very least so you can evaluate the arguments presented by different commentators. See the Further Reading section at the end of this chapter for resources to help in this area. In conclusion, it should be remembered that though there are differences in translations and

---

[10] *Prevenient Grace: An Investigation into Arminianism*, 2nd Ed (Teleioteti, 2020), 189-192.

manuscripts, there is far more agreement than disagreement and the most common differences between copies are insignificant for meaning and interpretation. There is good reason to trust the Old Testament text we have and the New Testament critical text that stands behind our English translations.

E. (5) Observe the text

At this point, we have prepared our hearts, identified our passage and its context, and begun to resolve differences between translations of the text. With this foundation laid, it is now time to turn and consider the text itself. The best thing to do is read, read, and read some more. Read in several translations or work to translate the text yourself, which will help you clarify what you think the text is saying. As you read, observe connections between the text, what words are repeated, themes are revisited. Consider if the author is using quotations from or allusions to the Old Testament; if so, read those texts and ask yourself why he is drawing on these texts. Some of us find it helpful to mark up our Bibles—draw lines between repeated or connected words, highlight or mark different words and their relationships, etc.—or to print out the passage on a piece of paper and do the same.

The point is to pay careful attention to the text, to make sure you understand what is being said and why it is being said. It is only by understanding clearly what is being said that you will know how to make an application of your passage. This step should take the most amount of time. There are several tools that you can use to read better, depending on the type of passage you are reading (poetry, narrative, or letter); I will discuss these tools in the following chapter. At this point, all I want to do is hammer in how important it is to read the text well, to read it carefully, and do so repeatedly. A good technique for looking well is asking good questions; instead of staring blankly at the text, ask why this word is used instead of that one, ask why this sentence follows that one or this conjunction is used. Asking good questions will reveal far more than just looking will do.

In our culture, we are used to quick fixes—5-minute oil changes, 30-second commercials, and Google searches. We are not trained to work our way patiently and slowly through a text to ensure we understand it. If we are going to be good readers of the Bible, we need to train ourselves to do this. When I was taught exegesis in Bible College, my teacher used the following story to illustrate this:

a. Agassiz and the Fish

It was more than fifteen years ago that I entered the laboratory of Professor Agassiz, and told him I had enrolled my name in the scientific school as a student of natural history. He asked me a few questions about my object in coming, my antecedents generally, the mode in which I afterwards proposed to use the knowledge I might acquire, and finally, whether I wished to study any special branch. To the latter I replied that while I wished to be well grounded in all departments of zoology, I purposed to devote myself specially to insects.

"When do you wish to begin?" he asked.

"Now," I replied.

This seemed to please him, and with an energetic "Very well," he reached from a shelf a huge jar of specimens in yellow alcohol.

"Take this fish," he said, "and look at it; we call it a Haemulon; by and by I will ask what you have seen."

With that he left me.... I was conscious of a passing feeling of disappointment, for gazing at a fish did not commend itself to an ardent entomologist....

In ten minutes I had seen all that could be seen in that fish, and started in search of the professor, who had, however, left the museum; and when I returned, after lingering over some of the odd animals stored in the upper apartment, my specimen was dry all over. I dashed the fluid over the fish as if to resuscitate it from a fainting-fit, and looked with anxiety for a return of a normal, sloppy appearance. This little excitement over, nothing was to be done but return to a steadfast gaze at my mute companion. Half an hour passed, an hour, another hour; the fish began to look loathsome. I turned it over and around; looked it in the face—ghastly; from behind, beneath, above, sideways, at a three-quarters view—just as ghastly. I was in despair; at an early hour, I concluded that lunch was necessary; so with infinite relief, the fish was carefully replaced in the jar, and for an hour I was free.

On my return, I learned that Professor Agassiz had been at the museum, but had gone and would not return for several hours. My fellow students were too busy to be disturbed by continued conversation. Slowly I drew forth that hideous fish, and with a feeling of desperation again looked at it. I might not use a magnifying glass; instruments of all kinds were interdicted. My two hands, my two eyes, and the fish; it seemed a most limited field. I pushed my fingers down its throat to see how sharp its teeth were. I began to count the scales in the different rows until I was convinced that that was nonsense. At last a happy thought struck me—I would draw the fish; and now with surprise I began to discover new features in the creature. Just then the professor returned.

"That is right," said he, "a pencil is one of the best eyes. I am glad to notice, too, that you keep your specimen wet and your bottle corked."

With these encouraging words he added—

"Well, what is it like?"

He listened attentively to my brief rehearsal of the structure of parts whose names were still unknown to me; the fringed gill-arches and movable operculum; the pores of the head, fleshly lips, and lidless eyes; the lateral line, the spinous fin, and forked tail; the compressed and arched body. When I had finished, he waited as if expecting more, and then, with an air of disappointment:

"You have not looked very carefully; why," he continued, more earnestly, "you haven't seen one of the most conspicuous features of the animal, which is as plainly before your eyes as the fish itself. Look again; look again!" And he left me to my misery.

I was piqued; I was mortified. Still more of that wretched fish? But now I set myself to the task with a will, and discovered one new thing after another, until I saw how just the professor's criticism had been. The afternoon passed quickly, and when, towards its close, the professor inquired,

"Do you see it yet?"

"No," I replied. "I am certain I do not, but I see how little I saw before."

"That is next best," said he earnestly, "but I won't hear you now; put away your fish and go home; perhaps you will be ready with a better answer in the morning. I will examine you before you look at the fish."

This was disconcerting; not only must I think of my fish all night, studying, without the object before me, what this unknown but most visible feature might be, but also, without reviewing my new discoveries, I must give an exact account of them the next day. I had a bad memory; so I walked home by Charles River in a distracted state, with my two perplexities.

The cordial greeting from the professor the next morning was reassuring; here was a man who seemed to be quite as anxious as I that I should see for myself what he saw.

"Do you perhaps mean," I asked, "that the fish has symmetrical sides with paired organs?"

His thoroughly pleased, "Of course, of course!" repaid the wakeful hours of the previous night. After he had discoursed most happily and enthusiastically—as he always did—upon the importance of this point, I ventured to ask what I should do next.

"Oh, look at your fish!" he said, and left me again to my own devices. In a little more than an hour he returned and heard my new catalogue.

"That is good, that is good!" he repeated, "but that is not all; go on." And so for three long days, he placed that fish before my eyes, forbidding me to look at anything else, or to use any artificial aid. "Look, look, look," was his repeated injunction.

This was the best entomological lesson I ever had—a lesson whose influence was extended to the details of every subsequent study; a legacy the professor has left to me, as he left it to many others, of inestimable value, which we could not buy, with which we cannot part....

The fourth day a second fish of the same group was placed beside the first, and I was bidden to point out the resemblances and differences between the two; another and another followed, until the entire family lay before me, and a whole legion of jars covered the table and surrounding shelves; the odor had become a pleasant perfume; and even now, the sight of an old six-inch worm-eaten cork brings fragrant memories!

The whole group of Haemulons was thus brought into review; and whether engaged upon the dissection of the internal organs, preparation and examination of the bony framework, or the description of the various parts, Agassiz's training in the method of observing facts in their orderly arrangement, was ever accompanied by the urgent exhortation not to be content with them.

"Facts are stupid things," he would say, "until brought into connection with some general law."

At the end of eight months, it was almost with reluctance that I left these friends and turned to insects; but what I gained by this outside experience has been of greater value than years of later investigation in my favorite groups.[11]

F. (6) Identify the passage's relation to the surrounding contexts

In step 4, I suggested that you identify the contexts in which the text is found before beginning to study the passage itself. At that point, you learned about the context, then in steps 4 and 5, you learned about the passage. Now it is important to bring these two together. In this sixth step, we identify why our passage is where it is. For example, why does Paul begin the main argument of Romans with an exposition of the fallen state of humanity (Rom 1:18-

---

[11] There are several versions of this story available around the web, this one is from the Gospel Coalition, https://www.thegospelcoalition.org/blogs/justin-taylor/agassiz-and-the-fish/.

3:20)? Or why does Mark tell the story of Jesus cleansing the temple between the cursing of the fig tree and its effect (Mark 11:12-25, cf. Matt 21:19-22)? Why does it matter that you study Mark's account of an event and not Matthews? Does Mark have a different purpose that will affect your understanding of the passage? Answering such questions will teach you more about your passage and reveal some of its significance, ways in which it applies.

Consider Romans 1:18-3:20; by thinking about its place in the book of Romans, we see that it has a fundamental role in establishing the truth that all humans need the salvation God makes available through the Cross. We understand, then, that the negative picture Paul paints of God's wrath against sin is intended to point Jews and Gentiles alike—all people—to their need for Jesus Christ. On such a foundation, there is no legitimate ground for Jews or Gentiles to look down on one another. The following passages (3:21-4:25, 5:1-21) show us that on the day "God judges the secrets of men by Christ Jesus" (Rom 2:16, cf. 6-11), our hope for a positive verdict will be in what Christ has accomplished and not in any works we have done (Rom 3:21-5:21; cf. Rev. 13:8, 20:11-15). For the passage in Mark, studying the context of Mark 11:12-25 would reveal that Mark frequently splices a story in the midst of another (forming an A1, B, A2 pattern) in order that the middle story would interpret the surrounding material or vice versa. In this case, the cursing of the fig tree—a tree which appeared to have fruit but had none—reveals God's verdict upon the temple, which ought to have produced the fruit of righteousness but was instead found to be a den of robbers (Mark 11:17). In Habakkuk, the location of Chapter 3 at the end of the dialogue between God and Habakkuk in chapters 1-2 leads us to interpret this song (chapter 3) as a response to God's revelation of the Chaldean invasion, given in 1:5-11 and discussed in 1:12-2:20. For this reason, the "anointed" in 3:12[12] is best understand as the Chaldean leader raised up by God (1:5), and the "work" mentioned in 3:2 is to be correlated with the other two instances of this word root in 1:5 ("For *I am doing* a *work* in your days").

In addition to questions of the immediate context, also identify what difference the greater canonical context makes. You may ask, for example,

---

[12] This verse ought to be translated, as in the KJV and my commentary on Habakkuk, "You went out for the salvation of your people, for salvation with your anointed."

what difference it makes that the Psalms are in the Old Testament and not the New. How will your application have to take into account its location? Also, why is Chronicles in the third section of the Old Testament (the Writings)? Does this shed light on its purpose and give you ideas on how it applies? Why does the phrase "worthy woman" appear only in Proverbs and the book of Ruth? Does the close connection between Proverbs 31 and the book of Ruth shed light on the application of the latter? For passages appearing in the Old Testament, we will have to consider what has changed between the Old and New Covenants in order to make an appropriate application.

Interpreting Chronicles in light of the 3rd section of the Old Testament explains why it differs in its presentation from Samuel and Kings and may point us to more explicitly ethical applications, using the stories of righteousness reward and unrighteousness punished to illustrate God's faithfulness to uphold his promises to bless and to curse certain behaviours. However, we will also have to take into account the difference between Testaments and the rest of the biblical teaching. Doing so, we may see instances of a curse as ultimately pointing to final judgment and blessing pointing to our hope in God's faithfulness, whether we see it fulfilled to some extent in this life or wait for the fulness of his promises fulfilled in the new heavens and the new earth.

Considering the differences between covenants will lead us to apply the passages in Exodus, Leviticus, and Deuteronomy about physical separation from unbelieving nations as examples and illustrations of the spiritual separation we are called to under the New Covenant (2 Cor 6:14-7:1). Though God's will and character remain the same across both Testaments, the difference in the covenant community (cf. Ch. 4) will lead us to apply texts concerning God's promises and his will differently than the ancient Israelites would have. We may eat bacon, but we will be reminded that God cares about the purity of his people, that they would not be a mixture of holy and unholy, torn between the Kingdom of God and Satan's kingdom (cf. Lev 11:2-33).

Intertextual connections such as that between Proverbs 31 and the book of Ruth will draw our attention to the exemplary behaviour of Ruth of Boaz. Though the idealization of the faithful woman in Proverbs 31 seems unattainable, Ruth and Boaz illustrate how the godly characteristics extolled in these proverbs play out in real-life circumstances.

G. (7) Apply the passage

Once you are satisfied that you have understood the passage—not exhausted it but have enough understanding of what it is saying—apply it to yourself or those to whom you are ministering. Ask questions like; how does God want me to change my thinking in light of this passage? For example, Romans 9 may require you to reconsider your understanding of how you were saved. Ask, how does God want me to act in response to this passage? Maybe Paul's conviction to remember the poor in Galatians 2:10 will lead you to use your wealth to meet the needs of those in your congregation who are lacking. Or ask, how does God want me to change my attitude, the way I feel? In reading the Psalms, the appropriate response may be mourning over sin or rejoicing over salvation. Reading Philippians 4, the response may be to battle anxiety with thanksgiving and the truth of God's Word.

As you seek to apply the text, remember the categories we discussed in Chapter 5 (validity, appropriateness, and fittingness). Make sure that your application is valid in light of the text's wording, appropriate to its intent, and fitting for its referent—e.g. that you are not applying an injunction solely for Israel to the Church today. As you formulate and clarify your application of the passage, it often happens that you come to a better understanding of the text and must revise your application. This is part of the process of understanding the text well.

H. (8) Check your understanding

The last step in interpretation is to check your understanding. So far, you should have been checking your work against the text itself and your application against your previous study of the text. Now, seek the input of others to verify or challenge your work. This can often happen effectively in dialogue with someone else studying the same passage. It can also be helpful to talk to your pastor or lay leaders, if they have time, about your understanding of the text.

In addition to those in your church or school community, commentaries, theological studies, and good web resources can help you better understand the text, see things that you missed, and revise or confirm your application. We will discuss these resources further in Chapter 10, but now is the time when you would use them.

I. Conclusion

Though I have divided exegesis, or Bible study, into these eight steps, you will probably discover that you would do it a little differently. You will also discover that this list is more of a circle than a line; each step often forces you to go back to the beginning and move through the steps again. The important thing is that we must be good readers of the text; each of these steps is necessary, though you may do them a little bit differently than I do. We must also never leave our work at step 6, understanding what the text says; we must always press on to application, asking why it matters that the text says this. It is our responsibility as those seeking to be faithful to Jesus Christ to read closely and respond appropriately. Only when we have responded to the text in a right manner have we completed our task.

Further Reading

Fee, Gordon – *New Testament Exegesis: A Handbook for Student's and Pastors* [I]

Stuart, Douglas – *Old Testament Exegesis: A Handbook for Student's and Pastors* [I]

Text Criticism[13]

Black, David Alan – *Rethinking New Testament Textual Criticism* [A]
*Jongkind, Dirk – *An Introduction to the Greek New Testament* [B]
Wurthwein, Ernst – *The Text of the Old Testament* [I]
Metzger, Bruce M. & Bart D. Ehrman – *The Text of the New Testament: Its Transmission, Corruption, and Restoration* [I]

---

[13] Many of resources on this subject are not written by Evangelical Christians and need to be approached with considerable care. Dirk Jongkind's book is a good place to start for an Evangelical perspective.

7

KNOWING THE STYLES OF BIBLICAL WRITING

"Hear my words: If there is a prophet among you, I the Lord make myself known to him in a vision; I speak with him in a dream. Not so with my servant Moses. He is faithful in all my house. With him I speak mouth to mouth, clearly, and not in riddles, and he beholds the form of the Lord. Why then were you not afraid to speak against my servant Moses?" – Numbers 12:6-8

As we read texts—books, essays, blog posts, etc.—we learn quickly to identify relationships between related types of text. For example, we classify books as fiction and non-fiction according to their intent. We can relate essays according to the style of writing and the amount of knowledge they assume. Technical essays assume a lot of pre-understanding and often involve difficult style; popular essays, on the other hand, do not assume the reader is fluent in the topic and try to write in a more common vernacular.[1]

Beyond these general types or genres of literature (books and essays;

---

[1] The reader who has previously studied Biblical exegesis and hermeneutics will notice that some divergence in this chapter from the standard evangelical approaches to "genre." I explain in *The Gift of Reading – Part 2* why I take issue with contemporary genre theory and how the approach taken here is helpful. The second section of this series ("God's Gifts for the Christian Life") will provide much of the content concerning genre usually found in hermeneutics textbooks. What is said here is meant to lay a foundation for interacting with these other resources and the Biblical text.

popular and technical), we can also identify styles of writing shared among bodies of writing. For example, though it is difficult to draw a solid line between them, poetry and narrative texts can be distinguished. In English, the former are identified by their rhythm and often vivid imagery, the latter by its coordinating style (where events are relayed one after another with explanatory detail revolving around these events). Furthermore, we can distinguish broadly didactic prose texts, texts that communicate hypotactically—that is, they use lots of conjunctions to subordinate sentences (e.g. because, for, therefore, so that, etc.)—and favour logical organization rather than temporal (they relate ideas logically not events in temporal order).

This book is an example of didactic prose (though the story of Agassiz and the Fish was narrative, and the prayer in the introduction was poetry). In the Bible, we can identify four broad text styles used by the authors to communicate. There are narrative, poetic, didactic prose,[2] and prophetic styles. It is usually the case that a book will mix these styles, having both narrative and poetic texts, for example. In this chapter, we will consider key features of these styles and techniques that can help us observe texts of a particular style better. Having categories for recognizing different styles of texts will help us in many of the steps outlined in the previous chapter. I cannot hope in a book this size to give a sufficient account of the following styles found in the Bible; instead, I intend to lay a foundation upon which the reader may build with online and print literature or by learning from a mentor or teacher. However, like every aspect of exegesis, knowledge of the styles of biblical texts emerges from careful attention to the texts themselves, so readers who have not had formal training yet have spent much time in the Word may very well recognize the various textual features I group together as "styles."

---

[2] The term "discourse" is often used for what I am calling "didactic prose." I admit that discourse is a lot less clumsy and technical sounding, yet "discourse" is in many ways too broad of a category. All communication is "discourse," not just one style of it. My terminology is weak because outside of Biblical literature, "didactic prose" does not need to be a form of teaching (such as a love letter). However, I think this accurately captures the style as it is found in the Bible.

A. Narrative[3]

Now when they had departed, behold, an angel of the Lord appeared to Joseph in a dream and said, "Rise, take the child and his mother, and flee to Egypt, and remain there until I tell you, for Herod is about to search for the child, to destroy him." And he rose and took the child and his mother by night and departed to Egypt and remained there until the death of Herod. This was to fulfil what the Lord had spoken by the prophet, "Out of Egypt I called my son." – Matthew 2:13-15

The most common style in the Bible may be narrative; many books are narratives, and many books that are not narratives contain narrative segments (e.g. Job 1-2; Isa 36-39). We could define a narrative as a text that is characterized by a narrator and a plot.[4] That is, it is characterized by a person telling a story—a narrator—and progressing set of events. A plot has elements of progression—it moves somewhere—and this progression is based on the temporal succession of events. Narratives will predominantly use a narrative style, as discussed below, yet will integrate sections of didactic prose and poetry. For example, the book of Samuel is a narrative; it has a single narrator and a plot. Yet the book contains texts in non-narrative style, such as the songs in 1 Samuel 2:1-10 and 2 Samuel 1:19-27. For this reason, we need to distinguish narrative texts, characterized by plot and a narrator, from narrative style, the predominant style of writing within narrative texts. The same distinction is true for didactic prose texts and style; a didactic prose text, such as an epistle, will often contain sections written in narrative, poetic, or prophetic style (e.g. Galatians 2:11-16).[5]

---

[3] Some of the content and many of the examples in what follows are adapted from my master's thesis on 1 & 2 Samuel, *God's Kingdom through his Priest-King*.

[4] This is based on the definition employed by Jean Louis Ska, *"Our Fathers Have Told Us": Introduction to the Analysis of Hebrew Narratives*, Subsidia Biblica 13 (Roma: Editrice Pontificio Instituto Biblico, 1990), 6.

[5] In such cases, these texts need to be analysed according to their style; so a poem embedded in a narrative needs to be analysed as a poetic text. However, a poem will play a role in the narrative in which it is embedded. They will often provide a narrator or a character's interpretation of the surrounding events. For example,

Every style uses basic units to communicate—for example, didactic prose (such as this book) is driven by sentences organized into paragraphs. The basic building blocks of a narrative are actions and scenes, a set of actions accompanied at times by a setting or interpretation. In the example above (Matt 2:13-15), there are seven actions that comprise the scene. The final sentence is an example of a narrator interpreting the scene. Narrative is also distinct from other styles in the way it communicates its message. Instead of directly explaining what is meant or using symbolism and metaphor, narrative employs description. In literary theory, it is often said that narratives *show;* they do not tell. If, for example, the narrator wants to impress upon the reader the seriousness of murder and its consequences, he would not say, "You shall not murder" (Exod 20:13). Instead, he would tell a story showing the severity and consequences of murder (Gen 4:1-16).

Recognizing these basic features of narrative (its temporally based plot, descriptive character, and basic division into scenes) helps us learn to read specific narratives better. For the rest of this section, we will consider how the author of a narrative uses plot and the order of scenes to communicate, how an author uses description to convey meaning, and how the technique of storyboarding can help us look closer at narratives.

a. How Narratives Communicate: Plot and Scene Arrangement

Though a narrative is based on a linear series of events (Bob leaves the house, shuts the door, locks the door, walks to his car, and drives to work), narratives are not necessarily told in a linear fashion. Sometimes the narrator will rearrange a series of events to communicate something, to make his point. There are many examples of this throughout the Bible, but a particularly prevalent device used is called "interpolation" (this is especially common in the Gospel of Mark, earning it the nickname "the Markan sandwich").

Interpolation occurs when an author begins a scene but introduces another scene or segment of narrative before concluding the first scene. This forms an A1 – B – A2 pattern, where A1 is the first part and A2 the second part of a scene interrupted by B. An example of a significant interpolation is

---

Hannah's song in 1 Sam 2:1-10 provides a lens through which to interpret all the following events.

found in 2 Samuel 11 and 12. In 2 Samuel 11:1, the narrator introduces the siege of the Ammonite city Rabbah. The success of this siege is not recorded until 12:26-31. This raises a significant question: is the author merely interested in plot, recording events in their proper order, or is he making a point by separating the beginning of the siege from its conclusion? If you read the events that occur between this sandwich, you might observe their significance. 2 Samuel 11:2-12:25 recounts David's adultery with Bathsheba, a key point in the story of David. More significantly, this incident is closely related to God's promise to David in 2 Samuel 7. God promises to give David peace from his enemies and an offspring who would rule forever after him. Implicit in the covenant God makes with David is the demand for obedience. When we read of David's horrific acts, we should be drawn back to the covenant and wonder how David's behaviour will affect it. Indeed, the author invites us to do so by putting off the record of the defeat of the Ammonites until after the crisis resolves. By splitting the account of the defeat of the Ammonites, the author of Samuel places the promise of rest from David's enemies in danger. Careful attention to the structure of the narrative, and the technique of interpolation, helps us understand what an author is telling with his story.[6]

Authors use the arrangement of their narratives to teach the reader in many ways; interpolation is only one of them. Another arrangement to be aware of is a chiasm, where an author creates an A-B-C-B'-A' pattern by shaping his later material to reflect the first part of his narrative. In such an arrangement, the emphasis lays on the central point, C. Learning to identify and interpret such devices will only come with practice, but some basic principles can guide us in identifying them. If plot is the linear succession of events that lays behind a narrative (Plot = events A, B, C, D, E, F: Bob leaves the house, shuts the door, locks the door, walks to his car, and drives to work), we can discern the use of narrative devices when this temporal arrangement is changed. Narrators must necessarily exclude some events of a plot from their story (e.g. the story may only have events A, D, E, and F), for they cannot recount everything that happens; sometimes, these omissions are important. For example, in our story of Bob leaving his house to go to work, omitting the action "he locked the door" may foreshadow a future event, such as a home robbery. It is also significant when the narrator

---

[6] This example is taken from Rutherford, *God's Kingdom*.

deliberately changes the order (Plot = A, B, C, D, E, F : Narrative = A, C, B, D, E1, F, E2). Sometimes a narrator will recount an event and then revisit it from another angle, shedding further light on its significance (Genesis 1, cf. Genesis 2). When this happens, we need to ask why the narrator has changed the order of events? What is he trying to communicate? What tension is he trying to create?

b. How Narratives Communicate: Description

The use of narrative arrangement could be called a macro-level tool narrators use to tell their stories; it involves the arrangement of scenes.[7] But zooming in to the scenes themselves, the narrator also has several tools at their disposal to tell the story.

When a narrator tells a story, he or she is not able to recount every detail of an event; to do so would be impossible and would make for horrible reading. Instead, they offer an interpretation of an event. They are selective about which details they include and which they exclude. Because they are selective about the details, carefully reading a narrative is key to understanding it. We must observe what the author includes—nothing is by accident—and what he excludes.

For example, consider the description the author of Samuel provides for Saul. In 1 Samuel 9, he includes, among other details, that Saul is the son of a wealthy man named Kish (9:1), a handsome young man (9:2)—indeed, the most handsome (9:2). Furthermore, he is tall (9:2). Coincidently, this tall (גָּבֹהַּ, *gābōah*) man is also from Gibeah (גִּבְעָה, *Gibʿāh*), a tall place (10:26). The details about his height may seem pointless and disconnected from the details about his status, yet after closer examination, they may not be after all. Consider, first, that the word גָּבֹהַּ only occurs four times in 1 & 2 Samuel, all in 1 Samuel. In explicit contrast to 1 Samuel 9:2, God tells Samuel not to anoint a future king on the basis of "the *height* of his stature" (16:7, emphasis added). The most significant instances are in 1 Samuel 2:3, "Talk no more *so very proudly*," literally "very highly" (גְּבֹהָה גְבֹהָה, *gᵉbōhāh gᵉbōhāh*). In context,

---

[7] Scene, as I am using it, is an imprecise descriptor. A scene is a complete narrative unit, composed of one or more major narrative actions and usually distinguished by some sort of scene transition or descriptor (e.g. 2 Samuel 11:2, 11:6, 11:14).

this line begins a contrast between the rich and lofty who are brought low and the lowly who are exalted by Yahweh. The point of the song in which 2:3 is found is to anticipate the work of God to exalt a future of king of Israel from a lowly state to the throne (cf. 2:10). For this reason, the way the narrator portrays Saul in 1 Samuel 9-10 is incredibly significant. By portraying Saul as a man of prominent physical presence and social status, the narrator subtly demonstrates that this man will not be the king God intends to give his people.

Paying attention to the details of a narrative takes time and practice, but there are several things to look for. Look for repeated words in scenes and across entire narratives; consider which characters the narrator describes and names—they are probably important—and which are barely considered, for they are often just part of the scenery (e.g. 2 Sam 11:2-5); and identify key themes that are repeated (e.g. Gen 11:30, 25:21; Judg 13:2; 1 Sam 1:5-6; Luke 1:7) or events that are closely related (e.g. Gen 12:1-20; 20:1-18; 26:6-11). Pay particular attention to the comments the narrator makes. If a narrator takes time to provide a comment evaluating the behaviour or motives of a character, it will be highly significant (e.g. 2 Sam 11:1).

Entire books are dedicated to the different techniques narrators use to communicate. We do not have space to explore these techniques, but I have provided several resources at the end of this chapter that do so. Though there are many books that will lay out different features to pay attention to, the best approach I have found is to read lots of narrative texts, getting a feel for how different narrators tell their stories. To breakdown a scene in a narrative and pay closer attention to its details, the technique of storyboarding may be helpful.

c. Study Strategy: Storyboarding[8]

Storyboarding is a technique for visually breaking a narrative down into its basic parts and thinking more slowly and carefully about it. To start, you need to identify the scope of your narrative. If you are dealing with a single scene, you will map out each major action of the scene. If you are dealing with a

---

[8] I have adapted the idea of storyboarding for Biblical narratives and the format below from my teacher, Brad Copp.

string of scenes, you will map out each scene. The idea is to identify those main actions or events that drive the story and how the narrator recounts these actions or events. The main action of a scene will often be accompanied by sideline actions; for example, for Jesus to heal someone, he sometimes stretches out and touches them (e.g. Mark 1:41). There will often be an introduction to a scene, presenting the circumstances in which the main actions occur or introducing the characters (e.g. Job 1:6). Sometimes individual actions are given background, such as a narrator's description of the circumstances preceding the action (Mark 4:38a). Place dialogue or clause of direct perception (he saw *that they were there*) beside your storyboard; the board is focusing on the actions themselves. However, dialogue is often

---

Background information: here you will put any information concerning the setting of the main action (Hebrew: often nominal clauses, clauses beginning with a noun, or ויהי (*vayhi*, and it happened)

Main actions: e.g. they saw that, they said, he touched, they fought (Greek: indicatives)

Sideline actions: e.g. they got up, packed up, embarked, walked (Greek: participles, infinitives)

Narrative Clues: Record any implicit or explicit clues the narrator provides for interpreting the scene. Implicitly, does this scene have repeated words, does it juxtapose with a preceding or following scene? Explicitly, does the narrator offer any evaluation of the events, any comment on their nature or purpose (e.g. Mark 1:41a)?

---

essential to interpreting the actions of the scene. Here is a template:

Consider the account of David and Bathsheba (2 Sam 11:1-27). We could break this narrative down into five major scenes or moments (each made of several scenes) and an introduction (or exposition). The exposition or introduction is a narrative scene that serves to set the background for the events to follow; in these verses, it is verse 1. Storyboarding the exposition (2 Sam 11:1) and the three scenes (2 Sam 11:2-3, 4, 5) of the first narrative section (2 Sam 11:1-5) might look like this:[9]

---

[9] We could divide 2 Sam 11:2-5 into 3 scenes. 2 Sam 11:2-3 gives the introduction and initial action of David. 2 Sam 11:4 gives the narrative climax of the

Verse 1

Background information: Time: "In the spring of the year, the time when kings go out to battle" (1a-b)	
Main actions: David sent Joab… They ravaged… And besieged them…	**Sideline actions:**
Narrative Clues: "the time when *kings go out to battle*" - David, the king, does not go out to battle (1b). "David sent Joab, and his servants with him, and all Israel…. *But David* remained at Jerusalem" (1c-e). The last sentence (1e) focuses on the status of David; it is not a main action. The narrator is alerting us to a key piece of the story: everyone BUT David went to battle.	

Verse 2-3

Background information: <u>Time and circumstance</u>: late one afternoon, David was walking on the roof. <u>Inciting incident</u>: he saw a woman bathing. <u>Characterization</u>: she was very beautiful (11:2).	
Main actions: David sent And inquired (11:3) One said (11:3)	**Dialogue:** said "is not this Bathsheba, the daughter of Eliam, the wife of Uriah the Hittite?"
Narrative Clues: repetition of *sent* (11:3) from verse 1. 11:3 anticipates Uriah, a major character in the following narrative (11:6-13). We are shown that David knew she was married, highlighting his sin. In 11:2, the narrator notes that the woman was bathing, anticipating the narrators explanation of her bathing in 11:4.	

Verse 4

Main actions:
So David sent messenges
And took her
And she came to him
And he lay with her
Then she returned to her house.
Narrative Clues: "sent" appears again, perhaps portraying David as aloof, separate from the rest of the characters (cf. 12:15-23). The narrator tells us, "She had been purifying herself from her uncleanness." That he provides this information indicates it is of some interpretive importance. Elsewhere, the narrator draws attention to ways David breaks the Torah; this may be one such instance (cf. Lev 18:19).

account. 2 Sam 11:5 provides the conclusion of the narrative, the result. This transitions to the next narrative, in which David responds to the resulting situation. 2 Samuel 11:1 could also be divided into three small scenes.

Verse 5

Main actions:	
The woman conceived	Dialogue: told David, "I am pregnant."
She sent	
And she told David	
Narrative Clues: "sent" appears again. Though we have been given a name, the narrator identifies her as "the woman." This is consistent with the way the narrator characterizes Bathsheba throughout the narrative.	

A few notes should be made on these storyboards. The narrator indicates something is wrong in the introduction (or exposition) by contrasting the custom of the day, "kings go out to battle," with David's inaction. This is emphasized by the contrast between David and his troops in 1c-e, "But David remained…." Our suspicion, aroused by the narrator's comments, is confirmed by the following story. I have not marked any sideline actions in these narratives; Hebrew often presents all actions as coordinated, on the same narrative level, even where one action is logically more prominent.

In verses 2-3, David viewing Bathsheba bathing is part of the setting for the main actions David takes to pursue adultery. That the narrator gives us information about Bathsheba, both her name and her husband's name, indicates the importance of both characters for the following narrative. In contrast, the messenger David sends is merely "one."

In verse 4, the author mentions that Bathsheba was cleansing herself from impurity; we need to ask why he would include this information. Some commentators suggest that the narrator is indicating she is fertile, thus anticipating the statements in verse 5, but this hardly seems worthy of the narrator's attention. However, throughout the book of Samuel, the narrator holds Saul and David up to the standard of the Law revealed in the Torah, a pattern that fits here. If Bathsheba was cleansing herself from her menstrual impurity (11:4), it would have been against the Torah to sleep with her (Lev 18:19). This hardly seems worth mentioning in light of the adultery and murder, which are the focus of the narrative, yet that David would transgress in the minutiae of the Law underscores the point that David is not at this time acting as God's king ought to (cf. Deut 17:18-20), a point that the author repeatedly makes.

In verse 5, we also see Bathsheba treated as a secondary character, merely "the woman." She is presented primarily in relation to David and Uriah. When she is finally identified as "[David's] wife, Bathsheba" in 12:24, this serves to indicate the resolution of the tension throughout the narrative. So it appears that the author's reluctance to name her and identify her as David's wife from 11:2-12:23 is a tool he uses, perhaps to focus on David as the narrative's focus and to reveal the favourable outcome of the incident in 12:24, where God recognizes their marriage and grants them a son.

B. Poetry[10]

How lovely is your dwelling place,
    O LORD of hosts!
My soul longs, yes, faints
    for the courts of the LORD;
my heart and flesh sing for joy
    to the living God.

Even the sparrow finds a home,
    and the swallow a nest for herself,
    where she may lay her young,
at your altars, O LORD of hosts,
    my King and my God.
Blessed are those who dwell in your house,
    ever singing your praise! *Selah*
– Psalm 84:1-4

Poetry permeates Scripture. The longest book in the Bible consists of poetry, as does most of the third part of the Old Testament. Many of the narratives, epistles, and prophetic books in Scripture also contain texts written in poetic style. Though they come in many different forms (such as song, poem, and proverb), all the poetic texts in the Bible share several basic features that help

---

[10] Some of what follows is adapted from my study guide, *Believe the Unbelievable* (Teleioteti, 2018), and commentary (Teleioteti, 2020) on the book of Habakkuk. Habakkuk is one of the most poetic books of Hebrew prophecy, making it well suited for poetic analysis. Many of the examples that follow will be taken from Habakkuk, especially chapter 3, but the reader can see the same sort of features in other poetry, such as Psalm 23 and 84. Habakkuk 3 is explicitly a Hebrew poem, not an example of prophetic style.

us identify and interpret them. Understanding the basics of biblical poetry is essential to reading the Bible well. Even in narratives, poetic texts are often key to interpreting the work (e.g. 1 Sam 2:1-10).[11]

Poetry comes in many shapes and sizes, and the lines between poetry and prose are at times blurred (especially in prophetic literature). However, I think we can distinguish poetry as a style of literature that uses various devices to create a *conceptual rhythm*, often to great emotional effect. Whereas prose strikes the reader with its profundity and narrative draws the reader into its tensions, poetry incites the passions of the reader with despair and hope, anger and joy, etc. By "conceptual rhythm," I intend to distinguish the poetic style of biblical poetry from English poetry. English poetry is characterized mainly by meter; Hebrew poetry is not. Meter is found in biblical poetry, but only as one device among many used to achieve a conceptual rhythm. We could define conceptual rhythm as the presentation and explanation of ideas and events through the interplay of lines. Hebrew poetry uses a variety of features, including wordplay and metaphor, to create a rhythm of ideas, not sound. The desired emotional and cognitive effects of this conceptual rhythm are achieved through the use of parallel lines and text units to juxtapose ideas along with various sonic and visual devices that tie together and bring out the meaning of the lines. As a piece of poetry unfolds, it presents the same idea from several different angles presenting a cohesive whole. It circles a topic, achieving a sort of 3D presentation of ideas in contrast with the 2d presentation of prose. Another way to describe poetry is to say that it moves from ambiguity, from initially vague and ambiguous ideas and imagery, to clarity by expanding upon the initial idea or image, looking at it from several different angles.

The three main features of biblical poetry are terseness, literary devices, and parallelism. Terseness describes the intentional minimalism of Hebrew poetry. Hebrew poets keep their words to a minimum: even if the result is ambiguous, they will use three words instead of ten. Like English poetry, biblical poetry also employs vivid imagery, which is usually concrete imagery taken from everyday life (this contrasts with the symbolic imagery of prophecy), and poetic devices such as onomatopoeia, alliteration, assonance,

---

[11] What follows is mainly a description of Hebrew poetry; traditional Greek poetry is distinctly different. However, what poetry is found in the New Testament is heavily influenced by the Hebrew Old Testament and thus bears great similarity to Hebrew poetry.

etc. to communicate. Parallelism describes the use of groups of poetic lines to communicate a single idea or image. For the rest of our discussion of poetry, I want to briefly discuss the way biblical poets use terseness, poetic devices, and parallelism, and then consider a way we can think through poetic texts more closely.

a. How Poetry Communicates: Terseness and Poetic Devices

Biblical poetry employs many of the same literary features as English: there are metaphors (Hab 1:12), hyperbole (Hab 3:16a-d), onomatopoeia (Hab 2:20), simile (Hab 2:5c-d),[12] alliteration (Hab 3:16e-g), assonance (Hab 1:6b), and acrostics (Ps 119)—among others.[13] Rhyme is not as common as in English poetry, but wordplay and assonance are much more so. Wordplay and assonance are often achieved by using words of the same root (Hab. 1:5) or words spelled similarly (1:6).[14] Words with similar or very different meanings, yet similar spellings, are frequently employed for poetic value. Important to note is also the frequent use of ellipsis, the omission of a necessary word—verb or noun—to be supplied by the parallel lines.[15]

Ellipsis, along with other features, contributes to the terseness of biblical poetry. "Terseness" describes the intentional minimalism of Hebrew poetry. Words are kept to a minimum: even if the result is ambiguous, Hebrew poets

---

[12] In poetry, a letter following a verse number specifies the line in question.

[13] Though only Habakkuk 3 is written in what I have identified as poetic style, it is the book I am most familiar with and even its prophetic portions serve well to illustrate the devices found in Hebrew poetry. This is because, as we will see under prophetic style, many prophetic texts employ the language pattern of poetry though using a different manner of communication. All of Habakkuk is written in a poetic language pattern, though Habakkuk 3 is explicitly a song and employs a fully poetic style.

[14] Assonance may not be the proper word here, for written Hebrew consists only of consonants and this is primarily what is emphasized in these poetic devices. That being said, I will continue to use assonance to refer to the poetic device of playing off similar sounds, whether consonantal or vocalic.

[15] Wilfred G. E. Watson, "Poetry, Biblical Hebrew," ed. Geoffrey Khan, *Encyclopedia of Hebrew Language and Linguistics* (Leiden; Boston: Brill, 2013), 152; Andrew E. Hill and John H. Walton, *A Survey of the Old Testament*, 2nd ed. (Grand Rapids: Zondervan Publishing House, 2000), 383.

will use three words instead of ten.

It appears that Hebrew poets do sometimes employ meter in their poems, yet it is only one of many tools used by the Hebrew poet to achieve a conceptual rhythm.[16] When meter is employed, this sonic rhythm is achieved by patterns of syllables, accents, or words. In the first case, a series of sets of lines (a colon) may contain a pattern of syllables that is repeated in each colon or with a rhythmic variation. There may also be a pattern of accents per line or the number of words in each line. Alliteration or assonance also contribute to this sonic rhythm.[17]

Many of the devices used to create a poetic effect in Hebrew are not reproducible in English, yet the genius of Hebrew poetry (including its New Testament counterparts) is its ability to achieve its intended effect even in translation. Because so many devices are used and because the essence of Hebrew poetry is conceptual—focused on making an idea or picture clear—it is easy for the English reader to get the poetic effect of the text. Parallelism, the workhorse of Hebrew poetry, is largely responsible for this, but the use of vivid imagery also helps biblical poetry communicate across languages. Psalm 23, for example, employs the life of a shepherd to powerful effect, communicating God's care; Psalm 84 draws on scenes from the religious life of Israel, from its geography, and its royal court to effectively communicate the blessedness of life with God. The use of vivid, comprehensible imagery to communicate is a hallmark of Hebrew poetry and is one of the ways it can be distinguished from prophetic style, which we will consider below. Instead of drawing on everyday experience, prophetic imagery is otherworldly, it draws on everyday life but uses these experiences in ways that require thought and wisdom—even Divine interpretation—to understand. It is in a sense abstract, for the relationship between the imagery and its intended reference is not immediately discernible, for example, the use of specific materials to indicate different earthly empires in Daniel's vision of a statue (Dan 2). We will consider prophetic style below, but for now we will turn to consider poetic parallelism.

---

[16] Cf. Hill and Walton, *A Survey*, 387; David L. Petersen and Kent Harold Richards, *Interpreting Hebrew Poetry*, Guides to Biblical Scholarship (Minneapolis: Fortress, 1992), 37–39; Watson, "Poetry, Biblical Hebrew," 152.

[17] Hill and Walton, *A Survey*, 383.

The substance of Hebrew poetry, that of which it consists, is series of parallel lines—each set known as a colon. A sort of rhythm is sometimes associated with the number of lines in a colon (*bicolon*, two lines; *tricolon*, three lines), but even here there is no uniformity: using varying numbers of lines is again a tool for achieving poetic rhythm, but not the whole of it.[18] The primary tool used to achieve conceptual rhythm in Hebrew poetry is the parallelism of ideas.

b. How Poetry Communicates: Lines and Parallelism

Each series of lines balances an idea in various ways. Usually, lines will parallel each other in their members as well; that is, they may not have the exact correspondence in the number of words but will correspond in word order, absence or presence of nouns, and the use of modifiers.[19] Parallelism employs, as the name suggests, parallel lines—poetic lines related grammatically, phonetically, semantically—to communicate in richer ways than prose. We could describe Hebrew Parallelism as the use of closely related lines for evocation—engaging the affections—and disambiguation. Disambiguation describes the way poets use parallel lines to resolve ambiguity resulting from the terseness and imagery of poetry, the way they use additional lines to bring another perspective and resolve ambiguity.[20]

Thus Hebrew poetry can be considered as analogous to a holograph: it is three dimensional language, not two-dimensional language. The poet will present an idea and revisit it in the following lines; sometimes an entire poem looks at the same idea from various perspectives. Each line, then, gives a complementary perspective on the ideas the author wishes to communicate, painting a three-dimensional picture. This combination of ambiguity followed by disambiguation produces a sense of elation in us, the readers, as we move from confusion to realization of the meaning. There is a sense of discovery as a poem progresses. The use of multiple perspectives and

---

[18] Petersen and Richards, *Interpreting Hebrew Poetry*, 41.

[19] Hill and Walton, *A Survey*, 383.

[20] The language of ambiguity and disambiguation is borrowed from Adele Berlin's work on Hebrew Poetry. As with the authors cited above, I have not followed her work completely or closely in this section, but I have profited from her analysis. Adele Berlin, *The Dynamics of Biblical Parallelism* (Bloomington: Indiana University Press, 1985).

compact language, as well as liberal use of metaphor, contributes to the rich emotional impact Hebrew poetry has.

Here are several examples from Habakkuk Chapter 3 and Psalm 84:

Example 1 (Hab 3:13):

You come forth for the salvation of your people,
    for salvation with your anointed;

Example 2 (Hab 3:11):

The sun and the moon stand in their exalted abode,
    to make your arrows that fly gleam,
    to brighten your flashing spears.

Example 3 (Ps 84:9):

Behold our shield, O God;
    look on the face of your anointed!

Example 4 (Ps 84:10):

For a day in your courts is better
    than a thousand elsewhere.
I would rather be a doorkeeper in the house of my God
    than dwell in the tents of wickedness.

These examples serve to illustrate some of the various ways in which parallelism is used in the Old Testament. In example one, the second line is used to explain how God is going to save his people; he will do so through his anointed, Chaldea. In example 2, the second and third line (11b & 11c) explain why the heavenly bodies are standing tall in the sky, in order to highlight the weapons God will use to achieve salvation for his people. In example 3, the second line explains what is meant by the first: "Behold our shield" could mean a million different things, yet the second line identifies this shield as the king and "behold" is a call for God to consider and show favour to the king, the protector of God's people (hence, "shield"). In example 4, the first colon (the first two lines, 10a-b) uses the second line only to finish the thought of the first. In the second colon (10c-d), the second line is used to make a powerful contrast between the pleasures of even the lowliest position in God's temple and the most luxurious one apart from him.

By understanding a few of the ground rules of Hebrew poetry—that we should expect terseness and parallelism resulting in initial ambiguity that is clarified as we read on—we can better appreciate the beauty of this art and see more clearly the meaning God intends through it.

c. Study Strategy: Mapping Parallelism

As with narrative, there is a technique we can use to visually display a poetic text and think through the relationships of its pieces. We could call this *mapping parallelism*; it is similar to the technique we will see below for prose, called arcing. Mapping parallelism forces us to think through the relationships between lines and identify what lines should be read and interpreted together. To begin, we must select the text we will use. Going through the text, break the text into discrete lines of text. There is no clear guide for doing this; it is more of an art than a science. However, English translation or Hebrew bibles will often break the text into lines; studying their divisions can help identify what is poetry and then how lines can be identified. Most often, a line will represent a complete grammatical thought—though the author may ellipse a word or two. The exception is the use of enjambment, where a sentence is continued in the next line (cf. Ps 84:10a-b; Hab 1:8b-c).

If you read Hebrew, another indicator of line divisions is the use of ו (v^e, and) with no clear conjunctive or adverbial function (i.e. it does not clearly mean "and" or "but" or have an adverbial function, "even"). Though it often has a conjunctive meaning, connecting verbal clauses, ו also often indicates line division (e.g. Hab 1:16, 2:5). Your initial division of lines will not be perfect, but this step is necessary as we begin to analyse the text.

Next, take a blank piece of paper or a document and write out each line in a vertical row (some might prefer to write the whole line, others just the verse and line number, e.g. 1a). Having identified lines, we now need to identify colons—groups of lines. Poetry is most often divided into bi-cola (plural of bicolon), groups of two lines, but will also use tricola (groups of three lines) and the occasional tetracolon (a group of four lines). Sometimes translations or commentators will identify a monocolon (an independent line), but in many cases, these are better seen as parts of a tricolon. Begin by identifying lines that most clearly belong together; an example would be two lines where one has a word ellipsed (is missing a word) and the other supplies it. In many cases, lines that share synonymous, antithetical, or closely related words should also be grouped together (e.g. love and beneficence, righteousness and wickedness, joy and blessedness). Enjambment or verbal clauses connected by a ו (v^e, and) are also important clues for identifying groups of lines. Draw an arc or box connecting the cola (groups of lines) you have identified (see the illustration below).

Once you have discovered the most prominent sets of lines, go back through your list and identify whether the remaining lines are most closely related to another ungrouped line or to one of the more evident groups of lines. Again, draw lines connecting the grouped lines together. After doing this several times, every line should be grouped with another line or several others.

Having identified the groups of lines that make up a poetic text, the next step is to identify larger groups of text—groups of bicola, tricola, and tetracola. Most poems, except the largest and smallest, can be divided into two larger groupings, stanzas and strophes. In my terminology, strophe refers to the largest unit of poem, made up of several stanzas, and stanzas to the next largest unit of a poem, made up of groups of bicola, tricola, and tetracola. Sometimes these larger divisions can be identified by thematic unity or the use of keywords, but there are several explicit devices uses by poets to divide their texts at these large levels. One of these is the Hebrew word סֶלָה (*selāh*), used in songs to indicate a musical transition of some sort (cf. Psalm 84, Habakkuk 3). At other times, there will be the repetition of a key word once every several lines, such as the word הוֹי (*hōy*, which can have the sense "woe") (cf. Hab 2:6-20; Ps 84:4, 5, 12) or a repeated set of lines that form a refrain (e.g. Hab 2:8c-d, 17c-d; Ps 42:5, 12, 43:5).

Once a poem is divided into these various groups of lines, identify the basic relationship displayed between the lines. You can do this by describing each group on the same or a separate piece of paper. Alternatively, you could come up with a series of abbreviations such as those used in arcing (see below) to communicate the relationship between lines and groups of lines. I am not providing a list of such relationships because there is an indefinite number of possible relations; in the past, scholars have attempted to group all these relations into three broad categories, but these categories proved too broad to be useful.[21] I will note several possible relations, but this is by no means exhaustive.

Lines could be grouped together in antithesis. That is, one line could give an idea and the next its opposite or a juxtaposing idea (Ps 84:10). One line could be grammatically subordinate or related to another and so complete or expand it (Hab 3:11). Sometimes lines will display logical progression, such as is found in prose (Hab 1:4). Lines can be simply descriptive of the noun or verb in the first line (Hab 1:6). A set of lines can function like a narrative to expound a temporal series of actions (Exod 15:10). Sometimes a whole group of lines clearly communicates the same idea from different perspectives (Exod 15:8). More complex relations can also be found, such as a chiasm (a-b-b'-a' pattern; Hab 2:15-16). It is common in the proverbs for lines to present several distinct yet related ideas, the thing they share in common being the point (e.g. Prov 30:18-19).

Putting all this together, grouping lines, cola, and stanzas with annotation will look something like the example below, which diagrams Habakkuk 2:6e-11b. As will be seen, a lot is left unsaid by such a diagram. For this reason, it is helpful to write out below the diagram or on the back of the diagram an explanation of each relation, asking, for example, what it means for Habakkuk 2:6e-g (labelled a-b below) to be a series interrupted with an exclamation. Generally, these lines give different perspectives on Babylon's ravaging of the nations; from the perspective of the conquered, it is described in terms of both what they take and how God perceives their theft—it is a heavy debt they will not be able to pay.

---

[21] Many scholars have worked to revise this understanding. E.g. James L. Kugel, *The Idea of Biblical Poetry: Parallelism and Its History* (New Haven: Yale University Press, 1981); Berlin, *The Dynamics of Biblical Parallelism*; Robert Alter, *The Art of Biblical Poetry* (New York: Basic Books, 1985); J.P. Fokkelman, *Reading Biblical Poetry: An Introductory Guide*, trans. Ineke Smit, First edition. (Louisville: Westminster John Knox, 2001).

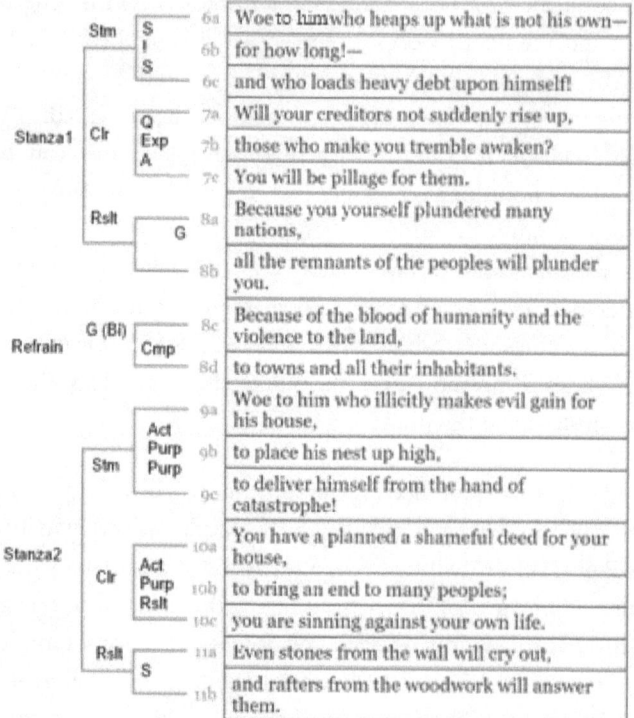

The section of Habakkuk I have selected is two stanzas with a refrain between them. The first stanza consists of two tricola (6a-c, 7a-c) and a bicolon (8a-b). The first three lines present a simple series (S) interrupted by an exclamation (!). Together the tricolon (the three lines as a group) gives a statement (Stm) that will be clarified (Clr) in the next lines. These next three lines present a question (Q), expanded upon in 7b (Exp) and then affirmed or answered in 7c (A). 8a-b gives the result of the first two tricola, with 8a giving the ground (G) for the statement in 8b.

The refrain in 8c-d gives the ground (G) for both Stanza 1 & 2; hence, it is bilateral (Bi). 8d completes the statement in 8c (Cmp).

Stanza 2 has the same structure as Stanza 1, two tricola followed by a bicolon, giving a statement (Stm, 9a-c), its clarification (Clr, 10a-c), and the result (Rslt, 11a-b). Lines 9a-c and 10a-c have a similar pattern. 9a-c gives an action followed by two lines explaining the Chaldeans intent with this act. 10a-b presents an action with its purpose, but 10c gives the result of this action. 11a-b is a series, describing how the peoples whom Chaldea subdued and used to build their "house" (9a) will indict them.

Because of the variety of possible connections lines of poetry may have and because their force is found not in their logic but in the collective picture they paint and their emotive effect, such an analysis is often not very helpful. However, when you are struggling to figure out what the text means or are seeking to translate the passage and want to understand how the units of text are related to one another, such an analysis can be quite useful.

C. Didactic Prose

Poetry and narrative engage our hearts and draw us into the world they present, but neither communicates to our minds quite like didactic prose. When it comes to making an argument or spelling out in careful detail truth or instruction, nothing beats didactic prose. Prose, broadly, forms an opposition with verse or poetry. Without a rhythm scheme or line structure, prose is composed of sentences and paragraphs. Narrative, direct speech, and theological treatises are all examples of prose, broadly conceived. However, we can distinguish within this broader category a non-narrative form of prose. "Didactic" refers specifically to teaching, yet I think it is a fitting term to describe the non-narrative prose of Scripture found in prophetic books, direct speech, and especially the New Testament epistles. When used in this way, "didactic prose" refers to the non-narrative and non-poetic texts of Scripture that are used to communicate truth or description and instruction to God's people.

Didactic prose shares several features that distinguish it from narrative and poetry. Like narrative and unlike poetry, didactic prose uses sentences instead of lines and paragraphs instead of strophes or stanzas. Unlike narrative, didactic prose does not follow a temporal plot: it does not relay events that follow one another in time. Thus, it is not *paratactic*, stringing sentences along in a coordinating fashion (and... and... but... and). Instead, didactic prose is structured logically and rhetorically. Logically, it communicates through *hypotaxis*, using conjunctions (and, but, however, for, etc.) to indicate the logical relationship between clauses and sentences. Rhetorically, didactic prose often follows a standard structure of communication, such as the typical letter form of the epistles or the lawsuit form of the prophetic books. Unlike poetry, didactic prose tends to be very concrete and literal, though it occasionally incorporates strong metaphor and symbolism. For the rest of our discussion of prose, I want to consider how it uses grammar and logic to communicate and the interchange of indicative and imperative found in much didactic prose. To conclude this section, we will briefly consider two tools to help us better analyse didactic prose.

a. How Prose Communicates: Grammar and Logic

In poetry, grammar is often sacrificed for the sake of art, and the logic behind a text is often implicit, rarely made explicit. In narrative, relatively few types of clauses are used, and the structure is not driven by logic but by narrative progress, thus "and" and "but" are common but clauses indicating logical result ("therefore"), purpose ("in order that"), and explanation ("for") are relatively rare. What is absent from poetry and narrative forms the backbone of didactic prose. It is in prose that in-depth grammatical study and logical precision become invaluable tools for understanding an author's thought.

In English, translators have endeavoured to simplify complex Greek grammar in a manner that is clear for English readers. Primarily, for the English reader, the grammar needed is knowledge of different clause types, how they are formed, and how they function. A clause is a part of a sentence that contains a complete predication, a verb plus its complement (*I ate food* is a clause; *ate* is the verb and *food* the complement). A clause may be modified in various ways by prepositional phrases ("*for* dinner," "*in* the bedroom," etc.) or adverbs ("quickly," "hesitantly"). Its constituent nouns (in this case, "I" and "food") may be described with various adjectival phrases (large, tall, tasty, wonderful, which was just cooked, etc.). Clauses come in two forms, independent (which stand on their own) and dependent (which require another clause to make sense). Conjunctions are used to connect clauses to one another and are essential to understanding the logic of a prose text. In Greek and Hebrew, these same units of grammar are present but are indicated in different ways. The biblical languages are very good at making clear the relationships between the various parts of a clause and sentence. In both languages, specific verbal forms (infinitives and participles) and prepositions take on a much more significant role in indicating logical connection than they do in English. For the English reader, these connections are often made explicit in translation, but different translations may understand the relationships differently. This is where knowledge of the original languages is very helpful; such knowledge will help you understand the range of possibilities and what makes the best sense in context. In the last part of this section, we will briefly consider two methods for thinking carefully about the grammar of a didactic text and the logic behind it. Before that, we can consider the broader logic of didactic prose texts.

b. How Prose Communicates: Indicative and Imperative

None of the books of the Bible are intended to be a bare philosophical or theological treatise. That is, none of them is interested in merely describing or explaining a truth or aspect of the world. On the contrary, they are circumstantial and intended to bring about some sort of response in the reader. To say that they are circumstantial is to say that every biblical text is written to specific people to address specific circumstances. We saw in the first part of the book how we are part of the audience of Scripture, but the method God has used to instruct and guide us is to teach us through instances where he addressed his people in history to guide and correct them. For this reason, no biblical text is an abstract treatise but is intended to bring the truths God has revealed about himself and his world to bear on real-life issues. It does so to draw forth a response, to bring the unbeliever to faith (e.g. John), to challenge the stagnating Christian to persevere (e.g. Hebrew), to correct false teaching (e.g. Galatians, 1 John), or to encourage right behaviour among God's people (e.g. Romans, James).

This means that truth is put in service of exhortation: think rightly about God so that you will respond rightly towards him, his people, and his world. There is, therefore, a common pattern in didactic prose, indicative followed by imperative. Indicative refers to clauses and sentences that make statements, describing something or presenting a truth. Imperative refers to exhortations and commands. Didactic texts in the Bible root their commands in truth, whether it is in God's authority, character, or truth about his ways and his creation (e.g. Matt 5:48; Rom 5:1-5). Therefore, as we read didactic texts, we need to ask the questions, "why is this truth given?"—i.e. what should we do about it—and, "what truth undergirds this command?"

c. Study Strategy: Arcing and Sentence Diagramming

To understand both these questions, we need to get a firm grasp on the grammar of a text, how all the pieces come together, and the logic of paragraph or unit of text—how sentences and units of sentences relate to one another. There are several tools to do this, but there are two that I have found most helpful. We do not have space to go to great depth with either of these tools, but there are several great resources to further your understanding of them.

For sentence diagramming, a basic tool for looking carefully at clauses, Thomas R. Schreiner's *Interpreting the Pauline Epistles* is an excellent guide. Additionally, <u>Biblearc.com</u> is a free online platform that facilitates sentence diagramming and offers some instructional videos for doing it and using the program. Basically, to diagram a clause, you identify its specific parts (the verb, nouns, pronouns, adjectival phrases, adverbs, prepositional phrases, etc.) and visually represent the relationships the pieces have with one another. A usual method to do this is to identify the verb and put it in the centre of a line on a piece of paper. To the left of the verb, write out the subject and to the right the object. On the far left of the same line, write out the conjunction where present. Then, write out all adjectives and adverbs or adverbial phrases indented beneath the word they modify (see the example below).

Review of English Grammar

For various reasons, many of us do not know English grammar as well as we should. Even at a seminary level, I have found it necessary to review the basics of English grammar in order to facilitate sentence diagramming and arcing in language and exegesis tutorials. Here is an overview of basic grammatical units that are important for using these tools:

Verb: the main component of a sentence, describe an action or a state. (is, was, run)

Adjective: modifies a noun, specifying it (which man? The *green* man).

Adverb: modifies a noun, verb, or adjective, specifying the modified word in various ways (*when, as, too, not*).

Noun: describes a person, place, or thing. A pronoun replaces a noun.

Object: receives the action of the verb (he threw *the ball*).

Subject: performs the verbal action or is predicated (he threw, he was tall). In the passive, is acted upon (*She* was chosen).

Indirect object: receives the action of the verb secondarily (he passed *him* the ball).

Clause: A clause is complete grammatical unit, containing both a verb

> (more technically, a predicate: verbless clauses are quite frequent in Greek and Hebrew and occur occasionally in English) and its complements (minimally, a subject). "He ran," "She quickly drove to the store," "because the dog ran."
> **Independent clause**: An independent clause is a clause that contains a completed thought, and so could be a sentence by itself (e.g. "He ran").
> **Dependent clause**: A dependent clause is a clause that cannot stand on its own; it needs to be connected to a dependent clause (*because the dog ran*, he caught the car).
> **Proposition**: Especially in the context of arcing, discussed below, a "proposition" refers to a clause, a grammatical unit consisting minimally of a predicate and subject.

Sentence diagramming forces us to slow down and consider carefully how an author has communicated and why he has done so. It forces us to think carefully about what we usually do intuitively. This tool is especially helpful when a sentence is ambiguous.[22] For example, sentence diagramming may force you to ask whether "like a dove" in Matthew 3:16 refers to the manner of the Spirit's descent or the physical manifestation he takes (though I cannot identify a significant difference in meaning). Matthew is not clear either way, and maybe both are intended (though cf. Luke 3:22), but such a question will probably lead you to ponder the significance of the Holy Spirit descending as a *dove*. More significantly, sentence diagramming will force you to think through the connection between the pieces of Revelation 13:8 and the phrase "before the foundation of the world." Theologically, the text cannot mean that Christ was slain before the foundation of the world, yet some have argued it is elliptical and means "Book of the life of the lamb whose slaughter was ordained from before the foundations of the world."[23]

---

[22] Some exegetes use a related tool, creating a sentence flow, to identify the key themes and terms and the progression of the argument of a passage. I find arcing, discussed below to be a better tool for the latter and marking up a passage on paper or in a Bible best for the former. However, see Gordon D. Fee, *New Testament Exegesis: A Handbook for Students and Pastors*, 3rd ed. (Louisville: Westminster John Knox Press, 2002), 41–48.

[23] E.g. Mounce writes "It is better in this case to follow the order of the Greek syntax and read, 'the Lamb that hath been slain from the foundation of the world.'"

Otherwise, it could be connected to "written," "whose name has not been written from the foundation of the world in the book of life of the lamb who was slain." Whatever the case may be, sentence diagramming will force you to make a decision about what is intended and think through the theological implications of this decision. For Revelation 13:8, a sentence diagram might look like this:

Subject	Verb	Object
name	has been written	
whose	not	
	before the foundation	
	of the world	
	in the book	
	of the life	
	of the Lamb	
	who was slain	

The resources mentioned above will also guide you in the use of our second tool, *arcing*. Schreiner's *Interpreting the Pauline Epistles* has a fantastic chapter on "Tracing the Argument," using arcing to identify the logic of a passage.[24] Biblearc.com, as the name implies, provides a platform for arcing the argument of a text in various modern translations as well as the Greek and Hebrew text. Various free lessons and paid lectures are offered for learning how to arc a text. Arcing is a way of visually diagramming and thinking through the relationships of clauses and paragraphs within a chosen text. My instructions on mapping parallelism in the last section are inspired by arcing, so it is very similar. However, because didactic texts relate clauses logically, we can be much more precise about the possible relationships clauses will have to one another, so most instructions on how to arc a passage

---

However, to anticipate a later chapter, one should take this judgment with a grain of salt. Greek syntax is notoriously flexible and there are good reasons why the phrase "from the foundation of the world" may be put at the end of the Greek sentence. Robert H. Mounce, *The Book of Revelation*, NICNT (Grand Rapids: Eerdmans, 1977); G.K. Beale, *The Book of Revelation: A Commentary on the Greek Text*, NIGTC (Grand Rapids; Carlisle: Eerdmans; Paternoster, 1999).

[24] This document on biblicaltraining.org is adapted from Schreiner's chapter, http://nt504.biblicaltraining.org/Flow_and_Tracing.pdf. The full chapter is available through this link https://blog.biblearc.com/blog/tracing-the-argument/.

will provide a list of possible relationships clauses can have to one another. Schreiner writes,

> All propositions relate in either a *coordinate* or *subordinate* way to previous propositions. We can see the relation between propositions in sentences. For instance, coordinate propositions are found in compound sentences. Compound sentences have two or more independent clauses joined together. The sentence 'I listened to the radio, and I washed my car' is a compound sentence. Both of these clauses are independent and could be separate sentences. Also, there is no dependent relationship between the two clauses. Two separate activities were performed: washing the car and listening to the radio. However, these two clauses can easily be rewritten so that one clause is a *subordinate* clause. If I write, I listened to the radio while I washed my car," then the sentence is now a complex sentence (containing at least one subordinate clause) instead of a compound sentence. The clause "while I washed my car" is not an independent clause but a subordinate one.[25]

In brief, this method is exactly like mapping parallelism in the last section. But instead of dividing the text into lines, it is necessary to break the text into its constituent clauses (the main verb with a complement, such as an object or subject, and various modifiers). After identifying the clauses or propositions (in Schreiner's terminology) that make up your passage, lay out the propositions on a vertical or horizontal line (either using the full clause written out or its verse and clause reference [e.g. 1a, 1b, 1c; 2a, 2b, 2c], see the example below). To trace out the argument of the passage, identify the clauses that are most closely related and indicate their relationship by connecting them with an arc. Continue to identify relationships between clauses and groups of clauses and indicate these relationships with further arcs. Do this until you have one arc that encompasses the whole text. Then, using the list of possible relationships clauses could have with one another, identify how each clause and group of clauses is related and mark it with the pertinent symbol. When you have finished, explain in writing each relationship and the reason you have identified it as such. Using biblearc.com

---

[25] Thomas R. Schreiner, *Interpreting the Pauline Epistles*, 2nd ed. (Grand Rapids: Baker Academic, 2011), 99.

and its system of reference, an arc of Romans 5:1-5 might look like this:

	Romans 5:1-5
	ESV
1a	Therefore, since we have been justified by faith,
1b	we have peace with God through our Lord Jesus Christ.
2a	Through him we have also obtained access by faith into this grace in which we stand,
2b	and we rejoice in hope of the glory of God.
3a	Not only that, but we rejoice in our sufferings,
3b	knowing that suffering produces endurance,
4a	and endurance produces character,
4b	and character produces hope,
5a	and hope does not put us to shame,
5b	because God's love has been poured into our hearts through the Holy Spirit who has been given to us.

Though I am not convinced that this exhausts all possible relationships that could be identified between clauses, the list Thomas Schreiner provides is quite helpful. He lays out the possible relationships between clauses in the following way (we do not have space to thoroughly explore each relationship, but his chapter, available through the link above, and the website biblearc.com, explains each category):[26]

    I. Coordinate Relationships – in a coordinate relationship, each clause presents a different action that is not grammatically dependent on the others
        A. Series (S) – in a series, actions are presented sequentially without logical dependence.
        B. Progression (P) – unlike a series, actions in a progression build upon one another, often they are logically dependent on the previous action though grammatically coordinated (e.g. "I tied my shoes, I opened the door, and I left the building": each action is grammatically coordinate yet there is logical progression).

---

[26] The brief explanations provided are my own. See also, http://www.bradcopp.com/PTH223/propositions.pdf.

C. Alternative (A) – when actions or states are alternatives, they present two or more alternatives, none of which are dependent on the others. For example, "we could go to the store or to the theatre"; "for dinner we could cook steak, eat out, or order Chinese food."

II. Subordinate Relationships – subordinate clauses (or propositions) do not stand alone but relate in some way to the main clause; they provide further specification (time, manner in which the action was performed, motive, etc.) or give more information for background.

    A. Support by Restatement
        1. Action-Manner (Ac/Mn) – an action is given, then the subordinate clause explains the manner in which the action was performed.
        2. Comparison (Cf) – a clause is explained by providing a comparable situation or action.
        3. Negative – Positive (-/+) – two antithetical statements are provided, alternatives that juxtapose sharply (cf. Eph 5:17)
        4. Idea-Explanation (Id/exp) – The idea or statement given in the main clause is explained by a subordinate clause.
        5. Question-Answer (Q/A) – One clause presents a question which is then answered in another.

    B. Support by Distinct Statement
        1. Ground (G) – A clause is a ground when it presents the logical reason for or cause of the main clause.
        2. Inference ($\therefore$) - A clause is an inference when it presents the logical result or conclusion to be drawn from the main clause.
        3. Action-Result (Ac/Res) – the main clause presents an action and another clause the result.
        4. Action-Purpose (Ac/Pur) – the main clause presents an action and another clause the reason the action was performed or its goal.
        5. Conditional (If/Th) – One clause presents a condition ("if," the protasis) and another clause the result if that condition is met ("then," the apodosis).

6. Temporal (T) – the subordinate situates the main clause temporally.
7. Locative (L) – the subordinate clause situates the main clause in a location, giving the physical/geographic setting.
8. Bilateral (BL) – a bilateral proposition is a bridge between a preceding proposition or group of propositions and one that follows, closely connected to both. It could perform any of the above functions for the preceding and following propositions (cf. Eph 5:21).

C. Support by Contrary Statement
1. Concessive (Csv) – The supporting clause presents a contrasting situation by which the main clause is to be understood. E.g. *"although the journey was difficult*, they sailed all the way home" (cf. Heb 5:8, 1 Cor 4:15).
2. Situation-Response (Sit/R) – One clause presents a response given to a situation presented in another clause (or series of clauses), e.g. "'Rabbi, when did you come here?' *Jesus answered them*, "…." (John 6:25-26).[27]

Often the relations are indicated by specific conjunctions or verbal types, so knowledge of the underlying Greek or Hebrew text can be very helpful in identifying the specific relationship a clause or group of clauses has/have with one another (the resources above provide some of the most frequent Greek conjunctions used to indicate these relationships). Using these categories, we can explain the arc of Romans 5:1-5 like this:

> **Verses 5:1a-2b**: in these first two verses, Paul draws three ideas from the truth that we have been justified by faith; since we have been justified, we have *peace, grace*, and *hope*. This is a series: they do not explain each other but are three inferences drawn from the truth of justification (argued for in the previous chapters of Romans, as indicated by *therefore*).
> **Verses 2b-5b**: 3a-5b expand upon the *hope* Christians have because of justification; Paul draws forth the implications of this hope for the Christian life. He does this through a series of

---

[27] The explanations are my own, informed by Schreiner's work and others. Schreiner, *Interpreting the Pauline Epistles*, 111–112.

progressing coordinate relationships. In 5:1a-2b, the coordinated clauses are a series; they are on the same level, each an inference from the statement in 1a. However, in 2b-3a and 3b-5b, the coordinate clauses are a progression: each clause builds upon the preceding result of hope until it reaches a climax in 5a-b.

Verses 2b-3a: 3a presents an unlikely way that rejoicing expresses itself in the Christian life: rejoicing in the hope of the glory of God means rejoicing even in suffering. It presents a coordinating action—"not only doing this but also"—yet the second action serves to specify and explain the first. So, though grammatically coordinated, it is in a sense subordinate (a specific example of a general idea, rejoicing in hope).

Verse 3b-5b: In the following clauses, Paul gives the reason that the Christian can rejoice in suffering; it is because they know that the end of suffering is glory—that hope will not be put to shame. 3b-5a is a progression, giving a step-by-step analysis of how suffering produces as a result worthy of rejoicing.

Verse 5a-b: in the final verse of this text, the progression of hope is fulfilled in glory. The Christian will not be shamed because God's love will ensure they receive the object of their hope (cf. Romans 8). 5b provides the ground for 5a: because God's love has been poured out through the Spirit, the Christian is sure that their hope will be realized.

One could go to a further depth than I did here, identifying the relationships the various prepositional phrases (e.g. "in which we stand," "through our Lord Jesus Christ") have to the clause they modify. But this should suffice to give you an idea of what arcing might look like. "It may appear," writes Thomas Schreiner,

> that tracing the logic in this way is a very laborious way to state what was obvious from the beginning. Even in short texts, however, this method is valuable because it constrains the reader to slow down and to note the function of every proposition in the text. The reader then begins to observe more closely what is in the text, and then proceeds to ask questions about how the text coheres. In addition, the longer the text, the more such an analysis is necessary. It may be easy to consider the relationship between only two verses, but tracing the entire argument for extended paragraphs or even the entire letter can easily slip from our grasp unless we have some way of holding before our mind the logic of

the text.[28]

The point of this chapter is not to teach these methods in detail; there are many books and free resources that do a better job than I could. Instead, I hope only to introduce these techniques and show how they fit into the method I am unpacking in this work.

D. Prophecy

The last type of biblical text we will look at is prophecy. To say a text is prophetic does not refer to a text type in the same way as poetry, narrative, or didactic prose. Those three categories involve the stylistic categories I call in *The Gift of Reading – Part 2* "language pattern" and "manner of communication." *Language pattern* refers to the distinct way these styles of text connect units of thought, e.g. whether through sentences (prose) or lines (poetry) and coordination (narrative prose) or subordination (didactic prose). *Manner of communication* refers to the way the language pattern they use communicates, such as through a story involving a narrator and plot (narrative), logical argumentation and explanation (didactic prose), or conceptual rhythm through the use of imagery in conjunction with poetic devices and parallelism (poetry). What I am calling prophetic texts do not have a distinct language pattern. Instead, prophetic texts can usually be classified as poetry or didactic prose—often blurring the lines between these two. However, because of the distinct way prophetic texts communicate, both as prose and as poetry, it is worth considering it separately. That is, what I am calling prophetic texts have a distinct manner of communication.

At times, prophetic texts can be divided into lines and poetic units. In these cases, we can analyse a prophetic text by mapping its parallelism. At other times, prophetic texts can be divided into sentences and paragraphs. In these cases, we can use arcing to identify the relationships between clauses and sentence diagramming to understand what is being said precisely. What makes prophetic texts distinctive is the symbolic imagery that they use.

a. How Prophecy Communicates: Symbolic Imagery

---

[28] Ibid., 103.

As I observed above, poetry often uses concrete metaphors. To be concrete, a metaphor must relate to human experience. These are metaphors that draw on our memories and shared experience to provide their emotional force. Psalm 84, for example, uses common imagery to incite the imagination of those singing it. Lines like verse 3 would resonate with the experience of many Israelites,

> Even the sparrow finds a home,
> > and the swallow a nest for herself,
> > where she may lay her young,
> at your altars, O LORD of hosts,
> > my king and my God.

More familiar to many of us will be the imagery of Psalm 23. Though drawn from a culture different from ours, we can still see the concreteness of its shepherd imagery.

The reader of biblical prophecy, such as is found in the Old Testament prophetic books, in Daniel, and in Revelation, will immediately notice that its imagery is often of a different sort. In Numbers 12:8, God himself identifies prophecy as riddles or ambiguous sayings in contrast with the Law delivered to Moses, which is a clear word. Consider the following examples:

> Even stones from the wall will cry out,
> > and rafters from the woodwork will answer them (Hab 2:11)

> The cup of YHWH's right hand is coming around to you,
> > and disgrace will come upon your glory. (Hab 2:16)

> "And though a tenth remain in it,
> > it will be burned again,
> like a terebinth or an oak,
> > whose stump remains
> > when it is felled."
> The holy seed is its stump (Isa 6:13)

> I saw in my vision by night, and behold, the four winds of heaven were stirring up the great sea. And four great beasts came up out of the sea, different from one another. The first was like a lion and had eagles' wings… (Dan 7:2-4)

> Then came one of the seven angels… and spoke to me, saying,

"Come, I will show you the Bride, the wife of the Lamb. And he carried me away in the Spirit… and showed me the holy city Jerusalem coming down out of heaven from God, having the glory of God, its radiance like a most rare jewel, like a jasper, clear as crystal. (Rev 21:9-11).

Like the imagery of the psalms, prophecy obviously draws on the experience of its readers and hearers. Yet, there is often a greater distance between the experience and the intended meaning of the imagery in prophecy than in poetry. In each of the above examples, the experiential basis for the imagery is recognizable, but the meaning is not so readily apparent. In such cases, we are heavily reliant on the interpretation provided by the author in context or by a heavenly messenger recorded in the text to make sense of the text.

In Habakkuk 2:11, we see from the context that the stones and rafters represent the peoples Babylon has conquered to build their empire. These people groups are crying out to God for vengeance in the very song in which this line is written. In Habakkuk 2:16, we can make sense of "The cup in YHWH's right hand" from the use of this image in the rest of the Bible; it represents the wrath of God. Isaiah 6:13 only makes sense in light of the last line, from which we see that the stump is a sign of hope remaining in a future Davidic king. We only know the meaning of Daniel 7 because an angel interprets it later in the chapter (7:15-18). In Revelation 21, the angel's words introducing the vision present the explanatory key; the holy city is the people of God united with God in their midst. The text goes to a great length to describe the future glory of this people as endowed by God; notice the parallels between the description of the city's appearance and the throne of God earlier in Revelation, where the beauty of jewels is also used to describe the glory of God (Rev 4:3-6). If the imagery of prophecy is generally more symbolic than regular poetry, the imagery of the so-called "apocalyptic" books, Daniel, Revelation, parts of Ezekiel, and Zechariah, are more so. They represent "an intensification of prophecy."[29]

i. Apocalyptic and Prophecy

Some readers may find it problematic that I have identified apocalyptic literature with the prophecy, for in New Testament and Biblical studies,

---

[29] Beale, *The Book of Revelation: A Commentary on the Greek Text*, 37.

these are not considered the same (indeed, Apocalyptic is considered a genre; prophecy is not always recognized as a distinct genre). I discuss genre in *The Gift of Reading – Part 2* and argue for a better way of understanding it, as a way of grouping similar texts in order to better see their commonalities. In terms of what I have presented so far in this work and my argument in the latter work, grouping apocalyptic texts with prophetic texts makes sense. The particular common ground they share is in their manner of communication. Prophetic texts (as defined above) and apocalyptic texts both take a stance of revelation, revealing something told to them or shown to them by God. The Book of Revelation, for example, is identified as a prophecy revealed by the Lord Jesus Christ (1:1-3). The manner in which these prophetic revelations communicate is similar in both prophetic texts—such as Habakkuk 2, Jeremiah 51, and Ezekiel 32:1-8—and apocalyptic texts, such as Revelation 6 and 19.

However, G.K. Beale is right to identify the latter as intensified; both prophetic texts and apocalyptic texts share a similar symbolic nature, yet the symbolism of the latter texts is of a greater magnitude in both quantity—apocalyptic having more symbolism—and quality—the symbols being more complicated and abstract, disconnected from their intended referent (such as a beast representing the kingdoms of earth, Dan 7:1-8). Yet clear continuity is seen in the way symbols are used to reveal truths about God and his ways, how we are to interpret this symbolic communication (through context and intertextuality), and even in the symbols themselves (cf. Hab 2:6, Rev 16:19). Beale writes of Revelation,

> Though there are many definitions of apocalyptic (according to either form, thematic content, or function), it is best to understand apocalyptic as an intensification of prophecy. Too much distinction has typically been drawn between the apocalyptic and prophetic genres…. Apocalyptic should not be seen as too different from prophecy, though it contains a heightening and more intense clustering of literary and thematic traits found in prophecy. That this is the case especially in Revelation is borne out by its self-description as a "prophecy" In 1:3, as well as in 22:6-7, 10, where verbatim parallels with 1:1, 3 are found (see also "prophets" in 22:6…).

> The word "apocalypse" in 1:1 is a direct allusion to Daniel 2, where the word is used of the prophetic revelation communicated form God to the prophet Daniel....[i]
>
> In the Gift of Reading – Part 2, I argue that the common understanding of genre, reflected in Beale's analysis, is flawed, yet the insight that the style of revelation is similar to prophecy, an intensification of it, is very helpful and helps us begin to interpret so-called apocalyptic texts.
>
> ---
>
> [i] Beale, The Book of Revelation: A Commentary on the Greek Text, 37.

b. Study Strategy: Intertextuality

Because the imagery in prophecy is often so detached from its experiential basis, we must pay careful attention to the context to determine what the symbolism means. Reading prophecy, for this reason, is often a whole Bible endeavour. To understand the imagery in Revelation, for example, we need to pay careful attention to the book of Daniel and the interpretations provided there. Understanding Jesus's Olivet discourse in Matthew 24 requires a background understanding of the imagery used in Jeremiah and Isaiah for the end of Babylon and the nations, the embodiments of opposition to God (e.g. Isa 34, Jer 51). Symbolism, as found throughout prophetic texts and intensified in so-called apocalyptic texts, uses a symbol, such as an object (Hab 2:16) or number (Rev 20:3), in order to tell us something about the idea, event, or person/thing that is signified by the symbol. The meaning of the symbol is found in the comparison made between the signified and the signifier, the symbol.[30] For example, in Revelation 20:3, the use of "the thousand years" is symbolic of an indefinite but lengthy period of time in which (according to my interpretation of the

---

[30] "There are three crucial parts of a metaphor: the literal subject (tenor), the figurative subject (vehicle), and the resulting point of comparison. The figurative subject always explains the literal subject in some way. The figurative subject is a filter or lens through which the main point (or points) of comparison is (or are) deduced and applied to the literal subject. The point of comparison usually carries both cognitive and emotional elements. If "George is a wolf" is said in a context in which George is understood to be a dangerous criminal, then we understand better through the picture of wolf [sic] that George is someone who hurts people, and this image evokes a feeling of fear." Ibid., 55.

passage) Christ reigns over the earth before his return. As a symbol, "1,000" is like the period of Christ's reign in the sense that it is lengthy. The number 1,000 is a regular symbol in the Bible for a lengthy period of time (cf. 2 Pet 3:8). The symbol "cup" in Habakkuk and elsewhere in the Bible is a part of a greater image of the wrath of God like an intoxicating drink, overwhelming and destroying its recipient. The comparison lies in the destructive effect that both God's wrath and strong drink have on the one who receives them. Our best tool for figuring out the significance of the symbols used in prophecy is the Bible itself. By turning to other passages where the same symbol is used, we can learn from the context or from a specific interpretation given by God how the symbol ought to be interpreted. Sometimes many comparisons may be drawn between the symbol and the object or idea it is signifying or pointing to.

Prophetic texts in the Bible use rich symbolism to communicate; they bring the subject of the text into relation with something else, the symbol, in order to teach us. The relationship between the subject and the symbol, their similarities or dissimilarities, teaches us what we are to learn about the subject.[31]

Further Reading[32]

* Adele Berlin – *Poetics and Interpretation of Biblical Narrative* [B-I]
Jean Louis Ska – *"Our Fathers Have Told Us": Introduction to the Analysis of Hebrew Narratives* [I]
Robert Alter – *The Art of Biblical Narrative* [B-I][33]
* V. Phillips Long - *The Art of Biblical History* [B-I]
Douglas Stuart – *Old Testament Exegesis: A Handbook for Student's and*

---

[31] In this way, prophetic symbolism is exactly like abstraction in other fields, as I have unpacked in the first volume and will unpack further in the third volume.

[32] I do not recommend any poetry books below because most of them are ultimately not helpful in actually reading Biblical poetry. My approach is a synthesis resulting from a survey of the classic and contemporary approaches to Biblical poetry mediated through my own experience studying Hebrew poetry. The bibliography contains books I have used and found of some help in this regard.

[33] Alter and Berlin are Jewish, so they come to the text with a different theology of Scripture than a Christian would. With Alter this is particularly evident; he is good at observing things in the text, but his interpretations are usually way out in left field.

Pastors 4th edition [I-A]
    * Gordon Fee – *New Testament Exegesis: A Handbook for Student's and Pastors 3rd Edition* [I-A]
    * Thomas R. Schreiner – *Interpreting the Pauline Epistles* [I-A]

8

KNOWING BIBLE TRANSLATIONS

⁵Look, all of you, among the nations and behold—
 and be astonished and astounded!
For a deed I am doing in your day;
 you would not believe it though it were told.
– Habakkuk 1:5

⁴¹"Look, you scoffers,
 be astounded and perish;
for I am doing a work in your days,
 a work that you will not believe, even if one tells it to you."
– Acts 13:41

So far in this part of the book, we have considered the act of reading the Bible and the features of the Bible that we need to be aware of, with some consideration of tools we can use to read the various styles of biblical writings. For the rest of part 2, we will consider various tools we have available in our reading of Scripture. We will consider bible translations in this chapter and the biblical languages in the next chapter. In Chapter 10, we will consider the use of various secondary resources to check our interpretation of a text. We will conclude in Chapter 11 with a consideration of how we can evaluate our own interpretation and the interpretations of others.

Whether we like it or not, we are all indebted to and reliant upon Bible translations in our study of the Bible. Even for those who will be reading in the original languages, it is often Bible translations that serve as our first recourse for interpretive help. It is essential, then, that we have a firm understanding of Bible translation in general and the translations we will be using. First, we will consider Bible translation in general, its nature and limitations. Second, we will consider general approaches to Bible translation as exhibited in the major English translations. Finally, I will offer an evaluation of several of the most prominent English translations, considering their value and limitations.

A. Bible Translation

What is a Bible translation? Our answer to this question will have a significant impact on how we translate the Bible or how we interact with Bible translations. For example, if we say that a Bible translation presents the *content* of the original Greek and Hebrew text, we may produce or seek a very free translation that aims at communicating the ideas and truths of a text without attention to the way it communicates them. As an answer to this question, I want to show that a translation is a specific use or interpretation of the original texts and that there are two broad types of translation that are commonly used.

In our discussion above, I suggested that when we speak of the "meaning" of a text, we are thinking of specific ways that text could be used. "You shall not murder" means "it is wrong to murder," "it is wrong to kill another person without God-given authority," etc. We could say that these are all meanings of לֹא תִרְצָח (*lōʾ tirṣāḥ*) (Exod 20:13). It may be helpful to consider a translation as the communication of the meaning of a text from one language to another. Texts may mean countless things, for they apply to innumerable situations. However, there is no one-to-one correspondence between an original language from which we are translating and the receptor language into which we are translating. Therefore, in its attempt to communicate the meaning of a text, a translation by necessity restricts the meanings of a text.

Consider our example above, "You shall not murder" translates more of the text's meaning than "You shall not shoot a person indiscriminately," yet it does not replace the original Hebrew. "You shall not murder" employs the English word "murder," which is similar to but not identical with the

Hebrew רצח (*rṣḥ*); it will thus have a similar but not identical range of meanings. For example, the Hebrew command includes what we would call "manslaughter," killing without pre-mediation. It also covers criminal negligence, accidental killing or negligence that results in death. The English translation "you shall not murder" captures one set of meanings indicated by the Hebrew but excludes others. Like application, translation attempts to communicate the meaning of a text to an audience, yet it attempts to do so in a way that is analogous or as close as possible to the original. A translation may attempt to follow the word order and style of the original as much as possible, but even when this is not attempted, a translation will attempt to communicate with the same text type: we translate poetry as poetry, narrative as narrative, etc. Like an application, translation necessarily restricts the meaning of a text to communicate it to an audience, to a specific culture and language, yet it generally attempts to retain as much of the **meaning potential** of the original text as possible and tries to mirror its form to some extent.[1]

This is an important point for us to see. If a translation is by necessity a restriction of meaning, an application, no translation will ever replace the need for the original texts. Even if we could guarantee that every translation would be perfect, there would need to be new translations as language changes and new translations as new ways we need to apply the text become apparent. In theory, then, there can be many legitimate and helpful translations in the same language; they may even complement each other where they differ (they may choose different yet equally legitimate ways of translating a text). Consider, for example, the way Paul uses Habakkuk 1:5 in Acts 13:41. Paul quotes from the Septuagint (LXX), the Greek translation of the Old Testament. It is clearly different from the Hebrew represented in English translations, yet Paul's use of it indicates that it is a valid translation in one way or another. If we consider what Habakkuk 1:5 means in context, we see that it is both a declaration of God's salvific intent (e.g. Hab 3:18) and

---

[1] Meaning potential refers to all the possible applications a text could have. This is natural extension from our discussion in Chapter 5. If meaning refers to the different ways a text may apply, then any text has many meanings, as many as there are possible circumstances to which it could apply. Furthermore, these meanings are only potential, or latent, until they are met with a circumstance to which they apply. Thus, we may rightfully speak of a text's "meaning potential."

a revelation of his coming judgment (Hab 1:12). A general translation, one that seeks to convey as best as possible the full meaning potential of a text, will translate the text in such a way that allows for the text to be applied in both senses. However, a translation that seeks to make a more specific application of the text may narrow it down to either the salvific or the judgmental aspect of the text:

> The LXX ... here correctly (though restrictively) conveys the sense of the Hebrew text. If we judge the LXX here as a word for word translation, it fails. But if we consider it an application [a specific translation], it succeeds and is ideal for Paul's intended application of this text. In Hab 1:5, the Septuagint focuses on the judgment aspect of God's vision, ignoring the salvific side. Paul uses it because he is preaching that same aspect, though elsewhere he preaches Habakkuk with the salvific aspect in view (Rom 1:17).[2]

The Septuagint here is an adequate, even helpful, translation of Habakkuk 1:5, but it is not sufficient to convey all the possible meanings or applications of the Hebrew text. Other translations will be required to communicate all that God intends for his people from this text.

B. Translation Theories

In the history of Bible translation, both general and specific translations have been produced. The Latin Vulgate, Luther's German Bible, and the English King James Version represent *general translations* of the Bible. They attempt to communicate as much of the meaning potential of the original texts as they can. These translations are designed to be used in preaching, teaching, and general reading of the Word of God.

However, at times pastors and teachers have seen fit to produce their own translations of biblical texts. Sometimes errors in the general translations have required it, but at other times, this has been necessary because they have needed to communicate a specific nuance or application of the original text that the broader translations do not communicate. Sometimes these individual translations are *general translations*, trying to present the fullness of the original meaning, but often they are paraphrases or *specific translations* that

---

[2] Rutherford, *Habakkuk*.

attempt to narrow the meaning to a specific application.³ In our day, this is seen especially in paraphrase or loose translations of the Bible, such as *The Message*.

In modern translation theory, general translations are the goal, yet there are two broad approaches taken to produce general translations. On the one hand, there are translations that attempt to achieve formal equivalency. These translations try to convey the form and meaning of the original text; "in its stricter form, this theory of translation espouses reproducing even the syntax and word order of the original."⁴ The NASB and ESV—among others—are contemporary attempts to attain different degrees of formal equivalency. On the other hand, some translations seek dynamic or functional equivalency; they are not so concerned with the form of the original text (its shape, size, emphasis) but with its meaning (usually conceived of as singular) and force (its intended effect). Formal equivalence does not attempt to close the historical distance between the ancient biblical texts and the modern culture; it will attempt to retain the impression of ancientness a reader of the original languages will experience. On the other hand, dynamic or functional equivalence is

> the attempt to keep the meaning of the Hebrew or Greek but to put their words and idioms into what would be the normal way of saying the same thing in English…. Such translations keep historical distance on all historical and factual matters but 'update' matters of language, grammar, and style.⁵

All contemporary translations fall somewhere between these two extremes, with wooden literalness on the one hand and loose paraphrase on the other. The formal equivalency and functional equivalency of contemporary translations fall right and left of centre.

We will consider how this looks in the following section, how

---

³ I have defended the appropriateness of such individual translations elsewhere. https://teleioteti.ca/2017/12/05/a-defence-of-an-authors-translation-part-1/

⁴ Leland Ryken, *The Word of God in English: Criteria for Excellence in Bible Translation* (Wheaton: Crossway, 2002), 19.

⁵ Gordon D. Fee and Douglas K. Stuart, *How to Read the Bible for All Its Worth*, 3rd ed. (Grand Rapids: Zondervan, 2003), 41.

translation theory plays out in specific translations. However, as far as theory goes, I think neither one of these theories is ideal. If our goal is to produce general translations—translations that are readable and useable for daily devotions, teaching, and preaching—then our goal should not be driven by a bare theory of how to translate but be adaptive towards the goal of translation. The goal should be to convey as much of the meaning-potential of the original text as possible to a contemporary audience. The word of God is sufficient for all the Christian life; a general translation should seek to facilitate its function in this way for the reader. This necessitates the balance both formal and functional equivalency are trying to reach. If a translation is too awkward and foreign for the reader of English, they may not understand any of the meaning intended by the text. However, if the text is too loose and specific, the reader may not hear the specific application the Holy Spirit would have for them.

I would endorse, then, a form of what Leland Ryken calls "essential literalness." Ryken defines essential literalness as "a translation that strives to translate the exact words of the original-language text… but not in such a rigid way as to violate the normal rules of language and syntax in the receptor language."[6] Paraphrasing this, I would say that a general translation should seek to retain the maximum possible meaning potential of the original text by retaining its wording and emphasis—its form—, its clarity, and its literary force (beauty, rhythm, technicality, simplicity, etc.) in a translation that conforms to the rules of the receptor language. The goal is to stay as close to the original as possible—lest you lose some of the ways it might apply to the reader—while maintaining its ability to be understood and the more subjective effects reading produces.

These theories of translation are worked out in the many translations with which God has blessed the English-speaking world. No translation adequately communicates the full meaning potential of the original texts, so we need to employ a variety of translations in our study if we are to see all that God has for us. If we are reading in the original languages, the variety of modern translations will help us to grasp better what is being said and help us learn to read and understand the original languages.

---

[6] Ryken, *The Word of God*, 19.

C. Bible Translations

There are dozens of English Bible translations available; I have chosen only to discuss below those that are most commonly used and, in my estimation, the most helpful. It should be observed that there are many unhelpful "translations" out there, those produced by various cults or by individuals without a considered approach to translation and without sufficient knowledge of the original languages. For this reason, it is good to research where a translation comes from if it is not one of the more commonly recognized Bible translations. Some of those produced by individual scholars are quite helpful, but the number of bad translations out there necessitates a comment.

From our discussion so far, it will probably not be a surprise that I recommend the more formal equivalent translations for study while suggesting that translations on the functional equivalence side are valuable for gaining insight into the meaning and application of specific texts. The following translations are given in alphabetical order, not in any way reflecting my estimation of their merit.

a. ESV

The English Standard Version is the translation I have chosen to employ throughout this book and other projects. The ESV is generally an attempt at formal equivalence but one which seeks to maintain the literary nature of the original texts at the same time. In the translators own words, "we have sought to be 'as literal as possible' while maintaining clarity of expression and literary excellence…. As an essentially literal translation, then, the ESV seeks to carry over every possible nuance of meaning in the original words of Scripture into our own language."[7] This effort leads them, for example, to maintain cultural and historical difference where it is present in the original text.

Because of its emphasis on both the literary quality of the translation and faithfulness to the original meaning, the ESV is a great study resource. Its strength is in its preservation of the meaning potential of the original text, not only in what it says but also in the effect its literary art conveys, such as the way narrative can draw you in and poetry can evoke various emotions.

---

[7] ESV Preface

Textually, the ESV is based on the latest critical editions of the New Testament and on the Masoretic text of the Old, as much as the translators deemed possible.[8]

b. KJV

The King James Version is old; it has gone through several revisions but is rooted in the early days of the reformation. I include it on this list both because it remains a commonly used translation and has some, though limited, value for contemporary study. In its day, it represented the height of biblical scholarship and literary quality. Though seeking to be literal in many ways, it nevertheless succeeded in communicating the beauty of Hebrew poetry, for example, in a way many modern translations fail to do. Its main value for contemporary study is the way it offers access to a different era of biblical scholarship. Though the translators did not have access to many of the tools we have today—and this is at times evident—they also had a great knowledge of the Bible and translated on the basis of the tools they had access to and their understanding of language. For all the advances we have made in philosophy and the study of language in the modern age, we have not left the historical tradition of these things in the dust. In many ways, the beliefs that have informed modern translations are as influenced by our own culture and its deficiencies as the KJV translators were influenced by theirs. For this reason, the KJV sometimes offers a superior perspective on how to interpret a text (such as is the case in Hab 3:13). However, because of its evident deficiencies, the KJV needs to be used carefully.

There are two major issues presented by the KJV to the modern reader. The first is that its language is outdated. That is, the English language has evolved significantly since the King James Version was produced, even since its latest revisions. This means that words and grammatical structures that were once clear and understandable are no longer so, words have fallen out of our vocabulary, and some words have changed meaning (e.g. Phil 4:6, Rom 13:13, Psalm 37:14). The second issue is the quality of its underlying text.

---

[8] Though I am not too familiar with it, the preface of the Holman Christian Standard Bible expresses a translation theory similar to the ESV. However it does not present itself as part of the KJV tradition, so it is a new translation based on the MT text presented in the BHS and the Greek critical text presented in the NA27. From my limited experience, I find the HCSB closer to the NASB in its final result as far as readability/eloquence is concerned.

That is, though it is based on most of the same Old Testament texts as we use today (MT, LXX, and Vulgate), its New Testament text is based on a single tradition of the Greek text that today is not thought to be highly reliable. Therefore, though the KJV could conceivably have some use in study, it is not better than or to be preferred to contemporary translations.

c. NASB

If you were looking for a very literal translation of the Bible based on the best scholarship of the years prior to its latest update in 1995, the NASB is where you would go. The goal of the NASB was to preserve the legacy of the KJV and its significant American version, the ASV, "by incorporating recent discoveries of Hebrew and Greek sources and by rendering it into more current English."[9] Thus, it sought to remedy the two significant issues that face the contemporary reader of the KJV. It is probably the closest to formal equivalency among the major contemporary Bible translations. Its close adherence to the wording of the original texts makes the NASB an invaluable tool for those beginning their journey with the original languages. It is often easy to identify how the NASB is translating the underlying Hebrew or Greek words without having to use an interlinear Bible. For these reasons, it is a valuable tool for study. I have often found in my own study that it also presents an alternative Evangelical perspective on difficult texts than that which the ESV offers, so it is useful for comparing and contrasting translations.

As compared to the ESV or even the KJV in its own day, the NASB does not do as good of a job (in my opinion) of conveying the rich literary beauty of the original language texts. This is not an insignificant issue, for the artistry of the biblical texts is essential to understanding their message. The skilled use of poetry and narrative in the Bible is intended to lead the reader to the appropriate understanding and response to the text.

d. NET

Compared to the others, the NET is a relative newcomer to the translation scene, a whole new translation (not a revision) published in 2005. The goal of the NET is to produce a translation that is "accurate, readable, and

---

[9] From the Preface of the NASB 1995 update.

elegant."[10] It seeks to preserve the meaning intended by the original authors in an understandable manner and to maintain the literary elegance of the original. Like the NIV, the NET attempts to achieve functional or dynamic equivalency in its printed text. However, it is accompanied by extensive footnotes that explain the literal readings of texts and why they were translated the way they were.

The use of extensive translators' notes makes the NET a tremendous asset to students of the Bible. For those using the original languages, its insight into the difficulties of grammar and text criticism is invaluable. For those who are not using the languages, its explanation of how they got to their translation from the original text can be helpful for resolving or at least identifying the reasons for differences between translations. The NET was produced by Evangelical scholars and so is informed by a broadly Evangelical theology in its translating choices. Though its notes are helpful for getting beyond the problems with dynamic equivalency, it still suffers from a similar problem as the NIV. That is, the text is sufficiently specified for our culture today to remove much of the meaning potential the more literal translations are attempting to preserve. For this reason, the NET is a great study asset, but I would recommend using a translation like the ESV or NASB as the basis for your study and Bible reading.

e. NIV

The NIV is the standard translation for the dynamic or functional equivalence approach to translation. It has been produced by a top-notch group of over a hundred scholars representing many different protestant denominations. The NIV has been translated wholly from the original Greek and Hebrew texts, so it is not a revision of a previous English Bible (as the ESV, NASB, and NRSV are). It was first published in 1978 and has seen several revisions since then.[11] The NIV has sought to prioritize "accuracy, clarity and literary quality" with the purpose of creating a multi-purpose Bible translation (a *general translation* in my terminology). The translators that make up the Committee on Bible Translation, which stands behind the NIV, believe that the best way to attain this goal is through the functional

---

[10] From the preface of the first edition of the NET.

[11] The edition I am using is from 2011.

equivalence model of translation.

The NIV is based on the latest biblical scholarship and often represents keen insight into the meaning of the biblical texts. For this reason, it is a great study resource, especially for checking your interpretation and seeing if other interpreters are seeing the same thing. However, as I have suggested above, it seems to me that the principles of functional or dynamic equivalency do not retain the meaning potential of the original text to the same extent a more formally equivalent translation is able. The nature of a translation philosophy that seeks to be intelligible and clear throughout while communicating the author's meaning accurately often necessitates moving from the generality I have argued for to specificity, narrowing down possible and potential meanings. By "possible meanings," I mean that such a translation must often choose between mutually exclusive interpretations of a phrase or sentence in cases where an essentially literal translation will do its best to maintain the ambiguity. By potential meaning, I refer to the innumerable applications a text may legitimately have. All translations will narrow this range, but functional equivalency often narrows this range beyond what is necessary for communicating the text in English. Consider a few of these examples:

> For on him God the Father has placed his seal of approval. – John 6:27 (NIV 2011)

> for on him the Father, God, has set his seal. – John 6:27 (NASB, cf. ESV)

> For it seems to me that God has put us apostles on display at the end of the procession, like those condemned to die in the arena. We have been made a spectacle to the whole universe, to angels as well as to human beings. – 1 Cor 4:9 (NIV 2011)

> For I think that God has exhibited us apostles as last of all, like men sentenced to death, because we have become a spectacle to the world, to angels, and to men. – 1 Cor 4:9 (ESV, cf. NASB)

> to call all the Gentiles to the obedience that comes from faith for his name's sake. – Rom 1:5 (NIV 2011)

> to bring about *the* obedience of faith among all the Gentiles for his name's sake. – Rom 1:5 (NASB, cf. ESV)

I am not suggesting that the NIV is wrong in the interpretation it presents in these passages, only that it is clearly presenting a greater restriction—a further specification—of the text than is necessary to communicate in English. Consider Romans 1:5, to translate "obedience of faith" as the NASB or ESV have communicates roughly the same range of possible meanings as the Greek phrase that stands behind it. The NIV's translation makes the meaning clear, yet the meaning they make clear is only one possible interpretation among several. 1 Corinthians 4:9 adds additional interpretive comments that are thought to be invoked by the word the ESV translates "exhibited," yet this is not what the text says, nor is it certain that the word would carry those connotations. Therefore, the translation is more specific than the text justifies. Similarly, in John, "seal of approval" interprets the significance of the act of sealing.

A particularly significant area where this is evident is the debate over so-called "gender-neutral" terminology. There are many places in the Bible where a term can mean *either* a male or a human in general; accordingly, most Bible translations will translate one or the other (man or human being). However, there are specific words that have a component of meaning that is particularly male and yet are used to refer to both men and women. For example, υἱός (*uios*, son) means a male child yet is used to refer to male and female Christians. Should we, then, translate it "son" or "child"? It may seem common sense to translated "child" because it *refers* to men and women, yet this makes the interpretive judgment that the male component does not affect the meaning of the passages in question. Therefore, if we are to leave open possible and potential meaning, we should translate what the text says (sons), not what we think it means (child). Furthermore, in many cases in the New Testament, the use of the word υἱός meaning "son" is *intentional*, for example, in Romans 8:14. That is, it is the son who inherits from the Father; it may very well be—and probably—is the case that by calling men and women together sons, the biblical authors intend to say that all Christians are inheritors of God's good promises to his children. Furthermore, Doug Moo suggests that "son" in Romans 8:14 makes an explicit connection between our status as Children and Christ's status as God's Son, a connection lost by translating υἱός as "son" in one case and "child" in another.[12] Schreiner also

---

[12] Douglas J. Moo, *The Epistle to the Romans*, NICNT (Grand Rapids: Eerdmans, 1996), 499–500.

suggests that the use of son echoes the description of Israel as God's son.[13] For whatever reason, Paul chooses to use the more general term τέκνα (*tekna*), children, in latter verses (Rom 8:17); so if we are to honour his intent—whether meaningful or stylistic—we should render the two words with their more formal English equivalents (υἱός as son, τέκνον as child).[14]

f. NLT

So far, the translations we have considered are all around the centre of the spectrum, with the NIV on the dynamic side and the ESV on the formal side. The New Living Translation moves us farther down the line of dynamic equivalency. The NLT translators sought to "render the message of the original texts of Scripture into clear, contemporary English."[15] The goal was to be "faithful to the ancient texts and eminently readable." Where the original text was clear, this meant taking an approach that was more formally equivalent, but where the text was more difficult, they took a more dynamic approach. The resulting translation is quite a bit more dynamic than the NIV. Like the NIV, a strong team of Evangelical scholars stand behind the NLT.

The NLT has much the same strengths as the NIV, though it is harder to use for translating and understanding the original texts. In its weaknesses, it is generally the same, though by taking a more dynamic approach, these weaknesses are magnified. Thus, the NLT is useful for reference in your studies but would not serve well as the basis for study or the primary translation for comparing translations.

g. NRSV

With the NRSV, we are back towards the centre. The NRSV follows in the same English Bible tradition as the ESV and NASB but moves towards the dynamic side of things. The NRSV fares much the same as the NIV and NLT, though closer to the NIV. It is the least evangelical of the translations,

---

[13] Thomas R. Schreiner, *Romans*, Baker Exegetical Commentary on the New Testament 6 (Grand Rapids: Baker Books, 1998), 423.

[14] Cf. Vern S. Poythress and Wayne A. Grudem, *The Gender-Neutral Bible Controversy: Muting the Masculinity of God's Words* (Nashville: Broadman & Holman Publishers, 2000), 247–250.

[15] From the preface of the 2015 edition.

and this is at times evident in its translations. Overall, it makes a helpful reference but not a good basis for your study or reading.

h. The Message

The Message is the most dynamic of all the translations we have considered here. It is the product of the late Eugene Peterson, a popular pastor who was extensively trained in the original languages. *The Message* offers the most specified of these general translations; in an effort to communicate to a contemporary audience, it restricts most possible and potential meanings. This makes it unhelpful for primary use in study or for reading the Bible and should not be used in these ways. Furthermore, in dozens of places, the translation adopted is, in fact, unhelpful and does not reflect the original text (e.g. Rom 1:26-27). However, given Peterson's writing abilities, it is probably the most readable and poetic of the translations considered. The main use to be made of *The Message* in Bible study is as a reference, to get an idea how someone has made an application of the text.

Further Reading

Gordon Fee – *How to Read the Bible for All Its Worth*, 33-53 (B)
* Leland Ryken – *The Word of God in English* (B-I)
Vern S. Poythress & Wayne A. Grudem – *The Gender-Neutral Bible Controversy* (B-I)

9

KNOWING BIBLICAL LANGUAGES

לֹא־יָמוּשׁ סֵפֶר הַתּוֹרָה הַזֶּה מִפִּיךָ וְהָגִיתָ בּוֹ יוֹמָם וָלַיְלָה לְמַעַן תִּשְׁמֹר
לַעֲשׂוֹת כְּכָל־הַכָּתוּב בּוֹ כִּי־אָז תַּצְלִיחַ אֶת־דְּרָכֶךָ וְאָז תַּשְׂכִּיל:

The book of this law must not depart from your lips, but you shall meditate on it day and night so that you may be careful to act according to all that is written in it, for then you will succeed in your ways, and then you will have wisdom.[1] – Joshua 1:8

From my time learning Hebrew and Greek and serving as a teacher's assistant for language classes, I have observed two responses students have towards learning the biblical languages. On the one hand, some students rise to the challenge of the languages and begin to delight in reading the Bible in a whole new way. On the other hand, some students find the languages too difficult to manage or do not give the adequate time necessary to really learn them. I think that everyone can learn Hebrew and Greek—it is not so different from learning French, Spanish, German, or Arabic. And if you learn Hebrew, you can learn Aramaic—the third biblical language. However, to learn these languages takes a tremendous commitment of time and a lot of effort, time and effort not all of us are able to give.

For this reason, I have two purposes in this chapter. First, I hope to underscore the importance of the biblical languages, especially the *proper use* of the languages. Second, I want to outline two ways the biblical languages

---

[1] My translation.

often relate to Bible study, namely word and grammar studies. I hope that this chapter would encourage those of us with the ability, namely the time and diligence, to learn the languages to do so. For the rest of us, I hope that it has been clear so far in this book—and I hope that it will remain clear throughout this chapter—that the biblical languages are tremendously important, yet not all of us have to learn these languages to reap their benefit. God has gifted the church with many people who are able to competently handle the challenges of language study and translation so that the rest of us may reap the benefit. It is necessary that some of us learn the languages but not all of us. For the reader who will not be undertaking the task of learning the languages, the discussion in this chapter will be best used as a primer for evaluating the claims of secondary resources (e.g. commentaries) you will use in study.

A. The Importance of the Biblical Languages

Not many of us take the biblical languages—Hebrew, Aramaic, and Greek—as seriously as Martin Luther did. Luther was adamant that the very Gospel itself was at stake when it came to studying the biblical languages,

> Let us be sure of this: we will not long preserve the gospel without the languages. The languages are the sheath in which this sword of the Spirit is contained; they are the casket in which this jewel is enshrined; they are the vessel in which this wine is held; they are the larder in which this food is stored…. If through our neglect we let the languages go (which God forbid!), we shall … lose the gospel.[2]

Was Luther correct in his assessment? Everything we have seen so far, especially the last chapter, suggests that he was indeed correct. And history confirms it. Church history is full of minor (and major) errors made in doctrine and teaching because people did not have access to the languages, errors resulting from either mistaken or unclear translations or sloppy handling of the original language texts. If what I have argued so far is true, namely that translations necessarily restrict the **meaning potential** of the biblical texts and that there is and will be a continued need for new Bible

---

[2] From his letter "To the Councilmen of All Cities in Germany That They Establish and Maintain Christian Schools."

translations, then there is now and will always be a need for Christians who are well trained in the biblical language.

First, it is essential that we have *Christians* trained in the languages. For all sorts of reasons, many people who do not proclaim Jesus Christ as Lord have learned Greek and Hebrew and have positions as biblical scholars. But translating is by no means a neutral endeavour; it involves interpretation. Therefore, we need many men and women committed to Christ who will learn the languages and use them to serve the Church.

Second, if translations by their very nature restrict the meaning potential of a text, then pastors and teachers must—wherever possible—learn the languages. That is, if they are to preach the full counsel of God and be equipped to address every need their congregations have, pastors and teachers need to have at their disposal everything God has given them—access to all the potential applications Scripture has. Though using multiple different Bible translations addresses this issue to some extent, this still does not replace careful interaction with the original text. Thus, wherever possible, present and future leaders of the church should seek to acquire competence in at least biblical Greek and Hebrew.

Third, not only is there a need for languages in the context of local church ministry, but there is also a continual need for translating the Bible into English and other languages. So long as cultures and languages change, we will need revisions of old Bible translations and sometimes entirely new ones. There will always be a need for Christians willing to take up the arduous task of carefully translating the original languages for contemporary audiences.

In addition to these practical necessities that demonstrate the importance of the biblical languages, knowledge of the biblical languages is also important for correcting faulty interpretations of the Bible. Because the original texts are the final standard for meaning, adjudication between competing interpretations of texts must at some point have recourse to the original texts. This may come through means such as dictionaries, commentaries, and computer software, but those using these tools must have sufficient knowledge to do so, and there must be others with the requisite knowledge to produce such resources. Furthermore, as observed above, if we Christians do not produce resources for using the languages well, others who do not share our commitments about Scripture will.[3] Therefore, there is a great need for Christians today to carefully study and become competent in the original languages.

As I have argued throughout this book, all believers are able to read the Bible—whether they have the languages or not. But I think it is has been clear in each chapter that there is a certain measure of clarity that comes from studying the original languages that is not possible without them. My first teacher of Hebrew, Brad Copp, suggested that reading the Bible in the biblical languages was like switching from black and white to colour TV, or standard definition to HD. The content is the same, yet you begin to see things you did not see before. This is true in addition to what we have already seen concerning the way translations limit the meaning potential of a text. For this reason, the biblical languages are not necessary for every individual Christian, yet everyone who learns to read them will profit and the Church as a whole needs Christians who read the languages.

B. The Appropriate use of the Biblical Languages

So what goes into learning and using Greek, Hebrew, and Aramaic? Let's be clear about one thing: it is not simply a matter of learning how to navigate Bible software! Bible software such as Logos and Accordance has made way for those with enough money to access high-quality language resources and to view the original language source behind many contemporary translations. This is in many ways a blessing, yet it also harbours a curse. With easy access comes the temptation of sloppiness and laziness. When it comes to learning and maintaining a language, such habits can be deadly.

There are two routes for learning to use Greek, Hebrew, and Aramaic in Bible study. The first is learning the tools for word and grammar studies. For many of us who do not have the privilege of studying the Bible as a full-time job, this will be our primary option. The second is to learn to read the languages. In my estimation, the latter option is both the hardest and the most beneficial. To learn to read takes dedication and a daily effort to engage

---

[3] In the first book of this series, *The Gift of Knowing*, I show how commitment to Christ is essential to all human knowledge and knowing. This implies the point I am making here, that Christian commitments are essential to studying the Biblical languages. I make this point in different language throughout this book.

with the Greek and Hebrew Bible. For the rest of this chapter, I want to focus on the use of the biblical languages in Bible study for those who have enough of a foundation to engage in such a study (I would recommend the equivalent of an introduction to biblical Languages course or first-year Greek or Hebrew course, the equivalent being *Greek for the Rest of Us* or *The Basics of Biblical Greek* and their Hebrew equivalents). For those without such a foundation, the following guidelines may help you evaluate the discussion in commentaries and other study aids. At the end of the chapter, I will provide resources I have found helpful for learning to read the languages, including free online classes to do so.

The two main uses of the biblical languages other than textual criticism are word studies and grammar studies. Let's first consider some broad rules for study using the biblical languages and then consider word and grammar studies.

a. *Ground Rules for Language Study*

Greek and Hebrew are not simple languages, nor is it a simple matter to move from one language to another. The work of translation is a noble endeavour, and we ought to be deeply grateful for the translators of our Bibles. They have laboured a lifetime to learn the languages and have put great thought into how they might best translate Greek, Hebrew, and Aramaic texts into English. For this reason, we ought to have great humility when we attempt to use the languages for biblical study.

Now, translators are not inerrant; they make mistakes. Sometimes the mistakes they make are their own or result from the resources they have used. Also, the English language changes, so we may not be sure what was intended by a specific translation. Furthermore, studying the original languages may reveal that a specific translation is acceptable but does not present the best interpretation of a text. For these reasons, I think it is appropriate to dig beneath translations and look at the original texts; however, we must do so with great humility. Whatever our background is, we are all standing on the shoulders of giants as we use Greek, Hebrew, and Aramaic language tools. We may conclude that some of them were wrong and that there is a better interpretation available. However, we must come to these conclusions with careful thought and due diligence. So our first rule for language study is humility; if you come to a conclusion that no one else has reached or one that is vastly different from what others are saying, check yourself. You are more likely to make a mistake than those who have spent a lifetime reading the biblical texts.

Along with humility, we also need to remember that as much as translating is an art, it is also a science. That is, there is a certain amount of subjective intuition necessary to produce a beautiful translation, yet languages behave according to certain patterns that need to be observed in translation. I highly recommend D. A. Carson's *Exegetical Fallacies* in this regard.[4] The first two chapters, addressing word study and grammatical fallacies, respectively, provide a necessary corrective to many common mistakes that are made when using the biblical languages in Bible study. His writing is dense, but the book rewards careful study. In addition to familiarizing yourself with Carson's book, it will also be important to gain a working knowledge of the Hebrew and Greek alphabet and some of the differences between English and these languages. For this purpose, two books by Zondervan will be helpful; *Hebrew for the Rest of Us* and *Greek for the Rest of Us*.[5]

b. Word Studies

The way Greek and Hebrew are most commonly used in Bible Study is for word studies. A word study investigates the meaning of the original language term rendered in an English translation. Word studies are helpful when we are looking to see how a term is used throughout the Bible or in a particular set of writings. They are also helpful for identifying the exact meaning of an ambiguous English word used in translation.

Word studies will not reveal any profound insight into theology or the meaning of a text, but they bring precision to our study and help us to better interpret Scripture by Scripture. Regarding clarity, they help us identify what exactly is intended by our English translations. Consider, for example, Joshua 1:8. The seventh word in this verse, הָגָה (*hāgāh*), is translated "meditate." This may bring confusion to a reader at first glance, for in modern English

---

[4] D. A. Carson, *Exegetical Fallacies* (Grand Rapids: Baker Books, 1996).

[5] Lee M. Fields, *Hebrew for the Rest of Us: Using Hebrew Tools without Mastering Biblical Hebrew* (Grand Rapids: Zondervan, 2008); William D. Mounce, *Greek for the Rest of Us: The Essentials of Biblical Greek*, Second Edition. (Grand Rapids: Zondervan, 2013).

meditate has at least two meanings. On the one hand, "meditate" usually means to empty oneself of thought in order to achieve inner peace and clarity, or something of this sort. However, an older meaning of meditate is to think carefully and repeatedly about something. The translators of our Bibles only intend one of these meanings. We have two tools to figure out what is intended. The first is context: words only have meaning from their context, so we must ask how the word is being used. Joshua 1:8 clearly indicates the second meaning, for the first part of the sentence calls Joshua to not let "the book of this Law" depart from his lips. The verse is not about a mystical inner peace (though a different sort of peace will result from meditation on the Word), instead it is about grounding oneself in God's revelation. If we remain unsure or want to be more certain, we can do a word study to see how the Hebrew term is used throughout the rest of the Bible.

If we search for הָגָה in Hebrew Bible, we will see that it is used 25 times. The most recent English language lexicon of Hebrew (lexicon = dictionary) lists five different ways the "Qal" stem of הגה is used.[6] In some texts, it refers to the noise an animal makes (Isa 59:11, Ezek 7:16), in other texts to the moans of mourning (Isa 16:7), to human communication (Isa 50:3, Ps 35:28), in several texts to the act of meditation, and in three texts to plotting or imagining (Ps 2:1, 38:13; Pr 24:2). Our text is clearly an example of "meditating." The contexts in which this word is used, along with the range of meanings (these five different things it could mean) suggest that in our context the word means to think carefully and repeatedly upon something. Our study confirms what we can see from the context of our English translation.

In another situation, we may not need clarity on the basic meaning of a word but how the author is using it. This tends to be the case for words used technically, that is, words that are used frequently with a specific connotation (such as the word αναστασις, *anastasis*, which generally means "the act of rising" but is often used in the New Testament specifically for a resurrection). Now, we must not confuse concepts with terms; though an author may frequently use a specific term (αναστασις) to refer to a concept, such as a resurrection from the dead, this does not mean that the term only means

---

[6] Qal is one of several forms a Hebrew verb may take. Many Hebrew verbs will take on a different meaning depending on what stem they are found in.

"resurrection" or that we can learn all we need to know about a "resurrection" from this term. It can be helpful to study each occurrence of a word, but this only tells us how a word is used, not what a concept such as *justification* or *resurrection* means. To learn about a concept, we need to understand the context in which the term is used and how that concept is treated in other passages, where other words may be used for the same idea.

For example, it would be a fruitful study to identify how the word translated justification, δικαιόω (*dikaioō*), is used in Paul's writing and the New Testament in general. This would help us identify key texts for the doctrine of justification by faith. This would not, however, reveal all the texts involved. Such a word study would confirm that the word means "to be declared righteous," but we would need to dig further to discover what is meant by "righteous." This might lead us to study the whole word group,[7] the nouns δικαιοσύνη (*dikaiosunē*; righteousness) and ἀδικία (*adikia*; unrighteousness); the adjectives δίκαιος (*dikaios*; right, righteous) and ἄδικος (*adikos*; unjust, unrighteous); and the Old Testament words that are related, namely the צדק word group (*ṣdq*; to be righteous). This may lead us to the conclusion that "righteousness" within the Bible is both a legal and covenantal term; that is, the term refers to a right standing within God's covenants. It refers to both a status of not-guilty, so free from covenant curses, and of being in the right, as such a recipient of covenant blessing. Δικαιόω means "to declare someone to be in the right or to be righteous," yet a word study will lead us to explore how the Bible deals with the topic of righteousness. We may then conclude that when Paul uses the word δικαιόω and its relatives, he intends the covenantal idea of righteousness expounded throughout the Old Testament.

To do a word study, we first need to identify which Greek or Hebrew

---

[7] Word groups are found in all languages but are prominent especially in the study of Hebrew. Words are often formed from the same basic form, or *root*, to form verbs, nouns, adjectives, adverbs, etc. For example, in English, deity, divine, divinity, to deify, and deification are all from the same word group. In languages such as Greek and English, where the language has evolved for a long period of time in many different contexts, it can often be dangerous to assume that words from the same word group will have the same meaning. However, this is sometimes the case in Greek and English and more so in Hebrew.

word is being translated in our English translation.[8] A generation or so ago, two tools you could use for this purpose would be an English concordance or an interlinear Bible. Web resources and Bible software have essentially made these tools obsolete. There are several free Bible study resources online that will show you what Greek word is being translated with the click of a mouse. On Netbible.org, you can use the NET translation and a Greek parallel text to identify the word in question. To do so, navigate to your passage and open the "Greek" panel on the right side of the interface. Hovering over a word in either the NET or the original language text will automatically highlight the word being translated on the one side and its translation on the other. If you search for your text in your desired translation on BlueletterBible.org (BLB), the "tools" option contains an interlinear that will display a list of every English word in a selected passage and the corresponding Greek word. On BLB, the Greek is given in its lexical form, what they (inaccurately) call a root.[9] Similarly, on Netbible.org, you can click on a word in the Greek text, and a box will appear giving you relevant information about it, including the lexical form, again called a "root." This is the form you will need to search for in the Bible and to look up in a lexicon.

If you are studying a Hebrew word, especially a verb, things get a little more complicated. It is important if you are studying a Hebrew verb to also note what stem it is in. The Hebrew verbal system is quite complicated, but a single verb will have different meanings depending on which stem it is in; thus, a word study cannot be on the verb but only on the verb in a specific stem.[10] The only online resource I am aware of for finding the Hebrew stem and lexical form is biblehub.com/interlinear/.[11] Select under the heading

---

[8] You can find diagrams of the following procedures online at https://teleioteti.ca/2019/08/09/word-study-guide/.

[9] In language study, "root" refers to a basic set of letters that are modified to become nouns, verbs, adjectives, etc. For example, the root of δικαιόω and ἀδικία is *δικ. The lexical form, what is necessary for a word study, simply means the form of the word without any morphological changes—it is not changed for gender, number, possession, tense, etc. A lexical form, therefore, is the form of the word you would find in a lexicon: in English, you look for "see" not "saw" in a dictionary.

[10] If you study Hebrew to a greater depth, you will begin to see how the stems relate and benefit from a broader study, but this requires an advanced knowledge of the Hebrew language.

[11] As of 2021, Esv.org offers similar resources based on the ESV translation.

"Hebrew interlinear" the option "interlinear verses." Navigate to your passage; you will be presented with a slew of information. It will present the Strong's number, transliteration, Hebrew word, translation, and parsing.[12] For Josh 1:8, the word translated "meditate" is described as V-Qal-ConjPerf-2ms. What is relevant for our purposes is the stem, in this case, *Qal*. The most common Hebrew stems that will be given are *Qal, Niphal, Piel, Pual, Hithpael, Hiphil,* and *Hophal*.[13] To find the lexical form, the form you need to search for, select the Strong's number at the top. Most of the information presented on the page that appears is concordance data; I do not recommend using it for a word study.[14] All we need on this page is the "Original Word," by which they mean the lexical form (what BLB and Netbible.org call a root). In this case, it is הָגָה (*hāgāh*). Alternatively, you can download a Logos 8 basic package for free (as of May 2019); this product contains the Lexham English Bible (LEB) and the KJV. If you hover the cursor over a word in either Bible, it will show you the lexical form and parsing. You can also right-click on the word and see this data displayed.

With the lexical form of a Greek or Hebrew word, and the stem of a Hebrew verb, we can then do a word study. The goal of a wordy study is to come to a better understanding of an original language word as it is used in the Bible, and sometimes by a specific author. The next step is to produce a list of every use of your word in the Bible using a search platform. I recommend using Biblearc's "scholar search," though Logos' search is good.[15] In Logos, you can use right click on a word and select "morph" under the search options. You will need to deselect every search option but stem

---

[12] Parsing is a description of the inflections of the word in the text. In English, we may parse "the horses'" as a definite, plural noun. In the discussion below, I presuppose that you will use Bible software or a website for parsing. However, there is a print way to discover the parsing of a Hebrew or Greek word, known as an analytical lexicon.

[13] There are variations of these stems, yet a consideration of these is beyond the scope of this book.

[14] Concordance definitions do not tell you what a word means but how a specific translation has translated it.

[15] Biblearc is actually faster and will display results in NASB and ESV translations. The free Logos package will only show search results in the KJV or LEB.

for a Hebrew verb. For a Hebrew verb, your search option should look like "Lemma:הגה@va" (a = Qal, other stems will be represented by a different letter). For every other word, Greek or Hebrew, it should be "lemma:" followed by the word.[16] On Biblearc, you cannot choose to select a specific Hebrew verb stem, so only use it for Hebrew noun/adjective searches or Greek word searches. To search on Biblearc, open a scholar search tab. Select the WLC Hebrew text or NA28 Greek text (depending on the language of your search). Select "word" on the bottom left-hand side of the screen and select "Lemma/Strong's" from the box that appears. Either use the provided on-screen keyboard to type out the word you will search for or copy the word into the bar.[17] From the options available, select the word you want to search for. Close the box with "update" and press enter or select the magnifying glass to perform the search. The results for both Biblearc and Logos will be in both English and the original language. On Biblearc you can select the English translation with the box marked by default +ESV under the search bar.

For many words, they will only appear several times, so you will want to consult the entire Bible. For more common words, it is good to search the whole Bible, but it will be more practical to focus on the way an author or even a specific book uses the word. For instance, you may consider how John uses the Greek word κόσμος (kosmos, world or universe): this word often takes on a specific theological connotation in his writings, referring to the whole world conceived of as in opposition to God.

With all the passages displayed, your next step is to write out all the ways the word in question is used. I recommend that you provide the English translation and jot beside it what is meant by that specific English word in its context, e.g. "meditate," to think repeatedly and intently about (Josh 1:8). This will provide you with the range of meanings for your word. Consider how other translations have translated the same verse to get a better handle on what the word means. Then consult the standard lexicons for the language

---

[16] "Lemma" indicates that you are searching for the lexical form.

[17] Alternatively, you can use the Strong's number provided in the online resources mentioned above.

in question.[18] See if they provide any further senses of the word that you do not have or if they provide alternative translations or meaning for the word in a specific context. Though these resources are produced by men and women who have laboured hard to understand how different terms in the Bible are used, they are not inerrant and free from error. Though we approach these resources from a posture of humility, "we must remember that these resources are created by fallible human beings who sometimes show their mental frailty or theological biases."[19] Indeed, at every point these resources are dependent on the theological biases of their authors and this at times leads them to conclusions that are contrary to the teaching of Scripture.[20]

The final step is to bring the insights of a word study to bear on the study of your passage. After ascertaining the range of meanings your word could have, you must then ask how it is being used in your specific passage. That is, words have a range of meanings or senses, but authors only intend one of these senses at a time. There are exceptions where an author employs intentional ambiguity that plays on two senses a word may have. Such is probably the case in John 3:3, where "born *again"* probably means "born *again & from above*," two possible senses of ἄνωθεν (*anōthen*).[21] However, such cases are exceptions; far more frequently, only one sense will be intended. Therefore, it is important to summarize the results of your word study as it impacts your passage; how is הָגָה (*hāgāh*) being used in Josh 1:8 or how is δικαιόω (*dikaioō*) being used in Gal 2:16? If your word study is broader—

---

[18] We will consider in the following chapter the standard works in this regard. They are all quite expensive, so having access to an academic library, well-equipped church library, or a language package for Bible software will probably be necessary.

[19] Andreas J. Köstenberger, Benjamin L. Merkle, and Robert L. Plummer, *Going Deeper with New Testament Greek: An Intermediate Study of the Grammar and Syntax of the New Testament* (Nashville: B&H Academic, 2016), 480.

[20] For example, the authors of *Going Deeper* rightly observe that Louw & Nida are wrongly led by their theology to exclude "propitiation" from the senses that the Greek word ἱλασμός (*ilasmos*; propitiation, place of propitiation) can have. Cf. Johannes P. Louw and Eugene A. Nida, eds., *Greek-English Lexicon of the New Testament: Based on Semantic Domains*, 2nd ed., vol. 1 (New York: United Bible Society, 1989), 40.12.

[21] Cf. D. A. Carson, *The Gospel According to John*, The Pillar New Testament Commentary (Leicester; Grand Rapids: IVP; Eerdmans, 1991).

for example, to understand how *Paul* uses δικαιόω—still summarize how he uses it in each passage where it occurs, for it will be used for different purposes and nuances in each case.[22]

c. Grammar Studies

In addition to word studies, it may also be useful to study the grammar of a passage in the original languages. Sometimes we need to do a grammar study. Such a study might consider the nature of a verb used, perhaps to explain why my translation of Habakkuk 3:3 has "God *comes in* from Teman" but the ESV has "God *came* from Teman." It may also consider the role of a specific clause, such as the clause introduced by לְמַעַן (*lᵉma'an*, "so that") in Joshua 1:8. A grammar study could also be used to investigate the difference between the translations of the NET, "the faithfulness of Christ," and the ESV, "faith in Christ," in Galatians 2:16. Whereas word studies deal with the meaning or sense of a word, a grammar study deals with the meaning of clauses and phrases or the translation of grammatical details such as verbal tense. Because grammar does not have as close a correspondence between original and receptor languages as words, a grammar study will require a greater understanding of the languages. For this reason, only experienced students of the biblical languages should pursue grammar studies. If you do not have experience with the languages but have a grammatical question, it would be wise to seek the assistance of someone in your church with such experience.

When you have identified a grammatical detail you want to investigate, such as a difference in translations that goes beyond word meaning, you will first need to identify the grammatical construction that is responsible for the difference. If you have your first year of Greek or Hebrew under your belt, the best way to do this is to attempt to translate the passage for yourself and identify where the difficulty lies. Alternatively, you may find a discussion of details of grammar in a commentary or study Bible and use this as your starting point for a study. Whether you use a secondary resource or your own

---

[22] Fee's *New Testament Exegesis*, Stuart's *Old Testament Exegesis*, and Köstenberger's *Going Deeper* go to a bit more depth than I have, but I have intentionally diverged from them on minor points. This accords with the greater argument of this book. Carson's *Exegetical Fallacies* chapter 1 provides greater insight into the technical details behind word studies and will help the exegete avoid common errors.

study of the text, a grammar study begins with identifying the particular grammatical feature involved.

In the cases cited above, the differences in Habakkuk 3:3 will not be resolved by grammar alone, for the verbal form used could indicate either tense depending on the context. In Joshua 1:8, a study of the function of לְמַעַן in different clauses will need to be studied. In Galatians, the general relationship between a head noun and a genitive noun will need to be studied, and particularly those instances where the head noun is verbal noun (where it has a corresponding verb; πίστις [*pistis*], faith, is related to πιστεύω [*pisteuō*], to believe) and the genitive is a personal noun (a pronoun or name). When you study a specific word that has a syntactical function (to indicate different clauses), you can use both grammars and lexicons to do your study. You will want to look up the specific word and identify how it is broadly used. When it comes to conjunctions or prepositions, a lexicon and grammar will tell you what the marker means when used with specific grammatical forms. For example, for לְמַעַן (*lᵉmaʿan*), *William's Hebrew Syntax* tells us that it could be used with a personal noun to indicate "for the advantage of"; it could be used with an object to indicate cause, "because of"; with an infinitive construct or an imperfect verb, it could indicate purpose, "in order to"; and it could be used for result, often with an infinite construct, "so that."[23] The Dictionary of Classical Hebrew (DCH) only tells us that it could mean "in order that" or "so that" with an infinitive construct or imperfect verb.

In the case of Galatians 3:16, Bible software or a Greek Bible will show that the phrase "the faithfulness of Christ" or "faith in Christ" are translating πιστεώς Χριστοῦ (*pisteōs Christou*). This is a verbal noun, πίστις (faith or faithfulness) with a personal noun Χριστός (Christ) in the Greek genitive case. The NET and the ESV disagree on how the genitive Χριστοῦ should be related to the head noun πιστεώς. Looking up the genitive case in a reference grammar like Wallace's *Greek Grammar Beyond the Basics* or in *Going Deeper* will reveal all the different ways that a genitive could function with a noun. Several of these, namely the subjective and objective genitive, only occur when a genitive noun is connected to a verbal head noun, as in this case. Knowing that Christ is a proper name (i.e. a personal noun), we can see

---

[23] Ronald J. Williams and John C. Beckman, *Williams' Hebrew Syntax*, 3rd ed. (Toronto: University of Toronto Press, 2007), 134–135.

if a grammar gives specific details on how a personal genitive is used with a verbal noun. Bible software actually enables us to search for the specific combination of a verbal noun with a personal genitive, yielding the different ways that this construction could be used. As in a word study, such a grammatical study of a phrase, such as πιστεώς Χριστοῦ, or a clause marker, such as לְמַעַן in Joshua 1:8, will yield a range of possible functions a phrase or clausal marker could have.

At this stage, you will have a list of possible functions the specific grammatical combination or clause you are studying could have, much like a word study yields a range of meanings a word could have. The next step is to identify the particular function the grammatical feature you are studying has in context. In Habakkuk 3:3, I have come to the conclusion that the imperfect verbs used throughout the chapter are best translated as English present tense verbs, for they set the reader immanent events before the eyes of. That is, though the events are properly future (describing the coming Chaldean invasion), the song is intended to relate the events immediately as the object of reflection.

In Joshua 1:8, I have followed the ESV in rendering the לְמַעַן clause as a result clause, "so that you may be careful to act according to all that is written in it." Though *William's* does not explicitly say that result clauses are found with imperfect verbs, this is evident from the uses of the combination (consider DCH's list) and is implicit in his statement that result clauses are "often" found with the infinitive construct—not exclusively. Context leads to the conclusion that result is intended, not purpose. However, our study also reveals that there is a more subtle interpretive choice being made in this translation; English forces us to choose whether we think the result is cause-effect, "so that you *will* be careful to act," or an action that is made possible, "so that you *may* be careful to act." The latter seems more likely in light of the passage in general and the biblical teaching about the necessity of human effort in right action (e.g. Phil 2:12-13).

Concerning Galatians 3:16, your study may reveal that both the NET and ESV provide acceptable translations in terms of conventional grammar and the meaning of the terms. The ESV's "faith in Christ" understands Χριστοῦ (*Christou*) to be an objective genitive, providing the object of a verbal noun. The NET's "faithfulness of Christ" understands Χριστοῦ to be a subjective genitive, that Christ is the one who acts with faithfulness. There are examples throughout the New Testament of both objective and subjective genitives, and both are found with personal nouns. In fact, there are more subjective genitives that occur with personal nouns. However, because both combinations are possible, we must turn to context to decide which reading is better. Much has been written on this question, but I am convinced that the traditional Reformed reading—that it is an objective genitive ("faith in Christ")—makes the best sense of the various uses of the phrase. Namely, I would argue that "faithfulness" is never used in the Old or New Testament for covenant obedience or status, as it must be interpreted if it is a subjective genitive, but it is used for loyalty or faithfulness directed towards another party. Among many reasons, this is why I would say that "faith in Christ" is the best translation of this phrase.[24]

In this chapter we have considered the importance of biblical languages and considered two significant ways that the biblical languages are employed in Bible Study. This supplements the discussion of translation and text criticism in previous chapters. Overall, we have seen that the knowledge of the biblical languages is invaluable and essential to the healthy use of Scripture within the Church. However, we have also seen that those who do not have the time or ability to learn Hebrew, Aramaic, and Greek can have confidence in their Bible translations and make some use of the languages in their studies. God has provided us with those gifted in the languages in order that the rest of us can profit and have confidence in our access to God's Word, but those of us who are able must pursue the languages for the benefit of our own study and the rest of the Church. At the end of the day, however much or little we use the languages in our study, a good rule to remember is this: "the pastor's study of the Greek text should be like undergarments—providing support but not publicly visible."[25]

---

[24] So Moo, *The Epistle to the Romans*; Douglas J. Moo, *Galatians*, Baker Exegetical Commentary on the New Testament (Grand Rapids: Baker Academic, 2013); Schreiner, *Romans*; Thomas R. Schreiner, "Galatians," ed. Clinton E. Arnold, Zondervan Exegetical Commentary on the New Testament 9 (Grand Rapids, MI: Zondervan, 2010). Though many academic commentaries and journal articles argue the opposite point.

[25] Köstenberger, Merkle, and Plummer, *Going Deeper*, 477.

Further Reading

D. A. Carson – *Exegetical Fallacies* (I)
John Piper – *Brothers, We Are Not Professionals* (pgs. 98-105) (B)
Vern Poythress – *In the Beginning Was the Word: A God-Centered Approach* (I-A)
Moises Silva - *Biblical Words and Their Meaning* (I)

Using the Languages

Lee M. Fields – *Hebrew for the Rest of Us* (B)
William D. Mounce – *Greek for the Rest of Us* (B)
Logos Bible Software
Accordance Bible Software
Daniel B. Wallace – *Greek Grammar: Beyond the Basics* (I-A)
Ronald J. Williams & John C. Beckman – *William's Hebrew Syntax* 3rd Edition (I)
Bruce K. Waltke and M. O'Connor – *An Introduction to Biblical Hebrew Syntax* (I-A)

Reading the Languages

Gary D. Pratico and Miles V. Van Pelt – *Basics of Biblical Hebrew* (B)
Andreas J. Köstenberger, Benjamin L. Merkle, and Robert L. Plummer – *Going Deeper with New Testament Greek* (I)
Mile V. Van Pelt – *Basics of Biblical Aramaic* (I)
William D. Mounce – *Basics of Biblical Greek* (B)

Reader's Bibles[26]

German Bible Society - *Biblia Hebraica Stuttgartensia: A Reader's Edition* (I)
German Bible Society - *UBS Greek New Testament: Reader's Edition* (I)

---

[26] A reader's Bible assumes a first-year knowledge of the relevant language. It aids the reader by providing footnotes explaining relatively rare vocabulary (beyond what you would learn in a first-year class) and parsing difficult or rare verbs. Because it facilitates the first-year student getting into the Bible and beginning to read, these may be the most helpful tool for learning to read and for acquiring and retaining vocabulary. See my review of these bibles on Teleioteti.ca, https://teleioteti.ca/2019/05/20/a-review-of-hebrew-and-greek-readers-bibles/.

Richard J. Goodrich and Albert L. Lukaszewski – *A Reader's Greek and Hebrew Bible* – 2nd Edition (I)

Dirk Jongkind, ed. – *The Greek New Testament: Reader's Edition*, Produced at Tyndale House, Cambridge (I)

Web Resources

Biblicaltraining.org
Concordia Seminary - offers video lectures on Hebrew and Greek through iTunes.

10

KNOWING TOOLS FOR READING BETTER

> Now a Jew named Apollos, a native of Alexandria, came to Ephesus. He was an eloquent man, competent in the Scriptures. He had been instructed in the way of the Lord. And being fervent in spirit, he spoke and taught accurately the things concerning Jesus, though he knew only the baptism of John. He began to speak boldly in the synagogue, but when Priscilla and Aquila heard him, they took him aside and explained to him the way of God more accurately. – Acts 18:24-26

With the last chapter, we have concluded our discussion of the practice of exegesis, how we go about studying the Bible. What we have yet to consider are the various resources that will aid us in our study. I have recommended books that are similar to this one, which discuss the theory and practice of exegesis or reading the Bible, but I have yet to talk about the resources that will help us when we look at specific texts. There is a wealth of information available online in this regard; in fact, some print resources traditionally used have been replaced by the various free computer-based resources we have talked about. There remain some tools that you will need to purchase or find access to if you want to wrestle deeply with the biblical text and its interpretation.

A chapter like this could be lengthened without end, but I want to restrict our discussion to several of the resources that I believe will be most helpful for our studies. I want us to consider, first, the tools for understanding specific biblical books and texts; these are broad introductions to the Bible and its books, Bible dictionaries, and commentaries that offer close insight into texts. Then, we will consider some resources for reading the Bible as a whole, several helpful volumes on biblical Theology. Lastly, we will consider the primary tools for using the languages, namely Lexicons and Bible software. My goal in this chapter is to familiarize you with significant resources to be aware of and to introduce broader types of Bible study tools that are available and their purpose.

A. Tools for Understanding Biblical Books and Passages

It is impossible for any of us to attain an exhaustive understanding of the Bible—it is just too big! It would be years of work, starting from scratch, to outline the thought of and explain the broad contours of any individual biblical book. But if we need to know the context of a passage to understand it, we cannot dispense with this step; we cannot avoid our need to come to an understanding of whole books of the Bible. However, we do not have to do this alone. Christians have been studying the Bible since it was first penned, and they have passed on the fruit of their labours for generations to follow. The result of almost 2000 years of study is a body of resources to help us come to an understanding of the Bible. This can be a daunting thought at first, yet 2000 years of study—at its best—has not produced anything that is not already to be found in the text. We, therefore, do not *need* to wrestle with the history of Christian interpretation to understand a biblical text, but we have the blessing of looking to this wealth of insight for wisdom when we are struggling.

On the other hand, every generation faces its own challenges and it needs to confront its own presuppositions, so turning to secondary resources (resources that help us understand the Bible) can provide its own challenge. Sometimes these resources will spend pages expounding an issue that has no relevance to the needs of our churches and society today; other resources will spend pages lost in details that are ultimately useless for understanding the text before us. I will offer some advice in the following chapter for navigating these challenges and have written a companion volume to this book, *The Gift of Reading – Part 2*, that will examine the hermeneutical assumptions, or beliefs about interpreting the Bible, that produce much error (or at least distraction) in Bible study resources.

My advice when using these tools is as follows; the needs of God's people change throughout the ages, but the text stays the same, so insights into the text itself are timeless, but sometimes particular applications are unnecessary for us and our churches. Furthermore, because we are concerned with how the text is speaking to us and to our churches, do not get caught up in academic discussions about source material and ancient situations that are not mentioned in the text (more on this in the following chapter, in the first part of this book, and the companion volume). Lastly, there are many insights that are historically interesting and may very well be true, but they do not help us see the text and its meaning, so do not trouble yourself with them.

a. Introductions to the Bible

Generally, an "Introduction" or "Synopsis" provides an overview of the content and academic discussion around a book of the Bible. Usually, an introduction of this sort will deal with either the Old or New Testament, but there are interpretive handbooks or introductions that address a specific body of biblical writing, such as the Pentateuch, Gospels, or Pauline letters. Introductions are good for giving you an overview of a book and providing key interpretive details for making sense of its parts. When it comes to an introduction, not all are of the same quality, nor do all have the same purpose. There are introductions from all over the theological spectrum, including from non-Christians and atheists, and there are more or less popular treatments as well as academic ones.

Generally, there are theological, historical (or "special"), and critical introductions to the Bible. The two former types are often Evangelical, while the latter is not. I do not find much use for critical introductions to the Bible: they tend to focus on purely academic issues, often with an explicitly non-Christian perspective. Of the other two types, both have their place. Theological introductions focus on the major themes, literary forms, and theological contributions of biblical books. Historical introductions are the most common; they focus on the traditional question of Evangelical Historical-Grammatical Exegesis; who is the author? who and where is he writing to? where did he write from? what is the date of the letter? what sources did he employ? and what was his purpose? I have suggested—and will argue at length in *Part 2*—that much of this data is unnecessary for interpreting the Bible. Often these details distract us from what the Bible is actually saying. Nevertheless, these volumes regularly yield helpful insights into the structure of biblical books and their purpose. There are also more general introductions that cover theological, historical, and sometimes even critical perspectives. Here are several biblical introductions I have found useful in my own studies:

i. General

Bill T. Arnold, Bryan E. Beyer — *Encountering the Old Testament*

Walter A. Elwell & Robert W. Yarbrough — *Encountering the New Testament*

ii. Historical

Tremper Longman III & Raymond B. Dillard — *An Introduction to the Old Testament*

D. A. Carson & Douglas J. Moo — *An Introduction to the New Testament*

iii. Theological

J. Ligon Duncan and Richard Belcher — *A Biblical-Theological Introduction to the Old Testament*

J. Ligon Duncan and William B. Barcley — *A Biblical-Theological Introduction to the New Testament*

b. Bible Dictionaries

Sometimes there is a particular theme you may want to explore, or you may have a more general question about a concept that appears in your studies. For example, you may want to more about "apostles" beyond just the meaning of the word, which is what a word study reveals. Or you may want to know more about parables, what crucifixion was like beyond what the Bible tells us, what the Bible tells us about the fall of Babylon, or you may want to have an outline of the history of Israel as recounted in the Bible. Such questions can often be answered by looking up articles in a good Bible dictionary.

A Bible dictionary is an example of a tertiary source in academic studies: it does not teach something new or present an interpretation of a primary source. Instead, it offers a summary of the more detailed studies that are available. They are most helpful for finding a bibliography for more in-depth study but will often suffice for our Bible study purposes. There are several single-volume Bible dictionaries that are readily available, but for the most part, they are not very helpful. The Lexham Bible Dictionary that comes with most Logos packages is somewhat helpful, but the most helpful Bible Dictionaries are devoted to specific areas of biblical studies or specific sections of the Bible. The IVP Bible Dictionary set is a particularly helpful resource for Bible questions, but it is expensive and on the academic side of things.

c. Commentaries

Commentaries can be the most helpful and most confusing or distracting tools at our disposal. The good use of a commentary can sharpen our exegesis and application, but the bad use can lead us far away from the text. A commentary is concerned with providing an interpretation of a text, so there are as many commentaries as there are interpretations and interpretive approaches to the Bible. Now, there is something to be learned from any commentary, but many of them are written by authors who do not accept a basic Evangelical bibliology as necessary for interpreting it (see part one of this book). So, though there may be value in wrestling through a classic liberal commentary, your time would be best invested in Evangelical commentaries written by authors who are committed to the Bible as it presents itself.

There are many commentaries that fall into this category. As you engage in biblical study, it is a good idea to keep track of good commentary series and good commentators, those that most often answer the questions you are asking. Even the best series has volumes that miss the mark, and many great authors write in otherwise mediocre series, so it is important to pay attention to both series and the authors who write within them.

Commentaries generally come in several different types. First, there are technical, semi-technical, and popular level commentaries. Technical commentaries are concerned with wrestling through the academic questions of biblical studies and focus on the original language texts. Semi-technical commentaries are based on the original languages and offer comments on them but do so in a way that is accessible to those without language training. Popular level commentaries focus on helping the untrained Christian reader understand the Bible.

Second, we can identify three broad categories of commentaries among these. Most technical and semi-technical commentaries offer a verse-by-verse analysis of the text, sometimes accompanied by a unique translation of the text. Most popular commentaries and some semi-technical ones offer a unit-by-unit, or paragraph-by-paragraph, summary of the meaning of the text. Lastly, some commentaries focus on application, with or without verse by verse and unit-by-unit comment. The most helpful commentaries combine all these approaches in one. Whatever approach a commentary takes, it will often begin with a lengthy introduction to the book in question, providing the same type of information as a more general Bible introduction but to a greater depth. The following are some of my suggestions for helpful technical, semi-technical, and popular Bible commentaries. I am focusing on series, but as I observed above, the individual authors of commentaries are more determinative of quality than the series. It should also be noted that there are some single-volume Bible commentaries, but I have not found these of much use in my study.

i. Popular

The two best popular-level Bible commentary series I have found useful are the Tyndale Bible Commentaries and The Bible Speaks Today. The Tyndale Bible Commentaries come from various theological spectrums, though all generally Evangelical, and features some outstanding biblical scholars among its authors. The usefulness of each volume varies, some being so focused on historical matters that they do not really give any insights into the text. But overall, this is a helpful verse-by-verse series that is accessible to the interested reader. The primary use of this volume will be in understanding the specific meanings of words, grammatical constructions, and wrestling with significant text-critical issues. It offers some theological reflection, but not as much as the following series.

The Bible Speaks Today series focuses more on theology and units of thought than the Tyndale commentaries, making it better for understanding the meaning and application of a text than the Tyndale series. This series also features many outstanding biblical scholars and theologians, so it offers many insights.

ii. Semi-Technical

In my estimation, some of the best commentaries available today fall into this general audience, addressing students, pastors, and scholars. These commentaries assume a bit more understanding than popular level commentaries, but if you have made it this far in this book, they should prove to be no problem for you. I particularly recommend many of the volumes in the New International Commentary on the New Testament (NICNT) and Old Testament Series (NICOT), the Zondervan Exegetical Commentaries (ZEC) series, and the Baker Exegetical Commentaries on the New Testament (ECNT). Though it was discontinued before it was finished, many of the volumes in the Wycliffe Exegetical Commentary Series are also great. The Expositor's Bible Commentary is an affordable yet helpful option as well.

Each of these will comment on the original languages, text-critical issues, and interact with the theological implications of the text. The Zondervan Exegetical Commentary has an explicit section devoted to application—addressing the contemporary relevance of the text—but the NICOT and ECNT will also draw explicit attention to the way the text speaks to our contemporary culture.

iii. Technical

As far as Technical commentaries go, I do not have many to recommend. For the New Testament, I have found the New International Greek Testament Commentary (NIGTC) a reliable guide for understanding the technical intricacies of the New Testament. This series also pays attention to the theological implications of the text, so it is quite helpful across the board. I have yet to find an equivalent series for the Old Testament. On a purely linguistic basis, Baylor University's series "Handbooks on the Greek/Hebrew Text" is very helpful. Unfortunately, this series will not deal with the broader meaning and application of the text.

For text criticism, the Biblia Hebraica Quinta series (which is not yet finished) provides a thorough commentary on text-critical issues in each volume, however it is coming from broadly atheistic presuppositions (the editors are from various theological and religious backgrounds). On the New Testament, the United Bible Society's *Textual Commentary on the Greek Text* is helpful, though the UBS committee and author Bruce M. Metzger are not working from the same presuppositions concerning Scripture as I have argued for in this and other books.

B. Tools for Grasping the Unity of Scripture

I argued in the first part of this book that reading the Bible is a whole Bible endeavour; we need to understand the story and content of the whole Bible to understand its parts. I also argued that understanding how the Bible interprets itself is essential to read it well. The commentaries and introductions discussed above will do this to some extent, especially the *Biblical-Theological Introduction to the New Testament* and *to the Old Testament*. However, there will be many times when you may want a more in-depth treatment of the New Testament's use of the Old or of the metanarrative recounted in and unifying themes of Scripture. There are many significant works in this department, but I will draw attention to only a few.

The book I have found most helpful for grasping the big picture of Scripture may be Peter J. Gentry and Stephen J. Wellum's *Kingdom through Covenant*. This is a technical volume that is available in a more popular form as *God's Kingdom through God's Covenants*. The work of Graeme Goldsworthy is also quite insightful, specifically his books *According to Plan* and *The Goldsworthy Trilogy*. Regarding the Old Testament, the book *Dominion and Dynasty* by Stephen G. Dempster is a helpful overview of significant themes in the Old Testament. The series of which it is apart, *New Studies in Biblical Theology*, is very helpful but quite academic. *An Old Testament Theology* by Bruce Waltke is also helpful, especially its discussion of the Old Testament cultus (pattern of religious ritual) established in the Pentateuch. Regarding the New Testament, G.K. Beale and Thomas Schreiner have great New Testament biblical theologies that are worth consulting. Many of their insights have made their way into this and other books I have written, but these volumes will reward careful study.

All the books cited above deal with the use of the New Testament in the Old to some extent. However, for a more detailed study, G.K. Beale's *Handbook on the New Testament Use of the Old Testament: Exegesis and Interpretation*, is particularly valuable. In addition, the *Commentary on the New Testament use of the Old Testament* edited by G.K. Beale and D. A. Carson is a treasure trove of insight.

This area, understanding how the Bible is put together and how the New Testament uses the Old Testament, is an area of particular interest for me as a New Testament believer academically trained in the Old Testament. I have benefitted greatly from each of the above works but have struck a slightly different path in the introduction to this book and in my work on Habakkuk, namely my *Believe the Unbelievable: A Study in Habakkuk* and my commentary *The Book of Habakkuk: An Exegetical-Theological Commentary on the Hebrew Text*. I would suggest using the general approach I have offered and using these resources for in depth study on specific themes and issues that I have not had space to unpack in these pages. In the coming years, as the Lord wills, I hope to write another part to this series dealing with the Bible itself. The first volume, a theology of the Bible, and the second, an introduction to the Bible, will take the general approach and argument of the first part of this book and expand them across book-length treatments.

C. Tools for Original Language Study

The last set of tools we will discuss in this chapter are those that aid us in language study. In the previous chapter, I suggested some grammars that will suffice for studying the grammar and syntax of Hebrew for most readers. I also introduced several online resources that will help with basic language study. In this part, I want to outline the significant lexicons (i.e. original language dictionaries) that will be essential for doing word studies or reading the Bible in these languages. I also want to consider the two major bible software programs.[1]

a. Lexicons

When doing a word study or translating, the most useful tool may be a good lexicon. The key word here is "good." There are lots of lexicons available, but not all of them are of equal quality. As a rule of thumb, do not use a concordance-based lexicon, such as a *Strong's* lexicon. These do not tell you what a word means; they only give the range of translation glosses given by

---

[1] There are several free Bible programs available. I do not have much experience with these, yet I assume you will get what you paid for. They will usually have open-source resources; these are not the best quality and are usually open source for a reason (usually outdated). It may also be the case that these programs will not have the highest standards of proof checking (a problem found even in purchased Bible software). Other software is community based and has many pirated resources.

a particular English translation.² What you want is lexicon that will provide you translational glosses (single word or phrase equivalents for the original language word) accompanied by a definition, an explanation of what it means. The major scholarly lexicons for Greek and Hebrew (usually including Aramaic) will provide a combination of gloss and definitions, along with a sample of uses.

When studying Greek, the major lexicons to use are *A Greek-English Lexicon Of the New Testament and Other Early Christian Literature* (BDAG) and *Greek-English Lexicon of the New Testament* by Louw and Nida (L&N or simply Louw and Nida). The latter is organized according to meaning, so it will require an index; the former is the most extensive biblical Greek lexicon and is organized alphabetically. There are two other lexicons to be aware of. Sometimes free software will come with an older Greek lexicon known as Thayer's. It may be of some use, but it is rather outdated and should not be relied upon. You will also find many references to the massive volume produced by Liddell and Scott (LSJ). Liddell and Scott's *A Greek-English Lexicon* covers ancient Greek up to and beyond the New Testament. It is of some help yet is outdated like Thayer's. Furthermore, it provides mostly glosses, not definitions, and is too broad in its scope to be of immediate value for our purposes. That is, LSJ has many uses for scholars and academics but should not be depended on for a basic word study; our focus should be on the language of the New Testament—which is an example of the Koine Greek dialect. Another lexicon to be aware of is the *New International Dictionary of New Testament Theology and Exegesis*, edited by Moises Silva. This is a helpful reference work that presents extensive word studies on key Greek terms.³

When studying Hebrew, the major lexicons to use are the *Hebrew and Aramaic Lexicon of the Old Testament* (HALOT) and the *Dictionary of Classical Hebrew* (DCH). These are the scholarly standards, yet the older work known as the Brown, Driver, and Brigg's Lexicon (BDB) is still helpful, though it

---

[2] A gloss is a single word equivalent for an original language word. For example, "faith" is often offered as the translation of πίστις (*pistis*). A definition will explain what the word actually means and which sense of an English equivalent is relevant.

[3] The older *Theological Dictionary of the New Testament* should be avoided unless you have familiarized yourself with word studies and have digested Carson's *Exegetical Fallacies*. This volume comes from a broadly liberal theological background and is riddled with lexical fallacies.

should be employed in conjunction with the former works. HALOT and DCH are both organized alphabetically; BDB is organized instead by root words, so the beginning student of Hebrew will need to use an index or software version to find a word. HALOT contains an Aramaic dictionary, but DCH does not. HALOT has been the scholarly standard for many years; the price of DCH hinders it from overtaking HALOT in this regard. All three of these lexicons come from a critical background of Hebrew scholarship, so discernment is necessary when using each of them. They will often point to emendations of the text that should not be followed without a text-critical basis, for which you will need to consult the BHS or BHQ apparatus—both of which also offer emendations of the text.[4] DCH is also a dictionary for all classic Hebrew literature, including the Dead Sea Scrolls and the Hebrew inscriptions. When using DCH, look for the way the language is used by the biblical authors more than its use among the extra-biblical sources.[5] I should also mention that DCH and HALOT both have concise abridgments available: Holladay's short Hebrew lexicon is based on HALOT, and the *Concise Dictionary of Classical Hebrew* is based on DCH. These are helpful tools and are far cheaper, yet they do not contain the extensive treatment of biblical usage found in the larger works.

When using any lexicon, use discernment. The authors are governed by philosophical presuppositions concerning language and by theological presuppositions in their work. Always compare what you read in a lexicon with what you find in a text. Especially in word studies, use the lexicons to supplement and check your work but do not rely on them alone. I have mentioned some of the presuppositions behind the major lexicons in this and previous sections, but take the time to read the prefaces of these lexicons to learn about their methodology and research the authors a bit: this will give you an idea of where the lexicon is coming from and potentially why it comes

---

[4] An emendation refers to an intentional correction of the consonantal text of the Hebrew Bible, usually done in an effort to "make sense" of the text.

[5] In a paper on Job 30, I present several reasons against accepting these scholarly emendations and also why the Hebrew language of the Bible should be given priority over extra-Biblical Hebrew and Semitic texts. Some of this has made its way into *The Gift of Reading – Part* 2. Cf. J. Alexander Rutherford, "Lament of the Afflicted: A Translation of Job 30" (Teleioteti, 2017), accessed January 8, 2018, https://teleioteti.ca/2017/12/15/the-lament-of-the-afflicted-a-translation-of-job-30/.

to different conclusions than another.

b. Bible Software

The last resources we will consider in this chapter are paid Bible software, specifically Accordance and Logos. Both have pros and cons; you cannot really go wrong with either. Both programs contain an extensive suite of language study tools; this is probably what they are most useful for. Until recently, Accordance and the now discontinued Bible Works were the scholarly standards, yet Logos is growing in its reputation for quality. In my experience, both programs contain more errors than the print edition of study resources, so beware of the potential for such errors. Both Logos and Accordance provide competitive pricing for language study resources, such as grammar and lexicons, when compared to the print editions. You will not save a ton of money if you want to get the best lexicons, for example, yet the digital format makes their use far more practical. Accordance continues to have a strong scholarly reputation and contains powerful language study resources, yet it is less intuitive than Logos.

Both programs have a large selection of resources for purchase; Logos is, from my experience, more feature-driven than Accordance. That is, with Logos, there is a new edition with a new study feature available every year or so. The presence of so many features means that Logos has a steep learning curve if you want to make use of its full potential.

In my opinion, Logos' feature-driven focus is one of its greatest weaknesses. Every few years, Logos releases a new edition of its software, featuring several new books and features. To access these new features, you usually are required to spend another $100 to $200 dollars for the minimum base package required to use these features. This means that in addition to whatever package you originally bought (mine cost me about $1200) you are required to spend an additional $100-200 every few years to take advantage of the new features Logos continually releases. This can quickly make Logos an expensive option. Another thing to note with Logos is that the volume of resources given does not necessarily reflect their value (I am not sure how Accordance fairs in this regard). A basic package may give you several hundred resources, yet many of them are not high quality or are open source. That is, they may not be very helpful, and if they are helpful, they may be accessible for free elsewhere. For this reason, when weighing a package to buy, see if it contains the resources you need and will use and consider if it is worth it just for those resources; you may never use the rest.

Another consideration to make before investing in an expensive Bible software program is the stability of the medium. That is, computers have only emerged in the last 50 or so years and have seen a tremendous amount of change since they first appeared. What was cutting edge in the 90s appears ridiculous today. If computers as we know them today go the way of the floppy disk, it is legitimate to ask if the software we invest in now will remain usable in 10 or 20 years. Also, if either company goes out of business, there is the danger that their product will no longer be supported as technology develops. For this reason, investing several hundred dollars now in Bible software may entail greater costs in the long run.

That said, both Accordance and Logos can make Bible study quicker and easier. They are not essential for studying the Bible but are a great resource to make life a little easier.

Further Reading

G. K. Beale – *Handbook on the New Testament use of the Old Testament: Exegesis and Interpretation* (I)

D. A. Carson – *New Testament Commentary Survey* (B)

Gordon D. Fee & Douglas Stuart – *How to Read the Bible for All its Worth* (B)

Gordon D. Fee – *New Testament Exegesis, 3rd Edition* (I)

Tremper Longman III – *Old Testament Commentary Survey* (B)

Thomas R. Schreiner – *Interpreting the Pauline Epistles* (B – I)

Douglas Stuart – *Old Testament Exegesis, 4th Edition* (I)

11

EVALUATING EXEGESIS AND APPLICATION

> Do your best to present yourself to God as one approved, a worker who has no need to be ashamed, rightly handling the word of truth. – 2 Timothy 2:15

If we are to read the Bible and respond as God would have us, we need ears to hear. We need to be attentive and know how to discern his voice, how to interpret the Word he gives us. In these last six chapters, we have considered the practical side of studying the Bible, how we may pay close attention to hear it well. In chapter 5, we looked at the purpose of reading the Bible (what we are aiming for in our reading) and how we recognize that we have achieved this goal. Essentially, we listen to God's word so we may know him and submit to him. To do this, we need to understand what the text means and how we are to respond to it. We looked at three different criteria by which we can identify if an application is justified or not. To conclude this second part of the book, I want to revisit these three criteria. In our labour to understand the Bible, we encounter varying interpretations of biblical texts. For this reason, we need to have an idea of how to evaluate the interpretations of the commentaries and resources we use and to check our own interpretations at the end of our study. Applying what we have already seen, I want to suggest three ways we can check whether an interpretation is justified or not: we can ask if it is a justified use of the text through the criteria of validity, appropriateness, and fittingness; we can ask if it is justified by asking if it can be argued from the text in its biblical context; and we can ask if it involves a misuse of extra-biblical background material.

A. Is It Valid, Appropriate, and Fitting?

Everything we have considered so far in this section has given us tools to evaluate the interpretations of other readers. Pursuing some of the resources I suggested, such as D.A. Carson's *Exegetical Fallacies*, will equip us further to identify methodological mistakes we and others might make. In addition, the criteria of *validity*, *appropriateness*, and *fittingness* provide a good way to analyse other interpretations. We ask, does the interpretation correspond to the words and grammar of the text (validity)? Does it fit the tone or intent of the text, not twisting the purpose of a text (appropriateness)? Does the interpretation fit with the referents of the text, identifying not only the appropriate historical entity involved but also the audience to which statements and commands are directed (fittingness)?

Regarding fittingness, we must be diligent in asking if the appropriate audience has been understood, especially when reading the Old Testaments and narrative texts—in which characters speak to audiences that do not always include the reader. In addition to these questions, I think the most important question to ask of ourselves and the work of others is, "If they listened well, would other interpreters hear what I think the text is saying?"

B. Can It Be Argued from the Text?

If the text of Scripture is the standard by which our interpretations are considered right or wrong, then it is a standard available to each reader. Assuming they have the same presuppositions concerning the nature of Scripture and its Author—that we are reading within the same worldview—would another interpreter see what I am seeing? Asking this question will often reveal to us where we have entered speculation. We should be able to explain why our interpretation of Scripture is correct from the text before us, including reference to the rest of Scripture. If we base our interpretation on the meaning of a word, we should be able to appeal to other places in Scripture that show how it means that—whether by example (other uses) or analogy (uses of related words or the same grammatical construction). So, ask yourself if you could show someone else what you think the text means. Not being able to do so does not necessarily mean your interpretation is wrong, but it should force us to evaluate why we think it means this.

When it comes to commentaries and related resources, they have the burden to show us that what they say is what the text means. Sometimes the meaning of the text is obvious to both you and the resource you are reading, so you find their application of the text convincing. However, if they claim it says something that you do not see in the text, look for the reasons they provide. Why do they think it says this? If they do not point you back to the text, if they do not show you how the text means what they say it does, there is no reason to accept their interpretation.

The area where this disconnect appears most often, where the interpretation does not seem evident from the text, is in appeals to extra-biblical material.[1]

C. Does It Illegitimately Appeal to Extra-Biblical Data?

This is ultimately an application of the last question we asked: if a valid interpretation is one that can be argued from the text as read in the biblical context, then extra-biblical data (i.e. archaeological data, extra-biblical Greek and Hebrew texts, historical records, etc.) can only serve a supporting role. Ultimately, such data can help us illustrate the text in our preaching, it can reveal things in the text that we did not notice before, and it can give supporting evidence for an interpretation of the text. That historical data can serve no greater role than this is implicit throughout the argument of this book. However, because appeals to extra-biblical data play a central role in both Evangelical and non-Christian approaches to biblical exegesis, I will address this issue to a greater extent in *The Gift of Reading – Part 2*. To conclude this chapter and so the second part of this book, I want to argue very briefly for this point and then explain what I see as the three legitimate uses of extra-biblical data.

I think my point about extra-biblical data can be made by thinking about the implications of rejecting it. I am claiming that "when a historical parallel is used to explain a text, the evidence necessary to establish a link between a piece of extra-biblical data and the text needs to be sufficient to make the point independently."[2] That is, to legitimately use extra-biblical data, you

---

[1] What follows is adapted from my article, The Problem of Extra-Biblical Data. https://teleioteti.ca/2018/08/15/the-problem-of-extra-biblical-data/. I expand upon this in *The Gift of Reading – Part 2*, in which I consider alternate approaches to reading the Bible.

[2] ibid.

must first show that it is relevant to the text you are interpreting. You can only do this if the text already says what you want to say with your extra-biblical data. Rejecting this claim leads to some destructive conclusions.

First, a rejection of this claim accepts that extra-biblical data can make the text mean something it does not say. Among conservative Evangelicals, this is called *eisegesis*, reading a meaning into the text that is not there in the first place. This also implicitly rejects the clarity of Scripture and sufficiency, as argued for in the first part of this book.

Second, the most significant implication of this is that extra-biblical data is necessary to interpret the biblical text. This would not have been a problem for some of the original readers of the texts, yet we cannot guarantee that every reader would have had access to all the necessary data. Furthermore, we cannot guarantee that 1st century Christians had the necessary data to interpret the Old Testament, the first parts of which were written over 1400 years before them. Lastly, much of the data used in scholarly literature to explain the biblical text is from recent archaeological discoveries, discoveries that were not available to the majority of the church over the last 2000 years. If this data is *necessary* for reading the Scriptures, and it was not available to the Christians for whom the Bible was intended to guide, then Scripture would be unable to function in its God-ordained manner until this data was recovered. I think this is a theologically untenable position.

Third, if an appeal to extra-biblical data produces meaning that is not discernible from a biblical text read within the biblical context, then such an appeal is an instance of a fallacy sometimes called "illegitimate totality transfer." That is, all words have a range of meaning; they do not mean only one thing but can mean many things depending on the context. However, as we discussed earlier in Chapter 9, words mean only one thing from this range of meanings when they are used. It is, therefore, a fallacy to bring this whole range of meanings into a context. Similarly, phrases and ideas could have many different functions, but they have a specific function in their context. We cannot, then, read into a text all the possible functions or connotations a phrase, idea, or word has in another context; we must ask how the author is using it here (the criteria of validity). This should suffice for our purposes to show why extra-biblical data cannot be used to say more than the text says. If this is the case, we must ask what use can be made of extra-biblical data.

As I mentioned above, I see three general uses of such data that are legitimate. First, it can be used to illustrate our application of a text. I suspect that this is how most people intend to use extra-biblical data. Sometimes the meaning of a text is not fully appreciated, sometimes it is not felt by an audience, until it is brought to life through an illustration or story. Sometimes contemporary events and life experiences, or a little imagination, do the trick. However, using illustrations from the practices and history of the biblical peoples can make a point powerfully. For example, we can use Ancient Near Eastern accounts of sieges to illustrate just what Jeremiah and Habakkuk have in mind when they talk about piling mounds of dirt to take a city. This is helpful. However, we must always make clear that we are using this data to illustrate, not to create meaning. If we do not make this clear, we risk teaching those who hear us that the Bible is a text reserved for the experts with the knowledge of and access to extra-biblical archaeology and data.

Second, extra-biblical data can be used to illuminate the text. Sometimes studying extra-biblical accounts or language helps us see things that were before our eyes the whole time. By way of example, archaeological evidence has helped scholars re-examine the meaning of 1 Samuel 13:21 (compare the KJV and ESV) and conclude that the Hebrew word פִּים (*pîm*) is a monetary unit, not a "file."[3] However, there is nothing in the context to suggest פִּים is intended to indicate that the Hebrews were being ripped off by the Philistines, an argument made by some commentators. This may very well be the case, but nothing the author says indicates that he meant this.[4]

Third, extra-biblical data can be used to confirm our interpretations. Sometimes we are in a position where we need to argue for one interpretation over another. The final decision and most decisive argument must come from Scripture. However, there is no reason why we cannot make the argument from Scripture and then confirm it by appealing to extra-biblical data that is consistent with our interpretation and not the other.

Hopefully these questions will be of some help in discerning the validity of our own interpretations and the interpretations of others. However, as much as skill and reason is a key aspect of reading our Bibles, it is not the only aspect. No matter how clear our vision and attuned our ears, if our hearts

---

[3] The KJV's "file" is actually their attempt to explain the phrase "the charge was a pim" (my translation).

[4] It could be argued that by using the word "פִּים" he intends this, however this is a circle.

are made of stone, we will not hear God's voice. For this reason, we must now consider the role of the heart in biblical interpretation.

—Part 3—
We Need Hearts to Understand

12

BEGINNING WITH FAITH IN GOD

> And he said, "Go, and say to this people:
>   'Keep on hearing, but do not understand;
>   keep on seeing, but do not perceive.'
> Make the heart of this people dull,
>   and their ears heavy,
>   and blind their eyes;
> lest they see with their eyes,
>   and hear with their ears,
>   and understand with their hearts,
>   and turn and be healed."
> – Isaiah 6:9-10, cf. Matthew 13:10-17

It is a common misunderstanding that the preaching of God's Word and the reading of God's Word has one function, to bring us to faith and lead us in obedience to God (Matt 28:18-20, Rom 1:5). As we have seen, the Bible does do this. It is a covenant document given to lead his people to faith, to give them the knowledge of him, and to lead them in obedience. However, it also has another function.

When God charged Isaiah to preach, it was not to bring salvation; instead, it was to bring judgment. The preaching of God's will would only harden the hearers in their rebellion against him. Instead of turning from their wicked ways, they would double down and sin all the more. This was not only true of Isaiah's ministry. Jesus himself identified the purpose of his parables as hardening the hearts of those who heard them. Jesus speaks in parables because those who heard him already had hard hearts; the preaching of the Word would only seal their judgment (Matt 13:10-17, cf. John 12:36-43). There is, therefore, great danger in coming to the Bible in the wrong way. It may be the means God uses to open our eyes to his glory shining in the face of Jesus Christ (2 Cor 4:6), or it may be the tool he uses to cement our hearts fast in sin. The preaching of the word magnifies the content of the heart; in soil that is tilled and ready, the sowing of the Word yields an abundant crop. In the soil that is shallow and hard, the sowing of the Word leaves the ground worse off than before (Matt 13:1-9, 18-23). Thus, the heart matters when we read the Bible; a right state of heart is essential if we are to read the word rightly. If we are going to read the Bible as God has intended for us to do, then we need to approach it in the right way, with the right heart. We could summarize the biblical posture towards God's Word in this way: beginning with faith in God, we submit ourselves before him to learn with humility. We can divide this into three segments. In this chapter, we will look at "beginning with faith in God," in the next "we submit ourselves before him, and in Chapter 14 "to learn with humility."

We need a right heart to read the Word. Though it is ultimately God through the Spirit that prepares our hearts to receive his word (cf. John 6:44-45), our responsibility is to approach the Word, first, with faith.

Our confession of faith is the result of a changed heart produced by God, of God's Word landing on tilled soil. Our faith lived out is the product of the Spirit at work in us as we labour to persevere in the faith and obey the Lord (Phil 2:12-13). Coming to the Word in faith, believing in God and trusting him for all that he has accomplished in Jesus Christ, is thus the necessary condition of reading the Bible. Without faith, humble dependence on the Lord, we will not read the Word rightly and may find ourselves under the judgment of God.

How does this work, you may be thinking? If our interpretation of Scripture is rooted in the text before our eyes, how is it that the lack of or presence of faith could change the result of our interpretation? In light of what we saw in Chapter 1, I think there are three clear ways a lack of faith blinds us. Without faith, we will not adopt the Bible's own methods for reading it, we will not read the Bible according to what it says about itself, and we will not arrive at the right conclusions because we cannot obey God while in rebellion against him.

We have seen a bit in this book, and I have argued at length in Volume

1 of this series, that no use of our minds (including reading) is a morally neutral act. We approach every task—especially reading and learning—with assumptions about the way the world is, assumptions that determine how we interact with it. To read the Bible rightly—indeed, to do anything rightly—we need a Christian worldview: we need to accept what God says about the creation and act in accord with this. However, if we do not have faith in God, we will not submit to him and learn his ways. This is the fundamental error Paul identifies with the Pagan rejection of the Gospel, "we preach Christ crucified, a stumbling block to Jews and folly to Gentiles, but to those who are called, both Jews and Greeks, Christ is the power of God and the wisdom of God" (1 Cor 1:23-24). He goes on in 1 Corinthians 2, "The natural person does not accept the things of the Spirit of God, for they are folly to him, and he is not able to understand them because they are spiritually discerned" (14). Only by adopting God's perspective on the world, which we do through faith, will we see God's ways as "wisdom" and not "folly." Not only are Christian presuppositions necessary, presuppositions which only come through faith resulting from a changed heart, but we also need to read the Bible as the Bible.

What I mean is this; if we read the Bible as a historical document, as the rants of erring men—i.e. as a fallible document—we will not read it rightly. With these beliefs we may care enough to read the Bible, but we will pick and choose what seems right to us in the Bible.[1] No longer will it be our absolute authority and guide for life in obedience to God; it will only be another sourcebook for us to piece together our own way of life. If we read the Bible primarily as a historical document, we may or may not credit it with authority, depending on the significance of the history it represents, but we will certainly read it according to the canons of modern historical science. Instead of asking what the Bible says about itself and how to read it, we will assume that we should read it like we would any other historical document. This would be to miss its own claims to self-sufficiency, to clarity, and its claims that it is written specifically for the New Covenant people of God throughout the age between Christ's first and second comings. Without faith, we will not approach the Bible as the Word of God, as an authoritative covenant document, as self-attesting, self-sufficient, clear, inerrant, etc. So, without

---

[1] This is evident in the works of classic Liberal scholarship in the 19-20th centuries and in some recent bestsellers, such as Jordan Peterson's *12 Rules for Life*.

faith, we will not approach the Bible with the essential presuppositions to understand it.

Finally, apart from faith, a reader of the Bible has no reason to read it rightly and a great reason to misinterpret it. As Christians, we have every reason to seek to understand what the Bible is saying. We believe that it is the Word of our good God who cares for us, so we know we need to hear what he says. Furthermore, it is the word of our sovereign Lord, our king; we are therefore obligated to obey him and need to know what he is asking of us. It is a serious matter to disobey one who has authority over us, to disobey the ruler of the universe, so it is necessary for us as covenant servants to seek the proper understanding of our Lord's will. We also know that God is present with us, that he knows what we are reading and how we are applying it, so we cannot get away with twisting and distorting his words. To honour him, to love him, to obey him, to serve him, to enjoy him, we need to hear what he is saying.

An unbeliever, on the other hand, has no such reasons. He does not want to obey God, to love him, to serve him, or to enjoy him. Indeed, by suppressing the truth of God in unrighteousness, every unbeliever demonstrates that their fundamental desire is to be their own God and escape the rule of their creator (Rom 1:18-25). This means that they have every reason to avoid a right interpretation of Scripture. They do not want to hear what God desires of them, let alone obey it. Instead, if they give any value to Scripture, it must be as a document that serves their rebellious purposes. So the Bible becomes a record of human insight, man's path, not God's. Or it becomes the fictional accounts of a despicable being that humanity once worshipped. Maybe it is a revelation from a god, but this god is bound by human reason, so every objectionable piece of Scripture must be lopped off. Many unbelievers have learned from reading the Bible and have said true things about it, but these factors will always influence their interpretation.

"Without faith," writes the author of Hebrews, "it is impossible to please him, for whoever would draw near to God must believe that he exists and that he rewards those who seek him" (Heb 11:6). The author of Hebrews has in mind the life of the patriarchs, yet this holds true for all humanity. If someone is said to please God and this requires that they had faith, then it follows that if anyone does not have faith, they cannot please God. Surely reading the Bible, obeying God by listening to his voice and submitting to him to understand it correctly, is pleasing to God. Surely it is pleasing to God to take careful time to discern his voice. Without faith there is no pleasing God, and thus there is no right reading of Scripture. *Beginning with faith in God,* we submit ourselves before him to learn with humility.

13

WE SUBMIT OURSELVES BEFORE HIM

> "Seek the LORD while he may be found;
>   call upon him while he is near;
> let the wicked forsake his way,
>   and the unrighteous man his thoughts;
> let him return to the LORD, that he may have compassion on him,
>   and to our God, for he will abundantly pardon.
> For my thoughts are not your thoughts,
>   neither are your ways my ways, declares the LORD.
> For as the heavens are higher than the earth,
>   so are my ways higher than your ways
>   and my thoughts than your thoughts. – Isaiah 55:6-9

Beginning with faith sets the tone for our reading of Scripture. We start with the assumptions of the Christian Bible, that God exists, that he has spoken, and that he rewards those who seek him—that obedience is worth it. Faith is the foundation, but it takes a specific expression as we live out the Christian life. In Romans 10, Paul describes the fundamental acts taken to become a Christian, to enjoy God's salvation, as "[believing] in your heart that God raised [Jesus] from the dead" and "[confessing] with your mouth that Jesus is Lord" (Rom 10:9). Faith in God's existence and salvific acts manifests in the confession of submission to Jesus Christ as Lord, the covenant king over all creation. A true confession of Jesus as Lord will manifest in a life of submission to this Lord. Similarly, as we read Scripture, a foundation of faith in the God of the Bible will manifest in a way of reading that submits to this

God. Beginning with faith in God, *we submit ourselves before him* to learn with humility.

Among many implications, that the God who authored Scripture is our Lord means that we must trust his judgment over our judgment—concerning right and wrong, true and false—and that we must respond to the commands and rebukes of Scripture. Obedience is not optional for a Christian. To be a Christian is to be someone who follows Christ, and to follow Jesus who is Lord is to submit to and obey Jesus as he has revealed himself.

This obedience is not only manifest in dos and don'ts but also in demands upon our reason and moral sensibilities. Scripture calls us to believe in things other worldviews reject and to accept behaviour that other faiths repudiate. Scripture tells us that God created the heavens and the earth and made them good; thus, to deny the reality of matter or its goodness, or to suggest that it is eternal, is not an option for the Christian. The Bible teaches that God created humanity specially, that he created them from two original humans, and that they are distinct from the animals and other aspects of creation. Indeed, the Bible teaches that God created humanity as the pinnacle of his creation. Therefore, any worldview that rejects these claims—such as the evolutionary explanation of speciation and the creation of man—cannot be held consistently by a Christian.[1] If the Bible teaches that the creation of humanity, and so the rest of creation, is a relatively recent occurrence, then it would be inconsistent for a Christian to hold to contrary claims of a far more distant emergence of humanity and the creation. Philosophically, a Christian cannot believe that there are standards of right and wrong or true and false by which God and humans are both judged, for this would mean that these standards are independent of and higher than God and that humans and God are on equal footing. In each of these cases, if God our Lord—and the Creator and Sovereign who knows something about his creation—tells us something is true or false, we are obligated to obediently accept his Word.[2]

This also applies to our moral sensibilities. We have no right, as covenant servants, to stand in a position of judgment over God and believe that something he declares to be just and good is unrighteous and evil. Now,

---

[1] See the Crossway volume, James Porter Moreland et al., eds., *Theistic Evolution: A Scientific, Philosophical, and Theological Critique* (Wheaton: Crossway, 2017).

[2] On this point and how it is the salvation of reason, Vol. 1.

I am not saying that there are no difficult cases where it is hard to see *why* something is just and good, yet we are obligated nevertheless to accept that they are. This, in fact, gives us great freedom. We can trust that God is good, true, and right even when we do not exactly see how. Our hope is that when we see God in glory, our struggles with Hell, with the conquest of Canaan, with the imprecatory Psalms, etc., will fade away as we behold face to face the one true and good God. For now, we know that God himself is the standard of what is right and wrong, so we are in no position to pass judgment upon him and his Word. Indeed,

> who are you, O man, to answer back to God? Will what is molded say to its molder, "Why have you made me like this?" Has the potter no right over the clay, to make out of the same lump one vessel for honorable use and another for dishonorable use? (Rom 9:20-21)

There are answers to some if not all our most difficult questions, yet even with the right answer, we may not like the truth. However, in such circumstances, and in every case where a biblical teaching troubles us, we are confronted with a question, will we trust God or ourselves? Fundamentally, do we believe that God is wiser and better than we are? For if he is, we can trust him even with the most difficult of issues. Isaiah recounts God's compassion and thoughts towards humans as being of a fundamentally different nature than humanities—they are above and beyond ours (Isa 55:6-9). This means that our thought must be accommodated to his, our sensibility and reason subjected to his ultimate reason and moral standards.[3]

To submit ourselves before God as we read Scripture is fundamental to receiving his Word and rightly understanding it. None of us enjoys submitting to someone above us, so we are naturally inclined to twist and ignore difficult things. We simplify or simply ignore difficult teachings for the sake of our reason and sensibilities. Yet Scripture declares such actions sin, to put ourselves in place of God, to exchange the Creator and his standard for ourselves—the creature. If we are going to read Scripture rightly and truly know God, then we must do so with a posture of submission, to accept the teaching of Scripture no matter where it may lead us. Beginning

---

[3] I explore this to a greater depth in the first volume of this series.

with faith in God, *we submit ourselves before him* to learn with Humility.

14

TO LEARN WITH HUMILITY

> Now a Jew named Apollos, a native of Alexandria, came to Ephesus. He was an eloquent man, competent in the Scriptures. He had been instructed in the way of the Lord. And being fervent in spirit, he spoke and taught accurately the things concerning Jesus, though he knew only the baptism of John. He began to speak boldly in the synagogue, but when Priscilla and Aquila heard him, they took him aside and explained to him the way of God more accurately. – Acts 18:24-26

Our posture towards God as we read Scripture is one of faith and submission, of trust acted out in humility. We accept his Word even when it offends and troubles us. He is God; we are not. This is essential to reading God's word but not the whole story. The end of our submission is that we might learn from God, implying that we do not have all that we need to know already. We approach Scripture because there is something we need to learn; we do not have sufficient wisdom or all truth. Indeed, we approach Scripture believing some things to be true that are actually false. This necessitates the last heart posture we will consider. Beginning with faith in God, we submit ourselves before him *to learn with humility*.

Faith is ultimately a confession of our inadequacy and evidence of humility. By believing in Christ Jesus for salvation, we admit that we are inadequate. We admit that we have fallen short of God's standard and earned only a curse, that we are not deserving of favour or blessing. We admit that we have not and cannot earn God's favour and that we need him to live an obedient life conforming to his purposes. This same humility is an essential aspect of reading the Bible well.

First, humility is manifest in the confession that we need God to understand his word. We need God to act in our heart so that we do submit when we are challenged. As we discussed in Chapter 5, we need God's Spirit to quicken our sluggish senses and intellects and to soften our stubborn hearts in order that we might perceive and receive God's Word. To learn with humility means that we approach Scripture with Philippians 2:12-13 on our minds, "work out your own salvation with fear and trembling, for it is God who works in you, both to will and to work for his good pleasure."

Second, humility manifests in the way we consider ourselves. None of us has mastered God's word; none of us has exhausted all that it has to say or accurately interpreted every part. Part of the problem is that we are sinful, yet being sinful does not mean that we sin and err in everything we do. We get things right sometimes, even often! Given infinite time and the truth that the Bible is clear, it is possible that someone could rightly understand every part of Scripture. However, none of us has infinite time. For this reason, we need to be humble about our inadequacies; we need to acknowledge that we do not have it all together, that we do not have every answer. We must, therefore, approach Scripture as those who have much yet to learn. We must approach commentaries and secondary resources as those who have much left to learn. And we must approach others in conversation with the self-awareness that we still have much to learn—no matter our experience or education. This leads to the final way we need to see humility manifest in our reading.

Third, humility manifests in the way we conduct ourselves with others in the reading of Scripture. I hope it has been clear throughout this book that the Bible does not present Bible study as a private effort. Bible study is done for the people of God by the people of God in the presence of the people of God. We need one another if we are going to read the Bible well. This is necessary because we all have blind spots, areas in our life that require the insight of others. This is necessary because we all have errors that only others will correct. This is especially true of errors shrouded in pride. Finally, this is necessary because none of us has exhaustive understanding of Scripture or all the ways it could apply. We need the input of others to see how the Bible applies to our lives and the lives of others and that we might come to a right understanding of Scripture. We must enter into discussion with others and must approach the resources others produce with the humility to learn from them, to listen well and receive correction where necessary. Like Apollos in Acts 18, there are instances where we need brothers and sisters to come alongside of us and explain "to [us] the way of God more accurately" (Acts 18:26). If we do not have this posture as we come to Scripture, we will not hear all that God has for us to hear.

This is not to say that there will not be times when we will have to batten down the hatches and fight for our convictions. We will be confronted often in our study by positions with which we rightly disagree. We will need courage and perseverance to hold fast the truth against opposition. However, I suspect that we are more susceptible to the temptation of holding to our own ideas without regard for the insights of others, to the temptation of pride rather than humility. So this is what I have chosen to emphasise.

Reading the Bible is not just knowing what the Bible is and having the skills to figure out difficulties. Reading the Bible engages our minds and affections, our intellect and the posture of our heart. We must come to the Bible prepared to work hard, to think well, and to submit ourselves to God. Our heart must be oriented towards God with faith, reading to submit to him in order to learn with humility.

CONCLUSION

> This Book of the Law shall not depart from your mouth, but you shall meditate on it day and night, so that you may be careful to do according to all that is written in it. For then you will make your way prosperous, and then you will have good success. – Joshua 1:8

We began this book with a question, the most pressing question of our day; "Can I understand the Bible?" I have argued that our answer as Christians should be a resounding YES. I have argued that we can and must understand the Bible yet doing so will not be easy. It means devoting ourselves to the lifelong study of God's Word, meditating on it and reading it continually. I identified three things that are necessary to reading Scripture as God has intended us to read it: we need eyes to see, ears to hear, and hearts to understand.

In Part 1 we considered the eyes or worldview we need to see Scripture. We considered the nature of the Bible (ch. 1), the story and theology taught in Scripture (chs. 2-3), and the two people groups that Scripture is addressed to—the Old and New Covenant people of God (ch. 4). This gave us a foundation by which we could approach Scripture; it offered us a glimpse at the whole teaching of Scripture so that we may interpret its parts.

In Part 2 we considered how we might listen well or have ears to hear God's Word. This proved to be the lengthiest part of our project, extending over about 130 pages and seven chapters. In chapters 5 & 6, we looked at our goal as we read Scripture—namely, justified application—and a method by which we could reach this goal. In the following chapters, we considered various tools and skills that help us look carefully at Scripture. In the final chapter of Part 2, we considered how we could evaluate our interpretations and those of others to determine if they are justified.

In Part 3, by far the shortest of the books three parts, we considered the function of the heart in reading Scripture. I hope it is clear that the size of this section by no means reflects its importance. A right heart is the *sine qua non* of good Bible reading—the condition without which reading will not happen. I capture the role of the human heart with this sentence: beginning with faith in God, we submit ourselves before him to learn with humility. Each of this section's three chapters took one part of this phrase and unpacked what I intend. The foundation of our reading is faith, a right heart produced by God and a resulting belief in and dependence upon God. This posture of faith produces submission in our hearts and minds; as we read Scripture, faith should lead us to accept God's Word over humanity's and his judgments over our own. This posture of faith also produces a posture of humility towards our own understanding and towards that of our peers. With humility, we approach Scripture ready to always learn and be rebuked; with humility, we approach our peers ready to learn from them and be strengthened in our understanding and faith.

We have been on a long journey. It is my hope that those readers who came to this book convinced they could not understand God's word will now see how God in his mercy has enabled us to read his Scripture and know him through it. For those who were already convinced of this point, it is my prayer that the approach of this book has strengthened your reading skills, challenged your assumptions about the nature of hermeneutics, and strengthened your confidence in the sufficiency and clarity of God's word. For all of us, I hope we have seen our deep need for God and his people if we are to read Scripture well. Ultimately, it is my prayer that we have seen how reading itself is a gift from God. Christians will gladly proclaim that Scripture is God's gift, but how often do we confess that our very ability to read it is a gift from our heavenly Father? That we live among people who are able to teach us about the whole of Scripture is God's gift that we might understand its parts. That the manuscripts and knowledge of the biblical languages have been preserved over 2000 years is God's gift so that we might ever return to the sources of our faith and grow in our knowledge of him. The fact that Scripture is comprehensive in its scope and clear in its teaching is God's gift so that we may truly know him and obey him in this life. From beginning to end, reading the Bible is a gift enabled by our gracious Father. It is his gift so that we might be fully equipped to know his will and obey him, that we might know him more clearly and enjoy the fullness of life he has promised us through Jesus Christ (2 Tim 3:16-17; 2 Pet 1:3-4). The charge of this book is that which Joshua received; we must meditate on the Word of God day and night "so that [we] may be careful to do according to all that is written in it." This same charge is picked up at the end of the second section of the Hebrew Bible, Malachi 4, and in the first verses of the final section, in Psalm 1. It is with this, the words of our God in Psalm 1, that we will conclude:

> Blessed is the man
> > who walks not in the counsel of the wicked,
> nor stands in the way of sinners,
> > nor sits in the seat of scoffers;
> but his delight is in the law of the LORD,
> > and on his law he meditates day and night.
> He is like a tree
> > planted by streams of water
> that yields its fruit in its season,
> > and its leaf does not wither.
> In all that he does, he prospers.
> The wicked are not so,
> > but are like chaff that the wind drives away.
> Therefore the wicked will not stand in the judgment,
> > nor sinners in the congregation of the righteous;
> for the LORD knows the way of the righteous,
> > but the way of the wicked will perish. (Psalm 1:1-6)

Volume 2b:
The Gift of Reading
– Part 2
A Biblical Perspective on Hermeneutics

INTRODUCTION

If the Bible is God's gift to guide his people, then no more important question can be asked than this: "how do we interpret it?" If the Bible is God's gift so that we may know him and his world, we need to have an answer. For this reason, I wrote *The Gift of Reading – Part 1*. However, it was beyond the scope of that work to address many secondary questions it would raise, especially for those who have studied hermeneutics before. My goal in that book was to give a foundation for a life-long reading of Scripture rooted in the idea that God gave us a clear word—that Scripture is perspicuous. I argued this point from the explicit teachings and the implications of Scripture. However, most approaches to hermeneutics today, far from supporting the perspicuity of Scripture, explicitly or implicitly deny it.[1] They make reading the Bible far more difficult than the Bible indicates it should be. That is not to say Scripture claims to be an easy read, it does not (e.g. 2 Pet 3:16), but Scripture does teach that it is written for all Christians and intended by God to be understood by them. It is this claim that I believe

---

[1] In his essay "Is the Doctrine of *Claritas Scripturae* Still Relevant Today?" D. A. A. Carson argues that perspicuity is important but sees the primary challenge to this doctrine coming from Postmodern trends. Though D. A. Carson has done much to make the Word of God accessible to pastors and students worldwide, I will argue below that his own approach to interpretation—Grammatical Historical Exegesis—is equally a danger for this doctrine. D. A. Carson, "Is the Doctrine of Claritas Scripturae Still Relevant Today?," in *Collected Writings on Scripture*, ed. Andrew David Naselli (Wheaton: Crossway, 2010), 179–193.

many approaches to hermeneutics today deny, that God intends his Scriptures to be understood by all his people, not just scholars in the 21st century.

Consider the words of the Christian scholar George H. Guthrie, discussing the work of biblical scholarship,

> The process of learning, at its most basic, involves a deep study of the text of Scripture itself, and for the scholar, a deep study of Scripture calls for the hard work of biblical studies research…. To begin with, we must be able to engage the biblical languages with competence, as well as modern languages that facilitate our dialogue with others in the field. The study of the history of the ancient Near East and the Roman Empire, as well as a wide variety of cultural backgrounds, is mandatory. Since we are dealing with texts in a world of other texts, the ability to access and analyze ancient Near Eastern literature for Old Testament scholars or Second Temple Jewish literature and Greco-Roman literature for those studying the New Testament is mandatory, and increasingly, various aspects of modern linguistic theory play a part in our work as well. To understand and enter into dialogue with others in the field, we also must have some familiarity with the dizzying array of "criticisms," both higher and lower, in the history of investigating the biblical literature. Further, since texts are always interpreted, we need an awareness of what is going on in the areas of philosophical hermeneutics and biblical theology. On top of all this, we must keep up with developments in our own areas of focus—and bibliography has become daunting in almost all specializations.[2]

There are few scholars who have laboured more than George Guthrie in furthering the understanding of the Bible among Christians outside of Academia,[3] and his zeal for God and his Word is clear in his work. However, the methodology Guthrie has adopted in his reading of Scripture subtly undermines this labour. In this quote, Guthrie is discussing the work of the Christian biblical scholar, not the average Christian reading their Bible, yet it is disingenuous to think that such work is necessary for the scholar alone and

---

[2] George H. Guthrie, "The Study of Holy Scripture and the Work of Christian Higher Education," in *Christian Higher Education*, eds. David S. Dockery and Christopher W. Morgan, (Crossway, 2018), 83.

[3] Cf. https://georgehguthrie.com/.

not for everyone else.

Christian biblical scholars do all this work because they want to properly understand the text before them. They study modern languages so they can interact with the relevant scholarship in other fields. Among these other fields, they must study the history of the Ancient Near East, the Roman Empire, and other cultures because the biblical texts were written within these cultures. To understand and dialogue with these and other fields, the scholar must learn the various criticisms used to analyse the production and meaning of the biblical text. Indeed, the very question of the possibility of interpretation and the appropriate way to do it must be investigated: how can anyone hope to interpret the text if they do not have an idea of what "interpretation" means? Moreover, they need to study the ins and outs of Old Testament studies, New Testament Studies, of each book, of each corpus (The Torah, Prophets, Gospels, etc.), and of the relevant extra-biblical literature. This is a mountain of work, but the Christian scholar only undertakes it because they think it will help them understand the text. In some fields, the Bible might be studied in conjunction with these fields in order to learn more about the Ancient Near East or the Roman World, but Guthrie is claiming that the biblical scholar needs to study these things to learn more about the Bible—to interpret it. If God has given Scripture to guide his people and this guidance only comes through the right interpretation of Scripture, then every Christian needs to do what is necessary to properly interpret the Scriptures. Think about the implications if this is true.[4]

If pastors and lay Christians cannot hope to learn and master the materials necessary for sound biblical studies, they are left dependent on the scholarly commentaries. Yet there are dozens of commentaries on each biblical book, commentaries that not only disagree in the details but in their entire approach to interpreting a book. How can anyone—including the scholars themselves—have sufficient understanding of the necessary materials to properly weigh the arguments presented for specific interpretive approaches and then for a particular interpretation of a passage. And the lay Christian cannot just rely on their pastor's preaching alone for access to the Word of God. Pastors have a limited time each week and an entire

---

[4] I address some of the problems with such thinking in Vol. 1, but I intend to address it more thoroughly in an upcoming book on training Christian teachers.

congregation to whom they minister, but Christians are called to teach their children the word of God and to live their entire lives in light of Scripture. The preaching of the Word plays an essential role in the life of a Christian, but it cannot be the only access a believer has to God's Word.

If this is truly what is necessary to interpret Scripture properly, no one—not even the scholar—has a hope of arriving at a confident conclusion concerning the text's meaning. This is disastrous if the Bible is our only hope to know anything in this world, as I argue in *The Gift of Knowing*. If the Bible is our only access to the saving Gospel of Jesus Christ, then a failure to understand it means that we have lost access to the very message that can save us. If the Bible is God's guide for life before him, equipping us for every good work (2 Tim 3:16-17), but is inaccessible, what hope do we have for living a life pleasing before him?

If this is true, if the present approach(es) to biblical interpretation leads to nihilism concerning the text's meaning, then we need an alternative approach to reading the Bible, a way of reading the Bible that is rooted in its own authority. I have argued for such an approach in *The Gift of Reading Part I*.

In this book, I do not intend to revisit that same territory; instead, I hope to consider more closely the alternate approaches to hermeneutics among Evangelicals and biblical scholars. First, in doing so I hope to prove the above assertions, namely, that present approaches to hermeneutics undermine the perspicuity of Scripture and lay impassible barriers before the interpreter. Second, I hope to unpack some of the theory behind the hermeneutical approach presented in the first book. Namely, I hope to address to a greater extent the questions of the Bible's role in its own interpretation, of meaning, and of the Bible's relation to history.

To do this, to show the hopelessness of the contemporary hermeneutical endeavour and to flush out the approach of the first book, we will first survey the history of hermeneutics. This will be an unfortunately brief survey, for my strengths lie elsewhere, yet I hope it will lay a solid foundation for the following discussion. In the three main parts of the book, we will consider the role of the Bible (Part 1), particularly the question of authority and the textual aspect of meaning; the role of the reader (Part 2), particularly the nature of the biblical audience and the reader's contribution to meaning; and the role of the author (Part 3), particularly the author's role in meaning and the relationship between the Bible and history.

I pray that this book will help us to better understand our contemporary circumstances and point us back to the Word of God as a firm anchor for our lives. It is my prayer that this book would point us back to Scripture as a clear, sufficient, and authoritative foundation for life and ministry. Scripture has such a breadth and depth that it demands from the scholar a life of rigorous study yet simultaneously beckons the thirsty child of God, come, be quenched with the glory of God shining forth and his all-sufficient wisdom graciously given to his people. May God grant to us the blessings that come from being firmly rooted in his Word:

> Blessed is the man
>   who walks not in the counsel of the wicked,
> nor stands in the way of sinners,
>   nor sits in the seat of scoffers;
> but his delight is in the law of the LORD,
>   and on his law he meditates day and night.
>
> He is like a tree
>   planted by streams of water
> that yields its fruit in its season,
>   and its leaf does not wither.
> In all that he does, he prospers.
> The wicked are not so,
>   but are like chaff that the wind drives away.
>
> Therefore the wicked will not stand in the judgment,
>   nor sinners in the congregation of the righteous;
> for the LORD knows the way of the righteous,
>   but the way of the wicked will perish. (Ps 1:1-6)

1

APPROACHES TO HERMENEUTICS

Throughout the history of the Church, Christians (and the Jews before them) have wrestled with God's authoritative revelation in Scripture and how to interpret it. They have wrestled with how to apply God's words to and through the Old Testament prophets and New Testament apostles to a people living hundreds—even thousands—of years later. It can be disheartening to consider all the different approaches that have been taken to biblical interpretation (to hermeneutics) throughout the history of the Church.

However, despite the dozens of approaches we witness in the literature, it is encouraging to observe that throughout the ages, the Bible has been understood. That is, whether the method consciously adopted was "allegorical" or "literal," Christians have consistently confessed the teaching of Scripture, that Jesus is fully God and fully man, that there will be a resurrection from the dead when Christ returns, that Jesus was crucified under Pontius Pilate and rose again on the 3rd day, etc. There is debate, yet it is clear when we study the history of God's people that his Word is getting through, that it is being understood and responded to. That is, whatever our method may or may not say about the clarity (or perspicuity) of Scripture and our ability to read it, men, women, and children have understood the Word of God read and proclaimed for several millennia. Indeed, until recent years, the debate over the interpretation of Scripture has not been whether the words on the page can be understood but whether or not there is additional meaning beyond these words.

Closely related to this debate over additional meaning is the question of application, namely, how do we relate the words of Scripture to our lives? What do we do with them? Specifically, what do we do with difficult texts or those that are hard to apply? This is where, in my judgment, the confusion begins, yet this is also where Scripture speaks most clearly.

The Bible does not provide us with a definition of "meaning," though it has implications for our definitions. It does not give us a treatise on its relationship to history, though it does give us ample guidance in this regard. Yet, Scripture is clear on whom it was written for and how they are to respond to it—as I have attempted to show in *The Gift of Reading – Part 1* and will continue to argue here. Furthermore, Scripture is clear that it bears ultimate authority, authority to define good and bad, right and wrong (see *The Gift of Knowing*). Thus, Scripture is abundantly clear concerning how it ought to be used, concerning its application. More often than naught, the diversity of hermeneutical approaches throughout the history of the church emerges out of confusion over these two points, the authority and audience of Scripture. It seems, therefore, that Scripture has something to say on the topics where interpretation is most contentious.

As we briefly survey the history of hermeneutics, keep these things in mind, the question of audience and authority. For convenience's sake, we will consider the various approaches to hermeneutics according to their relationship to three major movements in Western philosophy, Premodernity, dominated by the Greek philosophers; Modernity, dominated by the empirical sciences and enlightenment philosophy; and Postmodernity, dominated by relativism or the authority of the thinking person.[1]

A. Hermeneutics in Pre-Modernity

We could begin our discussion with the early Jewish forms of interpretation, such as is found in the early Pesher commentaries and later Midrash, but I think it will be more fruitful to begin with early Christian hermeneutics.

---

[1] It may be appropriate to observe a certain chronological arrogance in the way contemporary philosophy and historical studies consider the world, as if Modernity is the defining moment in the history of the world. Modernity is not so different from pre-modernity and is guilty of as much ignorance and wrong as its predecessors. Nevertheless, these categories remain useful.

Among the many reasons for this, the Christian writers are more explicit about what they are doing, so it is easier to discuss their methods, and much of what the 1st century Jews did in interpretation is echoed in later Christian works.[2]

a. Irenaeus and the Rule of Truth

There was much fruitful discussion among the apostolic and early church fathers about particular hermeneutical issues, such as how the Old Testament relates to the New—specifically prophecy and typology (an issue we considered briefly in *The Gift of Reading – Part 1*). Attention was particularly given to the role of Scripture in its own interpretation. The early Church Fathers were quick to identify and emphasize the importance of Scripture for its own interpretation, namely, its authority over us to lead us in interpreting it. Irenaeus argued that Scripture functioned as a "rule of truth," a guide to its own interpretation; he argued that the Valentinian Gnostics missed the meaning of the Scriptures by arguing from individual snippets of text and in doing so disregarding "the order and connection of the Scriptures, and so far as in them lies, dismember[ing] and destroy[ing] the truth."[3] he describes their practice like this,

> Their manner of acting is just as if one, when a beautiful image of a king has been constructed by some skilful artist out of precious jewels, should then take this likeness of man all to pieces, should rearrange the gems, and so fit them together as to make them into the form of a dog or of a fox, and even that but poorly executed; and should then maintain and declare that *this* was the beautiful image of the king which the skilful artist constructed, pointing to the jewels which had been admirably fitted together by the first artist to form the image of the king, but have been with bad effect transferred by the latter one to the shape of a dog, and by thus exhibiting the jewels, should deceive the ignorant who had no conception what a king's form was like, and persuade them that that miserable likeness of the fox was, in fact, the beautiful image of the king. In like manner do these persons patch together old

---

[2] E.g. Philo practiced allegorical interpretation like many church fathers. Both are dependent on the Greek allegorical tradition for their methods.

[3] This is from *Against Heresies*, 1.8.1 according to the translation in Philip Schaff's *Ante-Nicene Fathers*.

wives' fables, and then endeavour, by violently drawing away from their proper connection, words, expressions, and parables whenever found, to adapt the oracles of God to their baseless fiction.[4]

Here, Irenaeus charges the Valentinians with wrenching the Scriptures from their textual connections—from the context in which they should be read—and jamming them together to prove their point.[5]

Later in the work, he speaks of the need to interpret the parables in light of the clear teaching of Scripture, by doing so he "he who explains [the parables] will do so without danger, and the parables will receive a like interpretation from all, and the body of truth will remain entire, with a harmonious adaptation of its members, and without any collision [of its several parts]."[6] Elsewhere, in his *Demonstration of the Apostolic Preaching*, he summarizes this rule according to various doctrines concerning the Father, Son, and Holy Spirit (par. 6). Adriani Rodrigues is surely right when he summarizes Irenaeus thought in this way;

> In these considerations, the rule of faith seems to be described as a framework or system that serves as the correct set of presuppositions or preunderstanding for the activity of biblical interpretation. However, this rule does not appear to be distinguished from Scripture.[7]

This rule seems to be the Scripture, its canonical shape and teaching, applied to its own interpretation. This is a profound insight into the function of Scripture in its own interpretation, an insight that lies at the heart of my project in these two books. In Irenaeus and many of the early fathers, Scripture was given a preeminent role in its own interpretation.

---

[4] Ibid.

[5] Their twisting of Scripture would be like taking Jesus' words, "relax, eat, drink, be merry" as a command to be practiced instead of the foolish words of the rich man in Jesus' parable (Luke 12:19).

[6] The first note is my own, the second is from Schaff. This is again taken from Schaff's *Ante-Nicene Fathers*.

[7] From his article, "The Rule of Faith and Biblical Interpretation in Evangelical Theological Interpretation of Scripture," Themelios 43.2 (2018), 259-260.

In the following centuries, the rule of Scripture interpreting Scripture continued to be employed, yet it sometimes took on a function that undermined Scripture's own authority to confront and challenge the presuppositions of its readers.[8] Moving past Irenaeus, we see this in the most (in)famous approach to interpreting Scripture among the early Christians, allegorical or spiritual interpretation.

b. Allegorical Interpretation

Allegorical interpretation is often associated with the Alexandrian Catechetical school (its most prominent figures being Clement of Alexandria and Origen) but can be found throughout the writings of the Church Fathers. Moisés Silva reminds us that it is too simplistic to associate allegorical interpretation with the Alexandrians alone, but it is also simplistic to think that allegorical interpretation was the only hermeneutic used by these Fathers. To the contrary, even Origin—infamous as he is for his allegorizing—believed that much of the biblical narrative is historical and that there is a literal meaning. However, as we will see, this literal sense was for the simple believer; allegorical interpretation was for the more spiritual Christian.[9]

Allegorical interpretation was a practice the early Christians and 1st-century Jews adopted from the Greek philosophical schools. For the Greeks, allegorizing was a way to find the principles of their philosophy in the ancient Greek epics; for the Philo the Jew, it was a way of finding Platonic philosophy in the writings of Moses and the Old Testament. For the Christians, allegory was a tool used to find Spiritual truths of Christianity and Christianised Greek philosophy in Scripture. Loosely, allegorical interpretation mirrored the Greek philosophy it evolved out of, "in Platonic thought, earthly things are inferior to the heavenly forms and only shadows of them. In the same way, the literal sense of the Bible is inferior to the spiritual sense."[10] I would add,

---

[8] I deal with presuppositions in *The Gift of Knowing*. We could define a presupposition as, "one of our foundational beliefs by which we automatically—without deliberate thought—interpret all our experience and from which we do all our reasoning" (16).

[9] Moisés Silva, *Has the Church Misread the Bible?* in Moisés Silva, ed., *Foundations of Contemporary Interpretation* (Grand Rapids: Zondervan, 1996), 48–54.

[10] Graeme Goldsworthy, *Gospel-Centered Hermeneutics: Foundations and Principles of Evangelical Biblical Interpretation* (Downers Grove: InterVarsity Press, 2006), 95.

"and the literal sense is a shadow of the spiritual sense." Allegorical interpretation sought to look through the historical or literal sense to a greater spiritual or philosophical truth. Clement, for example, was able to identify in the story of the prodigal son several spiritual truths, such that "the robe that the father gave to the prodigal represents immortality; the shoe represent the upward progress of the soul; and the fatted calf represents Christ as the source of spiritual nourishment for Christians."[11] In particular, allegorical interpretation was seen as a way to resolve apparent difficulties in Scripture. In fact, not all passages of Scripture were to be interpreted allegorically.

Saint Augustine was a careful reader of Scripture and argued that careful attention to the text would yield its meaning. Indeed, he was so bold as to claim that it is "very rare and very difficult to find any ambiguity in the case of proper words, as far at least as Holy Scripture is concerned, which neither the context, showing the design of the writer, nor a comparison of translations, nor a reference to the original tongue, will suffice to explain."[12] However, there are places in Scripture where "figurative words" are used and where taking them as literal, or according to their normal historical sense, would be dangerous. From the example he uses and the evidence of his practice, what he intends is not metaphorical speech, which is probably considered part of the ambiguous language made clear in context, but texts meant to be read allegorically:

> For he who follows the letter takes figurative words as if they were proper, and does not carry out what is indicated by a proper word into its secondary signification; but, if he hears of the Sabbath, for example, thinks of nothing but the one day out of seven which recurs in constant succession; and when he hears of a sacrifice, does not carry his thoughts beyond the customary offerings of victims from the flock, and of the fruits of the earth. Now it is surely a miserable slavery of the soul to take signs for things, and to be unable to lift the eye of the mind above what is corporeal and

---

[11] William W Klein, Craig L. Blomberg, and Robert L. Hubbard Jr., *Introduction to Biblical Interpretation*, ed. Kermit A. Ecklebarger (Dallas: Word Publishing, 1993), 34.

[12] Saint Augustine, *On Doctrine*, Book 3, chapter 4 in Philip Schaff, *A Select Library of the Nicene and Post-Nicene Fathers of the Christian Church: St Augustin's City of God and Christian Doctrine*, vol. 2, A Select Library of the Nicene and Post-Nicene Fathers of the Christian Church (Buffalo: The Christian Literature Company, 1887).

created, that it may drink in eternal light.[13]

For Origen and Augustine, allegory was not a hermeneutic for reading all Scripture but a writing strategy used by the biblical authors, a writing strategy that only the more spiritual and learned readers of Scripture would discern.

They thought that allegorical reading was recognized by difficulties in the text, by moral truths that seemed unpalatable or historical events that could not have happened, according to their judgment. "Allegorical reading is pursued in addition to the literal exegesis, which is seldom wholly eliminated. It is almost never applied to whole biblical books; rather, it is used only for problematic, that is incomprehensible, morally objectionable or seemingly nonsensical passages."[14]

This is ultimately a problematic approach, for by addressing apparent difficulties in Scripture with such a hermeneutic, the reader is able to avoid submitting his or her intellect and judgment to Scripture in the very place it is being challenged. A similar phenomenon happens today when readers committed to naturalism read the miracles of Scripture in terms of purely natural phenomenon: because God—if he exists—cannot interfere in the natural world, miracles must be merely coincidental events explained by the regular working of the world.[15] In his book *On the First Principles*, Origen explains the phenomenon that revealed to him an allegorical passage in some detail:

> But since, if the usefulness of the legislation, and the sequence and beauty of the history, were universally evident of itself, we should not believe that any other thing could be understood in the Scriptures save what was obvious, the word of God has arranged that certain stumbling blocks, as it were, and offences, and impossibilities, should be introduced into the midst of the law and the history, in order that we may not, through being drawn away

---

[13] Ibid, Book 3, chapter 5. Notice the Platonic language here.

[14] Therese Fuhrer, "Allegorical Reading and Writing in Augustine's Confessions," in *In Search of Truth. Augustine, Manichaeism and Other Gnosticism*, ed. Jacob Albert van den Berg et al. (Leiden, The Netherlands: Brill, 2010), 27.

[15] One thinks of cable documentaries on biblical events, one of which attempted to explain the pillar of fire by which God led his people in the Exodus as oil fields burning.

in all directions by the merely attractive nature of the language, either altogether fall away from the (true) doctrines, as learning nothing worthy of God, or, by not departing from the letter, come to the knowledge of nothing more divine… the Scripture interwove in the history (the account of) some event that did not take place, sometimes what could not have happened; sometimes what could, but did not. And sometimes a few words are interpolated which are not true in their literal acceptation, and sometimes a larger number. And a similar practice also is to be noticed with regard to the legislation, in which is often to be found what is useful in itself, and appropriate to the times of the legislation; and sometimes also what does not appear to be of utility; and at other times impossibilities are recorded for the sake of the more skilful and inquisitive, in order that they may give themselves to the toil of investigating what is written, and thus attain to a becoming conviction of the manner in which a meaning worthy of God must be sought out in such subjects.[16]

Two things should be observed in Origen's argument here. First, interestingly enough, his argument presupposes Scripture's inerrancy while apparently undermining it. That is, he assumes that Scripture cannot make errors, so when he discerns an error, it must be an intentional cue to seek a deeper meaning. This reveals a more serious concern: for Origen, Augustine, and those who adopt a similar approach to discerning an error in Scripture, they must assume they have authority over Scripture to determine its truthfulness. That is, they must have a standard other than Scripture by which to discern what is tenable in their reading. If Scripture were their standard, it would be impossible to observe an error or incongruity, for if Scripture is the highest authority, then apparent errors reveal error only in the reader.[17]

In sum, though they rightly identified a literal sense in Scripture and even confessed that this literal sense was almost always attainable, Origen and Augustine struggled with some areas of application and subtly rejected the Scriptures own claims to absolute authority with their allegorical interpretation.

---

[16] Origen, *De Principiis* (Greek), Book 4, chapter 15 in A. Roberts and J. Donaldson, *Ante-Nicene Christian Library: Translations of the Writings of the Fathers Down to A.D. 325*, Ante-Nicene Christian Library: Translations of the Writings of the Fathers Down to A.D. 325 v. 10 (T&T Clark, 1895).

[17] See further *The Gift of Knowing*.

c. The Reformation

The same trends observed in the church fathers continued throughout the middle ages; centuries of Christian teachers continued to interpret the Scriptures allegorically, yet they often maintained that their allegories must be grounded in the literal sense of Scripture. There was at this time push back against allegorizing, with some significant teachers elevating the literal sense of Scripture above the allegorical sense.[18] Albert the Great and Thomas Aquinas both moved away from allegorical interpretation towards the words of Scripture:

> Albert assumed that "that [sic] there was but one genuine exegesis worthy of the name; that which explains the sense intended by the author and is indicated by the text itself": the literal sense, therefore, provided the basis for the three spiritual senses, which Albert understood as pedagogical extensions of the letter. Aquinas built on this assumption and moved away from the method of the postils or annotations toward an analysis of the text in terms of its logical divisions and their relationship to one another.... Aquinas' commentaries are "almost exclusively occupied" with the exposition of the literal sense, which he also identified as the *fundamentum historiae* [the sense based in history]. Indeed, Aquinas commented with some frequency that the *primus sensus* [the first sense] and *prima expositio* [the best explanation] was *magis litteralis*

---

[18] Klein, et al., claim that Thomas Aquinas argued for the literal sense of Scripture. Klein, Blomberg, and Hubbard Jr., *Introduction to Biblical Interpretation*, 39.

During the middle ages, the view appears to have emerged of a fourfold sense of Scripture; in addition to the literal or historical, there was also the moral and anagogical senses. A short rhyme supposedly circulating at this time expresses what is intended by these quite clearly; "The letter shows us what God and our fathers did; the allegory shows us where our faith is hid; the moral meaning gives us rules of daily life; the anagogy shows us where we end our strife." Ibid., 38.

In the work *Glossa ordinaria*, the senses where defined in this manner, "*historia*, which tells what happened (*res gestae*); *allegoria*, in which one thing is understood through another; *tropologia*, which is moral declaration, and which deals with the ordering of behavior; *anagoge*, through which we are led to higher things that we might be drawn to the highest and heavenly." Richard A. Muller, *Post-Reformation Reformed Dogmatics Volume 2: Holy Scripture: The Cognitive Foundation of Theology*, vol. 2 (Grand Rapids: Baker Book House, 1987), 17.

[the more literal],[19] and that the purpose of exegesis was to identify the "intention" of the words, of the book, or of the writer.[20]

In the pre-reformation ages, we see that the so-called "literal" sense remained important, though allegorizing was frequent. The rules for attaining the literal sense were much the same as those Augustine expressed in *On Doctrine*, yet Aquinas added that this literal sense was singular and associated with "intention." These ideas prove to be highly influential in the modern era yet are fraught with difficulties. However, for Aquinas these are firmly rooted in the grammatical or literal sense of the text. Continuing with our brief history, it was in the Reformation that the literal sense rose to forefront of biblical interpretation, though allegorizing was still present.

Steeped as he was in the monastic traditions, it was hard for Luther to set aside allegorical interpretation completely, and so it is present in his work. However, with the other reformers, his teaching concerning biblical interpretation set aside allegorical interpretation for the literal meaning. Where he did allegorize, he sought to find truths about Christ and the Gospel in the Old Testament. Setting aside the practice of allegorizing among Luther and the reformers, I want to consider their development of the interpretation of the literal sense of Scripture.

At this point, we should probably clarify what we mean by "literal sense." As I believe is clear from Origen and Augustine, the literal sense does not mean "literal" as opposed to "metaphorical," but literal as the plain sense of the words of Scripture. The literal sense is what is said, interpreted appropriately in its context, not anything we might discern behind or above the words of the text. "Literal" may thus encompass literary conventions such as symbolism, intentional allegory, or metaphor but excludes all meaning that is not indicated by the written context of words, phrases, sentences, paragraphs, etc., which are the object of our interpretation. Luther's allegories are not "literal" in this sense because there is nothing in the context to

---

[19] "Literal" here means something like my definition below, the clear sense of the text whether it is metaphorical or plain.

[20] Muller, *Post-Reformation Reformed Dogmatics Volume 2: Holy Scripture: The Cognitive Foundation of Theology*, 2:18–19.

connect his interpretations with the text,[21] unlike, for example, Paul's "allegorical" argument in Galatians 4. We could define the literal sense as the meaning of the text as determined by its linguistic and literary context.[22] We will consider "meaning" to a greater depth in a later chapter.

Returning our attention to the reformers, several key emphases emerge in their writings concerning Scripture and interpretation. For both Calvin and Luther, the Holy Spirit had an essential role in guiding the reader in the right reading of Scripture and confirming it to them. This was called by Luther "internal perspicuity," whereby the Spirit's internal witness allows the Christian to discern and recognize God's voice in Scripture and to evaluate the teaching of humans.[23] This internal work was necessary but not sufficient; Scripture also had an external perspicuity. The radical reformers, from whom the Anabaptist tradition derives, went farther than the magisterial reformers in arguing that the Spirit was the sole arbiter of meaning, even claiming that the Spirit revealed meaning beyond the letter of the text. The reformers responded that the Spirit helped the believer discern the meaning that was clear in the text.[24] Thus, external perspicuity was a partial answer to the extremes of the radical reformers: Luther considered Scripture to be reasonably clear in its meaning so that Christians—those who have the

---

[21] Consider his allegory of the doves in Genesis 8:6-12, which can be read here http://henrycenter.tiu.edu/2016/01/luther-allegory-doves/. Luther interprets the raven and doves sent forth by Noah as pictures of the Law and Gospel, respectively.

[22] Following Kevin J. Vanhoozer, Iain Provan brings authorial action into the definition of "literal." Against the sort of literalism that misses the point of a text, Provan argues that a "truly literal reading pays attention to the 'speech acts' of the author, and not just the words themselves... The literal sense of a text is discovered, then, not only by consulting a dictionary about what a word... typically means in the language spoken by the author (which is indeed important), but also by paying attention to how the word is used in a particularly speech act." As will become clear later, the language of "speech act" is less than helpful for understanding the meaning of biblical texts. However, this understanding of literal is very similar to what I have proposed, in that "literal" encompasses all forms of literary communication. Iain W. Provan, *The Reformation and the Right Reading of Scripture* (Waco, Texas: Baylor University Press, 2017), 87–88.

[23] Luther, *The Bondage*, 124; Klein, Blomberg, and Hubbard Jr., *Introduction to Biblical Interpretation*, 41.

[24] Cf. Kevin J. Vanhoozer, *Biblical Authority after Babel: Retrieving the Solas in the Spirit of Mere Protestant Christianity* (Grand Rapids: Brazos, 2016), 116; Provan, *The Reformation and the Right Reading of Scripture*, 286.

internal testimony of the Spirit—can argue and resolve disputes of the meaning of Scripture.[25]

Over-against the Catholic counter-reformers' emphasis on Tradition as the interpreter of Scripture, Luther and the rest of the Reformers also reaffirmed the early church teaching that Scripture interprets Scripture, which we saw in Irenaeus.[26] The later English Puritan, William Ames, wrote that the Scriptures "give light to themselves, which should be uncovered diligently by men and communicated to others according to their calling."[27] In the Westminster Confession, the English divines wrote that "The infallible rule of interpretation of Scripture, is the Scripture itself; and therefore, when there is a question about the true and full sense of any scripture (which is not manifold, but one), it may be searched and known by other places that speak more clearly" (1.9). One of the key ways the later reformers unpacked this "infallible rule," was through a biblical theology of covenants, through which the relationship between New and Old Testaments could be understood.

Lastly, they appealed to the text of Scripture, interpreted in the context of Scripture and according to its grammar and context, as the basis of meaning. According to Ames, "Some knowledge, at least, of [the original languages] is necessary for a precise understanding of the Scriptures, for they are to be understood by the same means required for other human writings, i.e. skill and experience in logic, rhetoric, grammar, and the languages."[28] The Scriptures, according to Luther, are clear in their meaning, in its literal sense; any unclarity comes from our own confusion or lack of knowledge.[29] At least

---

[25] Luther, *The Bondage*, 125. Cf. William Ames, *The Marrow of Theology*, trans. John D. Eusden (Grand Rapids: Baker Books, 1997), 188.

[26] Cf. Luther's letter to the Catholic Emers, "Dr. Martin Luther's Answer to the Superchristian, Superspiritual, Superlearned Book of Goat Emser of Leipzig."

[27] Ames, *The Marrow of Theology*, 188.

[28] Ibid., he makes the exception that the Spirit is necessary.

[29] Ibid., 125. Cf. Martin Luther, *Sermons by Martin Luther: Volume 1; Sermons on Gospel Texts for Advent, Christmas, and Epiphany*, ed. John Nicholas Lenker, vol. 1 (Albany, Ore: AGES Bible Software, 1997), 330; Martin Luther, "Dr. Martin Luther's Answer to the Superchristian, Superspiritual, Superlearned Book of Goat Emser of Leipzig," in *Works of Martin Luther*, trans. A. Steimle, vol. 3 (Albany, Ore: AGES Bible Software, 1997), 255–256; Mark D. Thompson, *A Sure Ground on Which to Stand: The Relation of Authority and Interpretive Method in Luther's Approach to Scripture* (Carlisle; Waynesboro, GA: Paternoster, 2004), 204, 208.

for Ames, this literal sense was singular; "there is only one meaning for every place in Scripture. Otherwise, the meaning of Scripture would not only be unclear and uncertain, but there would be no meaning at all—for anything which does not mean one thing surely means nothing."[30]

B. Hermeneutics in Modernity

After the Reformation, the Western world underwent tremendous change. When the ashes settled, a new movement came on the scene. Out of the Renaissance and Reformation emerged the Enlightenment (17th-18th centuries) and the worldview of Modernity after that. During the Enlightenment, philosophy and the scientific revolution were transforming the world. Within the scientific and philosophical world, there was a significant departure from the biblical presuppositions of the Reformation—that the Bible was the ultimate authority for all human life—and a renewed commitment to the autonomy and rationality of humans. As the Modern world emerged after the Enlightenment, there was an intense interest in the scientific study of history or "historical criticism," the objective study of the history behind texts. (I have covered this period to some extent in *The Gift of Knowing* and in *The Gift of Seeing;* the philosophical movements covered there shed light on the related evolution of biblical studies at this time.)

Biblical studies became the subject not only of Christian study but of intense scholarly scrutiny from both the orthodox and non-orthodox, the Christian and atheist (or deist). The variety of approaches to the biblical text that developed during this time are too numerous to account for here, but we can consider three broad trends of biblical interpretation during the Modern period (19th-20th centuries). There was the critical approach that flourished among rationalistic Protestantism and atheistic biblical studies; the Evangelical or orthodox approach that followed the Reformers and culminated in the so-called "Grammatical-Historical" approach; and various anti-modern views, such as the anti-rationalist approach taken by Martin Kähler and his disciples.

a. Critical Hermeneutics

---

[30] Ames, *The Marrow of Theology*, 188.

Among the universities in post-reformation Europe, the default approach to studying the Bible was that of historical criticism, the objective study of the text and the world in which it was formed. As an "objective study," historical criticism was to be done apart from theological commitments, without prejudicing the potential outcomes of biblical study. This represents the first time in "Christian" (loosely conceived of course) biblical studies that the principle of "Scripture interprets Scripture" was outright rejected. Richard N. and R. Kendall Soulen in their *Handbook of Biblical Criticism* outline the presuppositions of this model as follows;

> (1) that reality is uniform and universal; (2) that it is accessible to human reason and investigation; (3) that all events historical and natural occurring within it are in principle interconnected and comparable by analogy; and (4) that humanity's contemporary experience of reality can provide objective criteria by which what could or could not have happened in the past can be determined.[31]

This approach was not really the "objective" study of Scripture but the atheistic study of Scripture, the study of the Bible and the events it records on the presuppositions that God either does not exist or that he does not interfere in his creation (i.e. deism). Not only did the historical-critical approach reject the principle of Scripture interpreting Scripture, but it also rejected the necessity of the Spirit for interpreting Scripture rightly and the search for the literal meaning of the text.

That is, no longer were scholars interested in the meaning—singular or plural—of the text and its contemporary application; they were interested in the events recorded in the text and the history of the text's formation. Biblical studies thus moved away from application (whether theological or practical) to description. Commentaries at this time and onward came to be dominated with the description of text history, the background of the text, and the nuances of language and text criticism (the study of what manuscript reading represents the original).

This broad approach of historical criticism generated a myriad of criticisms, specific approaches to the historical study of the Bible. "Criticism"

---

[31] Richard N. Soulen and R. Kendall Soulen, *Handbook of Biblical Criticism: Now Includes Precritical and Postcritical Interpretation*, 3rd Revised and Expanded. (Louisville; London: Westminster John Knox, 2001), 78.

in biblical studies after this point has come to refer to a specific scholarly approach to the Bible (such as feminist criticism, rhetorical criticism, etc.). Considering three of the early approaches to historical criticism should serve to illustrate this general approach.

i. Source Criticism

Source Criticism may be the preeminent form of historical criticism in the history of biblical studies. Many theorists in the 19th century contributed to this approach, but its most significant contributor may be Julius Wellhausen, whose *Prolegomena to the History Israel* set the agenda for Historical Criticism for the next century. By reading the biblical text carefully, primarily the Pentateuch (Genesis – Deuteronomy), source critics thought they could delineate the original sources that were used to compile the Pentateuch. Classically, critics identified four sources behind the Pentateuch, each source named after its distinguishing features; J, the Jehovist or Yahwist; E, the Elohist; D, the Deuteronomist; and P, the Priestly source. For example, J was supposed to use the divine name Jehovah (or Yahweh) while E employed the divine name Elohim. It was thought that two sources were indicated by the interweaving of these names throughout the biblical text. In other cases, supposedly contradictory accounts were thought to betray different sources.

It was argued, for example, that Genesis 1 and 2 represented two creation accounts from different sources juxtaposed in the final source. Source criticism, especially JEDP, loomed over the following century of biblical studies, only going out of fashion in the 80s and 90s. In some circles, it still finds favour (e.g. some volumes of The Word Biblical Commentary). Source criticism sometimes appears in New Testament studies as a tool for textual criticism in the Gospels, but its Modernist and unorthodox starting assumptions have led to its rejection by secular postmodern interpreters and orthodox Christian interpreters.[32]

---

[32] Many of its assumptions are also plainly false. In addition to the atheistic presuppositions quoted from the Soulens above, OT source critics also rejected inerrancy and biblical authority—which is how they could view Genesis 1 & 2 as contradictory—and gave the biblical authors far less credit than is due. Many of the supposed contradictions and discrepancies are actual rhetorical and literary devices used to recount the biblical narrative, other supposed contradictions simply do not exist. This view also does not see Scripture as an authoritative document delivered by God and addressed to present believers.

ii. Form & Tradition Criticism

Another historical-critical movement that has loomed large over the history of interpretation is that of Form Criticism and its child Tradition Criticism. Essentially, Form Criticism seeks to delineate the different types of literary forms used by the biblical authors—such as legendary stories, myths, legal cases, etc. Herman Gunkel, for example, argues that Genesis is composed of "legends." A legend is a poetic and subjective account of a historical event that begins orally; it is a crafted historical account meant to teach an idea. Because legends originated as oral traditions, interpretation must concern the original oral form, not the final written form.[33]

Tradition criticism sought to trace the evolution of literature through the process of its oral transmission. While neither of these criticisms necessarily rests on atheistic presuppositions, their value for Christian biblical studies is questionable. Regarding Tradition criticism, even if its starting presupposition that biblical literature began in an oral form were true and the outline of its transmission accurate—a very big if—this would not have any effect on Christian biblical interpretation, which involves interpreting Scripture as a canonical document written by God to govern his covenant people. Form criticism can be helpful at times, but as we will see in chapter 3, "form" and "genre" are slippery terms. Though their study has yielded some fruit, much of the product of form criticism is speculative and unhelpful for the study of the Bible as God has given it to his people.

In New Testament Studies, form criticism became associated with the existential interpretative approach of Rudolf Bultmann. Bultmann argued that the biblical stories could not be the substance of God's revelation, for the progress of science in the modern age has revealed a world far different from that described in the New Testament; "We cannot use electric lights and radios and, in the event of illness, avail ourselves of modern medical and clinical means and at the same time believe in the spirit and wonder world of the New Testament."[34] his brand of form criticism involved identifying the form of the text and performing demythologization, looking through the objectifying presentation of the NT—i.e. the way it cloths existential truths

---

[33] Cf. Herman Gunkel, *Genesis*, trans. of the 1910 ed. (Macon: Mercer University, 1997).

[34] Rudolf Bultmann, *New Testament and Mythology and Other Basic Writings*, trans. Schubert Miles Ogden (Philadelphia: Fortress Press, 1989), 4.

in mythological language—for the "understanding of existence that expresses itself in them."³⁵ Only in this way would the message of the NT be accepted in the modern scientific age.³⁶

Though the outcomes of historical criticism have sometimes been adopted by more conservative biblical interpreters, such approaches could not serve as the basis for theology and church teaching. For this, the biblical text needed to be read to discern how God was speaking to his people through it. Continuing in the same interpretive tradition as the reformers, conservative biblical scholars formulated the rules of interpretation more clearly in response to historical criticism and its bedfellows. This arc of serious conservative engagement with Scripture reached its peak in what is often called grammatical-historical interpretation.

b. Grammatical-Historical Exegesis (GHE)

The growing debate over the historicity of the biblical text, its accuracy, and the proper interpretation of difficult passages and language led to the production of technical commentaries among conservatives as much as it did among liberal or atheistic scholars. Conservatives approached the Bible with generally conservative theological presuppositions, so their conclusions were significantly different than their contemporaries, yet the style of technical commentary—commenting on the historical background and linguistic nature of the text—grew to be the predominant scholarly genre of commentary, differing from the more theological and application-oriented Reformation era commentaries (such as Calvin's biblical commentaries).³⁷ In the mid to late 20th century, the principles of a conservative scholarly approach to biblical interpretation were expressed in various ways under the heading "grammatical-historical interpretation."

As the name indicates, such an interpretation revolves around two major

---

[35] Ibid., 10.

[36] This interpretive approach seems to have made a minor resurgence in the teaching of Psychologist Jordan Peterson, see my review of his *12 Rules for Life*. https://teleioteti.ca/2018/10/11/review-of-12-rules-for-life/.

[37] A helpful example of this conservative critical commentary is the commentary series written by Karl Fredreich Keil and Franz Delitzsch, which remains helpful today.

axes, the text and history. Originating as it has among conservative scholars, grammatical-historical interpreters also tend to employ the ancient principle of the analogy of faith, or Scripture interprets Scripture.[38] We could thus summarize this approach to Scripture as a theologically informed, historical investigation of the meaning of the text. The goal for evangelical grammatical-historical interpretation is to apply the meaning of the text to contemporary circumstances. Let us consider, first, this goal of GHE Interpretation and, second, the method usually used to attain it.

i. The Goal of Grammatical-Historical Exegesis

The goal of GHE is to identify the *meaning* of the text, often with the goal of then applying the meaning of the text to our contemporary context. At the core of what makes GHE unique is its view of meaning, from which its method is derived. If a text's meaning is found in the reader, then the study of a text would focus on a reader; if it is found in the text, it would focus on the text alone. Proponents of GHE argue that there is only one meaning for each text, the same meaning for any reader; that it is propositional; and that this meaning is equivalent to the author's intention.[39] Thus, the meaning of a text is historical because it is the intention of a historical author. However, the only access we have to the author's intention is the text he has given understood as a product of the world within which it was produced—in its cultural context. By studying a text in interaction with what we can reconstruct of the thought-world and events of its historical context, it is

---

[38] This principle is used to differing degrees among such exegetes. The work by Goldsworthy places a particularly strong emphasis on this aspect of Grammatical-Historical Exegesis. Goldsworthy, *Gospel-Centered Hermeneutics*.

[39] Though not an Evangelical, Benjamin Jowett summarized this well when he wrote in 1869, "Scripture has one meaning—the meaning which it had in the mind of the Prophet or Evangelist who first uttered or wrote, to the hearers or readers who first received it." Quoted in David C. Steinmetz, "The Superiority of Precritical Exegesis," in *A Guide to Contemporary Hermeneutics: Major Trends in Biblical Interpretation*, ed. Donald K. McKim (Grand Rapids: Eerdmans, 1986), 65. Francis Watson writes that the literal sense of Scripture consists of "verbal meaning, (ii) illocutionary and perlocutionary force, and (iii) the relation to the centre." "Illocutionary" and "perlocutionary" force are terms borrowed from speech-act theory, meaning what one does by the act of speaking (i.e. warning, answering a question) and the effect one intends to achieve with an act of speaking. The "centre" here is the canonical context focusing on Jesus Christ. Francis Watson, *Text and Truth: Redefining Biblical Theology* (Edinburgh: T&T Clark, 1997), 123.

possible to uncover the intention of the author, or at least that is the claim of GHE proponents.

ii. The Method of Grammatical-Historical Exegesis

We could identify the Grammatical Historical school as a moderate or conservative form of what John Sailhamer calls "event-centered" exegetical method.[40] That is, Grammatical-Historical interpreters are concerned with the historical communicative event, or speech-act, represented by the text.[41] A book is the creation of an author who seeks to communicate something to an audience. The author's intention is that which he wants to communicate to this audience. On this view, the text is the code by which the author transmits his intended communication. It is assumed his audience would have the necessary knowledge to decode this communication, a position we cannot presume to share by default. We must work to decode the transmission in the text we have because of our cultural distance and roles as observers of this communicative act.

i. Mirror Reading

Andreas Köstenberger and Richard Patterson define mirror-reading as, "the (often doubtful) interpretive practice of inferring the circumstances surrounding the writing of a given text from explicit statements made in the text."[i] As a staple of historical critical methodology, mirror-reading is often criticized and even rejected outright. However, despite Patterson

---

[40] John H. Sailhamer, *Introduction to Old Testament Theology: A Canonical Approach* (Grand Rapids: Zondervan, 1995), 36–85.

[41] "Speech-act" is a specific phrase use by some philosophers to describe the nature of human communication. This analysis focuses on language as an action, as such meaning is found in the context of communicative action and not just the text—which is only a piece of a speech-act. Kevin J. Vanhoozer may be the most prominent Evangelical to employ speech-act theory in his hermeneutical and theological theory. Yet even where this language is not present, speech-act provides a good summary of the way GHE views communication. Kevin J. Vanhoozer, *Is There a Meaning in This Text?: The Bible, the Reader, and the Morality of Literary Knowledge* (Grand Rapids: Zondervan, 1998); Kevin J. Vanhoozer, *The Drama of Doctrine: A Canonical-Linguistic Approach to Christian Theology*, 1st ed. (Louisville: Westminster John Knox, 2005). Cf. Watson, *Text and Truth*, 98–106.

and Köstenberger's rightful caution towards the excesses of this approach, it seems to me that all historically rooted methodologies involve an element of mirror reading: as the scholar attempts to identify a correspondence between the text and known circumstances, they are forced to identify circumstances implied by the text to test against the historical data. Clinton Arnold, another Evangelical interpreter, seems admit this—though rejecting the title "mirror-reading"—in an interview with Andrew Naselli, "It is not 'mirror reading,' however, to examine explicit features of the so-called heresy in light of the religious and cultural environment. In other words, when Paul says, 'Let no one disqualify you, insisting on asceticism and worship of angels, going on in detail about visions' (Col 2:18), this is a specific indicator of what the opponents were teaching that calls out for historical examination. We need to look at all such explicit indicators and attempt to discern what the church was facing."[ii] It seems that some level of understanding concerning the circumstances against which the author writes is required in order to understand his intentions, and this implies some level of reading the text to discern such circumstances. But the excesses are evident when authors create elaborate background scenarios to explain the meaning of a text—as exemplified in several works in recent memory.[iii] So, though qualifying it against some excess, GHE implies a form of mirror-reading as an aspect of its historical methodology. The difference is that GHE measures its mirror reading by history, comparing what is said and implied by a text with historical data. I have argued elsewhere that even this form of mirror reading is unhelpful; in its place, I suggested mirror-reading as a tool for better reading texts—as a form of the analogy of faith:

> Mirror reading, when used this way, takes the data from a reading of the letter and then correlates it with the rest: it asks, what in the letter best explains this feature? What features of the letter fit together? Reading [Colossians] this way, we see a correlation between Christ's creation of and authority over the rulers, their defeat, the elemental spirits (note the inclusio in 2:8, 20), and the worship of angels. These details are mutually interpreting, making sense of each other when read together. Therefore, this form of mirror reading is not an attempt to read each individual part against a reconstructed background but each part against each other. To read the parts by the whole is a normal part of

interpretation; mirror reading is a tool for doing this. With it, we correlate the parts and use the resulting synthesis in our reading of the letter (e.g. that Christ created the rulers in 1:16 is probably meant to address the problem of spirit worship in 2:18).[iv]

---

[i] Andreas J. Köstenberger and Richard Duane Patterson, *Invitation to Biblical Interpretation: Exploring the Hermeneutical Triad of History, Literature, and Theology* (Grand Rapids: Kregel Publications, 2011), 842.

[ii] Quoted from "Mirror Reading," *Andy Naselli*, last modified May 30, 2011, accessed April 26, 2019, http://andynaselli.com/mirror-reading.

[iii] E.g. Richard Clark Kroeger and Catherine Clark Kroeger, *I Suffer Not a Woman: Rethinking 1 Timothy 2:11-15 in Light of Ancient Evidence* (Grand Rapids: Baker, 1992).

[iv] James Alexander Rutherford, "Christ Is Preeminent over False Religion: An Investigation of the Colossian False Teaching," August 29, 2016, https://teleioteti.ca/resources/papers.

This involves the threefold study of the author, text, and audience. Because we do not have direct access to the author and audience, the method to regain their perspective is again threefold. We can read the text and attempt to discern the events and positions that have necessitated it (an effort known as *mirror reading*), we can read the rest of the Bible to learn more about the author and his audience, and we can study extra-biblical accounts of the culture and thought world in which the text was composed. For the biblical authors, a scholar could understand them better by studying all their writings (e.g. "The Pauline corpus," Paul's letters) and the 3rd and 1st person accounts given of them in the rest of Scripture (we can learn more about Paul from Acts and autobiographical comments such as Gal 1:11-24 and Phil 3:1-11). For the audience, the primary way a scholar could understand them better is through mirror reading and by studying the cultural context. Broadly, this context would be the Ancient Near East (Old Testament) or the Greco-Roman world (New Testament). Narrowly, this involves the study of the particular geography, social climate, and thought world where the audience of the biblical books lived (e.g. Thessalonica, Galatia, Ephesus, Philippi, etc.). Such study is thought to help us understand the thought world presupposed by the text.

Thus, grammatical study tells us what the text says, and historical study helps us to understand what that would have meant when the original author wrote it. For example, Craig Blomberg, in his commentary on 1 Corinthians, argues concerning 1 Corinthians 11:2-16 that Paul may be referring to a shawl or covering but probably hair length; this is the grammatical aspect of interpretation, what the text says. On the other hand, he argues that in light of the 1st-century world in which Paul wrote this letter, Paul's intention was to instruct men to act in culturally appropriate ways as males and women as females, not to use their freedom in Christ as an opportunity cast of traditional values. He offers many suggestions as to why long hair on a man or short hair on a woman would have been culturally inappropriate.[42] he writes, "most interpreters agree that one timeless principle that may be deduced from this passage is that Christians should not try to blur all distinctions between the sexes."[43] he then argues that none of the verses commands a specific "timeless" custom, such that hair length or a heading covering should be used, only

> When in a particular culture, appropriate honor to God and husband cannot be maintained without certain head coverings, such coverings must be used. When covered or uncovered heads and long or short hair imply nothing about one's religious commitment or marital faithfulness, worrying about the appearance of one's physical head in these ways becomes unnecessary.[44]

Having identified the probable meaning of the words and the syntax of the text, Blomberg then uses historical background to explain why Paul says what he says and is used to guide application.

One college-level textbook uses the analogy of a journey to explain this method. First, the interpreter grasps the text in the "town" of the original audience, using grammar and historical context to discern what it would have

---

[42] Eg. Craig L. Blomberg, *1 Corinthians*, NIVAC (Grand Rapids: Zondervan, 1994), 210–211.

[43] Ibid., 214.

[44] Ibid., 215. I argue for a different approach in my article, https://teleioteti.ca/2018/02/15/is-a-covering-long-hair-or-veil-interpreting-1-corinthians11/.

meant to them.⁴⁵ Second, the interpreter identifies the width of the river separating that "town" from their own: they seek to identify the differences between the original audience and themselves (e.g. redemptive-historical context, cultural, historical setting, situation, linguistic background, etc.).⁴⁶ Third, the interpreter "crosses the principlizing bridge," identifying the universal theological truth that connects their town to the interpreters. "As God gives specific expressions to specific biblical audiences, he is also giving universal theological teachings for all of his people through these same texts."⁴⁷ Fourth, this theological principle is then applied in the interpreter's own town; the journey is complete when the meaning is brought from the audience's town to the interpreter's—when the text is applied to its contemporary audience.⁴⁸

Though Conservatives responded to the challenge of Modernist historical criticism by becoming better historians and linguists, studying the history behind the biblical texts and the languages in which they were written to counter the challenge of Modernity, not all scholars adopted this response. Others retaliated against Modernity by seeking to separate God's revelation in Scripture from the sphere of history and grammar within which the challenges of historical criticism were raised.

c. Existential Hermeneutics

This is the approach taken by a school of interpretation we could call "Existential." By existential I do not mean to identify these thinkers with the Existentialist school of Philosophy (identified with Heidegger, Sartre, Bultmann and Tillich), though there are significant parallels in their thinking

---

⁴⁵ Grammatical Historical exegetes often interchange what the author intended with what the audience would have understood. Though practically these are not identical, in hermeneutical theory they are treated as the same.

⁴⁶ D.A. Carson describes the step of leaving one's own town as "distanciation." Distanciation describes the act of critically examining a text and oneself as a reader, discerning the differences in presuppositions between the two so that the text can be read on its own terms. In *Exegetical Fallacies*, 22–24.

⁴⁷ J. Scott Duvall and J. Daniel Hays, *Grasping God's Word: A Hands-On Approach to Reading, Interpreting, and Applying the Bible*, 2nd Ed (Zondervan, 2005), 23.

⁴⁸ Ibid. 21-25

and a common historical root. Instead, I identify them as an "existentialist" school of hermeneutics because they identify God's revelation (which is the goal of Christian biblical interpretation) with a personal experience and not the text's meaning, however that may be conceived.

The originator of this approach was a German theologian name Martin Kähler. In his book, *The So-Called Historical Christ and the Historic Biblical Christ*, Kähler attempts to guard Christian theology against the attack of historical criticism by separating God's revelation in Christ from the historical events and grammatical meaning of the text.[49] *Historie*, the events and people of history which are the subject of historical-critical science, was to be distinguished from the way people receive or are affected by historical events, *Geschichte*.[50] Against historical criticism, Kähler argued that their goal of an unbiased picture of history—*Historie*—was unattainable: the historical task is itself interpretive and employs historical materials which are themselves interpreted. Because *Historie* was unattainable, the historical-critical task of rooting Christianity in objective facts was doomed to fail. Furthermore, the conservative approach, as embodied in Grammatical-Historical Exegesis, was likewise doomed to fail. On the one hand, it depended on vast theological structures or systems that were beyond the grasp of the average Christian, and by competing with historical-critical scholars to show that the Bible is indeed factual, they anchored their theology to *Historie*, which was unattainable. A better way was needed, an approach that recognized the Gospels as subjective responses to the historical events of Christ's life—as *Geschichte*—and grounded theology in this. In the place of these historical approaches, Kähler offers an existential hermeneutic. God does not use

---

[49] Martin Kähler, *The So-Called Historical Jesus and the Historic, Biblical Christ* (Vancouver: Regent College Pub., 1998).

[50] Students of philosophy will notice striking parallels between the position developed by Kähler and Barth and the philosophy of Immanuel Kant. To protect the hard sciences from the scepticism of David Hume, Kant developed a two-fold picture of the world. On the one hand, there was the *phenomenal* world, the world of our experience. This realm is wholly subjective, created by our minds, yet it is completely knowable and subject to consistent laws; it is the realm of science, where we can attain knowledge. On the other hand, there was the *noumenal* world, the world that actually exists apart from our mind's interpretation. This world is wholly unknowable. Its existence is the presupposition of the sciences and knowledge, but it cannot actually be known. In the same way, *historie* is the real events of history that must have happened for *geschichte*, our interpretation, yet we cannot know anything about *historie*: is not accessible to us.

Scripture to communicate propositions (statements of truth) or theological systems to Christians. Instead, Scripture paints a picture of Christ. We see Christ in Scripture and so recognize the Bible as authoritative, as God's revelation. The whole Bible is needed for us to get this picture, yet this picture does not rest on any detail; whether Scripture errs or not, it infallibly presents a picture of the "historic" (*geschichtlich*) Christ. Thus, our reading of Scripture concerns our subjective perception of Christ in Scripture and does not involve wrestling with the grammar and history of the text.[51] Kähler himself is not well known today, but his students are some of the most influential scholars who wrote under the banner "Christian" in the 20th century, including Karl Barth and Paul Tillich. Karl Barth is the author that most obviously and most influentially represents an existentialist hermeneutic.

To vastly simplify Karl Barth's approach,[52] we could say that for him, Scripture is God's chosen avenue of revelation. God has freely chosen to use this one book to reveal himself to man. Yet God has not bound himself to this book, as if humans were able to grasp and manipulate his revelation as they see fit. Instead, God reveals himself in Scripture at his pleasure through a personal, existential encounter. To say the Bible is the Word of God is to say that the Bible becomes the Word of God in so far as and when God allows it to be so.[53] The Christian meets God as he or she reads Scripture; this encounter is, as with Kähler, non-propositional (it does not reveal anything *about* God). Instead, it is personal.[54] Textual meaning and authorial intent are not, therefore, the subjects of Christian theological investigation; they are the objects of historical-critical study. Therefore, despite what the historical critics may say, God's revelation through Scripture is unhampered, for it does not rest on what is said but in God's free decision to encounter

---

[51] This is based on my review of Kähler's book on Teleioteti, "Review of the So-Called Historical Jesus and the Historic Biblical Christ," *Teleioteti*, July 25, 2018, accessed April 27, 2019, https://teleioteti.ca/2018/07/25/review-of-the-so-called-historical-jesus-and-the-historic-biblical-christ/.

[52] In my opinion, Karl Barth's theology is on the whole unclear and confused.

[53] Karl Barth, *Church Dogmatics*, vol. 1.1 (Peabody, Mass: Hendricksen, 2010), 11–17, 115–124, 174–175.

[54] We would, of course, debate the bifurcation of propositional and personal knowledge or encounters, as if you could meet and know someone without knowing anything about them. Though, it is true that we can know things about someone without being able to succinctly express them. Cf. *The Gift of Seeing*.

his people there.[55]

In some ways, existential interpretation anticipates postmodern interpretation in the second half of the 20th century, but a key difference is evident. Though Postmodern interpretation rejects objective truth in significant ways, it does not deny that a reader comes away from a text with a meaning or with meanings—with statements that can be formulated as propositions. Instead, it makes this meaning dependent on the reader and separates it from the text and author who wrote it. Existential interpretation, on the one hand, has gone farther than Postmodern interpretation by saying that the biblical text does not communicate *anything*. But, on the other hand, in moving meaning into the reader, Postmodern interpretations often go further than existential interpreters like Barth and even Kähler, denying not only the possibility of accessing historical events but also the ability of texts or authors to communicate.[56] That is, we can walk away from a text with propositional knowledge, yet this knowledge is a product of our own activity as we interact with the text not the text or the author's intentional activity.

C. Hermeneutics in Postmodern

In the 20th century, philosophy entered a new movement, known as Postmodernity. Though it is sometimes thought that Postmodernity is a response to Modernity, it appears to be Modernity come of age. In Modernist philosophy, there was an irreconcilable tension between the objective world and the subjective interpreter. Postmodernity drew out this tension and drove

---

[55] Cf. Karl Barth, *The Word of God and the Word of Man* (New York: Harper & Row, 1957); John M. Frame, *A History of Western Philosophy and Theology* (Phillipsburg: P&R Publishing, 2015), 364–383; Cornelius Van Til, "Has Karl Barth Become Orthodox," *The Westminster Theological Journal* 16, no. 2 (May 1954): 135–181.

Barth does not argue for a "special hermeneutic," a unique way of reading the Bible over against all other literature. Instead, the differences between the interpretation of the Bible and every other book rest in the difference of subject matter. Because the subject matter of the Bible is the sovereign Lord Jesus Christ, who is ultimately free, the meaning of the text can only be grasped if and when the sovereign subject allows this to happen. See Thomas E. Provence, "The Sovereign Subject Matter: Hermeneutics in the Church Dogmatics," in *A Guide to Contemporary Hermeneutics: Major Trends in Biblical Interpretation*, ed. Donald K. McKim (Grand Rapids: Eerdmans, 1986), 241–262.

[56] I address this briefly in the previous volume in this series, *The Gift of Knowing*.

it to its extremes, turning the emphasis from the objective world to the subjective interpreter.[57] In language, this produced several different movements. As far as its impact on biblical hermeneutics, the most significant impact of Postmodernity has been expressed in the flourishing of "exegeses," of which Structural Interpretation and reader-response criticism are worthy of notice.

Before the 20th century, the question biblical hermeneutics sought to answer was, "How do we properly interpret the Bible?" This implies, of course, that there are right and wrong ways to read the Bible, that there are right and wrong interpretations and, therefore, right and wrong interpretative methods. Within Postmodernity the emphasis is not on how to properly interpret the Bible but how we can interpret the Bible. That is, the Bible can be studied historically, to understand how it was shaped and its historical role (historical criticism and sociology of religion). The Bible can be studied as a product of a community, understanding how it functions to shape the life of and came to be as a product of a particular society (Canonical criticism, analysis of the interpretive community).[58] The Bible can be studied as a product of and a tool for the flourishing of Patriarchy but also as an agent for the liberation of women (Feminist criticism).[59] A socio-literary, political reading of the Bible might use the opposition of "empire," those in power, and "periphery," those exploited, as the lenses through which to read and apply Scripture, as Ched Myers has in his commentary on Mark.[60] The list goes on and on, but it is important to observe that in postmodernity, these differing exegeses are not mutually exclusive; they are all legitimate approaches to the text.

Because of the mutual toleration these exegeses have for one another and their almost unanimous focus on the reader, we could identify behind postmodern exegeses a unified Postmodern hermeneutic. For the most part,

---

[57] Cf. *The Gift of Knowing*, 9-20; Frame, *A History*, 500–504; Goldsworthy, *Gospel-Centered Hermeneutics*, 130–138.

[58] Cf. Brevard S. Childs, *Introduction to the Old Testament as Scripture* (Philadelphia: Fortress, 1979).

[59] Cf. Letty M. Russell, ed., *Feminist Interpretation of the Bible* (Philadelphia: Westminster John Knox, 1985).

[60] Ched Myers, *Binding the Strong Man: A Political Reading of Mark's Story of Jesus* (Maryknoll, N.Y.: Orbis, 1988).

the question of "how do texts communicate" and "what is meaning" are answered by looking at the reader. The reader of a text is, in one way or another, the arbiter of meaning.[61] The various approaches of exegesis are only different ways that a reader or recipient of the text might respond to or interact with the text they study. An example of this is some forms of Structural exegesis.[62]

a. Structural Exegesis

Structural exegesis takes its cues from Structuralism, a movement in linguistics deriving from the work of the Swiss linguist Ferdinand de Saussure (1857-1913). The ways structural linguistics has been applied to biblical exegesis are manifold, but it fits into the Postmodern turn in hermeneutics as one of many different exegetical approaches that are considered compatible.[63] It also fits into the Postmodern turn in philosophy in that meaning is moved away from history, even the author. However, the role of the reader in Structural exegesis is not creating meaning but discovering the meaning found in the text. In some forms of Structuralism, meaning (or signification) is imposed upon the author rather than a creation of the

---

[61] Jonathan Culler writes, "If the reader always rewrites the text and if the attempt to reconstruct an author's intention is only a particular, highly restricted case of rewriting, then a Marxist reading, for example, is not an illegitimate distortion, but one species of production." Jonathan Culler, *On Deconstructionism: Theory and Criticism after Structuralism* (Ithaca, N.Y.: Cornell University, 1982), 38. That is, once the arguments of scholars like Kähler is accepted, that all attempts to recover *historie*— in this case, the author's intention—are actually *geschichte* (interpretation or subjective reception), then it makes sense to argue that various interpretations or subjective receptions (reader responses) are acceptable. If the "author's intent" is a subjective interpretation—even a creation of the interpreting mind—then what claim to pre-eminence can it have over explicitly ideological interpretations such as Marxist reading? If *historie* is inaccessible—if the author's intention is lost—then it seems to follow that all sorts of reader responses are acceptable.

[62] Structuralism is in some ways a predecessor of Postmodernity more than an example itself, for it places meaning in the text not the reader. However, there is greater continuity than is sometimes granted. Cf. Ibid., 17–30.

[63] Cf. K. Lawson Younger, *Ancient Conquest Accounts*, Journal for the Study of the Old Testament Supplement 98 (Sheffield: Sheffield Academic Press, 1990), 57; Daniel Patte, *What Is Structural Exegesis?* (Philadelphia: Fortress, 1976), 1–3.

author.⁶⁴ However, more Evangelical approaches to structural exegesis identify the author as the originator of meaning. In such approaches, meaning is identified with the deeper structure of a text. The Evangelical Old Testament scholar K. Lawson Younger serves as a good example of this form of structural exegesis.

In his book *Ancient Conquest Accounts*, Younger argues that the conquest accounts in Joshua can be understood as a form of ideological communication. That is, they are carefully structured to communicate an ideological message shared among other Ancient Near Eastern conquest accounts of the same form.⁶⁵ What distinguishes his approach from other exegeses is that he wants to look beyond the details of the text to the underlying structure, the *trellis*, which he claims communicates meaning.⁶⁶ he argues that this communicative structure is made up of a series of syntagms or individual syntactic entities (phrases, clauses, etc.—textual units—understood to have stereotyped functions) structured in a specific way.⁶⁷ Thus, by identifying a parallel structure of such syntactic entities (syntagms), Younger claims to identify the same *trellis*, or form, in similar Ancient Near Eastern conquest accounts, arguing that this structure communicates the same ideological message in all these accounts. Though he does not reject the historicity of the events recounted, he does argue that the existence of an underlying ideological structure should make exegetes cautious about coming to historical conclusions about the details of the text.⁶⁸ Furthermore, he contends that this ideological pattern is the meaning of the text; whatever historical details may be present are secondary. That is, the historical events

---

⁶⁴ Daniel Patte explains that Structural exegesis presupposes a dialectical view of humans and language, where a person is both the creator of signification (or meaning) and has signification imposed upon him by the very nature of language. Ibid., 3.

⁶⁵ For Younger, "ideology" is a pattern of beliefs and facts claimed to be explanatory of a range of social phenomena. Cf. Younger, *Ancient*, 46, 51, 56.

⁶⁶ Ibid., 55–56, 63.

⁶⁷ Cf. Ibid., 70.. I examine Younger's approach to a greater extent in my paper, "Not a Single Survivor," available at https://teleioteti.ca/resources/papers/.

⁶⁸ he explicitly brackets out or ignores the historical aspect of the text from his investigation, but he then says, "The fact that there are figurative and ideological underpins [sic] to the accounts should not make us call them into question *per se*—it [sic] should only force us to be cautious!" Ibid., 256.

are merely an opportunity for textual performance, for the ideological message to be communicated.

This implies that the events themselves are not meaningful apart from the meaning given to them by the human interpreter; meaning is found in the structural form into which the events are fit.[69] This allows Younger to dismiss some of the details of the text as products of the underlying structural pattern. Particularly, he claims that the statements of complete destruction found in Joshua 9-12 (e.g. Josh 10:28-43) are instances of stereotyped language used in conquest accounts: the language serves a structural function as part of the underlying *trellis* that communicates the text's meaning.[70] Therefore, the reader is not to understand these statements as literal descriptions of what happened.[71] In this way, the historical emphasis of Modernity gives way to an emphasis on suprahistorical communication, history as a means of communicating and not the communication itself.

More extreme than structuralism are the various forms of criticism that separate meaning from both the author and the text, placing it in the interpreter. Feminist interpretation is a significant reader-response and deconstructionist literary movement today that does this.

b. Feminist Interpretation

In the book *Feminist Interpretation of the Bible*, edited by Letty M. Russell,[72] the authors provide a litany of examples of such exegesis. In her essay, "Feminist Interpretation: A Method of Correlation," Rosemary Radford Reuther seeks to explain what is meant when feminist theology is said to draw upon women's experience as a source of knowledge.[73] She delineates "women's experience" and its relevance for interpretation. Against traditional theology, she defends experience as ultimately authoritative. Tradition is verified by its

---

[69] Ibid., 55–56, 63.

[70] Ibid., 227–228, 323.

[71] Ibid., 243.

[72] Russell, *Feminist Interpretation of the Bible*.

[73] Rosemary Radford Ruether, "Feminist Interpretation: A Method of Correlation," in *Feminist Interpretation of the Bible*, ed. Letty M. Russell (Philadelphia: Westminster John Knox, 1985), 111.

explanation of experience; experience collects and provides interpretive keys (tradition) that are, dialectically, further refined by experience.[74] Feminist hermeneutic is new not because it asserts the authority of experience, for all interpretation does this (the presupposition of reader-response hermeneutics). Instead, it is new because it invokes the experience of women.[75] She defines women's experience as that experience of women in a patriarchal society with its interpretation of their distinctive biology. This experience is interpretive when women become aware of this society's false paradigm and take a differing stance rooted in their experience: they begin to interpret texts and reality not according to the pattern of the reigning society but according to the paradigm provided by "women's experience." As an interpretive principle, she posits that only what affirms the full humanity of women is authoritative. This interpretive principle denies every form of chauvinism in interpretation. To give biblical sanction to her approach, she correlates the feminist hermeneutic with Scripture's prophetic-messianic tradition. For Ruether, this is Scripture's process of ever reconsidering what is truly liberating (the Word of God) and discarding what was distorted in tradition. This prophetic tradition faces similar distortion and so requires refinement also. This, she writes, affirms feminist principles, which measures Scripture by their experience of oppression to discern in it what is truly liberating and so authoritative.[76]

With Feminist interpretation, we touch upon the extremes of

---

[74] Ibid., 111–112. "Dialectically" refers to the back-and-forth interchange characterized by this interaction. Tradition is an accumulation of experience which is interpreted by further experience.

[75] A particularly confusing point in feminist interpretation is what is meant by "women's experience." Feminists do not mean the experiences of particular women; instead, what is intend is an abstract "women experience" that is not equivalent to every experience of women. Some experiences are consistent with and thus embody this "women's experience," yet not all things a woman experiences are characteristic of "women's experience." This "experience" is thus a scholarly abstraction. Jonathan Culler describes it like this (revealing the incoherence of the idea), "For a woman to read as a woman is not to repeat an identity or an experience that is given but to play a role she constructs with reference to her identity as a woman, which is also a construct, so that the series can continue: a woman reading as a woman reading as a woman." Culler, *Deconstructionism*, 64. "Construct" here refers to an abstraction, an identity that is not equivalent to any specific experiences of a particular person

[76] Ruether, "Feminist Interpretation: A Method of Correlation," 111–124.

Postmodern hermeneutical approaches. To conclude this chapter, let us pull back from the fringes and turn to a final hermeneutical approach that has far more of a following among Evangelicals, theological interpretation.

c. Theological Interpretation

Theological interpretation does not refer to any single approach to interpreting the Bible but to a group of approaches that share some similarities. Theological Interpretation rejects the myth of neutrality perpetuated by historical criticism, that interpretation of the Bible could be done from a neutral, unbiased perspective. Instead, it recognises that all interpretation is "theological," that it is influenced by the theology of the interpreter. Theological interpretation seeks to be explicit about these presuppositions and—among its Evangelical proponents—seeks to be explicitly confessional, rooted in the tradition or traditions of the church (that is, the so-called "great tradition" or different denominational traditions). In this broad sense, the exegetical approach I am developing in this series is a form of theological interpretation. Indeed, there are some brands of theological interpretation that operate within the confines of Grammatical-Historical Exegesis, as discussed above. But many theological interpreters identify themselves with the pre-critical or pre-modern allegorical interpretation, which we also considered above. David C. Steinmetz, for example, wrote an essay arguing for the superiority of pre-critical exegesis over Grammatical-Historical Exegesis that focuses on a single meaning for biblical texts.[77] Because our discussion above has already covered these two branches of theological interpretation, I want to discuss theological interpretation as it is practised in ways distinctly Postmodern.

As we saw above, the pre-modern approach of the Early Church was not radically different than that practised by the reformers and even shared many similarities with the Grammatical-Historical approach of Modernity. In my opinion, the reformers and Protestant's rejection of allegorizing practised by the Fathers was merely taking the bibliology of the Fathers and allowing it to reform their hermeneutical practice, rejecting any external authority that could identify a Scriptural passage or teaching as "difficult." Even the focus on the single meaning and authorial intention among Grammatical-Historical

---

[77] Steinmetz, "The Superiority of Precritical Exegesis," 65–77.

Exegesis was anticipated in Thomas Aquinas and Albert the Great. However, theological interpretation, in its most postmodern form, has not followed this stream of biblical exegesis but has taken the excesses of Medieval Exegesis and run with them. As an example of this tendency, we could look at what we could call dogmatic allegorical interpretation.

Allegorical interpretation, as we saw earlier, was reading scripture as an allegory, where events and persons signified another reality. For Augustine and Origen, allegory was a form of writing the biblical authors used. The biblical authors signalled the presence of an allegory through the insertion of difficult doctrines or events. This could be called allegory as a genre, which fits into the overall textual approach these interpreters took. However, what I am calling "dogmatic allegory" is allegory of a different sort. Instead of looking for places where authors intended allegory, this form of allegory is free to find additional meaning in every text. For example, Hans Boersma writes in his book *Heavenly Participation* that he does not believe that there is any "objectively given, historical meaning that one can discover and solve as one does scientific problems" in the biblical text.[78] He does not reject the insights of historical-critical study but points to spiritual or theological interpretation as a way of going beyond historical-critical exegesis and avoiding the Postmodern scepticism towards meaning.[79]

The literal sense or senses are the starting point for this interpretation, but spiritual interpretation will look for the greater Christological reality that this sense points to. The difference between this approach and genre-based allegorising lies in the rejection of any objective meaning or basis for the allegory. For Augustine and Origen, they thought that the authors intended to write allegorically, so they looked for clues to the allegorical meaning in the text. Boersma, on the other hand, writes approvingly of the approach taken by Henri de Lubac,

> He recognizes that different readers might well come up with different interpretations *within* the same level. In other words, two exegetes might well present two (or more) different allegorical or Christological readings of the same passage. This hardly presents a

---

[78] Hans Boersma, *Heavenly Participation: The Weaving of a Sacramental Tapestry* (Grand Rapids: Eerdmans, 2011), 152..

[79] Ibid. Cf. Hans Boersma, *Sacramental Preaching: Sermons on the Hidden Presence of Christ* (Grand Rapids: Baker Academic, 2016).

problem for de Lubac. Convinced that interpretation is a sacramental entry into the infinity of the spiritual realm, he maintains that the sacramental reality (*res*) of the biblical text cannot possibility be captured by one particular allegorical rendering of the text. Therefore, plurality of meaning is not a danger to be avoided and does not constitute an argument against spiritual exegesis; plurality of meaning is something to be *expected*, precisely because exegesis is the Spirit-guided means that enables human participation in heavenly realities.[80]

This multiplicity of meaning is not bound by the author's intention but is bound up in the reception of the text by the reader. There is an interchange between the text and tradition, allowing further meaning to be identified over time. Indeed, "the church's historical interpretation of the text has entered into its meaning, sometimes in enormously significant ways."[81] Because the meaning of a text is bound up in Christ, as the one to whom it points, the meaning of any text is infinite. Christ and his actions have infinite implications for the Christian life, so the interpretation explores this wealth of meaning. Tradition sets the trajectory of this exploration; "As long as (1) allegory centered on Christ and his church and (2) one allowed for real participation of the historical in the spiritual, one could hardly go wrong with allegory."[82]

---

[80] Boersma, *Heavenly Participation*, 140.

[81] Ibid., 141.

[82] Ibid., 151. For a further discussion of the language of "participation" and "sacrament," see my paper "Sacramental Ontology and Augustine's Platonism" on https://teleioteti.ca/resources/papers.

The parallels between this approach and postmodernity are, I think, clear. As with postmodern interpretations, Boersma conceives of meaning as plural, not singular; he identifies meaning in the reader (here it is the reader's imaginative exploration of the Christological anchor of Scripture); and he sees his approach as parallel to and not in conflict with other exegeses.

ii. The Narrative Turn

It is worth observing that there has been a turn in recent interpretation towards the importance of narrative in Biblical interpretation. On the one hand, there is the Reformed emphasis on Redemptive History, which I discussed as an essential part of interpretation in *The Gift of Reading Part 1*. But there has been another emphasis on narrative that has emerged in recent years, what we might call sociological or epistemological narrative. There has been an increasing interest in narrative as a key aspect, if not the key aspect, of human self-understanding. In the early chapters of his book *The New Testament and the People of God*, N.T. Wright states that "Stories are one of the most basic modes of human life" and that "the stories which characterize the worldview itself are thus located, on the map of human knowing, at a more fundamental level than explicitly formulated beliefs, including theological beliefs."[i]

In Biblical studies, the role of this emphasis on narrative or story has come to the forefront in two ways. First, the Bible has been identified as a narrative and so narrative becomes the primary lens through which to read it. Second, and closely related, many scholars have attributed narrative (more precisely, story) with prominence in the formation and content of a worldview. In *The Gift of Reading Part 1* I acknowledged the essential role of narrative for understanding the Bible and the Christian life, something I intend to expound further in the third volume of this series (*The Gift of Seeing*). However, I want to take issue with some aspects of this narrative turn in theology and interpretation.

First, regarding the significance of the Biblical narratives in Christian spiritual formation, I am not qualified to comment on the merits of the psychology present here (that story is essential to human identity and self-understanding) but in as much as this emphasis detracts from the non-narrative parts of Scripture and the non-narrative role of narrative, I think this is a danger. That is, narrative is important yet so are the didactic prose and prophetic—i.e. non-narrative—parts of Scripture. Some scholars claim that the Bible is a narrative, yet I have seen no compelling evidence in this regard nor is it evident to me that this is the case. As I discuss in *The Gift of Reading Part 1*, the Bible tells a narrative (i.e. it explains the true meaning of history) but does so as a covenant document, not a narrative. It does not do justice to the unique ways the different parts of Scripture inform and shape Christian life and doctrine to subsume them all under the overarching category of narrative—as both Reformed and narrative-theological interpretations are sometimes guilty of doing.

Furthermore, as I believe V. Phillips Long has argued persuasively, narrative has a profoundly didactic function. Phil shows that narratives are artfully shaped to convey interpretations of historical events, to give an interpretation of what happened.[ii] That is, sometimes this narrative focus is used to diminish the propositional authority of Scripture, its ability to tell us true and false and to teach truth about God and man. This is contrary to the very nature of narrative; the difference between didactic prose—such as this book—and narrative is not that one communicates truth that can be summarized as propositional statements (i.e. God is all-powerful) but that they represent two different approaches to teaching truth and eliciting different responses to it. Narrative has the power to show us truth in a way logical arguments cannot and to make us feel the emotive import of these truths. It is also uniquely suited to telling us *what happened*. Didactic prose, on the other hand, is especially suited to convince us of truth, to debunk falsehood, and to explain *why something happened*. Thus, didactic prose and narrative—as well as poetry—are complementary approaches to teaching truth.

Second, I think the epistemology presupposed in this narrative turn is questionable. These are issues I have touched upon already in *The Gift of Knowing* and will deal with more thoroughly in *The Gift of Seeing*, but a few words would be fitting here. I believe that the use of "story" is confused in these views, that the role of "stories" in knowledge is misunderstood, and that the idea of story in Biblical studies is used—whether intentionally or unintentionally—to undermine the authority of Scripture over every aspect of our thinking. Regarding the use of "story," what is intended is not clear. "Narrative" refers the literary form used to tell stories, where a story is developed through a temporal succession of events (a plot) recounted by a narrator.[iii] "Story" naturally refers to "plot," or the basic—that is, non-literary—interpretation of the relationship between temporally successive events, or history. "Story" is an interpretation of these events and narrative the recounting of this story.[iv] According to Wright, "story" is irreducible to anything else, such as a proposition, and is the essential nature of Scripture.[v] However, story begins to be stretched beyond reasonable bounds in these examples. Scripture is clearly not narrative, and though it tells stories, it is not a story. Paul's letters draw on the Biblical metanarrative, or interpretation of history and events, yet does not tell many "stories." Paul's ability to interpret and apply events, which naturally fit a story form, in prose seems to me to lay bare the epistemological weakness of Wright's position.

That is, Wright argues that theological "abstractions," such as "Monotheism," are shorthand for stories. He also dismisses the ability for stories to be reduced to anything else. To anticipate the argument I will present in *The Gift of Seeing*, and have anticipated in *The Gift of Knowing*, stories—and their narrative presentations—are better understood as one part of the subject's interpretation of objects—namely events. That is, we can look at an event and deduce truths from it and we can interpret in relation to other events. This is what a story is, an interpretation of events in relation to one another. Narratives presuppose a story, for they recount a specific relation between events. Narrative is the natural form for recounting a story and a story may be the best way to interpret the relationships between events; however, it is not the only way. We can also interpret these relations as confirmation of universal laws; we interpret the cause-effect relationship between two pool balls as confirmation of the laws of motion and causality. Furthermore, stories are often used not only to interpret the relationships between events but also to teach the meaning of things and to illustrate or prove abstract ideas such as laws. I can illustrate what is meant by causality by telling a story about events that demonstrate causality. I can illustrate what is meant by God's power through stories about God's actions. Stories are essential to human knowledge, for we experience a temporal succession of events throughout our lives and interpret them. And stories are indispensable for pedagogy, for teaching truth. But stories are not irreducible; the fact that we can talk about stories in non-narrative forms and discuss them demonstrates this to some extent. Furthermore, to embrace story at the expense of the role of abstraction in human thinking is to stumble into the same epistemological dilemma as Empiricism. Empiricism bases all knowledge upon the senses, so all knowledge is limited to telling what has happened. Such knowledge cannot guarantee what will happen or will always happen; it can only say what has happened (the objects of experience). Such an epistemological position can tell you what it means for God to have acted faithfully but cannot tell you that God's faithfulness means he will always act in this manner. It can tell you that God is powerful but not that God is all-powerful. Indeed, abstractions such as laws are more ultimate than stories in the sense that they are the principles by which we interpret events, producing stories. All that to say, human knowledge is complex and cannot be reduced to "story," no matter how significant that category proves to be and how pedagogically effective narrative is.

Which brings us to one final point concerning the narrative turn. Wright, and others to different extents,[vi] have sought to explain the authority of narratives or the role of theology in new terms, terms other than that of epistemic normativity (ability to tell us what is right and wrong, good and bad, etc.).[vii] Wright argues that the authority of Scripture is like an unfinished play, setting the trajectory and establishing the parameters and characters for later actors—us—to improvise with. He disavows the ability to "look up the right answers" in Scripture.[viii] However, as I argued in *The Gift of Knowing* and *The Gift of Reading Part 1*, the Bible makes no such claims. Indeed, the Bible claims complete normative authority over all areas of our life and is a covenant document meant to *legislate* the Christian life. That narratives can have normative authority in this sense is demonstrated by the Old Testament case laws, which were not merely suggestions for improvisation but concrete examples to use in making future judgments. There is an aspect of improvisation to be sure, for we must draw analogies. Yet this improvisation is grounded in normative commands and truths that shape our perspective of the world. I think John Frame is right when he writes, "To base ethics on a narrative devoid of revealed commands leaves us with no ethical standards except those derived from would-be autonomous thought."[ix] I do not find Wright's suggestions helpful at all for understanding the Christian life and the role of Scripture within it.[x]

[i] N.T. Wright, *The New Testament and the People of God*, Christian Origins and the Question of God 1 (Minneapolis: Fortress, 1992), 38.

[ii] V. Philips Long, "The Art of Biblical History," in *Foundations of Contemporary Interpretation*, ed. Moisés Silva (Grand Rapids: Zondervan, 1996).

[iii] Jean Louis Ska, *"Our Fathers Have Told Us": Introduction to the Analysis of Hebrew Narratives*, Subsidia Biblica 13 (Roma: Editrice Pontificio Instituto Biblico, 1990), 21.

[iv] This is something I will unpack further in my book *The Gift of Seeing*, but seems congruent with Wright's presentation of "story," cf. Wright, *The New Testament*, 79.

[v] Ibid., 38, 79, 139–143, 371; cf. N. T. Wright, *Scripture and the Authority of God* (Society for Promoting Christian Knowledge, 2005).

[vi] Cf. Vanhoozer, *The Drama of Doctrine*; Kevin J. Vanhoozer, *Faith Speaking Understanding: Performing the Drama of Doctrine*, First edition. (Louisville: Westminster John Knox Press, 2014). Vanhoozer's model of theodrama is very similar to Wright's understanding of the authority of narrative.

[vii] Wright, *The New Testament*, 139–144.

[viii] Ibid. 141. Cf. Wright, *Scripture and the Authority of God*.

[ix] John M. Frame, *The Doctrine of the Christian Life*, A Theology of Lordship 4 (Phillipsburg: P&R Publishing, 2008), 326. n. 2.

[x] Cf. John M. Frame, *The Doctrine of the Word of God*, A Theology of Lordship (Phillipsburg: P&R Publishing, 2010), 517–524.

D. Conclusion

Throughout the history of the Church, Christians have been reading the Bible. Despite the different ways they have approached the Scriptures, every generation has arrived at and confirmed the same doctrines. Despite the hermeneutical obfuscation, God's voice has been heard clearly. A significant reason for this, I believe, is that we have all been looking at *the text*. Though we differ in our approach to reading, we cannot deny what is before our eyes. Though the Bible admits that it contains difficult texts, even here the emphasis falls on the corruption of those who stumble over these hard-to-understand passages (2 Pet 2:9).

I think this much has been clear in our survey: through each generation, some Christians have often fallen into the trap of reading the Bible according to the agenda of the culture. For the early Church fathers, their philosophy occasionally influenced their perception of textual difficulties and justified their allegorical readings. For the Reformers, the temptation was to read their struggles into the text, such as identifying the Pope as the Antichrist. Under Modernity, the Church fought to justify the historicity and moral authority of the text in light of the progress of the Enlightenment. Under Postmodernity, Christians have fought to maintain the universal authority of Scripture against the relativizing tendencies of Postmodernity. I suggested in the introduction to this chapter that it is worth observing the role of audience and authority in these different hermeneutical approaches. Sometimes in subtle ways and at other times in explicit ones, the different approaches we have seen have let the ultimate authority of the Bible slip.

Some among the Early Church Fathers relied on external standards of morality and philosophy to judge what was a difficult teaching or text. For the Modernist interpreters, the canon of human reason was dominant in epistemology, giving the standard of morality and truth by which the Bible was to be read and judged. The influence of this thinking has even been seen within the Grammatical Historical camp, as proponents have sought to justify the Bible's inerrancy and authority on the basis of human reason as their epistemological authority.[83] In Postmodernity, the authority of the Bible has been radically dismissed by those who claim that it cannot even speak apart from a reader giving it meaning, that it cannot communicate and so cannot have authority, or that its authority is not the sort that can tell us what to believe and what not to believe. Alongside these struggles with the question of biblical authority has been confusion over the audience of the Bible.

Though it is present to some extent in the early church, the struggle over

---

[83] In *The Gift of Knowing*, I try to show that a key tension throughout human history has been the authority of God versus the authority of man. Christian theology and philosophy, even by those who are otherwise orthodox, has been heavily influenced by non-Christian philosophy which has attempted to interpret the world form the standpoint of autonomous, human authority.

the question of the audience has come to the fore since the Reformation. Under Modernity, the historical nature of the Bible came under close scrutiny, and great attention was paid to the original context of the individual books of which it is composed. Specifically, by looking at the Bible as a historical document recording a communicative act—a transmission from an author to an audience—much thought was given to the role of the original audiences in this communication. When Modernity matured into Postmodernity, the role of the audience was almost entirely eclipsed by the reader. That is, the intended audience of the author and his intentions were eschewed in exchange for the response of the present reader. In its most extreme forms, the text becomes merely an opportunity for a reading performance—for the reader to imaginatively create meaning. The questions of authority and audience—along with the author, meaning, and text—will play a key role in my hermeneutical proposal. In the following pages, I am striving to acknowledge the Bible's authority over every area of the hermeneutical task, as I attempted in *The Gift of Reading Part 1*. By doing so, I think we can see why God's Word has always been heard despite the din of hermeneutical theories, and we can see how God has equipped us through the Word with the tools necessary to read it well. We will begin here, with the role of biblical authority in the hermeneutical task in Part 1. We will look at the role of the Bible in its own reading. Then we will consider the role of the reader in Part 2. Finally, in Part 3, we will consider the role of the author.

Further Reading

Graeme Goldsworthy - *Gospel-Centered Hermeneutics*, 87-180
Moises Silva – *Has the Church Misread the Bible*

—Part 1—
The Role of the Bible

2

THE BIBLE AS SELF-INTERPRETING

> When your son asks you in time to come, "What is the meaning of the testimonies and the statutes and the rules that the Lord our God has commanded you?" then you shall say to your son, "We were Pharaoh's slaves in Egypt. And the Lord brought us out of Egypt with a mighty hand. And the Lord showed signs and wonders, great and grievous, against Egypt and against Pharaoh and all his household, before our eyes. And he brought us out from there, that he might bring us in and give us the land that he swore to give to our fathers. And the Lord commanded us to do all these statutes, to fear the Lord our God, for our good always, that he might preserve us alive, as we are this day. And it will be righteousness for us, if we are careful to do all this commandment before the Lord our God, as he has commanded us." – Deuteronomy 6:20-25

Throughout this series, I have argued that the Bible is the ultimate authority for a Christian. As God's very words given to govern and guide his people, Christians are obligated to obey the Bible. In *The Gift of Knowing*, I argued that the rejection of God's authority undermines any claim to knowledge, that submission to God as he has spoken through the Scriptures is essential to the task of living within and understanding God's world. In *The Gift of Reading Part 1*, I argued that the Bible is shaped as a covenant document, explicitly communicating with God's authority. The authority of God expressed in the Bible is not a word for bygone generations nor a word for this generation alone; the Bible was intended by God to govern his covenant people until his return. God breathed out the Scriptures in order that they might be useful, available to equip his people for the good works for which he created them (2 Tim 3:16-17, cf. Eph 2:10). Surely Yahweh—the God who created the heavens and the earth by his very words (Genesis 1), who struck Egypt with might plagues (Exodus 1-12), and who raised Jesus Christ from the dead (Eph 1:19-21)—could ensure such an end if that were truly what he desired. Isaiah affirms that when God sets his mind to do something, when he speaks to accomplish a goal, it is accomplished (Isa 55:10-11).

If God truly intended his Word to govern his people and equip them for the very purpose he created them—as Paul affirms in 2 Timothy 3:16-17—then surely he will have given his people not only a text but a means to interpret this text. And if he has invested the Bible with ultimate authority, the authority of his own word, then it must be self-interpreting—for if interpretation relied on another court of appeal, that interpreter would be the ultimate authority. This is an issue I take with many of the hermeneutical approaches we saw in the previous chapter: they have not taken into consideration the Bible's own claims and have produced hermeneutical models that imply one generation—either the first generation or us today—has a privileged position for interpreting the Bible. But if God has given us the Bible to be read and profited from, we must presuppose in our hermeneutic that the Bible is self-interpreting. I want to outline in this chapter several ways God has shaped the Bible to be self-interpreting. But first, let's look closer at the problem that would emerge if the Bible was not self-interpreting.

The goal of the Bible is truly ambitious, to govern God's people over a period of roughly 3300-3400 years and counting. When the Torah was first written, it was intended to legislate the Old Testament people of God. This covenant remained in effect until the 1st century AD. The New Testament was finished by the end of the 1st century AD and was given to govern God's people until Christ's return—almost 2000 years now. To illustrate the difficulties that are involved in such a project, think of all the cultural changes that have happened in Western Culture over the last 600 years. Roman Catholicism has lost its dominance in Europe, Protestantism became a force to be reckoned with, North America and South America were colonised by European countries, most Western monarchies have been replaced by alternate forms of government or have been radically transformed, the influence of Christianity on public life is waning, technology has exploded in unimaginable ways, etc. Not only has culture shifted, but language has also shifted, consider the preface to John Owen's *The Doctrine of the Saints Perseverance* (1654),

> *The Wife man tells us, that* no man knoweth Love or hatred, by all that is before him. *The great variety wherein God difpenfeth outward things in the World, with the many changes and alterations,* which according to the counfell of his will, *he continually works in the difpenfations of them, will not all them nakedly in themfelves, to be evidences of the fountaine from whence they flow. Seeing alfo, that the* want, *or* abundance *of them, may equally by the Goodneffe and Wifdome of God, be ordered and caft into an ufefull* fubferviency, *to a Good* infinitely tranfcending *what is, or may be contained in them, there is no receffity*....[1]

In the 360 or so years since this edition was printed, the English "f" has been replaced by the "s," at least one word has passed out of usage (I do not know what "fubferviency" means), verbal forms and spelling has changed, and stylistic standards have also changed (though Owen was never exemplary in his time). This is, nevertheless, recognizably English. Imagine trying to learn 17th century French today; you would not only be wrestling with the changes in language but also the challenges of moving from one language to another. This is similar to what we find in the Old and New Testaments. The Old Testament was written in Hebrew and Aramaic, intended to be read by an audience for hundreds of years. But by the 1st century, Hebrew was replaced as the common language in Judea with Aramaic and Greek. So readers in the 1st century were dealing with texts in a non-native tongue written up to 1,400 years prior. From the time of the New Testament until now, the Greek language has undergone massive changes as well, and Hebrew was not a living language until it was resurrected recently. So a challenge has faced interpreters since the Bible was penned, understanding the language of the Bible as those who are fluent in an altogether different language or a language that has changed significantly.[2] If the original texts or *autographa* are authoritative, then

---

[1] Taken from the digitized copy on the John Richard Allison Library website, see The Puritan Project.

[2] Though I think the differences are less significant than are often claimed, Hebrew scholars differentiate between Archaic, Classical (Pre-exilic), and Late Biblical Hebrew (Post-exilic). These categories describe the Hebrew found in

we need a way to be sure that we can understand the language of the Bible to interpret it correctly—despite the differences.[3]

In addition to the problem of language-distance, there is also a problem created by the size and scope of the Bible. As we discussed in *The Gift of Reading Part 1*, to read any part of the Bible we need to understand the whole teaching of Scripture. We saw earlier in this book that the early church practised such contextual reading (reading parts in light of the whole) in the form of the analogy of faith. The Bible is massive and complex; it would be a lifelong endeavour to come to a sufficient understanding of the whole Bible by oneself. So, for the Bible to be self-interpreting in the sense discussed above, it must be able to function as its own standard for its language, it must be sufficient to allow us to learn its languages and verify our interpretations,[4] and it must be sufficient in scope to present an interpretive lens for the parts.

However, sufficiency in this internal sense is not enough: even if the Bible were perfectly sufficient in its content, this would not ensure that it was self-interpreting. If we had no knowledge of the Bible and, given internal sufficiency, it fell from heaven into the midst of our culture, we would still not be able to interpret it. That is, we would have no knowledge of the language to begin interpreting, and without knowledge of the whole, we would not have a solid beginning point to interpret it.[5] To be self-interpreting, the Bible also needs to have what we could call *external sufficiency*. What I mean by external sufficiency is this: it must have the capacity and means in itself to create an interpreting community through which an understanding of the whole can be passed on to succeeding generations.

So in our discussion of the sufficiency of Scripture for its own self-

---

different parts of the Bible; the Hebrew texts found in Qumran also demonstrate differences and the Rabbinic Hebrew of the Mishnah even more so.

[3] Translations do not solve the problem, for we need to be able to have confidence that our translators can accurately understand the original texts to produce accurate translations.

[4] "Verify" corresponds to the category of validity developed in *The Gift of Reading Part 1*.

[5] If, somehow, we knew the languages in which it was written, we could eventually come to an understanding of whole by reading and re-reading, constantly re-evaluating our understanding of each part. Yet, as mentioned above, given the scope and complexity of the Bible, this would take far more than a single lifetime.

interpretation, we can distinguish between *external* and *internal* sufficiency. For the rest of this chapter, I want to consider several features of the Bible that provide internal sufficiency and the role of external sufficiency, how the Bible creates an interpreting community sufficient to ensure its interpretation throughout the generations. Regarding internal sufficiency, I want to consider the role of the analogy of faith, the role of narrative/textual closure, and linguistic sufficiency.

A. Analogy of Faith

We saw earlier how the analogy of faith was the appeal made by the earlier church fathers, such as Irenaeus, to all the Scriptures in interpreting the parts. The emphasis of the analogy of faith today often focuses on the role of the narrative told by Scriptures (its interpretation of the created world's past, present, and future)[6] and the role of systematic theology in interpretation (e.g. we interpret the biblical passages in which God is said to change his mind in light of those passages where he is said not to change his mind and vice versa, coming to a more nuanced understanding of God).[7] Both of these approaches are seen throughout this series; I have argued so far that we need to read the Bible according to its own theology and worldview—the worldview it teaches—and that we need to interpret it and the world through its metanarrative, or interpretation of all history. These are important aspects of the analogy of faith, but we can point to two other ways Scripture interprets itself. It provides a robust context for interpretation and is often explicitly self-interpreting.

Beginning with context, consider what would happen if you only had the beginning and the ending of a book. You may understand the argument of the book, but you will not know whether to believe it or not or understand what any specialized terms mean, for these are often defined and worked out in the body of a book. Alternatively, consider if you found the middle chapter

---

[6] E.g. Peter John Gentry and Stephen J. Wellum, *Kingdom through Covenant: A Biblical-Theological Understanding of the Covenants* (Wheaton: Crossway, 2012); Goldsworthy, *Gospel-Centered Hermeneutics*.

[7] E.g. Vern S. Poythress, *Reading the Word of God in the Presence of God: A Handbook for Biblical Interpretation* (Wheaton: Crossway, 2016), 36–37; Goldsworthy, *Gospel-Centered Hermeneutics*.

of a book. What could you understand of it? You would not know the necessary details about the characters, you would not know where they came from, why their present circumstances are important, and what end this is all working towards. Furthermore, you may be missing key details about the setting, language, or others features that are only revealed when you read the whole book. To put it simply, a text deprived of context is meaningless. It is not meaningless because it says nothing, but it is meaningless because it could mean anything.[8]

Without the author telling you what you should think about the circumstances and characters in the story, you are "free" to create all manner of circumstances, scenarios, storylines, and details. However, such freedom is ultimately a curse, for you will never understand what the author wanted you to know. To understand a text as it is meant to be understood, we need context—a beginning, middle, and end. We need to know the vocabulary an author is using, his characters, and his story. This is not only true of novels, but it is also true of books that recount historical events. In these cases, there are characters—nations and individuals—and circumstances that the reader must be familiar with.

Consider the book of Revelation; what would Revelation 20-22 communicate if we were missing the rest of the Bible? What would we think of final judgment and Satan if we did not understand the nature of sin and the enemy of God's people? What would we make of the massive city descending from heaven if we did not have the rest of the Scriptures to identify Jerusalem with the people of God? What would we do with Jesus's promise to come quickly? Would we assume that he already came or broke his promise? Only context, the rest of Scripture, can answer these questions. God has shaped Scripture as a cohesive whole to provide such a context, a sufficient context to interpret all the events and characters involved so that we might understand them. This enables us to rightly understand the parts of Scripture by reading them in light of the whole Bible, in light of what has come before and what comes after.

This is the case for symbolism as well. A reader of the Gospels for the first time, for example, would probably be lost as to the significance of Jesus referring to the "cup" his Father has prepared for him (e.g. Luke 22:42, John 18:11). However, someone familiar with the Old Testament will recognize in

---

[8] We will look at this further in the chapters on meaning.

this language—especially in the context of the crucifixion—the symbolic use of "cup" in the Old Testament. In the prophets, God's judgment against nations and people was often expressed as drinking from the cup of God's wrath (Isa 51:17, 22; Jer 25:15; Hab 2:15-17; Job 21:20; Rev 14:10). Thus, reading Jesus words in the context of the Bible, we understand that Jesus is about to drink full the wrath of God towards the sins of his people.

Having a context that explains the features of a text is important if it is to be self-interpreting, yet knowing the context—knowing the story and characters—will not necessarily help us resolve pressing difficulties in an individual text. Sometimes we need a word from the author, a little bit of a hint or help to resolve a pressing difficulty.

A good author is aware of this. A good author pays attention to the clarity of his or her work and anticipates confusion, providing interpretive clues along the way to help the reader grasp the point. It is a serious understatement to say this, but God is a good author. He is the best author. He knows that his children are going to get confused over some point or another, so he has provided us with the canon to give us clarity. There is a lot of overlap with the previous category, for context often provides this interpretive clarity. Often, reading a bit further reveals the necessary details to understand what came before. But, at other times, the Bible specifically comments on itself to help us understand it. This is frequent in books of prophecy, where the prophets provide God's interpretation of their vision (e.g. Dan 7:15-28, Dan 8:15-27; Rev 7:14). These interpretations often serve double duty because the imagery is shared between books—e.g. the interpretation of Daniel's visions helps us understand the visions in Revelation. More significantly, the revelation of Jesus Christ in the New Testament sheds immense light on the Old Testament (e.g. Luke 24:25-27, Acts 8:25-35). The New Testament authors often quote the Old Testament; by doing so, they help us understand what was meant: this goes both ways, for the Old Testament also helps us understand what the New intends (e.g. Hab 2:4 sheds light on Rom 1:16-17, Gal 3:11, and Heb 10:36-39 and vice versa; Gen 15 helps us understand Rom 4 and Gal 3, and vice versa; etc.). God has given us the canon we have in order that it might be self-clarifying, that is, in order that it would give us all the tools necessary to interpret difficult texts.

The analogy of faith describes the role of the teaching and context of

Scripture for interpreting the parts. Scripture provides a sufficient context to be self-interpreting so that we might understand the persons, events, symbols, etc. in order to apply Scripture to our lives. Now, as we saw in *The Gift of Reading Part 1*, Scripture is sufficient to interpret it as God intended but not to indulge all our curiosities. There are passages in Scripture that hint at events and persons about which I would love to know more, such as the responses of people to the mass resurrection when Jesus died and what happened to those resurrected, but it gives no more details than is necessary to understand the role of these events in their context—the resurrection of these saints testifies to the new reality that began with Christ's death and resurrection, namely that the new creation and end times resurrection have begun (cf. Matthew 27:52-53).[9]

The analogy of faith has functioned since the Scriptures were first delivered in order that God's people would be able to interpret and apply God's word. Yet throughout the Old Testament period, revelation continued. Scripture had a sort of sufficiency, but because of rebellion, God's people required continual rebuke and reminders: they needed continuing prophetic words. Full sufficiency for interpretation can only be attributed to a final document, one that will not receive any more supplementation. Thus, in its full sense, it is only an attribute of the completed Bible, New and Old Testaments together. Not only is finality a precondition for something to be "sufficient" and so self-interpreting, but it is also a condition that makes it self-interpreting.

B. Closure

Though the Bible began with a core set of covenant documents—the Torah, Genesis through Deuteronomy—it expanded throughout the Old Covenant period. This period ended with the death of Jesus, at which time a New Covenant was inaugurated. This covenant was accompanied by a new revelation from God, a new covenant document to supplement the Old Testament. Only this final product, the Bible—the Old and New Testaments together in one covenant document—could be called final. This is God's final

---

[9] That is, the new creation and end times resurrection have begun with Christ but will not be finished until his return. In New Testament studies this is called inaugurated eschatology: the end times have begun but have not fully arrived.

word for his people until Christ returns. Theologians will often say that Canon is "closed"; this closure is necessary for Scripture to be self-interpreting for God's people from the 1st century until Christ returns.

Let me try to illustrate this point. Imagine finding a novel lying on a bench outside your home. It is a book you have never read before, and it is missing the last chapter. Ignoring the existence of the internet and bookstores, what would happen if you read through the whole book only to discover that the last chapter was missing? Besides your frustration, several consequences would result. On the one hand, you would be deprived of the ending you longed for. But more significantly, you would not understand what you had read. Your mind might go wild imagining all the possible endings the story could have, but you would never have certainty as to which of these possible endings was intended—was true. If it were a good story, you would not really understand anything at all. That is, many good stories wait until the very end to supply the key interpretive insight that sheds light on all that preceded it. When you reach the end of a good story, your mind speeds back over all that you have read and re-interprets it in light of the final revelation or twist (think of the movie, *The Sixth Sense*). In the case of such a story, the lack of an ending—of closure—means that the rest of the story is ultimately shrouded in mystery, awaiting the revelation that will reveal its meaning.

What if the ending of your book was missing, yet it was cut off at such a point that you were unsure if it was missing or not? What if you got to the end and were left questioning if that was all there was? You are forced to decide; do you interpret the book in light of the ending you have or conclude that you are missing the ultimate interpretive key to the book?[10]

In both cases, what is needed is closure. To rightly interpret a book, you

---

[10] The book of Mark provides an interesting illustration of this point. The book of Mark ends on a cliff-hanger, it recounts the angels' report of Christ's resurrection but ends there. At some point, it appears that scribes were not satisfied with this cliff-hanger and tried to fill in the ending of Mark from the other Gospels and Acts. The several endings that appear in the manuscripts provide different interpretations of the whole book, with the short ending printed in our English Bibles strongly supported by the rest of the book and our manuscript evidence. The point is this: if you read Mark with the short ending, you interpret the book one way; if you read it with the long ending, another interpretation presents itself. Only one is correct, so having a right knowledge of the ending is highly important.

need to have its ending and know that what you have is, in fact, the ending. The canon as we have it provides the necessary closure we need to interpret it. Scholars will argue from various pieces of evidence throughout the New Testament to show this, but the most significant evidence is the very shape of the canon itself. Good stories, good books, share many things in common. One of these things is resolution: the tension invoked in the beginning is resolved in the end. There are various ways of presenting this, but two significant ways are *mirroring* and *summarising*. As you may remember from High School or college, the way to understand a book is to study its beginning and its end. A book that makes an argument will present a thesis or a question at the beginning, raising a problem or stating its solution to a problem; throughout the book, various arguments will be made; and in the conclusion, these arguments will be summarised and the thesis or problem restated. The beginning and end give you two different perspectives on the same thing, the meaning of the book.

Sometimes, especially in a narrative, this is done artfully by mirroring. The conclusion will reverse the structure and content presented in the introduction, providing answers instead of questions. The book of Revelation both mirrors and summarises Genesis. A careful reading of the last chapters of Revelation and the first chapters of Genesis reveals that the problems raised in the beginning are answered in the end, and the language and structure mirror their counterpart. Genesis recounts God creating humanity for a garden and being exiled from it because of the Fall; Revelation recounts the answer to the Fall and the return of the exiles to a new Eden, a holy city occupied by God himself. Because the Bible is closed, we can expect to find a resolution to its narrative tensions, to the problems it raises. Knowing that the Bible is closed or completed should lead us to seek answers to problems we find in our reading, expecting them to be resolved later in the Bible. Closure is necessary for a book to be understood, providing both the ground for believing that tensions are resolved and the motivation to seek their resolution. Where such an endeavour concludes in an apparent paradox, we are led by canonical closure to accept that this is the resolution God intended for us to have. Canonical closure, along with the analogy of faith, describe significant ways by which God has made Scripture self-interpreting. Before turning to *external sufficiency*, I want to consider a specific application of the analogy of faith, how the Bible is linguistically sufficient.

C. Linguistic Sufficiency

I raised at the beginning of this chapter the problems for the sufficiency of Scripture and interpretation when it comes to language. To some extent, these problems are resolved by Scripture's external sufficiency, a tradition of interpreting Scripture in light of the original languages that has continued throughout the history of the Church. However, this sense of sufficiency does not make Scripture self-interpreting unless Scripture also has an internal sufficiency such that it can be the authority for its linguistic interpretation—for interpreting the words, grammar, and syntax of the original text. Some readers might be thinking at this time that I, as a student of the biblical languages—especially Hebrew—should know better. Archaeological discoveries and extra-biblical textual traditions have shed much light on the languages of the Bible, allowing us to interpret them better. I will postpone a discussion of the role of such discoveries until a later chapter, but I will say at this time that I am not convinced that these discoveries have or can have any normative value for interpreting the Bible: they cannot tell us what a word or grammatical construction mean. Whatever role they have, they will be supplementary to the content of the Bible. We will look at the roles they have later, but let's argue for the linguistic sufficiency of Scripture here.

I argued above that this must be the case theologically. If Scripture is not sufficient to lead us in the interpretation of the grammar, syntax, and meaning of the original language text, then it will not be self-interpreting, for interpretation is built on this foundation. We have seen that the Bible's claims to authority and sufficiency demand that it be self-interpreting, so from this starting point, we must ask how it is so linguistically. I believe we can argue for this in two ways, by showing briefly how the Bible has epistemological priority in its own interpretation—implying what we have already seen—and by considering the scope of the Bible as it has been given to us.

First, consider the epistemic priority of Scripture. To say that the Bible has epistemic priority is to say that the Bible has the ultimate say in its own interpretation. That is, if external evidence suggests one or more interpretations of a text and the piece of literature in which the text is found offers one interpretation, the interpretation provided by the text's context will always have precedence—for textual context is the primary consideration for interpretation (we explored this in *The Gift of Reading Part 1* and will look at it from a different perspective in a later chapter). When it comes to interpreting the Bible, the main difficulties are presented by rare words—including words that only occur once in the Bible (*hapax legomena*)—and difficult syntactic or grammatical constructions (i.e. difficulties in understanding the relationships between grammatical clauses and words). If there is an explanation of any of these difficulties that can be argued from the Bible itself, this explanation takes precedence over any other explanation given from extra-biblical evidence. We can give several reasons for this. First, the Bible is the context given to us for interpreting the text, of which words and clauses are a part. In this sense, it has epistemic priority. Second, textual context gives immediate credibility to an explanation coming from the Bible; extra-biblical explanations are far harder—maybe even impossible—to prove. That is, if you are explaining the meaning of a word from an extra-biblical text, you must show how this text is relevant to the interpretation of the biblical book—how it is geographically, linguistically, culturally, and temporally related (for language changes given different locations, dialects, worldviews, and times). Third—positively—the Bible also takes evidential priority in explaining itself because it provides three bodies of intelligible language that have exerted a shaping influence on themselves.

That is, first, whatever truth is found in the distinction between different stages of Hebrew in the Bible (archaic, classical, late), these involve stylistic changes. The vocabulary and grammar of Biblical Hebrew remain consistent: if you can read archaic Biblical Hebrew, there is a good chance you can read the classical and late Biblical Hebrew and vice versa.[11] So the Bible is demonstrability a single corpus of language, whereas appeals to different Hebrew inscriptions do not necessarily represent the same form of Hebrew (consider the differences between Christian literature from the American South and atheistic literature from England).[12] Considering the New Testament, though different styles are present (compare John with Acts and

---

[11] Comparing modern English to Old English is not even a good comparison, for the spelling of words is almost identical across these different Hebrew styles. There are some noticeable changes, yet they are encountered once or twice a reader quickly adjusts (e.g. the use of הוא in the place of היא, "she," in Archaic Hebrew, Gen 2:12). The biggest change maybe the preference for different verb types in Classical Hebrew vs Late Hebrew, though even here I believe the differences are sometimes overstated.

[12] Though different dialects existed between the tribes of Israel, especially in pronunciation (cf. Judges 12:5-6), the Old Testament largely comes from the perspective of Judah.

Hebrews), all the books of the New Testament are examples of the common dialect of the 1st-century world, Koine Greek. I am not an expert in Biblical Aramaic, but from my encounters with the Aramaic sections of the Bible, I believe the same can be said for these sections of the Bible as well. In this way, the Hebrew and Aramaic (for they are closely related) and the Greek sections of the Bible represent two or three bodies of intelligible literature.

Second, it should be un-objectionable to say that the Bible has exerted a shaping influence on itself. The entire Old Testament is shaped by the Torah, which provides its foundations;[13] the New Testament is shaped by the Old Testament; and the letters are shaped by the Gospels, or at least the teachings of Jesus found in the Gospels. Even stylistically, it has often been argued that the writing styles of the New Testament authors demonstrate the influence of the Hebrew Old Testament. As it is relevant to our argument, that the authors of the Bible are consciously and unconsciously influenced by the rest of the Bible suggests that we should seek to explain not only the meaning of their texts but also the decisions they make in writing by the texts that have shaped them. When we add to these considerations the theological argument that God has intentionally shaped Scripture to be self-interpreting, I think we have a strong case to suggest that this extends to the language in which it is written.

One last observation to make in this regard concerns the scope of Scripture. What I have argued so far would be hard to believe if it were said about any other single text. It is not so preposterous given a large body of texts—a corpus, such as Shakespeare's works, or maybe early 20th century English literature—but not many, if any, single texts could justify such a claim. Unlike the other books, the Bible is massive in its scope and size. Considering its scope, it covers the beginning of the creation to its end, documenting every major event God has deemed essential to interpreting history. It provides an interpretation of all history and of all the creation—giving a lens by which we can see everything (cf. *The Gift of Knowing* and *The Gift of Seeing*). Not only does it have such a broad scope, but it is also very large and is written in many different ways—such as narrative, didactic prose,

---

[13] I have argued elsewhere, for example, that the Torah provides a lens for interpreting the events of Samuel and Judges. Cf. J. Alexander Rutherford, *God's Kingdom Through his Priest King: An Analysis of the Book of Samuel in Light of the Davidic Covenant* (Teleioteti, 2019); "Not a Single Survivor," teleioteti.ca/resources/papers.

poetry, and prophecy. Its scope is relevant to the first part of internal sufficiency—the analogy of faith—and its size relevant to the second part—linguistic sufficiency. The Bible provides many examples of grammar, syntax, and word usage to which we can compare difficult passages in order to resolve them.[14]

Having considered the analogy of faith, canonical closure, and linguistic sufficiency, I think we have seen how God has created the Bible to be internally sufficient for self-interpretation. But as I suggested above, for a text to be self-interpreting, it needs external sufficiency in addition to internal sufficiency.

D. External Sufficiency

By externally sufficient, I refer to the necessity of an interpreting community to realize the self-interpreting nature of a text. That is, unless a text is very small, it is almost impossible to start from scratch—without any knowledge of its language, meaning, story, structure, etc.—and come to a full understanding of it. What is needed is a community that already understands the content and possess the tools to interpret the text so that new interpreters can be equipped to understand it. What separates a self-interpreting text from a non-self-interpreting text is the ability of the former to create and sustain an interpretive community and to serve as the final standard of its own interpretation (it must be internally sufficient for self-interpretation).

First, if a text fails to sustain the interpretive interests of people, after several generations, the meaning of the text will be lost—maybe even the text itself. Second, a self-interpreting text must have the ability to refine and challenge the understanding of the community it creates. That is, it provides the tools and content necessary for its own interpretation by constantly shaping and refining the tools of the community so that they understand it rightly. This process of refining means that the text itself is the ultimate standard of what tools and interpretive lens are appropriate for its own interpretation: this is the distinguishing mark of a self-interpreting text. This process, of coming to the Bible with a pre-understanding (an understanding

---

[14] See *The Gift of Reading Part 1* for my introductory guide to resolving such difficulties. To see how this works, see the essays in the appendices of this volume and my commentary *The Book of Habakkuk: An Exegetical-Theological Commentary*.

of the whole) and having it refined under the authority of the text is often called "the hermeneutical spiral."[15] Beginning with some level of understanding, the interpreter finds their interpretation of the Bible challenged and refined every time they attempt to interpret individual texts in light of the whole.[16]

This is the significance of the passage I quoted at the beginning of this chapter (Deut 6:20-25). Christians, and God's Old Covenant people before them, are profoundly text-centred people. The Bible, as God's very words, places a vital role in personal, family, work, and Church life. Every facet of life is to be brought into conformity with the Bible, so every Christian ought to be able to understand the Word when they read it or hear it read. In the Old Testament, the society of the Israelites was shaped to teach them the proper interpretation of God's word. The festivals—especially the Passover—were lived out parables or celebrations of God's past deeds, meant to point forward towards the demands of the Law (Deut 6:20-25). They provide both a reminder of what happened and an opportunity to reflect upon and learn the significance of the events recounted. The sabbath was a reminder not only of God's initial creation rest but also of the rest God promised his people when he brought them out from Egypt (Exod 20:8-11, 31:12; Deut 5:12). For New Testament Christians, baptism and the Lord's supper have a similar function.

Furthermore, reading Scripture was a regular practice in the Old Testament, demanded especially of the leadership (e.g. Deut 17:18-20; Josh 1:8). In the New Testament, the Apostles and the churches they founded devoted themselves regularly to the reading of the Scriptures (1 Tim 4:13).

---

[15] Grant Osborne named his 1991 introduction to biblical hermeneutics after this process, *The Hermeneutical Spiral: A Comprehensive Introduction to Biblical Interpretation* (IVP).

[16] J.I. Packer describes this spiral (though he uses "circle") in this way, "I use the phrase 'hermeneutical circle' to express the truth (for truth it is) that our exegesis, synthesis, and application is determined by a hermeneutic—that is, a view of the interpretative process—that is determined by an overall theology, a theology that in its turn rests on and supports itself by exegesis, synthesis, and application.... From this standpoint it might be better to speak of the hermeneutical *spiral*, whereby we rise from less exact and well-tested understanding to one that is more so." J.I. Packer, "Infallible Scripture and the Role of Hermeneutics," in *Scripture and Truth*, ed. D. A. Carson and John D. Woodbridge (Grand Rapids: Baker, 1992), 348.

As amazing evidence to this fact, many of Paul's letters were written to largely Gentile churches—churches full of those who had not grown up with the Old Testament Scriptures—yet he constantly quotes the Old Testament assuming that his Gentile hearers would understand the quotations (cf. Galatians, Ephesians, Philippians, Colossians, 1 & 2 Thessalonians). In the short time since their conversion, he expects them to have learned—or have access to those who would teach them—the Old Testament. Through its symbolic life and its mandate for the church (cf. Matt 28:18-20), the Bible sustains an interpretive community with the tools necessary to interpret it.

Throughout the history of the Church, those who become Christians are taught the faith that they confess; they receive from pastors and teachers a sketch of the biblical teaching by which they can interpret it when they read it or hear it read.[17] When God created the Church in the 1st century, calling forth Jews and Gentiles into a new covenant community instituted through the blood of Christ, he created an interpreting community that was shaped by the Apostolic teaching canonized in Scripture and was so equipped with a knowledge of its teaching in order to begin the hermeneutical spiral. This is the external sufficiency of Scripture: it was given into and was written to sustain a community that would use its own tools to interpret it. I discuss the role of the Church and tradition more in *The Gift of Knowing* and *The Gift of Reading Part 1*, but it is worth reiterating that Scripture, as the canonized teaching of God's prophets and apostles, is the foundation of Christian life and doctrine. Tradition is a record of the Christian interaction with and application of Scripture to their own cultures and times. It is invaluable—even necessary—for interpreting Scripture but only because it represents the whole counsel of God revealed in Scripture as it has been taught to his people.

---

[17] Many catholic interprets or supporters of the normative function of tradition point to Philip's encounter with the Ethiopian Eunuch in the Acts 8:26-40 as an example of the necessity of tradition to interpret Scripture. I would suggest that this is an example of the people of God functioning as an interpretive community, not adding anything to Scripture but helping those unfamiliar to make the connections that already exist. The New Testament does what Philip did in this passage, makes the connection between the Old Testament and Jesus; God's people throughout the ages help us to see clearly how Scripture does this.

E. Conclusion

In this chapter, we began our discussion of the hermeneutical issues concerning the Bible's role in interpretation. Starting with the Bible's role as authority for interpretation, I have argued that the Bible needs to be self-interpreting and have attempted to demonstrate several ways God has shaped the Bible to be so. With this as a foundation, I want to begin our discussion of "meaning" with the contribution the Bible, or the text, has in meaning.

3

THE BIBLE AND MEANING

> The "meaning of meaning" is a subject that has frequently been discussed by linguists, philosophers, theologians, and others. As with most terms, there is no single correct definition of *meaning*. Some types of definitions, however, promote misunderstandings and others help to alleviate them. – John Frame[1]

Behind the many different approaches to interpreting the Bible we saw in chapter 1, the question "What is 'meaning'?" or better, "where does meaning reside?" has stood behind their differences. For Postmodern interpreters, meaning rests solely in the text or the reader; for Modernists, meaning rests in the historical communicative act of which the text is a part. In different ways, all the approaches we have seen emphasize either the role of the reader, the author, or the text in meaning. In my attempt to answer these two questions—which are really two different ways of asking the same question—I want to suggest that the author, reader, and text all have a role to play in "meaning." In this chapter, we will consider the role of the text for meaning. In chapter 5, we will consider the role of the Reader, and in chapter 7, the role of the author. In summary, the author is the originator of meaning, the text is the standard or norm for meaning, and the reader is agent in making meaning. In this chapter, we will look at what I mean when I speak of "meaning" and then the role of the text as a standard for meaning in this

---

[1] Frame, *The Doctrine of the Knowledge*, 93.

specific sense.[2]

A. The Meaning of Meaning

When it comes to the definition of terms, there are no right or wrong answers, only helpful and unhelpful ones. When an author uses a word in a non-standard way and fails to explain what is meant, this is unhelpful; but if words are used in their normal way or their use is appropriately explained, there is nothing wrong with different definitions.[3] So I am not arguing that a specific meaning for the word "meaning" is correct; instead, I want to explain why I use "meaning" in specific way and why this is, in my opinion, the best way to use it in the context of hermeneutics.

Of the many ways the word "meaning" is used, I think two are most relevant to our discussion. On the one hand, people will sometimes say "that is not what I meant," "that is not what it means," or "what I meant to say is…." In these cases, "meaning" refers to an application or implication of what someone said. When someone draws a false conclusion from what is said, this conclusion is not what was meant. When people have competing explanations of the text, they debate over which one is what "the text means." Here, meaning is something other than the text; meaning is a right explanation of it. When someone clarifies what they *meant* to say, they often provide the conclusion—the action or belief—they wanted you to draw from what they said. They express the meaning they wanted you to take away from what they said. In all these senses, meaning appears to be an application or use of the text, the result of drawing from it an explanation, an action to take, an idea to believe, etc. John Frame argues, based on the later work of Ludwig

---

[2] Our discussion in this and following chapters is dependent on work published in my Master's Thesis, *God's Kingdom Through his Priest King* (Teleioteti, 2019), in *The Gift of Reading Part 1* (Teleioteti, 2019), and in a paper and an article available through Teleioteti.ca. J. Alexander Rutherford, "Towards an Evangelical Hermeneutic: A Critique of the Chicago Statement on Hermeneutics (1982)" (Teleioteti, December 2016), accessed January 23, 2018, https://teleioteti.ca/resources/papers/; J. Alexander Rutherford, "An Investigation into the Role of Context in Interpretation," *Teleioteti*, January 16, 2018, accessed January 24, 2018, https://teleioteti.ca/2018/01/16/investigation-role-context-interpretation/.

[3] Consider the discussion of meaning and terminology in general in Vern S. Poythress, *Symphonic Theology: The Validity of Multiple Perspectives in Theology* (Grand Rapids: Academie Books, 1987); Frame, *The Doctrine of the Knowledge*, 93–98.

Wittgenstein, that "meaning" as the use of a text makes the best sense of how we use the word and is the most helpful for discussions of hermeneutics. "We must say," he writes, "that the meaning of an expression is its *God-ordained* use."[4] he summarizes his discussion like this,

> To ask for the meaning of an expression is to ask for an application. When we ask to know the meaning of a word or sentence, we are expressing a problem. We are indicating that we are not able to *use* the language in question. The problem may be relieved in a wide variety of way: synonymous expressions, ostensive definition, references to mental images, intentions, methods of verification, and so forth may all be of help. The goal, however, is not merely to supply one of those; the goal is to relieve the problem, to help the questioner use the language in question.[5]

I generally adhere to this sense of the word "meaning" in what follows: "meaning" refers to a justified use of a text. Because there are many justified uses of a text, we can rightly speak of the *meanings* of a text. I will use the phrase "meaning potential" to refer to all the potential uses a text may have.[6]

However, when it comes to hermeneutics, "meaning" is often used to refer to what the author intended. E.D. Hirsch, Jr. famously defined meaning in contrast with significance. Meaning was "fixed and immutable," but significance or application changed.[7] This "fixed and immutable" meaning

---

[4] Frame, *The Doctrine of the Knowledge*, 97..

[5] Ibid., 98. This is the definition I (loosely) followed in the first part of this volume. Cf. Ibid., 62–64.

[6] "Meaning-potential is a justified use of the text, as determined by the criteria of validity, fittingness, and appropriateness. When a new context is added, the text remains the same, but the field of reference, function, linguistic understanding will be affected. Some referents for "redemption" from "Egypt," for example, are removed from the realm of possibility (what may be "fitting" is narrowed). Yet, the justified uses of a text are increased. Without context to provide the fitting referent of "redemption" and "Egypt," a use that assumes the referent is the Exodus of Israel achieved by God is possible but not fitting, and so not justified. But with the addition of context that makes clear the referent, many possible uses are excluded, but this possible use is justified." Rutherford, *God's Kingdom*, 99. On justification and its criteria, see *The Gift of Reading Part 1*.

[7] This is Hirsch's own summary from the article "Meaning and Significance Reinterpreted"; his original work was *Validity in Interpretation*. Eric D. Hirsch, Jr.,

was equivalent to the historical intent of the author when he originally spoke or wrote. An immediate problem emerges with such a definition of meaning: what is intended by "intention?" Is it a mental picture the author had, a propositional statement of truth, or a goal he or she hoped to achieve with their communicative act?[8] Furthermore, is it conscious or unconscious intent? To be honest, I cannot tell you what the single, fixed "intent" is of what I am writing here. These are common criticism of such a definition.[9]

There is another problem with this definition that is often not considered; where do we draw the boundaries for a text with a single meaning? I pointed out in my paper "Toward an Evangelical Hermeneutic" that intention could refer to a propositional statement or goal for every word, sentence, paragraph, chapter, and book in the Bible. For a text to communicate, an author intends—at some level—for a metaphor to be interpreted properly, for a syntactic relationship to have a certain function, for a reader to come to believe or do something, etc.[10] So for every element of a text, we can rightly speak of the "author's intention." In which intention, then, does the single meaning lie? Hirsch sought with his definition to uphold the reader's intuitive belief that there are right and wrong meanings or interpretations of texts. His definition of meaning attempted to identify the normative aspect of meaning—that standard by which we judge the validity of interpretations—with something behind the text, with the author's original

---

"Meaning and Significance Reinterpreted," *Critical Inquiry* 11, no. 2 (1984): 202–225; Eric D. Hirsch, Jr., *Validity in Interpretation*, 9. print. (New Haven: Yale Univ. Press, 1979). Cf. Walter C. Kaiser, "The Single Intent of Scripture," in *The Right Doctrine from the Wrong Texts?: Essays on the Use of the Old Testament in the New*, ed. G. K. Beale (Grand Rapids: Baker Books, 1994); Earl D. Radmacher and Robert D. Preus, eds., "Appendix A: The Chicago Statement on Biblical Hermeneutics," in *Hermeneutics, Inerrancy, and the Bible* (Grand Rapids: Zondervan, 1984); Norman L. Geisler, "Appendix B: Explaining Hermeneutics: A Commentary on the Chicago Statement on Biblical Hermeneutics Articles of Affirmation and Denial," in *Hermeneutics, Inerrancy, and the Bible*, ed. Earl D. Radmacher and Robert D. Preus (Grand Rapids: Zondervan, 1984), 163–190.

[8] Cf. Frame, *The Doctrine of the Knowledge*, 98.

[9] Cf. C. S. Lewis, "Modern Theology and Biblical Criticism," in *Christian Reflections* (Eerdmans, 1967), 152–166; Philip Barton Payne, "The Fallacy of Equating Meaning with the Human Author's Intention," in *The Right Doctrine from the Wrong Texts?: Essays on the Use of the Old Testament in the New*, ed. G. K. Beale (Grand Rapids: Baker Books, 1994); Hirsch, Jr., "Meaning and Significance Reinterpreted."

[10] Cf. Rutherford, "Towards an Evangelical Hermeneutic."

intentions. But as John Frame has observed, this raises more problems than it solves. Placing the normative aspect of the text beyond the text, as with Hirsch's "meaning," is an attempt to guard the intuition that there are right and wrong meanings, yet "Instead of increasing the objectivity of our knowledge," Frame perceives, "such an intermediary is a subjective construct that inevitably clouds our understanding of the text itself."[11]

However, we know that texts mean some things and not others, that there is some sort of standard by which we can judge whether a particular use or meaning of a text is right or wrong.[12] If there is no normative meaning, such as Hirsch postulated in his 1967 book, then we are left with the text as the standard for judging whether a meaning is justified or not. With Frame I contend that the text (whether a sentence, paragraph, chapter, or book) is the anchor of meaning; it is the standard by which we evaluate if a meaning or use is justified.[13] I refer to the text, limited by context, as either the text or "what is said." "What is said" brings in the added element of intentionality, which we will discuss in chapter 8. As we will see below, a word or sentence taken on its own could say many things, but when placed in a robust context, it says something specific. This is the ground for meaning—words constrained by context. Meaning is the use of "what is said."

Later, when we consider the reader and meaning in chapter 5, we will consider the Reader's role in making and judging meanings. In what follows, I want to discuss how texts possess meaning, laying a foundation for our later discussion of recognizing meaning. In what follows, I will distinguish between "what is said" and meaning.

B. The Text and Meaning[14]

I argued above that context plays an essential role in the way Scripture self-interprets. The study of language and how it works in the 20th century has led

---

[11] Frame, *The Doctrine of the Knowledge*, 98.

[12] We are of course assuming that texts have communicated meaning in the past and do so today in the same way. Cf. Vern S. Poythress, *In the Beginning Was the Word: Language: A God-Centered Approach* (Wheaton: Crossway Books, 2009), 37–38.

[13] Frame, *The Doctrine of the Knowledge*, 98.

[14] This is adapted from my article on Teleioteti.ca, "An Investigation into the Role of Context in Interpretation."

to the common view that context is essential to understanding all communication. It will be advantageous for us to discuss here why this is the case. By considering how context creates meaning, we will see how texts are normative for meaning, how they contain a finite meaning potential.

Context, I argue, both limits and reveals textual meaning so that texts can be used. Texts of every sort are "multivalent"; they have a wealth of *meaning potential*. A text says something but could be used in an infinite number of ways; it has numerous potential applications or meanings. A commandment, such as "You shall not kill," can be used to create legislation, command behaviour, describe God's character, state a moral principle ("killing is wrong"), govern one's choices, etc. Texts are thus multivalent in the sense of "use." The words that make up texts, considered on their own, are also multivalent in the sense that they could be used to say many different things.

That texts are multivalent in this sense can be wonderful! The multivalence of biblical texts is the reason they apply to cultures and situations far beyond those in which they were originally written. However, misunderstood, a text's multivalence can lead to its abuse or neglect. If a text has infinite meaning potential, for example, it is practically meaningless. That is, all its meaning is derived from the reader and not the text itself. For example, the three symbols "רוץ" on their own are meaningless; what good would it do to have a document with only "רוץ" written on it? For the person who does not read Hebrew, it could mean anything they want it to—for nothing constrains their reading. For the person who reads Hebrew, it could mean any number of things (to run, flow; one running, something flowing; etc.). Without an appropriate restraint on meaning potential, a text can be used for any purpose or no purpose at all. For any word or text to have meaning, it needs *context*; it needs a larger unit of text in addition to the language with which to understand combinations of symbols (such as רוץ).

Context constrains the meaning of a text, reduces infinite meaning potential to finite meaning potential. This is how texts *mean*: they use symbols to make words in specific morphological forms and give them meaning by putting them into combinations. For a language to have meaning, it needs context. Context constrains the meaning of words and syntactical combinations, producing a text with a finite meaning potential. It is by constraining meaning that context gives meaning.[15]

Where there is context, and therefore meaning, there are valid and invalid interpretations of a text.[16] For example, careful attention to the context of the Ten Commandments, especially the word I rendered "kill" above, reveals that the meaning "killing is wrong" is an invalid meaning of the commandment (deriving the proposition "killing is wrong" is an invalid use of the text). The Hebrew word refers more specifically to "murder."

Because there can be valid and invalid meanings of a text, and these are given by the context, context is essential for understanding and using a text. Context—the surrounding texts and thought in which a text is found—hedges the meaning potential of a text.

Context tells the reader what is being said by restricting the meaning potential a text would otherwise have. Context also excludes potential uses of a text and guides the reader to those that are most relevant.[17] Context can also illuminate for a reader meaning potential that is originally obscure, such as revealing a shade of meaning for a word or structure previously unknown

---

[15] This account of the function of context is from the perspective of the reader, recognizing meaning or justified uses of the text. From the perspective of the author, writing a text is functional—selecting words and syntax in combinations for specific communicative functions, to communicate an argument, a truth, a picture, compel an emotion. Only a small fraction of potential uses is recognized by the author; sometimes a text implies things that the author would otherwise not want, yet this is nevertheless a valid use of the text—often revealing a flaw in the author's own thinking.

[16] It should be observed that not all context is explicit. For example, one liners and short quotes presuppose—if they are to have meaning—a shared context of meaning, such as a similar experience (experience of the same T.V. show) or a worldview in which the words used have the same meaning for the speaker and the listener.

[17] The idea of relevancy qualifies what we mean by valid interpretations. It is possible to have a valid interpretation that is not relevant. For example, it is valid to use the text "you shall not murder" to formulate the proposition, "'murder' is the fourth word in the command 'you shall not murder.'" This is true, yet it is irrelevant to the author's purpose in giving the command: it is a trivial use of the text, an inconsequential and so an interpretation that is irrelevant. Relevancy is not a measure of justification for an application but its worth. (If justification describes the legitimacy of an application, relevancy describes its usefulness.)

or alerting one to a detail that went previously unnoticed.

Consider the following. The four symbols "h-e-a-t" could be one of two words, each with a wealth of meaning potential (1. to cook, warm up, prepare; 2. the attribute hotness or a manifestation of hotness). The sentence, "Tim enfolded an empanada in tin foil in order to heat it up," limits the potential meanings of "heat" substantially. It is now clear what these four symbols (h-e-a-t) mean here. However, though what is being said is clear enough, how it could be used ("application") is vague: who is Tim, and why does it matter that he heated his empanada in tin foil? The uses at this moment are near infinite: any Tim may be the subject of the action, and his action could have infinite applications. Adding further context, however, will restrict the uses we could make of this sentence significantly and illumine the relevant uses (I concede that the following is preposterous):

> A doctor is treating a victim with substantial burns over his upper body. Readying the admission form, he reads the description of the incident that led to this hospital visit as recorded by Tim's mother. Apparently, during his lunch break, "after coming home, Tim enfolded an empanada in tin foil in order to heat it up; he then put it in the microwave for 10 minutes!! Shortly thereafter, Tim opened the microwave to investigate his food and flames and sparks burst forth, covering the poor boy!"

This sheds much light on the word "heat" and on the sentence as a whole. We now know how it can be used and how we should not use it. We can imagine another scenario where "heat up" indicates that the action in a basketball game is intensifying. For one who is unfamiliar with this idiomatic use of "heat," the context of a sports game will reveal what was, up to this point, unknown meaning potential.

Therefore, the primary function of context is limiting: it restricts meaning (as in the case of Tim and the empanada). A secondary function is illuminating: it reveals meaning (as in the case of a sports game). Reading within properly defined contextual boundaries will achieve both purposes. Because context has such control over meaning, placing a text within a new context can have significant effects on its meaning potential. We will consider this further when we consider the relationship between the author and meaning.

C. Conclusion[18]

In sum, as John Frame observes, in practical use, we use meaning in a way indistinguishable from application.[19] Therefore, meaning naturally refers not to the propositional "sense" behind the text but all the legitimate uses we make of a text, uses that (when justified) demonstrate our understanding of the text.[20] As an example, someone has only understood or grasped the meaning of "you shall not murder" when they can explicate the appropriate situation in which this command applies: he only understands it when he can use it.[21]

Instead of the single-proposition view of meaning, we can build on

---

[18] This is adapted, with permission, from an excurses in my Master's thesis, Rutherford, *God's Kingdom*, 93–102.

[19] Not being too much of a stickler for terminology, Frame offers as an alternative to identifying meaning with application the possibility of identifying meaning with the text and application with its uses. Frame, *The Doctrine of the Knowledge*, 98.

[20] Vern Poythress's account of meaning, which has some similarities to Frame's, reveals the fundamentally confused nature of the propositional or single-sense view of meaning. Poythress argues for a position that is both similar to yet more sophisticated than the usual single-sense view: he contends that the "sense" of a text is the objective anchor of application which can be paraphrased or communicated in different languages. It is this objective basis that leads us to conclude when we compare a paraphrase with the original that "they say the same thing." Yet he concedes that such a paraphrase represents a loss: it can never communicate the fullness of the original text. Yet, if meaning is this objective sense and the sense is appropriately embodied in both the paraphrase and the original, what is lost? The answer is that we lose some of the potential applications of the original. Thus, we are faced with a loss of meaning: the paraphrase is not as usable or rich as the original.

We can make more sense of this situation if we adopt Frame's view. We recognize in an accurate paraphrase continuity with the original: this text has been applied appropriately to a new context. In the case of a paraphrase, someone has explained part of the original. Yet as an application, the paraphrase is a restriction of the original; it cannot be used in as many ways as the original. In fact, it is impossible to recapture the full range of a text's appropriate applications by recommunicating a text in any other manner—that is, without reproducing the text in its full context. Thus, it is the text as restricted by its context that is the objective anchor of meaning, defined as legitimate uses of the text. Vern S. Poythress, *God Centered Biblical Interpretation* (Phillipsburg, N.J.: P&R Publishing, 1999), 69–92; Poythress, *In the Beginning Was the Word*, 163–185.

[21] Frame, *The Doctrine of the Knowledge*, 66–67.

Frame's conclusion and posit that meaning is not a singular objective universal idea that can be instantiated in new contexts and languages but the sum-total of the possible legitimate or justified uses one could make of a text. That is, the "objective" aspect of a text is the text itself delimited by its context, not a mysterious proposition that lies behind it.[22] On this understanding, we could define meaning as *every justified use of a text as determined by its literary and linguistic context*.[23] The question that remains yet

---

[22] We could argue, in addition, that there is no reason to believe God's thoughts about a text are propositions; it would cohere more with our experience of texts (we read texts and use them) to think that God perfectly knows the text in its context and all the real and potential implications that derive from the text. There is no reason to believe that behind the text there lies a singular proposition, either in the mind of an author (I can assure you none of what I am saying can be fully summarised in a proposition) or in the mind of God. This is significant if, as I contended in *The Gift of Knowing*, truth is correspondence between our interpretation of the creation and its Creator and God's interpretation.

[23] "Literary" refers to the textual body (book, anthology, etc.) in which a text is to be read and "linguistic" to the rules and nature of the language in which it was composed. Where does this leave history? As it regards the text—not situations to which the text will be applied—historiography (encompassing social history) and archaeology could be understood as parts of the linguistic context. That is, they help us to better understand the language of the text and the texts field of reference (referential meaning). However, caution must be taken in both regards.

Consider reference: though texts have what we could call "implied referents"— that is, referents that are described within the textual body—textual reference also extends beyond bounds of a text to the actual objects, persons, and events it recounts. A similar relationship exists between implied and historical referents as with implied and historical authors. Though an implied referent corresponds in the case of historical narrative to a historical referent, it is an intentional representation of the latter. Therefore, one must be careful about reading extra-textual knowledge of the historical referent into the implied referent. We will address this issue more in chapter 9. Cf. Carson, *Exegetical Fallacies*, 63–64; Moisés Silva, *Biblical Words and Their Meaning: An Introduction to Lexical Semantics*, rev. and expanded ed. (Grand Rapids: Zondervan, 1994); Rutherford, *God's Kingdom*, 115–116.

Linguistic understanding—specifically vocabulary and grammar—can be considered similarly. There exists a historical Hebrew language that has a close relationship with the historic languages of Ugarit, Syria, Aram, Egypt, and other peoples. Yet, the language of the Bible (and, indeed, the language of each author) is an implied language. That is, no author has a full understanding of his or her own language, therefore we must reckon in interpretation not with the historical language to which they were related but the implied language that they used. Consider, for example, the apostle John: he uses grammar in Rev 1:4 that does not reflect appropriate Greek usage (ἀπό ὁ ὤν, *apo o ōn*, from he who is). The "error" is part

unanswered is, what qualifies as a justified use of a text? A meaning would be justified if it makes a valid use that is appropriate to the function of the text and fitting for its field of reference.[24] A use is valid if it is part of the text's meaning potential as delimited by context; it is appropriate if it corresponds to the function of the text so that it would be inappropriate to use a text intended to lead one in right behaviour to counsel wrong behaviour (because God says murder is wrong, go murder!); and it is fitting if the use does not equivocate on the relationships between the text and referents (thus, to use a text about Israel's exodus from Egypt to make historical conclusions about the going forth of an unrelated people group from an unrelated location named Egypt would not be *fitting*). Validity, appropriateness, and fittingness in these senses are co-inherent and thus different perspectives by which the whole meaning potential of a text could be viewed, each depending upon the others and determined by a text's context.[25]

---

of the implied language of John but not the historical language of Koine Greek. See further our discuss of linguistic sufficiency above.

That God has exhaustive knowledge of each valid use of a text means that there is a true boundary to all textual meaning; it is not potentially infinite from a divine perspective. Poythress observes that at some point, a consideration of application "must somewhere along the way appeal directly to God's knowledge, authority, and presence." Vern S. Poythress, "Divine Meaning of Scripture," in *The Right Doctrine from the Wrong Texts?: Essays on the Use of the Old Testament in the New*, ed. G. K. Beale (Grand Rapids: Baker Books, 1994), 87–88.

[24] "Validity," "appropriateness," and "fittingness," are similar to Poythress's three perspectives on textual meaning—sense, application, and import. Poythress, *God Centered Biblical Interpretation*, 72–74. They differ in that, with Frame, I identify sense with the original text itself and not something that could be equally expressed by a paraphrase. Therefore, I extend "application" to cover re-expression of the text, such as paraphrase or translation. Cf. Frame, *Doctrine of Knowledge*, 93–98; Poythress, *God Centered Biblical Interpretation*, 72.

[25] That each of these is a co-inherent perspective on the meaning of a text means that the entire meaning potential of a text could be described from each of these perspectives. If a list of every valid use were provided, it would imply every appropriate and fitting use. The same is true of an exhaustive list of appropriate or fitting uses. On the use of "perspective" in this sense, see Frame, *The Doctrine of the Knowledge*, 89–90, 191–193; John M. Frame, *Perspectives on the Word of God: An Introduction to Christian Ethics* (Eugene, Or.: Wipf and Stock, 1999); John M. Frame, *The Doctrine of the Christian Life*, A Theology of Lordship 4 (Phillipsburg: P&R

Each text, therefore—whether it is a symbol, word, syntagm, sentence, etc.—has finite meaning potential (or a semantic range) that is delimited by the relevant contexts (textual, linguistic, cultural, etc.). If a context is expanded, there is a change to the meaning potential of a text, as I explained above.

According to the single-proposition view of meaning, meaning is in the text and discovered through the context. Therefore, context is only able to reveal the meaning of the text—what the author intended when he composed it. With reference to the biblical canon, this context is only capable of illuminating the meaning already in a text. In contrast, on the meaning-potential view of meaning, a consideration of the canonical context expands the meaning-potential of a text. No longer are the appearances of gentiles among David's mighty men (e.g. Uriah the Hittite) or reference to the redemption from Egypt (2 Sam 7:23) merely descriptive of historical events or the self-understanding of Samuel's characters, but they become rich with the meaning of the redemptive-historical story they reflect (e.g. Gen 12:1-3; Exod 15). The context does not change what the author said but expands greatly the potential uses of what he said. We will probe the implications of this view further in chapter 8. There remains, however, one more hermeneutical issue pertaining to the role of the Bible that we must address before turning to the role of the reader, namely, the relationship between meaning or interpretation and genre.

Publishing, 2008), 33–37; Poythress, *Symphonic Theology: The Validity of Multiple Perspectives in Theology*.

From a human perspective, which does not simultaneously grasp the whole range of validity-appropriateness-fittingness, it could be said that meaning is found at the nexus of validity, appropriateness, and fittingness. Yet from a divine perspective, these are co-inherent, thus their nexus excludes no valid, appropriate, or fitting uses of a text.

THE BIBLE AND GENRE

> That same day Jesus went out of the house and sat beside the sea. And great crowds gathered about him, so that he got into a boat and sat down. And the whole crowd stood on the beach. And he told them many things in parables, saying: "A sower went out to sow. And as he sowed, some seeds fell along the path, and the birds came and devoured them. Other seeds fell on rocky ground, where they did not have much soil, and immediately they sprang up, since they had no depth of soil, but when the sun rose they were scorched. And since they had no root, they withered away. Other seeds fell among thorns, and the thorns grew up and choked them. Other seeds fell on good soil and produced grain, some a hundredfold, some sixty, some thirty. He who has ears, let him hear." – Matthew 13:1-9

If you open most introductions to biblical interpretation written in the last 50 years, you will find a large section on the genres of the biblical texts and the role of these genres in interpretation. Grant R. Osborne, in his work *The Hermeneutical Spiral*, devotes an entire part (110 pages) to "genre analysis." Klein, Blomberg, and Hubbard devote 115 pages to the subject. Despite the significance granted to it, the question of what genre is, let alone its function in exegesis, is not an easy one to answer. Among evangelical works, the definitions of "genre" are not always compatible, if the word is even defined. A glance at the history of genre study, especially in the last 100 years, reveals that it is far more complicated than it might appear. From Plato to the

Postmodern study of literature, genre has been analysed, yet no consistent definition or understanding of the concept has emerged.[1] The loose consensus that exists among Evangelical interpreters emphasises the historical side of grammatical-historical hermeneutics and raises a challenge for the form of biblical sufficiency I have argued for it in this book. I have argued so far that the Bible is our ultimate authority for reading and presents itself as self-interpreting. In this chapter, I want to raise several theoretical problems I see in the present emphasis on genre and suggest that the insights of genre criticism are properly subsumed under what we have been discussing so far as the analogy of faith, reading Scripture in light of Scripture.

A. Genre and Its Problems

We can consider genre according to its definition and the features of a text to which it refers. In the contemporary discussion of genre, a genre is a specialized form of communication that presupposes specific hermeneutical rules. We have discussed general rules of reading so far in this and the previous work; in addition to these rules, genre is thought to provide specialized interpretive rules for specific types of literature. The analogy often used today, taken from Ludwig Wittgenstein (an influential 20th-century philosopher) is that of a game: "genre provides a set of rules that further refine the general exegetical principles ... and allow the interpreter greater precision in uncovering the author's intended meaning,"[2] "Literary genres, then, are like language games. The interpreter's task is to determine which game (e.g. epic, history, chronology, prophecy, parable, etc.) is being played; only then will the individual 'moves' make sense. Hirsch agrees, 'Coming to understand the meaning of an utterance is like learning the rules of a game.'"[3]

Genres function on several different levels; there are genres for book-sized literature and genres employed within these books. Poythress defines the classificational side of genres—how a genre is recognized—as "a group

---

[1] Cf. Osborne's helpful though very brief survey in his essay, Grant R Osborne, "Genre Criticism: Sensus Literalis," *Trinity Journal* 4, no. 2 (1983): 1–27.

[2] Grant R. Osborne, *The Hermeneutical Spiral: A Comprehensive Introduction to Biblical Interpretation* (Downers Grove, Ill.: InterVarsity Press, 1991), 151.

[3] Vanhoozer, *Is There a Meaning in This Text?*, 338. Quoting from E.D. Hirsch, Jr., *Validity in Interpretation*. Cf. Klein, Blomberg, and Hubbard Jr., *Introduction to Biblical Interpretation*, 260.

of pieces of literature with similar organization or style."[4] This classificational aspect of genre (the features which define it) appears to this author to be at odds with the function genre is thought to have, to govern reading.

"Style" and "organization" may have interpretive implications, but they may not. For example, while writing this book, dozens of different organization schemes have bounced around in my head, all of which would lead to the same result. My choice of this particular organization was purely pedagogical, how best to communicate the content I hoped to communicate and to make the argument I am trying to make—supporting the hermeneutic of biblical self-interpretation argued for in *The Gift of Reading – Part 1*. On the other hand, style may have interpretive implications, as we saw in that book, yet other elements of style—such as style of language (e.g. popular or academic)—do not require specialized rules of interpretation.

From the literature concerning genre and those things that are identified as genres, it becomes clear that more than style and organization are involved in generic categories. We could add to style and organization (or *form* as it is usually called) *function*, what a text is intended to do. For example, a *rîb* prophecy is supposed to be a legal indictment or prophetic lawsuit; a thanksgiving psalm is defined by its function to give thanksgiving; a historical narrative communicates historical events, but a parable does not seem to do so. We could also be more specific with "style," dividing this into *language pattern*—prose (whether narrative or didactic) and poetry—and *manner of communication*, consider whether it communicates through logical argument, description, or symbolism. These four considerations (form, function, language pattern, manner of communication) cover the various textual features that make up generic categories. An outlier here is the so-called "apocalyptic" genre, which is thought not only to include style and function but theological perspective—the worldview by which world events are interpreted.[5]

---

[4] Poythress, *Reading the Word of God in the Presence of God*, 207.

[5] As mentioned in *The Gift of Reading Part 1*, a better way to understand the distinctive aspect of "apocalyptic" literature in the Bible is to see it as heightened or intensified prophecy. It bears continuity with the prophetic books in its use of symbolism and metaphor and the weaving together of poetry, didactic prose, and narrative. However, symbolism and metaphor are so intensified that the work of an

Having considered how genre is defined and the features thought to characterize a genre, we must consider the function it is supposed to have. As a "language game," genre is said to be a shared interpretive framework between the reader and the author. The author uses a genre to communicate and assumes the audience will recognize the genre in the text they read and interpret it accordingly. This raises several problems that I want to consider here. First, if the intended audience of Scripture as we have received it is not the audience for which they were originally penned but believers today, as I have contended and will argue further in a chapter 6, then the intended readership does not know the language games under which the text was composed. This presents a problem for Scripture as self-interpreting. Indeed, most Evangelical authors argue that it is necessary to study generic categories within their historical context to get a firm grasp of the rules involved.[6] But this raises another problem, what explains the similarities found in different examples of a genre; that is, how does genre function in an author's composition of a work? I believe a consideration of compositional issues requires a revising of the usual understanding of genre. Lastly, genre as defined above falls under the same critique that I will raise in chapter 9 concerning the use of historical background material; to identify a specific text as part of a genre, there needs to be enough features present to prove the same thing an appeal to genre would accomplish. That is, if you are arguing that *Text A*, as an example of *Genre B*, needs to be interpreted according to *Principle C*, you must have enough evidence within *Text A* to justify your use of *Principle C*. Thus, an appeal to *Genre B* is redundant; it can only confirm or reveal what was always present in *Text A*. Let's consider these issues more closely.

a. The Issue of Genre and Audience

The first issues are those of genre and audience. Among evangelical authors, genre is part of the historical aspect of grammatical-historical exegesis. This raises a problem as far as our argument so far is concerned. If genre theory

---

interpreter is greatly increased with apocalyptic literature verses run-of-the-mill prophecy. Cf. Beale, *The Book of Revelation: A Commentary on the Greek Text*, 37–69.

[6] E.g. Osborne, "Genre Criticism," 24.

as addressed here is correct, there must be a high level of shared literary heritage between the author and audience for a text to be understood properly. We may be able to assume this is true when an act of communication is intended for someone from the same area and time, but it cannot be assumed across cultural, geographical, and temporal gaps.

The Bible was written to communicate over thousands of years and across the world, so if genre is a necessary category of interpretation, and God has intended the Bible to be read across this geographical-temporal chasm, then genre has to be something identifiable within the text itself. That is, "genre" must refer to the cues texts give to guide their own reading. We must firmly locate genre in the realm of text, its features, and not in the realm of culture—in a shared understanding between the author and audience. But if we follow this route, identifying generic categories as textual categories not extra-textual interpretative categories, we must re-consider their role in authorial composition and in interpretation.

b. The Issue of Composition

What, we must ask, is the relationship between the author and generic categories? Our answer to this question is very important. At the risk of being overly simplistic, I want to consider two possible answers to this question. The first answer is that genre, like rules for a game, is normative for an author's writing. If genre is normative, it means that an author is under obligation—conscious or unconscious—to conform to the standards of the genre. Once an author selects a genre or the choice of intended communicative function necessitates a certain genre, the style, form, and function of the text are a given. We could call such a view genre-realism, the idea that "genre" refers to an actual thing—a set of rules or perfect example—that is reflected in every instantiation or concrete text. If this were the case, knowing genre would reveal the meaning of the text, for by knowing the rules we could figure out exactly what was intended (cf. the approach of K. Lawson Younger mentioned in chapter 1 under Structural Exegesis). Though genre is often treated as if it were real in this philosophical sense, the problems with such a view are numerous. For one, genres have historical origins and change throughout time (e.g. the emergence of the *Nouveau Roman* style novel in France during the 20th century).[7]

Also, unless someone wanted to suggest that every genre exists in the mind of God and therefore can be truly "real" (again, in the philosophical sense), the idea of genre-realism is absurd (the only option would be that they exist in their own separate world, free-floating ideas beyond time and space). Finally, such a view could not explain why genres are frequently violated, in addition to changing. For example, it is said that epistles in the 1st-century Roman world are examples of a specific genre.[8] This genre has a specific form, yet Galatians—an otherwise perfect example of this genre—violates this form by omitting the thanksgiving section of a Greco-Roman epistle. Furthermore, the book of Hebrews has some epistolary features yet otherwise breaks from this genre. It seems to be a mixed genre, part letter and part sermon, leading to the often-used moniker "sermonic-epistle."[9]

There is a lesser form of realism I think we can also reject, what we could call "textbook realism." That is, there is no evidence for (and it is quite clear that there were no) style books prescribing genre rules for apocalyptic, 1st-century historical narrative, gospel, epistle, etc. Ruling out realism in either sense, we cannot treat "genre" as if it actually exists, as if there is an abstract body of rules embodied in every related text that can be extracted and used to read similar literature. Instead, we must look for another view for the relation between the author and genre.

In the place of realism, I think imitation is a good term to use for describing the role of genre in composition.[10] Texts are similar to one another because no text emerges in a vacuum. Texts are produced by authors, and authors are influenced by other authors—indeed, they are influenced by the history of literature. At the very least, this truth would produce unconscious similarities between texts. However, we can go further.

---

[7] Cf. Osborne, "Genre Criticism."

[8] J. Scott Duvall and J. Daniel Hays, *Grasping God's Word: A Hands-on Approach to Reading, Interpreting, and Applying the Bible*, 3rd ed. (Grand Rapids: Zondervan, 2012), 227–243; Osborne, *The Hermeneutical Spiral*, 252–260.

[9] E.g. Walter A. Elwell and Robert W. Yarbrough, *Encountering the New Testament: A Historical and Theological Survey*, 2nd ed., Encountering biblical studies (Grand Rapids: Baker Academic, 2005), 348.

[10] I do not mean "imitation" in the technical realist or Postmodern sense of *mimesis*.

When we write or speak, we want to communicate, so we pay attention to how we communicate. We think of what will best communicate our purposes, what will best achieve our purpose. If I wanted to be a successful comedian, I would study the performances of other comedians; if I wanted to write gripping novels, I would study those novelists I appreciate the most. The same goes for writing a dictionary; there is no rulebook that says I could not write a dictionary using the conventions of a novel, but it would be inefficient and unsuccessful to do so. Instead, if I wanted to write a dictionary, I would imitate the practice of those who have come before me. The same is true for history books, textbooks, and books like this one. In writing this book and my previous books, I did not consult a rule book for how to properly format a book; instead, I considered those books I found most effective in their communication and studied what they did. Even style books, which give the rules of how to write a good book or thesis, are based on imitation: they ask how a good thesis or book has been written in the past and consider how to teach others to write in that way.

Moreover, a text is not only an imitation; it is also a creative imitation. When we study other books to learn from them, we must decide between different approaches to determine which one is best for the purpose at hand. We may, in fact, contribute our own insight to the genre within which we are writing, creating a unique text that bears similarities to but is not identical with its predecessors. Imitation seems to me to be the best way to describe genre as it functions for the author.

If generic composition involves creative imitation, an issue emerges for the genre theory. Genre cannot be the rules for rightly reading a body of texts, for both elements—imitation and creativity—involve the breaking and invention of reading conventions. The rules for reading a specific genre only work if one text follows the same rules as another, but the "rules" do not exist outside of any individual text; they are bound up with and unique to every text an author produces. This leads us to our last problem with genre before we consider its positive function.

c. *The Issue of Identification*

The implicit realism of present genre theory yields further issues when it comes to identifying genre in texts and interpreting them accordingly. For example, consider The Book of Jonah. Some authors consider Jonah to be an example of the genre "satire." Part of their definition of satire is the fact that satires are not intended to communicate history. So it is argued that this interpretive principle—satires do not communicate historical events—must be applied to Jonah. Therefore, the book is not meant to teach us about historical events. The problem is this: their definition of "satire" begs the question. If Jonah is satirical and also communicates historical events, then the definition of satire must be expanded to include historical events. Otherwise, Jonah must not be satirical. To argue that Jonah is ahistorical because it is satirical, one must show from the book of Jonah that it is satirical *because it is ahistorical.* That is, the feature that one is trying to prove by an appeal to genre must be observable in the text itself, making an appeal to genre redundant. The problem is this; if genres are a body of rules, then we would expect very little variation from the rules; the presence of significant variation would invalidate their function. However, in practice, we do not find pure genres; we find narratives with satirical elements and satires with historical elements; letters with sermonic elements and sermons with epistolary elements; etc. Any interpretive rule to be used must therefore be clearly present in the text at hand, for only with evidence of its presence can we be sure that this is a generic feature the author chose to include.

Another example regards the narratives in Genesis. Authors sometimes have argued that the first chapters of Genesis show a stylized form and highly poetic nature; therefore, they cannot be historical. That is, because style and form from an ahistorical genre are present, the function must be ahistorical. Their arguments are usually overstated, but even if they were accurate in their observations, the conclusion does not follow. That is, there is no rule that says one cannot communicate historical events using poetic style; this is done many times in Scripture (e.g. Exod 15, Judg 5). The fact that style does not determine function and that form does not fix interpretation argues against the view that genre describes shared interpretive rules between authors and audiences. Yet the observations made under discussions of genre are often quite helpful—I made many in *The Gift of Reading Part 1*—so we must look for another model for explaining the insights of genre.

B. Classification and Interpretation

As can be seen from the first part of this chapter, there is a lot of overlap between Genre discussions and those of philosophy. Genres are often treated as philosophical abstractions, so it makes sense that the criticisms raised above are quite similar to those raised in Volume 1 of this series, *The Gift of Knowing* and the lengthier criticism I will raise in Volume 3, *The Gift of Seeing*. It also makes sense that my answer to the question, "what is genre" looks the same as my answer to the question "what is an abstraction." I will reserve the term "genre" for book-level literature types, such as dictionaries, novels, math textbooks, academic papers, theology dissertations, etc. Such book-level literary types, or text-types, are classifications used to describe related pieces of literature, literature that share similarities in the areas of *form, function, language pattern,* and *manner of communication.* Adapting my definition of abstraction from *The Gift of Knowing,* we can identify "genre" as a relationship identified between particular pieces of literature (Thesis A, Thesis B, etc.) that allows us to better understand other particular pieces of literature that share these commonalities. The relationships in view are those mentioned above (e.g. form); each of these features can likewise be identified as a relationship identified among the particular features of particular pieces of literature.[11] For the rest of this chapter, I want to consider these four categories we can use to see literature better and how they function as part of the analogy of faith.

C. The Generic Categories

a. Language Patterns

In *The Gift of Reading – Part 1,* we spent a chapter considering "Styles of Biblical Writing" (239-276); as the title of that chapter suggests, we considered the stylistic generic categories, namely, language pattern and manner of communication. I identified four broad styles of biblical writing, Narrative, Poetry, Didactic Prose, and Prophecy. In line with our previous discussion, I eschewed the term "genre" in referring to these classes of literature,[12] preferring the more specialised classification of "style." Specifically, these are groups of biblical writings that share a common pattern

---

[11] Cf. *The Gift of Knowing,* 102-104; "What is Abstraction? – Part 1 & 2, https://teleioteti.ca/2018/09/06/abstraction-part1/, https://teleioteti.ca/2018/09/20/what-is-abstraction-part-2/; and *The Gift of Seeing* (Airdrie AB, Teleioteti 2021).

[12] These are sometimes identified as genres, but this is rarer than identifying what I have called "text-types" (e.g. letter, historical narrative, covenant document) as genres. Cf. Ska, *Our Fathers Have Told Us,* 6.

of language and manner of communication. By pattern of language, I intend the way a literary work, a text, strings together words and clauses (the constituents of sentences) and sentences in order to make a cohesive text.

On the one hand, narrative in the Bible is characterized by coordinating ("paratactic") syntax and actions within scenes. That is, biblical narratives do not often provide logical explanation through subordinating conjunctions such as "for" or "in order that"; instead, scenes are connected with the coordinating and contrasting conjunctions usually translated "and" and "but." This is closely related to the way narrative structures units of text; instead of being grouped in thought units like a prose book or letter, biblical narratives present scenes that are based on actions. Sentences are either explanatory of or provide an action; an action with its circumstances and any explanatory material make a scene. Together, coordination and the action/scene syntax constitute the language pattern "narrative."

This can be contrasted with didactic prose, such as is found in Paul's epistles, which uses a pattern of subordination ("hypotaxis") and sentence/paragraph syntax. In didactic prose, subordination is favoured over coordination; "and" is rarer than in narrative, but "for" and "in order that" (among many other conjunctions) become much more common. Subordinating conjunctions are found because they make explicit logical connections; they function to make an argument and provide explanation. In the place of actions, didactic prose employs a broad range of sentences—such as statements and imperatives—connected by an implicit logical relation ("asyndeton") or explicit logical relation (indicated by conjunctions). This is what I mean by a pattern of language; I go to a greater depth with narrative and didactic prose—along with poetry and prophecy—in *The Gift of Reading Part 2*. Along with such patterns of language, I include in these stylistic classifications the manner of communication favoured in a text.

b. Manner of Communication

One early reader of these books found it odd that I would include "prophecy" along with narrative and didactic prose in my discussion of style, for prophecy does not exhibit any one pattern of language. This is true enough: as I discussed in *Part 1*, Prophecy switches between poetry and didactic prose freely, often blending the two. This blending justifies to some degree my decision to consider Prophecy as its own style, but language pattern alone does not constitute a style—as I am using the term. In addition to language pattern, there is the manner of communication a text favours; it is here that prose prophecy and poetic prophecy cohere and so become identifiable as a single style. By manner of communication, I intend the predominant means a text uses to communicate. In this book—an example of didactic prose—I am mainly communicating through argument and description. This is the standard manner of communication for didactic prose. At times I will use metaphor and story to make my points clearer, yet these are rare enough to be exceptions. Hence, manner of communication refers to the favoured or default means of communication.

In a narrative, the primary manner of communication is showing or displaying events. That is, a narrative portrays events in such a way that leads the reader to a conclusion: it usually does not tell the reader what to think; it shows them.[13] Poetry favours metaphor and picturesque language in its communication, yet we can be more specific here. Biblical poetry often employs concrete imagery, imagery that has a strong correspondence with the experience of the reader (e.g. Psalms 23; 84:3, 6). Prophecy similarly uses metaphorical language, yet the language of prophecy is far more abstract or symbolic.[14]

We witness the extreme form of this more abstract metaphor in apocalyptic literature, such as Revelation and Daniel (cf. Daniel 2:31-45). It takes more than wisdom to interpret such imagery, so interpretations are often provided. Prophecies such those found within Isaiah and Jeremiah are less abstract than the apocalyptic books, yet they are still distinct from poetry in their abstract symbolism.[15] Whether employing a poetic or didactic prose language pattern, this manner of communication remains prominent in Prophetic literature, hence why I identify it as its own style.

Now, caution is in order here. When we speak of narrative style, we are not talking about the style found in narrative text-types; we are talking about

---

[13] Literary theorists often of state that narratives "show," they do not "tell."

[14] By "abstract" I refer to the fact that the referents and meaning of the symbols used in prophecy are not as readily discernible as in poetry. Poetry is intended to elicit an immediate emotive response, to carry you along with its rhythm. Prophecy, on the other hand, is didactic; it is meant to teach significant truths about the world, the events of history, and God. The symbolism it uses to communicate sometimes requires careful thought; at other times, interpreting prophetic symbolism requires an explicit word from God.

[15] See the discussion in *The Gift of Reading – Part 1*.

a specific style that is prominent in such text-types, yet narratives such as Samuel include poetic and didactic prose sections (e.g. 1 Sam 2; 2 Sam 7). The same can be said of the prophetic books such as Isaiah; it contains prophetic style, but it also contains didactic prose and narrative. Habakkuk is a prophecy, yet its style is more poetic than prophetic, especially in chapter 3. In Isaiah and Habakkuk, prophetic style, as I have defined it, is present in those areas that combine poetic and didactic prose language patterns with abstract symbolism.

c. Form

The next generic category, text form or organization, has received a lot of attention over the last 100 years. In the late 19th century, form-criticism emerged, giving significant attention to literary form; afterwards, rhetorical criticism turned the spotlight onto the organization of material according to rhetorical patterns. More recently, narrative criticism has given significant attention to the organization and form of narratives. "Form" can be considered on several levels; there is the macro-structure of large text units, such as a book, and there are the smaller structures that characterize text units within a larger text. These small structures may be the forms of psalms or story-types. Despite the emphasis form has received in recent literature, I do not think form is critical to understanding many texts, though it remains very important for some text-types.

All texts have some form of structure; the demands of writing require that some thought be given to structure. However, though there will always be structure in a text (a form to its material), not all form has interpretive significance. The primary area where form has great significance is in narrative. Form matters in narratives because there is a standard against which to measure deviation. That is, narratives are based on a plot, a linear-temporal progression. When the form of a narrative deviates from the plot—when it skips a thousand years and focuses on 10, when it re-arranges material (called dischronologization) or interpolates material (when a story is spliced in between another story, such as in 2 Sam 10:1-12:31)—this yields great interpretive insight. However, in letters and many Psalms, the structure is less significant. There is no interpretive significance in placing thanksgiving sections before the body of a letter; this is often the case because of imitation (as discussed above). In many Psalms, their sections are thematically organized. There are some types of Psalms that share a similar structure, yet even in these cases, to rearrange the material would not change the meaning or interpretation of the psalm. For these reasons, because every text has a form and because form is not always of great significance for interpretation, I find it valuable to consider form under two heads—with a bit of a grey area in-between—as indispensable or variable.

In a novel or narrative, form is indispensable; it is fundamental to the text and its communication. However, in a dictionary, form is product of pedagogy, how best to communicate its content to the reader; you could conceivably organize a dictionary in dozens of different ways without changing its meaning (cf. the differences between the BDB and HALOT Hebrew lexicons). In didactic prose, the structure is a way of organizing and putting together an argument; the structure itself is not meaningful but often reveals the train of thought that makes up an argument. I thought about dozens of different ways to organize this book; in the end, the structure I chose was what I deemed best for communicating the content I wanted to communicate in a persuasive manner. If I chose a different structure, the argument may have been less clear or clearer and the book less or more readable, but the meaning potential would largely have remained the same. In between literary works with dispensable structure and those with indispensable structures are those for which structure affects interpretation but the loss of such structure is not catastrophic. I argued in *The Gift of Reading Part 1* that the Bible falls into this category, that the Bible has form and that this form is meaningful, yet if one or two books are rearranged, or the whole thing is shuffled, it is still possible to interpret the Bible correctly. Here, the order has significance for revealing meaning potential but does not create meaning potential.

In light of these considerations, form can be a helpful perspective with which to look at texts, but the most important question will be whether or not form is indispensable. On the one hand, when it comes to a narrative, it is very important to have a right understanding of how the story unfolds and how the author uses form to communicate his intent. But on the other hand, when commentators differ on the form of an epistle, such as Romans, we should not be overly concerned. We can still follow the thought well enough even if we have not divided it into the same sections as last reader. A clue to whether the form is indispensable or not is often given by the text itself. In a narrative, there are various markers that indicate the beginning and end of units and help organize sections of a book: there are clues to the structure given by the author. Such markers are also present in other literature. For example, in Habakkuk, there are two content headings that lead us to break the book into two sections (Hab 1:1, 3:1). But in the early manuscripts of biblical epistles, there were no paragraph breaks, and they did not have section headings; without such visible breaks and without significant syntactic markers of sections, the structure of an epistle's argument given in a commentary represents an effort to help the reader grasp the progression of an author's argument.

d. Function

The last generic category that is often considered in discussions of genre is function, what a specific text attempts to achieve. "Function" is often a category of distinction, affirming that a text does one thing instead of another. Every text has many functions, but those that are usually considered under genre are dichotomies: a text may teach theology and history simultaneously, but it cannot be both historical and ahistorical at the same time. Thus, some genres—such as historical narrative—are said to teach history, while others, such as parables, are non-historical narratives. However, because it is possible to use the form and style found in non-historical narratives—such as novels—to tell a historical story, the category of function is not the most helpful.

Function as an aspect of genre is also sometimes used for the way an utterance is used; a *rîb* oracle, for example, is thought to be a formalized prophecy that brings a charge of covenant sin against God's people.[16] But because of the variability implied in the function of genre in composition, we should not assume apart from textual evidence that two prophecies with the same form and style have the same function—to bring a covenant lawsuit. As with all other genre considerations, then, function needs to be identified from the features of the text and not as a corollary of form or style.

D. The Function of Generic Categories

Though I have attempted so far in this chapter to offer a criticism of genre

---

[16] Willem VanGemeren, *Interpreting the Prophetic Word: An Introduction to the Prophetic Literature of the Old Testament* (Grand Rapids: Zondervan, 1996), 400–407.

theory as it functions within Evangelical biblical interpretation, I do not want to disregard the insights that have been revealed through the study of genre. What I suggested above was that we need to reframe the role of genre in interpretation. Instead of interpreting genre in terms of realist categories and historical contexts, I suggested above that the categories usually discussed under genre are better seen as part of the analogy of faith, the way Scripture leads us in its own interpretation. This is where I want to conclude this chapter.

Because there are stylistic, formal, and functional similarities between the texts of the Bible, it is reasonable to believe the in-depth study of one text will help us understand similar texts better. For example, during my studies on the books of Samuel and Habakkuk over the last five years, I have learned much about the way the authors of these books communicate. Turning to other narratives, I see many of the same structural tools used by the author of Samuel in other narratives. By reading the narratives of Kings and Chronicles in light of my in-depth study of Samuel, I have been able to see more clearly how the authors have shaped their stories to communicate a particular view of history and a lesson for their readers. The same is true of Habakkuk; by studying the style used by Habakkuk, I have been able to better understand the similar prophetic language employed in the other prophetic books, especially Jeremiah, and the poetic style Habakkuk shares with the Psalms. This is the strength of genre discussions found in most introductions to hermeneutics: they are the result of careful attention paid to particular texts in search of similarities. The resulting categories and generalizations help us to see better features of these texts that we may have otherwise missed (which is the same function abstractions have in other parts of life).

This is how I see the fruits of genre study functioning in biblical interpretation: generic categories are not straight-jackets or hard and fast rules that tell us how to interpret texts or what to expect from them. Instead, genres provide glasses that help us to see better what is there in the text. Because of this understanding of genre, not as interpretive rules but as a product of and aid in the exegesis of texts, I believe that genre considerations are not the topic of hermeneutics but of biblical study. Therefore, I intend to include the insights of genre study in the 2nd part of this series, in which I will present a theology of the Bible and an overview of its contents (usually found in NT & OT introductions or surveys).

J. Alexander Rutherford

—Part 2—
The Role of the Reader

5

THE READER AND MEANING

> I charge you in the presence of God and of Christ Jesus, who is to judge the living and the dead, and by his appearing and his kingdom: preach the word; be ready in season and out of season; reprove, rebuke, and exhort, with complete patience and teaching. For the time is coming when people will not endure sound teaching, but having itching ears they will accumulate for themselves teachers to suit their own passions, and will turn away from listening to the truth and wander off into myths. – 2 Timothy 4:1-4

In the last four chapters, we have seen that there is much good in the history of the interpretation of the Bible but also some error that has crept in, a tendency to accommodate the Church's approach to reading the bible to an external authority, to the philosophical spirit of the time. Against this trend, I have argued that we need a method and theory of biblical interpretation that is rooted in the Bible's own authority. *The Gift of Reading – Part 1* presented such a method; here in *Part 2*, I am establishing the theory that upholds that method. In the last three chapters (part one of this book), we looked at the role of the Bible in its own interpretation and the relationship between the biblical text and meaning. In this section, part two of this book, I want to turn to the role of the reader in interpretation.

This section and the one that follows are intentional asymmetrical with the first; that is, I intend parts two and three to be together shorter than part one. The reason for this is simple: the theory unpacked in this book is text-centred, so our discussion will predominantly concern the text. However, the reader and the author still have an important role to play, so we will consider these roles in this and the following part. Here, in chapter 5, I want to consider the contribution of the reader to meaning, as we have defined it in chapter 3. Namely, I want to consider what it means for the reader to be the maker of meaning and how this creative production is governed by the text. In the following chapter (6), I want to consider for whom the Bible was written and the impact this has on interpretation.

To say that the reader is the maker of meaning may be a dangerous line to take, yet I think it is a helpful way to look at the reader's role in light of our definition of meaning in chapter 3. If meaning is a justified use of a text, then texts do not have meaning until they are read; what they have is meaning potential. A reader makes meaning by actualizing the potential of the text, by rightly applying it to specific circumstances and questions. This is the sense in which I identify the reader as a maker of meaning and the way I conceive the role of the reader in interpretation. Their job is not to decode the Bible, to recreate its history. Instead, their job is to use it. In the many passages concerning the role of Scripture in the believer's life, this is its role; it is used by the reader under the guidance of the Holy Spirit to change actions, perceptions, and even hearts (e.g. Rom 10:14-21; 2 Tim 3:16-17, 4:1-4). Because of the Spirit at work in our lives, the Scriptures are active in their own right, convicting us of sin (e.g. Heb 4:12-13), yet the primary emphasis is on how through careful thought we use the Scriptures in our own lives and in the lives of others, for encouragement, rebuke, instruction, teaching, etc. We are called to be meaning makers, using the Bible for the glory of God.

This role requires much creativity to anticipate and perceive how the Bible applies to our own lives and the world around us. Sometimes the application is direct and easy; at other times, it takes much effort to discern how the situations before us are analogous to and fall under the purview of the Bible. We do so, however, with the assurance that Scripture is indeed useful so that we might be fully equipped for the good works for which we were created (2 Tim 3:16-17, cf. Eph 2:10).

By identifying the reader as a maker of meaning (in the sense defined above), we are coming close to the Postmodern approaches to biblical interpretation, yet we are not entirely in agreement with them. Postmodernity has done some good in showing us that the reader has an important role to play in reading, yet it has done so within a philosophical paradigm that rejects God's authority and the authority of texts. As Christians, we do not share these assumptions. We are self-consciously submitted to the Lordship of Christ and are obligated to honour not only him but the men and women who have written texts. That is, we have a moral obligation to submit ourselves to God and, as an extension of this submission, to seek a proper understanding of the texts and utterances of men and women created in the image of God.[1] One of the ways we do this, and here I am particularly thinking of our reading of Scripture as an act of submission to God, is to ensure that the uses we make of the text are justified. In chapter 3 and in *The Gift of Reading – Part 1*, I discussed three criteria we use to determine whether a text is justified; it must be valid, appropriate, and fitting. The reader is responsible for doing their due diligence in order to use the text in a justified manner, to creatively make meaning in submission to God. *The Gift of Reading – Part 1* was my attempt to show how this is practically done, how we read Scripture in a way that yields justified meaning—how we use it in submission to God. We can be confident that we will be able to use the Bible in a justified manner because, as we saw in the last section, God has written the Bible to be used by and useful for his people. However, this claim is contested explicitly or implicitly among many approaches to reading the Bible, so we need to consider it to a greater depth in order to uphold our argument so far.

---

[1] See further, *The Gift of Knowing*, esp. 78-81.

THE AUDIENCE OF SCRIPTURE

> For whatever was written in former days was written for our instruction, that through endurance and through the encouragement of the Scriptures we might have hope. – Romans 15:4

For whom was the Bible written? This question is very important, for if the Bible was written for a distant people—separated from us by time, space, and culture—how can we be sure that what was clear for them will be clear for us? So far, I have assumed (with some proof-text evidence) that Christians today and throughout history are the intended audience of the Bible. However, the most common analyses of the Bible today do not share this assumption. For example, in their textbook *Grasping God's Word*, J. Scott Duvall and J. Daniel Hays argue that we must first understand the text within the thought-world of its *original audience* before we can apply it to us;[1] and in his book *Exegetical Fallacies*, D.A. Carson argues that we must undergo "distanciation"—an act of comprehending our distance from the original audience of Scripture—in order properly interpret Scripture.[2] Most commentaries and introductions to the Old and New Testaments by Evangelical Christians spend much time discussing the original audience of the biblical books.[3] This gets at the heart of the question: in biblical

---

[1] Duvall and Hays, *Grasping God's Word*.

[2] Carson, *Exegetical Fallacies*, 23–24.

[3] E.g. D. A. Carson and Douglas J. Moo, *An Introduction to the New Testament*, Second Edition. (Grand Rapids: Zondervan, 2005).

interpretation, are we concerned with the books of which the Bible is composed or the Bible, which can be subdivided into books? That is, is the Bible a unity that can be divided into books or books that are packaged and distributed together?

A. The Audience of the Bible

If our answer is the latter—that the Bible is a package of many different books—then our answer to the question of the audience will be varied. We can look at Romans and identify the audience as the 1st century Roman Christians; for Galatians, we can identify the audience as the 1st century Galatian Christians, etc. Even though we do not know the exact audience of Hebrews, Samuel, and Job, we can still say that these books were originally written for an audience other than us.

This is all true, but I have contended and will contend again that this is not all the Bible says about itself. It is true that the Bible originated as individual works authored by men under the inspiration of the Spirit, works addressed to specific groups of God's people in specific situations. Yet, to say that that this is how the Bible originated is not to say that this is an adequate description of what it is now. Already in our discussion, we have seen that to put a text in a new context is transformative; from the moment a letter or book of the Bible became part of the Bible, the authoritative canon God has given his church, it has taken on a new nature. We will see in the next chapter that there is strong continuity between the original and final form of these documents, but we can no longer consider them individual books that are part of the Bible; instead, they must be considered as pieces of the canonical book God has entrusted to his people. From this perspective, we need to re-evaluate the question of the audience. Fortunately, the Bible has much to say in this regard.

I argued in *The Gift of Reading – Part 1* that the bible is a unified literary work that is intended to govern God's people, a covenant document. It is not a collection of historical documents that give us insight into a past act of revelation nor a record of a revelatory act that we can access; to the contrary, it is a direct word from God to his covenant people. To see this, consider with me the way the biblical authors talk about the Old Testament and even—here and there—about the New Testament. Paul is clear that "whatever was written in former days was written for our instruction, that through endurance and through the encouragement of the Scriptures we might have hope" (Rom 15:4). For Paul, the Old Testament Scriptures were written for all Christians. This is repeated in Timothy and Corinthians;

> All Scripture is breathed out by God and profitable for teaching, for reproof, for correction, and for training in righteousness, that the man of God may be complete, equipped for every good work (2 Tim 3:16-17)

> It is written in the Law of Moses, 'You shall not muzzle an ox when it treads out the grain.' Is it for oxen that God is concerned? Does he not certainly speak for our sake? It was written for our sake.... (1 Cor 9:9-10)

> Now these things [i.e. the events recounted Exodus and Numbers] took place as examples for us, that we might not desire evil as they did.... Now these things happened to them as an example, but they were written down for our instruction, on whom the end of the age has come. (1 Cor 10:6, 11, cf. Heb 1:1)

Lest we think this only applies to the Old Testament—though that is phenomenal in and of itself—the New Testament speaks about itself in a similar way. Paul, in Colossians, indicates that his letters were not to be kept solely for a single church but to be read by the other churches (Col 4:16).[4] Peter, in 2 Peter, indicates that Paul's letters were being read by his audience as well—even that they were written for them—and equates them with Scripture, which Paul himself indicates was for all Christians to be equipped (2 Pet 3:14-16; 2 Tim 3:16-17). According to the Bible's own testimony, it was written for us on whom the end of the age has come, for Christians—those who live between the first and second coming of Christ.

The New Testament does not treat the Old Testament as an assortment of books written to other people; it treats the Old Testament as a unified document, as the abiding Word of God, written for Christians. The New Testament authors likewise treat each other's letters as messages to all Christians. As I argued in *Part 1* by analogy with the Old Testament, the Bible

---

[4] It is interesting that the manuscript evidence for Ephesians suggests that it may have been a cyclical letter, with that edition written to the Ephesians and other editions of the same letter addressed to other churches.

should be read as a single unified document; it follows from this analogy and from the explicit statements of the New Testament that it is a document written for Christians. We can be confident, therefore, that the Bible is addressed to us as much as it was addressed to them, that its audience includes us alongside the ancient Jewish and 1st century Christian people.

B. Our Distance from the Text

If this is true, if this is how the Bible addresses the question of audience, we must then consider what we should do about the appearance or perception of distance we experience when we read the Bible. That is, there is a reason why Carson and others discuss distanciation: there does seem to be an identifiable distance between us and the content of the text. I think we can resolve this issue, of perceived distance, with an appeal to the setting of the text, the analogy of faith, and the Christian worldview.

To begin with, consider the setting of the text. Though we are the audience of the Bible, the Bible is set across thousands of years. Genesis covers the beginning of the world until the 2nd millennium BC, so we should expect to feel some distance between ourselves and the stories there. Even Revelation, the last book of the Bible, is separated from us by 2000 years. Because the Bible is set in different times, the customs recounted within, the societal problems, and the cultures recounted are vastly different from our own. If we do not feel the distance, we are not reading the Bible rightly. Yet, if we are the intended audience of the Bible, then this distance is not an impediment to our reading. Instead, this is the setting God has chosen—and chosen because it represents the history of his people—to communicate to *us*. We can be sure that though we are distant, these situations are analogous to our own and that they are intended to teach us how to live in our own day. We may not, therefore, understand every detail as a person of that time would—the value of a *"pim"* (1 Sam 13:20), the appearance of an Ashtoreth pole, etc.—yet we can be sure that we will understand enough to receive the message God is communicating to us. I can understand what is meant in context by a *"pim"*—a unit of measure—without learning from archaeology that it means two-thirds of a shekel. I can understand from context that the Israelites erected wooden poles to worship Ashtoreth, the false goddess of the Sidonians, and that this was a visible reflection of their idolatry without understanding the dimensions or cultic function of such a pole. That we are the intended audience, and that God has given Scripture to be used for and by us, is our assurance of this fact.

The historical distance caused by the setting should be no more of a hindrance to our understanding than the mythical settings of Star Wars and the Lord of the Rings. With such novels and movies, we expect them to give us enough details of their world in order to understand what is going on. For the Bible, the analogy of faith as set out in the first section of this book indicates how the Bible functions to facilitate our interpretation of it. The Bible is vast enough in its content to give us the necessary pieces to interpret its stories and events in order to profit from them. In addition to the analogy of faith, the shared worldview of God's people brings the unity we need to interpret the Bible rightly.

If you took a 1st-century pagan Roman citizen and 21st-century person from almost anywhere in the world, the differences between them would be outstanding. Their religious practices, way of viewing the world, understanding of their purpose in life, their relationship to everyone else in society, their obligations to the state, the nature and origin of the natural world, etc. would all be very different. But a different answer would have to be given if we considered the differences between a 1st-century Greek convert in Ephesus and a 21st century convert in Vancouver, granting that they both have a firm grasp of Christianity. We could still identify things that separate them—their positions in society, their understanding of the natural world, etc.—but we would find that there is a lot more uniting them than separating them.

Both live within "the world," a kingdom consisting of all human persons, rebelling spiritual persons, and institutions who are united under Satan in futile opposition to God. Their relationship to the unbelieving world is defined by this opposition; they are called to be holy and spiritually separate from the purposes of the World. They are called to act in such a way as to point those in the world towards the Kingdom of God and its proclamation, the Gospel. Furthermore, participation in the life of the local church will have a significant role in their life, sometimes at the expense of relationships with biological family. They will worship the same God, worship on the same day where possible, and read the same Scriptures. They would have (relatively) the same understanding of the origins of the world and the way it will end. They would have the same understanding of their purpose in the world.

Essentially, in as much as their beliefs conformed to the Bible (their mutual standard for faith and practice), they would have the same worldview—the same ethic, the same epistemology, the same understanding of the world in relation to God.

It is, of course, true that no Christian has a perfect understanding of God and his world, but in whatever right understanding they have, Christians throughout the generations are united. Furthermore, they are united in their efforts to ever submit their beliefs to God through Scripture, so their unity will only grow throughout their lifetime.

Because the actions commanded of and rightly performed in Scripture come forth from the same worldview we are called to have today, there is great commonality between us as the audience of the Bible and the 1st-century Christians and ancient Jewish people who originally received biblical revelation. Furthermore, because the practices and beliefs of the culture in which they lived are shaped by the same fundamental posture against God that our culture today possesses, the challenges they faced are very similar to those we face. Even though the form of idols differs, and the sins of the day may not be the same, we readily find analogous circumstances in our culture to those faced by the original recipients of biblical revelation. Together with the considerations of text setting and the analogy of faith, along with the stated audience of Scripture, we have a firm footing for reading the text as an address to us, God's covenant people.

—Part 3—
The Role of the Author

7

THE AUTHOR AND MEANING

> We have the prophetic word more fully confirmed, to which you will do well to pay attention as to a lamp shining in a dark place, until the day dawns and the morning star rises in your hearts, knowing this first of all, that no prophecy of Scripture comes from someone's own interpretation. For no prophecy was ever produced by the will of man, but men spoke from God as they were carried along by the Holy Spirit. – 2 Peter 1:20-21

In the last two chapters, we turned from considering the role of the text in reading the Bible to the role of the reader. Now, in these final two chapters, we will consider issues related to the author, namely, how the author is the originator of meaning and what it means to speak of authorship with regard to Scripture (chapter 7) and how the text and meaning relate to historical background (chapter 8)—the authors' circumstances. In this chapter, we will first consider how the author relates to meaning and who is/are the author(s) of Scripture.

A. The Author as Originator

We saw in chapter one that under Modernity, the author and his or her intentions became the most significant consideration in meaning. Under Postmodernity, the reader tends to be credited with the most significance. In the first two parts of this book, we saw that the text is rightly considered the ground or standard for meaning—which is the role given to the author under

Modernity—and that Postmodernity is partially correct in identifying the reader as a key player in making meaning. It might seem, then, that the author has no role in meaning—at least as we have defined it. Yet this would go against common sense, for we intuitively perceive that intentional authorship is an essential condition for texts to mean anything.

For example, if we observed water carving out letters in a mountainside to form a sentence, such as "Bob's store is down the road," we would not give any effort to identify the meaning or usefulness of this statement; it would be pure coincidence that the rock formation resembles a coherent sentence—and maybe a case of reading more into formations than is actually there. Indeed, if there was a store down the road named after or owned by a man named Bob, we would immediately draw the conclusion that what we thought was a mindless, accidental process was actually the work of an author. Therefore, where meaning is present, we rightly infer the activity of an author; and if there is no author, we rightly infer that all semblance of meaning is an illusion.

So we know that authors have a role in meaning, yet they are not the standard of meaning—for we have no access to their mind other than the text they produced.[1] Furthermore, they are not the makers of meaning in that they do not define and intentionally prescribe every use their text may have; the reader is the maker of meaning by using the text. What is left is the role of originator or origin of meaning, or more accurately, meaning-potential. That is, when an author says something—whether it is writing a text or speaking an utterance—they create a finite body of meaning potential. Their communication (in this case, a text) is spoken in a context to say something specific. This contextually bound communication has a fixed potential for meaning—as we saw in chapter 3. Without an author acting, there would be no meaning potential and, therefore, no meaning. As the originator of meaning, the author's role is a presupposition for meaning rather than an agent in the making of meaning. We cannot understate the significance of this role: it is because an author wrote something that we have meaning at all. So by defining meaning as the product of a reader's interaction with a text, we are not excluding or diminishing the role of an author in communication.

---

[1] Cf. Lewis, "Modern Theology and Biblical Criticism."

Of specific relevance to the reading of Scripture, we can also say that the author is the seal of a text's authority. That is, no text bears authority in and of itself; authority is something possessed by persons. A text may state many things, but our judgment of the value of these statements depends on the author. For example, if a reputable and trustworthy historian releases a book, we will trust that the text, when properly interpreted, will tell us something about the world. However, if a known forger and liar releases a history book, we know that no amount of careful study will reveal truths about past events and people. Again, it would make a big difference whether a letter came from our spouse or from our enemy—even if it said the very same thing. If a document is sent to us concerning parking on the street in front of our house and is authored by a government official with the capacity to legally bind us, we would treat this text with much more authority than the same document drafted by a neighbour with no such authority. In this way, the author as originator of meaning is also the seal of its authority. Because the Bible is authored by God himself through his chosen representatives, the Bible carries his ultimate authority in every statement, in every claim, in every command and demand. To conclude this chapter, it is worth spending a moment discussing this, for the so-called "dual authorship" of Scripture has proven to be a stumbling block for many in the discussion of hermeneutics.

B. The Authorship of Scripture

If we were to take the position of Modernity described in chapter 1, the question of authorship would be of profound importance, for meaning rests in what the author intended to achieve by his specific communicative act to a specific people. Moreover, the question of dual-authorship of the Bible—the Divine and human authors of its constituent documents—would prove to be quite difficult to answer. That is, if the meaning is the authorial intention, are we looking for the earthly or Divine author's intentions? Furthermore, if the meaning is singular, what do we do with situations where the text apparently said more than the human author could have reasonably intended? If, however, the approach I have offered is correct, I think these problems disappear. After considering what the Bible says about its authorship, I will outline how its claims to dual authorship do not prove problematic in light of our argument so far.

The standard Evangelical position concerning the Bible is that Scripture was written by human authors under the inspiration of the Holy Spirit with the result that every word of Scripture is that which God wanted to be written.[2] The result is a text that is fully human, bearing the stylistic variety of a human work, and also fully divine, being God's very words. That God is the author of all of Scripture is evident from hundreds of passages in the Bible. Some of the more significant are 2 Timothy 3:16-17, where all Scripture is said to be "breathed out" by God (leading to the theological term, *inspiration*), and 2 Peter 1:20-21, quoted above, in which Peter says that the writers of Scripture "spoke from God as they were carried along by the Holy Spirit." Several times through the Bible (e.g. Hebrews 4:7), the Holy Spirit is identified as the author of words that are ascribed to men (cf. Acts 4:25). These texts are significant in that God is not identified as the author only of passages where his direct speech is quoted (such as in Exodus and Deuteronomy) but also of psalms and narratives where the author or narrator are speaking. Now, in many of these texts, a human author is explicitly given. Therefore, there are human authors of Scripture, yet they are not its only authors; God is the ultimate author who "carried them along" in their writing in order that the product would be his very words—breathed out by him and carrying his authority (2 Tim 3:16-17; 2 Pet 1:20-21). The mechanism by which he led their writing is unknown to us, but we do not need to know it in order to confess this truth.

Now, if the meaning of a text were singular, then we would need to legitimately ask, could God have inspired a text to have a meaning that the original author did not intend when he wrote? However, this question is irrelevant on our account of meaning.

That is, the meaning potential of a text is fixed by its context, including the words of which it consists and the textual context within which it is embedded. This means that when a biblical text became part of the canon, this change in context may have enlarged its meaning potential, yet this by no means entails that there is a change in the definitions, syntax, and grammatical relationships of the text as originally penned. Because God orchestrated the writing of the original text, I think it is safe to assume that the meaning potential of a text now found in the Bible is enlarged yet in continuity with

---

[2] This is often called "verbal plenary inspiration," God has inspired every word of Scripture.

that which the earthly author originally penned.³ The question of the original author's intention may be relevant for historical study but not for interpreting a text. Furthermore, it is not relevant for interpreting the Bible as we have received it; the final interpretive context is not the original situation in which the writing was penned but its final canonical context, the context of the Bible as an authoritative covenant document written for our sake. If this is the case, the most significant ramification it may have is on our understanding of the role of historical evidence (extra-biblical literature, archaeological finds, etc.) on our reading of Scripture.

---

³ On the other hand, because meaning potential is changed by context, it may not be wise to attempt to read between the lines of the final text we have and deduce conclusions about the original author and audience to which it was first written. We need to be careful here; this is not because the texts are ahistorical but because their new context is different then their original. This is only a danger to certain forms of historical-critical study, for as we have seen, God intends the final form as we have received it to be the final interpretive context within which we ascertain what is a justified reading or not. Footnote 23 on page 428-429 is relevant in this regard.

THE BIBLE IN HISTORY

Now these things happened to them as an example, but they were written down for our instruction, on whom the end of the ages has come. – 1 Corinthians 10:11

Much of modern biblical interpretation revolves around the study of the Ancient Near Eastern and 1st-century Roman world in which the biblical texts were written. In the study of the Old Testament, much time is given to the study of the Hebrew Language within its context as an ancient Semitic language; there is also lots of attention given to the literary milieu in which it was written—to the Babylonian, Ugaritic, Egyptian, Assyrian, etc. texts from a similar time. In the study of the New Testament, much attention is given to the Greek literature of the late 1st century BC and the 1st Century AD to better understand Koine Greek, the dialect in which the New Testament was written. Furthermore, much attention is given to the literature of Second Temple Judaism and of the Roman world at this time to better understand the worldviews of the biblical authors, their audiences, and the circumstances which the biblical letters were meant to address. If the argument of the books in this series *(The Gift of Knowing; The Gift of Reading Part 1 & 2)* has been cogent so far, then this approach to the Bible needs to be radically revised.

First, the intention and thought-world of the author are not the basis for meaning; the text interpreted in its biblical context is the basis for meaning. Second, the audience for which Scripture was written was not the original audiences of each biblical text, an audience that might approach the text with 1st century or ANE assumptions; instead, we—Christian throughout the ages, those "on whom the end of the age has come" (1 Cor

10:11)—are its intended audience. Third, the worldview of the authors who wrote Scripture, of its original audience, and of us today are not radically different from one another—as the worldviews of the ANE, of the 1st-century Roman Empire, and of any 21st-century culture are. On the contrary, we all share the worldview revealed by the Bible and delivered to us through the community of faith that has shaped us. We are all subject to the reforming work of Scripture and bear to greater and lesser degrees its worldview, over against the worldviews that characterize the kingdom of Satan—with its assumptions of the autonomy of persons and opposition to God. We cannot, therefore, assume that an understanding of the ancient world and its languages will have the impact on our studies that it is thought to have. However, we cannot throw out this evidence either. We know from the history of interpreting the Bible that this evidence—the evidence of extra-biblical literature and archaeology—has helped us grow in our understanding of the Bible. What we need is not a wholesale rejection of extra-biblical resources but a proper understanding of their place, an understanding that appropriately relates them to the Bible as it declares itself to be—authoritative, self-interpreting, and universally relevant. For the rest of this chapter, I want to briefly outline what role I think such evidence should take in our study of the Bible.[1]

To re-phrase the problem of using extra-biblical evidence in biblical interpretation and to frame our discussion for the rest of this chapter, consider the following statement and its implications: *when a historical parallel is used to explain a text, the evidence necessary to establish a link between a piece of extra-biblical data and the text needs to be sufficient to make the point independently.*[2] That is, if the extra-biblical data is said to say something the text itself does not say, this is called imposition or eisegesis—reading into the text something that is not there. Meaning is no longer found in the text; it is found in the author's mind, in his thought processes that led to the text he wrote. However, as I have argued above, this is an inadequate view of meaning. Meaning is the use of a text governed by the text itself. If this is true, historical material is not necessary to understand a biblical *text*, which is the object of our interpretive

---

[1] What follows is adapted from my article "The Problem with the Use of Extra-Biblical Data in Interpretation," from https://teleioteti.ca/2018/08/15/the-problem-of-extra-biblical-data/.

[2] This is the same principle used in our discussion of genre in chapter 4.

endeavours. Historical evidence may help us to better understand the thought process of the author (if that is possible) and the original audience's reception of the document. It cannot, however, be used to make the text say anything that is not already there. If sufficient evidence to justify the use of historical material is only present when the text says as much as the evidence is used to say, historical material is in a significant sense redundant. If we cannot appeal to historical evidence to find meaning, for the meaning we would find is no longer that of the text, then all this evidence can really do is help us see better what the text has been saying all along. So we need to ask, what good is extra-biblical evidence after all?

Before we give an answer, a secondary point needs to be made. Much use of extra-biblical material is a fallacy sometimes called *illegitimate totality transfer*.[3] That is, every word or symbol has a semantic range that is narrowed by context to indicate something specific. When a true parallel is made between an extra-biblical item and the text, this does not justify reading the whole semantic range of that item into the text. The connection is made between two specific points on the semantic range of the text and the item; such a connection does not justify expanding from there to the whole range. For example, one may argue that Paul is using the word-group παιδεια (*paideia*, education) in Galatians 3-4 in relation to the Roman views of adoption and inheritance, of which this is a key word-group. Granted that this connection is legitimate, it would be fallacious to read any more about Roman views of adoption and inheritance into the text than Paul makes clear.

If we do not allow such a jump, from one point of the semantic context to its entirety, we are then left with our initial proposition: the text must be able to make any point extra-biblical data is used to establish.

A. The Uses of Extra-Biblical Evidence

Our discussion so far leaves us with an obvious question: What then is extra-biblical data useful for? I want to argue that it is useful for illustration, illumination, confirmation, and application. First, it is useful for illustration, helping us preach the text. That is, we can understand how Paul used the word παιδαγωγός (*paidagōgos*, guardian) in Galatians by examining the

---

[3] Cf. Carson, *Exegetical Fallacies*, 60–61.

word's range of meanings within the Bible. But by drawing the connection to the broader social context of the word, we are provided with rich illustrative material to make clear Paul's point. If a preacher or teacher can make such an illustration without implicitly teaching his audience that this material is necessary for interpreting the text (a danger this series of books have been trying to avoid) such illustrations can be very effective.

Second, extra-biblical background material is useful for illumination, useful for helping us to see the text. This is needed at times because we have cultural blinders inherited from our culture and upbringing or other limitations that prevent us from seeing what was present in the text the whole time. Historical material can unearth such things. For example, in the 19th and 20th centuries, it became popular to view the language of the New Testament as a divine language, a special Greek dialect given by God to communicate the unique content of the New Testament. However, the discovery of hundreds of Greek papyrus texts in the 20th century—letters, government documents, shopping lists, etc.—revealed that the language of the New Testament was not a divine language; it was the common language of the day, hence "Koine" or common Greek. This discovery revealed that the theories of a by-gone generation were wrong, that these theories were not rooted in anything the Bible said. This discovery was a corrective on arguing theological ideas from the absence of evidence—of violating the rule that the absence of evidence is not the evidence of absence.

Third, extra-biblical material is useful for confirmation. Sometimes there is heated debate over specific stances on interpreting a passage. There may be a case where the argument reaches a standstill and producing a piece of extra-biblical evidence will tilt the case one way or another. One instance is 1 Samuel 13:21. After telling us that the Israelites went to the Philistines to have their tools sharpened, for there was no blacksmith, we are told וְהָיְתָה הַפְּצִירָה פִים לַמַּחֲרֵשֹׁת (vᵉhāytāh happᵉsîrāh pîm lammahărēsōt). The meaning of this verse is not immediately evident, for "פְּצִירָה" (pṣîrāh) and "פִים" (pîm) occur only here in the Hebrew Bible. The syntax, along with the probable meaning of פְּצִירָה ("fee," from פצר, pṣr, to urge), suggests the following rendering: "and the charge was a *pim* for the plowshare...." However, the translators of the KJV attempted read פִים with פְּצִירָה to mean "a double-edged (lit. double-mouthed) file," translating it simply as "a file"; this translation indicates that Israel had the ability to sharpen some of their tools themselves. However, this does not quite conform with the previous verse, which says that Israelites went to Palestine to have these same weapons sharpened (v. 20). Archaeological evidence confirms that פִּים should be understood as a Philistine measurement, weighing about two-thirds of a shekel. This supports the first interpretation over-against the KJV. The implication is that Israel was dependent on the Philistines even for their tools, showing that they had no weapons. Some commentators argue that the price suggests they were being gouged, but this is not necessary to understand the use of the term in its context.[4] Thus, extra-biblical data helps us follow one interpretation over another; it may also have functioned in this case for illumination.

Lastly, it is useful for application. By bringing forth extra-biblical material, we expand the sphere of application for a text: we can let the item and the text interact to shed insight on, for example, a historical question. For example, by bringing forth the discovery of an inscription reading "house of David," we can use the bible to shed light on the meaning of that phrase and its relevance.

B. The Challenge of Using Extra-Biblical Data

There remains a challenge in our use of such data, namely, how we can be sure that our extra-biblical evidence is being used rightly? I want to propose one test we can use and then some challenges that need to be overcome if we are to use this data rightly.

First, the test: an interpreter must ask if they could make the point for which they are using extra-biblical evidence from the text alone. This is another implication of the statement with which we began. If the historical evidence disappeared, can you convince someone from the data available in the text? If not, this is an invalid use of extra-biblical data.

Second, the use of background data is fraught with more troubles than

---

[4] Cf. V. Philips Long, "1 and 2 Samuel," in *Zondervan Illustrated Bible Background Commentary: Old Testament: Volume 2, Joshua, Judges, Ruth, 1 and 2 Samuel*, ed. John H. Walton, vol. 2 (Grand Rapids: Zondervan, 2009).

is commonly acknowledged. 1) There needs to be a sure connection between the data and the text, but how can one establish this? What evidence can be produced to establish this connection? Many times, dating and locating are uncertain; how then can it be known that the author or audience was even aware of this particular piece of background data someone wishes to employ? The problem is compounded when we add that we are unsure of the social stratification of author and audience: if the data is right concerning time and place, how do we know they had access to and then used it?

2) This data itself needs interpretation. Because the Bible claims illumination, self-sufficiency, and truth for itself, it is a better tool in interpretation than any other piece of data. Therefore, it is more appropriate to interpret extra-biblical data by the Bible than the other way around.

3) I would raise again the problem that the extra-biblical evidence can add nothing to the text. If we judge the meaning of a text by its context and the meaning of the evidence by its context, by what do we judge our construal of their relationship? The only judge is the hypothesized mind of the author or audience, which is itself derived from one of the above. We are thus left with no standard of verification for our interpretation. We have no way of knowing if our construal of the relationship between the Bible and a piece of extra-biblical evidence is correct. However, if our use of extra-biblical data passes the test I proposed, then these challenges are no longer a problem, for our point rests in the text. Now, I can imagine that there might be some objections to the point I am making in this chapter, so in conclusion, I want to consider what I think will be the most common objections.[5]

D. Objections

First, someone might say, "the author originally wrote to an audience; do we not need to understand what this original audience would have understood?" This same argument could be made about the author. We could answer this in two ways. First, if we accept this assumption, this does not invalidate our point. The reason is this: the text is our standard of verification, so our conception of the author or audience's interpretation must always conform to the words of the text in their literary context. Thus, such an interpretation is subject to our test for verifying extra-biblical data given above. If our

---

[5] These reflect objections I have encountered in discussions with my peers, pastors, professors, and in various articles and books concerning interpretation.

understanding of "what they would have understood' does not pass this test, it is invalid. If it passes this test, it is redundant: we are just rephrasing "what the text says" as "what the author said" or "what the audience would hear." Second, as we have seen, the Bible was written for our sake. Thus, we are the ultimate audience of the Bible and our standard for interpreting Scripture itself, so we are back with what the text says.

Second, someone may object that such an approach de-historicizes the text. By severing its relation to the external data, have we not de-historicized the Bible, made it merely an interpretation that says nothing about the facts of history? This conclusion is unwarranted. The text speaks about history from within the flow of history—it provides the true interpretation of history—and so applies to history. Yet, it is self-interpreting, written in such a way that it fully interprets history without needing external data to interpret it. It was produced in history, speaks to history, yet was shaped by God to be interpreted throughout history.

Third and finally, someone might suggest that this "disembodies" the text. That is, they might suggest that the approach given here treats the Bible as if it has fallen from heaven, free from the historical processes by which texts are usually formed. In response, we can say, first, that the points I am making are universal points of interpretation. Given a cogent text (a text not meant for insiders with extensive extra-textual knowledge), the best interpretation is the one that corresponds to the words of the text. Second, though the Bible began its life in the same way as many documents written in various circumstances, these documents were reconstituted— "reembodied"—as a New Covenant document written for a community stretching 2000 years, written to be understood and used throughout the ages. Therefore, we are not disembodying the text, making it an unearthly entity, but properly considering the way God has chosen to embody it.

CONCLUSION

I began this book with a challenge I believe all Christians, especially pastors and teachers, face today, the erosion of the perspicuity of Scripture in contemporary biblical studies. In *The Gift of Reading – Part 1*, I set out to present an exegetical method that was derived from the Scripture's own claims to authority and intelligibility. In this second part, I have attempted to support and uphold that method by explaining at length the theory and theology behind it. In chapter 1, we briefly surveyed the history of biblical interpretation among Christians and the post-Christian world. In the following chapters, we interacted with the challenges raised in this survey.

In Part 1, we considered the role of the Bible, how it is the standard by which we measure meaning (i.e. a justified use of Scripture) and the way Scripture is self-interpreting. In Part 2, we considered the role of the reader in interpretation. We looked at the reader as the maker of meaning, the one who puts the Scripture to use, and we saw how the Bible is addressed to Christians throughout the ages, including us today. In Part 3, we considered the role of the author as the originator of meaning, the one who says something with a text and from whom a text derives its authority. In the final chapter, we considered how extra-biblical evidence plays a role in interpretation.

In the end, I believe we have seen how Scripture not only presents itself as self-interpreting but also how it functions in this way. We have seen that God has not left us without hope for hearing his voice. He has granted us a clear text that contains within itself the resources necessary to interpret and use it throughout the ages. We, like the 1st-century Christians, are those upon whom the end of the age has come, those who live as members of the new creation living within the old creation. To live for God's kingdom, to make his glory known and expand the sphere of those who confess his rule, we are deeply in need of a divine word. We need certainty amid our society's relativity; we need of hope in the place of our society's nihilism; we are in need of confidence that we are indeed united with Christ and recipients of his salvific work; and we are in need of wisdom, wisdom to make decisions every day concerning faithfulness to God and the success of his commission. Thanks be to God that he has not left us without a witness; he has provided us with all these things and more in the Scriptures. The Bible is a treasure granted to us and to our children; God in his kindness has not left us without a way to access and use this treasure. He has granted us all things pertaining to life and godliness, including the ability and resources necessary to make use of his Word.

To illustrate how this works in application, especially with problematic texts, I have included six exegetical essays (3 Old Testament, 3 New Testament) illustrating the use of biblical background material (Appendices 2 & 3), use of the Bible to resolve translations issues (Appendices 1, 2, 3, & 5), and the use of the Bible for theology (Appendices 5 & 6). In addition, my commentary on Habakkuk illustrates the theory and method of *The Gift of Reading – Part 1 & Part 2* through the exposition of an entire biblical book.

In conclusion, we must thank the Lord with the Psalmist for the great gift that is his Word. We must seek ever to grow in our understanding and application of it;

> Oh how I love your law!
> > It is my meditation all the day.
>
> Your commandment makes me wiser than my enemies,
> > for it is ever with me.
>
> I have more understanding than all my teachers,
> > for your testimonies are my meditation.
>
> I understand more than the aged,
> > for I keep your precepts.
>
> I hold back my feet from every evil way,
> > in order to keep your word.
>
> I do not turn aside from your rules,

for you have taught me.
How sweet are your words to my taste,
    sweeter than honey to my mouth!
Through your precepts I get understanding;
    therefore I hate every false way.

Your word is a lamp to my feet
    and a light to my path.
I have sworn an oath and confirmed it,
    to keep your righteous rules.
I am severely afflicted;
    give me life, O Lord, according to your word!
Accept my freewill offerings of praise, O Lord,
    and teach me your rules.
I hold my life in my hand continually,
    but I do not forget your law.
The wicked have laid a snare for me,
    but I do not stray from your precepts.
Your testimonies are my heritage forever,
    for they are the joy of my heart.
I incline my heart to perform your statutes
    forever, to the end. (Psalm 119:97-112)

—Appendices—
Theory in Application:
Exegetical Essays

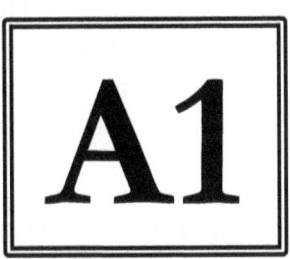

THE SOVEREIGNTY OF GOD OVER THE REPENTANCE OF MAN: RE-READING DEUTERONOMY 30:1-14

This paper was originally prepared as an appendix to my book, *Prevenient Grace*.[1] It appears here with some adaptation. It argues against the standard translation of Deuteronomy 30:1-14. It is argued that in its context, this passage speaks of a future day when God would grant his people new hearts to believe in and love him as he had commanded them to. It is therefore a prophecy of the New Covenant and the fount of most New Covenant prophecies in the Old Testament.

The attentive reader, following along in his or her Bible, may have noticed that my interpretation of Deuteronomy 30:1-14 differs significantly from most English translations. I want to briefly defend my reading and offer a provisional translation that follows the contours of the interpretation I am suggesting. Three main issues confront the exegete in this passage; first, one must determine where the protasis (if...) ends and the apodosis (then...) begins.[2] Then the functions of the many uses of כִּי (*kî*; for) need to be

---

[1] Rutherford, *Prevenient Grace*.

[2] In a conditional sentence (if...then), the apodosis is the main clause—what will happen (then). The protasis is the condition—when or in what circumstances this will happen (if).

determined. Finally, one must arrive at a conclusion on the tense of verses 11-14, namely, are they referring to the same time as the previous verses (future) or to the situation of those to whom Moses first wrote (present).

From the syntax of the chapter and its context—both immediate and greater—I will argue that the text should be translated as follows,[3]

> ¹And *when* all these things come upon you—the blessing and the curse, which I have placed before you—then you will <u>return</u> these things to your heart[4] among all the nations where Yahweh your God scattered you. ²And you, you and your sons, will <u>return</u> to Yahweh your God and obey his voice with all your heart and with all your soul, according to all I have commanded you today. ³And Yahweh your God will <u>turn</u> your fortune[5] and he will have

---

[3] Stylistically smooth English has not been my primary focus with this translation. My translation philosophy for this passage has been somewhat akin to the ESV, attempting to be as close to the text as possible while accommodating for foreign idioms. For the sake of the following arguments, I have underlined the keyword שׁוּב and italicized the conjunction כִּי.

[4] Idiomatically, this means something like "call to mind" or "remember." I have retained the clumsier wording because of its parallels throughout the rest of the passage. Cf. ESV, NASB.

[5] This is the probable meaning of this interesting phrase; a literal rendering would be, "to turn your turning." The Vulgate and Septuagint seem to have read the Hebrew word rendered "your fortune"—שְׁבוּתְךָ ($š^eb\hat{u}t^ek\bar{a}$)—as a derivative from שׁבה ($šbh$), to take captive. God would then be turning their captivity. The LXX has rendered it as "your sin", τας ἁμαρτιας σου (*tas harmatias sou*), and the Vulgate as *captivitatem tuam*, "your captivity." Study of a cognate Aramaic phrase, from the Sefire inscription, suggests strongly that this word is indeed derived from שׁוּב ($š\hat{u}b$), to turn. Further support for this is found in our context, where *šûb* is a key word. Though God's turning of their turning—in light of history, the greater canonical context, and the immediate context—has in view his restoration of their fortunes via a return from exile, the idea of captivity is not to be derived from the word itself. With Driver, it seems best to understand the word to refer to a "*turn*, or change, in a people's fortune." With the same meaning in context, Christensen and Tigay identify it as an idiom with the specific meaning "restore," that is turn one's fortune by restoring a previous, and positive, state. Cf. Jb. 42:10.

Jeffrey H. Tigay, *Deuteronomy [Devarim]: The Traditional Hebrew Text with the New JPS Translation*, 1st ed., The JPS Torah commentary (Philadelphia, Penn.: Jewish Publication Society, 1996), 284, 399; Francis Brown et al., *The Brown-Driver-Briggs Hebrew and English Lexicon* (Peabody: Hendrickson, 1996), 986; Ludwig Koehler et al., *The Hebrew and Aramaic Lexicon of the Old Testament*, electronic ed. (Leiden; New York: Brill, 1999), 1385–1386; Duane L. Christensen, *Deuteronomy 21:10-34:12*, vol. 6B,

compassion on you; he will <u>turn</u> and gather you from all the people among whom Yahweh your God has scattered you. ⁴Even if your exiles are at the edge of the heavens, from there Yahweh your God will gather you and he will take you from there. ⁵And Yahweh your God will bring you into the land which your fathers possessed and you shall possess it, and he will do good to you and make you more numerous than your fathers.

⁶And Yahweh your God will circumcise your heart and the heart of your offspring so that you will love Yahweh your God with all your heart and all your soul, so that you may live. ⁷And Yahweh your God will lay all these curses upon your enemies and upon those hating you, who persecuted you. ⁸And you will <u>turn</u> and obey the voice of Yahweh and do all his commands, which I have commanded you today.

⁹And Yahweh your God will prosper you in all the works of your hand, in the fruit of your womb, and in the fruit of your cattle and in the fruit of your land. *For* Yahweh will <u>turn</u> to rejoice over you for good, as he rejoiced over your fathers. ¹⁰*For* you will obey the voice of Yahweh your God, to keep his commandments and his precepts, the ones written in this book of the law. *For* you will <u>return</u> to Yahweh your God with all your heart and with all your soul. ¹¹*For* this commandment, which I have commanded you today, will not be too difficult for you and it will not be far away. ¹²It will not be in the heavens, that you should say, "Who will go up to the heavens and retrieve it for us and make us hear it so that we may do it?" ¹³And it will not be beyond the sea, that you should say, "Who will cross to the other side of the sea and retrieve it for us and make us hear it so that we may obey it?" ¹⁴*For* it will be very near to you, in your mouth and in your heart, so that you will do it.

To defend this translation, I will briefly address the three translation issues mentioned above. There are two main interpretations of this passage found among commentators, each reading sharing similar translations for each issue. One reading emphasizes Israel's response as the condition for God's

---

Word Biblical Commentary (Nashville: Thomas Nelson Publishers, 2002), 738; S. R. Driver, *A Critical and Exegetical Commentary on Deuteronomy*, 3rd ed., The International Critical Commentary (Edinburgh: T. & T. Clark, 1895), 329; Joseph A. Fitzmyer, *The Aramaic Inscriptions of Sefire*, Biblica Et Orientalia 19 (Rome: Pontifical Biblical Institute, 1967), 119–120; R. Laird Harris, Gleason L Archer, and Bruce K Waltke, *Theological Wordbook of the Old Testament*, vol. 2 (Chicago, Ill.: Moody Press, 1980), 896.

actions—so the apodosis is understood to begin in verse 3, and the multiple instances of כִּי *(kî)* are understood to be strongly causal or conditional (because, if).⁶ The other understands the whole passage as prophetic and sees verse 6 as key; God's action is emphasized.⁷ My translation follows this later reading. The first reason for this is the identification of the apodosis.

A. Identifying the Apodosis of The Condition in Verse 1

In the former reading, prioritizing Israel, the apodosis is usually identified as starting in verse 3, when Yahweh is said to turn Israel's fortune. Verses 1b-2 are then understood as conditions for Yahweh's actions; he will restore Israel when the nation turns back to him. Though this reading is syntactically possible, there is not much evidence in context favouring it. The unit of verses 1b-9 is composed of a series of vav+perfect constructions (and you/he will…); in theory, any of these vavs could begin the apodosis (then clause),⁸ but it is best to read the first vav as beginning the apodosis. A few reasons for this are as follows.

First, there is no discernible reason to start the apodosis at the third vav and not the first. Brettler shows that considering the syntax alone, neither the first nor the third vav clause is favoured as the beginning of the apodosis.⁹

---

⁶ On these readings, Kyle B. Wells, *Grace and Agency in Paul and Second Temple Judaism: Interpreting the Transformation of the Heart,* Supplements to Novum Testamentum 157 (Leiden; Boston, Mass.: Brill, 2015), 39. Block and, seemingly, Wright follow this first reading, at least to some extent. Daniel Isaac Block, *Deuteronomy,* The NIV Application Commentary (Grand Rapids: Zondervan, 2012), 695, 700; N.T. Wright, *The New Testament and the People of God,* Christian Origins and the Question of God 1 (Minneapolis: Fortress, 1992), 289.

⁷ Wells, for example, provides possible arguments for this interpretation. Wells, *Grace and Agency in Paul and Second Temple Judaism,* 29–33. Coxhead, Brettler, and Sailhammer, for differing reasons, read it as a promise of the New Covenant. Marc Zvi Brettler, "Predestination in Deuteronomy 30:1-10," in *Those Elusive Deuteronomists* (Sheffield: Sheffield Academic Press, 1999), 171–188; Steven R. Coxhead, "Deuteronomy 30:11-14 as a Prophecy of the New Covenant in Christ," *Westminster Theological Journal* 68 (2006): 305–320; John H. Sailhamer, *The Pentateuch as Narrative* (Grand Rapids: Zondervan, 1992).

⁸ Williams and Beckman, *Williams' Hebrew Syntax,* 181.

⁹ Brettler, "Predestination in Deuteronomy 30:1-10," 176–177.

Moreover, sometimes the subject shift from "you" to "Yahweh" is identified as a reason for taking verse 3 as the beginning of the apodosis. This is not convincing, for the subject first changes between 1a and 1b—from "these things" to "you."[10] If a subject change is our clue to the beginning of the apodosis, then it should begin in 1b. Subject changes aside, we must determine the beginning of the apodosis from context.

There is nothing in context that would favour suspending the apodosis until verse 3, but there are good contextual reasons to identify the shift at verse 1b. Turning from the coming of the curses in chapter 29, chapter 30 begins by casting a prophecy for the future; "when all these things have happened...." Taking verse 1b as the apodosis starts the prophecy with the promise of a time when Israel will turn back to God. They will finally be obedient, and God will prosper them. No cause would then be given for why Israel turns, just that they most assuredly will after God brings the curses upon them. The reader is immediately confronted with a tension: what has made it so that the negativity of chapter 29 changes to such a positive hope in 30? Chapter 30 verse 6, the heart of this passage, will give us the answer.

In 29:1-4, Moses laments the state of the people, they have seen all the miraculous signs God has done, yet God has not given them the heart to understand it all (v. 4). The eventual rebellion and the coming of the curses in this chapter flow right out of this state (cf. 29:19). This has already been foreshadowed in Deuteronomy 5:29. Here, the people vow to follow Yahweh, but he responds with the desire that they would have this heart always, for then it would go well for them. However, the problem is that they do not have this heart always. If Israel's disobedience stems out of stubborn hearts that God has yet to change, the sudden obedience prophesied in Deuteronomy 30 should automatically beg us to ask what has changed: has God acted?[11]

This is exactly what the structure of the chapter and verse 6 point to. The syntax of verses 1b-9a, reading the apodosis in 1b with the first vav, links together a series of events that will all happen in the future, after the blessings and the curses come upon Israel. They could all be simultaneous: the syntax does not suggest that one is dependent on another. However, syntax is not our only guide; the macro-structure of the chapter and the context we have

---

[10] Wells, *Grace and Agency in Paul and Second Temple Judaism*, 29.

[11] Wells makes a similar point. Ibid., 38.

just looked at suggests that verse 6 is the key to all the prophesied future events. Many commentators have pointed out a chiasmic structure in this passage, ending it at v. 10, but there seems to me to be a few points that are forced in these structures.[12] Taking vv. 11-14 to be part of the prophecy in verses 1-10, the structure they are seeing becomes a closer parallel. With my translation, it looks like this:

> (A) and you will <u>return</u> these things to your heart... (v. 1b)
> (B) And you will <u>return</u> to Yahweh your God and obey (v. 2)
>   (C) and Yahweh will <u>turn</u> your fortunes... <u>turn</u> and gather you... do good to you and make you more numerous than your fathers (vv. 3-5)
>   (D) *⁶And Yahweh your God will circumcise your heart and the heart of your offspring, so that you will love Yahweh your God with all your heart and all your soul, so that you may live... and you will <u>turn</u> and you will obey the voice of Yahweh and you will do his commands* (vv. 6-8)
>   (C') And Yahweh your God will prosper you... *for* Yahweh will <u>turn</u> to rejoice over you... as he rejoiced over your fathers. (9)
> (B') *For* you will obey the voice of Yahweh your God. *For* you will <u>return</u> to Yahweh your God with all your heart and with all your soul. (v. 10)[13]
> (A') ¹¹*For* this commandment... will not be too difficult for you and it will not be far away... ¹⁴*For* it will be very near to you, in your mouth and in your heart so that you will do it." (v. 11-14)[14]

---

[12] E.g. in Block's chiasm, v. 8 is attached to v.9 as echoing vv. 3-5, but v. 7 need to be ignored in his diagramming of the chiasm for it to make sense. his chiasm also must begin at 2a, though we are seeing that 1b is the clearest beginning for the apodosis. 2a is also an even more awkward point to begin the apodosis than 3. The biggest issue is the severing of vv. 12-14 from the preceding passages, which we will examine with the use of כִּי (ki). Ibid., 32; Block, *Deuteronomy*, 695; Wright, *The New Testament and the People of God*, 289.

[13] This verse is directly dependent upon v. 6, as the repetition of "all your heart and with all your soul" suggests. It is because God has worked that this is possible; the parallelism suggests that the act in v. 2 would also be dependent upon God's act in v. 6. Cf. Wright, *The New Testament and the People of God*, 289.

[14] The day will come when the people will turn to the commandments God has revealed to them, remembering them (v. 1). The parallel also emphasizes the same

The heart of a chiasm is the point it is meant to emphasize: here it is the work of God to change the heart of his people with the result that they "will love Yahweh [their] God with all [their] heart and all [their] soul." Love is the heart of covenant faithfulness, and so this act is what enables them to be covenantally faithful; as verse 8 makes clear, this is what enables the Israelites to then return to God and obey him. In Deuteronomy 5:29, God exclaimed, "Oh that they had such a heart as this always, that it might go well with them and with their descendants forever." Here, Moses prophesies that a day will come when this is true; the cause of this change is God, working to change their hearts.

Understanding verse 1b as the apodosis makes this future prophecy parallel in structure and emphasises what the context has already demanded be emphasised: God needs to act so that Israel can be faithful.

B. Translating the Conjunction Ki

The second translation issue is the use of כִּי (*kî*) in verses 9-11. כִּי in Hebrew encompasses functions that English expresses with many different words: there is no one-one equivalence in translating this word. In a helpful and much-cited paper, Aejmelaeus examines the various functions כִּי has in Hebrew, classifying them according to whether they follow or precede the main clause.[15] When כִּי (*kî*) precedes the clause, it usually has a function like a subordinate clause in English: Aejmelaeus classifies these uses as circumstantial. In these situations, the conjunction can communicate the ideas of condition (if), temporal condition (when), or causation (for/because).[16] This is seen in verse 1, where כִּי has a subordinate temporal value, functioning as the protasis of a conditional construction. However, all

---

thing, but from a different perspective. Here, we see that it is because of God's work that the day will come when the commandments will be inside the hearts of the people.

[15] She uses main clause in a slightly idiosyncratic way: "The term 'main clause' will, however, be used in the following discussion to designate the clause to which the כִּי clause is joined, regardless of the distinction between subordination and coordination." Anneli Aejmelaeus, "Function and Interpretation of כי in Biblical Hebrew," *Journal of Biblical Literature* 105, no. 2 (1986): 196.

[16] Cause is used in the broadest possible sense, for כִּי can communicate cause, motivation, reason, explanation. Ibid., 196–198, 201–202.

the occurrences of כִּי in verses 9-14 follow their main clause, and so—according to Aejmelaeus—need to be considered separately from those that precede the main clause.

From Aejmelaeus' analysis of these uses, it appears that כִּי following its main clause has a causal sense most of the time (in the broad sense noted above). Exceptions to this are the odd temporal or conditional occurrence, though the temporal use of כִּי following a main clause is always linked to a temporal correlate in the main clause. The only example she has of a conditional use after the main clause is earlier in Deuteronomy, where Israel's obedience is demanded by context as the condition (e.g. in the account of covenantal blessings).[17] Some have argued for the temporal reading of כִּי in our passage, suggesting that the temporal use of כִּי in verse 1 and the temporality of the main clause (and… will…) allow for this.[18] I must agree with Block that this seems forced, but a causal sense needs to be nuanced and not treated as equivalent to a condition.[19]

Each of the uses of כִּי carries a strong causal sense, explaining the action in the previous clause. In 9b, Yahweh's act of prospering his people is the result of his turning to them and rejoicing over them. God rejoices over his people because they will finally obey his commandments (10). This is not a condition, for it is sure to happen, but it is also more than temporal. They will obey *because* they will turn to Yahweh with all their heart and soul (8). As I mentioned earlier, this verse is dependent on God's work in verse 6, as are verses 11-14. The resulting idea is that even though the cause of God's rejoicing is Israel's obedience, they turned to him because he acted first to circumcise their heart. Verses 11-14 gives the reason that Israel will finally obey and return to Yahweh: they will obey because in that future day the commandments of Moses will no longer be external and distant; the commandments will then be inside of them. This is a direct result of God's act of circumcision (30:6), and as we have seen earlier [this is a reference to

---

[17] Ibid., 207–208.

[18] E.g. Coxhead, "Deuteronomy 30:11-14 as a Prophecy of the New Covenant in Christ," 307–308.

[19] Block, *Deuteronomy*, 700. his translation in the chiasm, following the NIV, is conditional. Ibid., 695.

the book, *Prevenient Grace: An Investigation into Arminianism*], the rest of the Old Testament and New Testament interpret it as such (cf. Jer. 31, Isa. 54:13, Rom 10:7-9). This brings us to our last translational issue, the timing of verses 11-14.

C. The Time of Verses 11-14

The NIV, NET, NASB, ESV, and LXX all translate verses 11-14 with verse 15ff and so separate them from what preceded, seeing a shift from the future back to the present. The breaks marked in the MT may also support his reading (with an open break [פ] between verses 10 and 11 and a closed one [ס] between vv. 14 and 15). Despite this consensus, there are good reasons to doubt this division of paragraphs.

First, verses 11-14 are made up of adjectives, participles, pronouns, and prepositional phrases, none of which communicate a time value in Hebrew. So any judgment about the timing of these verses needs to come from context.[20] This immediately lays the burden of proof upon those claiming that these verses return to the present, for everything preceding them was looking to the future. We must ask, then, if there any indications of a shift in timing. Other than the external testimony of the LXX and MT, the only other argument available is to suggest that הַיּוֹם (*hayyôm*; the day, today) in v. 11 calls the reader back to the present.[21] This is not convincing for two reasons. First, הַיּוֹם is not functioning adverbially to indicate when the commandment will be close (as in "today the commandment is close") but is part of an adjectival clause clarifying what commandment is in view: it is Yahweh's law, which Moses has delivered to the people that day, that will be close to them in the future. Second, in verses 2 and 8—both of which look to the future— הַיּוֹם (*hayyôm*) is used in the exact same way. So the use of הַיּוֹם does not

---

[20] Coxhead, "Deuteronomy 30:11-14 as a Prophecy of the New Covenant in Christ," 306; Thomas O. Lambdin, *Introduction to Biblical Hebrew* (New York, N.Y.: Charles Scribner's Sons, 1971), 19.

[21] I am not spending time on the argument that this passage is directly connected to what follows, for it is begging the question to argue that because this is connected to what follows, it should be translated in the present. If the tenses are translated present, then vv. 11-14 surely goes with vv. 15ff. But if there are good reasons to take the tenses as future—such as no evidence to the contrary and both the syntax and flow of thought which suggests this—then it must go with vv. 1-10. Wells, *Grace and Agency in Paul and Second Temple Judaism*, 37.

anchor this text in the time of Moses.

The arguments for taking verses 11-14 with what precedes it are numerous. Wells points out that the very problem Israel suffered from in chapter 29 (that God had not yet given them hearts to understand) is said to be remedied in this passage, so it must refer to Israel after God has given them a heart to understand (i.e. after 30:6).[22] There is also the coordination of כִּי (*kî*) clauses throughout the later verses of this chapter. Most English translations do not show this sequence of כִּי stretching from verses 9-14, a sequence without any syntactical clues that would suggest they should not be understood together. It makes most sense to take כִּי in verse 11 as marking a causal clause occurring at the same time as verse 10, as I have suggested in my explanations of the uses of כִּי above.[23] Furthermore, Paul quotes this passage in Romans 10:7-8 and understands them to be fulfilled in the New Covenant through Christ. If we read Deuteronomy 30:11-14 as referring to the future, this explains his interpretation.[24]

Lastly, Sailhamer has demonstrated that the internal clues of verses 11-14 point away from Sinai to a New Covenant—as later prophesied by the prophets. The two question Moses says do not need to be asked are: "Who will go up to the heavens and retrieve it for us and make us hear it so that we may do it," and "Who will cross to the other side of the sea and retrieve it for us and make us hear it so that we may obey it?" Some may take these as generic references, expressing the difficulty and length of the task needing to be done. Sailhamer, in contrast, argues that in these verses the prophesied New Covenant seen in verses 1-10 is compared with the Covenant at Sinai.[25] These are not generic references then; they are references to the nature of the Old Covenant. Under the New Covenant, no one will have to go up to the heavens to get God's commandments—as Moses ascended Sinai to receive

---

[22] Ibid., 38. The rest of the OT, as we saw earlier, also anticipates this as a future act of God. Coxhead, "Deuteronomy 30:11-14 as a Prophecy of the New Covenant in Christ," 309.

[23] Coxhead, "Deuteronomy 30:11-14 as a Prophecy of the New Covenant in Christ," 306–308. I disagree with his conclusion that כִּי in v. 11 should be taken temporally, but his arguments do show that כִּי should be joined with what came before it (v. 1-10).

[24] Ibid., 311–319; Sailhamer, *Pentateuch*, 474. See my paper reproduced as Appendices 4.

[25] Sailhamer, *Pentateuch*, 473.

them from God. Showing this parallel, he writes, "At Sinai, for example, God spoke directly to the people "from heaven" (Deut. 4:36). Moses' words here also reflect the words of the people at Mount Sinai, 'You [Moses] go near and listen to all that the Lord our God says, Then tell us whatever the LORD our God tells you' (5:27; cf. Exod 20:18-21)."[26] What was under the Old Covenant written upon stone tablets will now be etched in the hearts of God's people (Deut 30:6, 14; Ezek 36:26).[27] "Who will cross over the sea" would then be a reference to the crossing of the Red Sea on the way to Sinai.[28] Reading 30:11-14 as referring to the future also picks up the natural transition in verse 15, were "today" shifts from telling us about the commandments to focus on the present actions of Moses.[29]

I have argued here that Deuteronomy 30 should be read as a prophecy of a coming New Covenant, when God will enable his sinful people to obey and follow him by giving them a new heart. Israel's actions, their faithfulness, are not what precipitate God's actions; it is God's merciful act of heart circumcision that brings about their covenant faithfulness. Deuteronomy 30:11-14 is not, then, Moses' affirmation of the people's ability to follow the law as they were. These verses are his promise that in the future God would act as he had not yet acted (cf. 29:4) so that the people would finally be able to follow and obey him from their hearts.

---

[26] It is true that Moses does not explicitly make this connection, but there is enough evidence to show that it is intended. When God meet Moses at the mountain, God speaks to the people from heaven (Exod 20:22; Deut 4:36; Neh 9:13). In Deut 4:36, God is also said reveal himself on earth in fire and to speak from it, God comes in clouds and fire and Sinai becomes the place where heaven and earth meet (Deut 5:22-27). Furthermore, the words of Deut. 30:12-13 allude to Deut 5:27, where the people ask Moses to mediate for them (Deut 5:27, cf. Exod 20:18-22). Ibid., 474.

[27] Ibid., 473–474.

[28] Ibid., 474; Coxhead, "Deuteronomy 30:11-14 as a Prophecy of the New Covenant in Christ," 310–311.

[29] Sailhamer, *Pentateuch*, 474.

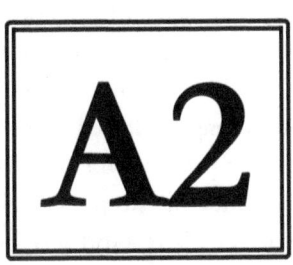

I WILL MAKE THEM LIKE THE CALF: AN EXAMINATION OF JEREMIAH 34:17-22 IN ITS LITERARY CONTEXT

This paper was originally prepared for a study on Jeremiah with Professor Tremper Longman III. It serves to illustrate the use of Scripture to resolve grammatical difficulties and how appeals to context can resolve issues that are usually resolved with appeals to archaeological material, as is the case with the self-maledictory covenant ceremony recounted in this passage.

Called from a young age, Jeremiah was God's prophet to apostate Judah. For decades he spoke of the coming judgement of God against the unrighteousness of his people. He was given the difficult task of speaking for God to a people hardened in their disobedience towards him. Yet the book of Jeremiah is not just a giant judgment oracle; the many texts concerning judgment are punctuated by glimmers of hope and accounts of the sins that have led to Judah's dire situation. It is in the juxtaposition of hope and judgment, of God's faithfulness in fulfilling his promises and his people's adultery, that the substance of the message of Jeremiah emerges. Jeremiah, following Deuteronomy (esp., 30:1-14), presents God and his sovereign mercy as the only hope for Israel. God is consistently free, merciful, and faithful: he brings the judgment he promises yet grants mercy to the repentant; he tears down and overthrows yet will build and plant. These juxtapositions are significant for the passage that this paper will explore,

34:17-22.

In these verses we read an account of momentary repentance among the Judahites. Around the time of a short respite from Babylon's attack on Jerusalem, the leaders and people of Jerusalem covenant before God to free their slaves, in accord with a long-neglected command from Deuteronomy. Yet, shortly after fulfilling their promise, the owners of the slaves go back on the promise and repossess their slaves, possibly in response to Babylon's withdrawal.[1] In response, in 34:17-22, God pronounces judgment on these covenant breakers. The purpose of this paper will be to examine these five verses. We will look at this passage in its literary context, following God's promises (chs. 30-33) and preceding the obedience of the Rechabites (ch. 35), to see how it contributes to the theology of Jeremiah and how its placement accents the various themes found within it. To accomplish this purpose we will first look at 34:1-16 to understand the necessary context for 34:17-22, then we will take a closer look at verses 17-22, finally we will set these verses in their greater literary context and draw out some of the implications this context has for our reading of the passage. In conclusion, I will offer some ways this passage relates to the New Testament and speaks to our contemporary circumstances.

A. Jeremiah 34:1-16

Jeremiah 34 comes as somewhat of a downer after the heights of hope expressed in 30-33. Returning to the narrative under the reign of Zedekiah (28-29, 32:1-35), Jeremiah presents a message about the end of Zedekiah and Jerusalem: Zedekiah will be captured by Babylon and the city will be burned with fire (34:2-3). Yet, though Zedekiah will meet his end, a measure of mercy is found in God's prophecy concerning his future. Regarding Jehoiakim, God shows Jeremiah that there will be no royal burial or lament (22:18-19), but it is said of Zedekiah, "You shall die in peace. And as spices were burned for your fathers, the former kings who were before you, so people shall burn

---

[1] R. K. Harrison, *Jeremiah and Lamentations*, Reprinted., Tyndale Old Testament Commentary 21 (Downers Grove, Ill.; England: Inter-Varsity Press, 2009), 148; Tremper Longman III, *Jeremiah, Lamentations*, NIBC (Peabody; United Kingdom: Hendrickson; Paternoster, 2008), 229; J. A. Thompson, *The Book of Jeremiah*, NICOT (Grand Rapids, Mich.: WM. B. Eerdmans Publishing Co., 1980), 611.

spices for you and lament for you, saying, 'Alas, Lord!'" (5).[2]

The following verses then revisit the same period (cf. 34:1, 6) from a different perspective. We are now told of a brief moment of repentance, initiated by Zedekiah, in which the people of Jerusalem move to fulfill obligations God had laid upon them in Deuteronomy 15:12. They were to set free their Hebrew slaves every 7 years, yet this had not been done (Jer 34:13); those who covenanted with Zedekiah in the presence of God were to set free the slaves they had kept far past these prescribed years (34:8). They went back on this covenant (11), so God sent Jeremiah with a message for these covenant breakers. In verses 13-16, God recounts his faithfulness and the basis for the covenant they had made: he had made a covenant with their fathers; he had taken them out of slavery in Egypt and instructed them to set their slaves free regularly. Verses 17-22 continue this message from God, giving his response to the disobedience of those who made the covenant with Zedekiah.

B. Jeremiah 34:17-22

Having recounted in 34:16 what they had done—"but then you turned and profaned my name when each of you took back his male and female slaves"—Jeremiah then presents them with the consequences of their covenant breaking:

> [17]Therefore, this is what YHWH has to say, "You yourselves have not obeyed me to proclaim liberty, each man to his brother, and each man to his neighbour." "Behold, I am proclaiming for you liberty," says the Lord, "liberty unto the sword, unto pestilence, unto famine, and I will make you a horror to all the kingdoms of the earth. [18]And I will make the men who transgressed the covenant, who did not establish the words of the covenant that they cut before me, like the calf they cut in two and between whose pieces they walked—[19]the officials of Judah and the officials of Jerusalem, the eunuchs, the priests, and all the people of the land who passed between the pieces of the calf. [20] I will give them into the hand of their enemies, into the hand of those seeking their life, and their carcasses will be food for the birds of the heavens and

---

[2] All Scripture quotations except Jer. 34:17-22 are taken from the ESV. It is noteworthy that הוֹי אָדוֹן (*hôy 'ādôn*; Alas, lord!) is found in the MT only here and in Jer. 22:18.

the beasts of the earth. ²¹And I will give Zedekiah, the king of Judah, and his officials into the hand of their enemies, into the hand of those seeking their life, into the hand of the army of the king of Babylon, which has gone up from against you." ²²"Behold, I am giving the command," says YHWH, "and I will bring them back to this city and they will wage war against it and capture it and burn it with fire. I will make the cities of Judah a desolation without inhabitants."³

In this fascinating passage, the consequences for covenant failure are seen to be dire. Significantly, we are given in this passage a glimpse of covenant making in Israel: the consequences of covenant failure are given in terms of a covenant making ritual the people of Jerusalem underwent (18-19).

Verse 17 reiterates the failure of these covenanters, furthering the message of judgment with a play on the liberty they said they would give. They said they would proclaim liberty but took it back; God, on the other hand, would not waver in granting them liberty, though it would be a liberty to death by various means (cf. 14:12, 24:10, 32:24). Their feigned repentance had bought them no mercy; their fate remained what it had always been, if not worse (18-20).

Verses 18-19 make this judgment more specific. What is clear in these verses is the basic nature of the ritual these covenanters underwent: they cut a calf in half (18) and walked between the halves (18, 19). The meaning of the latter half of verse 18, and so the consequences they faced for their failure, is more debated.⁴ The MT text does not have an equivalent to "like" in this verse; the MT reads "I will make [lit. give, נָתַן] the men... the calf which...." To make sense of the text, the BHS suggests an emendation of הָעֵגֶל (*hā 'ēgel;* the calf) to כָּעֵגֶל (*kā 'ēgel;* like the calf), others reject a comparison and suggest alternate ways to understand the relation of "the calf" to the rest of

---

³ This is my translation of Jeremiah 34:17-22. It is translated from the MT as represented in the BHS. No emendations were followed.

⁴ Kapelrud argues that Jeremiah has reinterpreted a non-threatening covenant ratification in a self-maledictory manner. Harrison thinks that self-imprecation is implied, but that the idea "like the calf" should not be supplied. Arvid S Kapelrud, "The Interpretation of Jeremiah 34:18ff," *Journal for the Study of the Old Testament* 22 (1982): 138–141; Harrison, *Jeremiah and Lamentations*, 149.

the sentence.⁵ It seems to this author that neither option is optimal; instead, it is best to read the text as it stands with the comparative idea implied. The reasons for doing so are based on the syntax and sense of the passage.

Beginning with the syntax, an implied comparative is rare but not unheard of in prose (frequent in poetry). In Exodus 7:1, when God reassures Moses, he tells him that he has made (נָתַן, *nāṯan*) him "אֱלֹהִים לְפַרְעֹה" (*'ĕlōhîm lᵉp̄ar'ōh*; God to Pharaoh). No one reads this as YHWH's pledge to make Moses one of Pharaoh's gods, nor in the generic sense "a mighty one." The sense here is "I have made you like God to Pharaoh" (ESV; cf. NASB, NRSV).⁶ Though "like" in Exodus 7:1 is not semantically equivalent to "like" in our passage—for in 7:1 the idea is "in the place of God as a representative" and in Jer. 34:18 as "sharing the same fate as" (in the place of)—these ideas are close enough in Hebrew, as in English, to see in this passage justification for unmarked comparisons.⁷ Furthermore, without אֶת (*'eṯ*) attached, "calf" is most likely not functioning as a direct object, for Jeremiah uses the marker of the DDO consistently—especially in prose.⁸

Considering the sense of the passage, נָתַן (*nāṯan*; "make") requires some sort of complement and הָעֵגֶל (*hā'ēgel*; the calf) is appropriate. Semantically, נָתַן involves transference: sometimes נָתַן is spatial, with the subject giving the object to someone or setting the object on or in something; in other instances, נָתַן is transformative, with the subject making the object to be something. In the latter case, a woman is given as a wife, Moses is made to be like God, and Abraham is made to be the father of many nations.

---

⁵ The LXX has translated הָעֵגֶל as an accusative, which the NETS understands to be equivalent to the Hebrew sense: "render them as the bull calf" (41:18). The vulgate follows suit, translating with the accusative *vitulum*; this may allow for a similar ad sensum construction but is rendered by Douay-Rheims adverbially ("when they cut"), with a resumptive verb in verse 20 ("And I will give the men… I will give them into…").

⁶ That Moses represents YHWH, the אֱלֹהִים, and that the text has the plural for singular אֱלֹהִים not אֵל (*'ēl*) or אֱלוֹהַּ (*ĕlôah*) suggest that Moses will be like YHWH, the God, to Pharaoh

⁷ The closest discussion I could find of this in the major grammars is the instances of understood prepositions with a verb when clarity is unaffected. Paul Joüon and Takamitsu Muraoka, *A Grammar of Biblical Hebrew*, Revised English Edition. (Pontificio Istituto Biblico, 2006), 462.

⁸ Contra Harrison, *Jeremiah and Lamentations*, 149.

Transference, whether spatial or transformative, requires a complement in the sense that what is receiving the object or what the object becomes needs to be implied or explicitly indicated. When we read in the passage that God "will make the men who transgressed...," we naturally look for that which they are to be made into. The only possible complement to אֶת־הָאֲנָשִׁים (*'eṯ-hā'ănāsîm;* the men) is הָעֵגֶל (*hā'ēgel;* the calf), for every other part of the sentence is part of an adjectival clause. Apart from נָתַן (*nāṯan;* "make"), there is no clause in which הָעֵגֶל could function: it is not connected to the preceding relative ("the words of the covenant which they cut before me") and the following relative modifies it adjectivally (the calf "they cut in two and whose pieces they walked between"). If we take הָעֵגֶל as part of the נָתַן clause, it is clear Yahweh is not going to turn these men into the calf. Apart from the ridiculousness of that reading, the article and the following relative clause indicate that the calf to which they are to be made like is the one they cut in half. Therefore, there is very good reason to read the text, without need of emendation, as "and I will make the men... like the calf...."

We should then understand the ceremony these men performed as one of self-malediction: by walking through the severed halves of the calf, these men indicated that they will fulfill their vow and that failure will result in their own dismembering.[9] They made this vow before God; because they failed, God now says through Jeremiah that he will be faithful on his part: they will be made like that calf; their lives will be forfeit.

Verses 20-22 then explicates the nature of the judgment they will receive. All who passed through the calf will be given into the hand of their enemies. Their bodies will be slaughtered and become a feast for the birds—a death notably worse than that promised to Zedekiah in 34:1-16. The Babylonians at this time appear to have withdrawn (21-22), yet in tremendous irony, these pagans will be obedient to YHWH's command and return to take the disobedient Zedekiah and his officials captive and to burn the city.

In summary of these verses, the repentance initiated by Zedekiah failed: the people went back on their covenant and incurred God's wrath further. Instead of receiving blessing for obedience, they would receive cursing for disobedience. The officials and the people would be made like the calf whose

---

[9] So Longman III, *Jeremiah, Lamentations*, 230; Hetty Lalleman, *Jeremiah and Lamentations*, Tyndale Old Testament Commentaries 21 (Downers Grove, Ill.: InterVarsity Press, 2013), 248–249; Thompson, *The Book of Jeremiah*, 612–613.

pieces they walked through to affirm their covenant, Zedekiah would be given into the hand of the Babylonians, and the city would burn.

C. Verses 17-22 in Context

Now, with an understanding of verses 17-22, let us consider these verses in their greater literary context, in relation to verses 1-16, chapters 30-33, and chapter 35. Beginning with the most immediately connected, it is important to note how verses 17-22 contrast the death of the covenanters with Zedekiah's promised death in verses 3-5. There is an inclusio here; the section begins and ends with Jeremiah's word that Jerusalem would be burned by the Babylonians (vv. 2, 22), his word that Zedekiah and (in the second text) his officials would be captured (vv. 3, 20-21), and a contrast between the fate of Zedekiah (vv. 4-5) and his officials (vv. 18-20). Lying between these bookends is the narrative of Zedekiah's failed attempt at initiating repentance. This suggests that part of the reason Zedekiah receives mercy whereas Jehoiakim did not is at least this attempt (cf. Jeremiah 36). Zedekiah is still to be judged, for he is consistently considered an unfaithful king, yet the portrait Jeremiah paints is of a weak and cowardly king, who seeks God's will but does not have the guts to follow it (cf. 37:2, 20-21, 38:13-28). This contributes to the greater tension within Jeremiah between God's promises to David (23:1-8, 33:14-26) and his judgment upon the Davidic line (cf. 34:1-16, 22:11-30). The act of mercy here, in contrast with judgment pronounced on Jehoiakim's line, makes it even more shocking when all of Zedekiah's children are slaughtered before his eyes (39:6) and God reveals hope in the preservation of Jeconiah, Jehoiakim's son, at the conclusion of the book (52:31-34). This contrast demonstrates the theme of Jeremiah's ministry—God's sovereign freedom and his purpose to "pluck up and to break down, to destroy and to overthrow, to build and to plant" (1:9-10)—in relation to his promises to David.

This tension with regard to the Davidic covenant is especially heightened by the placement of this passage following the restoration oracles in chapters 30-33. In 33:14-26, God promises to raise his righteous branch from the line of David (cf. 23:1-8), concluding with his purpose to "restore their fortunes and [to] have mercy on" the offspring of Jacob and David. That the following account has a faint glimmer of mercy regarding the Davidic line is surely intentional.

The greater significance of the location of 34:1-22 in relation to chapters

30-33 is the reinforcement the latter account provides for the promises preceding it. This is first achieved negatively; God's faithfulness is contrasted with the unfaithfulness of Judah. The actions of the wicked Judeans in breaking their covenant provides a foil for the revelation of God's enduring purpose to be faithful to his covenants with David and the patriarchs (33:23-26). In concluding the restoration promises, God compares his faithfulness to this covenant with his faithfulness to the covenant he made with creation and affirmed with Noah (as the day and night endured, so would these promises). In the account of 34:1-22, this is set against the background of Judah's inability to maintain even the most basic commitments of their covenant with God: they promise to make up for their neglect and only reap further condemnation.

The reinforcement of the promises made in 30-33 is also achieved positively in this passage. In contrast with the faithfulness of the officials of Judah, God through Jeremiah reminds them of the reason for the command to release the slaves: God was faithful to deliver his people from slavery as he had covenanted[10] and proceeded to make a covenant with their fathers to do the same. God's faithfulness was demonstrated in Egypt and became the foundation for the requirement to release Hebrew slaves regularly. Furthermore, those who passed through the calf did so before YHWH in his temple (34:15, 18); they vowed that they would do this or pay the consequences. When they failed to keep up their end of the deal, God demonstrated his faithfulness in judgment, revealing that the Babylonians will return and that the unfaithful covenanters will pay the consequences of their broken oath. This account of a covenant made under Zedekiah is, then, perfectly placed after the promises of restoration in 30-33 to draw attention to Judah's failure, continue Judah's indictment, and emphasize even more God's faithfulness and trustworthy character.

We have considered our passage in relation to some of the greater themes unpacked across Jeremiah and in light of what precedes, all that remains is to consider 34:17-22 with what follows in chapter 35. Chapter 35 takes us back to the days of Jehoiakim; we are given an account of Jeremiah's

---

[10] It is surely not coincidental that when God performs the self-malediction ceremony on behalf of his servant Abraham (Genesis 15), he promises to deliver his people from slavery in Egypt, as this ceremony involves their vow to release the slaves.

interaction with the Rechabites. In short, Jeremiah contrasts the disobedience of Judah with the obedience demonstrated by the Rechabites. The Rechabites are a family of Jews who undertook an oath from their fathers to abstain from certain practices, such as drinking or building and living in a house. When Jeremiah places before them wine, they are obedient to their oath and refuse (35:5-6). This family is faithful to the words of men, says Jeremiah, how much more should Judah be faithful to God's covenant? The folly of Judah's disobedience is magnified when set next to the faithfulness this family showed to their fathers.

The result for the Rechabites is God's promise to preserve them, "Jonadab the son of Rechab shall never lack a man to stand before me" (35:19). But concerning Jerusalem God says, "I am bringing upon Judah and all the inhabitants of Jerusalem all the disaster that I have pronounced against them" (35:17). This example of obedience provides, of course, a sharp contrast with the disobedience of Judah displayed in 34.[11] God's mercy and faithfulness are also demonstrated in that he blesses the Rechabites for their obedience. The message received by the reader is that Judah has no one to blame for their end but themselves. God is ever faithful to bless obedience but equally faithful to curse disobedience; God will tear down Judah for their disobedience, but he will build up the Rechabites for their obedience.

D. Conclusion

The purpose of this paper was to examine Jeremiah 34:17-22 in its literary context. We first examined the words of Jeremiah given in 34:1-16, an account of the making and breaking of covenant made by the people of Jerusalem to set free Hebrew slaves. This prepared us for our discussion of verses 17-22, in which God's judgment on the covenant breakers is pronounced. There, after weighing the evidence, we saw that the people undertook a self-maledictory covenant ceremony and, after failing to keep their promise, brought upon themselves God's sure judgment: they would be made like the calf they cut in two, slaughtered at the hands of their enemies. Considering these verses in their literary context, we then saw how the account in 34:1-22 was perfectly placed to emphasize Jeremiah's themes

---

[11] Only Kidner explicitly comments on this literary contrast. Derek Kidner, *The Message of Jeremiah: Against Wind and Tide*, The Bible Speaks Today (Leicester, England ; Downers Grove: Inter-Varsity Press, 1987), 116–119.

through a contrast and comparison of God's faithfulness in the promises of restoration (chs. 30-33) and the Rechabites' obedience (ch. 35) with Judah's unfaithfulness is chapter 34. Having understood Jeremiah 34 in its context, we must now ask how it relates to the New Testament and our contemporary situation.

Regarding our text and the New Testament, the faithfulness of God that Jeremiah is eager to emphasize ultimately finds its fulfillment in Christ. In our passage, God was seen to be faithful in cursing disobedience and his faithfulness to his promises was highlighted in context; both facets of God's faithfulness find their consummation on the Cross, as does the promise of blessing contrasted in chapter 35. On the Cross, God is shown to be perfectly faithful in his justice, poured out on Christ in our stead; he is also shown to be faithful with regard to his promises of restoration, providing in Christ the new heart his people needed (John 6:44-45), and raising up the Righteous Branch and true Davidic Messiah (shockingly, a descendent of Jeconiah). With regard to blessing, God is faithful to honour Jesus' perfect covenantal obedience, rendering to his people the benefits of right covenant relationship achieved by him.

Regarding our contemporary situation, we are in as much need as the original recipients of Jeremiah of the faithfulness of God, who is consistent in fulfilling his promises and blessing obedience. Concerning the former, we as Christians are a people waiting for the fulfillment of God's promises. In Christ, he has given the new heart and provided the forgiveness of sin promised (31:31-34), but we still await Christ's return and the fullness of the kingdom of God in the new creation. That God is ever faithful is the encouragement we need to stay vigilant as we wait for Jesus' return. Concerning the latter, that God rewards obedience and punishes disobedience is a reminder of what Christ accomplished in his life and death. Because he took our disobedience upon himself, we can have assurance and we can praise God that there is now no condemnation for those in Christ Jesus: the curse has been removed. Because he fulfilled all obedience, we can be assured that we now take part in and will soon experience the fullness of the covenant blessings God has prepared for those in right covenant with him. Lastly, though it would be wrong to reduce this text to a moralistic passage about keeping our promises, surely in our pursuit of Christlikeness, God would ask nothing less of us than mirroring his faithful character in being people of our word, fulfilling our commitments, oaths, and promises.

A3

THE LAMENT OF THE AFFLICTED: A TRANSLATION OF JOB 30

This paper was originally prepared for Professor Andrew Lewis to meet the requirements for a graduate level advanced Hebrew course. It has been adapted for this context. It explores the issues of translation and the sufficiency of Scripture for textual/linguistic challenges in interpretation.

In a matter of days, Job lost his children and his wealth; at the hands of Satan—by God's permission—Job lost everything. Compounding this, the friends who came to comfort him fail to reckon that Job may not be suffering for his wickedness. For chapter after chapter, we read the accusations and self-styled remedies proffered by these friends. As these speeches draw to an end with the poem to wisdom in chapter 28, the narrator presents three final speeches from Job in chapters 29-31. Job moves from contemplating his past condition in chapter 29 to his present state in chapter 30; chapter 31 concludes this series of speeches with a defence of his innocence. Though each of these chapters is worthy of study, the present paper will focus on chapter 30, presenting a translation which aims to communicate the meaning potential of the Hebrew text with as much of the poetic effect of the original as possible. Thus, an effort will be made to follow the form and particular emphasis of the Hebrew text in readable English, the goal not being good English literature but Hebrew literature that is comprehensible to the English reader and that achieves the emotive effect of the original.

Before considering my translation, a word on the form of evidence and argumentation employed is necessary. Like many books of the Hebrew Bible, scholarly translation and interpretation of Job regularly involves significant emendation of the Masoretic Text.[1] By their very nature, such emendations are speculative. Even on the level of explicit reasoning, without addressing theological presuppositions, one may take issue with this approach.[2]

An emendation is only invoked when the present text is considered suspect to the interpreter, yet what is suspect to one interpreter may not be so for another. Such suspicions may be a product of the reader rather than the text, of unfamiliarity with Hebrew, or of an overly constrictive understanding of language (e.g. an author is not credited with the freedom to create new constructions and grammatical combinations using rules exhibited elsewhere).

Because of the speculative nature of emendation, the practice of the present author is to seek an explanation in the possible sense "awkward" texts may have when considered in light of similar grammatical and syntactical combinations found elsewhere in Scripture. Because we have no a-priori reason to doubt the Masoretic text we have received, and we have significant a-posteriori evidence to trust it, this author will accord the MT the benefit of the doubt, leaving the burden of proof on the one who seeks to prove that their emendation is better than the received text. The principle of parsimony also favours any reading that explains the text as it stands, without need of multiplying explanations. Furthermore, because it is impossible to prove that the present text is unintelligible, no one being fluent enough in ancient Hebrew to make such a definitive judgment, any proof resting on "better sense" will be rejected, for this is a subjective judgment based on limited knowledge (i.e. that it makes no sense to us says nothing about its

---

[1] "Emendation," as used here, encompasses everything from the subtle changes of revocalization to the insertion of consonants and supposedly missing words *without manuscript warrant*. Emendation does not encompass the comparison of variant readings, which are measured by the canons of textual criticism.

[2] Of course, to not talk about such presuppositions is not to say they do not matter nor that they are not influencing the following discussion. It is only to say that I will not explicitly argue for the beliefs presupposed below, though I have in the present book, and will not directly address the presuppositions of those who disagree. Cf. J. Alexander Rutherford, *The Gift of Knowing: A Biblical Perspective on Knowing and Truth*, God's Gifts for the Christian Life - Part 1 1 (Vancouver: Teleioteti, 2019).

comprehensibility for the original author or audience). According to the definition of emendation given above, such claims of awkwardness or incomprehensibility are the only possible evidence in favour of consonantal emendation, so such emendations will be rejected.

Proposed revocalisations will be considered not on the basis of "better sense," for the reasons stated above, but on the basis of analogous misreadings in the present tradition and alternative textual evidence, thus being considered on the basis of a textual criticism as with consonantal emendation. For these reasons, the Masoretic Text will be given priority.[3]

Concerning lexica, evidential priority for the interpretation of *hapax legomena* and other rare words will be given, in order of priority, to the canonical biblical text, other Hebrew texts, Aramaic texts, and then other Semitic language texts. The canonical text will be given priority, for it forms a single body of intelligible language and exerted an influence on itself over the course of its writing (e.g. the Pentateuch and its language influenced the following works). Because extra-biblical Hebrew texts share the same language and vocabulary where they can be compared, appeals to words that are present in these texts to explain those rare in the biblical corpus are substantiated by this shared lexical stock. Aramaic clearly influenced the authors of the biblical texts, including demonstrable borrowing of vocabulary, and is present in the biblical text, so appeals to Aramaic of relatively the same period as the text under consideration are considered legitimate. Other Semitic languages yield many insightful parallels in lexical stock, yet one must tread carefully for it is impossible to be certain of the influence of a particular language and its vocabulary on the author or audience of a particular book, an issue compounded when the provenance and date of a book such as Job is unknown—despite the best speculations concerning the nature of its language.[4] On the basis of these considerations,

---

[3] A full text critical analysis of the text falls beyond the scope of this paper, yet it should be noted that many of the appeals made to alternate manuscripts and translations violate the canon of *lectio difficilior*.

[4] Cf. Aaron Hornkohl, "Periodization," in *Encyclopedia of Hebrew Language and Linguistics: Volume 1; A-F*, ed. Geoffrey Khan, vol. 1, 4 vols. (Leiden; Boston: Brill, 2013); Jan Joosten, "The Distinction Between Classical and Late Biblical Hebrew as Reflected in Syntax," *Hebrew Studies* 46 (2005): 327–339; Choon Leong Seow, "Orthography, Textual Criticism, and the Poetry of Job.," *Journal of Biblical Literature*

an interpretation is to be preferred when it can be supported by the context, analogous uses of syntax and grammar,[5] and inter-biblical lexical appeals. On this basis, the following translation is proposed.

A. Job 30

a. Strophe 1 – I Am Mocked by Wretches[6]

Stanza 1
[1]But now, men younger[7] than I laugh at me,
    whose fathers I refused
    to put with the dogs of my flock.[8]
[2]Yes, the strength of their hands, what use was it to me?
    men whose vigour had perished![9]

130, no. 1 (2011): 63–85; Ian Young, "Is the Prose Tale of Job in Late Biblical Hebrew?," *Vetus Testamentum* 59, no. 4 (2009): 606–629.

[5] "Analogy" is not restricted to identical grammatical and syntactical combinations (syntagms) but comparable uses of the same morphological (e.g. noun patterns), grammatical (clause level: e.g. a noun in a construct relationship with an adjective), or syntactical (sentence level: e.g. כִּי functioning to subordinate a clause) patterns.

[6] "I will employ the terms 'strophe' and 'stanza' in a particular way…: I employ these terms to describe greater and lesser sense units, respectively, made up of groups of colons (the smallest sense unit of poetry, a grouping of lines). Strophe in my use would be roughly equivalent to a 'verse' in contemporary lyrical poetry, the broadest division of a poem or song. Stanzas are the smaller units that make up a strophe." Rutherford, *Habakkuk*, 52.

[7] צָעִיר can have connotations of social inferiority, which appears to be the case here (cf. DCH, HALOT).

[8] This is read as enjambment, with the infinitive completing מָאַס.

[9] This line appears to be describing further the "fathers" in the previous lines, so a past tense is appropriate in translation. Two problems concern us here; the first is the meaning of כֶּלַח ("vigour"). כֶּלַח occurs only here and in Job 5:26. In Job 5:26, Eliphaz expounds the rewards of one who responds rightly to God's corrective discipline; this man will "go to the grave in *kelaḥ*." The idea would be that he will die while he still has strength, or vigour. HALOT identifies it as a collocation of לֵחַ and כֹּל, supporting this, contra David J. A. Clines, *Job 21 - 37*, ed. Bruce Manning Metzger et al., Word Biblical Commentary 18a (Nashville: Nelson, 2007), 944.. The following

Stanza 2

³Because of want and barren hunger,[10]
    they were those who gnawed[11] at the parched land
    —only yesterday it was ruined and devastated—[12]
⁴who broke off the mallow from its bush,
    and the root of shrubs for their food.[13]

---

line uses the imagery of a sheaf gathered at the appropriate time, supporting the English idiom used by the ESV "ripe old age." What this means, though, appears to be the same as the previous line: "you will die at a good time, not too early nor will your life stretch on unnecessarily." This idea of vigour, the vitality of life, thus works in 5:26 and here in 30:2—these men are useless, their vitality is long gone. כֶּלַח is used for its assonance with the initial כֹּח.

The second problem concerns the use of עַל here. Hartley, in agreement with DCH, suggests it means "from"; yet the lexical evidence for this meaning is lacking. John E. Hartley, *The Book of Job*, NICOT (Grand Rapids: Eerdmans, 1988), 396. Clines argues that it is better understood according to the so called "pathetic" sense (advantage/disadvantage), yet the meaning this yields is not readily apparent to this author (a problem Clines acknowledges when he identifies it as "untranslatable"). Clines, *Job 21 - 37*, 944. Clines' interpretation further requires an implied possessive connecting "them" to "vigour," a connection which עַל suffices to make. By analogy with אֶל (concerning), with which עַל is often interchanged, עַל here means "concerning them, vigour has perished." This is equivalent semantically and emphatically with "men whose vigour had perished."

[10] "Barren" seems to emphasize their hunger while adding the idea of hopelessness, that it will not be satisfied.

[11] The article on the participles in vv. 3 and 4 indicates that they are functioning substantivally, further describing the fathers of those who now mock Job. ערק only appears twice (also in Job 30:17), yet the meaning "gnaw" seems clear from context and is supported by Syriac and Arabic cognates (cf. the Vulgate's *rodo*). The LXX's "flee" is contextually unlikely. Similarly, Clines, *Job 21 - 37*, 945.

[12] The pair of nouns here appears to be in apposition with צִיָּה ("parched land"), describing it as it was when these men were alive. אֶמֶשׁ ("yesterday"), which usually refers specifically to the previous night or generally to the previous day, is being used much like the English idiomatic use of "yesterday" for a period some time ago that seems much more recent. The land was at this time—as if only yesterday—ruined and devastated.

[13] לָחְמָם is either a verbal form "to warm themselves" (חמם) or לֶחֶם with a 3mp pronominal suffix. The verbal form would require a revocalization or it would be an anomalous infinitive form (Isaiah 47:14 has the same form; HALOT suggests a revocalization, yet the line could be read as "this [fire] is no hot coal fire for *their food*,

Stanza 3

⁵They were driven from the community
  —they shouted against them as thieves!¹⁴
⁶So they dwelt in the slopes of wadis,¹⁵
  in holes of the ground and among rocks.¹⁶
⁷In the midst of bushes they bray,
  under nettle they huddle together.
⁸Sons of lowly wretches,¹⁷
  —yes, they are men without names—

---

no fire to sit before!" that is, it is no campfire). The form in the MT is a standard form for לֶחֶם and is best read as such.

"Shrub" is usually identified as "broom," the roots of which are inedible, yet this should not be used either to dismiss the possibility that the root could be food (contra Clines, *Job 21 - 37*, 946; Marvin H. Pope, *Job: Introduction, Translation, and Notes* (Garden City: Doubleday, 1973), 220.) or to read too much into the line—such that the inedibility of broom-root emphasizes their desperate state. Either of the two possibilities above is plausible, yet it is not clear in context that either is intended. Whether mallow or saltwort, מַלּוּחַ is not a preferable food option; the context indicates that the root of this broom shrub—inedible or not—was likewise not preferable (cf. Franz Delitzsch, *Job: Two Volumes in One*, Commentary on the Old Testament in Ten Volumes IV (Grand Rapids: Eerdmans, 1978), 142–143.).

¹⁴ The shift in verbal subject in the second line creates a disjunction, a rapid change of perspective, best communicated with an emphatic parenthesis.

¹⁵ "Wadi" refers to stream beds that are dry until the rainy season, when heavy rains fill them.

¹⁶ Neither הֹר ("hole") nor כֵּף ("rock") has a preposition: the בְּ from the first line is assumed. This could be read as "in holes of dust and of rocks" or "in holes of the dust and in rocks." A decision here is difficult, yet the second reading seems slightly more likely because the collocation of rocks and holes in the ground as hiding places for the destitute appears elsewhere (cf. 1 Sam. 13:6, 14:11; Isaiah 1:19).

¹⁷ בֶּן plus a noun is often used attributively or substantively; with an adjective, this construct makes the adjective a substantive. When בֵּן is in a construct relationship with an adjective, it is almost always with a gentilic adjective (15/18 times). In two other cases, the adjective is an indefinite substantive (אֶבְיוֹן, one who is needy [Ps. 72:4]; עֶלְיוֹן, (the) Most High [Ps. 82:6]). This leaves only Job. As with the two instances in the psalms, the adjective is indefinite, suggesting that it should be read as substantive genitive of relationship: "children of lowly wretches." נָבָל has usually been understood as "fool" (senseless, unwise), yet it is employed elsewhere in opposition with נָדִיב (noble; Pr. 17:7, Isa. 32:5): the sense seems to be "lowly of status" with negative connotations of the dregs of society (Isa. 32:6) or foolish people (Deut. 32:6), depending on the context.

they were violently driven from the land.[18]

b. Strophe 2 – I Am a Byword to the Unrestrained

Stanza 1
[9]But now I have become their sons' song[19]
   I am a byword to them.
[10]They abhor me and keep themselves far from me;
   yet from my face they withhold not their spit.[20]

Stanza 2
[11]Because he loosed my cord[21] and humbled me,
   they cast off all restraint in my presence.[22]
[12]At my right hand the rabble arises;
      they shove my feet
      and raise against me

---

[18] נָכָא is an alternate form for the more common נָכָה (to strike; cf. DCH, HALOT). An adjective נָכֵא (stricken) with these consonants is found in Proverbs 15:13, 17:22, and 18:44, with a meaning related to נָכָה (cf. the adj. נָכֵה). נָכָא in the Niphal, therefore, means "to be struck"; followed by מִן, the idea is to be struck resulting in movement away, thus "to be violently driven from."

[19] נְגִינָה, a musical composition, doesn't necessarily have negative connotations; yet elsewhere it is contextually clear that a "mocking song" is intended (Lam. 3:14, 3:63). Heb., "their," referring not to the fathers that were being described previously but their sons introduced in v. 1.

[20] Clines objects that it is logically incoherent to say that they keep themselves far from Job but also spit on his face. This is not necessarily the case: both spitting and keeping their distance are actions of disdain and disrespect; Job envisions the young mockers at times giving him a wide berth and at others drawing near only to spit upon him. Therefore, the uses of מִן concluding the first line and opening the second are visually and semantically parallel. Clines, *Job 21 - 37*, 948.

[21] יֶתֶר refers to a piece of material used for various functions for which we would use a "string" or a "cord" (e.g. "bowstrings" Ps. 11:2). The idea here is not readily apparent to the contemporary reader, yet we can surmise from context that for God to loose Job's "cord" was to bring about the humiliating and oppressing circumstances under which he now finds himself.

[22] Lit., "they cast off reins in my presence": because God has afflicted Job, these young men act towards him without any sort of restraint.

their calamitous ways²³
¹³They break up²⁴ the path before me²⁵
and profit from my destruction—
they have no need of help.²⁶
¹⁴As through a wide gap they come,
beneath a calamity²⁷ they roll on.²⁸
¹⁵Sudden terrors are turned upon me,²⁹

---

²³ Clines describes סלל ארחות as "technical language for throwing up a siege-ramp"; I was unable to find any evidence for this contention. A noun from the root סלל (סֹלְלָה) does mean "siege ramp," yet this noun is never used with the verb. The verbal form is used elsewhere with synonyms of אָרַח (Job 19:12, Isa. 62:10) and is used absolutely for building a road (Isa. 57:13, 62:10). Another use of סלל describes the piling up of corpses (Jer. 50:26), which is similar in idea if "building a road" involves the piling of stones. Cf. the verbs used for siege ramps in Hab. 1:10 and Ezek 4:2. It is probable, then, that the idea here and in Job 19:12 is not the making of a siege ramp but of establishing a way of acting towards someone that is intent on their destruction (corresponding to the well-established metaphorical extension of אֹרַח and דֶּרֶךְ as a way of behaviour). "The paths of their calamity" is "their paths of calamity," a descriptive genitive, and so equivalent to "their calamitous paths." Clines, *Job 21 - 37*, 950.

Each of these four lines is brief, forming an almost staccato description; this echoes the unrestrained, rebellious "rabble" it describes.

²⁴ נָתַס (break up) is a hapax, best explained as an alternate form of נָתַץ, cf. HALOT, DCH, BDB.

²⁵ Lit., "my path."

²⁶ Lit., "there is no helper for them": contextually the idea is not that they have no helper and need one, but that they have no helper because they are succeeding so well in the afflictions they administer.

²⁷ DCH lists שֹׁאָה as a hapax, yet it is better taken as a defectively written form of שׁוֹאָה (cf. v. 3; so HALOT). The sense of "roll on" is obscure, but in light of use of גלל to describe the movement of rocks and the flowing of water, it probably has a sense of unyielding power.

²⁸ At first these lines are opaque, but it seems that "calamity" and "wide gap" are parallel: Job envisions these young men assailing him during or after a disaster has wrought its destruction.

²⁹ The written form is a Hophal, the only such instance for this verb; some conjecture a Niphal, yet the Hophal makes contextual sense. It emphasizes the terror while keeping the subject doing the turning in the background, fitting for a context in which Job expounds his suffering with reference to those who are assaulting him.

they chase away my nobility like the wind;³⁰
my salvation passes away like a cloud.

c. Strophe 3 – I Am Afflicted by God

Stanza 1

¹⁶And now my life is poured out before me,
days of affliction seize me!
¹⁷The night digs out my bones from me,
and my gnawing pains do not sleep;
¹⁸With great violence it disguises itself as my garment;³¹
like the neck of my tunic, it clings tightly to me.³²

Stanza 2

¹⁹He throws me to the mud,
I become like dust and ashes.
²⁰I cry to you for help and you do not answer me,
I stand to my feet and you just look on me;

---

³⁰ Some emend תרדך, a Qal 3fs verb, to a Niphal, "my nobility is chased away." E.g. Hartley, *The Book of Job*, 399. This is, however, unnecessary: though it is awkward to have a plural subject in the first line ("terrors") paired with a singular verb in the second ("it chases away"), this is not unheard of and is to be preferred over the suggested emendation. The resulting sense would be, "Sudden terrors are turned upon me, the terrors chase away my nobility like the wind."

³¹ לְבוּשׁ (garment) is translated with a comparative value. This function is often marked by the preposition כְּ; there are, however, exceptions where the comparative is unmarked. In poetry, unmarked comparisons are common and in prose at least two examples can be presented (e.g. Jer. 34:18, Exod 7:1; cf. Appendix 2). Reading the first line in this way allows us to make sense of the following line, which is often translated at odds with the first line (cf. ESV, NET). The masculine subject probably refers neither to "night" (a feminine noun) nor God (contra NET), but the night personified and collocated with עָרְקַי (my pains): the night-pain, equivalent to v. 16's "affliction," wraps close like his garments.

³² These two lines are difficult, yet the second line seems to presuppose as its subject not לְבוּשׁ (garment) but לַיְלָה or עָרְקַי. Neither of these readings is ideal, yet the idea is clear enough: "the afflictions (associated with the night) cling close to me, like my very garment they force themselves on me." The usual reading (ignoring emendations) that his clothing disguises itself—i.e. distorts itself—is lexically difficult (the word does not have this extension elsewhere) and one struggles to make sense of it with the following line (though the image of tossed clothing fits well with the previous lines).

²¹You have changed, become cruel towards me;
   with your powerful hand, you harass me!
²²On the wind you raise me and cause me to ride;
   you attain success causing me to melt.³³

Stanza 3
²³But I know that you will turn me to death,³⁴
   to the home appointed for all the living—
²⁴surely he would not stretch a hand against a ruinous heap,
   if in his misfortune he utters a cry for these things!³⁵
²⁵Though I did not weep for the man facing a difficult day,³⁶
   my soul now³⁷ grieves as a needy man.
²⁶For I hoped for good,
   but calamity has come

---

³³ Or "with great competence (or wisdom) you melt me." This follows the qere, תּוּשִׁיָה (sound wisdom or success), translated as an adverbial accusative, "with success." Many translations and commentators reject the qere as nonsensical; e.g. Robert L. Alden, *Job*, The New American Commentary v. 11 (Nashville: Broadman & Holman, 1993), 293–294; Clines, *Job 21 - 37*, 956; Delitzsch, *Job: Two Volumes in One*, 161–163; Hartley, *The Book of Job*, 402; Pope, *Job: Introduction, Translation, and Notes*, 223.

"Cause me to melt" translates the verb מוּג: the meaning is either that Job is like earth washed away by the wind and rain (cf. Ps. 65:11) or that God's attack melts away Job's courage, his strength, his resolve (cf. Isa. 14:31, Jer. 49:23, Ezek 21:20). The latter fits well with Job's contemplation of death in the following verses.

³⁴ שׁוּב does not mean here "bring me to where I once was" but " turn me towards a new place."

³⁵ The identity of "these things" is the pressing question of this line. It seems that the cry uttered by Job, describing himself as a "ruinous heap," is directed to "death" and "home" in the previous verse. Cf. Alden, *Job*, 295, ft. 53.

³⁶ Lit: "difficult of day," functioning substantively. A few possibilities present themselves for these two lines: looking back on a difficult day, Job remembers his endurance, yet now as things have soured even further, he is broken; or, the initial *lamed* indicates the object for which one weeps and the second a comparison with one who grieves. Cf. v. 4, Deut. 9:21; Bruce K. Waltke and Michael Patrick O'Connor, *An Introduction to Hebrew Syntax* (Winona Lake, Ind.: Eisenbrauns, 1990), 206–207. On the second approach, interpreting "difficult" as a substantive, Job's position has been reversed.

³⁷ Though not explicit, the apodosis functions as a temporal contrast with "the difficult day" in the previous line.

and I waited for light,
>but darkness has come.

Stanza 4
27My bowels are in turmoil and are not silent,
>days of affliction meet me;
28I go about blackened, but not by the heat of the sun;
>I get up in the assembly and cry for help,
29But I have become a brother to the jackals
>and a neighbour to the ostrich's children.[38]
30The skin upon my flesh has blackened,
>my bones burn with heat.
31My lyre is now for mourning,
>my flute for the sound of those weeping.

---

[38] The Hebrew does not have a conjunction opening v. 29, yet the relationship with what precedes and what follows implies the adversative relationship provided by "but." The sense is that the blackening of his skin, his diseased state, results in his cries for help falling on deaf ears: he is rather like the animals of the wild deserts, alone and rejected.

DO NOT SAY IN YOUR HEART: AN EXPOSITION OF ROMANS 10:1-8 IN THE CONTEXT OF 10:1-13

This paper was originally prepared for Professor Doug Moo to meet the requirements of graduate-level study on Romans. The parameters of this assignment restrained the amount of conversation partners with which I could dialogue, yet this does not take away from the strength of the arguments presented herein. This paper illustrates the theory and method unpacked above with particular attention to the question of the New Testament's use of the Old.

In a pluralistic society like ours, nothing is more offensive than the proclamation of Christ as Lord, the sole King and way to God. Christ as *the* way to God precludes any other. Despite the 1st century's own pluralism, the offense of Jesus was not his exclusivity over against other religions, but the exclusivity, the superiority, of Christ over the Old Covenant. Jesus' exclusiveness is offensive to all societies, yet the problem was particularly compounded for Paul in light of God's promises to Israel—how can they not be saved? Paul, in Romans 9-11, takes on this challenge: he wrestles with the question of what God's ultimate work in Jesus means for Israel.

At the middle of this section, in 9:30-10:13, Paul looks at the culpable failure of Israel that resulted in their condition. Paul expounds how in ignorance they rejected God's climactic work in Christ and so needed salvation (10:1-13). This section is important, yet difficult. In 10:5-8, Paul boldly juxtaposes Moses' own words in Leviticus and Deuteronomy to show that the Jews, in seeking their own righteousness, repudiated God's ultimate provision of righteousness in Christ.

This paper will seek to expound this most difficult section. It is broadly acknowledged that 9:30-10:13 is a single unit in Paul's argument.[1] I, with some commentators, recognize a further subdivision between 9:30-33 and 10:1-13.[2] For the purposes of this paper, I intend to concentrate on verses 1-8 in this subsection. It is my intent to expound the argument and unity of this text, with particular attention paid to Paul's use of Deuteronomy 30:11-14.[3] To relate my exposition, I will offer my proposed outline and then present my exegesis of Romans 9:1-8, with an excursus on Deuteronomy 30:11-14.

Before turning to our text, let us consider the argument's flow in 30:1-13:

I. <u>Israel's Need for Salvation (10:1-13)</u>
   1. **Israel Needs Salvation, Having Rejected God's Righteousness (10:1-4)**
   2. **God's Righteousness Is Not the Law-Righteousness Israel Seeks: It is by Faith through Jesus (10:5-13)**
      A. *Moses wrote of a law-righteousness (10:5)*
      B. *Faith-righteousness is God's near, New Covenant, work, received by faith and confession (10:6-13)*
         i. God's faith-righteousness is not of the distant Old Covenant but the near New Covenant (10:6-8)
            a. *Faith-righteousness is not the distant law (10:6-7)*

---

[1] Douglas J. Moo, *Encountering the Book of Romans: A Theological Survey*, 2nd ed., Encountering Biblical Studies (Grand Rapids, Mich.: Baker Academic, 2014), vii; Schreiner, *Romans*, 533.

[2] F. F Bruce, *The Epistle of Paul to the Romans: An Introduction and Commentary* (Grand Rapids: Eerdmans, 1963), 68; Moo, *Encountering*, 144; Schreiner, *Romans*, 534.

[3] Cf. Appendix 1.

                          b.   Faith-righteousness stands upon New Covenant faith (10:8)

           ii.   Confession and faith are the way for all to receive salvation. (10:9-13)

A. Exegesis

a. Israel Needs Salvation, Having Rejected God's Righteousness (10:1-4)

Brothers, my heart's desire and prayer to God for them is that they may be saved. ²For I bear them witness that they have a zeal for God, but not according to knowledge. ³For, being ignorant of the righteousness of God, and seeking to establish their own, they did not submit to God's righteousness. ⁴For Christ is the end of the law for righteousness to everyone who believes.[4]

Verse 1. Paul's use of the vocative "Brothers" signals a shift to another facet of the present topic.[5] Having explained Israel's failure to attain righteousness in the preceding verses, Paul now reiterates his heart concerning Israel, first expressed in 9:1-4,[6] in light of this failure: he desires their salvation. He focuses on the human cause of their apostasy, further explaining Israel's failed pursuit of a law leading to righteousness (9:30-33).

Verse 2. In verse 2 we encounter the first occurrence of the conjunction γαρ (for) in these verses (also 3, 4, 5, 10, 11, 12, 13). Most of these uses are explanatory. Here, Paul begins to explain his desire for Israel's salvation: they are not saved; their zeal for God is in ignorance of his accomplishment. Paul testifies that they have zeal, yet it is misplaced. Their ignorance is expounded in what follows.

Verse 3. Paul now provides further explanation (γαρ) on verse 2.

---

[4] Scripture quotations are from the ESV. Quotations from Deut. 30 are my translation.

[5] Douglas J. Moo, *The Epistle to the Romans*, NICNT (Grand Rapids: Eerdmans, 1996), 631.

[6] Here, with anguish over their damnation.

"[B]eing ignorant" (ἀγνοοῦντες) and "seeking" (ζητοῦντες) translate two participles that explain Israel's failure to submit.

First, they were ignorant of God's righteousness: it is not that they did not have access to the truth but that they disregarded it. Though Paul often uses this word ἀγνοέω to refer to a lack of knowledge (Rom. 1:13, 1 Cor. 10:1, 12:1), he also uses it with the sense of the culpable rejection of truth (Acts 13:27, 1 Cor. 14:38). This latter sense is intended here (cf. vv. 5-8, 14-21).

Second, this wilful ignorance is coupled with the pursuit of personal righteousness. In light of Paul's salvific focus, individual—not corporate—righteousness is surely in view (cf. 10:1, 9, 10, 13).[7] From the rest of Paul's argument, it is law-righteousness (cf. 1:16-17, 3:21-4:12). So Paul continues a series of contrasts begun in 9:30-31 between law-righteousness and faith-righteousness.[8] Law-righteousness is not God's faith-righteousness, to which they have failed to submit (3). The righteousness they seek is by works (5), God's is by faith (6); the first is distant, of the Old Covenant (5), God's is near, of the New (6-13).

Verse 4. Paul now explains how Jews have failed to submit to God's righteousness, and so are in need of salvation. In Paul's compact argument, the connection between vv. 3-4 is not immediately clear.[9] Unpacking his argument, he is saying that the Jews have no righteousness and, therefore, are not saved (10:1, 3), because "Christ is the end of the law for righteousness to everyone who believes." It is because they reject Jesus and the New Covenant in his blood that they are without righteousness and damned. The righteousness of God in verse 3 is then that which God has made available through faith in Jesus. The introduction of the law here prepares us for the following contrast between law-righteousness (5) and faith-righteousness (6-13). However, the controversies over this text must detain us a moment

---

[7] Personal faith and confession in context also support an individual reading. Moo, *The Epistle to the Romans*, 634; James R. Lowther, "Paul's Use of Deuteronomy 30:11-14 in Romans 10:5-8 as a Locus Primus on Paul's Understanding of the Law in Romans" (Doctoral Dissertation, Southwestern Baptist Theological Seminary, 2001), 101–102..

[8] Moo, *Encountering*, 142

[9] Schreiner, *Romans*, 547.

longer.

In which sense Christ is the "end of the law" and the relation of "for righteousness" to this sentence are controversial. Beginning with the former, the semantic range of τέλος, translated "end," suggests that Jesus is the goal of the law or that he ends it—some argue that both senses coincide in this word. Because both are true theologically (Matt 5:17-20, Luke 24:44, Rom 7, Gal 3:24-25, Heb 8), context is our only guide. Following Moo, I interpret τέλος to refer to Jesus completing the law in that he is the goal towards which it moved. As a race has the finish line for its goal and end, so also the law has Christ. With the finish line reached, the Law has ended.[10]

My main reason for this interpretation is Paul's argument in the following verses. In 10:5-8, we will see that Deuteronomy 30:11-14 anticipates the end of the Sinai covenant and its Law. Furthermore, through his Christological application, he shows that this text—and so the Law as written revelation and the Law as an inadequate covenant—anticipates the need for and the coming of Christ (Christ as its goal). To this we can append Moo's arguments: first, the language of "attaining" and "pursuing" in 9:31-32a suggests that *end* refers to the *goal*. Christ, as the righteousness to which the law would lead, is that goal which Israel was pursuing with the law but missed. Second, in support of the temporal aspect ("it has ended"), Paul is consistent in his focus on the salvation-historical transition from Law to Christ resulting in the Law's end (3:21ff; 6:14, 15; 7:1-6): here, he maintains discontinuity between the law-righteousness sought by the Jews and God's righteousness.[11] Last, Moo argues that many similar New Testament uses of τέλος bear this dual nuance of "an end that is the natural or inevitable result of something else."[12]

Against this, Schreiner identifies the emphasis to be on Israel's subjective failure (v. 3): the law, then, has not had a complete, objective end but has ended subjectively, ended as a way for righteousness.[13] However, though the Jews are seeking their own righteousness, this is part of the wilful

---

[10] Moo, *Encountering*, 144–145; James D. G Dunn, *Romans 9-16*, Word Biblical Commentary 38b (Dallas, Tex.: Word Books, 1988), 589.

[11] Moo, *The Epistle to the Romans*, 622–626, 640.

[12] Ibid., 641.

[13] Schreiner, *Romans*, 547.

rejection of God's righteousness: they have rejected the salvation-historical shift.

We would be remiss if we did not now address the debate over what "for righteousness" modifies. Our discussion above assumes, and is evidence, that "for righteousness" modifies the whole initial clause.[14] We can add as evidence for our interpretation that it is supported by the contextual arguments made above and by verses 5-13, where Christ has made righteousness available through faith by ending the law.[15]

In summary, Paul shows the need for Israel's salvation by juxtaposing their sinful pursuit of law-righteousness with God's provision of righteousness in Christ as the Law's goal and end. In verses 5-8, Paul will now explain this by contrasting two OT passages.

b. God's New Covenant Righteousness Ended the Law (10:5-8)

> ⁵For Moses writes about the righteousness that is based on the law, that the person who does the commandments shall live by them. ⁶But the righteousness based on faith says, "Do not say in your heart, 'Who will ascend into heaven?'" (that is, to bring Christ down) ⁷"or 'Who will descend into the abyss?'" (that is, to bring Christ up from the dead). ⁸But what does it say? "The word is near you, in your mouth and in your heart" (that is, the word of faith that we proclaim).

Verse 5. Paul connects this verse as an explanation of what has preceded with γαρ (for). Moo interprets this verse as the grounds for verse 4 only—Christ as the end of the law.[16] I take verses 5-13 as an explanation of all of verses 1-4, that is, it shows the nature of Israel's ignorance in missing Christ as the end of the law and so their culpability and need for salvation. This is unavoidable if my interpretation of verse 4 as the summary and conclusion of 1-4 is maintained.

---

[14] Contra Ibid.

[15] Moo, *The Epistle to the Romans*, 637–638.

[16] Ibid., 645.

Paul begins this section (5-8) by showing what Moses said about law-righteousness, which the Jews sought. With a quotation from Lev. 18:5, it is seen that law-righteousness is by works: the one who *does* will live—in context, be saved.[17] This verse invokes one side of a tension in the OT between God's gracious promise (Gen 12:1-7; 26:4-5) and the need for Israel's obedience (e.g. Gen 19:5-6, Deut 3:26). Having already shown that life by works is impossible (1:18-3:20), it is by faith (1:17), Paul introduces Leviticus 18:5 as a foil for God's ultimate act of grace in Christ, ending the tension. The Law pointed beyond itself; it was penultimate: the ultimate has come in Christ. In what follows, Paul will demonstrate this. To do so, Paul

---

[17] Paul's use is supported in the OT. Habakkuk 2:4, juxtaposing Gen. 15:6 and Lev. 18:5 with regard to covenant life—not just physical blessing—shows that life could be regarded in an extended manner in the OT. See Rutherford, *Habakkuk*. cf. Moo, *Galatians*, s.v. Gal 3:11; Moo, *The Epistle to the Romans*, s.v. Rom 1:17.

turns to Deuteronomy 30:11-14.

iii. Excursus: Deuteronomy 30:11-14 in Context

Because most interpreters argue that these verses refer to the Law, Paul's quotation is obscured: has he used the Law to combat the Law? When understood in its context, I argue that this text is not a challenge to obey the Law: it is a prophecy of the New Covenant.[i]

Occurring in Moses' third speech, between accounts of the curses Israel will incur, Deuteronomy 30 is the glimmer of hope amidst the darkness of Israel's future.[ii] Assuming the failure of Israel, Moses looks to the future (30:1) and sees a day when Israel will turn to YHWH and prosper. By carefully using a chiasm, Moses identifies God's act to circumcise their hearts (30:6-8, reversing 29:4) as the reason for this turning of fortunes (30:3). Deuteronomy 30:11-14 concludes this chiasm: echoing 1b, it identifies Israel's remembrance as the result of a future heart-circumcision provided by God. These verses look to this future, gracious work of God. No longer would there be a distant, mediated covenant (vv. 12-13). Instead, God would circumcise their hearts and they would have the commandment close to heart and mouth.

Moo mentions this interpretation but rejects it. He gives as evidence for rejecting it "a clear transition" from the future restoration in 30:1-10 to the present situation of Israel in 30:11ff, signaled by the end of the waw+perfect pattern in verse 11.[iii]

I have argued elsewhere for reading verses 11-14 with 1-10; here I will summarize two of those arguments.[iv] First, verses 11-14 are made up of nominal and participle clauses; these do not convey time, adopting it from context. Those who argue for a return to the present in verses 11-14 need to provide evidence for a significant disjunction between verses 10-11, justifying this temporal shift. Evidence against this shift is found in the sequence of the Hebrew word כִּי (*kî, for*) through verses 9b, 10a, 10b, 11a, and 14. The end of the chain is not in verse 10 but in verses 11 and 14. Moses grounds the future return of Israel in verses 11-14, connecting these verses with God's circumcising work in verse 6. Second, heart circumcision, the very thing needed (29:4) and which God will provide (30:6), is seen to be fulfilled here (30:11-14, cf. Jer. 31:31-34). However, does the shift in verb usage introduce the needed disjunction?

For two reasons I argue that it does not. First, Moses has not begun to use the perfect conjugation as he does in other present addresses (e.g. ch. 29, 30:15ff); he employs nominal and participle clauses throughout these verses, with indicatives only in direct speech (vv. 12-13). Second, the nature of the clauses argues against an intentional disjunction. The clauses making up these verses (excepting the direct speech) are all describing the commandment, clauses which, in Hebrew, are most naturally expressed with predication. Furthermore, Moses would not have used waw+הָיָה (*hāyāh*, to-be) for predication in future time: nominal clauses are equally adequate to indicate future time, and הָיָה is not used as regularly for predication (in Deut. 30, הָיָה is only used twice).[v] So, our interpretation is well within the boundaries of Hebrew syntax.

In conclusion, there is sufficient evidence to conclude that Moses intends verses 11-14 to continue 1-10: the present is only reintroduced in verses 15 with the use of an imperative and a perfect verb. We can then suggest, for our reading of Romans 10:6-8, that Paul has identified this text as a New Covenant prophecy.[vi]

---

[i] Cf. Christopher Wright, Deuteronomy, NIBC (Peabody, Mass.: Hendrickson Publishers, 1996), 290; Eugene H. Merrill, Deuteronomy, The New American Commentary 4 (USA: Broadman & Holman Publishers, 1994), 390–391; Daniel Isaac Block, Deuteronomy, The NIV Application Commentary (Grand Rapids, Mich.: Zondervan, 2012), 706.

[ii] Chs. 28-29, 31-32; N.T. Wright, "Romans," in *The New Interpreter's Bible*, ed. Robert W Wall and J. Paul Sampley, vol. X (Nashville: Abingdon Press,

2002), 659.

iii Moo, *The Epistle to the Romans*, 652.

iv See appendix 1.

v Once as a predicate in a condition.

vi One may inquire why Paul has quoted the LXX in v. 8 if he reads it in this manner. Often the NT writers will quote the Septuagint when it disagrees with MT if it makes an appropriate application of the Hebrew for their circumstances, as it does here. E.g. Acts 13:41, Heb. 10:37-38.

Verses 6-7. Paul, in verses 6-13, intends to explain the righteousness of God as the righteousness available through Jesus, ending the Law and bringing the New Covenant, in contrast with the law-righteousness Israel pursued. Paul begins this contrast here, using the common minor adversative conjunction δὲ (*de*). In verses 5-8, Paul will focus on Jesus as the end of the law, connecting this to faith-righteousness in verses 8-13. He has already shown throughout Romans that faith, even in the Old Testament (1:17, 4:1ff), is the means by which one is righteous before God: here he will tie this truth into the New Covenant through Deuteronomy 30:11-14, demonstrating that faith-righteousness is the goal and end of the Old Covenant Law. This will then demonstrate Israel's dire state, for in pursuing the hopeless demand of Leviticus 18:5, Israel has missed God's very provision for salvation, the goal to which the Law has pointed all along.

To make this point, Paul personifies faith-righteousness and places in its mouth four quotes from Deuteronomy. The first three describe faith-righteousness by saying what it is not. Paul's first quote, "Do not say in your heart..." (Deut 9:4), is perfectly matched to his present purposes.[18] In Deuteronomy 9:4, Moses warns the Israelites: they are not to think that their righteousness has earned them life; they have stubborn hearts. They are receiving the land because of the nations' wickedness and God's faithfulness (9:4-5). By introducing Deuteronomy 30 with this quote from 9:4, Paul wants us to read what follows in terms of this rebuke against earned righteousness.[19]

Paul's quote from Deuteronomy 30 is less clear: with few exceptions, the various interpretations have all supposed that Deuteronomy 30:11-14

---

[18] Moo, *The Epistle to the Romans*, 652.

[19] Ibid., 651; Schreiner, *Romans*, 558. The connection between 9:4-6 and 10:12-22, 30:6-14 make it especially fitting.

describes the Law in Moses' day. Paul's thought is clarified by our interpretation of these verses. In Deuteronomy 30:12-13, the lines that Paul quotes describe the future "word" negatively. The New Covenant will not be like the Old:[20] "'It will not be in the heavens, that you should say, 'Who will go up....' And it will not be beyond the sea, that you should say, 'Who will cross to the other side of the sea....'" That is, this commandment will not be distant—there will be no need for a human mediator to go up Sinai. It will be near, easy. Paul interprets this Christologically: "'Who will ascend into heaven' (That is, to bring Christ down) or 'Who will descend into the abyss?' (that is, to bring Christ up from the dead)."[21]

Paul's Christological interpretation indicates that the New Covenant has come through Jesus's incarnation and resurrection. With the arrival of the New Covenant, Paul shows that the Old has ended (no longer will they say, "Who will go up?"), and he equates Moses' commandment with Jesus; he is near through God's work. This thought is finished in verse 8 with another quote from Deuteronomy.

Verse 8. In verse 8, faith-righteousness speaks again, describing the present reality: "But what does it say? 'The word is near you, in your mouth and in your heart' (that is, the word of faith that we proclaim)." Having equated Jesus with the commandment in verses 6-7, Paul effectively equates Jesus here with "the word," which is "the word of faith that we proclaim." Jesus, and the whole of his accomplished work, is the message Paul preaches, one that calls for faith, not works.[22] The Law's goal was Christ; now that he

---

[20] In Deuteronomy, it is not described as the New Covenant, but its interpretation and fulfillment throughout Scripture identifies it as such, e.g. Jer. 31:31-34, Ezek 36:22-37:28, Heb. 8. See further the first chapter of Rutherford, *Prevenient Grace*.

[21] The Septuagint likewise has "sea." Schreiner and Moo argue cogently that Sea and the Abyss (Hebrew, 'the deep') overlap in semantic range. Though the original context alludes to the crossing the Red Sea, the emphasis lays on the distance and difficulty it illustrates. Here, he has sacrificed this allusion in the second line to make clear his application. Moo, *The Epistle to the Romans*, 655–656; Schreiner, *Romans*, 558–559..

[22] That the message's content is faith is ruled out by the equation with Jesus in the previous verses and the following emphasis on faith as a response to the message. Schreiner argues that it is really a 'both-and;' this is true in as much as the message of Jesus has within it a message of faith (Hab. 2:4 in Rom. 1:17). Moo, *The Epistle to the Romans*, 656–657; Schreiner, *Romans*, 559.

is here, it is has become obsolete.

In these verses then, Paul has shown that Jesus has fulfilled Moses' prophecy of a future where God's word, his demands, would be internalized and his people would be able to follow him. In showing this, Paul has proved that Christ has ended the law and shown that Israel has wilfully rejected God's revelation to stubbornly pursue their own righteousness. Because of this, they are in need of salvation. Paul further connects this in verses 8-13 through the language of easiness, nearness, heart, and mouth to the Righteousness of God revealed in Christ—this is the ultimate fulfillment of the law and Moses' prophecy.

B. Conclusion

In this paper, I have only been able to scratch the surface of this passage, arguing for this exposition mostly through the demonstration of its explanatory value—how it makes coherent sense of the texts and contexts of Romans and Deuteronomy. The purpose of this paper has been achieved, shedding fresh light on this difficult passage via careful exegesis of the Deuteronomy quotations. Paul's pertinent use of Moses' prophecy substantiates his argument in verses 1-4 by showing the nature of Israel's culpable rejection of God's plan and explaining Israel's need for salvation. We may summarise these verses as an explanation of Israel's need for salvation, expounded in terms of their rejection of God's climatic and exclusive provision of righteousness through Christ (the end of the law) attained by faith.

This passage, interpreted in this manner, offers many insights. For our pluralistic society, this passage reinforces the exclusiveness of the Gospel. If anyone were to be saved apart from Christ, it would be Israel. Paul testifies that they are zealous, yet the Jews are in need of salvation because their zeal is misplaced. With a misplaced object, zeal achieves nothing. God has made his righteousness easily available in Jesus, yet this is also the only source of righteousness. For the Church, the exclusiveness of Christ testifies to the great treasure of the salvation God has given us—we should give everything to pursue it. It also speaks to the urgency of our mission: with Paul, we must pray and seek the salvation of all who are perishing apart from Christ the saviour. This is a challenge for me as it is for the Church generally—to give my all for Jesus and seek the salvation of the lost.

This passage also provides an intellectual challenge for the Christian. If my proposed exposition holds true, it serves as reminder that God knows better than us: instead of supposing with some that Paul was wrong in his uses of the OT, we see again that much thought and diligent prayer in submission to God's Word and his Spirit can show us the true genius of his Scriptures. Paul's intertextuality is a vivid witness to the theological cohesion of God's revelation. Theologically, this text contributes to the greater biblical theology of the New Covenant in Christ and reveals further the intertextual web that contributes to our understanding of it (to Jeremiah, Isaiah, and Ezekiel, now Deuteronomy 30: to John and Hebrews, now Romans 10).

J. Alexander Rutherford

2 THESSALONIANS AND HELL: SEPARATION FROM OR WRATH COMING FORTH FROM GOD?

This paper was originally written for Teleioteti.ca. I wrote it to address a trend I was finding among Evangelicals as I researched and wrote on the doctrine of Hell. It appears that many evangelicals are adopting a view of Hell that is primarily characterized by absence from God and not his active presence for judgment. This paper was written to address one specific text used to uphold such a view.

Many writers and preachers today speak about Hell as, among other things, eternal separation from God. Hell, it is said, is receiving what the sinner wanted all along, freedom from God, the absence of his goodness. Such a state would be horrifying indeed—the One who is Goodness, Love, our Joy himself completely absent!—yet is this what the Bible pictures? The text often cited in this regard is 2 Thessalonians 1:9: "to those who do not know God and to those who do not submit to the gospel of our Lord Jesus, who will receive as punishment eternal destruction *from* the presence of the Lord and *from* the glory of his might."[1] The key word here is "from," the Greek preposition ἀπὸ (*apo*). It is often understood in terms of separation, "eternal destruction separated from the presence of the Lord and separated from the glory of his might." Though this is a valid and a common sense of ἀπὸ (e.g.

---

[1] My translation unless indicated otherwise

Matt 8:30, Matt 11:25, 1 Thess 4:3), I will argue that the immediate context, Paul's use of ἀπὸ (*apo*) elsewhere, and the greater perspective of Scripture indicates that the text means "coming forth from" (preposition indicating location from which something comes).[2]

Our first consideration is the context in which verse 9 is found: the context indicates overwhelmingly that this final judgment the unbeliever faces is the active judgment of God, the pouring out of his wrath. In 1 and 2 Thessalonians, Paul is interested in explaining the day of the Lord, arguing that God will repay those who presently afflict believers when Christ returns and that those who have died will not miss out on the resurrection. Thus, Paul is interested in the two sides of the Day of the Lord: the resurrection to eternal life and the final judgment, beginning with Christ return. In 1 Thessalonians, Paul explains that the day of the Lord, Christ's return, will come quickly and be inescapable. The salvation the Thessalonians await is contrasted with the wrath unbelievers await (5:9). Then in 2 Thessalonians, Paul explains further this "wrath." In 1:5-7 Paul explains that in the final judgment, God in justice will repay with affliction those who presently afflict the Thessalonians; this will begin when "the Lord Jesus will be revealed from heaven with his mighty angels[3] in flaming fire, dealing out retribution" (1:7-8 ESV). Thus, God's righteous wrath against unbelievers manifests in his active judgment against sinners, retribution. This then brings us to verse 9, which is expanding upon verse 8. The end of verse 8 tells us that Jesus is dealing out retribution to those who do not know God and to those who do not "submit to the Gospel of our Lord Jesus"; verse 9 then describes further the retribution they will receive: "[they] will receive as punishment eternal destruction *from* the presence of the Lord and *from* the glory of his might." In the context of Christ coming for judgment from the throne of God, ἀπὸ clearly does not indicate *separation from* God's presence but the horrifying truth of judgment pouring *forth from* God's presence. This is consistent with Paul's use of ἀπὸ throughout 1 and 2 Thessalonians.

Consider this (ridiculous) sentence, "to *bear* arms is part of the great

---

[2] Both uses of ἀπὸ indicate separation, but the former is static; the latter involves movement away from.

[3] Or "with the angels of his host (i.e. army)."

responsibility we, as citizens, *bear;* we *bear* many burdens in our lives as responsible citizens, this is why we *bear* resemblance to our forefather." The first three uses of "bear" represent the sense "to carry," the latter two of which do so metaphorically; the fourth has a different sense, "to bear resemblance." In this context, the switch in sense is quite obvious, but if it was more ambiguous ("this is why we bear the image of our forefather"), the consistent use of one sense of "bear" (to carry) would suggest that we read "bear" in this sense and not the other: "this is why we [carry] the image of forefather."[4] This idea, that a writer will avoid ambiguity if he is using a word in a different way than it was consistently used before, lies behind my first argument.

Paul uses ἀπὸ 15 times in 1 and 2 Thessalonians. Of the 8 uses in 1 Thessalonians, only 2 have the idea of separation without movement from—and both of these are signalled by the verb they accompany ("to abstain"). Of the seven uses in 2 Thessalonians, four uses (other than v. 9) indicate movement away from (1:2, 7; 2:2; 3:2). The first two of these come immediately before our verse and refer to the same subject or sphere (peace comes forth from God in v. 2, Jesus from heaven in v. 7). This suggests to me that, in the absence of any clear indication of a shift in sense, the "ambiguous" use in 1:9 should be taken in the same way—"[coming] forth from the presence of the Lord and from the glory of his might." That Hell is the experience of God's wrath and not his absence is consistently attested elsewhere in Scripture

Three other Scripture should serve to confirm this. In Matthew 10:28, Jesus instructs the Twelve not to fear man, but rather "fear him who can destroy both soul and body in hell" (ESV). That is, Jesus looks to hell as the place where God will actively (he will do something) destroy[5] the body and soul in Hell. Furthermore, in Romans 2:8 Paul contrasts eternal life with

---

[4] We of course do not read it in this manner because even in this example, it is not ambiguous—context makes it pretty clear—and the idea of carrying around an image of an ancestor or predecessor is not common.

[5] Some suggest that "destroy" here means that Hell will have an end, but the horrifying truth is that to destroy something immortal (resurrected for judgment) is to subject it eternally to the forces that would ordinarily end mortal life. Thus, the horror of hell is underscored: we must be passionate to rescue unbelievers from this fate through the preaching of the Gospel.

"wrath and fury" towards unbelievers: wrath and fury both are active, they are something inflicted. This is affirmed in Revelation 14:9-10,

> And another angel, a third, followed them, saying with a loud voice, "If anyone worships the beast and its image and receives a mark on his forehead or on his hand, he also will drink the wine of God's wrath, poured full strength into the cup of his anger, and he will be tormented with fire and sulfur in the presence of the holy angels and in the presence of the Lamb. And the smoke of their torment goes up forever and ever, and they have no rest, day or night, these worshipers of the beast and its image, and whoever receives the mark of its name. (ESV)

This is horrifying language, but it is consistent with 2 Thessalonians 1:9. In all three of these Scriptures we see that final judgment is not being left in one's own misery, to be finally separated from God, but to have God excruciatingly present in judgment: even in Sheol, God cannot be escaped (cf. Ps 139:8, Job 26:6).

This is no trivial issue; this is not merely academic discussions of the minute details: it is deadly serious! 1 and 2 Thessalonians, and the rest of Scripture, teach that Hell is horrifying: it is the place where God's wrath is poured out in judgment against both the body and the soul! This is what Scripture teaches, and it does so for a reason. The doctrine of Hell in all its horror underscores two key Christian teachings: the nature of our God and the necessity of vigorous evangelism.

God is just, all Scripture testifies to this. This means that God has to punish sin; Hell demonstrates the seriousness with which he takes sin. Yet God sent his Son to save us from that reality; therefore, to properly understand Hell is to properly understand the cross. When Jesus cried out to the Father, "My God, My God, why have you forsaken me," he was not lamenting the absence of his Father. Jesus was expressing the agony of his Father turning the weight of his wrath towards him, wrath which he had patiently withheld for thousands of years. Jesus was experiencing the Father orientated towards him with pure white-hot wrath against sin. He was experiencing there on the cross the equivalent of an eternity of burning fire, of darkness so deep it hurts. He was experiencing eternal destruction—

destruction pouring forth from the throne of God.[6] Jesus suffered that for you, for me: he suffered God's wrath against sin that we who believe might be forgiven and sanctified, glorified as members of his bride the Church.

Yet there are those of whom this cannot be said: members of my family and old friends face that fate. Everyone who has not confessed Jesus Christ as Lord, who has not believed that God raised him from the dead after he was crucified (Rom 10:5-17), faces this fate: that is why the great commission, to go out into all the world with the message of the Gospel, is as vital today as it was 2000 years ago. People need to hear God's truth desperately; their lives are on the line. But how can they hear if no one goes, if no one tells them? The doctrine of Hell is absolutely horrifying, yet it is the truth.

Jesus teaches it; Paul and John teach it. They teach it so that we would go out and fulfill this commission. 2 Thessalonians 1:9 teaches that God is active for judgment in Hell: this means that we must be active in our mission to save people from this fate through the preaching of the glorious good news that Jesus Christ came and gave his life for sinners on the Cross. We must be bold in proclaiming the good news that Christ rose again on the third day, victorious over death and the grave, and now reigns at the right hand of the Father and through his people on earth. People need to hear the good news that sin has an answer, his name is Jesus Christ. They need to hear that in him alone our hope, our joy, and our future is found—and found in him abundantly.

---

[6] The description comes from the language of Hell; that Christ bore our punishment in our place, the punishment we would have faced in Hell, is testified throughout Scripture: e.g. Isa. 53:4-6, 10-12; Rom. 3:25; 2 Cor. 5:21; Gal. 3:10-14; 1 John 2:2, 4:10.

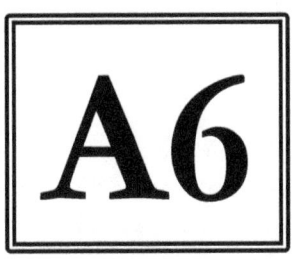

CONVINCED OF BETTER THINGS: AN EXPOSITION OF HEBREWS 6:1-12

This paper was originally prepared for professor Doug Moo for a graduate-level study on Hebrews. It contributes to this book by showing how we use the text to argue for theological truths and application.

Many of us have faced times of disinterest, of stagnation in our faith, when all that remains is a faint vestige of its once vibrant genesis. When we, or those we know, look away from the glory of God in the face of Jesus to the fake glory of worldly satisfaction, what are we to make of our state? Are we near unto damnation, drifting away into a state irreversible? Are we about to discover the faith we once held was a sham? Such questions surface when considering the difficult warning of Hebrews 6:1-12, a text where the author seems to teach that it is impossible for a Christian who falls away, whose faith snaps and breaks, to return. It appears that no one can restore such a person to repentance.

Many have sought to argue this impossibility is not universal—impossible for man but not for God—or to soften it to a "difficulty," still others have argued that true Christians are not the intended audience of this warning. The burden of this paper is show from the argument of the author of Hebrews (now abbreviated AOH) that Hebrews 6:1-12 is indeed addressed to Christians and that it teaches the impossibility of restoration for one who apostatises. I maintain, as the thesis of this paper, that the author exhorts his believing audience to press on to mature Christian faith through a warning grounded in the irreversible nature of apostasy and a statement of assurance grounded in the gracious provision of God. In this way, the author balances human responsibility with divine sovereignty in a warning that serves his audience's needs and coheres with the rest of the NT canon; that is, his exhortation is firmly grounded in the compatibilist worldview assumed throughout Scripture.[1]

To argue this, I will elucidate the context of Hebrews 6:1-12 and discuss the passage according to its three sections (vv. 1-3, 4-8, and 9-12) in dialogue with Wayne Grudem's essay *Perseverance of the Saints*.[2] In conclusion, I will offer a brief reflection on the passage's theological implications.

A. Exegesis

Some consider Hebrews to be one of the most difficult books in the NT, even comparing it to a puzzle: there is no certainty concerning the author, audience, date of writing, or necessitating circumstances.[3] The book's unique structure and pervasive use of the OT compounds its difficulty. Yet, despite such uncertainty, the letter's themes and argument are largely clear. We can determine that the author is exhorting a Jewish audience to press on to mature Christian faith and that the Hebrews faced three dangers; the subtle drift characterizing a lack of forward progress (2:4), possible rebellion against Christ and the New covenant (3:12-13; 10:26-29), and external trials

---

[1] Compatibilism, in Philosophy, is the belief that human responsibility is not negated when a free decision is determined (when the outcome is certain). It stands opposed to Libertarianism, which maintains that a responsible human decision must not be necessitated—it must be contingent, indeterminate. I have argued elsewhere the Bible assumes compatibilism, as have numerous Calvinist authors; cf. Rutherford, *Prevenient Grace*, 108–136, 280–286, 311–312; Jonathan Edwards, *Freedom of the Will* (Mineola, N.Y.: Dover Publications, 2012); Frame, *Doctrine of God*; D. A. Carson, *Divine Sovereignty and Human Responsibility* (Eugene, Ore.: Wipf and Stock Publishers, 2002).

[2] Wayne A. Grudem, "Perseverance of the Saints: A Case Study from the Warning Passages in Hebrews," in *Still Sovereign: Contemporary Perspectives on Election, Foreknowledge & Grace*, ed. Thomas R. Schreiner and Bruce A. Ware (Grand Rapids: Baker, 2000), 133–182.

[3] Donald Alfred Hagner, *Encountering the Book of Hebrews: An Exposition* (Grand Rapids: Baker Academic, 2002), 20; William L. Lane, *Hebrews 1-8*, ed. David A. Hubbard, Glenn W. Barker, and Ralph P. Martin, vol. 1, Word Biblical Commentary Vol. 47,A (Nashville: Word Books, 1991), xlvii.

exacerbating these dangers (2:18, 4:16).[4] The author mounts an extensive argument from the OT for the superiority of Jesus and the New Covenant inaugurated in his blood, interspersed with warnings and exhortations to move on to maturity. The author argues both from the superior nature of Jesus, the covenant representative, (1:4-4:13, 11:1-13:19) and from the New Covenant and its cult (4:14-7:38; 8:1-14; 9:1-10:39) for the superiority of the New Covenant salvation over against the Old Covenant.[5] The main idea of the book, then, is that the unmatchable Jesus, mediator of a superior covenant, ensures a superior salvation from which one dare not depart.

Our passage occurs at the beginning of the author's prolonged exposition of Psalm 110:4; AOH pauses his exposition to address the Hebrews' present spiritual state. In 5:11-14, the author explains that they are far from where they should be, given the time passed since their conversion (5:12). Though they should already be mature enough for a diet of solid spiritual food, they are infants still needing milk. One commentator explains this as irony: it is not that they are not mature, have not received mature teaching, but that they are acting like they are not.[6] I am not convinced this explanation does justice to the connection between 5:11-14 and 6:1-12. In 6:1, the author does not exhort them to return to a maturity they once had or live in a way fitting their true state (act mature, not infantile!). Instead, he exhorts them to press on to maturity: the warning, then, functions to move the audience from their infant stagnation into the maturity they must display. He has "much to say, and it is hard to explain" because of their present state (5:11),[7] but saying it is exactly what they need. Presenting them with solid food accompanied by exhortation and warning, is exactly the means by which he intends for them—with God's permission—to move on to maturity. Thus, AOH begins chapter 6 with the exhortation to move on with him to solid food.

---

[4] Paul Ellingworth, *The Epistle to the Hebrews: A Commentary on the Greek Text*, NIGTC (Grand Rapids: Carlisle: W.B. Eerdmans ; Paternoster, 1993), 78–80.

[5] Several exegetes recognize the centrality of covenant, including Philip Edgcumbe Hughes, *A Commentary on the Epistle to the Hebrews* (Grand Rapids: Eerdmans, 1977), 3; Ronaldo Guzman and Michael W. Martin, "Is Hebrews 5:11-6:20 Really a Disgression?," *Novum Testamentum* 57, no. 3 (2015): 303.

[6] Lane, *Hebrews*, 1:135.

[7] All quotations, unless otherwise stated, taken from the ESV.

a. Hebrews 6:1-3

With the exhortation in 6:1-3 to move on from milk to maturity, AOH indicates he does not intend to give them the milk they have heard so often but to press on to the hard-to-explain things. Before he does so, though, AOH begins a dire warning, extending from verse 1-12, intended to spur the Hebrews on to maturity. These beginning three verses introduce an exhortation to which the warning in verses 4-8 will add dreadful urgency.

Verse 1-2 By introducing this section with διο (*dio*, therefore), our author indicates a close logical connection between this exhortation and his indictment of the Hebrews in 5:11-14. Having identified them as spiritual infants who live on milk, he now calls them to move past this to the solid food more fitting their objective age. Within verse 1, ἀρχης (*archēs*) and θεμέλιον (*themelion*) are both semantically parallel, the former referring to a temporally early state ("beginning") and the latter a physically base state ("foundation"). They correspond clearly to chapter five's metaphorical "milk." The six items in verses 1-2 following "foundation" have engendered no small amount of scholarly debate over their precise nuances, yet it should suffice for our purposes to identify their collective function. The string of genitives is clearly dependent upon θεμέλιον, giving the author's outline of the "milk" upon which they have been living; these are, for AOH's purposes, the first things of Christianity. What deserves our further attention, though, are the author's exhortations to "leave" and "go on."

Within the semantic range of ἀφίημι (aphiēmi), translated "leave," are various senses communicating absolute departure ("leave behind"); yet this is, in context, not what the author has in mind. The author is not calling his audience to abandon the basics but to build upon the basis they have. To communicate this, that they are not to reject the basic teachings from which they are to move on, Lane translates ἀφίημι "leave standing."[8] That this is correct is supported by the use of θεμέλιον (*themelion*, "foundation") alongside the verb καταβαλλομενοι (*kataballomenoi*, lay [a foundation]) to describe these initial "elementary" teachings. AOH describes a foundation that is already in place and so can now be built upon; it needs no further

---

[8] Lane, *Hebrews*, 1:131, 139.

work. Therefore the sense here is, as a metaphorical extension of "leaving behind," "to stop concerning yourself with something"—to mentally leave it behind.⁹

Our last consideration in these first verses is the hortatory subjunctive φερώμεθα (pherōmetha, "let us... go on"), from which the participle ἀφίημι gets its hortatory force. Though many translations render φέρω (pherō) "go on" or some variation thereof (e.g. NASB, NIV 1984), many commentators follow the NIV 2011 in rendering φέρω as a passive of its regular sense "to bear," resulting in the translation, "let us... be taken forward."[10] The NIV's translation would suggest they are to surrender to God's work;[11] this is, however, contextually unlikely and not the only possible understanding of φέρω. Considering the context, the very charge levelled at the Hebrews is that they are being passive: they are in danger of "drifting away"; they are not pressing on to maturity. The exhortations are not framed as challenges to stop resisting God's Spirit but to pay closer attention to the message (2:1), to strive (4:11), to endure (10:36-39), and to run (12:1). Bruce describes the sense here, possibly drawing on 2 Kingdoms 18:27 (L manuscript), as "swift and energetic movement."[12] All examples of φέρω used intransitively suggest vigorous movement, so the force of the φέρω in this context is probably "let us press on [with vigour] to maturity!"

Verse 3. Having exhorted his audience to vigorous pursuit of maturity,

---

⁹ Frederick W. Danker, *A Greek-English Lexicon of the New Testament and Other Early Christian Literature*, 3rd ed. (Chicago: University of Chicago Press, 2000), 156–157.

¹⁰ R. T. France, "Hebrews," in *The Expositor's Bible Commentary*, ed. Tremper Longman and David E. Garland, Rev. ed. (Grand Rapids: Zondervan, 2006), 81; Brooke Foss Westcott, ed., *The Epistle to the Hebrews the Greek Text with Notes and Essays*, 3d ed. (London: Macmillan, 1903), 145; Hughes, *Hebrews*, 194.

¹¹ France, "Hebrews," 81.; cf. Daniel B Wallace, *Greek Grammar Beyond the Basics: An Exegetical Syntax of the New Testament with Scripture, Subject, and Greek Word Indexes* (Grand Rapids: Zondervan, 1996), 440–441.

¹² F. F. Bruce, *The Epistle to the Hebrews*, NICNT (Grand Rapids: Eerdmans, 1964), 110. Muraoka's LXX lexicon gives the same sense for this text and gives other examples of the passive functioning intransitively (e.g. Isa. 28:15, 18; Dan. 9:21; 2 Macc. 3:25, 14:45) T. Muraoka, *A Greek-English Lexicon of the Septuagint*, Rev. ed. (Louvain ; Walpole, MA: Peeters, 2009), 713.

AOH declares this is indeed what "we," himself and the Hebrews, "will do," given God's permission. He may have in mind the permission envisaged in James 4:15, but he predominately appears to be grounding their hope for a successful attainment of maturity in God's gracious provision, their dependence on which receives great emphasis from the emphatic marker of a condition in 6:3b (ἐάνπερ, *eanper*). This pressing on to maturity which God may permit includes, but should not be restricted to, the rest of the author's argument unpacked in chapters 6-7.[13] God's role is made clearer in verses 9-12 and is echoed in the benediction (13:20-21); the emphasis on God's gracious provision also coheres well with the emphasis provided by Jesus and Peter on God's role in perseverance (John 10:25-30; 1 Peter 1:3-7).[14]

b. Hebrews 6:4-8

Having concluded his initial exhortation with a sense of uncertainty, AOH now turns up the heat in these verses: he underscores the urgency of their situation by declaring the irreversible nature of falling away from the faith.

Verses 4-8. He intensifies the warning by introducing the main verb in verse 4 and withholding its infinitive complement until verse 6: the result is a rhetorical flourish emphasizing the identity of the verbal object, described by five participles. The Christian readers wait a foreboding moment to discover what is "impossible"; in that moment they are confronted by a picture of themselves as those who could, possibly, face this dire impossibility. Many would disagree with this interpretation in at least two ways: some would contend "impossible" really means difficult, and others would not agree that the participles describe Christians.

The first is the easiest disagreement to resolve. There is really no good reason to soften the usual force of ἀδύνατος (*adunatos*) to "difficult"; this would, in fact, defeat the author's rhetorical purpose. Though Louw and Nida define ἀδύνατος as "impossible," they explain the force in our text as "an instance of hyperbole" and so justify the translation "it is extremely difficult."

---

[13] Bruce, *Hebrews*, 118.

[14] In the 13:20, AOH identifies Jesus as "the great shepherd of the sheep," an image particularly associated with preservation (Ps 23; John 10:2, 11-16; 1 Pet 2:25).

They give no reason, however, why it should be read in this way.[15] Hagner similarly holds open the possibility God might restore an apostate, identifying the force here as "no return can be guaranteed."[16] Lexically, "impossible" is the obvious meaning; thus the burden of proof lays on those seeking to mitigate its force. Nothing in context does this; in fact, the urgency and severity of the warnings throughout the book (especially 10:26-39, 12:25-29) suggest his warning should be taken at face value. And, though it can hardly be debated that God *could* restore an apostate if he so desired, nothing in Scripture suggests he will; thus, there is no reason to soften the author's words on the basis of such a possibility.

The force of ἀδύνατος (*adunatos*) emphasizes the finality of abandoning their salvation, and thus the incredible danger of their current state.[17] This is reinforced in verse 6 when this impossibility is said to be because "they are crucifying once again the Son of God… and holding him up to contempt."[18] Thus, the author teaches the impossibility of repentance for one who falls away.

The second point of disagreement—the identity of those who face this impossibility—is more contentious. Are "those who have once been enlightened" Christians of genuine faith or do they merely look like Christians, having only apparent faith?[19] The standard Arminian view, and of

---

[15] Johannes P. Louw and Eugene Albert Nida, *Greek-English Lexicon of the New Testament: Based on Semantic Domains*, electronic ed. of the 2nd edition. (New York, N.Y.: United Bible Societies, 1996), 1:668.

[16] Hagner, *Encountering*, 90–91.

[17] Bruce, *Hebrews*, 118; Peter Thomas O'Brien, *The Letter to the Hebrews*, Pillar New Testament Commentary (Grand Rapids.; Nottingham: Eerdmans; Apollos, 2010), 219; Thomas R. Schreiner, *Commentary on Hebrews*, ed. Andreas J. Köstenberger, T. Desmond Alexander, and Thomas R. Schreiner, Biblical Theology for Christian Proclamation (Nashville: B&H, 2015), 180.

[18] Delitzsch and others have suggested this be interpreted temporally, yet the placement of the participles at the end of the clause and the context suggest a causal sense—"since" or "because." Bruce writes of Delitzsch's interpretation, "To say that they cannot be brought to repentance so long as they persist in their renunciation of Christ would be a truism hardly worth putting into words." Ellingworth seconds his judgment. Bruce, *Hebrews*, 124; Ellingworth, *Hebrews*, 323–325.

[19] Among so-called "free grace," theologians this passage is thought to challenge Christians with a potential loss of rewards, not salvation. On this position,

many others, is that the first four participles describe the experience of regenerate Christians in detail, with the last participle indicating the falling away of such people. Many Calvinists, on the other hand, understand this passage as describing those who by all appearances are Christians but are not truly regenerate.[20] Wayne Grudem does an admirable job representing this view.[21] The thrust of his argument is that *"the terms by themselves are inconclusive,"* are ambiguous; thus context is determinative as to whether these are true Christians or only apparent Christians.[22] Most commentators follow Grudem in giving much space to the exposition of each term. However, such an extensive task is beyond the scope of this paper and, I believe, unnecessary for understanding the author's point and seeing that these participles are meant (contra Grudem) to be a detailed description of a true Christian's experience. The phrases taken collectively, not abstracted from each other, and read in the present context give no reason to suppose these are not believers. That is, the burden of proof lies on those arguing that a group of terms that could describe genuine Christians and are found in a letter that has all appearances of being written to genuine Christians do not describe genuine Christians. Grudem offers three arguments for his view. Addressing

---

there is no distinction between "genuine faith," faith that endures (Heb 3:14) and produces fruit (Jas 2:14-26), and "apparent faith," bare assent that shows initial zeal but disappears quickly (Matt 13:20-22). All that is required for salvation is intellectual assent, but rewards are contingent upon conduct and perseverance (e.g. 1 Cor. 3:14-15). Space does not permit a thorough interaction with this position, but many works adequately address this position. E.g. Craig L. Blomberg and Mariam J. Kamell, *James: Zondevan Exegetical Commentary on the New Testament*, Zondervan Exegetical Commentary Series on the New Testament v. 16 (Grand Rapids: Zondervan, 2008), 125–141; D. A. Carson, "Reflections on Assurance," in *Still Sovereign: Contemporary Perspectives on Election, Foreknowledge & Grace*, ed. Thomas R. Schreiner and Bruce A. Ware (Grand Rapids: Baker, 2000), 247–276; D. A. Carson, *The Cross and Christian Ministry: Leadership Lessons from 1 Corinthians* (Grand Rapids: Baker Books, 2004); Thomas R. Schreiner and Ardel B. Caneday, *The Race Set before Us: A Biblical Theology of Perseverance & Assurance* (Downers Grove: InterVarsity, 2001).

[20] John Calvin, *The Epistle of Paul the Apostle to the Hebrews and the First and Second Epistles of St Peter*, ed. David W. Torrance and Thomas F. Torrance, trans. William B. Johnston, Calvin's Commentaries (Eerdmans: Grand Rapids, 1963); John M. Frame, *Systematic Theology: An Introduction to Christian Belief* (Phillipsburg: P&R Publishing, 2013), 1000–1001.

[21] Grudem, "Perseverance."

[22] Ibid., 152–153.

these in order, we shall see the context indicates no such thing.

He argues, firstly, that stating the impossibility of restoring one to repentance who has fallen away "does not necessarily imply that [AOH] thinks true Christians could fall away." Supporting this, he claims that the author is writing to those whose spiritual status is unclear.[23] Yet this is by no means evident; in fact, this assumes the very point Grudem is attempting to prove. He has moved from evidence for lexical ambiguity—that the four participles may describe a Christian or an apparent Christian—to actual ambiguity, that there is a question whether some of the Hebrews are Christians or only apparent Christians. However, the fact that the terminology by itself is ambiguous does not prove that actual ambiguity is being considered. Grudem takes these verses to present a test and challenge to the Hebrews: if they persevere, they are truly believers. If not, they are only apparent believers, thus they must strive for maturity so they may know their state. Yet, no evidence is given that the author questions the current salvific state of the Hebrews. Therefore, Grudem assumes by saying "he is especially writing to warn those whose spiritual status is not yet clear" that this is the question at hand and thus assumes without proof the burden of his interpretation. His following arguments build upon but do not provide proof for this assumption.[24]

Grudem argues, secondly, the illustration of the field in verses 7-8 demonstrates there was no initial saving faith. He contends that AOH uses this illustration to show that the response of the ground to the rain reveals what type of land it was: bad fruit reveals truly bad land. Against the supposition that the land once was good, he argues there is no indication the land once produced good fruit and the present participles suggest a continuous activity incompatible with land that once produced good but now produces bad fruit.[25] Again, Grudem's argument begs the question: he supposes the illustration is meant as a test, to reveal what the land was initially via its end result. This presupposes his interpretation of the passage, that it reveals endurance as the measure of true faith. He fails to give evidence that this is the purpose of the illustration. On the contrary, the author appears to illustrate with agricultural imagery two responses to God's blessing,

---

[23] Ibid., 154.

[24] Ibid.

[25] Ibid., 155–156.

explaining (γὰρ, *gar*, for) the warning: one response receives blessings (enlightenment, etc. from vv. 4-6) and produces the intended crop; the other receives the same blessings and produces thorns and thistles. The end of the latter is the point the author seeks to make: if they fall away, they will face eternal condemnation—being cursed and burned.[26] This illustration, then, heightens the warning with a vivid portrayal of the end of one who falls away.

Furthermore, Grudem fails to ask what the crop in context refers to, assuming it is—as in the Gospels—good works throughout a believer's life, such that a transition from belief to unbelief would involve the transition from producing good fruit to thorns and thistles. Though the author of Hebrews employs imagery similar to other texts, he may have a more restricted intent for the "crop" in context. The end which the author seeks for the Hebrews throughout this section and the letter is endurance until the end: read in this context, the image of "crop" in contrast with "thorns and thistles" suggests a contrast between maturity resulting in perseverance and unbelief that fails to press on. Therefore, this imagery may be consistent with Grudem's view, but cannot prove it. The imagery does not rule out that those considered in the previous verses are genuine Christians; it only illustrates the end of an apostate—one who does not prove useful for those for whom he or she is cultivated.

Grudem argues, thirdly, the better things in verse 9 of which the author has confidence for his readers are good fruits evidencing salvation, better evidence than the ambiguous experiences in verses 4-6. For this, he offers four supporting arguments. We will examine these arguments below when we consider verses 9-12, but for now we can point out that Grudem again begs the question: he supposes the author's description is intentionally ambiguous in verses 4-6, in need of supplementation to prove *these are true Christians*. It is this contention he has not yet proven: though the words themselves may be ambiguous, Grudem has not shown the author intends their collective force to be likewise ambiguous (he has not met the burden of proof). Furthermore, as I will argue below, Grudem's arguments and interpretation of verses 9-12 do not withstand scrutiny. If my reasoning below is sound, Grudem fails to demonstrate that the author intends verses

---

[26] The warnings elsewhere, especially in ch. 10, reinforce that eternal condemnation is indeed in sight. S. McKnight, "The Warning Passages of Hebrews: A Formal Analysis and Theological Conclusions," *Trinity Journal* 13, no. 1 (1992): 21–59.

4-6 to be ambiguous. We may, then, ask what the author does intend.

The first four participles describe a genuine conversion experience, for "*The* sign that one was a Christian in the NT was the Reception of the Holy Spirit.... the Spirit is 'center-stage' here."[27] Though the individual terminology may be ambiguous, their collective force is unavoidable: with no contextual clues contrariwise, the Hebrews would recognise themselves in this initial description. They would recognize themselves, that is, until the final participle, "and then have fallen away"; here is where the author's rhetorical suspension is felt. His suspension of the infinitive complement allows him to describe those facing the impossibility in terms that described the Hebrews, until this final descriptor: the warning invites them to see themselves in this danger if they only have this final experience. "Fall away" itself is being used to describe a decisive movement away from New Covenant faith, as demonstrated by the parallel warning passages and immediate context.[28] Though Hewitt suggests it is being used as a counter-factual condition—if they fall away, and they will not—it is syntactically functioning as an adjective grouped with the others under τους (*tous*, the) in verse 4.[29]

Thus the author, in verses 4-6, presents a terrifying proposition for the Hebrews to consider: to experience what they experienced and fall away, like they were in danger of doing (2:4, chs. 3-4), is irreversible, with no possibility to be renewed to repentance. They are challenged to press on to maturity, to pay close attention to what they heard, lest this become their reality. In verses 7-8, the author then illustrates this danger with a picture from agriculture: having received the rain of God, two options remain, to press on to maturity and produce the crop they were intended to produce, or to produce thorns and thistles and be utterly destroyed. To produce a crop, in this context, would be to enter into maturity; to produce thorns and thistles would be to fall away. At the moment it was their choice—God permitting of course

---

[27] Schreiner, *Hebrews*, 185.

[28] McKnight, "The Warning Passages"; Lane, *Hebrews*, 1:142.

[29] Thomas Hewitt, *The Epistle to the Hebrews, an Introduction and Commentary*, 1st ed., The Tyndale New Testament Commentaries (Grand Rapids: Eerdmans, 1960), 110–111; T. K. Oberholtzer, "The Warning Passages in Hebrews: Part 3 (of 5 Parts): The Thorn-Infested Ground in Hebrews 6:4-12," *Bibliotheca Sacra* 145, no. 579 (1988): 332.

(verse 3).

c. Hebrews 6:9-12

Having set out such serious stakes, AOH now revisits his statement in verse 3: will God permit them to press on to maturity? AOH has great confidence that God will not neglect the good works they have done, that they will obtain better things than fiery destruction (v. 8). Before transitioning in 6:12-20 back to the argument introduced in 5:10, AOH concludes his warning with an exhortation to show the same eagerness in the pursuit of maturity they have shown for good works.

Verse 9. The concessive statement opening this verse in the ESV describes the entire warning in verses 4-8.[30] The following clause is where Grudem's final argument comes into play: he argues "better things" should be understood as the resolution of the ambiguity in verses 4-6. The better things are the indisputable fruits of Christian living described in the following verses contrasted with the ambiguous terms in verses 4-6. He presents four arguments to demonstrate this: (1) "better" in Hebrews is usually used to contrast a good thing with something better; (2) a singular "a better thing" would be more suiting a contrast with final judgment; (3) the better things are present not future; (4) and AOH had "no need to assure them that they had not yet fallen away."[31] Verse 9, for Grudem, "provides a crucial key for understanding this whole passage." If "better things" are sure evidence of true faith contra the ambiguous experiences in verses 4-6, then those in verses 4-6 cannot be saved: there would be no need to be confident in sure signs of salvation for those who are saved.[32] Therefore verse 9 indicates those described in verses 4-6 are not believers, yet AOH is confident the Hebrews are true believers. None of these four arguments withstands close scrutiny, examining them shall serve to elucidate a more evident reading of verse 9.

Concerning his first argument, "better" is a key word in the book of Hebrews, frequently used to contrast Jesus and the New Covenant with the Old and its cult, and in many of its occurrences something good is contrasted

---

[30] Ellingworth, *Hebrews*, 329; Schreiner, *Hebrews*, 193.

[31] Grudem, "Perseverance," 158.

[32] Ibid., 159.

with something better. However, this is not so for every occurrence: in 7:7 κρείττων (*kreittōn*) offers neither a positive nor a negative comparison; instead, it is a substantive meaning "superior". In 11:16, the land the patriarchs left is contrasted with God's promise, with no evaluation given of the former land. In 12:24, "the better word" Jesus' blood speaks is one of promise whereas the "blood of Abel" is a cry for justice: the contrast is not between something good and something better, but something negative and something better because it is positive.[33] This last example is also instructive because it lies outside of the letter's main argument: contrasting Jesus' and Abel's blood does not further the New Covenant/Old Covenant contrast that is the main argument, showing that κρείττων does not necessarily compare something good with something better or an Old Covenant institution with a New Covenant one. 6:9 lies outside the main argument like 12:24 and, therefore, does not necessarily contrast something good with something better.

Grudem's second argument likewise fails. He contends that a singular "better thing" would be more suitable for a contrast with final judgment, that a singular adjective is more fitting if the author intends the better thing to be salvation. If the author were intending to contrast judgment with salvation, a singular adjective would indeed be more fitting, yet this is not the standard interpretation. The contrast is not between an abstract final judgment and final salvation, but between the ends of burning (v. 8) and of blessings (v. 7). The author is drawing explicitly on the previous illustration: he is convinced of better things than a curse and burning, using the article (τά) to refer to the end of the first field—which receives God's blessings.[34] The presence of the article rules out Grudem's interpretation.[35] The appositional phrase "things that belong to salvation" confirms this reading: these better things are not

---

[33] Bruce, *Hebrews*, 379.

[34] Εὐλογίας (*eulogias*, blessings) is probably an accusative plural. Μεταλαμβάνω (*metalambanō*, receive) can take an accusative or a genitive; with genitive it has the sense "take part in," "receive a share of"; with the accusative the sense is "to experience" or "receive" (L&N "experiences blessings from God"). In Heb. 12:10, when used with the genitive, the sense is quite different; this suggests the accusative should be read here. Cf. George Wesley Buchanan, ed., *To the Hebrews*, 1st ed., Anchor Bible 36 (Garden City, N.Y: Doubleday, 1972), 85; Ellingworth, *Hebrews*, 327; Louw and Nida, *Greek-English Lexicon*, 1:805.

[35] Ellingworth, *Hebrews*, 329.

those accompanying apostasy but the better blessings of salvation (the promises in v. 12).

Grudem argues, thirdly, from the present tense of ἐχόμενα (*echomena*, "that belong to") that these "better things" are present and not future experiences. There are at least two reasons why this argument does not succeed. Despite disagreements over the details, NT scholars agree time in the Greek verb is at the very least secondary, especially in the case of non-indicatives. Thus, the present tense here indicates only that the better things are contemporary with "salvation," they are pertaining to and accompanying it. Second, salvation in Hebrews is mainly considered a future concept (e.g. 9:28); therefore the better things accompany salvation is consistent with the imagery of verses 7-8, where the field is blessed when it produces the intended crop.

Grudem's fourth argument misses the point of alternative interpretations: the author is not telling his audience they have not yet fallen away; he is confident they *will not* fall away. The exegetes that differ from Grudem rely upon the future orientation of salvation in Hebrews. We see in this verse, then, AOH's confidence that the Hebrews will persevere, despite his warnings. In the following verses he grounds this confidence in God's justice.

Verse 10-12. In verse 3, the author suggested the Hebrews will only attain maturity if God permits it; here, with "for," he grounds his confidence that the Hebrews will do so in God's justice. He is confident that God will give permission. Verse 10, then, forms an inclusio with verse 3, resolving the earlier verse's uncertainty. Looking at their past good deeds, the author is confident that God is not unjust to neglect their faith evidenced by their works, implying that God will be just to do his part in ensuring they attain maturity. AOH concludes this section with a final exhortation to eagerly move on to maturity, being earnest "to have the full assurance of hope until the end." With a reference to those who inherited the promises before, the author begins a transition back to his main argument and anticipates the so called "hall of faith" in chapter 11.

B. Conclusion

We see, then, AOH is confident his readers will press on to maturity, to which he intends to lead them in the following chapters. Our passage contains a severe warning—falling away is irreversible—coupled with great confidence grounded in God's just recognition of their faith-filled response of good works. Bringing together the threads of our exegesis, the key idea of Hebrews 6:1-12 is "to fail to move forward is to move back towards the final and fatal state of apostasy": phrased as an exhortation, "press on to maturity lest your sluggish immaturity lead you to fall away and be lost forever." This is the author's main idea, yet he does not leave the Hebrews with an overwhelming sense of doom. Without diminishing the threat he has given, he encourages them with Divine sovereignty: God will indeed permit them to press on. By juxtaposing Divine sovereignty and human responsibility, AOH places himself firmly within the compatibilist worldview shared by the rest of the NT, offering us a potential solution to the theological tension this passage, and those like it, introduce.

While the rest of the NT will not allow us to follow Arminianism here, exegesis will not allow us to go the typical Calvinist direction. Our exegesis reveals, though, a third solution, one which allows us to affirm the rest of the NT evidence without softening the hard words of the text. The problem, I contend, with Calvinists and their exegesis is they are not consistent with their own worldview: by accepting the Arminian argument that such a warning is merely "hypothetical," pointless, unless there is no guarantee of final perseverance, they fail to consider the solution compatibilism may provide to this exegetical-theological dilemma. The compatibilist view of free will allows us to hold together the genuine possibility of an action, such as believing or falling away, and the guarantee that an action will or will not be performed by a specific person in a specific situation: responsibility or freedom and determination (necessity) are compatible. Applied to our passage, then, compatibilism allows us to affirm both that true Christians are able to fall away and that God will never allow these—or any—Christians to do so. This is the point our author makes: press on, for falling away is devastating and irreversible; yet God is not unjust to neglect you.

I confess this interpretation is a reversal of previous printed support I have given Grudem's argument.[36] After careful examination of the passage, it is my judgment that the interpretation presented here better explains the

---

[36] Rutherford, J. Alexander, *Prevenient Grace: An Investigation into Arminianism*, 1st Edition (Vancouver; Teleioteti 2016), 250. This was removed from the 2nd Revised Edition (2020).

author of Hebrews' argument. For the complacent Christian, the one who is content to confess the faith but is not willing to press on to a deeper delight in and knowledge of God and his ways revealed in Scripture, Hebrews 6:1-12 offers a dire warning: press on or drift away. There is no alternative. To turn away from the faith is a decisive and permanent decision, a decision which stagnation will bring to reality. The only option is to press ever onwards towards the great promises God has given in Christ Jesus our Lord.

Volume 3:
The Gift of Seeing
A Biblical Perspective on Ontology

INTRODUCTION

The fear of the LORD is the beginning of knowledge; fools despise wisdom and instruction. – Proverbs 1:7

"All is water," the words of one of the earliest philosophers, Thales (c. 624-546 BC). They were apparently his attempt to explain what the world really is. For most of us, it perfectly captures the madness of the philosophers—those who attempt to figure out the nature of our world. Such a claim seems patently absurd. Thales proposal was creative to be sure—and knowing that over 70% percent of our world's surface is water, it even makes a tiny bit of sense—yet it failed in its simplicity to capture the magnificent variety of our experience. He was not the first to propose a crazy idea. The German Philosopher Gottfreid Leibniz (1646-1716 AD) thought the world was made up of little minds: even a rock had thoughts! Is this all philosophy offers us, thought games detached from real life?

A. What Is Ontology?

It is hard to deny that much philosophical thought has been this way, and the pursuit of philosophical knowledge has often done great harm. One area where this is particularly true is called "ontology." Ontology is sometimes used interchangeably with "metaphysics" to describe the study of *"being qua being"* (the explanation of which would require far more space than it is worth).[1] Ontology has different connotations in different spheres of thought, often relating to categorization, that is, how things should be related, and the hierarchy of these relations (think: Animal – Mammal – Human – Nicole). I have found it helpful to summarise ontology as the exploration of two immensely important questions concerning our knowledge and its relation to the world outside of ourselves. The first question is the question of *what exists*: what is it that deserves the title "being"? Are they different degrees of being or does this describe all existing things indiscriminately? We will see why this question is important later. The second question is the question of what it means for a thing to be something: what does it mean to describe James as a "human" or a certain object as "James"? In the history of philosophy, this second question has been closely related to the first. At this point, you may be rolling your eyes, but I hope that the importance of these questions will become clear as we explore them throughout this book.

B. Why Bother with Ontology?

We will address some aspects of ontology in this book because knowing what God says on several key issues concerning ontology has profound implications for the way we think about doing theology and, more broadly, the way we think about the Christian life and ministry in the Western world. This will involve both deconstruction, showing how the Bible pushes us away from certain ontological positions, and construction, showing how the Bible makes several important affirmations.

Ontology is important for us because the Christian tradition, the reflection of God's people on Scripture for the last 2000 years, is deeply intertwined with ontology. The Scriptures are clearly not a philosophy textbook, and they do not go out of their way to discuss the sorts of questions philosophers have asked. However, Christians have long believed that ontology is closely intertwined with theology, and the history of philosophy has revealed that Christian theology has exerted a profound influence on the development of the ontologies of the modern world. Through its teaching about God and his creation, the Bible cautions us from embracing many ideas prominent in the history of philosophy and makes several important positive affirmations relevant for ontology.

---

[1] This is Aristotle's description of the height of philosophical exploration, described in the book we call *Metaphysics*.

That Scripture has implications for ontology is not reason alone to study it; I do not believe that knowledge for the sake of knowledge is a worthwhile pursuit. However, because the theology we proclaim is deeply intertwined with ontology and because every facet of our culture implies an ontology, it is worth addressing ontology from God's Word to hear what God himself says about these pressing issues. As a result, we may just come to worship God for the brilliance of his creation. Moreover, we may find ourselves better equipped to think through the challenges raised against our faith. Finally, we may find ourselves thinking more biblically about the task of theology and its expression.

In the following pages we will neither answer nor even raise every issue discussed in the name of ontology. Instead, we will focus on several crucial issues to which the Bible has something to say. As we unpack each issue, it should become apparent why these issues are relevant for Christian theology and thinking Christianly in Western culture.

C. How Will We Study Ontology?

I have tried to give the reason for studying ontology, the question that remains is, how? In *The Gift of Knowing* (volume 1 in this series) I sketched some features of a Christian epistemology, or view of knowledge. In it, I argued that the Bible is our ultimate norm or standard of truth. In the following argument, the Bible and its worldview will function as our ultimate presupposition, the foundational belief upon which the rest are built. In *The Gift of Knowing* I also argued that God has revealed himself in his world and given human beings reliable minds and senses. Therefore, we will also employ reason and our experience of God's creation. Some philosophers, as we will see, have doubted that our experience can tell us anything about the real world, so we will revisit some of the ground covered in the previous book. Our study of ontology will, therefore, involve considering the world in light of the Bible using the faculties of knowledge God has given us. One last factor remains, us. Every endeavour to know is ultimately ethical, asking the question "what ought I believe about this?" For this reason, we must conduct our study with an appropriate posture of humility and submission before God. As the Covenant Lord of all who believe in him, and the Lord of all the creation, all human beings—Christians especially—are obligated to think as creatures, as those under authority. This will not be study of ontology "within the limits of reason alone," as Immanuel Kant would have it, but ontology within the bounds of God's revelation.

D. The Foundations of Ontology

The Christian study of ontology is thoughtful reflection on knowledge, the objects of knowledge, and their relationships with one another performed in submission to God.

As we will see in the following chapters, the history of ontology is deeply intertwined with humanity's quest to have exhaustive knowledge of the universe. No single human being—nor the entire species for that matter—can know every detail of the universe, so philosophers took another route to exhaustive knowledge. They tried to identify that one thing (or the many most basic things) that explained everything. If they could not know every detail, they would discover the one general idea that explained everything. They called this idea "being," and ontology has often been thought of as the study of being, the study of the ultimate nature of reality. We will see that the Bible has something to say at this most basic point of ontology, so from the start we will set out on a different path than ontology has taken for the most part.

a. The Preconditions of Ontology

From the very beginning, the Christian is confronted with the truth that there is no single category by which she can exhaustively know reality; there is no "being in general," at least in the way the philosophers understood it. "In the beginning, God created the heavens and the earth" implies, among other things, that there are two distinct modes of existence in this world.[2] There is

---

[2] Some exegetes debate whether "the earth was without form and void" (v. 2) indicates that Genesis 1 describes God merely shaping pre-existing matter. My own reading of the text agrees that "God created the heavens and earth" introduces the whole section to follow (Gen. 1:2-2:3). However, it seems that by saying "God created the heavens and the earth," the author means more than just he "shaped" or "formed" them. Moses indicates that God is the originator or cause of everything. The following verses do not bother explaining how God brought the created universe into existence; it only details how God prepared the earth for humans, his representative kings. This is supported by the fact that the creation of the invisible world—including angels—is excluded from the discussion. I conclude, therefore, that "the heavens and the earth" is a merism: it means, God created *every single thing*. Then the narrative focuses on the thing in view, the earth.

Yahweh, the self-existent Creator, and "the heavens and the earth," the dependent creation. Though we may describe both God and his creation as existing, or having "being," God's existence is remarkably different than that of his creation.

For one, the creation is a dependent or derived existence: it comes from and depends on God. God's existence, in contrast, is independent and underived (theologians call this aseity). God is necessary, in that he relies on nothing to exist and the existence of everything else relies on him; the creation is contingent, in that it only exists because God willed it to exist.[3] For this reason, "being" with reference to the Creator and the creature does not mean the same thing (it is not *univocal*). Our ontology begins with this acknowledgment: the Creator and the creature are distinct. However, contrary to the beliefs of many philosophers and theologians, the rejection of being in general in this sense does not endanger our knowledge of God. Furthermore, God's transcendence (his utter difference from us) is not transgressed by the claim that he is rightfully said "to be" as we are said "to be." These points, though brief, have tremendous implications not only for ontology but also for the way language connects with reality.

Cornelius Van Til used to illustrate the Creator-creature distinction by drawing two circles, one above the other, with lines between the two. The separation of the two circles indicates their distinction, but the lines indicate communication between the circles: God interacts with his world. Because of this distinction, a Christian ontology will abandon the search for exhaustive knowledge. Such knowledge is impossible. The question is then raised, is ontology even possible? If there is complete distinction between the Creator and the Creature, can we really penetrate to the world beyond our minds? Can we dare say anything about a totally distinct being?

---

[3] Necessary in this context means that it is impossible for God not to exist. That is, there is no conceivable world in which God is not present, for without God there is nothing—a non-world. Thus, to conceive of a *world* is to conceive of a world with God. Contingent means that we can conceive of a world where the contingent entity does not exist. It is possible to conceive of—indeed there was—a "time" when the created order did not exist, before "in the beginning."

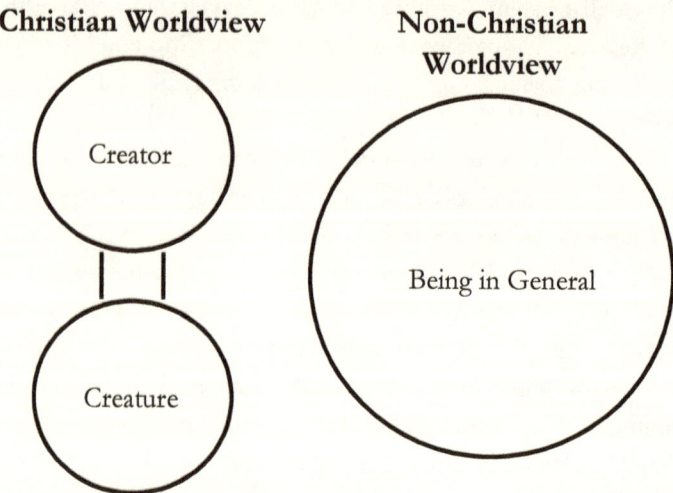

i. The Surrender of Autonomy

To these questions, the Bible gives a resounding yes—but by doing so it demands intellectual submission. That is, the Bible offers us the promise of true knowledge concerning God, our selves, and the world he has created, yet it offers them at a cost. The Bible is not a shopping centre from which we can choose the best bits and leave the rest; it is an all-or-nothing deal. If we want the answers the Bible gives us, we need to accept not only the truths we like but also the things we do not like so much.

The first thing taken from us is our pretence of autonomy. Reason is not our final authority according to the Bible; Yahweh is our final authority. He is supremely reasonable, in fact he is the source of reason itself, but his reason is above ours. That is, he has access to things we do not, so we will be stretched at times to accept things that we cannot verify by experience or logic. Indeed, we may be asked to accept things that *appear* to be contradictory.[4] If we accept God as our authority and are led to accept two apparently contradictory premises (i.e., God is three, God is one) on that ground, we can have the utmost certainty that the contradiction is only apparent, resulting from our finite understanding. Because of this, all our reasoning must proceed carefully in submission to God as he has revealed

---

[4] For more on this, see Vol. 1, *The Gift of Knowing*. From the Bible, we can surmise that no biblical teaching nor feature of reality is truly contradictory, yet it may appear so from a finite perspective.

himself, primarily in his Word but also in his world.[5]

ii. The Humility of Faith

The second thing the Bible takes from us is our pride. According to the Bible we are not capable of submitting to God on our own, not in our actions let alone our intellects (e.g., Rom 1:18-32; 8:5-8). So to do this, we need help; we need to look outside ourselves.

First, we need redemption. Our incapacity is not a problem in our being (we are not metaphysically incapable) but in our hearts. We have all fallen short of the glory of God and willingly engaged in rebellion against him (Rom 3:23, 8:5-7). In doing so, we have earned his wrath, a verdict of guilty and the resulting punishment. We have continually hardened our hearts so that we would never choose to willingly obey him. God's answer to both these problems, and so the necessary remedy for our intellectual rebellion, is redemption through Jesus Christ.

Through the life, death, and resurrection of God the Son, Yahweh has enacted a New Covenant with all who are and will be his people. Of the many promises of this Covenant, one is the enablement of our hearts: God promised to his people in the Old Testament that he would one day do a work in the hearts of his people so that they would be able to love and obey him (Deut 30:6; Isa 54:13; Jer 31:31-34). He would take their hardened hearts of stone and give them soft, fleshy, obedient hearts (Ezek 36:22-27). By God's grace, we receive this promise (John 3:1-7; John 6:35-45); we receive the regeneration of the Holy Spirit and thus the redemption of our intellect in addition to the redemption of our souls. We are equipped by the Holy Spirit for obedient worship and life before God. This is the precursor to right intellectual pursuit, and thus a necessity for our adventure in ontology.

Second, we need illumination. When we are redeemed, we are regenerated; we receive that initial heart-change that enables obedience to God. Unfortunately, this initial work does not end all our problems. We sit in a tension between already being transformed and not yet receiving the fullness of what God has promised us. We still have the capacity, even the

---

[5] On the authority and difference of these forms of revelation, see *The Gift of Knowing*.

tendency, to rebel against God and sinfully warp his Word and commandments. However, we are not without hope, for the Spirit of God not only initiates our redemption and enables faithful thinking in us, but he also continues this work.

Illumination is a term sometimes used to describe the work of the Spirit in our lives to overcome our sinful blindness and sharpen our abilities so that we would grasp and respond to the Word of God (cf. 1 Cor 2:6-16, Rom 12:1-2). We need this same work to illumine our understanding of God's words in creation. Because of the moral corruption of the human heart, our theological endeavour has these two preconditions: we need to be regenerated by Spirit and continually empowered by him to appropriately receive what God has clearly spoken.

b. The Possibility of Ontology

Early we raised two problems, the search for knowledge of everything and the knowability of God. With these preconditions in place, we can turn now to the way the Bible enables philosophical enquiry and justifies—indeed, demands—knowledge of God. For the Christian, ontology is possible, but the non-Christian finds himself stuck between a rock and a hard place. Neither empiricism nor rationalism yields any knowledge of reality.

i. The Non-Christian Dilemma

For the empiricist, bound to believe only what he experiences, certain knowledge—even probable knowledge—is impossible. That is, knowledge concerns objects, events, and their relationships; we know the features of things and how those things will respond in certain interactions. However, to know any of these things, the empiricist must know every detail of the universe. That is, an empiricist may repeatedly observe a connection between an action (e.g. hitting a pool ball) and an effect (the ball rolling), yet he cannot say from his experience that there is a necessary relationship between the action and the effect. He has no experience of necessity, so he cannot say it exists. Even more problematic, he has only a limited experience of this relationship, so he has no reasonable ground to claim that this will happen in every circumstance. He cannot claim *to know* that hitting a pool ball will result in the ball rolling. All he can say is that he has the experience that thus far, hitting a pool ball will start it rolling. Regarding the ball itself, what could he say about it? He observes a certain colour, a geometric shape, 3-dimensions, and weight. However, how can he know from his experience that this is not just a product of his mind? How does he know that there is actually a ball out there? Furthermore, given that he has reason to believe there is a ball, what can he know about this ball? He may know the above details, but he cannot know how the ball would feel in a different circumstance, how it would look in different lighting, or how it would react on a different surface. Indeed, he knows that as he moves farther away, he experiences the ball as smaller and if he gets nearer, the opposite occurs. Thus, it would seem that the size of the ball is conditioned by his mind, as is it colour—given that his colour-blind friend perceives it differently. If all he knows is his own experience of the ball, he really does not know anything about the ball at all!

He could spend his life with the ball and would not have exhaustive knowledge of it. Indeed, we may even question whether he has knowledge of the ball at all. The point is, even if an empiricist can gain knowledge of a particular thing, he cannot gain exhaustive knowledge of the universe. He cannot know from experience alone that another ball will have the same properties; he must then go on to investigate that ball fully. He must investigate every particular thing exhaustively to know everything. Such a task is impossible, so he is stuck with a very small body of knowledge, namely, his immediate experience.

The empiricist is stuck with limited experience of particulars and no knowledge of things in general (he knows a particular pool ball, but nothing about pool balls, or balls, or objects, or laws of motion). The Rationalist's attempt to exhaustively know everything results in the exact opposite situation. A rationalist will not use his senses to discern the details about a particular object but will seek to abstract from the particulars of his experience the unifying reality that lies behind it all. He moves from Fido, to pug, to dog, to animal, to living thing. The problem with "living thing" is that it is not at all helpful in understanding the particular "living thing" Fido: "living thing" tells us nothing about the features or character of this creature.

Going even further back, the Rationalist will arrive at "being," that thing which everything has in common. But what is being? If god, a dog, an amoeba, a black whole, space, dust, an imaginary flying spaghetti monster, or a cartoon on TV has "being" in some sense, what does "being" tell us? As Hegel observed, "being" is indistinguishable from "non-being": they are both empty terms! Because it must be infinitely flexible to cover every particular detail, it cannot have any details. Being itself is un-predicate-able; we cannot say anything about it. Yet, if we can say nothing about it, we cannot even say that it "is." The very postulation of a category "being" is self-contradictory, for to say anything about it is to describe it. If we cannot say anything about the thing that stands behind everything, what separates it from nothing? Imagine this "being"; if you remove every distinguishing feature of everything you know, what are you left with? You are left with nothing. Thus, the Rationalist seeks to know everything by coming up with an abstract explanation everything shares in common, yet the end result is no-thing—no knowledge at all.

ii. Biblical Ontology

The Bible brings us beyond this impasse. It does this in three ways; it qualifies the goal of ontology, it justifies the knowledge of the senses and the importance of particulars, and it gives us completely certain points of knowledge from which we can go about interpreting our world.

First, the Bible redefines the ontological task. Traditionally, ontology seeks certain knowledge of reality. Certain knowledge of reality must be exhaustive, so it seeks to come to know the essence of reality itself—being. Thus, ontology has been an end in itself. However, the Bible shows us that exhaustive knowledge of reality is impossible. The Creator-creature distinction indicates that there is no single point of knowledge ("being in general") that will give us knowledge of all things. Furthermore, we are shown in Scripture that we can have true knowledge of God but not exhaustive knowledge; even his thoughts are higher than ours (cf. Exod 33:17-23; Isa 55:8-9, Rom 11:33-36).[6] So exhaustive knowledge of the Creator is impossible.

What about the creature? The Bible teaches that there is an invisible realm beyond our experience, so a significant part of the created order is beyond our knowledge. There are spirits of all sorts, "Seraphim" and "Cherubim" (are these different or the same?), demons and angels, good spirits and bad spirits. We really have only a limited grasp of these beings and

---

[6] Theologians will often say that we can "apprehend" God, grasp him with our minds, yet we cannot "comprehend" God, know him exhaustively.

their abilities, for God has not chosen to give us much more than a glimpse. We know that they are active in our world, so our knowledge always touches upon the precipice of the unknown. However much we analyse and understand the regularities of our world, there are immensely powerful, personal beings active in the world, doing who-knows-what! Lastly, in the biblical picture of things, particular things matter, so we cannot have true knowledge without knowledge of particular things. We cannot, of course, know every particular created thing—even of the visible world—therefore exhaustive knowledge is impossible. What then is left of ontology?

For the Christian, ontology is not the search for "being in general." Ontology does not offer a way out of the difficult task of interpreting and living in light of experience. Instead, it is the exploration of the conditions of our knowledge that we might confidently engage in the task of knowing God and his world. Thus, *ontology is thoughtful reflection on knowledge, the objects of knowledge, and their relationships with one another that is performed in submission to God.* It is a fruitful endeavour because this knowledge is necessary for epistemology, knowing anything at all. It is particularly necessary for the sciences, studying the world in order to put it to use. It is also necessary for ethics, knowing how to act in and towards the world. In all these ways, it will aid us in the task of theology, applying the Bible in word and deed to our lives in the contemporary world.

Second, the Bible puts significant weight on particulars and so justifies the validity of experience for ontology. In several ways, the Bible shows us that particulars matter and validates the use of our senses to know reality. The Bible is not concerned with moving beyond particulars to a unifying idea; it places great value on particular objects and events. For example, "history" is not an abstract idea in the Bible, it is not merely the temporal flow within which the self-functions. History has a definite beginning, a definite end, and important moments that define it. That history has a goal means it is purposeful, meaningful; more importantly, the individual events of history have universal significance.[7]

---

[7] This is an important point, for in the Enlightenment, one of the most fundamental beliefs was the principle that the contingent truths of history cannot tell us anything about the necessary truths of reason. That is, historical events have no significance for knowledge and understanding reality. This is sometimes called Lessing's ditch, the claim that an uncrossable chasm separated reason from history.

We will consider this at greater length in Part 2, but consider Paul's words in 1 Corinthians 15: "And if Christ has not been raised, then our preaching is in vain and your faith is in vain" (15:14). If a particular event, the resurrection of Christ, did not happen, the hope for an end of history as we know it (the resurrection) is unfounded. The movement of history depends on this one event. Furthermore, a present state—namely, faith and hope—depends on the particular details of this event: Christ really must have died and he really must have been raised. Thus, a sort of abstract history like that proposed by Hegel (where the "resurrection" and other ideas are merely expressions of the idea of "freedom" working itself out as the world) is not valid. Particular details of the objects of these events also matter. It matters that Christ was physically present and physically resurrected. To Thomas who doubted, Jesus offered the evidence of his wounds; he said to him, "Put your finger here, and see my hands; and put out your hand, and place it in my side" (John 20:27). The reality of Jesus physical body (though resurrected) and the truth of his resurrection are here put to test by an empirical method. 1 John makes the same point:

> That which was from the beginning, which we have heard, which we have seen with our eyes, which we looked upon and have touched with our hands, concerning the word of life—the life was made manifest, and we have seen it, and testify to it and proclaim to you the eternal life, which was with the Father and was made manifest to us. (1 John 1:1-2)

See how John establishes the truth of his testimony about the Gospel of Jesus Christ and its implications: he emphasizes the physical nature of Jesus from sensory experience (cf. 1 John 4:2-3). Do not miss this: John appeals to sensory data for true knowledge of a particular object, the person Jesus Christ. He makes this appeal to uphold his teaching, his theology. In these ways, a mere sampling of the extensive testimony of Scripture, we see that biblical philosophy is interested in experience, that the senses do tell us about reality, and that particular events and objects are important. As we will see shortly, this focus on particularity without the loss of unity has immense significance. Because knowledge cannot dispense with particulars, we cannot have exhaustive knowledge of anything. However, because God, who has exhaustive knowledge of everything, has made himself and his world known, we can have true knowledge of somethings.

Third, the Bible gives us certain points of knowledge—unity and certainty—from which we can go about interpreting particular objects of our experience. If the biblical worldview is concerned with particulars, a comprehensive philosophy would be an exhaustive account of every detail of the created realm and God himself: it would be God's very mind. Unlike non-Christian ontology, knowing rooted in a Christian ontology does not search for exhaustive knowledge of everything. Instead, it is never ending growth in the knowledge of each thing: it is a way of life taken up by the individual. Ontology is, thus, not an end in itself but an invitation to wisdom, a framework to live our intellectual lives in submission to God and in the fear of him. A Christian is to interpret all experience in light of the Bible. Though we will pursue an ontology in this book, it will not be traditional "metaphysics," for we are not interested in those abstract questions such as knowing "being *qua* being." Instead, we are looking at how the Bible justifies and enables the Christian act of knowing; we are not outlining a particular individual's interpretation of reality—let alone God's exhaustive interpretation.

If experience were all there was, we would not be able to engage in ontology. However, God has not given us a world of "bare facts," or unrelated and meaningless things. Instead, he has given us a world infused with meaning, caught up in his plan for history, and revelatory of his glory and wisdom. The Bible is caught up in this dimension of knowledge, not just with things but with things *interpreted*, things brought into relation—even thought into existence (as we will see in chapter 9). Ontology is the study of particular *things*, the things that exist brought into relationship and thus interpreted. The point I want to make here is that the Bible does give us unity. The Bible not only justifies the use of our senses but also our minds. In Deuteronomy, Moses commands the people of God to love God not only with their actions and emotions but with their thinking (Deut 6:4-5). Further, Paul's writing is full of the use of logic (i.e. reasoning) and calls Christians to *think* about their faith and how they live it out (e.g. Rom 12:1-2, Col 3:1-3). The very fact that we have been given a book which is to be taught (e.g., 1 Tim 4:11-12) demonstrates that our minds are useful and thus to be used. Reading itself is a tremendous feat of reason. Psychologists and linguists in the 20th and 21st century have demonstrated the profound ability of our minds to naturally acquire competency in spoken languages. However, to read, to move from symbols on a page to understanding, is a far more complicated task, one that must be learned. Once taught, reading unlocks an untold world of understanding, but it is fundamentally a feat of reason, of our minds moving from meaningless symbols to a world of meaning through an intuited grasp of language. On these grounds, we are justified in using the tools of our minds and senses in the pursuit of knowledge, we may even find truth among the "rationalists" and "empiricists" who, despite their idolatrous use of these tools, nevertheless presumed upon their God-given reliability. We can and must use our minds and our senses, but we must do so only in submission to God.

In addition to justifying the tools of our knowledge, the Bible also validates the physical/sensible existence of the external world. It likewise teaches us about an invisible realm which must be factored into our life, not only in our study of psychology and nature (e.g., Mark 5:1-6) but also ethics (oddly enough, 1 Cor. 11:10). It teaches us to be humble about our study and keep the particulars in view, but it also teaches us that there is an overarching interpretation of reality that we must consider. God exists, he has knowledge of all things. This means, first, that we must measure our interpretation of any particular thing by his interpretation of it; we must go to the Bible.[8] Second, this means that all events, and thus the objects involved in those events, must be interpreted in light of the broad narrative of redemption and its individual details (we cannot ignore the crucifixion of Jesus, his resurrection, the re-creation to come, the original creation account, or Noah's flood). Lastly, it teaches that God is actively at work in the world, intervening miraculously and consistently upholding it at all times. The body of this volume will explore the conditions of our knowing, particularly in response to three challenges raised by the history of ontology.

This book is written for the interested—and potentially concerned—Christian, for those of us who have considered the worldviews around us and found them wanting or for those of us who simply desire to know more about the world God has created. Though we will be dealing with philosophy and philosophers, I will not assume a background in philosophy. I write to those who want to have an answer to the questions the world raises about Christianity and who desire a more biblical way of looking at the world. By the Lord's grace I hope to point you to the treasure trove that is Scripture so

---

[8] More on this point in *Gift of Knowing*.

that together we can be encouraged in our faith, be driven to worship of our heavenly Father, and be equipped to submit every thought to obey Christ (2 Cor 10:5).

Our discussion will be shaped around three significant challenges to the task of knowing raised by the history of ontology. The first is the problem of change, which we will explore in Part 1. The second is the problem of the one and the many, which we will explore in Part 2. The third is the problem of moving beyond the mind, which we will explore in Part 3. In each part, the first chapter (Chapters 1, 4, and 7 respectively) will introduce the problem by looking at several historical philosophers and their arguments. These problems build on each other, so there will be a natural progression from Part 1 to Part 3, moving from the early 1st millennium BC to the late 2nd millennium AD.

It is my earnest prayer that we would each come to see and truly believe that the fear of the Lord is the beginning of wisdom. To this end, I offer this prayer to the Lord for myself and for you, the reader,

> Father, you are the God who sees,
>   who looks on us in our weakness
>   and condescends to make yourself known.
> You have made yourself known,
>   and shaped us to know.
> Give us eyes to behold your glory,
>   hearts to submit to your ways.
> May we see with clarity the gift of your creation,
>   the intricate design of your revelatory work.
> In the name of your Son, Jesus Christ, Amen

Further Reading[9]

John Frame, *Cornelius Van Til: An Analysis of His Thought* [I-A]
John Frame, *The Doctrine of God* [B-I]
John Frame, *The Doctrine of the Knowledge of God* [B-I]
Cornelius Van Til, *A Christian Theory of Knowledge* [A]

---

[9] The following resources range from (relatively) easy to quite difficult in their readability, I mark the easier reads with a B, those a bit more difficult with an I, and the most difficult with A. I adduce difficulty on the basis of both the depth of content, knowledge presupposed by the author, and the clarity of the writing. An asterisk before a book indicates that it is especially recommended.

—Part 1—
The Problem of Change and Identity

ALL IS FLUX

For God knows that when you eat of it your eyes will be opened, and you will be like God, knowing good and evil. – Genesis 3:5

For his invisible attributes, namely, his eternal power and divine nature, have been clearly perceived, ever since the creation of the world, in the things that have been made. So they are without excuse. For although they knew God, they did not honor him as God or give thanks to him, but they became futile in their thinking, and their foolish hearts were darkened. Claiming to be wise, they became fools, and exchanged the glory of the immortal God for images resembling mortal man and birds and animals and creeping things. – Romans 1:20-23

The Bible begins with God: "In the beginning, God created…." Moses asserts three realities here: first, God existed at the beginning, and therefore was not part of that which began. Second, the God who is not part of the creation acted to bring about the creation. Third, besides him there is a creation that had a beginning at the hands of God. These realities have far reaching ontological implications. Genesis 1:1 separates the Creator from creature and identifies God as independent and personal, as an agent of creation. It also identifies the creation as a dependent and finite existence; it had a beginning.

But shortly after creation, this foundational distinction was blurred by

God's creatures: the Fall happened. The Fall is profoundly ethical—a rebellion against God—and epistemological—humans making themselves the ultimate standard of truth. It is also significant for ontology. Not only do human beings think they have the authority to judge right and wrong and true and false independently of God, but they also blur the distinction between God and his creatures.

This is, of course, the lie of the serpent: if you eat, you will be like God. At the heart of the rebellion in the garden was the claim that there was something human beings could do to become like God. Now, likeness unto God is not impossible in itself: humans were created in his image; they are fitting representations of him. However, in this, they remain dependent beings, receiving this likeness as a gift. In the fall, Adam and Eve believed the lie that they could break through their dependence and exalt themselves to equality with God. In doing so, they followed the foolish pride of Satan, the original rebel, who was doomed from the start by thinking he could somehow exalt himself above the heavens and be like God. His temptation to Eve, "when you eat of it, your eyes will be opened, and you will be like God, knowing good and evil," is an invitation to join in his own rebellious attempt to exalt himself to God's place.

The whole human predicament can be interpreted in light of this metaphysical rebellion: the creature attempts in futility to exalt itself to the place of the Creator. This is immediately evident in Adam and Eve's descendants, who begin to imitate God creative activity for their own sake (Gen 4:1-6:7). This is likewise clear early in the book of Genesis, before and after the flood. After God wipes out the sinful human race, sparing only eight human lives from his judgment (7:1-7:19), Noah's descendants immediately resume the sinful project of pre-flood humanity and build a tower. "Come," they called, "let us build ourselves a city and a tower with its top in the heavens, and let us make a name for ourselves" (11:4). With the tower of Babel, creatures once again attempted to exalt themselves to the place of the creator.

According to Romans 1, this describes the human predicament: every human being has wilfully dismissed God's existence and exalted the creature to his place (20-23). Paul describes it as futility and foolishness (21): knowing full well that God existed, humans have sought to interpret and define their world apart from him. Early in human history, even today, this took the form of idolatry. Idolatry exalts an object of the created order—often a human creation—to the place of God, attributing to a lifeless object the praise and glory due to God. Habakkuk captures in his poetry the foolishness of this endeavour:

> What benefit is an idol,
> > that its maker would hew it,
> > a cast image and a teacher of lies,
> for the maker trusts what he has made,
> > enough to craft speechless idols.
> Woe to him who says to wood, "wake up!"
> > "Awake!" to a dumb stone.
> Is it able to teach?
> > Behold, it is overlaid with gold and silver,
> > but there is no breath at all in it. (Hab 2:18-19)

In the 21st century, on this side of the "Enlightenment," we tend to look upon such idol worship with a sneer, wholeheartedly agreeing with Habakkuk's indictment. Yet are we so different? Paul says that all humans have ignored the existence of the true God and exalted the creature in his place. Nowhere is this more evident than philosophy. Philosophers eschew the humility of the idol worshiper and, divulging themselves of external gods, make themselves to be god.

As the Triune Creator of the Bible, Yahweh, is the Sovereign Lord and Judge, wielding authority and control over his created world, so humans once attributed these attributes to idols. The gods represented by idols were said to control the harvest and give humanity instruction, to have authority over them and exert control. The modern person has not jettisoned the idea of an authoritative and controlling being. They have only begun to consider themselves that being. The German philosopher Ludwig Feuerbach (AD 1804-1872) may have put it most bluntly when he wrote, "the being of man is alone the real being of God,—man is the real God."[1] Feuerbach argues that "God" is nothing more than the idealized human race: humanity considers the perfections of humanity and projects this ideal into a new being

---

[1] Ludwig Feuerbach, *The Essence of Christianity*, trans. George Eliot (Amherst, New York: Prometheus Books, 2010), 230.

altogether. For Feuerbach and the philosophers who followed him, "God" is the ultimate idol, a human creation. Humanity itself is the true god; it is the ultimate standard of right and wrong and the only being that controls this world.

Though Feuerbach may have been the bluntest in this regard, the whole history of ontology attests this same idolatry. From the pre-Socratic philosophers (c. 7th – 6th cent BC) to Richard Dawkins, philosophers have continually attempted to explain the world without reference to God and have, in doing so, made themselves to be gods. The key issues in ontology that we will address arose in this way, putting humanity in the place of God. The first issue is the problem of change. The problem is not change itself (though this is difficult enough to explain), but the relationship between change and knowledge: if everything changes, how can we know anything at all? We will trace this problem across early Western philosophy before summarising it at the end of this chapter. In the following chapter, we will consider change as a positive aspect of God's creation. In Chapter 3, we will argue that we can embrace change without abandoning knowledge.

A. Pre-Modernity – The World of Reason

Though not much remains of the early philosophical writings, what we know is that philosophy began as a rebellion against Greek religion. Greek polytheism attempted to explain the events of nature—good and bad harvests, storms and disasters—and the twists of fate, such as a loss in battle, with reference to a pantheon of gods. There were gods of nature and human institutions (such as war and wisdom). Human worship could manipulate these gods to gain an advantage, and a failure to do the necessary acts would result in physical consequences. The religious milieu in which Western philosophy was born was much like the religious world from which Yahweh called forth his chosen people. As our God called his people to cast off idols for the true worship of Yahweh, the philosophers called the people to cast off the gods in exchange for the world of human understanding. Thus, they set off in the opposite direction from the one on which Yahweh was leading his people. From the city of Miletus, the first Greek philosophers rebelled against this arbitrary system of religion, this system that attributed change and stability in nature and society to powerful "gods." In its place, they attempted to explain the world through reason alone. Greek society had already rejected the living God for idols; now the philosophers rejected the idols for themselves.

a. *The Pre-Socratics*

If we were to try to explain the world today, we would probably start with our senses, analysing what we perceive and trying to arrive at valid conclusions. This was not the Pre-Socratic philosophers' approach; their words are, as John Frame puts it, "the language of a man sitting in an armchair, dogmatically asserting what the whole universe must be like."[2] They did not go out into the world; they drilled down into their minds. They asked themselves what best explained their experience.

Some of the earliest thinkers tried to narrow the world down to one substance or ultimate material that unified all experience—maybe water or fire. Aristotle identified their focus as the "material cause" of change, the single thing that remained consistent across all change—whether, water, air, fire, or something else. Others focused on the changing nature of the world. That is, they noticed that things appear to change: water moves downstream, furniture wears out, and trees grow. Yet this change was problematic. If the water in a stream is always moving or changing, how can the Euphrates be the same river one moment and then the next. The water, the most prominent feature of the Euphrates, is no longer the same after a moment passes; the stream bed is constantly changing as water flows through it; even the Euphrates' location changes over time. If the identity of the Euphrates is its qualities, then it constantly being replaced with a new entity: its water, soil, and even location is changing every moment. Similarly, its colour will change given the changing light and the contents of its water. The life it sustains may change suddenly given the influx of pollutants, and its temperature will constantly be in flux. It would appear that if something's identity lies in the qualities it possesses, "No man ever steps in the same river twice."[3] That is, at each moment a new stream exists, with unique qualities different from that of the prior moment. Consider the Theseus paradox. Imagine a ship that is in service for an exceptionally long time, let's call it the Theseus. As the ship is damaged in war and over its long years of service, it will need continual

---

[2] Frame, *A History*, 53.

[3] This quote is attributed to Heraclitus by Plato in his dialogue *Cratylus* (402a); it represents his thought, though it may not be his original words.

maintenance. This maintenance may be very gradual, but timber by timber, we can imagine that the entire ship is refurbished. If not a single piece of the original Theseus remains, how can it be said to be the same ship that was first christened?

If things are constantly changing, how can there be any consistency to the world?[4] How can we really know what the world is? If every feature of the Euphrates has changed in the last 20 years, how is it still the Euphrates? If every cell in a human body has died over the course of someone's life, how is it the same person? The early Greek philosophers had two answers to this problem of change: either the world is wholly changing or wholly unchanging. They were what we would call "monists," they believed that the whole world was ultimately one substance (maybe water, or matter—whatever that is). Therefore, as monists, they sought to explain everything by one principle: this one substance was either always changing or never changing at all.

i. Heraclitus

One the one hand, there was Heraclitus of Ephesus (535-475 BC). Heraclitus taught that change was the ultimate nature of reality. He claimed that everything changes, yet this claim would eradicate reason: if everything changed, a person could not draw stable conclusions about anything.[5] For someone committed to reason like Heraclitus, this is an unacceptable conclusion. So he introduced another idea, a principle that he thought brought stability to the world. However, on close examination, his principle did not fix his problem. He suggested that all changes, so one must ask: does the principle of stability change?[6] If it does, it cannot provide the stability

---

[4] If we witness such change on the level of our observations, how much more change is going on where we cannot perceive it?

[5] If A equals B one day and A does not equal B the next, any possible conclusion could be drawn. More practically, if a house is a house one day and a horse the next, how can someone know the house? If a river is no longer the same river when you return to it, how can you possess knowledge of it?

[6] A few generations ago, much was made of the fact that Heraclitus and later Greek thinkers called this principle, ὁ λόγος (the logos). Some exegetes tried to argue that this idea of "the logos" as the ultimate principle of order in the universe stands behind the use of ὁ λόγος ("the Word") in the prologue of John's gospel. However, in context, there is no sense of this impersonal philosophical idea; instead, John

necessary for knowledge. If it does not change, then "everything changes" cannot be true; it does not explain the entire world. Furthermore, if the principle of stability does not change, how can we know that everything else is, in fact, changing? Heraclitus was struggling to explain how stability—the necessary condition of reason—and change—the way the world appears—could coexist. Reason led him to conclude that change was the fundamental nature of reality, yet this ruled out reason in the first place.

ii. Parmenides

Adopting the exact opposite approach was Parmenides (510-440 BC) and his (slightly) more famous pupil Zeno (490-430 BC). Parmenides argued that change was an illusion, that the real world is unchanging. Change, he reasoned, required something to move from being (e.g. "green") to nonbeing ("non-green"). Because non-being is a contradiction, reasoned Parmenides, change must be an illusion. "How is 'non-being' a contradiction?" you may be asking. Non-being does not exist by definition (it does not have *being*). However, the moment one employs the term to say anything, its existence is asserted. To say something that was once green is now red is tantamount to saying that "it *is* non-green" (or so thought many early Philosophers). "Is" is a predicate of existence; in Greek, "being" refers to that term. Thus, a sentence that involves both "is" and "non-green" asserts of the latter the very existence its meaning denies.

Parmenides' pupil Zeno is known for putting forth perplexing parables to prove that change is an illusion. One of his most famous asks us to consider a race between a turtle and a hare. "If we give the turtle a slight head start," he would ask us, "who would win the race?" At first, we would think that the head start makes no difference; the hare would win! "Ah-ha," Zeno would respond, "but that is impossible! You see, for the hare to catch the turtle, would it not first have to halve the difference between itself and the turtle? Would it then not also have to halve that distance? Again, would not that distance have to be halved?" That is, there would be an infinite number of steps the hare would have to take to cross the distance between itself and

---

identifies the speech of God by which he created the world as Jesus. John explicitly links his prologue to the Genesis account with his introduction, "in the beginning" (John 1:1, Gen 1:1), and goes on to draw out the significance of "the Word" as the one through whom and by whom the creation was created (John 1:3, 10).

the turtle, thus it would never reach the turtle.[7] Now, this is ridiculous: of course the hare would win! Yet, if our experience (a hare winning) contradicts reason, it must be illusory. Zeno's parable was intended to show that all change involves such a ridiculous scenario, thus it must be illusory.

To explain the world, Parmenides argued by reason that changelessness or stability was the true nature of the world. However, in doing so, he not only invalidated all his experiences but also ruled out the possibility of reason. Though truth and the laws of reason are stable, reasoning itself (at least for human beings) is a temporal process: we think one thought after another. In a sense, knowing is change. When we reason, we move from not-knowing to knowing, from some knowledge to more knowledge. If all is unchanging, then the learning process cannot happen. A person either knows or does not know; they cannot come to know. Therefore, all acquired knowledge requires both change and changelessness: an unchanging standard by which something may be true and the reasoning process.

These early philosophers illustrate a key struggle in ontology, to balance change and unchangingness (or stability). Throughout Western philosophy, there is tension between change and stability. Some philosophers argue that reality is wholly changing or wholly stable, yet the most sophisticated approaches have sought to balance both change and stability. Doing so is a crucial problem in ontology.

B. Summary of the Problem

In the history of philosophy, many treatises have been written on the causes and conditions of change, but this is not our interest here. Instead, the problems raised by the Pre-Socratic philosophers that interest us are the problem of change and identity, namely, how can something remain what it is through extensive change. We illustrated the problem with the picture of a river that is ever-changing or a ship that gradually has every part replaced. If every quality of the things we experience can change, we must deny that such

---

[7] This presupposes that it is impossible to finish an infinite number of events: from whatever point you begin, an infinite number of steps remains between you and the completion of the infinite set—an infinite set being the infinite distance, or other variable, considered as a whole. But is this necessarily true? Is there no case in which an infinite number of steps could be crossed?

qualities are the ground for identity (something being *this* thing) or deny the continuation of identity altogether (assert that I, James, am not the person who began writing this sentence). If we refuse to deny identity altogether, we are left searching for another ground of identity. For most of the Western Philosophical tradition, this ground was sought in the "form" or universal. That is, though the qualities that distinguish me from you change, my "humanness" remains throughout my life. "Humanness" is itself unchanging. Perhaps, therefore, identity lays not in what makes things unique, what distinguishes James from Marty, but in that which unites them, the form.

If we follow this line of thought, a correlated vision of knowledge emerges. That is, if what makes me "James" is ever shifting, it is not really a worthy object of knowledge. What you knew one day is no longer true nor useful the next. Instead, what is truly important to know is that unchanging core that defines me, in my case, "humanness" (for Fido, "dogness"). Moreover, the possibility of *knowing* the qualities that characterize me is called into question. If by "knowledge" we mean to know something about something, and if such knowledge may be true or false, the shear changeability of my qualities calls knowledge into question. That is, to know the feel of a specific part of the Euphrates at 5:30 PM on Sunday the 7th of March, 2021 says nothing about the feel of river at any other point or at any other time. Thus, I do not know something about the "Euphrates," instead, I know something about Point A of the Euphrates at 5:30 PM, 7 Mar 2021. This is brutally specific knowledge that really tells me nothing at all. Moreover, if truth is defined—as it historically has been—as correspondence between a proposition (a statement of belief) and reality, this statement cannot be said to be true. That is, there is no correspondence at his moment because "Point A of the Euphrates at 5:30 PM, 7 Mar 2021" no longer exists at 12:59 PM, 8 Mar 2021. Though it may have been true the moment I thought it, it is no longer verifiable, for the original correspondence ceased to exist the moment after the experience was registered. It would seem, therefore, that any knowledge of particular things, namely, of the distinguishing and particular qualities of each thing, is fleeting. What I know or do not know is changing each moment and the next. Because of such problems, many philosophers in the history of Western thought have chosen to make "universal" or unchanging truths the real objects of knowledge. For Plato, the true objects of knowledge were the eternal Forms, which we will consider in Part 2. Aristotle defined these forms in a very different way, yet they were likewise the true objects of philosophical knowledge. Aristotle did not argue this; instead, he asserted that what matters most when we know something is the "what it is."[8] Accidents—variable qualities such as colour, location, dimension, number, etc.—are "obviously" not objects of "science," "for all science is either of that which is always or of that which is for the most part. For how else is one to learn or teach another?"[9] Without much argument, he assumes that the contingent, what may not have been, has no universal significance or relevance for "knowledge."[10] The history of Christian theology has been performed as a "science" in this sense, pursuing the universal truths of reason. One recent theologian defined the knowledge pursued by Christian theology as "eternal and necessary truths."[11] This set of problems, the continuity of identity and the possibility of knowledge despite change, will be the topic of the following two chapters. First, in Chapter 2, we will see that the Bible does not have such a negative view of change; change does not endanger the possibility of identity or knowledge. In that chapter, we will merely outline the facts of the matter, that change does happen and this ought not be a problem. Second, in Chapter 3, we will then seek to show how this can be, how we might resolve the problems of identity and knowledge given God's revelation in the Bible.

---

[8] Cf. *Metaphysics* Book Z (7), ch. VI.

[9] Cf. *Metaphysics* Book E (6), ch. II.

[10] "it is opinion that deals with that which can be otherwise than as it is." Metaphysics Z ch. XV, cf. E ch. I-II, Z ch. I.

[11] John Webster, "What Makes Theology Theological?," in *God Without Measure: Working Papers in Christian Theology*, vol. I, T&T Clark Theology (London ; New York: Bloomsbury T&T Clark, 2016), 221.

Further Reading

Gordon Clark, *Thales to Dewey:* [I-A]
*John Frame, *A History of Western Philosophy and Theology* [B-I]
John Frame, *Cornelius Van Til: An Analysis of His Thought* [I]
Ronald Nash, *Life's ultimate Questions* [B]

HISTORY: EMBRACING CHANGE

All flesh is like grass
 and all its glory like the flower of grass.
The grass withers,
 and the flower falls,
 but the word of the Lord remains forever.
– 1 Peter 1:24

And we all, with unveiled face, beholding the glory of the Lord, are being transformed into the same image from one degree of glory to another. For this comes from the Lord who is the Spirit. – 2 Corinthians 3:18

In Chapter 1, we saw that change created a world of problems for the early philosophers. To simplify things, we can say that they were faced with three possible responses to the problem of change. First, they could deny that change happened, in doing so, they would reject experience but exalt reason. This was the approach of Parmenides and Zeno. Second, they could deny that knowledge was possible, rejecting reason, and deny the continuity of identity through time. This was an approach taken only by the most extreme sceptics. Third, they could find a way to maintain change alongside of stability, often exalting the latter at the expense of the former. In philosophy, the changing world was treated as a lesser object of knowledge (if it was knowable at all). However, the Bible would lead us in a different direction. In this chapter, we will see that instead of rejecting either change or stability or holding the two in an uneasy tension that favours the latter, the Bible would have us recognize the significance of the changing the world. The stability necessary for knowledge is not found apart from or in tension with change but is complementary to it: together they provide a holistic view of knowledge and the world. In this chapter, we will focus on change and its importance. In the following chapter, we will consider stability.

Let us start with the most basic of truths: the Bible affirms change. There was once a time when the creation was not, but "in the Beginning," God created it. However, God did not create it in an instant; he established it over the course of six days, with a seventh day rest. Even then, God did not complete his work: he commissioned humanity to continue his work of creating an earthly kingdom for his glory. Adam and Eve were entrusted with the task of populating God's creation and with bringing it under their rule, which represented his ultimate rule (Gen 1:26-30). Change is rooted not only in God's own activity but in the very nature of his creation. Moreover, God underwent a certain form of change in the process; he went from contemplating creation to achieving it, acting in a way he had yet to do. This was not the first movement God would undertake; he then entered his creation, enjoyed relationship with his creature, only to curse them for their disobedience. Later, he would promise himself to them in covenant. Then, when they broke that covenant, he descended as a man, "emptying himself" to become like his creatures to die in their place (Phil 2:5-11). Humans likewise change. Adam and Eve would have grown in their knowledge of God, each other, and his world if they had faithfully engaged in their God-given task. Instead, they grew in knowledge of each other and the world but became estranged from God. They were also cursed, along with the creation, with a sort of corrupting change: they would now die, have their bodies wither away and experience pain. In these ways, the Bible affirms *the experience of change*. We will consider in Part 3 how experience relates to the external world, but for the moment it should suffice to affirm that God and humans change in their experience and that this is hardly a bad thing. Indeed, God wired change into the very DNA of his creation: it was designed to be developed, to grow. Moreover, this experience is not illusory. God grants experience an important epistemic status. In the early narratives of the Bible, we are not given any hint that the world of experience, with all its flux, is a bad or untrustworthy thing. This is affirmed as the story of God's world unfolds. When Christ becomes incarnate, he is experienced as the very revelation of God (e.g. John 14:8). It is not reason through which God is most clearly shown, but through the Cross: it is a single moment of the most vivid change—from glory to shame, life to death—that God is most clearly revealed (1 Cor 1:18-2:13; 15:1-11). When Jesus is raised, he does not offer philosophical proofs of his resurrection but his gouged side and pierced hands (John 20:24-29). As John reflects on his experience with Jesus, he recounts what he "has seen, and heard, and touched" (1 John 1:1-4). Sensual experience, taste, sight, touch, smell, and hearing are integral to the Christian experience of fellowship, ministry, and life together, both in communion with Christ and the saints. The Bible thus affirms experience, and experience is in its very essence change.

A. History: The Medium of Change

The medium of change is "history," the unfolding of events. The Bible is profoundly event-centred; it is not interested in the abstract truths of reason but the contingent truths of history. That it is, it does not offer abstract explanation for why things happen, neither impersonal and unchanging laws nor abstract necessities. Consider the creation; there is no necessity in the seven days: this is pure contingency, a choice God made. He did not have to do the work in a series of moments rather than an instant, let alone 6 days. He did not have to create humans after the animals, nor a formless mass from which he would partition out the land and waters. The Bible gives no abstract reason why Christ became a man, such that this is the inevitable climax of creation. Instead, Christ's incarnation is presented as wholly determined and wholly contingent. That is, God's purpose in creation was to make known his glory through the demonstration of his mercy on the cross (e.g. Rom 9:22-24).[1] There was nothing accidental about the incarnation, crucifixion, resurrection, and exaltation (Acts 2:23-24, 3:18, 4:27-28). However, these events are themselves dependent on contingencies. Redemption was necessary because Adam chose to neglect his God given commission, letting Satan tempt Eve who in turn offered the fruit to Adam. The offering of God's own life was necessary because he chose to make a promise to Abraham, that God would take upon himself his people's covenant failure (Genesis 15:7-21). Jesus' death occurred at the hands of his own people, who chose to reject their shepherd and receive a criminal in his place. It was not

---

[1] Cf. J. Alexander Rutherford, *Revelation, Retribution, and Reminder: A Biblical Exposition of the Doctrine of Hell* (Airdrie, AB: Teleioteti, 2021).

necessary for them to nail him to a cross, but they did so, and in doing so fulfilled centuries of prophecy. Jesus' life consisted of hundreds of moments where he spoke, healed, and in doing so revealed his own glory and that of his Father. This is the grammar of Scripture: history.

History is the medium through which God has intercourse with his creation, covenanting, punishing, and rejoicing alongside of them. History is the medium through which God has made himself known. Whether in thunder and darkness, fire and smoke, a burning bush, a triad of men in front of a tent, or in the incarnation of his son, God has chosen to reveal his glory, his multifaceted character, and his enduring purpose through the medium of change. Change is, therefore, not something to be avoided. Events, because they are fleeting—here one moment and gone the next—are not to be shunned. Nor are individuals, because they change and pass away, to be ignored. Instead, individuals as the agents in events, which are the grammar of God's self-revelation, are the most important objects of knowledge. Knowing God in Scripture is knowing the agent (the person) who creates and destroys, who humbles and exalts. Knowing God means knowing the one who came in mercy and grace and who will return in judgment. Not only is the knowledge of God grounded in the individuality of history, but the community constituted by God's grace and love is radically individual.

B. Redemption: The Mode of Change

If history describes the medium of change, *redemption* describes its mode. That is, redemption is the eb and flow of history, the instrument by which the world is created and re-created and by which individuals are formed or destroyed. *Redemption* is not itself the goal of change but the means by which that goal is accomplished. Redemption describes what God is doing and what all other agents in the creation are doing in relationship to him.

When God created the heavens and earth, his commission to humanity was to build his kingdom. However, when humanity rebelled, a new reality emerged. No longer was the creation on a simple trajectory of unimpeded progress. Instead, two kingdoms were now at war. Those whom God had commissioned to create for his glory were now creating for their own glory. To build his kingdom, God would first need to redeem some of those who had fallen; indeed, kingdom building would now be defined in terms of redemption, the work of all of God's people to beckon those lost in darkness into the light and to then strengthen them in fellowship with God and one another. Thus, coming to know God, the expansion of God's kingdom, and the end of rebellion would be cast in terms of *redemption*, in terms of God's act to bring the lost to the light and to dispel the darkness. It is important to observe that the Fall and its corresponding redemption do not create change; instead, they dictate what sort of change must now occur. To attain glory—the fullness of God revealed and the perfection of his people—there must now be war and salvation. Redemption entails that change will not be from knowing to greater knowing alone, but also the changing of allegiance and the change from sinner to saint. Furthermore, God's people would always have acted towards one another and the creation, but now these actions are defined by the realities of Fall and redemption. They are acts not of neutral development but of healing and restoration.

The agents of redemption are not logical propositions or necessities but individuals. All changes involved in redemption are those wrought by and upon individuals. God is saving individuals to be a people for himself from the mass of individuals who are in rebellion against him. These individuals are not the faceless masses but certain persons with a unique contribution in God's redemptive purposes. Not all are hands or eyes, but each member has their own role to play in Christ's body so that his purpose in redemption will accomplished (cf. 1 Cor 12:1-31; Eph 4:1-14; Rom 12:1-8). Not only is change a necessary component of history and redemption, but the end of change is not itself changeless.

C. Glory: The End of Change

The end or goal of the change God has wired into creation is God's glory radiated among his people and a perfected creation. This is the end for which God has made the world and towards which redemption working across history will achieve. Change is not itself incidental to this end; it is change itself that accomplishes this goal. That is, if God forewent the complexities of history and simply created a perfected world, something would be missing, namely, the full revelation of his glory. The events and contingencies of history are the very means by which glory will be achieved. Far from being a problem, as the Greeks presumed, change is the meaning of the creation. It is through the give and take of human-divine relationships that God's glory is fully revealed. "What if," asks Paul, "desiring to show his wrath and to make known his power, has endured with much patience vessels of wrath prepared for destruction, in order to make known the riches of his glory for vessels of mercy, which he has prepared beforehand for glory" (Romans 9:22-23). Why did the fall happen? Because only through the destruction poured out on sin would "the riches of his glory" be revealed. Why has sin continued for millennia? That at the end of patience his "glory" would be revealed. I argue elsewhere that this passage points us back to the Cross, again connecting the contingencies of the crucifixion with the fundamental goal of the creation, the glory of God.[2] Or consider the book of Ezekiel, where the consistent refrain after every revelation of God's past and future actions is that "they may know that I am YHWH" (e.g. Ezek 6:10). So change is inextricably connected with the purpose of creation; the revelation of the glory of Yahweh, our God.

But will change cease when the creation is perfected? Once again, the answer would seem to be "no." The Bible offers no vision of perfection bereft of relationship, the intercourse of persons that defines history and which implies continual change. There may no longer be death and decay, significant forms of change that are characteristically negative. However, water will still surely flow, food will be eaten, vegetation will be consumed, experience will develop, and even knowledge will increase. We are not given an extensive vision of the New Heavens and the New Earth in Scripture, but we are shown enough to affirm continuity between this world and that. The characteristic nature of the future is not a lack of change but a lack of sin and its consequences, death and decay. The New Heavens and the New Earth are presented as the culmination of all that the earthly church pointed to, communion with God and man in the pursuit of his glory amid his creation.

D. Embracing Change

This is the first answer the Bible gives to the ontological problem of change. On the one hand, it affirms the reality of change with a resounding "amen!" Moreover, it does not reluctantly admit change despite its negative entailments; change is presented as fundamentally good, true, and beautiful. Change is what the creation is all about. Changes in knowledge, ability, experience, appearance, location, colour, quantity, and time are all inextricably connected with what it means to be human and what it means

---

[2] See my book *Revelation, Retribution, and Reminder* (Airdrie, AB; Teleioteti 2021)

for the creation to be all that it is. Change is something not only given to humanity but embraced by God in his communion with his people. Change is thus not a bad thing (a movement from being to non-being) or evidence of deficiency. Instead, change is a positive development in the communion of persons that develops what is already present, not filling in a deficiency but radiating excellence. The biblical view of change is not imperfection but perfection itself: perfection is the making known and exchanging the fullness of God's character shared with his people. However, if we affirm change in these various ways, must we abandon continuity of identity and the possibility of knowledge? Does everything merge into one indistinguishable mass of every moving thing which never experiences loss or addition?

Impassibility and the First Cause

Our argument thus far raises a significant issue in terms of classical Christian theology, which we will briefly address here. My goal with this book and all the books in this series is to argue by painting a portrait that is clearly dependent on God as revealed in Scripture, coherent with that revelation, and coherent with the world we experience. I intentionally do not engage with classic philosophy and theology at every point, for I think doing so is a futile endeavour that involves adopting the very presuppositions I am arguing are the problem. However, the issue of impassibility and its connection to Aristotle's causality argument is worth addressing.

A key pillar of so-called "Classical Theism" is the claim that God does not experience any change, including the sorts of changes I have attributed to him thus far in this chapter. There has been much written on the matter in recent literature, for and against the doctrines of immutability (God does not change), impassibility (God does not change emotionally), or simplicity (God is unmoved and unmoving, pure actuality with no parts). Though these doctrines capture some aspects of the biblical teaching—namely, that God is faithful and consistent, that he is not caught off guard or ever frustrated in his purposes, and that God is not dependent on a reality above or behind him—these doctrines are heavily reliant on the philosophical position we are criticising. That is, they presuppose that change is a bad thing or an imperfection. Because they assume with the early philosophers that change is negative, they can argue that God cannot change if he is perfect. We have already seen that the Bible never suggests that change is a bad thing. Several times the Bible affirms that God is unchanging in some sense (e.g. James 1:17), but it does so without ever denying God's actions in history or his "passions" (however we wish to qualify these). We will see in the next chapter that stability is an integral part of creation and central to who God is, so there is a very real sense that God is unchanging. He is unchangingly dependable, faithful, and consistent in his character. We can be sure that who he has revealed himself to be once is who he is today. He does not decay, grow weak, become feeble, or lose control; he is perfect yesterday, today, and forever. However, once we have jettisoned the assumption that all change is bad, none of these affirmations requires us to say that God does not change at all. God shows mercy, relenting from judgment he would otherwise have brought upon sinful beings. God responds with wrath towards sin. God created, revealed himself repeatedly throughout the creation, and became incarnate. Though God knows all things and is never learning new things, participation with the creation implies a sort of change in knowledge. God knew perfectly well that his Son would be crucified at a specific time on a particular day by specific creatures in a particular way, yet when the crucifixion happened, his perfect foreknowledge (this would happen) became perfect knowledge (this did happen). Such modal change is indeed change, but it does not imply imperfection.

Among the many objections raised against the claim that God changes, the most significant is perhaps the claim that God is pure actuality with the related first-cause argument. This argument dates to Aristotle but was most clearly articulated in Christian theology by Thomas Aquinas. On the one hand, it is claimed that for God to be perfect he must be pure actuality. In Aristotelian metaphysics, everything is a combination of potentiality (the potential to be something or have a certain property) and actuality, the reality of being something or having some quality. An acorn is potentially a tree; a green table is potentially a blue table; and a hot cup of coffee is potentially a cold cup of coffee. All change involves the move from potentiality to actuality. Potentiality is a deficiency or imperfection for Aristotle, for actuality is what all things move towards, potentiality being the possibilities of that thing being perfect. Accidental potentiality, such as colour, location, or temperature is also present in a thing: if a table could be green, then becoming green leaves open the potentiality that it could be red. Because accidents always imply potentiality, a perfect thing must have none. This leaves only the potential for substantial change, such as from an acorn to a tree. However, if a thing is moving towards its goal—if it still has unrealised potential—it is imperfect. God, therefore, as the most perfect being, must be completely changeless; it (for Aristotle's god is impersonal) must be pure actuality. Moreover, argued Aristotle and Aquinas, the created order requires a purely actual being to explain it. God cannot cause the world to come into existence directly, for he is unmoving (he cannot change in properties such moving from "potentially creating" to "having created"), but he can be the supreme end of all creation, that to which all things move (the telos or goal of creation). There must be, it is argued, an uncaused cause that stands behind all movement from potentiality to actuality.

The first thing to observe about this argument is that none of its claims are derived from the Bible. Therefore, if we have good biblical reason to believe God changes, then we are justified in dismissing the argument; we have seen that we do. But let's think about it further. Is change always from a negative state ("potentiality") to a positive state ("actuality")? It is not clear that this is the case. That my marriage will be seven years long instead of six years next year does not imply any qualitative difference (a negative-to-positive relationship) between these two lengths. The movement from "knowing it will happen" to "knowing it happened" likewise involves no negative-positive relationship. Moving from calm to righteous anger is only a negative movement if we presuppose that "calm" is better than "anger," yet this begs the question; we must first know that changelessness ("calm") is better to make such a claim. The Bible presents both calm and anger as perfect expression of God's glorious character: the change from calm to anger demonstrates that God's wrath is not irrational but a righteous response.

Second, it is not evident that all change requires an external cause, so it is not self-evident that the first cause necessary to explain physical change and the world's existence at any moment must be unmoving. Moreover, it is not clear that all forms of causation would violate God's aseity, or independence from creation—that he must by necessity be unmoved. In the first case, Aristotle, Aquinas, and many others have assumed that all change has a similar pattern. That is, they have assumed that physical change (from hot to cold) and what we would today call psychological change (from one state of knowledge to another) can be mapped onto the same explanatory schema. They do not argue for this assumption, and there is no good reason to accept it. For example, I believe that all human decisions have a cause. However, the cause of human decisions is not a cause in the same sense that one billiard ball causes another to move. In the case of a human decision, it is arguable that the causality involved is both internal and external. On the one hand, the decision is caused by a crisis, a moment that requires a decision. However, by definition, a crisis does not determine which decision is made only that a decision is made. The internal cause that leads someone to make one decision and not another is not analogous to billiard balls. Essentially, the internal cause is character, the collected habits and dispositions that characterise the self and its embodied expression. Already, it is clear that all change cannot be explained in the same way, so the necessity of an ultimate first cause for the physical universe that does not have its own cause does not immediately mean that God is unmoving, as Aristotle would have it, for God may experience other sorts of change with purely internal causation. Now, as Hume argued (see *Dialogues on Natural Religion*), we need to be careful in applying our experience of causality to God. However, biblical revelation invites us to make a more significant comparison between humanity and God than Hume allowed. For human decision making, for acts of will, there always appears to be the factor of crisis or the moment that requires decision making. If we analyse it closely enough, crisis always seems to have an aspect external to us. That is, I might be faced with the choice to write a book, yet there are dozens of experiences that have led to the moment where I am faced with that decision. Though this would always seem to be the case with humans, it is not logically necessary that a crisis must always have an external cause. Indeed, God is presented in Scripture as freely creating, so there appears to be at least one moment of decision (to create or not) that has no circumstantial cause outside of God himself. Having taken away the external aspect of crisis, we can see from the analogy of human decision making how God could make an utterly self-caused decision. Given this possibility, the first-cause argument does not lead to the conclusion that God cannot change.

This argument brings us to the second consideration raised above; namely, it is not clear that all causation violates God's independence from creation. A frequent objection raised against the claim that God changes (even in a limited sense) is that any change in relation to the creation would make God dependent on the creation. For example, in 2 Samuel 24:24-25 David offers sacrifices to God amid a terrible plague. God is said to respond to "the plea for the land," and he averts the plague (v. 25). On the surface, it would appear that David's actions have caused a change in God. It is claimed that such change (from wrath to mercy; from one passion to another with the accompanying change in their expressed behaviour) would not only make God imperfect because of change (the argument we addressed above) but would also make God dependent on his creation and, therefore, less than God. That is, if the creation in some sense causes God to change in his disposition or behaviour, then the resulting state depends on God's creation. At first, this objection appears powerful—none of us want to be caught saying God "depends" on the creation! However, the objection involves equivocation on key terms. That is, the sort of dependence implied in this argument is not clearly negative. If God were dependent on creation in the sense that he needed something from the creation or that his existence depended on creation, this would be unbiblical and clearly wrong (e.g. Acts 17:24-25; Ps 50:12). However, this is not what "dependent" means in the above objection. That God is currently angry at me because of my sin, and so his disposition is dependent on my sin, does not mean that he needs me or that his existence is dependent on me. Instead, it only means exactly what it seems to mean: God is rightly angry at specific actions I have taken, and thankfully shows me mercy because I repent and trust in his Son. Indeed, unless we accept the two premises that 1) all change is negative and that 2) all change is the same, there is no reason to object to the fact that God responds to specific situations and has different dispositions towards different behaviours. Indeed, the Bible claims this on almost every page. The Bible declares that God changes in these ways, so we should believe it. Furthermore, the arguments raised against the biblical claims to this effect are not nearly as strong as is often claimed.

FURTHER READING

Matthew Barrett, *None Greater* [I]
Craig A. Carter, *Contemplating God with the Great Tradition* [I]
James E. Dolezal, *All That is In God* [I]
James E. Dolezal, *God Without Parts* [A]
*John Frame, *The Doctrine of God* [B-I]
Jeffery D. Johnson, *The Failure of Natural Theology* [B-I]
*Rob Lister, *God Is Impassible and Impassioned* [I]
See my reviews of *All That Is in God*, *None Greater*, *Contemplating God*, and *The Failure of Natural Theology* on Teleioteti.ca.

CONSISTENCY: MIND AND IDENTITY

> All flesh is like grass
> and all its glory like the flower of grass.
> The grass withers,
> and the flower falls,
> but the word of the Lord remains forever. – 1 Peter 1:24

The biblical picture of change does not imply the cessation of identity nor the impossibility of particular knowledge, but is this mere naïveté? I do not believe this is the case. However, if we pursue an answer along the lines of the biblical vision of history, we must make certain sacrifices. If knowledge in the Bible is the contingent sort, knowledge of history in all its complicated glory, then we cannot appeal to abstractions (to the Forms or universals) as the anchor of stability amidst the sea of change. We will consider universals more thoroughly in the next part; for now we can say they are not the answer we are looking for. What is ruled out by the biblical picture thus far is a principle of stability that is abstract, such as the Forms, or materialistic, such as an unchanging world. The rejection of these two extremes suggests that we may benefit from investigating the opposite of both principles, particularity instead of universality and immaterial instead of material. We can picture this in the following way:

1 Material 2 Universality

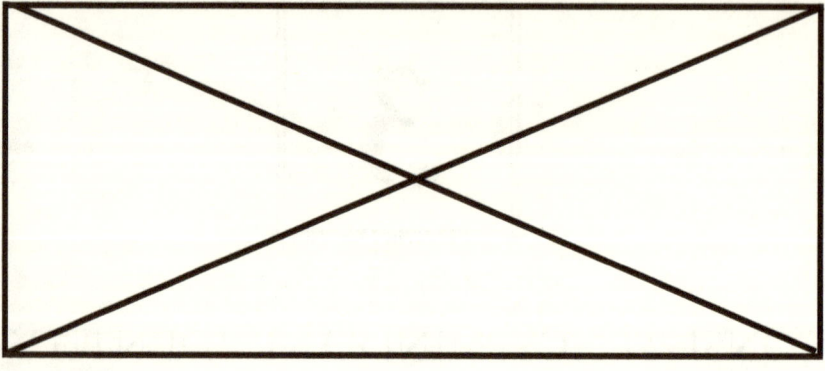

3 Particularity 4 Immaterial

Principle 1 is the claim that consistency derives from the stability of the thing-in-itself, therefore denying actual change. Principle 2 is the claim that consistency derives from a reality that stands behind multiple things themselves, the shared bit that never changes. If either is true, the other is redundant as a principle of stability. Principle 3 states that stability derives from the thing considered distinct from the universal shared by many things. Principle 3 is a possible interpretation of Principle 1, and if it is true, Principle 2 is false. Principle 4 states that stability derives from a non-material reality (a mental state or transcendent reality), not the material reality, which contradicts Principle 1. Principle 2 often implies principle 4, but not exclusively. The problems we considered and the biblical picture we saw in the last two chapters rule out Principle 1 and 2, thus leaving us with principles 3 and 4. If stability is rooted in the particular thing but not the particular thing as a material object, then we must take Principle 3 and 4 together. Therefore, stability is found in the particular things considered immaterially, which is another way of saying mentally. This can be viewed in two ways, subjectively and objectively. We will begin with the subjective perspective and then move to the objective.

Mind

The above argument does not rely on a particular view of the mind, only the rejection of physicalism. That is, we do not need to posit how exactly the mind is above the cause-effect world of the physical; all that needs to be conceded is that the "mind" is above matter. This is well supported by the cognitive sciences, which simultaneously demonstrate the interconnectivity between the mind and the body while illustrating the latter's relative independence. From the biblical perspective, we know that the self exists beyond the body's death, suggesting that the mind is not purely reducible to the body. Furthermore, the Bible indicates that humans are responsible and creative, able to make decisions and act in new ways. All these realities would seem to be an illusion if the mind does not transcend the body, for every "decision" would merely describe the subjective experience of a chain of physical cause-effect forces moving from external stimuli to internal neuronic processes. There would be no room for genuine "decision" making, where the subject acts according to a subjective force, such as desire. Moreover, the notion of "subjective experience" cannot be explained within physicalism.

FURTHER READING

Bradley L. Sickler, *God on the Brain*. [B-I]

A. Subjective Stability

If a stream has identity over time and yet its qualities are completely changed, then this identity cannot reside in the qualities themselves. However, there is another way to view identity. Individuals who view the Euphrates are not shocked by the changes they witness during their lifetime; they can still identify its continuity. Moreover, this continuity can be described in a book or orally, communicated beyond immediate experience. However, the consistent factor in each of these cases is an interpretation: a person has attached a name to an object of their experience and is able to describe and communicate that object to others. If the object itself is always changing, but it has a continuous identity, then the interpreting mind is the culprit. It is the interpreting mind which is responsible for creating identity. Identity is found in the particular thing, such as the Euphrates, but only in that particular thing as interpreted by a mind (see further, Part 3). We can see this working in the case of someone who loses their sense of identity, namely, their memories, relationships, and sense of continuity with the past or future. Even in extreme cases of dementia, the personal loss of identity does not entail the loss of identity in its entirety, for family, friends, and even doctors know the patient and interpret this person in terms of identity across time. They may also remind the person of his or her identity, which is recognized by others though eclipsed in his or her own mind. This identity is subjective because a person's experience of a river in the 19th century will differ from that of a person in the 20th century. They may not share any overlap in their experience. Thus, identity in this sense is *contingent*, variable from person to person. A man in the 4th century may have a concept of a river they call the ירדן and another in the 20th century of a river they call the Jordan, with no discernible overlap in their concepts. However, another person in the 21st century may correlate their own experience with that of individuals in the centuries between and develop a concept of the Jordan as it has developed from then until now, a single object which has undergone significant change but is identified by this historian as the same thing. Thus, we can see how the subjective identity created by an individual's interpretation can move towards an objective identity through communication. If we presume that the human mind itself is not subject to wholesale change such as we witness in nature, which is a point upheld throughout the Christian tradition on a firm biblical basis, then we can rightly maintain this subjective sense of identity (see the excurses above).

B. Objective Stability

Objective identity emerges once we acknowledge that humans are not the only ones doing the interpreting. We know from the Bible that history is not pure contingency; instead, it unfolds according to the foreknowledge and determination of God (e.g. Acts 2:23, 3:18, 4:28; Rom 8:28-30, Eph 1:2-23). God knows all that happens before it happens and works in his providence to bring all things to pass. Thus, there is no "bare fact," that is, uninterpreted thing. Every individual and aspect of this world is caught up in God's vision of and plan for the created order. God not only knows what I have done and am doing but also what I will do. He knows what I once was and will become. If the human mind can create subjective identity, then God's omnicomprehension (his grasp of all things) creates objective identity, an interpreted whole of all things as they are related, differentiated, and change across history. In response to the Theseus paradox, we can say that the shipbuilders and crew perceived continuity from one moment to the next.

Even if they died with no overlap in their experience, God nevertheless perceived and determined the ship's fate from its origin to end. The identity of the Theseus is ultimately grounded in God's determination of history, though it is experienced and communicated from the perspective of those humans that have encountered it. The collective human perception of continuous identity, whether of a ship or a river, are like the pieces of a puzzle that fit together into a picture God has painted. Thus, admitting God into the picture offers us an answer to the problem of identity.

The interpretation of objects by humans and, ultimately, God not only provides an answer to the problem of change and identity but also change and knowledge. A full exploration of the later problem will have to await Part 3. For now, it will suffice to say that the biblical vision of change shows us that knowledge is fundamentally caught up with the particulars; God's interpretation of all things enables us to affirm this is indeed "knowledge." First, that objects have continuous identity despite change means that knowledge of any object concerns not only their present but their past and their future. Thus, the location and feel of the Euphrates on March 8, 2021 is not insignificant; it is one aspect of a broader understanding of the river as it has evolved over thousands of years. Second, it is true that there is no correspondence outside of the present for a proposition and the reality it describes, but this need not impede truth. We have already seen that interpretation plays an integral part in what it means for something to be a thing. In Part 3, we will see that this is truer than is presently apparent. Because interpretation is fundamentally part of what it means to know anything—moreover, because knowledge is always interpretation—and God possesses the perfect knowledge of all things, his correct interpretation of reality becomes the standard by which our knowledge is measured as true or false. That is, because all knowledge is interpretation, an object is an essential part of the act of knowing but not its sum. Therefore, it is unable to be the standard of knowledge. Such a standard must be the perfect measure by which knowledge is compared, thus a perfect interpretation. Because God possesses the perfected interpretation of all things, his pre-interpretation is the standard for our re-interpretation. All knowledge is, therefore, thinking God's thoughts after him. We do not, of course, have direct access to God's mind, but we can further surmise that God, desiring us to know and use our knowledge, has created the world and our faculties in such a way that we can reliably arrive at truth within the bounds of his spoken revelation.[1]

---

[1] See further, *The Gift of Knowing*.

—Part 2—
The One and the Many

THE RATIONAL WORLD

In Part 1, we consider the problem of change. This problem was prevalent in the period of the so-called "Pre-Socratic" philosophers. In the following centuries, Plato, his student Aristotle, and their heirs continued to address this problem. However, it was caught up in a more elaborate problem often called "the One and the Many," also known as the problem of individuation. In response to the problem of change, Western philosophy from Plato onwards has posited a two-world or two-principal schema for recognizing the reality of change while salvaging knowledge. On the one hand, there is the "One," the world of reason and unity. On the other hand, there is the "Many," the world of experience and particular things with all their differences. For Plato and those after him, the "One" was what mattered; it was the real world. The "Many" were the problem, and they were in one way or another subordinate to the "One." We will consider this problem in the work of Plato and Aristotle and trace it briefly across the history of Western philosophy until the time of the Reformation. We will then reflect on the nature of the problem.

A. Plato and Aristotle

The Pre-Socratic philosophers we considered in Chapter 1 were monists, that is, they try to answer the question of what is (of what exists) by positing a single explanation for all reality: all is one.[1] For Thales, everything is fundamentally water. For Heraclitus, the fundamental reality is fire, and it is perpetually changing. For Parmenides, the fundamental reality is an unchanging, spherical thing. All these philosophers thought that a sufficient explanation of the world must reduce everything to their unifying factor: there must be a single explanation for everything. Heraclitus realized that one principle was not adequate to explain everything, so he introduced another principle in addition to pure change, the principle of stability. However, this idea was not fully thought out in Heraclitus. Over the next two centuries, this idea of two explanatory principles was adopted more consistently by a philosopher named Plato and his pupil, Aristotle.

a. Plato

Plato (427-347 BC) may be the most famous philosopher in Western thought. John Frame observes that the greatest philosophers tend to take the seemingly disparate ideas of their predecessors and achieve a synthesis.[2] This is what we see in Plato. Plato's predecessors wrestled with change and stability, arguing that one or the other was the ultimate explanation of reality. However, we saw that change and stability are both needed to explain the world, to justify human thinking about the world. Plato brought the tension of change and stability together by positing two ultimate realities that explain the world. On the one hand, there is matter or "the Receptacle." The Receptacle is imperfect, featureless: it is responsible for change. On the other hand, there is the world of forms. The world of forms is stable (i.e. unchanging), perfect, and immaterial. The world of our experience is a marriage of the Receptacle, or matter, with the world of the forms.

The Receptacle, whatever it may be, is the principle of change in Plato's metaphysic. Change for the Greek philosopher's is a sign of imperfection: it implies moving from a negative state (not being, not knowing) to a positive

---

[1] At this time, there was another group of thinkers called atomists who explained reality as consisting of indivisible entities called *atoms* ("atom" meaning indivisible). Atomism is form of pluralism, the belief that reality is not fundamentally one (as in monism) but fundamentally a plurality. We will not consider this view further, yet it is interesting to observe that atomism and monism are two manifestations of the problem of *the one and the many*, which we will consider here.

[2] In, *A History of Western Philosophy and Theology*.

one (being, knowing). The Receptacle is able to change into something meaningful—the sensible world—yet it resists perfection by nature. The world as we know it is not the Receptacle; it is the Receptacle shaped by the forms. The Receptacle itself is featureless (pure change) and thus unknowable. Yet we only experience it as a crude resemblance of the perfect world of the forms, as a shadow resembles the object casting it. Therefore, knowledge comes not by looking at the things we sense but by contemplating the perfect world, which gives the Receptacle meaning. This world is the world of the Forms.

The world of the Forms is rather odd to wrap our minds around. It is immaterial, so above this physical world, and contains the perfect ideas of the objects (such as trees) and concepts (such as justice, love, goodness). These ideas are not particulars; they are not the idea of *a* perfect tree, but pure abstractions. That is, they are the unity, "treeness," that particulars, such as individual "trees," share in. If you look out in the world and see various trees, you see particular objects: you may see an oak tree or an arbutus. More so, you may see the oak tree on the corner of Walnut St and Creelman Ave in Vancouver, Canada. This particular oak has a history. Yet, the specific arbutus and the specific oak tree have something in common, a "treeness."[3] *Treeness* is what makes certain things trees. For Plato, *Treeness* exists in the world of the Forms, independent of any tree. It is hard to find an analogy for what Plato intends, but one way to think of it is like a formula: any particular tree can be derived from *Treeness*, yet *Treeness* is not a tree. Treeness is a truly odd concept, for it is nothing like a "tree": because all trees partake of it, it is neither brown nor white, neither leaved nor un-leaved, indefinite in shape, size, behaviour, root structure, age, or medicinal benefit. In the end, it begins to resemble "non-being," nothing at all.

To illustrate what he intended, Plato used an allegory of a cave. Imagine being a prisoner shackled and facing the back wall of a dark cave. The only light you had shone from behind you and illuminated the wall before you. On this wall were cast various shadows, of a statue, of a jar, of a lion, etc. These shadows are like the particulars; particulars, such as a tree, are faint shadows of the Form's perfection. Finding your chains unlocked, imagine

---

[3] In philosophy, a noun or adjective with the ending "ness" refers to the unity that all the particulars of the noun partake of. For example, every good act partakes of *goodness*. *Goodness* is the standard by which an act is declared good.

turning around and discovering that various objects are casting the shadows you have known. You would know a statue or a jar in part from the shadow, yet true knowledge of the statue or jar is found not by contemplating the shadow but by looking upon the real objects.[4] For Plato, these real objects are the Forms. Thus, actual knowledge does not come from our senses, which sense the particulars, but by our intellect, which contemplates the Forms.

In Plato's ontology, we see Parmenides' stability and Heraclitus' change brought together. The world we sense is ultimately unreliable; it partakes of ever-changing matter or the Receptacle. It is unknowable. However, there is an unchanging world that lies behind this one; this world is knowable. In answer to the question "what exists?" Plato's answer is that the Forms are the most real of all things and all objects experienced in this world have a derivative existence, partaking of the being of the Form and the non-being of the Receptacle. In answer to the second question of ontology, "what does it mean for something to be a certain thing," Plato's answer is "participation." I, James, am a human because I partake of the Form Humanness; I am "individuated," made other than that Form and different from you or Aliyah by the Receptacle and its distortion of the Form's perfection. Because all that differentiates or "individuates" me from you is negative, is the distorting effect of non-being, the differences between you and me are not important as objects of knowledge. Instead, true knowledge is the Form's perfection. Therefore, knowing "James" is only valuable in as much as experience helps us to move intellectually towards the contemplation of the Form "Humanness."

Plato's ontology has had a profound effect on the Western World. Philosophers are still discussing the problems he attempted to answer, and some Christians today even see a return to Plato as the key to living faithfully in the modern world. Plato's ideas had a particularly strong influence on Christian philosophy, primarily through the post-New Testament Neo-Platonists. The most famous Christian Platonist was Augustine of Hippo

---

[4] If you are wondering where the light comes from, Plato gave the Form of the Good a particularly prominent position in the world of the Forms. The Good is the ultimate Form, it gives meaning to all the others. As all the particulars partake of a Form, all the Forms partake of the Good. This illustration is found in *The Republic* alongside the related illustration of "the divided line."

(354-430 AD), a North African bishop. Augustine's main contribution to philosophy is in the philosophy of history. But he also took a unique position on Plato's world of the Forms. Philosopher's call Plato a "realist," that is, he believes that the Universals or Forms have an extra-mental existence: they exist apart from any mind. Augustine was not a realist in the same sense as Plato; he expressed an early form of what would be called conceptualism. He taught that the forms (e.g., goodness, treeness, justice) were not free-floating immaterial ideas but ideas in the mind of God. The only way humans can know particulars, argued Augustine, is because God illumines their minds with his understanding of the forms. For Plato, and for Augustine nearly a millennium later, the forms existed apart from the objects of our perception. For Plato, this meant two worlds, a world of perfect changelessness and an utterly unknowable world of pure change. Plato's star pupil Aristotle also believed in a two-fold explanation for the world, yet he attempted to bring together these principles in a way that Plato did not.

b. Aristotle

Aristotle (384-322 BC) was a particularly sharp student of Plato—so sharp that he was the tutor of Alexander III of Macedon, later known as Alexander the Great! Aristotle took in many of Plato's ideas but reformulated them in what he thought was a more reasonable fashion. In his work called *Metaphysics*, he explicitly rejected Plato's external world of Forms.

Aristotle believed that there is one world, the sensible world we experience. Everything in this world is ultimately explained by two principles, form and matter. If you take a table, for instance, it has various accidental (that is, unessential) properties such as a black colour, 4 feet high, etc. None of these features makes it a table. What makes it a table is its form, yet form is not enough to make a table. A table is also made of *matter*. In the case of a table, its matter is wood. The wood would likewise consist of form and matter, the latter of which would be form and matter once more. At some point you arrive at a base or *prime matter* that undergirds all change and is not itself defined by form. Contemporary philosophers argue that Aristotle did not actually believe in *prime matter:* matter is never apart from form. Form and matter are always compounded. However, the basic point remains the same. Whether or not matter can be considered apart from form, it remains the principle of potentiality, that which remains constant even when one substance becomes another (such as wood to fire). *Matter* is one of two foundational principles in Aristotle's metaphysic. It is like Heraclitus's ever-changing fire. *Prime matter* for Aristotle is indeterminate: it is featureless, unknowable. It is no different than nothing (or in philosophical terms, non-being) except that it is the necessary counterpart to form. Because *matter* is non-descript, it could be described as pure potentiality: that is, it can become anything. Everything in our experience is partly potential because it partakes of matter and partly actual because it partakes of form. Actuality is the realization of form in something. An example sometimes used is an acorn: in a sense, an acorn has the potential to become a tree. As an acorn, it is potentially a tree; one day it will be an actual tree. I said earlier that Aristotle's metaphysic explained the world with two principles, form and matter. Pure matter, matter without form, would be pure potential: it would have no features. Thus it could become anything. Pure matter is fully changing and changeable. For Aristotle, matter never exists apart from "form:" everything that exists consists of matter and form, with one exception.

Aristotle's god is unchanging and thus has no matter; it is pure actuality with no potentiality. This god is sometimes called the Unmoved Mover. The Unmoved Mover is completely unchanging; it does not interact with nor is it affected by the world. In fact, it does not know of or think of the world. It has been described as "thought thinking thought." How, you may ask, does such an entity earn the title "Mover"? For Aristotle, the Unmoved Mover is responsible for all change in the world, for the transition from potentiality (matter) to actuality (form). The Mover does not achieve this by doing anything; instead, it is described as supremely attractive. Like a magnet, the Mover draws everything to itself.

To the question, "what exists," Aristotle's answer is only concrete objects. Things exist, not abstract definitions (humans exist; humanness does not exist, or only in a secondary sense). Everything has a form or essence, which explains what it is, and matter, which is shaped by the form into the multi-faced objects of our experience. A specific chunk of matter, "this" matter over against "that," differentiates one human from the next. However, when it comes to "form," it is identical across every human, animal, etc. Indeed, the "form" is what something actually is. In his book the *Categories*, Aristotle makes it clear that any object is always a *something*: everything is defined, as a *human, animal, plant, table*, etc. This is an important point for ontology. What makes each human, the form, is identical across all humans. Moreover, this is what they are.

Concerning "James," that he is a human is more important than the fact that he is a Canadian, born in the 20th century, 6 foot 3 inches tall, living in Australia, etc. These latter qualities are "accidents" that specify what human I am talking about but only exist in and around the "substance," which is "a human." If I want to know how to act towards an object, I need to know something about its accidents (its location, size, etc.). However, if I really want to know why it is the way it is and what is most important about it, I need to know the form. The important ontological takeaway from Aristotle is this: what fundamentally exists are "substances," definite things such a *human* or a *horse*. It is not right to speak of something that is a *horse*, for "horse" is the most fundamentally real thing about it. Moreover, the "universal" ("horseness") exists as that which has caused many particular things to be the way they are; it is that aspect that is identical in each of them. However, this universal is just this: the identity of all these particulars; it does not, as with Plato, exist in another realm apart from the particular.

We see, therefore, both similarities and differences between Aristotle and Plato. For both, form and matter are important; there are particulars and universals, the form that characterizes something (that oak tree is a particular; treeness is the form). Aristotle attempted to bring both of Plato's worlds together into one: form and matter (cf. Plato's Receptacle) do not exist in two separate worlds; they are found together in every object. Both thinkers move beyond their predecessors by explaining the world not with one but with two ultimate principles. Both Plato and Aristotle held to a principle of change (Receptacle/matter) and a principle of stability (Form/form). What unites them most is the very thing that makes them alien to our modern era. Both of them are concerned with particular things primarily for the sake of the universal to which they point.

B. Patristic and Medieval Philosophy

The state of ontology looked much the same for the following two millennia. In the years following Aristotle, Greek philosophy tended to seek harmonization between elements of Aristotle and Plato's thought. There were unique movements, such as Stoicism, but by the 4th century, Neo-Platonism was dominant. Neo-Platonism attempted to integrate the logic of Aristotle with the metaphysics of Plato, resulting in complex and innovative systems of thought. However, in terms of ontology, Neo-Platonism closely resembled Plato and Aristotle. Western philosophy stuck close to its Hellenistic origins for many centuries.

Things began to change in earnest just after the Reformation, though we cannot be certain why. Around the time of the Reformation, something happens. The study of philosophy turns from looking through the world or behind the world to looking at the world. Ontology became less about epistemology and more about reality. In his paper "The Christian Doctrine of Creation and the Rise of Modern Natural Science" (1934), Michael Foster argued that this revolution came out of the changes wrought by the Reformation.[5] Specifically, he observed that modern natural science depends on a uniquely un-Greek idea, that matter matters. Modern science is built on the idea that the physical world is valuable in its own right; it is a legitimate object of knowledge. Foster asked what accounted for the introduction of this un-Greek idea and identified the source as the Bible, specifically, the doctrine of creation. For Foster, what makes particular objects important is contingency, the fact that they are not exhaustively defined by reason. They are not reducible to a single idea such as "treeness." For the Greeks, a particular tree reduced to "treeness" as the sum of its intelligibility: to know treeness is to know the tree entirely. But for the post-reformation world, the uniqueness of particular trees become significant. Foster's study displays sharp insight into the shift that happened, but the cause of this shift may be traced significantly earlier. Nevertheless, the Bible is still the culprit.

In the 4th century, when the Church Fathers were hashing out the doctrine of the Trinity over against the many alternate positions, they drew heavily on the resources of Plato and Aristotle, mediated at times through their Neo-Platonic followers. When it came to the Trinity, the clear tension of God's oneness ("the Lord is one"; Deut 6:4) and his plurality ("...baptizing them in the name of the Father, and of the Son, and of the Holy Spirit"; Matt 28:19) was tantalizing similar to the ontological problem of the *one and the many*. For this reason, the so-called "pro-Nicene" Fathers (those who upheld the creeds of Nicaea and Constantinople) used the tools of the Greek ontology to resolve this dilemma. For the Basil the Great and his contemporaries, God was one in the same way that the universal was one, despite its many particulars. In his letter *To Ablabius: That There Are Not Three*

---

[5] M. B. Foster, "The Christian Doctrine of Creation and the Rise of Modern Natural Science," *Mind* 43, no. 172 (1934): 446–468.

Gods, Basil's brother Gregory of Nyssa made this connection definitively clear. In response to the argument that we say James, John, and Peter are "three humans," so the Trinity should be identified as "three gods," Nyssa countered that this use of language is wrong. There is only one "human," properly speaking, the "human nature" in which James, John, and Peter all participate. In the same way, there is only one "divine nature" (though we cannot speak of it), so it is improper to speak of "three gods." This solution is ontologically loaded, drawing heavily on the resources of Neo-Platonism. Athanasius and Apollinaris draw a similar conclusion, using the related resources from their Philosophical background. The problem with this line of thinking (at least as it concerns the development of ontology that we are tracing) is that it is, on the surface, incompatible with biblical Christology. That is, like their Hellenistic predecessors, the "universal," the one nature, is what fundamentally exists. The "many," the particulars, only exist in order to realize or "instantiate" the one. Yet in the Bible, Christ is said to be "made like his brothers in every respect" (Heb 2:17), and he is identified as God (e.g. John 1:1; John 20:28-29).

At the council of Chalcedon (AD 451), over a century of Christological conflict came to a head. The council incorporated the language of Pro-Nicene theology, that Christ was "consubstantial" (the same *nature*) as God, and of the later Christological debates, that Christ was "consubstantial" with humanity (of the same *nature*). "Nature" in these phrases refers to the universal or the "One"; thus, Christ is on the same ontological plane as both the Father and the Spirit, realising the one nature of God, and on the same ontological plane as James, John, and Peter, realising the one nature of man. What is not evident in the discussion at Chalcedon is the realisation that this Christological claim stands at odds with the Hellenistic ontology employed up to this point to explain the Trinity and other facets of theology. That is, if the "One" was primary and the sole purpose of the "Many" was to realise the One in the world, to give it reality, then it made no sense to claim that there was a person—even one person—who realised two distinct (and in many ways, contradictory) natures. This problem became the source of dramatic tensions in the following centuries of Christian theology. As Christians wrestled with Christology for and against Chalcedon, they came to similar conclusions concerning ontology.

a. *Maximus the Confessor*

The debates following Chalcedon, extending from the 5th through the 7th centuries, saw significant developments in the ways Christians understood ontology.[6] Though several of the fathers in the 6th and 7th centuries could be considered for their contribution to these developments, I have chosen to focus on Maximus the Confessor (AD 580-662). Maximus was an Eastern Father who became incredibly influential in the Eastern church after his death; he continues to have significant influence today. I have chosen to focus on Maximus not because of his unique contribution to ontology but because of his influence throughout church history. He is also the 7th-century father I have studied the most extensively. His ontology is exemplary of the developments that occurred at this time.

Maximus depended heavily upon Gregory of Nyssa; like Nyssa, Maximus developed a sweeping ontological vision of reality. In one sense, the nature was a concrete reality with great significance, yet unlike Nyssa, the essence was not what fundamentally existed. Essence was highly significant, but in Maximus we find it separated from existence. Nature or essence was not the thing that was most properly "being." Instead, nature was something that defined a thing: it was one of the properties that inhered in or around a thing. If that is not clear, neither was he (nor his predecessors). However, if we think about it a bit, we can get his point. When I say, "James is a man," it is possible to understand "James" as merely a sign substituting for the subject "a human" (as Aristotle would have it). However, it is also possible to say that "James" is the sign describing a fundamentally existing thing, a "substance" of which "a human" is the most basic thing that can be said about this "substance." This substance, "James," is Canadian, 6ft 3in tall, and, most importantly, "a human." In such statements, no matter how important the claim "he is a human" is, "humanness" has been put alongside the other "qualities" or "accidents" that describe a thing. The substance is not the nature; instead, it is an indescribable something that gives reality to the nature. Thus, theoretically, such a substance could "uphold" or "support" not just one but two natures. Specifically, in the case of Jesus, the pre-existent Son who was always "God" took upon himself the additional nature "Human."

The significance of this move was not truly seen for several centuries.

---

[6] Zachhuber argues for these developments. See his book for the development of ontology post-Chalcedon. Johannes Zachhuber, *The Rise of Christian Theology and the End of Ancient Metaphysics: Patristic Philosophy from the Cappadocian Fathers to John of Damascus* (Oxford University Press, 2020).

However, by severing "nature" from "substance," essence from existence, the nature or universal was rendered superfluous, or at least this was the claim of several Medieval philosophers.

b. William of Ockham

Centuries later, William of Ockham (AD 1287-1347) argued that everything for which the Greeks and Christian philosophers needed the Universal could be explained solely in terms of the mental act of relating particulars. Thus, the "universal" was solely a tool of the human mind: all that really existed were particulars. This move was only possible on the foundation laid by Maximus and others, such that the particular thing, not the form it embodied, was what fundamentally existed. This shift to the particular initiated by the Post-Chalcedonian philosophers and brought to a head by Ockham is exactly what Foster observed in his reflections on post-Reformation philosophy. In this way, Christian Christology led to the ontological revolution Foster identifies.[7] At the end of the day, particular things in all their strange and variegated beauty were the basic objects of our thought and knowledge and the only things that actually existed.

For Ockham and many philosophers after him, the God of the Bible had an essential role to play in philosophy and ontology. However, post-reformation philosophy turned in an autonomous direction for the most part: philosophers sought to explain the world apart from God and his revelation. The Bible opened a door for innovation in ontology, yet non-Christian philosophy proceeded to cut off the limb upon which it stood. Ironically,

> If the reason upon which they relied had been in fact what they took it for, a 'natural' faculty bereft of the enlightenment of the Christian revelation, it could have discovered no truths not discovered by reason to the Greeks, and could not therefore have laid down the foundations upon which modern science was raised.[8]

The Christian doctrine of Christ and, as Foster argues, the doctrine of

---

[7] Cf. Ibid.

[8] Foster, "The Christian Doctrine of Creation and the Rise of Modern Natural Science," 450.

creation give value to particulars (what Foster calls "contingency"). Furthermore, by laying the groundwork for the abolition of the realist "One," these doctrines also leave God as the only one who gives unity to all the particulars. Yet though philosophers unconsciously adopted the belief that particulars mattered, they rejected the truth that Yahweh's will ordered all the creation to various degrees. Thus, the Bible's influence was enough to change the trajectory of philosophy, yet it did not stop the philosophers' efforts to explain everything without reference to God and his revelation. The temptation to eat and be like God was too strong for modern philosophy to resist. We will see in Part 3 that this had catastrophic consequences for the modern world.

C. The One and the Many

In these ways, ontology today revolves around two quite different foci than Plato, Aristotle, and the Patristic philosophers. In the modern era, the primary concern of ontology has been scientific, understanding the world as it is so that we can use it. The other concern has been atheistic, arguing in such a way as to exclude God from the picture and to open the door for human autonomy, namely, the freedom to interpret the world and act in it as each person sees fit. The latter agenda is characteristic of so-called Postmodernity but is not altogether foreign to Modernity. Because this is the focus of ontology today, the ideas of Plato and Aristotle seem very foreign. They are not concerned with the sensible world, for it is not the true object of knowledge. They are concerned with the unchanging world that is somehow related to the world of space and time. Even though Aristotle thought that form resided in sensible things, knowledge did not concern a thing—a tree—for the sake of that thing; knowledge concerned the particular only for the sake of learning about its form.

Because of this epistemological focus, the primary concern of Plato and Aristotle is a problem known as *the one and the many*. This is, alongside the problem of change and stability, the second major problem in ontology. Philosophers are those who seek knowledge; they want to explain the objects of their thought or experience. Therefore, a critical question that is raised when a philosopher examines the world is, "How can I know anything? What about the world justifies me in claiming to know something?" The philosophers realized that to know something about anything, we must know something about everything. That is, no thought—be it about a tree or a virtue such as love—exists in a vacuum.

We know a tree in relation to other trees and non-trees; we know love in relation to acts of love and acts that are not loving. Knowledge is essentially relational in this fashion. If I want to have true knowledge about a tree, I must not only know the tree but other things as well: I need knowledge of brownness, the colour of its bark; greenness, the colour of its leaves; the sun, which illuminates it; the earth, which anchors it; etc. If I want certain knowledge, I must know everything. That is, how can I be sure I truly know a fact about the tree if I do not know that there is not something out there that disproves that fact? Maybe this unknown fact is that I am all that exists, and the tree is a figment of my imagination. Or, perhaps, what I think is a tree is a shape-shifting demon spying on me! That one piece of data would fundamentally change how I perceive the "tree" and what it is. Therefore, without knowledge of everything, it is impossible to be certain about anything. Because no human can know everything, knowledge would seem to be impossible.[9] Therefore, philosophers were left with two routes by which they could know something. They could either appeal to unity or plurality.

The universe we know consists—apparently—of both unity and plurality: we know of a wolf, a pug, a greyhound, and a bulldog (particulars) and of dogs (a universal). For Plato, Aristotle, and their heirs, the most important thing to know about anything was "what it is." It was thought that we know what something is by the process of abstraction: we abstract generalizations from the particulars we experience. Experiencing wolves, pugs, greyhounds, and bulldogs, I can generalize concerning each of these that they are "dogs." You would think that knowing that a pug is a "dog" would give more knowledge, but, in a sense, "dog" is a loss of information: it excludes the characteristic smooshed-face and stubby legs of the pug. It especially excludes the particularities of Fido, a specific pug. Plato and Aristotle, along with many others, thought that true knowledge of something was found in the abstraction: I know Fido most fully not because of his

---

[9] The alternative sometimes taken in more recent times would be to define knowledge differently. Instead of certain knowledge, one can be said to know even if that knowledge later proves to be wrong, what matters is warrant or the conditions for making a legitimate knowledge claim.

particular characteristics but because I know dogness. "Scientific" knowledge, the knowledge pursued by philosophers, concerns only "what" questions:

> That there is no science of the accidental is obvious; for all science is either of that which is always or of that which is for the most part. For how else is one to learn or to teach another? The thing must be determined as occurring either always or for the most part, e.g. that honey-water is useful for a patient in a fever is true for the most part.[10]

Thus, contingent knowledge (knowledge of what is but could not have been) is neither desirable nor useful. Furthermore, if knowledge concerns the "whatness" of things, and this is found through abstraction, it then follows that one knows the universe most fully if he can abstract to a generalization that encompasses everything. Everything is "being." "Being" represents pure unity: a concept so broad it encompasses everything.

On the other hand, one could try to explain everything by appealing to particularity, examining every feature of Fido. Fido is black and white, short, about 2 feet long, has a short tail, etc. These can be broken down further: blackness and whiteness, shortness and length all can be broken down until we reach an underlying plurality that explains Fido. If we have arrived at the most basic explanation of Fido, we could say he is made up of "atoms"—indivisible things.[11] If they are indivisible, they cannot be described any further (to describe something implies that it could be broken down further, explained with something more basic than itself). The ancient Atomists gave the "atoms" elementary properties that would, in combination, produce all known reality. However, the attribution of various properties to the atoms was utterly arbitrary. Moreover, the interactions between these atoms were completely arbitrary, meaning that everything happened by chance. If one went beyond atoms, one may arrive at pure or prime matter, about which

---

[10] Aristotle, *Metaphysics* Book E (VI), Ch. 2.

[11] The irony of modern physics is that they used the term "atom" for something that we now know can be broken up further.

"nothing could be said" if it were really the stuff from which all else comes.[12] Such matter must be able to take on every quality (if it is to explain every feature of Fido, the Earth, and the Sun), so it cannot have any qualities.[13] Thus, we see that a pure abstract plurality ("atoms" or "matter") is meaningless or arbitrary, as is a pure abstract unity ("being"): to reduce everything to a unifying or particularizing principle leads to no knowledge.

Plato and Aristotle are philosophers who attempted to uphold plurality and unity. For Plato, the Forms give unity to the world and are themselves unified by the Form of Good. The ultimate plurality of the world is found in the Receptacle. For Aristotle, the forms (with god as pure form) and prime matter (pure potentiality) served these roles. Ultimately, neither thinker was able to hold both principles together: both form and matter reduced to meaningless abstractions; in the final analysis, they yielded nothing any average person would call "knowledge," nor anything the Bible recognizes as "wisdom." How the two principles could be related remained a tension in Plato's system, as it does in Aristotle's. Both attempted to explain their relationship. Plato mythologized about a craftsman who united the forms with the receptacle, yet the craftsman would introduce a third principle at odds with the other two. For Aristotle, the Unmoved Mover attracted matter as its final goal, moving it from potentiality to actuality. In my opinion, this is hardly satisfactory an explanation.

The problem of the one and the many is thus a key problem in philosophy: is unity or plurality ultimate, and if both are somehow mutually exclusive, how do they relate? If the "One" is ultimate, what is its relation to the many which resemble it? If the "Many" are ultimate, what do we make of their commonality? At stake is the possibility of knowledge itself:

> How is it that this seemingly well-intentioned search for truth leads

---

[12] John M. Frame, *Cornelius Van Til: An Analysis of His Thought* (Phillipsburg: P&R Publishing, 1995), 73. "But if every particular, every individual, is his own law and meaning, his own universal [i.e. unity], then again there is no meaning. Communication is nullified, since every particular or individual is an autonomous universe. There is no universal, because everything, ever last particular thing, is its own universal." Rousas John Rushdoony, "The One and the Many Problem—The Contribution of Van Til," in *Jerusalem and Athens: Critical Discussions on the Theology and Apologetics of Cornelius Van Til*, ed. E. R. Geehan (USA: Presbyterian and Reformed, 1971), 340.

[13] This is a contradiction, for to say "it has no qualities" is to give it a quality.

up such a blind alley? Van Til's analysis is that essentially both [abstract unity and abstract particularity] are idols, and thus self-destructive. They are idols because they are the result of man's desire for an exhaustive understanding of the world, an understanding that only God can have. As is always the case in idolatry, we seek for an ultimate within the creation, and when we think we have found it, we discover in due course that it is utterly powerless.[14]

---

[14] Frame, *Cornelius*, 74.

5

THE MANY: THE PRIMACY OF THE PARTICULAR

In the beginning, God created the heavens and the earth. – Genesis 1:1

And God saw everything that he had made, and behold, it was very good. – Genesis 1:31a

by him all things were created, in heaven and on earth, visible and invisible, whether thrones or dominions or rulers or authorities—all things were created through him and for him. – Colossians 1:16

"What if this whole question is a red herring, a diversion or pointless pursuit?" Thus was the shocking thought that I had one day after years of trying to understand the problem of the one and the many. For many years, a dear friend of mine had maintained that this was the central or at least an important problem of philosophy, a claim to which many agree.[1] Following Cornelius Van Til, he believed that the Trinity provides the answer to this problem: both unity and plurality are ultimate; neither have precedence over the other. However, after I had read the arguments of Plato, Aristotle, and others, I still could not understand the problem—let alone speculate about the answer. Moreover, in 4th-century Trinitarian theology, the Fathers seemed

---

[1] See, for example, Adrian Pabst, *Metaphysics: The Creation of Hierarchy*, Interventions (Grand Rapids: Eerdmans, 2012).

to emphasise the One over the Many, as had Plato and Aristotle, so the traditional doctrine did not seem to solve the problem—whatever the problem might be! John Frame teased me in the right direction with his claim that Van Til did not *solve* the problem of the One and the Many but eradicated it.[2] What then was the problem in the first place—so I could understand how Van Til did away with it—? Then it hit me, the "problem" of the One and the Many was the nexus of several metaphysical problems with which the philosophers wrestled. On the one hand, there was the problem of change: how do we understand identity across time, and how can we claim knowledge of a world in flux? On the other hand, there was the problem of experience: how could we claim knowledge or attain a rational, scientific understanding of the universe if all we have access to is the tiny slice of the world which we experience, and no assurance that this offers a bridge to the rest of the universe? To attain knowledge of everything or to have a rational understanding of the world, there must be something behind the flux of the world. We could call this something the "logos," that is, reason or rationality.

This rationality must be that which brings unity to the diverse world. If this "rationality" is to render the world intelligible, it must have certain features. It must be unchanging, otherwise it could not itself be an object of knowledge. It must also be abstract, not an individual, concrete object of experience. If it were individual or concrete, it would not give unity to all things. If this abstract, rational unity is what gives order and meaning to the world, then it must be the object of knowledge instead of the changing flux of our experience. This is the kernel of the problem of the One and the Many, the postulate of an abstract unity that explains everything. The pre-Socratics, Plato, and Aristotle all took the "One" in different directions, as we saw above. However, once the One is raised to explain stability and reason, a problem emerges: how does it relate to the world of experience in all its plurality? For Plato, the physical world "participated" (whatever that means!) in the One—the Forms and ultimately the Good. The One individuated itself with "matter," the corrupting non-being of the receptacle. Thus, the particular is less than the unifying rationality. Indeed, the particular is a corruption of the universal! Particularity and experience were dubbed "opinion" and sacrificed on the altar of reason. For Aristotle, there is no

---

[2] He didn't say it in such words, but that is what I drew from his argument. Frame, *A History*, 544.

abstract form existing in another world; instead, the forms are abstract formulas that shape matter in specific, concrete ways. Every horse is a horse because of "horseness," the unifying, rational cause that results in it being what it is. All that makes it "this" horse and not "that" one, its accidents (colour, number, place, etc.), is irrelevant to knowledge, for knowledge concerns that abstract, rational form. Again, particularity was sacrificed for unity. For thousands of years, the One triumphed over the many, but imagine a world without the "One." If every particular was totally isolated, on its own, and irrational, then thought itself is meaningless. I cannot know what any other mind might think—if there are other minds—for every mind is its own, distinct world. Every event is irrational and unexpected, so I cannot predict what will happen even in the very same circumstances as before. "Human" is an empty term that does not describe actual commonality between you and me; it is an arbitrary name that someone has foisted on us but adds nothing to the knowledge of you or of me. We find that even the limited experience we have does not qualify as knowledge: we cannot hope to know anything, let alone everything!

But this is all a far cry from the world of the Bible, is it not? The Bible affirms particularity in all its glorious strangeness, yet it simultaneously affirms reason. What if the problem is not really a problem at all? What if it is a red herring? What if the problem arises out of the systems of the philosophers and not reality itself? I followed this thought for a bit and am now convinced that this is the case. The "One" as conceived by the philosophers does not exist, nor the "many" as they perceived it. In his *Parmenides*, Plato presumed that if there was no univocity, that is, if an idea and its corresponding sign did not remain stable and unchanging, communication was impossible! Is this really true? As will see in this and the following chapters, this by no means follows. Related to this claim, Plato, Aristotle, and their heirs believed that language corresponded to reality, such that the existence of the term εἰμί ("to be") meant that "being" existed, in some sense of another. Is this really true? The philosophers all agreed that the most important thing to know about anything was its whatness, but is this true? Knowing that my wife is a "human" surely means something, but is it more important than knowing her past, appearance, character, personality, and present relationships (e.g. that she is married to me)? Furthermore, what does saying "Nicole is a human" really mean? Is the latter an abstract formula that explains certain features of her? Or is it a sign that draws a conceptual relationship between her and other things so that by contrast and differentiation, she might be known better? Moreover, is change really a bad thing? Is abstract, universal knowledge really more desirable than concrete, personal knowledge? Finally, can we really explain the world's past, present, and future in terms of necessity—of abstract definitions and laws?

The Bible claims otherwise: God has acted and continues to act predictably but contingently, as do the innumerable spiritual beings acting behind the scenes! We saw in Chapter 3 that we do not need an abstract, impersonal reason to explain the endurance of things across time; this can be explained in terms of persons interpreting the world. The Hellenistic "One" and "Many" are a sham, an idol of human reason raised in the place of the living God but failing in the end to replace him. In this chapter, I want us to consider "particularity" or the "Many" in biblical perspective, not as something to be explained away but as the fundamental reality of God's world. In the following chapter, we consider the "One" in biblical perspective, or the function of universality in knowledge and the corresponding commonality of particulars.

Thinking biblically, when we speak of the "particular," we mean individual things and the events involving them. A "thing" may be a person, a dog, or a rock, and an "event" may be an action they perform or something that befalls them—even a moment of internal change, such as coming to know or a change in knowledge (from future expectation to present reality, for example). It will become clear in Part 3 that "things" are more complicated than are immediately apparent. Still, we will presume the conclusion reached there: despite complications, there are genuinely things outside ourselves. The Bible does not have a category for the Greek "Universal": this does not necessarily mean that it is incompatible with such a notion, though I have argued and will argue in the next chapter that this is so. Instead, what is crucial to observe is that as far as God has sought fit to reveal to us, the "Universals" are not a big deal. For Christians, this should have great significance: that thing which the Greeks said was everything is, in God's opinion, nothing. Instead of the Universal, the Bible is interested in the particular. In this chapter, I want to draw our attention to three groups of particulars with which the Bible is interested: individuals, actions, and events (in the sense of history).

A. Particular Individuals

The Modern era could be labelled the "dawning of the self," for it is at this time that a hitherto unseen interest in "interiority," or that existential core that makes you you and not me, emerges. At least in terms of philosophy, the ancient world was far less interested in personhood than our age. All sorts of reasons could be raised for these developments. On the one hand, we are a hyper-individualistic culture and not communal (then again, did interiority or individualism come first?). On the other hand, the ancient philosophers were solely interested in "what"s and not "who"s: "interiority" is by definition accidental, contingent, and individual, not universal. The Greek and Latin terms we translate "person" (ὑπόστασίς, πρόσωπον, *persona*) did not refer to "person" in any modern sense but to the individual, the particular or the Many over against the One. Christian theologian Boethius famously defined a person as "an individual substance of a rational nature,"[3] Leontius of Byzantium, followed by Maximus the confessor, defined it as a "bundle of properties around the substance."[4] However, the focus on mind and personhood would seem to be a natural development of the shift to the individual we observed above.

The Bible has no word that overlaps significantly with the modern concept of a "person," but the lack of a term does not mean the lack of a concept. If a concept is a relation between particulars, as I will argue in the following chapter, then a concept may exist wherever there is similarity between particulars. I will use the term "person" to describe the overlap between three sorts of beings in the Bible, humans, spirits, and God.

We could identify various similarities between these three categories. For example, they all have a sort of transcendence over the cause-effect materiality of this world. God is the creator and Lord over all the creation; spirits act in and on the physical world, yet they are invisible and possess powers that seem to transcend the regularity of the physical. Humans have minds, however we may understand that term: minimally, they are above bare

---

[3] *Persona est rationalis naturae individua substantia.* Boethius, *Liber de Persona et Duabus Naturis*, ch. 3

[4] Zachhuber, *The Rise of Christian Theology and the End of Ancient Metaphysics*, 278.

cause-effect physicalism, able to genuinely reason and make decisions. Personhood involves this basic transcendence (which we will call "mind"), the ability to think upon and react to the physical world without being determined by its material processes. Related to mind is *activity*, the ability to cause change in other things, to act upon them intentionally, in a way that a rock may not. Some might argue that animals have both these qualities, but the extent to which animals possess mind is debatable, and the Bible does not present them on the same plane in this regard as humans, spirits, and God.

Humans, spirits, and God—"persons"—share the ability to communicate with language: they are the only beings in the Bible and in our experience able to do this. Though many animals share our ability to develop concepts, language enables us to refine and communicate concepts, as I am attempting to do here with the concept "person."[5] Persons are thus active, communicative individuals (as opposed to abstract ideas or universals) with minds. Furthermore, these and only these are portrayed as "spiritual" individuals, in the sense of relating to God in a certain way. God is, of course, God, so he does not "relate" to himself, yet his character reflected in his will is the standard by which all creaturely relating is measured, so he is by definition "in right relation to God." Creaturely persons are in right or wrong relationship according to this standard. More concretely, God does relate to himself in the persons of the Trinity. Spirituality and communication get at another element of continuity between "persons," communality. This is obvious for humans. For God, he relates to humans as their Father and even friend, and he presides over and communions with his angels, even Satan (Job 1:6-12, 2:1-6; 1 Chron 21:1, cf. 2 Sam 24:1; 1 Kings 22:19-23). God also relates to himself as Father, Son, and Spirit (e.g. Matt 26:42; John 17:20-26; Rom 8:26-27). How about spirits? They commune with God (Job 1:6-12, 2:1-6; Rev), worship God together (Deut 32:43 [LXX]; Isa 6:1-5; Psalm 97:7; Rev 5:1-14), and communicate with humans (e.g. Dan 10:10-21; Luke 1:19-20, Heb 1:7, 14). Thus, "persons," as a concept capturing the relation between humans, spirits, and God, are active, spiritual, communicative, and communal individuals with minds.

Something interesting emerges from this concept of "person." The

---

[5] Cf. Michael Polanyi, *Personal Knowledge: Towards a Post-Critical Philosophy*, First Harper Torchbook Edition. (New York: Harper Torchbook, 1964), chap. 5.

Father, Son, and Holy Spirit are not hypostases in the Greek sense of manifestations of a universal (an ontological concept we have rejected), but they are persons in the sense we have just developed. Moreover, God as he is one would appear to be a person in this sense.[6] That is, the Spirit, Son, and Father are all identified at various times and in various ways as "Yahweh" (e.g. Matt 28:19; John 8:58; 2 Cor 3:17-18), and Yahweh is the one God (Deut 6:4). Thus, Yahweh, our God, as he acts throughout the Old Testament does not easily resolve into any one person of the Trinity, yet he communes with humans and spirits, is clearly transcendent (possessing "mind" in the sense above), is the standard and reference point of spirituality, communicates, and is active. God as he is one, Yahweh, is thus drawn into a concept of person alongside the three Trinitarian persons, humans, and spirits. Thus, all the major players are in the Bible are persons: God is so in a profoundly mysterious way, three persons who are also one person. When we say that the Bible is concerned with particular individuals, we mean with persons.

B. Particular Actions

The Bible is not concerned with persons as "persons," with the concept we have just sketched, but with persons as they act and interact. As it concerns God, the Bible is interested in making him known through his words and his deeds. God acts for and towards his creation; in particular, he acts for the sake of persons. God acts for the salvation of his people and the judgment of the rebellious. God's rich interiority (his character or personhood) is revealed in both acts: through them, we come to know him. Created persons are not just objects of God's actions but are actors in their own right; they are ethical beings. God created humans to represent him in the creation, to rule it and shape it in a way that would reveal and glorify him. After the Fall, redeemed persons were charged with building God's kingdom in a new way.

Under the New Covenant, God's people are to be like him and proclaim his good news to all the world. Through these contingent actions, God covenanting with humanity and their obedience towards him, God's glorious purposes are fulfilled. Not only are obedient persons and their actions involved in God's purpose revealed in Scripture, so are the rebels. Satan plays an integral part in the drama of redemption: his rebellious actions matter, as

---

[6] Cf. Cornelius Van Til, *An Introduction to Systematic Theology*, In Defense of the Faith V (Presbyterian and Reformed Pub. Co., 1974), 348, 362–363.

do those of demons. They are foils to God's good purpose, fulfilling through their foolishness the revelation of his fullness. In addition, God often furthers his purpose through sinful humans, such as Pharaoh, Nebuchadnezzar, and Cyrus (Rom 9, Hab 2:5, Isaiah 45). The Bible is concerned with persons and their actions; persons and actions meet in events, and the linear development of events is what we call history.

C. Particular Events

We discussed history in Chapter 2-3; we will reiterate here that events, particularly those involving persons (therefore, the events in question are contingent occurrences), are the focus of the Bible. Is not the crucifixion at the heart of history? What more contingent event could we imagine? Jesus prayed that it might be taken away from him, yet this was the Father's will, and he submitted to it (Matt 26:36-46). It was the Father's good pleasure to "crush him" (Isa 53:10). The Jewish leader's intended it for evil, but God brought it about to fulfil his good purpose (Acts 2, 4, cf. Gen 51). Pilate wanted to release Jesus but submitted to the will of the crowd (Luke 23:13-25). The crucifixion was not logically necessary; it is not the sort of thing "science" or philosophy deals with. Nevertheless, it is of the utmost importance for understanding everything. It is not alone.

God created all things intentionally and carefully, including the scope of history. Throughout history, God has entered into covenants; these covenants have driven all human history. When humans have failed these covenants, God has responded for salvation and judgment. With these examples and more, we see that the most important things to know about history and the world are contingent. The world begins with God's activity, "God created," its end is consummated by God again acting, "Then I saw heaven opened, and behold, a white horse! The one sitting on it is called Faithful and True, and in righteousness he judges and makes war," "Then I saw a new heaven and new earth…. And I saw the holy city, new Jerusalem, coming down out of heaven from God" (Gen 1:1; Rev 19:11, 21:1-2) Judgment will come because humans have rebelled against God; they have violated their covenantal obligations. Humans are saved because Christ came, died, and rose again and so established a new covenant within which sinners are declared right and enjoy fellowship with God forever.

Particular persons, actions, and events are what Scripture is all about. In each case, particularity implies contingency, which is the domain of experience, not reason (though contingency is far from irrational). The Bible is thoroughly oriented to the particular; thus, the particular is primary. However, biblical particularity does not come at the expense of reason and unity. Only godless reason and godless unity are jettisoned.

THE ONE: MAKING SENSE OF ABSTRACTION

Forever, O LORD, your word is firmly fixed in the heavens. Your faithfulness endures to all generations; you have established the earth, and its stands fast. By your appointment they stand this day, for all things are your servants. – Psalm 119:89-91

In the previous chapter we saw that particularity is primary in the Bible. Earlier, I argued that the "universal" as conceived by the philosophers does not exist; we will take that argument a bit further in this chapter. However, for the Greeks, such a conclusion is devastating. If contingency is dominant, if it is what matters most, how can we know anything at all? If all is change and uniqueness, is not knowledge itself futile and reason an illusion? This may have been the conclusion of the philosophers, but it is not the conclusion that the Bible would have us reach. We saw already in Chapter 3 that God's pre-interpretation gives unity to the changing world; we will see in this chapter that his interpretation of all things combined with his verbal revelation in Scripture gives us access to the unity we need to interpret the world rationally. The rational unity of God's world is not the One of the philosophers; instead, it is caught up in the particular without abandoning itself to irrationality. We can see this in three ways: first, unity comes from the orderliness of God's world upheld by his faithfulness; second, unity comes from genuine similarities among the creation and God himself; third, unity comes through concepts, the perception of relations between objects of knowledge, whether the Creator or the creation. We will briefly address the first two senses of unity, for they are not that difficult. We will then spend the bulk of this chapter on conceptual unity, which stands in the place of the philosopher's universals and explains the mental process of abstraction.

A. The Unity of God's Law

> Thus says the LORD, who gives the sun for light by day and the fixed order of the moon and the stars for light by night, who stirs up the sea so that its waves roar— the LORD of hosts is his name: If this fixed order departs from before me, declares the LORD, then shall the offspring of Israel cease from being a nation before me forever." – Jeremiah 31:35-36

> He is the radiance of the glory of God and the exact imprint of his nature, and he upholds the universe by the word of his power. – Hebrews 1:3

"Contingency," as I have been using the term, means something free from necessity. That is, something is contingent when it could have been other than it is, when there is no logical or physical necessity such that it would be impossible for it to be otherwise. The philosophers held that there was a certain necessity present in the world such that we could learn about everything by studying the rational framework (or *logos*) that explains everything. They did allow for contingency, but this was relegated to the accidents, the unimportant data of experience. We have already seen that the Bible prioritizes the contingent things of God's creation, but I have claimed thus far that biblical contingency does not rule out *rationality*. We have good biblical reasons for believing that God has granted his creatures rational minds and created a world that has a significant level of consistency. However, we are not permitted to believe that there is a rational cause for everything or even most things. We are constantly confronted by the twin realities of regularity and irregularity, of necessity (or better, determinism) and contingency.

In one sense, the world is utterly contingent, for every single thing results from personal and unnecessary actions. On the one hand, human actions throughout the created history have shaped the world as we know it, as have the unperceived actions of innumerable spiritual beings active in this world. On the other, the creation itself existed because God chose to create when he otherwise could have not created; he also made it in a way that was pleasing in his sight, not unreasonable but not necessary either. A fine distinction between the contingent and the necessary breaks down at this point, for we do not think of God's will, his acting, apart from the rest of his character, which is good, just, true, and perfectly wise. So, though we confess that God freely chose to create (contingency), we also confess that this choice was rooted in his character, making the choice he made the perfect choice to make as determined by his goodness, justice, wisdom, and righteousness (necessity). A similar dynamic is evident in human decision making, where we genuinely make free choices, yet we never do so without the internality of our character: all our choices are shaped by our past and present, our character, habits, desires, and fears.[1] This is where determinism, or "contingent necessity" (to introduce a rather paradoxical phrase) emerges. The entire world as we know it is dependent on God's decrees, yet these decrees are not arbitrary, they are informed by his character and are shaped by his ultimate purpose to make known his glory.

We expect, therefore, that the world is *rational*, that there are reasons things are the way they are, even if those reasons are obscured to us. The world is rational because God is supremely rational. However, the world cannot be exhausted by finite reason, for we do not perceive the whole counsel of God nor the actions of all the persons active in this world. We trust that God perceives—indeed, decreed—this complex web of forces that produce the world past, present, and future and rationally comprehends all things, but we are not permitted to think that we can have such knowledge in this life or the next. Therefore, whatever rationality we may possess, is dependent rationality; it is rationality only up to a point. We can penetrate to the reasons of the world in as much as God has revealed himself and, above all, his consistency.

The physical sciences work because God acts in consistent ways. We are never told explicitly in Scripture that God will always act one way and not another; indeed, this is false. God periodically acts within his creation in

---

[1] See further, J. Alexander Rutherford, *Prevenient Grace: An Investigation into Arminianism*, 2nd Revised Edition (Vancouver; Teleioteti, 2020).

unexpected, unanticipated ways! Such are miracles. However, we are told that God "upholds" the world by his powerful word (Heb 1:1-3). That is, we are told that there is a regular way God maintains the world. Psalm 119 reflects on God's Law and his Word in general; verses 89-91 speak of God's "word fixed in the heavens," correlated with the establishment of the earth and the continuity of the created order. This reflects the Genesis creation account, where we witness God speaking the world into being with all its attendant order, such as day and night cycles. When speaking of the New Covenant Yahweh will make with his people, Jeremiah points to the "fixed order" of creation and states that as this is consistent, so God will remain consistent towards his people (Jer 31:35-36). Thus, we ought to expect a consistent baseline of orderliness to the created world that was fixed by God. Against this baseline, the actions of non-divine persons stand out, and God's irregular activity appears spectacular.

In this way, God's law (his fixed order for the physical world and his consistent character reflected in his revelation by which our actions and thoughts are governed) gives unity to the particulars of this world such that rationality is possible. The task God originally entrusted to humans, to subdue and rule the world would, seem to imply harnessing our abilities of reason, our ability to interpret, communicate, and anticipate the world around us.

God's law is only one aspect of the unity God has built into the creation. Law permits us to anticipate changes according to patterns of consistent behaviour, but behaviour and change always involve individuals. If no individual had anything in common, then law would be useless to us, for there would be no consistency in the objects to which the law might apply. I would know what is morally right, for example, in one specific case—that it is not right to murder Tim—but there would be no similarity between that act prohibited and any other possible act nor between Tim and any other possible being such that I could apply that same law to any other case. Or, drawing a physical example, there would not be any similarity between various pool balls, cues, or tables—let alone players—to know that my experience of one ball moving at time A is applicable at Time B. All reason requires similarity among the things of the world so that what is true in one instance can be extrapolated to others.

B. The Unity of Created Likeness

When God created man, he made him in the likeness of God. Male and female he created them, and he blessed them and named them Man when they were created. When Adam had lived 130 years, he fathered a son in his own likeness, after his image, and named him Seth. – Genesis 5:1-3

The Bible does not so much teach the idea of created likeness introduced above as presuppose it. For example, God presumes that there is sufficient commonality in the world for the case laws given in the Torah to apply in endless situations (e.g. Exod 21:12-14, 28-32). Indeed, all ethical teaching in the Bible presupposes this, such as the ten commandments and the New Testament epistles. What the Bible does teach is that God has created the world with sufficient likeness that his people may know him and his world. This is especially true for humanity.

There have been endless treatises written on the "image and likeness" of God in Genesis 1:26-27, but several points do clearly emerge in the context of Genesis. In verses 26 and 27-28, "image and likeness" and "image" are connected with God's commission to Adam and Eve, that they would "be fruitful and multiply and fill the earth and subdue it, and have dominion" (Gen 1:28, cf. 26). Thus, part of this likeness is the ability to do to a limited extent what God does, to rule and create. Our reasoning faculties, namely, our senses and interpreting faculties necessary to make sense of experience, must be sufficient for this task; this implies a likeness to God's own faculties for (pre)interpreting his creation. Genesis 5 draws a parallel between God's likeness granted to Adam and the likeness shared between Adam and his descendants. This original likeness between humans and God is carried on through the family line of Adam and is analogous to the likeness which Seth has to Adam. With Adam, Eve, Seth, and God, there is thus a concept of likeness, a relationship shared between them. It would seem that as we can know something about Seth by perceiving Adam, and about Seth and Adam by perceiving Enosh, we can know something about God by perceiving Adam, Eve, Seth, and Enosh, for each shares a likeness with God in a manner analogous to their likeness with one another. This conclusion is sustained across the Bible, where God reveals himself in terms of his creation and humanity in particular, thereby assuming that there is adequate likeness to facilitate actual understanding.

That is, the Bible does not share the scepticism of the ancient philosophers or the modern philosophers of language concerning "god-talk." That is, from Plato to 21st-century philosophy, the ability for humans to speak about God has been called into question. God is very rarely an object of human experience, and when he is, he seems to reveal himself in very human ways (e.g. Genesis 19), which the classic theologians called "accommodation." So we never experience God "as he is in himself." If human language is fundamentally rooted in our experience, how can we adequately speak of a God who is beyond our experience or, in the philosophers' terms, whose essence is hidden from us? If there is truly a division between the Creator and creature, how can our language be adequate to speak of him? However, the Bible simply assumes that our language is thus competent. God reveals himself throughout the Bible in human words and human ways, and though we are continually reminded that there is a great difference between us and God, we are never led to believe that this chasm inhibits our knowledge of God. God repeatedly acts so that "they may know I am Yahweh," and this self-revelation is accomplished (E.g. Ezek 5:13, 11:10, etc., cf. Exod 14:4). This is not true at the expense of God's transcendence, his genuine difference from and authority over us, but through the wisdom of his creating work. God created humanity like himself and the world in such a way that we can adequately understand God through our understanding of the world. Thus, the likeness God has established between aspects of the created order and between himself and the created order gives unity, the foundation for rationality.

C. The Unity of Conceptual Relations

> And the LORD appeared to him by the oaks of Mamre, as he sat at the door of his tent in the heat of the day. He lifted up his eyes and looked, and behold, three men were standing in front of him. – Gen 18:1-2

The unity of Law and likeness gives a foundation for the last form of unity that upholds rationality amidst the flux of particularity, namely, concepts. The Greek philosopher rightly recognized that we use universal or *abstract* language all the time. However, with few exceptions, I will argue that they misunderstand *abstraction*. For the Greeks, the abstract was more real than the concrete, "treeness" was more real (or at least more epistemologically important) than "this Arbutus tree." They thought that reality represented by an abstract term (a universal reality, such as the Forms) was the most significant object of knowledge. There were several exceptions to this (such as several early Stoics who understood the abstract along the same lines we will develop), but this was true for the most part.

The problem is not abstract terms themselves; we use universal or abstract terms every day. Every time we identify that dog as a pug or that oak as a tree, we are involved in some level of abstract thought. However, I contend that a correct understanding of abstract thought does not identify "abstracts" as real things or as important objects of knowledge. Instead, abstracts or universals are "concepts," mental acts and related linguistic signs that facilitate our knowledge of particular things. We will explore this first by revisiting the function of abstraction in the philosophical tradition before turning to a conceptualist account.

a. Abstraction and the Greek Universals

Abstraction properly conceived is a necessary tool in coming to true knowledge of God and his created world. If we want to think intelligently in this world, we need to use abstract thought. Yet if we want to think faithfully, we must think abstractly in the biblical sense, not in the sense of the classic philosophical tradition.

i. Abstract Vs Concrete Thinking

For many philosophers, abstract thinking is set in opposition to concrete thinking. Concrete thought is concerned with the particular objects of our experience. It is not interested in knowing what "dogs" are like; it wants to know what Fido is like. Instead of studying anthropology, concrete thought wants to know about John, an individual human.

Abstract thought, in contrast, is concerned with general categories that encompass particular objects. Abstraction is a generalization (e.g. "Humanity") of related particular objects (e.g. Bill, Bob, Jane, Judy, etc.). Fido is only of interest to the abstract thinker in as much as he sheds light on "dogs." John is only important in as much as he reveals something about "humanity." For the early Greek Philosophers, abstract knowledge was the only thing that truly qualified as knowledge. For Plato and Aristotle, Fido or the oak tree out your front door do not matter. They are not the most important objects of knowledge. True knowledge is of "dogness" (that essential element that defines a dog) or "treeness." In this sense of abstract thought, the differentiating features of particular objects or persons (size, height, colour, pattern, behaviour, personality, history) are not objects of knowledge. Instead, abstract thought focuses on the unity of objects; true knowledge concerns the essence of a human being, a dog, or a tree. To truly know something is to know the essence, that without which it ceases to be (i.e. the definition and accompanying set of properties make something what it is and the absence of which disqualifies a person from being human or a dog from being a dog, for example).

ii. Abstraction and the Possibility of Knowledge

Why in the world, you may be asking yourself, would someone define knowledge in this way? Abstraction in this non-Christian sense, if possible, allows humanity to have autonomous knowledge of everything. That is, if knowledge is found in abstracting the irreducible essence of things, it follows that you will eventually arrive at something true for everything. However, if knowledge is of particular objects, we are doomed to know almost nothing—or at least this would be the result within the systems of the philosophers.

iii. The Result of Non-Christian Abstraction

Therefore, if you want to know anything apart from revelation—if you want to reason autonomously—you must maintain the priority of abstract thought. You must believe that you can know everything without knowing every particular thing. "It certainly seemed," for the Greeks, "that abstraction was the royal road to knowledge, even knowledge of concrete realities."[2] But once we have followed abstract thought to its end—abstract knowledge of everything—what is the knowledge that we have obtained?

What, we may ask, unifies "dogs" and "man?" They are both "animals" in opposition to plants and insects. But plants, insects and animals have in

---

[2] Frame, *The Doctrine of the Knowledge*, 173.

common "life." They are all living things. These have in common with certain materials an "organic" nature, so they are all organic things. With inorganic things, they are all potential objects of our experience. Like our own thoughts, objects of experience can be predicated with the attribute "existence." In this way, some philosophers say we have arrived at that category that describes all things, "being." If we know "being," we know everything.

Yet what is our knowledge of this "being?" If it is the bare unity that describes my ideas, rocks, gases, stars, planets, lizards, amoebae, and humans, what do we really know about it? If your thought of "being" contains any "beings" (a rock, element, idea, person, etc.), you are not thinking abstractly enough! Our knowledge of being cannot be of any being and cannot have any descriptive characteristics (colour, height, width, location, etc.). It is, essentially, nothing. As the philosopher Hegel once observed, we cannot distinguish being from non-being! Our ultimate abstract knowledge of everything is the knowledge of nothing. Regarding humanness, the abstraction of humans is nothing like any human, for it is absent of colour, facial patterns, size; it is absent of anything by which we differ and by which we regularly identify persons as like us. In this way, abstract knowledge yields absolutely no knowledge at all. In the chapter above, we have already raised problems with this view of abstraction and explained much of what the theory was introduced to explain. However, more problems abound.

Related to the above, imagine a "human" without particular features or a definition of "humanness." In the former case, it is impossible; in the latter, a definition adequate to capture our similarities simultaneously fails to tell us anything valuable about us, humans. Or consider the problems caused by language. For Plato and Aristotle, the abstracts or universals corresponded to language (at least in its positive uses, "righteousness" but not "sin," "cleanliness" but not "dirty"; "sin" and "dirty" are thought to be the negation or the contrary of the positive). "Accidental" terms, those that inhere in a subject and are not found apart from one (such as colour, place, size, etc.), were thought to refer to actual properties inhering in a thing. Aristotle rejected the existence of abstracts apart from things, so concepts corresponded to actual properties but only as they are found in things. However, Plato believed that the abstracts existed above things, that is, that they were more real than them and caused them to be the way they are (to be red is to participate in Redness). Nominal or "substantial" terms likewise referred to real things, horses, humans, etc. This belief led to a series of issues in Plato's theory and also for Aristotle, though the problems faced by Aristotle were different than those faced by Plato.[3] The problem with such thinking, that terms correspond exactly to reality, is that it does not work within a single language, let alone across multiple languages. Consider the English term "table"; it shares considerable overlap but is undoubtedly not identical with the Greek term τράπεζα (*trapeza*) and the Hebrew שׁוּלְחָן (šhûlḥān). There is no one abstract concept that corresponds to each of these terms.

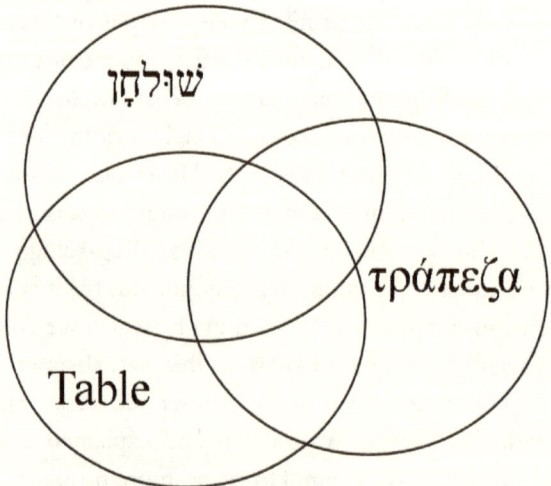

Overlapping Fields of Reference

Or consider the Hebrew word דָּג (*dāg*), translated "fish": it overlaps considerably with the English term "fish," yet refers to several things that would probably not be called a "fish" today (Jonah's "fish" for example). Consider the English term "love," which is used to translate the separate Greek words φιλέω (*phileō*), ἀγαπάω (*agapaō*), ἐράω (*eraō*), and στέργω (*stergō*). Some of these may be better translated with other English words, but they all overlap at some point with the everyday use of the term "love." Such a list could go on indefinitely: the point is, each word seems to refer to

---

[3] See Plato's *Parmenides*, especially the final section, and Aristotle's *Categories*. Problems or *aporia* with Aristotle's view are found throughout his works, especially *Physics, Generation and Corruption,* and *Metaphysics*.

a different totality of things, so we could say that each word has a different concept (though doing so makes things even more complicated!). There is surely not an abstract entity for each of these terms—*šûlḥan*-ness, tableness, *trapeza*-ness, etc. Yet they overlap significantly: what they have in common is their shared referents. The phenomena of linguistic diversity, such that different languages divide the world up in different ways (in one language, there might be less than ten words for colours, in another, upwards of 50), indicates that words do not correspond directly to reality (such that every word has a "right" meaning) and that they divide the experienced world in different but mutually compatible ways.[4] Not only is linguistic diversity a problem for the view that language connects directly to abstract, extra-mental realities, but there is also a significant body of evidence that animals have concepts, though they lack the advanced language skills of humans. This suggests that concepts precede language and are initially independent of it. However, the use of language creates and refines concepts, leading to the conclusions that concepts are mental equipment, as is language, but that the two have some measure of independent operation.[5] The problem with the philosopher's view of abstraction is that it is not evidently the way our minds work, nor how language works, nor a necessary implication of the world's structure, as we saw in the previous chapters.

---

[4] Cf. Poythress, *Symphonic Theology: The Validity of Multiple Perspectives in Theology*; Silva, *Biblical Words and Their Meaning: An Introduction to Lexical Semantics*; Poythress, *In the Beginning Was the Word*; Nicholas J. Ellis, "Biblical Exegesis and Linguistics: A Prodigal History," in *Linguistics and New Testament Greek: Key Issues in the Current Debate*, ed. David Alan Black and Benjamin L Merkle (Grand Rapids: Baker Publishing Group, 2020).

[5] Different studies work with different definitions of concepts, and there is a significant potential for an alternate interpretation in the tests regarding animals, but I think these points are still consistent with the evidence. Cf. Polanyi, *Personal Knowledge*, chaps. 5, passim; Kathleen Callow, *Man and Message: A Guide to Meaning-Based Text Analysis* (Lanham, Md: Summer Institute of Linguistics, University Press of America, 1998), 53; Thomas R. Zentall et al., "Concept Learning in Animals," *Comparative Cognition & Behavior Reviews* 3 (2008); Iain McGilchrist, *The Master and His Emissary: The Divided Brain and the Making of the Western World*, New expanded edition. (New Haven: Yale University Press, 2019), passim; Maximilian E. Kirschhock, Helen M. Ditz, and Andreas Nieder, "Behavioral and Neuronal Representation of Numerosity Zero in the Crow," *Journal of Neuroscience* 41, no. 22 (June 2, 2021): 4889–4896.

b. Abstraction from a Different Perspective

However, I think a better account of abstraction can be given, one that coheres well with what we have seen thus far. In the early 14th century, William of Ockham argued against various views of the universals that had been held up until his time. He argued against their metaphysical reality: they did not cause properties or change in extra-mental objects; they were not *real* in any extra-mental sense. However, they did have a role in human thought. He argued that universal concepts, or abstract cognitions, were mental acts that referred to multiple extra-mental objects according to their likeness. That is, James, John, and Peter have real similarities. I cognize each of them as individuals and develop a mental "sign" that refers to all of these individuals. This mental sign or act is not itself a thing, an idea or image, but a mental act that refers to all individuals that are most similar to these three men, that is, to anything that is "human." This linguistic sign itself represents the mental sign or concept. Ockham's view is complicated, but several important observations can be made from Ockham's thought. One the hand, he does not deny the existence of universal terms and concepts, such as "human." "Human" refers to particular individuals because they have something genuinely in common. I can thus use the term "human" in language and logic to communicate something of that commonality. Yet, for Ockham, this concept does not stand apart from the particulars I experience; it merely refers to them. That is, it is not a formula or image that is equally James, John, and Peter—taking away all their differences—but it is merely a placeholder for all such similar entities so that the mind may draw on its previous experience of such things in order to analyse new experience and communicate previous experience. A similar view has been developed and expressed by cognitive linguistics in recent decades. Kathleen Callows argues, "Rather than considering concepts as things, we should consider them habitual events."[6] That is, as we grow, we mentally group objects together, Peter, James, John, or Fido, Rex, and Fluffy. We develop a habit of automatically identifying those things that are similar and grouping them together. A concept is, therefore, not an abstract definition drawn from each of the particulars but is the act of connecting these particulars with one another.

---

[6] Callow, *Man and Message*, 53.

As we speak about "humans," we invoke or refer to a broad experience of things we have grouped together, often isolating one relation that obtains among them (such as their physical form, abilities, possession of mind, language, etc.). As a term, "human" refers to a concept, which isolates a specific group of things that are alike in certain ways. We could thus describe the abstraction signified by universal terms as a particular relationship between objects. Not all language functions in this way, but this holds for abstract qualities (e.g. colour), verbs and many abstract nouns (e.g. to love, love; to do good, goodness), and categorical nouns (e.g. human, animal, house).

As we will see in the following chapters, a colour is both definable and indefinable. We can identify the cause of our perception of colour so that we could define red as the perception of a certain wavelength of light. But this does not describe "red." "Red" is an experience that we know but cannot explain or define; all we can do is point to red things and identify other red things. "Red" as a colour—a perception—is always a red something. Indeed, we identify it as a specific relationship—a likeness—between many otherwise disparate objects.

Similarly, try as I may, I cannot define "love," either the act or the abstract. I can, however, identify acts of love. Acts that qualify as "love" meet in a rich concept that weaves together a complex set of factors, such as what is done, the motivations for it being done, the circumstances, and the reception of the act: all these are caught up in a kiss being an act of love and not merely a greeting, or in the giving of a gift. Surprisingly, the Bible never defines love in any philosophical sense: when Jesus wants to identify love, he points to his actions and sacrifice (John 13:34, 15:13; cf. 1 John 4:10); John points to God himself (1 John 4:16). However, love is central to the biblical ethic: the two greatest commands are love God and your neighbour as yourself (Mark 12:29-31). Instead of giving an abstract definition, the Bible repeatedly shows us what is not and is loving. In particular, the Bible shows us God's acts towards his people.

Finally, it should be clear how this is true for categorical nouns. The likeness between things varies: for many people, the concept of table revolves around function, namely, what a surface is used for. The concept of "human" changes depending on the context, but usually has the sense of common lineage: central to the biblical concept of humanity is its common descent from Adam. However, in other contexts, the term "human" merely refers to a concept of the human form, so that Yahweh and his angels may be called "men" (e.g. Gen 19).

A mental concept thus refers to the mental act of drawing together particular things according to their likeness. Such concepts are indefinite: there may be a mental concept for every relation that obtains between all particulars *I* experience. Thus, my concepts will differ in some ways from yours. However, God would possess every possible concept that his creatures may develop. As recognized by Ockham, concepts do not exist as mental acts alone; we also communicate concepts using language. All communication is by necessity restrictive: it predicates (i.e. so and so is *something*), drawing our focus on certain features or states of affairs and thus bracketing out others. Universal terms describe relationships we perceive between the particular objects of our experience. To say that "humans have minds" simultaneously restricts the concept "human" to certain things with minds and focuses on that very likeness. If I have never experienced humans before but have a concept of God and spirits as beings with minds ("persons"), the statement "humans have minds" incorporates humans into my previous concept of persons or things with "minds."

The relationships indicated by concepts are not themselves objects of knowledge but conceptual bridges that allow us to utilize the knowledge we already have in understanding new objects we experience. For example, the knowledge of Fido the poodle, Maximus Rex the pug, and Wolf the husky would allow someone to identify specific features and behaviours exhibited by the dog sitting outside the Blenz coffee shop on the corner of Cornwall Avenue and Walnut Street in Vancouver, Canada. So, concepts serve a rational function in our intellect. In a rich enough context, universal terms allow us to communicate new concepts to others. If I have never previously experienced a monkey, I may develop a concept of a monkey from certain animals at the zoo; by learning the term "monkey," I may then expand my knowledge of these animals by reading about other particulars in videos, images, and texts. My concept of a "monkey" will be different from yours, but will overlap in a significant way and so facilitate communication. However, in every case, concepts ultimately resolve into particulars. Because mental and communicative concepts refer to particulars, they are always to some extent concrete, not purely abstract. "Monkey" refers to certain objects according to what they have in common, so it indicates a specific likeness between them and indicates certain features held by these objects (such as prehensile tail). Yet no definition will suffice to capture the rich variety that is found across the many objects of a concept: though monkeys are all different in colour, the concept of monkey is not colourless. Such a variety of experiences juxtaposed with likeness cannot be captured in an abstract definition (which excises all differences in search of unity) but is upheld by our mental concepts. In sum, mental concepts are habitual events grouping objects, and communicative acts signify such events, often isolating particular relationships between objects.

i. An Abstraction is a Particular Relationship Between Objects

I have defined a concept as a mental act or "habitual event" of relating particulars; terms refer to concepts, presenting a particular relationship between objects with language. I think this is a definition of abstraction consistent with our experience as interpreted by the Bible. That we can talk about "humanity," "existence," "smallness," "largeness," etc. demonstrates that we use abstract thought.

Revisiting abstract nouns, I know that I have no definition of "love" or "goodness." But neither do I have a single exemplar of love in mind, an isolated event with no relation.[7] Instead, our concepts of love refer to a series of events that we deem exemplary of "love." If love is neither a floating abstract definition that lays behind these events nor a random assortment of events, what remains is that "love" is a relationship between these events. Love describes a particular feature of these events that is drawn out when they are viewed in relationship with one another. It is not a "part" of these events, as if you could take an instance of me saying "I love you" to Nicole and dissect it into parts—it is part speech, love, communication, respect, etc. Instead, love describes one way of looking at this event as it shares commonality with other similar events; it is a perspective by which all these events can be viewed.

---

[7] Withing cognitive linguistics, it is often supposed that concepts have a "prototype," or an exemplar to which other objects are related. I am not convinced that the data supports this theory nor that it has as much explanatory power as the view articulated above.

c. Problems with This View

I believe that such a definition of abstraction, as a particular relationship between objects (whether things or events) makes sense of what goes on with abstract thought. For our purposes, three problems emerge as concerns for this view. First, such a definition of love runs the risk of destroying communication: how do I know my perception of the relationship I call "love" is the same as yours? If there is no abstract definition of love by which we can compare our selection of examples of love, how do we know who is "right" or even that we agree? This then raises two more problems. Morality assumes that there is some standard by which we can determine which actions, thoughts, or attitudes are genuine examples of "love"; is that undermined by this definition? If morality is not undermined, how do humans access this standard—however it is now defined?

i. Problem One

First, there is indeed a sense in which all our abstract terms are subjective and arbitrary—yet this need not destroy the possibility of communication. That language is arbitrary and subjective is evident with a bit of thought: the symbol "d-o-g" is no more fitting for a dog than the symbol "c-a-t." In this sense, language is arbitrary. The fact that the definition of "love" among Christians differs from that of Atheists and that the very word "love" differs from the related words in other languages (e.g. ἔρως, ἀγάπη, φιλέω, אהב, *quiero, amo, adoro*) shows that "love" itself is a subjective term. But this does not necessarily destroy communication or morality. To the contrary, if we notice that the Spanish word *quiero* at times means "I love you" but can mean something more sexual, we do not say that "*quiero*" is being used wrongly because it does not equal our understanding of "love." Instead, we listen and learn the range of meanings *quiero* has. The point is this, everyone uses the word "love" or the equivalent in other languages to mean different things; to learn what someone else means by "love," we pay attention to how they use it. We identify the relationship that holds among all these uses, the similarities they all have. So, the subjectivity of our definition of abstraction does not destroy communication; to the contrary, it fits very well with how we learn a language and technical terms (i.e. particularly refined abstract terms). An implication of this is that humans must intentionally understand how others are using language to make communication possible. This means that communication is a moral act, one for which God will hold us accountable.[8]

ii. Problem Two

Our answer leads us to the second problem: for behaviour to be moral (judged good or bad), it must be measured by a standard that cannot be relative to each person. My definition of abstraction so far seems to endanger this, for it is usual to understand the moral standards as objective, abstract concepts. However, this is not a necessary conclusion. As we have seen, abstraction is a personal concept, the perception of relationships between objects. Therefore, an impersonal standard is out of the question. However, God—the true measure of right and wrong—is not an impersonal standard. We can define the standards of morality (moral goodness, love, truth, kindness, etc.) as God's perception of particular relationships between events (broadly defined to include actions, thoughts, feelings, etc.). "Love" as it matters for declaring something morally right or wrong is not my definition of love, nor the Greek definition of ἀγάπη (*agapē*, "love"), but God's definition of love. Our answer here brings us to the last problem.

iii. Problem Three

If the standard for truth and morality is God's interpretation of events, how do we have access to God's standards? We need to answer this in two ways, for we need to explain both the explicit standards for judging behaviour and the implicit "work of the law" that is imprinted on human hearts (cf. Rom 2:12-16). To explain the knowledge all human beings have of God's expectations, ultimately that they worship and obey him (Rom 2:18-32), we must appeal to something like innate ideas. As David Hume long ago showed, it is impossible to derive an "ought" statement from an "is": we cannot determine what we ought to think and do from our experience alone, so we need something by which to interpret our experience and declare it good or bad. Such a "something" cannot come from experience (a bare "is").[9]

---

[8] Cf. *The Gift of Knowing*.

[9] If every "is" implies an ought, then the reality of murder, assault, etc. would indicate the appropriateness or even the necessity of such things. If one were to discriminate and say that certain realities, such as what is "natural" as opposed to human-made, are morally normative, the problem remains. On the one hand, assault and killing are still normative (as they are present throughout the natural world); on

However, the Bible makes it clear that those without special revelation know what they ought to do: they recognize certain acts as wrong and others as right (e.g. Rom 1:18-3:8). Humans must, therefore, have the innate ability to identify moral acts, meaning they have the ability to develop moral concepts. In *The Gift of Knowing*, I suggested that this innateness may be explained as a sort of template: our minds are hardwired to identify certain features of the world and give them an appropriate evaluation, thus making these a normative concept. I still find this explanation necessary; I think our minds do have something like templates for building concepts of colours and things (giving unity to the cacophony of sensation we are confronted with; see Part 3). However, since writing *The Gift of Knowing*, I have developed my thinking on moral concepts. We have seen already that God himself is the standard of morality: his deeds and evaluations become the norms for our deeds and evaluations. At the heart of Romans 1-2, where Paul clearly asserts the universal knowledge of God's law, Paul first claims that all humans know God.[10] Therefore, it seems the claim that all humans know God's law is an implication of all people knowing God's "invisible attributes, namely, his eternal power and divine nature" (Rom 1:20a). If we know God, we will have some sense of how he will evaluate reality, including our actions and the actions of others. However, this adds another dimension to our problem: what do we do with this knowledge? Most people would not confess to knowing God in this way.

Our argument so far has opened space for a solution. By developing concepts in terms of mental acts and the fundamental objects of knowledge as particulars, we have broadened the concept of knowledge beyond propositions and explicit beliefs. The knowledge of persons, for example, cannot be reduced to propositions: it includes them but cannot be reduced to them.[11] I know Nicole, my wife, better than anyone else does (or so I would claim), yet her mom and sisters likely have more factual knowledge

---

the other, the principle used to differentiate between what realities are normative (natural vs. human-made) is arbitrary and needs justification. Thus, moral judgment requires a moral standard or principle by which the situation in question can be judged.

[10] Here, I discuss the function of the knowledge of God in conscious. We will look at this passage again shortly.

[11] Cf. Frame, *The Doctrine of the Knowledge*, 44–48.

about Nicole's life than I do. Knowledge of persons is complex, involving knowledge of their past and present with the result that we can anticipate their future, namely, how they will respond and what they may desire. Such knowledge facilitates communication, empathy, and relationships in general. This sort of knowledge (the knowledge of persons) is attendant in all my interactions with Nicole but is always tacit, part of the interpretive framework by which I interpret and construct the world around me.[12] If the knowledge of God possessed by all humans is propositional knowledge, we run into a problem: few people would consciously acknowledge this knowledge. However, if the knowledge of God we all possess is tacit, it may or may not correspond to conscious belief.

For someone who professes faith in the God of the Bible, this knowledge is analogous to the knowledge I have of my wife, Nicole: it is active in all my interpretive endeavours and is complemented by explicit association with Yahweh and propositional knowledge of his character and works (e.g. he is righteous, covenanted with his people, became incarnate, rules all things, etc.). However, for those without this conscious belief, the knowledge of Yahweh will still shape their interaction with his world: they will not consciously connect their perception of order and consistency in nature with God's faithfulness, but they will nevertheless interpret the world in light of this truth. Indeed, as Paul goes on to write, they may associate what they know of God—his "invisible attributes, namely, eternal power and divine nature" (Rom 1:20a)—with elements of the created order, deifying things that are not God, whether spiritual or human persons or even nature itself (Rom 1:21-25). As it concerns the innate sense of morality Paul identifies in these early chapters of Romans (often call conscience), person-knowledge of God (as described above on analogy with our knowledge of human persons) explains how we may innately know God's moral will concerning what we ought to and ought not to do (Rom 1:21, 32; 2:14-15). If, as I have argued, morality is rooted in God's nature reflected in verbal revelation and in his deeds, then knowing God enables us to anticipate what he approves of and disapproves of—as knowing Nicole allows me to anticipate what would please or displease her.

So, God has given all human beings the ability from birth to correlate

---

[12] See further, *The Gift of Knowing;* Polanyi, *Personal Knowledge*, 49–68, 69–195; Michael Polanyi, *The Tacit Dimension* (Chicago; London: University of Chicago Press, 2009).

specific experiences with his standards, judging them to be right or wrong. Whether we call an act ἀγαπή or love, we can judge it to be right or wrong. Yet this innate judge, our conscience, is not perfect: we twist and ignore it, leaving it marred (Rom 1:18-3:20). Therefore, we need an explicit revelation of God's moral standard by which we can correct our sinful distortions and be intentional in pursuing obedience to God.

I intend, of course, the Bible. If we learn what other people mean by "love" by studying what they identify as "love," we learn what God means by "love" by studying those things he identifies. Looking at Scripture, we are taught that God is love. We are taught that love is an essential way to understand who God is and that only by understanding who God is will we understand love (1 John 4:7-12). Everything we identify as "love" is only such, therefore, because it reflects this aspect of God's character. Love is a perspective by which we can view God's actions within his triune-self (e.g. John 17) and towards his creation. By looking at this pattern of God's activity, we can then identify what thoughts, actions, attitudes, etc. are loving or not. This pattern is sometimes described (1 Corinthians 13) and sometimes narrated (Exodus) but it is this, the character of God displayed through his actions (including word and deed) and revealed to us in Scripture that gives us a standard for what is and is not love. Therefore, the concept of "love," as our example for right loving, is a particular relationship that we identify between acts that are consistent with what God has shown us about his loving character. Thus, we have two ways to access God's perfect standard. First, all humans have person-knowledge of God, by which we intuitively identify right and wrong. However, this knowledge is marred by sin; we often need correction. Second, we have the revelation of God's character and his interpretation of many events and actions throughout history. This revelation corrects our knowledge of God and our evaluations of truth and goodness.

Before concluding, we can also observe how our argument explains how human language is adequate for speaking of God. That is, given that God is transcendent—utterly beyond us—and outside of our experience, how do our concepts, developed it would seem from our experience, allow us to speak and think rightly of him? Would not thoughts of the created order have to bring God down to the level of that order to speak rightly of him?

In response, we saw that God has structured the world to reflect his own faithfulness and has given us minds competent to discern consistency in the world. Given that we interpret the world with the presupposition of God's faithfulness (i.e. stability or consistency), our interpretation of the world as stable and consistent moves from God as he has made himself known to the world, not from the world to God. Furthermore, he has created humanity and the world with the adequate likeness that it might be an effective revelation of his character, as is evident throughout Scripture. This is clear both in its statements and the assumption that our language is adequate to speak of him. Finally, we are able to interpret actions and events as good or bad, right or wrong, loving or unloving *because* God has made himself personally known in our interpretive hardware: he has wired humanity with person-knowledge of himself. Thus, our concepts do not move from earthly analogies to God but from God to earthly things. If God is eternally triune, then it would not be preposterous to suppose that the person-knowledge of God contains knowledge of his triune-self, including his eternal fatherhood. Thus, we can discern a good father from a bad father because we know God who is the perfect father: our understanding of earthly fathers does not first inform our knowledge of God as father, but our knowledge of God informs our evaluation of earthly fatherhood. Of course, the impact of earthly fathers often does affect our interpretation of God as Father (cf. Rom 2:15), so we need Scripture to perfect our innate but distorted knowledge.

D. Conclusion

In this chapter, I have argued that the priority of the particular indicated by the Bible does not destroy reason or rationality, though it certainly limits it. We can interpret the world, have true and certain knowledge, and anticipate the regularity of our experience because God has carefully crafted his creation as the perfect medium of his self-revelation and for his creatures' creative obedience (i.e. ruling the earth as his representatives). His word upholds the consistent functioning of the world; the created world was created to be like God and like to itself so that humans could know God and his world; finally, the human mind was created with the ability to draw relations between things in order to better understand each thing in light of similar things. Ultimately, regularity, likeness, and conceptuality enable us to know God. We know God as Father because he has made earthly fathers like him; we know God as powerful because we encounter power in this world and his Word; etc. The biblical worldview upholds unity and plurality in a way the Greeks did not envision: the particular is primary, yet the particular is always mentally interpreted in relation to other things. This element of "interpretation" is ambiguous thus far: it will be the object of Part 3 to outline the significant ways in which the mind is involved in interpreting the world and the relationship between this interpretation, truth, and communication. It is fitting for us to respond to the beauty and wisdom of God's creation, so perfect for facilitating human understanding, as Paul once responded to God's wisdom in salvation:

> Oh, the depth of the riches and wisdom and knowledge of God! How unsearchable are his judgments and how inscrutable his ways!
>
> "For who has known the mind of the Lord,
>   or who has been his counselor?"
> "Or who has given a gift to him
>   that he might be repaid?"
>
> For from him and through him and to him are all things. To him be glory forever. Amen. (Romans 11:33-36)

—Part 3—
The Problem of the External World

7

THE END OF EMPIRICISM

A. Modernity – The World of the Senses

To say that "Modernity" is the "world of the senses" is not to say that all modern philosophy was supremely concerned with the sensible world. There were also idealists and rationalists who focused on the mind in one way or another, yet the overall concern of this time was to justify the scientific discipline.[1] The rationalists were concerned with building a foundation of certain knowledge from which other disciplines such as science could be performed; the empiricists attempted to probe the extent of what could be known through senses alone. The former school of philosophy, the rationalists, is primarily associated with Continental Europe; the latter school, the empiricists, with Britain.

The father of Modern philosophy is often thought to be Rene Descartes (1596-1650). Descartes considered himself a faithful Catholic. However, like the atheistic philosophers before him, Descartes starting point for philosophy is the self—the one thing of which he thought we could be most certain. Though Descartes is important in many respects, the British Empiricists are more important for our purposes.

---

[1] Idealism refers to a metaphysical view that reality is ultimately mental. That is, either what we perceive as physical is actually immaterial mental content or all we can know is our mental perception. Rationalism gives priority to the mind over the senses in attaining knowledge. Many rationalists would say that the senses yield no true knowledge.

a. George Berkeley

According to Immanuel Kant (one of the most influential philosophers in recent history), it was the British philosopher David Hume who "awoke" him from his "dogmatic slumber," from his philosophical rationalism. However, it was George Berkeley who developed many of the radical ideas that Hume would employ in pursuit of an atheistic agenda.

George Berkeley was an Anglican bishop in Ireland during the 17th century. He adopted a view of human knowledge much like that of William of Ockham, within which all human knowledge pertained to particular things. Berkeley went farther than Ockham by arguing that not only the universal but also the particular could be explained as mental activity. Instead of positing an extramental substance that could cause all our sense experience, such as a tree that caused our sense of rough, brown bark and green leaves, he argued that all experience could be explained by the direct activity of God, who was the cause of the various experiences we have. Berkely intended to rule out atheism and scepticism, but David Hume developed similar arguments in the opposite direction, toward scepticism.

b. David Hume

The most influential British Empiricist was, perhaps, David Hume (1711-1776). David Hume was ferociously consistent in his philosophy, to the extent that almost all knowledge was cast into doubt. Hume was no friend of Christianity, yet his writing shows just how hopeless is a philosophy built on reason alone.

As for ontology, Hume is most important in showing how hopeless the rational investigation of the connection between our mind and the outside world can become. For Hume, *analytic truths* can be known by the meaning of the words themselves, such as statements about mathematics and logic, but all other knowledge must be tested by the senses. Knowledge in the latter sense can be classified as impressions and ideas. Impressions are immediate sensory data. Ideas are mental concepts of objects derived from impressions, such as the concepts of that table or this house as found in our memory. For Hume, ideas are not 100% reliable and thus must be traced back to the impressions that created them for verification.

The assumption that all non-analytic truths (i.e. all truths that are not self-evident) must be tested by the senses rules out much of the ontological speculation of Hume's predecessors. Any search for a unifying "substance," such as a basic matter shared by all things, is impossible: we neither have nor can have experience of such a thing. Not only is it impossible to find an abstract concept that gives knowledge of everything, even the laws necessary to interpret the world have no basis in the senses. If we only sense diversity, we have no reason to believe that there is ultimate unity. Whereas Berkeley wanted to prevent scepticism by positing that God stood behind all human experience, thus making that experience consistent and trustworthy, Hume argued that we must be sceptical about the very existence of God.

If it is only reasonable to believe something demonstrated by the senses, the supernatural realm is ruled out as unreasonable. Hume did not make any metaphysical claim that God and miracles do not exist or cannot happen. He only claimed that there is no reasonable way to know that a miracle occurred or that God exists. We have no sense experience of God, so if someone tells us that God exists, how can we verify this claim? The same is true for miracles. Miracles are, by definition, rare events. As such, we will not have previous sense experiences of them. If we have never experienced a resurrection, it is only reasonable to doubt the idea of a resurrection. It is more reasonable to assume that any experience of a miracle is a false idea than to believe it without sense verification:

> Hume argues that there can never be sufficient evidence to affirm that a miracle has taken place. He begins by defining *miracle* as a violation of a law of nature. But that definition makes it impossible for us to believe that any event was a miracle. We always have more evidence, says Hume, for the normal course of nature than we have for any claimed exception to it. So when confronted with a strange event, we should always prefer natural explanations of it to supernatural explanations. Says Hume, it is always more likely that the witnesses misunderstood or misrepresented the event than that it was a violation of the laws of nature.[2]

By demanding a strict empirical standard for truth, Hume rules out many facets of ontology in general. In particular, he places God and the search for unity amidst the plurality of experience beyond the bounds of reason. If ontology seeks to explain knowledge and its relation both to

---

[2] Frame, *A History*, 202.

experience and truth, to our minds and the external world, Hume's scepticism rules it out. We have no access to the outside world nor to a God who would reveal anything about it. Furthermore, we have no access to a standard above ourselves to claim anything like transcendent truth (i.e. truth that is always valid for all people). The laws that appear to regulate our experience are reduced to psychology, and supernatural claims are purely claims of faith, not reason:[3]

> If we take in our hand any volume; of divinity or school metaphysics, for instance; let us ask, Does it contain any abstract reasoning concerning quantity or number [i.e., analytic truth]? No. Does it contain any experimental reasoning concerning matter of fact and existence [i.e., empirical truth]? No. Commit it then to the flames: for it can contain nothing but sophistry and illusion.[4]

c. Immanuel Kant

Before Immanuel Kant (1724-1804), philosophy evolved along different trajectories in continental Europe and Britain. The German thinker Kant changed this by bringing together the rationalism of the continent with the empiricism of Britain.

Where does one go after the scepticism of Hume? How could philosophy be pursued if everything must be subject to the test of experience? Kant's answer was something called the transcendental method. He reasoned not by deducing philosophical truths from several basic premises, as Descartes and the rationalists did, nor by deriving truth from sense experience. He argued instead from what must necessarily be so if knowledge is possible. That is, assuming that one can have knowledge, he asked, what must the world be

---

[3] This may sound like a twisted way of protecting Christian belief from science and philosophy, in a way similar to later protestant philosophers. However, Hume appears to be much more aggressively atheistic; though Christian belief is not proved wrong, it is shown to be utterly unreasonable. The conclusion of his *Dialogues Concerning Natural Religion* suggests that his goal is to show that after reason is done with it, Christianity is essentially meaningless.

[4] This is from Hume's *An Enquiry concerning Human Understanding*, 12.3.

like?⁵ What are the conditions that make knowledge possible? His answer was a two-world schema: there is the *noumenal* world and the *phenomenal* world.

The noumenal world is the world of what is, the actual. The phenomenal world is the world of the mind, of experience. We do not know anything about the noumenal world; our mind defines everything we experience. Our senses receive from the noumenal world something which Kant called *percepts*, bare "experience." *Percepts* have no content; our mind receives the percept and defines it with qualities such as treeness, brown, leafness, green, 8 feet tall, etc. There is something out there, but everything we know about the tree is imposed by our minds on the *percept* received. Therefore, we cannot know anything about reality; we can only know about our own mind. Nevertheless, the phenomenal world is the realm where science is safe to function apart from the criticism of philosophy. Now, someone may ask how we can even know that the noumenal exists if all our experience is mental. For Kant, the noumenal world must exist to explain our experience. Similarly, "god" must exist to explain ethics.

Thus, there is an external world in Kant's philosophy, but we cannot know anything about it. There is also a god, yet we cannot know anything about it. God exists merely as the goal of ethics; god is essentially the idea that appropriate ethical behaviour will be rewarded, justifying the effort to be virtuous. Kant was insistent that morality could not be done with any motive of self-benefit, yet for morality to make sense at all, there must be the promise that in the hereafter, good will be rewarded and evil punished. God is the necessary principle to this effect. We cannot know that this god exists, nor that the world exists, but we must nevertheless live "as if" they exist, for only in this way is a reasonable and ethical life possible.

With Kant we observe a significant shift. For Plato, the stable reality that made knowledge possible was the external world of the Forms. Kant

---

⁵ In the *Critique of Pure Reason*, Kant defines a certain form of knowledge he called "synthetic *a priori*" propositions, that is, truths which do not depend on sense experience and yet are not analytic. An analytic proposition such as "all bachelors are married" is self-evidently true, for the predicate ("married") is part of the subject ("bachelor"). A synthetic proposition, on the other hand, is one where the predicate is related to the subject but is not implied in it ("all bodies are heavy," that is, affected by gravity). The book then investigates whether synthetic a priori propositions are possible and how they can be so.

essentially reverses this: the stability necessary is imposed on the unknowable world by our minds. The forms do not exist beyond our minds but are an essential feature of our cognitive faculties. For Kant, ontology is absorbed into the thinking subject: it is all about the mind and what it must believe if reason is to be accepted. For Kant, the nature of reality is out of humanity's reach.

Kant and Hume leave us in an uncomfortable place regarding metaphysics; in different ways, they both argue that metaphysics is impossible. Their influence is still felt in modern philosophy, especially in certain forms of 20th-century liberal theology and in the Postmodern rejection of metaphysics. For ontology, Kant's position is similar to early Hellenistic philosophy in several ways. The extra-mental world is ultimately one, undifferentiated and unknowable; it is pure potentiality. The mind is the sole source of stability and form, giving shape to the potentiality of the world. The question of "universals" has faded from view, but if they exist, they are an imposition of our mind on the noumenal world. As with Berkeley, all qualities, such as location, colour, and all form (the similarity Plato and Aristotle identified as essence) are qualities of the mind, not of an external subject. It would thus seem that truth itself is lost, but this is not the position that Kant took. For Kant, the mental framework by which the noumenal world was interpreted was not individual but collective, the shared framework of humanity. However, there seems to be no compelling reason to accept this as the case. Furthermore, apart from revelation, Berkeley's claim that God upholds the unity of experience across all minds is similarly untenable.

B. Conclusion

Philosophy did not stop with Kant. Indeed, it has developed at a mind-boggling pace ever since. Space does not allow us to explore the developments leading up to our time. However, what we have seen thus far has set the tone for the contemporary discussion, at least as far as ontology is concerned. The conclusion of Berkeley, Hume, and Kant concerning the mind's power to form the world around us is widely acknowledged. The atheism of Kant and Hume is generally accepted, so positions within which God has a crucial function are not commonplace. The problem of the universal remains contentious, as does the nature of truth. However, in the work of Kant, Berkeley's claim that reality is mentally constructed was solidified and has become the basis for much contemporary philosophical discussion, both Christian and non-Christian.

Further Reading

George Berkeley, *Principles of Human Knowledge* [A]
George Berkeley, *Three Dialogues* [A][6]
Joshua R. Farris, S. Mark Hamilton, and James S. Spiegel, *Idealism and Christian Theology: Idealism and Christianity Volume 1* [A]
John Frame, *A History of Western Philosophy and Theology* [B-I]
David Hume, *Dialogues Concerning Natural Religion* [A]
David Hume, *An Enquiry into the Human Understanding* [A][7]
Michael Polanyi, *Personal Knowledge: Towards a Post-Critical Philosophy* [A]
Michael Polanyi, *The Tacit Dimension* [I][8]

---

[6] *Principles* is a highly abstract work. Berkeley wrote the *Three Dialogues* to present his main argument for subjective idealism in a more accessible and persuasive manner.

[7] The *Dialogues* argues against the possibility of natural religion; having dismissed the possibility of revelation elsewhere, the dialogue presumes that the question of God's existence is meaningless. In the end, we can have no answer and it makes no difference. The *Enquiry* summarises the main argument of Hume's larger *A Treatise on Human Nature* but is still a difficult work for those without a philosophical background.

[8] In *Personal Knowledge* and *The Tacit Dimension*, Polanyi agrees that objective knowledge is impossible, our minds are actively involved in presenting us the world we perceive in experience. However, this does not mean we cannot have truth or know the world outside of us. *Personal Knowledge* has many profound insights but settles on a decidedly unconvincing account of truth as personal assent. *The Tacit Dimension* presents many of what I would judge to be the most important theses in *Personal Knowledge* in an easier manner.

8

INTERPRETATION: BRING THE WORLD INTO BEING

And God said, "Let there be light," and there was light. And God saw that the light was good. And God separated the light from the darkness. God called the light Day, and the darkness he called Night. And there was evening and there was morning, the first day. – Genesis 1:3-5

The natural person does not accept the things of the Spirit of God, for they are folly to him, and he is not able to understand them because they are spiritually discerned. The spiritual person judges all things, but is himself to be judged by no one. "For who has understood the mind of the Lord so as to instruct him?" But we have the mind of Christ. – 1 Corinthians 2:14-16

How often have you thought of the mind's activity in presenting the world to you? For many Greek philosophers, the world of the senses was untrustworthy because it was always changing, and our minds were susceptible to illusion. However, the basic reality of the extra-mental world was not in question: there was a world out there constructed in a certain way, accessible to reason. With the rise of the empirical sciences in the mid-2nd millennium, it quickly became apparent that nature was not objectively presented to the human mind. Within philosophy, this was already being introduced in the 14th century with William of Ockham; it would be developed extensively by the British Empiricists and Immanuel Kant. In the world of the physical sciences, the subjectivity of the world was recognized by some, such as the philosophers Michael Polanyi and Thomas Kuhn, and ignored by many others, such as Richard Dawkins.

At some point, perhaps in high school, you probably heard the question, "If a tree falls in a forest with no one to hear it, does it make a sound?" At first this sounds sophistical (i.e. pointlessly sceptical), but it raises an important issue. Our reflexive response would be, "of course it does!" But, if we exclude for the moment the presence of God (whose existence means that there is always someone "hearing"), such an answer confuses the meaning of the term "sound." That is, if we acknowledge that a tree has indeed fallen, then it will, of course, create vibrations through the air. However, vibrations in the air *are not sound*; they are merely the cause of sound. That is, sound is *an interpretation* of vibrations, a mental construal as to their significance. Our ears receive the vibrations caused by the tree's fall and present them to us as the experience of sound. However, a deaf person will be acted on by the vibrations and yet not have the same experience, for their physical faculties did not present the sense data to their mental faculties. Someone who has perfectly functioning physical faculties may experience cognitive difficulties interpreting sound with the result that their experience is not the same as the average person. In these ways, "sound," as we usually construe it, does not exist outside of the mind and, therefore, does not exist without an interpreter. The cause of sound is present when the unobserved tree falls, but "sound" is not. Consider colour. Colour is the mental perception of specific wavelengths of light, but our perception of colour depends not only on functioning physical faculties but also corresponding mental faculties. Someone who is colour blind will have a different experience from someone who is not colour blind in response to the same stimuli.

Not only are traditional qualities like colour subjective, but even size also appears to be so. George Berkeley illustrated this point concerning size by asking us to picture a mite. We cannot even see a tiny mite, yet something that either possesses more precise vision or is of corresponding size can. The latter is an important point: size is heavily influenced by perspective. For a mite, a cat is enormous, but for a human, it is an average-sized animal. Even a spider is large for a mite though small for a human. A bear viewed from far away appear quite small, but up close it is large. In each case the stimuli is the same but perspective results in vastly different experiences. The same is true of taste, smell, and touch.

In each case, our experience of sound, sight, taste, smell, and physical sensation are all mental phenomena apparently caused by external stimuli but which do not correspond to that physical stimuli. This lack of correspondence is witnessed in the different experiences of those who receive the same perception, or the ability for the mind to misinterpret such external stimuli (leading us to believe light reflected from hot asphalt is water, for example). After carefully examining our senses, we must conclude that our experience is not a bare representation of the external world (a position called naïve realism): it is an interpretation of all sorts of apparently external stimuli. Our minds receive one thing and present to us another. This initial observation does not necessarily lead to scepticism: instead, we can marvel at the amazing complexity of the world God has created. It is mindboggling that our experience involves the perfectly synchronized interaction of external reality, physical senses, and mental interpretation. However, it does caution us against thinking that there is a one-to-one correlation between our experience and the external world. Indeed, it is impossible to imagine what the external world is actually like: if depth, proportion, shape, texture, colour, smell, taste, and touch are all the result of a careful balance of stimuli, reception, and interpretation, then the world before interpretation is impossible to imagine! Many studies have gone further to identify the variegated way interpretation "creates" the world we perceive: interpretation is not objective but is informed by our God-given faculties along with our conscious and tacit beliefs, so that in many ways we see the world as we want to see it.

Where does this leave us? At this point, some philosophers have dismissed the external world entirely (with sceptical or theistic conclusions offered in its place), or they have decried the pursuit of knowledge of the external world at all. However, we do not need to follow these paths. On the one hand, the "external world" is really not so external: it is a complex reality that involves interpretation in its creation but is, nevertheless, not subjective because of this. We reject subjectivity for two reasons: first, the world has been pre-interpreted by God, so there is a "right" interpretation or mental construction of the external world. Second, because God has structured the world and our senses that we may have knowledge of it and thrive within it for his glory, we can trust that our faculties offer us the world as we are meant to perceive it, at least they do so when functioning correctly. "Meant to perceive it" is not the world without perception at all: we have no reason to believe we were ever meant to know the world apart from perception. Instead, we have every reason to believe that God carefully constructed the creation so that it would be a coherent equilibrium between the unconstructed world and the constructing mind, working in tandem to present the "real," or the world of our experience. In many ways this is a team effort, for the fact that God has granted functioning faculties to humanity as a whole does not guarantee that every human possesses them: our experience abounds with evidence to the contrary. Some people experience physical impairment, others mental impairment, still others experience momentary impairment from physical trauma or substance abuse. However, working together, we can discern where malformed experience is occurring and submit to the judgment of others who are not experiencing the same distortions as we are. This is true not only of our basic faculties but also our belief systems.

In many ways, we see what we believe we will see. For example, if we are committed to the belief that resurrections are impossible, we will intuitively arrive at alternate conclusions when confronted with an apparent resurrection. Believing rightly is an important part of seeing rightly, as we saw in *The Gift of Knowing*. Therefore, we need others. Most importantly, we need God to construct the world of experience accurately. By submitting to others in our weakness and submitting to God as he has revealed himself in his Word, we can have confidence that we will see the world as he has intended us to see it and so be able to respond as he has intended us to respond.

All I have hoped to achieve in this chapter is raise the problem: our world is an interpreted world. There is no such thing as neutrality or objectivity. In addition, I have attempted to move us away from the conclusion that a lack of neutrality or objectivity leaves us with scepticism. God gives us a way beyond pure subjectivity, a way to uphold truth. It is to this that we must now turn.

Further Reading

George Berkeley, *Principles of Human Knowledge* [A]
George Berkeley, *Three Dialogues* [A][1]
*John Frame, *The Doctrine of the Knowledge of God* [B-I]
David Hume, *An Enquiry into the Human Understanding* [A][2]
Iain McGilchrist, *The Master and His Emissary* [A][3]
*Esther Meek, *Longing to Know* [B]
Esther Meek, *Loving to Know* [I][4]
*Michael Polanyi, *Personal Knowledge: Towards a Post-Critical Philosophy* [A]
*Michael Polanyi, *The Tacit Dimension* [I][5]
Sickler, Bradley L, *God on the Brain* [B]

---

[1] *Principles* is a highly abstract work. Berkeley wrote the *Three Dialogues* to present his main argument for subjective idealism in a more accessible and persuasive manner.

[2] *The Enquiry* summarises the main argument of Hume's larger *A Treatise on Human Nature* but is still a difficult work for those without a philosophical background.

[3] McGilchrist presents a fascinating account of the recent literature on the brain and the way it construes the world. I am not persuaded by his conclusions, and he is heavily influenced by the philosophical traditions of Phenomenalism and Existentialism, which I believe are extremely unhelpful. However, the book is fascinating and, for our purposes, presents the data for the subjectivity of experience persuasively. See my review, https://teleioteti.ca/2020/10/29/review-of-the-master-and-his-emissary/.

[4] See my review, https://teleioteti.ca/2020/11/18/review-of-loving-to-know/.

[5] In *Personal Knowledge* and *The Tacit Dimension*, Polanyi agrees that objective knowledge is impossible, our minds are actively involved in presenting us the world we perceive in experience. However, this does not mean we cannot have truth or know the world outside of us. *Personal Knowledge* has many profound insights but settles on a decidedly unconvincing account of truth as personal assent. *The Tacit Dimension* presents many of what I would judge to be the most important theses in *Personal Knowledge* in an easier manner.

9

TRUTH: THE FIRST INTERPRETER

Once again, the answer to the critical questions of ontology is seen to be Yahweh, the living God. He furnishes the world with continuous identity (Part 1), he created the worlds diversity while maintaining its unity through his interpreting word (Part 2), and he has created both the world that causes perception and the world of perception so that we might adequately perceive his world (Part 3). What remains for our purposes is to explore the last dimensions of God's work to ontologically sustain creation. Ontology, however it has been pursued, has concerned itself with truth. The philosophers have sought to identify the adequate objects of knowledge and the nature of that knowledge. In the Christian tradition, the view of truth as correspondence with reality has dominated. However, this view has relied on either Platonism, where truth is restricted to the world of the Forms and is a correspondence between human speech and the Forms, or objective empiricism, where there is somehow a correspondence between knowledge and the extra-mental world (the nature of mental content and so knowledge for such a position has been debated heavily). Our argument thus far has ruled out both these positions, but we need not give in to the sceptical alternatives. Our argument thus far gives a better ground for truth than either of these positions, namely, God himself.

As Van Til repeatedly stated throughout his life, there is no uninterpreted or brute fact.[1] Every facet of the creation is known and

---

[1] E.g. *A Christian Theory of Knowledge*.

interpreted—given value, meaning, and purpose—by God. God has pre-interpreted all things, so knowledge is merely thinking God's thoughts after him, and truth is a correspondence (however partial and finite) between our interpretation and his. Now, there will always be a qualitative difference between our thoughts and his, such that his are prior and ours follow, his create what they interpret and ours respond to his creation, his are the norm and our are normed. Nevertheless, there is a genuine correspondence. God is truth, as is his spoken Word: God's thoughts are the standard of truth itself by which any human thought is measured. What we have seen in this book is the extent to which this is true. God's thoughts uphold individual identity, so they are the standard for our perception of continuity. God's thoughts have exhausted every relation between himself and the creation and every created thing to everything else, thus acting as the standard for all universal concepts. Finally, the world itself exists to some extent as a mental construct. However, the real is not, therefore, purely subjective and relative, for it has always existed as it was meant to be perceived in God's interpretation. All thought, every perception, and each experience are wholly interpretative. Our interpretation is true when it corresponds to God's. However, "knowledge" is a complex thing, so how this works is complicated. We will consider here only three facets of knowledge, propositional knowledge, person-knowledge (with its analogues), and conceptual knowledge.

A. Propositional Knowledge

As far as classic philosophy was concerned, knowledge had one form, propositions. A proposition is a statement with, minimally, a subject and a predicate: "he is," for example. For Plato and Aristotle, knowledge concerned abstract things and the laws that governed their relations. A law can be expressed propositionally, e.g. when X then Y, as can the definition of a thing, e.g. a human is a rational animal. Logic, for Aristotle, governed the way we speak and reason about things. For the Stoics (another group of Greek philosophers), knowledge was still propositional but this time concerned states of affairs (e.g. it is raining). They developed a logic for relating propositions of this sort. In our view, Aristotle's view of logic is problematic, for there is no abstract definition of anything, and terms do not have the clear-cut boundaries that his logic requires (though his insights are still very valuable).² Propositional knowledge, especially in the Stoic sense, remains important in the biblical perspective. The Bible asserts many truths that are or may be articulated in propositional form (e.g. Jesus was crucified; Jesus rose again). A proposition may be true or false, but truth requires a standard or norm. However, unlike the Platonists, we have rejected the existence of abstract forms, so a statement such as "a human has a mind" is not true with reference to an abstract definition, a "form." Instead, several conditions relate to the truth or falsity of this statement. First, it is true if and only if the group of particulars indicated by the term "human" all possess "mind." Second, it may be true in one context and false in another. If uttered by Stan, who cognizes rocks with humans in his concept of "human," this statement is false. However, if such a statement were found in the Bible, where all "humans" (אָדָם, אִישׁ, אֱנוֹשׁ, ἄνθρωπος) possess a mind, it would be true. No such statement is thus categorically true, but is true or false depending on a given context. God has pre-interpreted all reality, including human cognition and utterance, so his mind is the standard by which any statement is made true or false. Similarly, in the case of states of affairs ("it is raining"), all such propositions are both temporally and subjectively contingent; that is, "raining" is dependent on a person's concept of rain (subjective) and is time-stamped (it is only true or false with reference to time and place). Thus, such a proposition is an interpretation of a particular experience and is made true or false with reference to God's interpretation. God's interpretation is, in this way, the truth-maker for all propositions. The objective truth status of a proposition is a different matter than its subjective status, as belief or knowledge. God's interpretation *makes* something true, but how can we be confident or justified in believing that it us true?

Several factors are at play in this question, namely, correspondence, coherence, and functionality. First, our belief must correspond to our experience *as created by right-functioning faculties*. That is, not all experiences warrant belief. Experiences derived from physical or mental handicaps or from temporary distortion (e.g. being high on drugs) or influenced by any other mechanism which causes false beliefs (such as illusion) are not a sufficient basis for belief. As discussed above, our faculties are basically trustworthy, but we need two or three "witnesses" (Deut 19:15) to confirm

---

² Cf. Vern S. Poythress, *Logic: A God-Centered Approach to the Foundation of Western Thought*, Electronic. (Wheaton: Crossway, 2013).

the reliability of our subjective interpretation. Thus, justified belief corresponds to experience for which we have good reason to trust (the basic trustworthiness of our faculties and the principle of external attestation, two or three witnesses). However, our physical/mental faculties are only one factor in interpretation: interpretation involves reading the world in light of our prior beliefs.

Thus, a justified belief must cohere with our worldview, or better, the correct worldview. Subjectively, if we are aware of tension, such a belief is not justified. For the most part, our worldview interacts with the world on an implicit level, so we are intuitively aware of contradictions, and our experience or framework is adjusted accordingly. However, there are times where we become consciously aware of dissonance, at which time a belief is justified when it coheres with our conscious beliefs. However, not any worldview will do: because God has revealed himself, we are obligated to bring our beliefs in line with his Word, so justification depends on coherence with a biblically shaped worldview or, in other words, the Bible's interpretation of everything.

Finally, a justified belief is functional. The belief that disease is unreal is not justified because it is unliveable: a person cannot consistently live with this belief. A proposition is true when it corresponds with God's interpretation; we believe it is true when it confirms with attested experience, a biblically shaped worldview, and life as informed by the Bible and experience. God is thus essential for truth making and subjective justification, for his Word gives us necessary access to the appropriate worldview for interpreting the world and the assurance that our faculties are basically reliable. Propositional knowledge is important, but it is neither the only nor the most common form of knowledge in our experience or in the Bible. More common, more important, is person-knowledge, or the knowledge of persons.

B. Person-Knowledge

Think of the statement, "I know X," where X represents any person, such as your mother, father, spouse, or friend. Clearly, the knowledge in question is not propositional knowledge—or at least it is not merely propositional knowledge. My claim to know Nicole, my wife, is not a claim to know the definition of the word "Nicole," nor any state of affair pertaining to Nicole. Yet, what is in view is certainly knowledge. Moreover, it is not less than propositional knowledge. That is, if I knew nothing about Nicole, such as her relationship status, family, anything about her, or any fact about her life, my claim to know her would certainly be false. However, no enumerated list of propositions can encompass my knowledge of Nicole. This knowledge is not only past but present; it informs my thoughts and actions towards her. This knowledge is also future-oriented, allowing me to anticipate her actions and feelings in countless circumstances. This is what I call person-knowledge.[3]

Before we explore the concept further, it is interesting to observe that person-knowledge extends beyond human and divine, even spiritual, persons—so perhaps I need to think of a better name for it! The closest analogue is the knowledge of animals: we know pets in an analogous way to our knowledge of persons. We may anticipate their future actions and decipher their present condition in terms of deep understanding of them. (There may be a similar but weaker analogy with our interactions with certain things, where we attribute significance that is not intrinsic to the thing (such as a child's pet rock); I am not yet convinced of this.)

Once we acknowledge that this is a form of knowing distinct from propositional knowledge, we are struck by three facts. First, this sort of knowledge is common in the Bible; second, this is the most common form of knowledge in our everyday lives; third, it is a form of knowledge neglected by the ancient philosophers. As for its commonness, every interaction with a familiar person involves it—and new interactions involve its development. Furthermore, we talk about knowing this or that person very frequently. In the Bible, propositional knowledge is often rendered with a particle indicating a state of affairs, knowing *that*. At other times, the words meaning "to know" (e.g. יָדַע, γινώσκω, ἐπιγνώσκω) have a direct object, indicating propositional knowledge (knowing the content associated with that object, e.g. "he knew the word [= what was said"]), an experience associated with the object, or conceptual knowledge, which we will consider below. However, the use of "know" with a personal subject, e.g. "He knew Yahweh," has distinct connotations. In many cases, to know a person of the opposite sex indicates

---

[3] I am avoiding "personal knowledge" despite its parallelism with "propositional knowledge" because "personal" suggests subjectivity and in his influential book *Personal Knowledge*, Michael Polanyi intends by "personal" the intricate subjective involvement of persons in every act of knowing. His work is of immense value but is not what I intend. Polanyi, *Personal Knowledge*.

sexual relations (e.g. Gen 4:1, 17, 25; Matt 1:25), and in non-sexual contexts, it often indicates an established relationship (e.g. Rom 8:29, 11:2). Thus, for the most part, the use of the term "to know" with a person in the Bible implies what I am calling person-knowledge but explicitly indicates a positive relationship with the person knowing (e.g. Gen 18:19, 29:5; 2 Sam 7:20; Isa 19:21; Matt 7:23; John 10:15, 27; Rom 8:29, 11:2).[4] To know Yahweh includes person-knowledge but also a commitment to Yahweh and the positive response to that knowledge. In English, we often speak of knowing a person without explicitly indicating a relationship (I may know someone who hates me). The Bible occasionally does so; for instance, Nathaniel expresses shock that Jesus knew him (John 1:48). Of Saul, those who "knew him previously" were shocked when he prophesied with a group of prophets (1 Sam 10:11). This seems to be the sense of Psalm 138:6b: God sees and so attends to the righteous, but he has no relationship with the wicked. Furthermore, as Christians, we come to know God (e.g. 1 John 2:3, 13), but all humans know God despite acting contrary to this knowledge (Rom 1:21). Thus, the use of "know" with the connotations of positive, intimate relationship seems to be a deeper extension of the basic sense of person-knowledge. This is particularly prominent with reference to God, who knows all people (e.g. John 2:24-25) and yet knows some people in a unique way (Matt 7:23; John 10:27; Rom 8:29, 11:2; 1 John 2:3, 13).

What, then, do we make of person-knowledge, this important but neglected form of understanding? I believe that it is closely connected to what I have called earlier "interiority," closely related to but not identical with "mind." The modern world is the age of the interior or the self; it is in the Modern and Post-Modern eras that the idea of interiority or the self has received the most attention and analysis. The self is the subjective centre of a person, the "I." That is, neither you nor I can be reduced to our bodies, senses, or brain activity. There are instruments for measuring our brain activity, neural activity, and different aspects of our physical nature, yet no matter how exhaustive the analysis, this data does not begin to approach what it means to be "me" or to explain my experience.

Part of self is consciousness, the awareness of a body as "ours" and the

---

[4] Matt 7:16-20, John 1:48 may be an instance where person-knowledge is intended but a relationship is not implied.

world in distinction from us.⁵ Part of the self is identity, our perception of ourselves in relation to and in distinction from other persons, the perception that though similar in appearance, I think, act, and have different experiences from other humans. Part of the self is knowledge and memory, accumulated experience and belief. I do not intend to give an exhaustive definition of the "self"—indeed, I believe that is impossible—but I hope this sketch of several features of the self indicate what I mean. So, by interiority I mean the subjective "I." The "I" is interior in that it is not visible nor exhaustively known to any other created being: it is distinctly mine.

Furthermore, it is not exhausted by the self; it is interior as our organs are interior, inextricably linked to everyday functioning and yet invisible. What I have called "mind" is one aspect of the self: "mind" describes the self in terms of transcendence, not bound by the cause-effect order of the physical realm. In the same way, I would describe the "body" as another perspective on or aspect of the self: the body is not something we "possess," merely an instrument as alien to us as a car or pen. Instead, our body is precisely ourselves as they are subject to the cause-effect immanence of the physical world. Mind and Body are thus not two different things, entirely distinct, nor the same thing (as physicalism would have it): instead, they are two essential ways of considered one thing, the self, considered as in the world (body) and above the world (mind).⁶ When we speak of identity, character, morality, habit, knowledge, memory, values, beliefs, relationships, etc., we are speaking of the self. The fact that we can and do speak of this interiority indicates that it is not unknown to ourselves nor others. How then, if it is suprasensible (more than we can access through our senses), do we come to know a "person"?

Thomas Aquinas once described our knowledge of God, given that his essence was supposed to be inaccessible to us, knowledge of his effects.⁷ I

---

⁵ This should not be taken for granted: it has been well established that different forms of brain trauma can cause someone to lose the sense of connection between the self and the body, indicating both the interconnectedness between the brain and the self and the distinction between us as our embodied whole and us as the experiencing subject. Cf. McGilchrist, *The Master and His Emissary*; Polanyi, *Personal Knowledge*, 1–17, 49–248.

⁶ I have benefited from but make no effort to follow the discussion of the human constitution in Frame, *Systematic Theology*, sec. 7.34.D-E.

⁷ Thomas Aquinas, *Summa Contra Gentiles* (2 XI-XII).

think Aquinas is wrong to give epistemological priority to the essence, as we have seen earlier in this book, and I think he is also wrong to separate the two as if knowing the effects of something can be separated from knowing the thing itself. But by drawing attention to the subject's activities as an avenue of knowledge (as Basil of Caesarea had done before him), Aquinas brings us close to the answer of how we know a person. We know persons like we know the wind: we cannot see it, but we see its effects everywhere. We feel it and experience its consequences.

In the same way, I can only directly perceive the external part of Nicole's self. Yet, through her expressions, actions, and words in various circumstances, a door is opened to her interiority. I begin to grasp the core that makes her who she is. As I grow in relationship with her, I begin to interpret her external behaviour in terms of her interiority. I can identify what is characteristic and out-of-character. I can identify habits and help her to overcome bad ones. I can discern subtle emotions that are not evident to others, associating subtle physical characteristics with her interior disposition.

The fascinating thing about person-knowledge is that it can be mediated over time and distance (even reality) through various visual and audio mediums. We can read the letters and books of historical figures and come to know them: we can anticipate why they did this or that and what they might have said or how they might have responded in another circumstance.[8] There is a degree of danger in overreading this sort of mediated person-knowledge into history, but we experience the same thing through various mediums of communication, such as video, SMS, email, letter, etc. Strange enough, when a novelist creates a compelling character, the reader acquires something analogous to person-knowledge, coming to anticipate that character's response in all sorts of circumstances.[9] Person-knowledge is

---

[8] Now, some critics take this too far and assume they can know with great precision the thought life and motivations of historical authors. There is great danger in pushing the partial knowledge we can access in literature. C.S. Lewis has some apt words on the subject in an essay in *Christian Reflections*. We could clarify that the person we come to know through literature is an "implied" person, who may or may not an accurate presentation of the real person. Cf. Lewis, "Modern Theology and Biblical Criticism"; Ska, *Our Fathers Have Told Us*, 41; Rutherford, *God's Kingdom*, 115–116. Cf. Tom Kindt and Hans-Harald Müller, *The Implied Author: Concept and Controversy* (Walter de Gruyter, 2008).

[9] Cf. Frame, *Doctrine of God*, 156–159.

fascinating and complex, yet essential to social life and self-understanding.

A key presupposition of this book has been that knowledge of God is presented in Scripture as this sort of knowledge: to know God is to know God as a person. I believe this claim needs little argument because it arises naturally from reading the biblical story and makes terrific sense of the Bible's insistence that we truly know God. It also explains why knowing God is a frequent refrain throughout Scripture that involves relational connotations without explicit (or with only minimal) propositional content.

We are discussing knowledge in relation to truth, so important questions are raised by person-knowledge: can it be true or false? what would this mean? It is undoubtedly the case that person-knowledge can be true or false. That is, if I claim to know Nicole and yet I am unable to understand or relate to her, that claim is surely false. However, there is a significant degree of variability between truth and falsehood when it comes to person-knowledge: I may know Stan to a certain degree, but not nearly as well as I know Nicole. My claim to know either is *true*, but the truth of this knowledge does not tell much about its degree. Furthermore, as the interiority of any person is unconscious to themselves, so our person-knowledge is unconsciousness to us. That is, I certainly know Nicole, but I cannot enumerate what that means—at least not to any exhaustive degree. Yet my knowledge is evident from the way we relate to one another. For his reason, I conclude that person-knowledge functions at a *tacit* level, part of the interpretive matrix we bring to the world. Person-knowledge is not the sort of knowledge we analyse and logically parse; instead, is the sort of knowledge that shapes our interpretation of our experience, constructs the world, and governs our behaviour (both intuitively and reflectively). In the latter case, when we consciously reflect on our relationship with and actions towards a person we know, we draw on person-knowledge without ever grasping the whole. Like an iceberg, we may access the tip of the knowledge we possess in rational processes but cannot discern the depths of the knowledge we possess. Once again, this account of person-knowledge fits remarkably well with Paul's account of the innate knowledge of God all persons have (Romans 1:18-3:20).

In the case of person-knowledge, it would appear at first glance that the truth-maker of our knowledge claim is a person's interiority. However, this raises several problems. First, the future-immortality of persons (that the righteous and the unrighteous will endure beyond physical death, be resurrected, and live forever) means that in any situation where we may know a person, there will always be a truth-maker, namely, the existing self. However, two problems emerge at this point: first, it would be impossible on this account to know a future self who has not yet existed; second, all such knowledge would carry an implicit time statement. In the first case, if the person themself makes a knowledge claim true (i.e. "I know Nicole" is true because my knowledge truly corresponds to Nicole's self), then knowledge of that person is impossible when they do not exist. Of course, the problem this raises is for God's foreknowledge, and it contradicts the explicit claims of Scripture (e.g. Jer 1:5; Rom 8:29; 11:2): God's knowledge could not be true on this account, for there was no truth-maker until that person was born. Second, "I know Nicole" would only be true for a moment, after which it would only be true that I knew Nicole. That is, if the truth-maker of my claim is Nicole herself, she is constantly changing. I may have known her on March 29th, 2021, but she has changed by March 30th, 2021. Several qualifications are, therefore, necessary.

First, no person-knowledge claim made by humans is an exhaustive claim: to say "I know Nicole" is not to say I have comprehended her interiority but that I know her well enough for the relationship I profess to have with her. Such truth claims are always claims to a degree and the truth of the statement depends on the relationship to which that claim pertains (to say one knows the grocery store cashier requires far less tacit content than to say one knows one's spouse). Only in the case of God's knowledge of persons is such a claim exhaustive. However, this does not threaten our knowledge of one another, so it should not threaten our knowledge of God. That is, that I only know Nicole to the degree appropriate for our relationship does not deny the veracity of my claim in any way. Similarly, that I know God only so much as he has permitted and as is appropriate for our relationship does not in any way deny the veracity of my claim. Thus, the unbeliever and believer both know God in truth, though the degree of that knowledge is relative to their relationship with him.

Second, as with propositional knowledge and (as we will see) conceptual knowledge, we must confess that person-knowledge is always an interpretation to any degree it exists. That is, my knowledge of Nicole is not an image of her interiority. I have no experience of what she experiences, with the particular inflections of her faculties and beliefs. Interiority is a complex of physical and mental operations, faculties, causes, etc. not recreated or mirrored in my person-knowledge, not even partially. Indeed, interiority is not reproduced even in a person's self-knowledge. Interiority, as observed above, is the consciousness, unconsciousness, and physicality of the body working in unison. As with every other aspect of reality, interiority is part extra-mental and part mental. A person's consciousness or mind is their interpretation of themselves; my tacit knowledge of that person is another interpretation of that same reality.

Thus, as with all other knowledge, the truth-maker for person-knowledge is God's exhaustive interpretation of a person, his knowledge of their own subjectivity and the reality that it interprets. My claim to know Nicole is true in as much as it partially but faithfully corresponds to God's exhaustive interpretation of Nicole, reflected faithfully in her own subjectivity. There is true continuity in Nicole's identity across time, represented by God's interpretation, her own subjectivity, and the extra-mental reality, such that my claim is always true though it never exhausts Nicole at all times nor at any one time. Given this account, we can resolve the first dilemma raised above concerning God's foreknowledge.

If the truth-maker is God's interpretation, then it predates the creation of everything, including that person. That is, if a person's subjectivity is their own interpretation of the complex of mind and body, thus being only a perspective on their self or interiority and not the interiority itself, it is not independent of the extra-mental reality which God has created. Moreover, because subjectivity is itself an interpretation of the self, the two are closely tied together, but the former can exist without the latter. For example, in a coma or deep sleep, the self still exists even if subjectivity is absent. God's exhaustive knowledge of the extra-subjective self allows him to know our subjectivity exhaustively, even before we experience it. Therefore, every person existed potentially in God's plan for creation and thus existed as an object of God's contemplation and interpretation alongside impersonal creation, like rocks, laws, and water. Therefore, person-knowledge is dependent on God's eternal plan and pre-interpretation.

Before turning to the final aspect of knowledge we will contemplate, conceptual knowledge, it is worth observing a rather unexpected conclusion that arises from the above discussion. Above, I drew attention to the analogy that obtains between a real person and a fictional character: both may be an object of person-knowledge. A well-written character takes on a life of their own, such that the author is not free to make of them whatever they will but are constrained by their initial vision for the character: once a character is established as faithful and true, God-fearing, and close to his family, it is incredulous that the same character would be portrayed as an atheist adulterer. We would cry foul! Either the original portrayal was *false*—and so the plot is perhaps a complex and psychologically provoking work—or the author has broken faith; they have broken the rules of good literature. Perhaps all that separates a good character in fiction and a real person is subjectivity, the ability to *experience* what is going on. One might object, what about free will! Free will is itself a complex issue; John Frame has tried to explain it on analogy with a narrative.[10]

Calvinists have long wrestled with the apparent tension between divine sovereignty and human responsibility, which the World (and various Christian theologies) call a contradiction. Their answer has been a position called compatibilism: compatibilism claims that free will really means humans are responsible for their actions and that responsibility is not contradicted by God's exhaustive sovereignty. I go to great length addressing this issue in my book *Prevenient Grace*, but it is important to consider the matter here.[11] For many, compatibilism means that free will means freedom from coercion: I am free when I do what I desire and I am not forced to do something. Things get complicated when we consider different kinds of desire, but this holds true despite the complexity.[12] Thus, freedom is linked with the subjectivity of a person, not the determinism of their circumstances (which the Bible tells us is exhaustive). Before the world was created, God ordained every single event that would happen. He planned and knew everything that would happen, as an author plans and knows everything about their novel. However, we know that God's determinism does not eliminate subjectivity or responsibility.

Following John Frame, we can picture this on analogy with the expert novelist: God foreknew every person he would make and created them as

---

[10] Ibid.

[11] Cf. Rutherford, *Prevenient Grace*.

[12] Concerning complexity, in one sense, I do not desire to give my life for my family, but in another I do and would, so though it conflicts with desire in one sense, I am still free when I make that choice

distinct persons. Given that personhood is an objective reality underlying a person's subjectivity, he could write their life's story without every violating the integrity of his vision for their personhood. On the one hand, they do what they do because God ordained for them to do it; on the other hand, they do what they do because they genuinely want to and make the subjective choice to do so. This may be a disconcerting thought at first. However, it coheres with the biblical vision of the compatibility of sovereignty and human responsibility. It also arises naturally out of our account of personhood or interiority and our knowledge of this reality.

C. Conceptual Knowledge

All that is left in our investigation of ontology on the biblical account is our knowledge of concepts, or conceptual knowledge. Conceptual knowledge is not propositional knowledge, for it cannot be expressed in a proposition (discussed in Chapter 6), nor is it person-knowledge, for it concerns many things and not any one person. In one sense, I would question whether it is rightly called *knowledge*, but we will see that this is true in a sense. That is, if a concept is primarily a mental act or habitual event for relating particulars, it is less like a proposition or that tacit interpretation of a person than it is like muscle memory or another habit by which we automatically respond to external and internal stimuli. Furthermore, it is hard to see how such an act can be true or false: if our mind draws two things into relation, then the concept of these things depends on their similarity, even if this similarity is minute. If a concept exists, it somehow corresponds to things, however useless this correspondence might be. Thus, concepts as mental habits may be more or less useful but are not true or false. However, we saw above that there is another perspective to be taken on concepts. A concept also refers to the relationship drawn between similar things: thus, I may have a concept which is the habit of relating all things with a similar colour; by calling this concept "redness," I isolate this relationship as an object of thought. It is in this sense that a concept is an object of knowledge. My thoughts *about* redness will be propositional and follow the rules identified above. However, the conceptual relationship will exist on the tacit level of interpretation, allowing me to interpret this or that object as red, a dog, a beagle, even if I cannot articulate what it means to be "red," a "dog," or a "beagle" in propositions. This implicit component of a concept is a form of knowledge employed in everyday life, even if it is rarely an object of direct thought.

This conceptual knowledge may be true or false in as much as the relationship that constitutes the concept actually obtains between all the objects of relevance. As discussed below, truth and falsehood with reference to concepts emerge primarily in the context of communication. That is, if my concept of "dog" builds on physical similarity, it may be false to include a human in that concept. It is possible for my concept of "dog" to include all the members of another concept, "human," in which case, the proposition "a human is a dog" would be true. However, if communicated in the context where humans were implicitly excluded from the concept dog, as with specific reference to the physiology of dogs, the proposition a "human is a dog" would be false, as would be the concept of "dog" that includes both humans and the idea of form or physical similarity. Of course, we could use the term "dog" for a concept that encompasses what we would conventionally call dogs and humans, but such a concept would only be true if it excluded the close similarity of form shared by "dogs" but not by "humans and dogs." It may be better to call the "truth" of a concept as accuracy, which sounds more natural to my ears. However, for our purposes, a concept is true when it rightly denotes a relationship obtaining between objects. Because that "relationship" only exists in mental interpretation, every concept is known to God and receives its truth value from him. Where the relationship is accurate, such that our concept corresponds to some extent without falsehood to God's pre-interpreted concepts, then that concept is true. Where this correspondence is not valid, then a concept is false.

Because concepts arise from habitual acts and are a tacit framework for relating objects, it unlikely that falsehood would emerge unintentionally. Given the basic trustworthiness of our faculties, attested in an individual's case by the presence of knowing community ("two or three witnesses"), we have every reason to believe our concepts to be true. However, when it comes to naming and communicating concepts, unintentional and intentional falsehood may enter. As it regards unintentional falsehood, if I use the term "dog" to communicate a concept of objects others call "books," I am liable to be misinterpreted. My choice of a sign, "d-o-g," has facilitated this falsehood. We could also unintentionally arrive at a false concept by misunderstanding a book. Thus, to facilitate communication, it is necessary to attend to the conventions of a given culture, to use the appropriate language in communication, and to read the works of others carefully in order to understand them and deal with them fairly.

Intentional falsehood may emerge because there is much rhetorical power in the use of concepts. For example, grouping a local pastor whom we dislike with those commonly recognized as false teachers amounts to portraying that pastor as a false teacher. If this were not the case, the attribution would be slanderous and the concept false. Calling certain humans "animals" or "barbarians" over against the rest of humanity would be similar, as would identifying unborn children as something other than persons, babies, or other terms that invoke the continuity between unborn and born life. Thus, in philosophy, when someone intentionally expounds the relationships between things, or in rhetoric, the possibility for false concepts is strong. However, where there is truth, it only exists because God has first thought it. All thought, conscious or unconscious, thus relies on the God who has pre-interpreted all things, created us to know as he has known, and revealed himself so that we might do so.

Further Reading

Michael Polanyi, *Personal Knowledge* [I-A]
*Michael Polanyi, *The Tacit Dimension* [I-A]
*John Frame, *The Doctrine of the Knowledge of God* [I]
John Frame, *The Doctrine of God* [I]
*John Frame, *Apologetics: A Justification of Christian Belief* [B-I]
Iain McGilchrist, *The Master and His Emissary: The Divided Brain and the Making of the Western World* [A]
Esther Meek, *Loving to Know: Introducing Covenant Epistemology* [B-I]
Vern Poythress, *Logic: A God-Centered Approach to the Foundation of Western Thought* [A]
Bradley L. Sickler, *God on the Brain* [B]

CONCLUSION

The fear of the LORD is the beginning of wisdom, and the knowledge of the Holy One is insight. – Proverbs 9:10

He is the radiance of the glory of God and the exact imprint of his nature, and he upholds the universe by the word of his power. – Hebrews 1:2

We set out in this volume to investigate ontology from a biblical perspective. We did not do so for the sake of knowledge itself; instead, we did so because ontology has historically been a critical battleground for Christian theology. It has frequently been an area where biblical teaching has come under attack. We have investigated the issue with the conviction that Scripture has something to say and can help us confidently go forth to understand God's word, God's world, and God himself. We approached the subject through three significant problems raised in the history of philosophy: the problems of change and identity, the one and the many, and the external world.

In Part 1, we saw that the concept of history and sense experience raises a problem for knowledge, yet the existence of minds and, more importantly, of the sovereign God who has pre-interpreted all things means that change is not the problem it was thought to be. Instead, change is a good thing in God's plan for creation: change and history are the means through which God has revealed himself to his creation. In Part 2, we considered the problem of the One and the Many. We discovered that the problem did not emerge out of the neutral observation of the world but out of certain preconceptions through which ancient and modern philosophers have interpreted the world. Instead of a problem, we saw that the Bible embraces the utterly contingent or particular world of our experience and that God gives ultimate unity to the world through his intentional, wise ordering or creation and interpretation of it. Finally, in Part 3, we considered the problem of the external world. That is, if our minds have a significant role in presenting the outside world to us, what can we really know about it? We saw that God created the world to exist as the equilibrium between mental interpretation and extra-mental reality. As such, truth never exists outside of the mind, nor do truth-makers. Instead, God is the standard of truth in its various senses and has enabled and continues to uphold our knowledge. Thus, far from being an arid and godless discipline, we have seen that ontology points consistently back to God, the creator of all things.

I believe we have witnessed the truth of the Proverbs, that "The fear of the LORD is the beginning of wisdom, and the knowledge of the Holy One is insight" (Prov 9:10). At each step, the possibility of knowledge is secured by God and our possession of it by his wise ordering of creation. Creation is utterly dependent on God while being distinct from him; it is always the creation, not the creator. Therefore, we are called to engage as creatures in all our knowing, humbled by our sheer dependence on the kindness and mercy of God, our creator. We have seen just a small glimmer of what it means for Jesus our Lord to uphold "the universe by the word of his power" (Heb 1:2).

God spoke all things into existence through his Son (Gen 1-2; John 1:1-5) and sustains its unity and rationality by his decree, pre-interpreting all things and governing the interactions of created things. Moreover, at some point, we discover that the world itself rests on God's word. This is true in the temporal sense: God's word is the cause of things coming into existence. It is also true in another sense. Philosophy and the physical sciences have sought to find the fundamental causes of all things in the natural world, that by which all else is explained. "Laws" orchestrate the ways things interact, but they do not cause the things themselves. There is the standard theory of particle physic in the natural sciences, which probes the causes of all macro-phenomenon at their elementary basis. The behavior of atoms is explained by appeal to their constituent pieces, neutrons, protons, and electrons. These, in turn, are explained by the various more basic elements, such as quarks, supposed to explain their properties. At some point, we must arrive at an explanation that is itself not explained by something else. What causes the quarks to vary from one another and gives them their own properties? If these are not the most basic explanation, what explains the substrate that explains them? The answer, whether at the level of the quark or deeper, must at some point be God. He is the only one who can uphold creation without himself being upheld. Thus, his word not only explains the origins of the created world but its present existence: it is his word that explains the most basic elements from which all else derives and for which the material world and its interacting forces depend. Spoken by God, the world is his creation and distinct from him, yet it is dependent on him in every way, past, present and future. Truly, "he upholds the universe by the word of his power" (Prov 9:10). "In him we live and move and have our being" (Acts 17:28).

Our first response can only be worship, crying out with the most powerful created beings, "Holy, Holy, Holy is the LORD of hosts; the whole earth is fully of his glory" (Isa 6:3), and proclaiming his wisdom with Paul,

> Oh, the depth of the riches and wisdom and knowledge of God! How unsearchable are his judgments and how inscrutable his ways! "For who has known the mind of the Lord, or who has been his counselor?" "Or who has given a gift to him that he might be repaid?" For from him and through him and to him are all things. To him be glory forever. Amen. (Rom 11:33-36)

God has made the world with intricate wisdom and made himself known so that we may know, love, and serve him. He calls all people to cast themselves on his mercy shown in Christ Jesus and to pursue him with all their lives. So, we must engage the world with the gifts God has given us for his glory, primarily seen in the expansion of his kingdom through the Church of his Son (Matt 28:18-20). However, for those who would question God's wisdom and think they can interpret the world apart from God who created it, his word is strong:

> Who is this that darkens counsel by words without knowledge?
>
> Dress for action like a man;
> I will question you, and you make it known to me.

J. Alexander Rutherford

Where were you when I laid the foundation of the earth?
   Tell me, if you have understanding.
Who determined its measurements—surely you know!
   Or who stretched the line upon it?
On what were its bases sunk,
      or who laid its cornerstone,
   when the morning stars sang together
      and all the sons of God shouted for joy?

Or who shut in the sea with doors
   when it burst out from the womb,
when I made clouds its garment
   and thick darkness its swaddling band,
and prescribed limits for it
   and set bars and doors,
and said, Thus far shall you come, and no farther,
   and here shall your proud waves be stayed'?

Have you commanded the morning since your days began,
     and caused the dawn to know its place,
   that it might take hold of the skirts of the earth,
     and the wicked be shaken out of it?
It is changed like clay under the seal,
   and its features stand out like a garment.
From the wicked their light is withheld,
   and their uplifted arm is broken. (Job 38:2-15)

WORKS CITED

Aejmelaeus, Anneli. "Function and Interpretation of כי in Biblical Hebrew." *Journal of Biblical Literature* 105, no. 2 (1986): 193–209.

Alden, Robert L. *Job*. The New American Commentary v. 11. Nashville: Broadman & Holman, 1993.

Alter, Robert. *The Art of Biblical Narrative*. New York: Basic Books, 1981.

Ames, William. *The Marrow of Theology*. Translated by John D. Eusden. Grand Rapids: Baker Books, 1997.

Anderson, James. *Paradox in Christian Theology: An Analysis of Its Presence, Character, and Epistemic Status*. Paternoster theological monographs. Milton Keynes: Paternoster, 2007.

Arnold, Bill T, and Bryan Beyer. *Encountering the Old Testament: A Christian Survey*. Grand Rapids: Baker Academic, 2008.

Bahnsen, Greg L. *Van Til's Apologetic: Readings and Analysis*. Phillipsburg: P&R Publishing, 1998.

Barth, Karl. *Church Dogmatics*. Vol. 1.1. Peabody, Mass: Hendricksen, 2010.

———. *The Word of God and the Word of Man*. New York: Harper & Row, 1957.

Beale, G. K. *Handbook on the New Testament Use of the Old Testament: Exegesis and Interpretation*. Grand Rapids: Baker Academic, 2012.

Beale, G. K., and D. A. Carson, eds. *Commentary on the New Testament Use of the Old Testament*. Grand Rapids: Baker Academic, 2007.

Beale, G.K. *The Book of Revelation: A Commentary on the Greek Text*. NIGTC. Grand Rapids; Carlisle: Eerdmans; Paternoster, 1999.

Beckwith, Roger T. *The Old Testament Canon of the New Testament Church and Its Background in Early Judaism*. Grand Rapids: Eerdmans, 1986.

Berkeley, George. *Principles of Human Knowledge and Three Dialogues*. Edited by Howard Robinson. Oxford World's Classics. Oxford: Oxford University Press, 2009.

Berlin, Adele. *Poetics and Interpretation of Biblical Narrative*. Winona Lake, Ind.: Eisenbrauns, 2005.

Black, David Alan, ed. *Rethinking New Testament Textual Criticism*. Grand Rapids: Baker Academic, 2002.

Block, Daniel Isaac. *Deuteronomy*. The NIV Application Commentary. Grand Rapids: Zondervan, 2012.

Blomberg, Craig L. *1 Corinthians*. NIVAC. Grand Rapids: Zondervan, 1994.

Blomberg, Craig L., and Mariam J. Kamell. *James: Zondevan Exegetical Commentary on the New Testament*. Zondervan Exegetical Commentary Series on the New Testament v. 16. Grand Rapids: Zondervan, 2008.

Boersma, Hans. *Heavenly Participation: The Weaving of a Sacramental Tapestry*. Grand Rapids: Eerdmans, 2011.

———. *Sacramental Preaching: Sermons on the Hidden Presence of Christ*. Grand Rapids: Baker Academic, 2016.

Brettler, Marc Zvi. "Predestination in Deuteronomy 30:1-10." In *Those Elusive Deuteronomists*, 171–188. Sheffield: Sheffield Academic Press, 1999.

Brown, Francis, S. R Driver, Charles A Briggs, James Strong, and Wilhelm Gesenius. *The Brown-Driver-Briggs Hebrew and English Lexicon*. Peabody: Hendrickson, 1996.

Bruce, F. F. *The Epistle of Paul to the Romans: An Introduction and Commentary*. Grand Rapids: Eerdmans, 1963.

Bruce, F. F. *The Epistle to the Hebrews*. NICNT. Grand Rapids: Eerdmans, 1964.

Buchanan, George Wesley, ed. *To the Hebrews*. 1st ed. Anchor Bible 36. Garden City, N.Y: Doubleday, 1972.

Bultmann, Rudolf. *New Testament and Mythology and Other Basic Writings*. Translated by Schubert Miles Ogden. Philadelphia: Fortress Press, 1989.

Callow, Kathleen. *Man and Message: A Guide to Meaning-Based Text Analysis.* Lanham, Md: Summer Institute of Linguistics, University Press of America, 1998.

Calvin, John. *Institutes of the Christian Religion.* Translated by Henry Beveridge. Peabody, Mass: Hendrickson Publishers, 2008.

———. *The Epistle of Paul the Apostle to the Hebrews and the First and Second Epistles of St Peter.* Edited by David W. Torrance and Thomas F. Torrance. Translated by William B. Johnston. Calvin's Commentaries. Eerdmans: Grand Rapids, 1963.

Carson, D. A. *Divine Sovereignty and Human Responsibility.* Eugene, Ore.: Wipf and Stock Publishers, 2002.

———. *Exegetical Fallacies.* Grand Rapids: Baker Books, 1996.

———. "Is the Doctrine of Claritas Scripturae Still Relevant Today?" In *Collected Writings on Scripture*, edited by Andrew David Naselli, 179–193. Wheaton: Crossway, 2010.

———. *New Testament Commentary Survey.* 7th Ed. Grand Rapids: Baker Academic, 2013.

———. "Reflections on Assurance." In *Still Sovereign: Contemporary Perspectives on Election, Foreknowledge & Grace*, edited by Thomas R. Schreiner and Bruce A. Ware, 247–276. Grand Rapids: Baker, 2000.

———. *The Cross and Christian Ministry: Leadership Lessons from 1 Corinthians.* Grand Rapids: Baker Books, 2004.

———. *The Gospel According to John.* The Pillar New Testament Commentary. Leicester; Grand Rapids: IVP; Eerdmans, 1991.

———. *The King James Version Debate: A Plea for Realism.* Grand Rapids: Baker Book House, 1979.

Carson, D. A., and Douglas J. Moo. *An Introduction to the New Testament.* Second Edition. Grand Rapids: Zondervan, 2005.

Carter, Craig A. *Contemplating God with the Great Tradition: Recovering Trinitarian Classical Theism.* Grand Rapids: Baker Academic, 2021.

Chamberlain, Paul. *Can We Be Good without God? A Conversation about Truth, Morality, Culture & a Few Other Things That Matter.* Downers Grove: InterVarsity Press, 1996.

Childs, Brevard S. *Introduction to the Old Testament as Scripture.* Philadelphia: Fortress, 1979.

Christensen, Duane L. *Deuteronomy 21:10-34:12.* Vol. 6B. Word Biblical

Commentary. Nashville: Thomas Nelson Publishers, 2002.

Clark, Gordon H. *Thales to Dewey: A History of Philosophy*. Cambridge, Massachusetts: The Riverside Press, 1957.

Clines, David J. A. *Job 21 - 37*. Edited by Bruce Manning Metzger, John D. W. Watts, Ralph Philip Martin, and David J. A. Clines. Word Biblical Commentary 18a. Nashville: Nelson, 2007.

———, ed. *The Dictionary of Classical Hebrew*. Vol. I–VIII. Sheffield: Sheffield Academic Press; Sheffield Phoenix Press, 1993.

Coxhead, Steven R. "Deuteronomy 30:11-14 as a Prophecy of the New Covenant in Christ." *Westminster Theological Journal* 68 (2006): 305–320.

Craig, William Lane. *On Guard: Defending Your Faith With Reason And Precision*. Colorado Springs, Colo.: David C. Cook, 2010.

———. *On Guard: Defending Your Faith with Reason and Precision*. Colorado Springs, Colo.: David C. Cook, 2010.

———. *The Kalam Cosmological Argument*. Eugene, OR: Wipf and Stock Publishers, 2000.

Culler, Jonathan. *On Deconstructionism: Theory and Criticism after Structuralism*. Ithaca, N.Y.: Cornell University, 1982.

Danker, Frederick W. *A Greek-English Lexicon of the New Testament and Other Early Christian Literature*. 3rd ed. Chicago: University of Chicago Press, 2000.

Delitzsch, Franz. *Job: Two Volumes in One*. Commentary on the Old Testament in Ten Volumes IV. Grand Rapids: Eerdmans, 1978.

Dempster, Stephen G. *Dominion and Dynasty: A Biblical Theology of the Hebrew Bible*. New Studies in Biblical Theology 15. Leicester: Downers Grove: Apollos; InterVarsity, 2003.

Driver, S. R. *A Critical and Exegetical Commentary on Deuteronomy*. 3rd ed. The International Critical Commentary. Edinburgh: T. & T. Clark, 1895.

Dunbar, David G. "The Biblical Canon." In *Hermeneutics, Authority, and Canon*, edited by D. A. Carson and John D. Woodbridge. Grand Rapids: Academie Books, 1986.

Dunn, James D. G. *Romans 9-16*. Word Biblical Commentary 38b. Dallas, Tex.: Word Books, 1988.

Dunn, John. "The Identity of the History of Ideas." *Philosophy* 43, no. 164 (1968): 85–104.

Duvall, J. Scott, and J. Daniel Hays. *Grasping God's Word: A Hands-on Approach to Reading, Interpreting, and Applying the Bible.* 3rd ed. Grand Rapids: Zondervan, 2012.

Edwards, Jonathan. *Freedom of the Will.* Mineola, N.Y.: Dover Publications, 2012.

Elliger, Karl, Wilhelm Rudolph, Adrian Schenker, Donald R. Vance, George Athas, and Yael Avrahami, eds. *Biblia Hebraica Stuttgartensia: a Reader's Edition.* 5., rev. Ed. Stuttgart: Dt. Bibelges, 2014.

Ellingworth, Paul. *The Epistle to the Hebrews: A Commentary on the Greek Text.* NIGTC. Grand Rapids: Carlisle: W.B. Eerdmans ; Paternoster, 1993.

Ellis, Nicholas J. "Biblical Exegesis and Linguistics: A Prodigal History." In *Linguistics and New Testament Greek: Key Issues in the Current Debate,* edited by David Alan Black and Benjamin L Merkle. Grand Rapids: Baker Publishing Group, 2020.

Elwell, Walter A., and Robert W. Yarbrough. *Encountering the New Testament: A Historical and Theological Survey.* 2nd ed. Encountering biblical studies. Grand Rapids: Baker Academic, 2005.

———. *Encountering the New Testament: A Historical and Theological Survey.* 2nd ed. Encountering biblical studies. Grand Rapids: Baker Academic, 2005.

Farris, Joshua R., S. Mark Hamilton, and James S. Spiegel. *Idealism and Christian Theology : Idealism and Christianity Volume 1.* Idealism and Christianity. New York: Bloomsbury Academic, 2016.

Fee, Gordon D. *New Testament Exegesis: A Handbook for Students and Pastors.* 3rd ed. Louisville: Westminster John Knox Press, 2002.

Fee, Gordon D., and Douglas K. Stuart. *How to Read the Bible for All Its Worth.* 3rd ed. Grand Rapids: Zondervan, 2003.

Feuerbach, Ludwig. *The Essence of Christianity.* Translated by George Eliot. Amherst, New York: Prometheus Books, 2010.

Fields, Lee M. *Hebrew for the Rest of Us: Using Hebrew Tools without Mastering Biblical Hebrew.* Grand Rapids: Zondervan, 2008.

Fitzmyer, Joseph A. *The Aramaic Inscriptions of Sefire.* Biblica Et Orientalia 19. Rome: Pontifical Biblical Institute, 1967.

Fokkelman, J.P. *Reading Biblical Poetry: An Introductory Guide.* Translated by Ineke Smit. First edition. Louisville: Westminster John Knox, 2001.

Foster, M. B. "The Christian Doctrine of Creation and the Rise of Modern

Natural Science." *Mind* 43, no. 172 (1934): 446–468.

Frame, John. "'Infinite Series.'" *Frame-Poythress.Org*. Last modified May 21, 2012. Accessed July 28, 2021. https://frame-poythress.org/infinite-series/.

Frame, John M. *A History of Western Philosophy and Theology*. Phillipsburg: P&R Publishing, 2015.

———. *Apologetics: A Justification of Christian Belief*. Edited by Joseph E. Torres. Second edition. Phillipsburg, New Jersey: P&R Publishing, 2015.

———. *Cornelius Van Til: An Analysis of His Thought*. Phillipsburg: P&R Publishing, 1995.

———. *Perspectives on the Word of God: An Introduction to Christian Ethics*. Eugene, Or.: Wipf and Stock, 1999.

———. *Systematic Theology: An Introduction to Christian Belief*. Phillipsburg: P&R Publishing, 2013.

———. "The Academic Captivity of Theology." In *John Frame's Selected Shorter Writings*. Vol. 2. Phillipsburg: P&R Pub, 2014.

———. *The Doctrine of God*. A Theology of Lordship. Phillipsburg: P&R Publishing, 2002.

———. *The Doctrine of the Christian Life*. A Theology of Lordship 4. Phillipsburg: P&R Publishing, 2008.

———. *The Doctrine of the Knowledge of God*. A Theology of Lordship. Phillipsburg: P&R Publishing, 1987.

———. *The Doctrine of the Word of God*. A Theology of Lordship. Phillipsburg: P&R Publishing, 2010.

———. *Van Til: The Theologian*. Phillipsburg: Pilgrim Publishing Company, 1976.

———. "Why Theology Needs Philosophy." In *John Frame's Selected Shorter Writings*. Vol. 2. Phillipsburg: P&R Pub, 2014.

France, R. T. "Hebrews." In *The Expositor's Bible Commentary*, edited by Tremper Longman and David E. Garland. Rev. ed. Grand Rapids: Zondervan, 2006.

Fuhrer, Therese. "Allegorical Reading and Writing in Augustine's Confessions." In *In Search of Truth. Augustine, Manichaeism and Other Gnosticism*, edited by Jacob Albert van den Berg, Annemaré Kotzé, Tobias Nicklas, and Madeleine Scopello. Leiden, The Netherlands:

Brill, 2010.

Geisler, Norman L. "Appendix B: Explaining Hermeneutics: A Commentary on the Chicago Statement on Biblical Hermeneutics Articles of Affirmation and Denial." In *Hermeneutics, Inerrancy, and the Bible*, edited by Earl D. Radmacher and Robert D. Preus, 163–190. Grand Rapids: Zondervan, 1984.

Gentry, Peter John, and Stephen J Wellum. *God's Kingdom through God's Covenants: A Concise Biblical Theology*, 2015. Accessed May 30, 2019. https://www.overdrive.com/search?q=0D8CDAE2-3760-4135-B741-B0C9022B879C.

Gentry, Peter John, and Stephen J. Wellum. *Kingdom through Covenant: A Biblical-Theological Understanding of the Covenants*. Wheaton: Crossway, 2012.

Gilbert, Greg. *What Is the Gospel?* Wheaton, IL: Crossway, 2010.

Goldsworthy, Graeme. *According to Plan: The Unfolding Revelation of God in the Bible*. Leicester: Inter-Varsity Press, 1991.

———. *Christ-Centered Biblical Theology: Hermeneutical Foundations and Principles*. Downers Grove: IVP Academic, 2012.

———. *Gospel-Centered Hermeneutics: Foundations and Principles of Evangelical Biblical Interpretation*. Downers Grove: InterVarsity Press, 2006.

———. *The Goldsworthy Trilogy*. Milton Keynes: Paternoster, 2012.

Goodrich, Richard J, and Albert L Lukaszewski. *A Reader's Greek New Testament*. Grand Rapids, Mich.: Zondervan, 2007.

Goodrich, Richard J, Albert L Lukaszewski, A. Philip Brown, and Bryan W Smith. *A Reader's Hebrew and Greek Bible*. Grand Rapids: Zondervan, 2010.

Grudem, Wayne. *Systematic Theology: An Introduction to Biblical Doctrine*. Leicester; Grand Rapids: Inter-Varsity Press ; Zondervan, 1994.

Grudem, Wayne A. "Perseverance of the Saints: A Case Study from the Warning Passages in Hebrews." In *Still Sovereign: Contemporary Perspectives on Election, Foreknowledge & Grace*, edited by Thomas R. Schreiner and Bruce A. Ware, 133–182. Grand Rapids: Baker, 2000.

Grudem, Wayne A., and Jeff Purswell. *Bible Doctrine: Essential Teachings of the Christian Faith*. Grand Rapids: Zondervan, 1999.

Gunkel, Herman. *Genesis*. Trans. of the 1910 ed. Macon: Mercer University, 1997.

Guzman, Ronaldo, and Michael W. Martin. "Is Hebrews 5:11-6:20 Really a Disgression?" *Novum Testamentum* 57, no. 3 (2015): 295–310.

Hagner, Donald Alfred. *Encountering the Book of Hebrews: An Exposition*. Grand Rapids: Baker Academic, 2002.

Harris, R. Laird, Gleason L Archer, and Bruce K Waltke. *Theological Wordbook of the Old Testament*. Vol. 2. 2 vols. Chicago, Ill.: Moody Press, 1980.

Harrison, R. K. *Jeremiah and Lamentations*. Reprinted. Tyndale Old Testament Commentary 21. Downers Grove, Ill.; England: Inter-Varsity Press, 2009.

Hartley, John E. *The Book of Job*. NICOT. Grand Rapids: Eerdmans, 1988.

Hewitt, Thomas. *The Epistle to the Hebrews, an Introduction and Commentary*. 1st ed. The Tyndale New Testament Commentaries. Grand Rapids: Eerdmans, 1960.

Hill, Andrew E., and John H. Walton. *A Survey of the Old Testament*. 2nd ed. Grand Rapids: Zondervan Publishing House, 2000.

Hirsch, Jr., Eric D. "Meaning and Significance Reinterpreted." *Critical Inquiry* 11, no. 2 (1984): 202–225.

———. *Validity in Interpretation*. 9. print. New Haven: Yale Univ. Press, 1979.

Hornkohl, Aaron. "Periodization." In *Encyclopedia of Hebrew Language and Linguistics: Volume 1; A-F*, edited by Geoffrey Khan. Vol. 1. Leiden; Boston: Brill, 2013.

Hughes, Philip Edgcumbe. *A Commentary on the Epistle to the Hebrews*. Grand Rapids: Eerdmans, 1977.

Hume, David. *A Treatise of Human Nature*. Edited by L. A. Selby-Bigge. The Clarendon Press, 1888.

———. *An Enquiry Concerning Human Understanding*. Edited by Tom L. Beauchamp. Oxford Philosophical Texts. Oxford: Oxford University Press, 1999.

———. *Dialogues Concerning Natural Religion*. Dover Philosophical Classics. Mineola, N.Y.: Dover Publications, 2006.

John Piper. *Think*. Wheaton: Crossway Books, 2011.

Johnson, Jeffery D. *The Failure of Natural Theology: A Critical Appraisal of the Philosophical Theology of Thomas Aquinas*. New Studies in Theology. Free Grace Press, 2021.

Jongkind, Dirk. *An Introduction to the Greek New Testament, Produced at Tyndale House, Cambridge.* Wheaton: Crossway, 2019.

Jongkind, Dirk, Peter J Williams, Peter M Head, and Patrick James. *The Greek New Testament, Produced at Tyndale House Cambridge.* Crossway, 2017.

Joosten, Jan. "The Distinction Between Classical and Late Biblical Hebrew as Reflected in Syntax." *Hebrew Studies* 46 (2005): 327–339.

Joüon, Paul, and Takamitsu Muraoka. *A Grammar of Biblical Hebrew.* Revised English Edition. Pontificio Istituto Biblico, 2006.

Kähler, Martin. *The So-Called Historical Jesus and the Historic, Biblical Christ.* Vancouver: Regent College Pub., 1998.

Kaiser, Walter C. "The Single Intent of Scripture." In *The Right Doctrine from the Wrong Texts?: Essays on the Use of the Old Testament in the New*, edited by G. K. Beale. Grand Rapids: Baker Books, 1994.

Kapelrud, Arvid S. "The Interpretation of Jeremiah 34:18ff." *Journal for the Study of the Old Testament* 22 (1982): 138–141.

Kidner, Derek. *The Message of Jeremiah: Against Wind and Tide.* The Bible Speaks Today. Leicester, England ; Downers Grove: Inter-Varsity Press, 1987.

Kindt, Tom, and Hans-Harald Müller. *The Implied Author: Concept and Controversy.* Walter de Gruyter, 2008.

Kirschhock, Maximilian E., Helen M. Ditz, and Andreas Nieder. "Behavioral and Neuronal Representation of Numerosity Zero in the Crow." *Journal of Neuroscience* 41, no. 22 (June 2, 2021): 4889–4896.

Klein, William W, Craig L. Blomberg, and Robert L. Hubbard Jr. *Introduction to Biblical Interpretation.* Edited by Kermit A. Ecklebarger. Dallas: Word Publishing, 1993.

Kline, Meredith G. *The Structure of Biblical Authority.* Rev. ed. Grand Rapids: Eerdmans, 1975.

———. *Treaty of the Great King: The Covenant Structure of Deuteronomy; Studies and Commentary.* Grand Rapids: Eerdmans, 1963.

Knuuttila, Simo. "Translation and Historical Semantics in Philosophy." *Collegium: Studies across Disciplines in the Humanities and Social Sciences* 12 (2012): 168–176.

Koehler, Ludwig, Walter Baumgartner, M. E. J. Richardson, and Johann Jakob Stamm. *The Hebrew and Aramaic Lexicon of the Old Testament.*

Electronic ed. Leiden; New York: Brill, 1999.

Köstenberger, Andreas J., Benjamin L. Merkle, and Robert L. Plummer. *Going Deeper with New Testament Greek: An Intermediate Study of the Grammar and Syntax of the New Testament.* Nashville: B&H Academic, 2016.

Kruger, Michael J., ed. *A Biblical-Theological Introduction to the New Testament: The Gospel Realized.* Wheaton: Crossway, 2016.

———. *Canon Revisited: Establishing the Origins and Authority of the New Testament Books.* Wheaton: Crossway, 2012.

———. *The Question of Canon: Challenging the Status Quo in the New Testament Debate.* Downers Grove: InterVarsity Press, 2013.

Kugel, James L. *The Idea of Biblical Poetry: Parallelism and Its History.* New Haven: Yale University Press, 1981.

Lalleman, Hetty. *Jeremiah and Lamentations.* Tyndale Old Testament Commentaries 21. Downers Grove, Ill.: InterVarsity Press, 2013.

Lambdin, Thomas O. *Introduction to Biblical Hebrew.* New York, N.Y.: Charles Scribner's Sons, 1971.

Lane, William L. *Hebrews 1-8.* Edited by David A. Hubbard, Glenn W. Barker, and Ralph P. Martin. Vol. 1. 3 vols. Word Biblical Commentary Vol. 47,A. Nashville: Word Books, 1991.

Lemmens, Willem. "Hume's Atheistic Agenda: Philo's Confession in Dialogues, 12." *Bijdragen* 73, no. 3 (2012): 281–303.

Lewis, C. S. *Miracles: A Preliminary Study.* New York: Harper Collins, 2011.

Lewis, C. S. "Modern Theology and Biblical Criticism." In *Christian Reflections,* 152–166. Eerdmans, 1967.

Lewontin, Richard C. "Billions and Billions of Demons." *The New York Review of Books.* Accessed March 15, 2016. http://www.nybooks.com/articles/1997/01/09/billions-and-billions-of-demons/.

Liddell, Henry George, Robert Scott, Henry Stuart Jones, and Roderick McKenzie. *A Greek-English Lexicon.* Oxford: Clarendon, 1996.

Long, V. Philips. "1 and 2 Samuel." In *Zondervan Illustrated Bible Background Commentary: Old Testament: Volume 2, Joshua, Judges, Ruth, 1 and 2 Samuel,* edited by John H. Walton. Vol. 2. Grand Rapids: Zondervan, 2009.

———. *The Art of Biblical History.* Foundations of Contemporary Interpretation v. 5. Grand Rapids: Zondervan, 1994.

Longman III, Tremper. *Jeremiah, Lamentations*. NIBC. Peabody; United Kingdom: Hendrickson; Paternoster, 2008.

———. *Old Testament Commentary Survey*. 5th Ed. Grand Rapids: Baker Academic, 2013.

———, and Raymond B. Dillard. *An Introduction to the Old Testament*. 2nd ed. Grand Rapids: Zondervan, 2006.

Louw, Johannes P., and Eugene Albert Nida. *Greek-English Lexicon of the New Testament: Based on Semantic Domains*. Electronic ed. of the 2nd edition. New York, N.Y.: United Bible Societies, 1996.

Lowther, James R. "Paul's Use of Deuteronomy 30:11-14 in Romans 10:5-8 as a Locus Primus on Paul's Understanding of the Law in Romans." Doctoral Dissertation, Southwestern Baptist Theological Seminary, 2001.

Luther, Martin. "Dr. Martin Luther's Answer to the Superchristian, Superspiritual, Superlearned Book of Goat Emser of Leipzig." In *Works of Martin Luther*, translated by A. Steimle. Vol. 3. Albany, Ore: AGES Bible Software, 1997.

———. *Sermons by Martin Luther: Volume 1; Sermons on Gospel Texts for Advent, Christmas, and Epiphany*. Edited by John Nicholas Lenker. Vol. 1. Albany, Ore: AGES Bible Software, 1997.

———. *The Bondage of the Will*. Edited by J. I Packer and O. R Johnston. Grand Rapids: Fleming H. Revell, 2003.

Manning, Robert John Sheffler. "David Hume's Dialogues Concerning Natural Religion: Otherness in History and in Text." *The Journal of Religion* 70, no. 4 (October 1990): 589–605.

McGilchrist, Iain. *The Master and His Emissary: The Divided Brain and the Making of the Western World*. New expanded edition. New Haven: Yale University Press, 2019.

McKnight, S. "The Warning Passages of Hebrews: A Formal Analysis and Theological Conclusions." *Trinity Journal* 13, no. 1 (1992): 21–59.

Meek, Esther L. *Longing to Know*. Grand Rapids: Brazos Press, 2003.

———. *Loving to Know: Introducing Covenant Epistemology*. Eugene, Ore: Cascade Books, 2011.

Moleski, Martin X. and The Polanyi Society. "Polanyi vs. Kuhn: Worldviews Apart." *Tradition and Discovery: The Polanyi Society Periodical* 33, no. 2 (2006): 8–24.

Moo, Douglas J. *Encountering the Book of Romans: A Theological Survey*. 2nd ed. Encountering Biblical Studies. Grand Rapids, Mich.: Baker Academic, 2014.

———. *Galatians*. Baker Exegetical Commentary on the New Testament. Grand Rapids: Baker Academic, 2013.

———. *The Epistle to the Romans*. NICNT. Grand Rapids: Eerdmans, 1996.

Moreland, James Porter, Stephen C. Meyer, Christopher Shaw, Ann K. Gauger, and Wayne Grudem, eds. *Theistic Evolution: A Scientific, Philosophical, and Theological Critique*. Wheaton: Crossway, 2017.

Mounce, Robert H. *The Book of Revelation*. NICNT. Grand Rapids: Eerdmans, 1977.

Mounce, William D. *Basics of Biblical Greek Grammar*. 3rd ed. Grand Rapids: Zondervan, 2009.

———. *Greek for the Rest of Us: The Essentials of Biblical Greek*. Second Edition. Grand Rapids: Zondervan, 2013.

Muller, Richard A. *Post-Reformation Reformed Dogmatics Volume 2: Holy Scripture: The Cognitive Foundation of Theology*. Vol. 2. Grand Rapids: Baker Book House, 1987.

Muraoka, T. *A Greek-English Lexicon of the Septuagint*. Rev. ed. Louvain ; Walpole, MA: Peeters, 2009.

Myers, Ched. *Binding the Strong Man: A Political Reading of Mark's Story of Jesus*. Maryknoll, N.Y.: Orbis, 1988.

Nash, Ronald H. *Life's Ultimate Questions: An Introduction to Philosophy*. Grand Rapids: Zondervan, 1999.

Nash, Ronald H. *Worldviews in Conflict : Choosing Christianity in a World of Ideas*. Grand Rapids: Zondervan, 1992.

Nietzsche, Friedrich Wilhelm, and Walter Kaufmann. *Basic Writings of Nietzsche*. Modern Library ed. New York: Modern Library, 2000.

———. *The Portable Nietzsche*. New York, N.Y.: Penguin Books, 1982.

Oberholtzer, T. K. "The Warning Passages in Hebrews: Part 3 (of 5 Parts): The Thorn-Infested Ground in Hebrews 6:4-12." *Bibliotheca Sacra* 145, no. 579 (1988): 319–328.

O'Brien, Peter Thomas. *The Letter to the Hebrews*. Pillar New Testament Commentary. Grand Rapids.; Nottingham: Eerdmans; Apollos, 2010.

Olshewsky, Thomas. "Demea's Dilemmas." *British Journal for the History of*

Philosophy 11, no. 3 (August 1, 2003): 473–492.

Osborne, Grant R. "Genre Criticism: Sensus Literalis." *Trinity Journal* 4, no. 2 (1983): 1–27.

Osborne, Grant R. *The Hermeneutical Spiral: A Comprehensive Introduction to Biblical Interpretation*. Downers Grove, Ill.: InterVarsity Press, 1991.

Pabst, Adrian. *Metaphysics: The Creation of Hierarchy*. Interventions. Grand Rapids: Eerdmans, 2012.

Packer, J. I. *Knowing God*. 20th anniversary ed. Downers Grove: InterVarsity Press, 1993.

Packer, J.I. "Infallible Scripture and the Role of Hermeneutics." In *Scripture and Truth*, edited by D. A. Carson and John D. Woodbridge, 321–356. Grand Rapids: Baker, 1992.

Patte, Daniel. *What Is Structural Exegesis?* Philadelphia: Fortress, 1976.

Payne, Philip Barton. "The Fallacy of Equating Meaning with the Human Author's Intention." In *The Right Doctrine from the Wrong Texts?: Essays on the Use of the Old Testament in the New*, edited by G. K. Beale. Grand Rapids: Baker Books, 1994.

Peckhaus, Volker. "The Contextualism of Philosophy." In *The Sociology of Philosophical Knowledge*, edited by Maren Kusch, 171–191. The New Synthese Historical Library 48. Springer Science & Business Media, 2013.

Petersen, David L., and Kent Harold Richards. *Interpreting Hebrew Poetry*. Guides to Biblical Scholarship. Minneapolis: Fortress, 1992.

Piper, John. *A Peculiar Glory: How the Christian Scriptures Reveal Their Complete Truthfulness*. Wheaton: Crossway, 2016.

———. *Brothers We Are Not Professionals A Plea to Pastors for Radical Ministry*. Updated&Expanded. Nashville: B&H, 2013.

———. *Desiring God: Meditations of a Christian Hedonist*. Rev. Ed. Colorado Springs: Multnomah, 2011.

———. *Reading the Bible Supernaturally: Seeing and Savoring the Glory of God in Scripture*, 2017.

Polanyi, Michael. "Knowing and Being." In *Knowing and Being: Essays by Michael Polanyi*, edited by Marjorie Grene, 123–137. Chicago: University of Chicago Press, 1969.

———. *Personal Knowledge: Towards a Post-Critical Philosophy*. First Harper Torchbook Edition. New York: Harper Torchbook, 1964.

———. *The Tacit Dimension*. Chicago; London: University of Chicago Press, 2009.

Pope, Marvin H. *Job: Introduction, Translation, and Notes*. Garden City: Doubleday, 1973.

Poythress, Vern S. "Divine Meaning of Scripture." In *The Right Doctrine from the Wrong Texts?: Essays on the Use of the Old Testament in the New*, edited by G. K. Beale. Grand Rapids: Baker Books, 1994.

———. *God Centered Biblical Interpretation*. Phillipsburg, N.J.: P&R Publishing, 1999.

———. *In the Beginning Was the Word: Language: A God-Centered Approach*. Wheaton: Crossway Books, 2009.

———. *Logic: A God-Centered Approach to the Foundation of Western Thought*. Electronic. Wheaton: Crossway, 2013.

———. *Reading the Word of God in the Presence of God: A Handbook for Biblical Interpretation*. Wheaton: Crossway, 2016.

———. *Redeeming Science: A God-Centered Approach*. Wheaton: Crossway Books, 2006.

———. "Reforming Ontology and Logic in the Light of the Trinity: An Application of Van Til's Idea of Analogy." *Westminster Theological Journal* 57 (1995): 187–219.

———. *Symphonic Theology: The Validity of Multiple Perspectives in Theology*. Grand Rapids: Academie Books, 1987.

Poythress, Vern S., and Wayne A. Grudem. *The Gender-Neutral Bible Controversy: Muting the Masculinity of God's Words*. Nashville: Broadman & Holman Publishers, 2000.

Pratico, Gary Davis, and Miles V Van Pelt. *Basics of Biblical Hebrew Grammar*. Grand Rapids: Zondervan, 2007.

Provan, Iain W. *The Reformation and the Right Reading of Scripture*. Waco, Texas: Baylor University Press, 2017.

Provence, Thomas E. "The Sovereign Subject Matter: Hermeneutics in the Church Dogmatics." In *A Guide to Contemporary Hermeneutics: Major Trends in Biblical Interpretation*, edited by Donald K. McKim. Grand Rapids: Eerdmans, 1986.

Radmacher, Earl D., and Robert D. Preus, eds. "Appendix A: The Chicago Statement on Biblical Hermeneutics." In *Hermeneutics, Inerrancy, and the Bible*. Grand Rapids: Zondervan, 1984.

Roberts, A., and J. Donaldson. *Ante-Nicene Christian Library: Translations of the Writings of the Fathers Down to A.D. 325*. Ante-Nicene Christian Library: Translations of the Writings of the Fathers Down to A.D. 325 v. 10. T&T Clark, 1895.

Roma, Emilio. "The Scope of the Intentional Fallacy." *The Monist* 50, no. 2 (1966): 250–266.

Rorty, Richard. "The Historiography of Philosophy: Four Genres." In *Philosophy in History: Essays in the Historiography of Philosophy*, edited by Richard Rorty, J. B. Schneewind, and Quentin Skinner. Cambridge University Press, 1984.

Ruether, Rosemary Radford. "Feminist Interpretation: A Method of Correlation." In *Feminist Interpretation of the Bible*, edited by Letty M. Russell, 111–124. Philadelphia: Westminster John Knox, 1985.

Rushdoony, Rousas John. "The One and the Many Problem—The Contribution of Van Til." In *Jerusalem and Athens: Critical Discussions on the Theology and Apologetics of Cornelius Van Til*, edited by E. R. Geehan. USA: Presbyterian and Reformed, 1971.

Russell, Letty M., ed. *Feminist Interpretation of the Bible*. Philadelphia: Westminster John Knox, 1985.

Rutherford, J. Alexander. "An Investigation into the Role of Context in Interpretation." *Teleioteti*, January 16, 2018. Accessed January 24, 2018. https://teleioteti.ca/2018/01/16/investigation-role-context-interpretation/.

———. *Believe the Unbelievable: A Study in Habakkuk*. Teleioteti Study Guides 1. Vancouver, BC: Teleioteti, 2018.

———. "Biblical Themes That Define Us (1): Two Kingdoms." *Teleioteti*, November 1, 2017. Accessed May 30, 2019. https://teleioteti.ca/2017/11/01/biblical-themes-that-define-us-two-kingdoms/.

———. "Christians and the World: The Ethics of a City on a Hill." *Teleioteti*, November 29, 2017. Accessed May 30, 2019. https://teleioteti.ca/2017/11/29/christians-and-the-world-the-ethics-of-a-city-on-a-hill/.

———. *God's Kingdom through His Priest-King: An Analysis of the Book of Samuel in Light of the Davidic Covenant*. Teleioteti Technical Studies 1. Vancouver: Teleioteti, 2019.

———. "Is There a Cultural Mandate for Christians?" *Teleioteti*, January 31, 2018. Accessed May 30, 2019.

https://teleioteti.ca/2018/01/31/2306/.

———. "Lament of the Afflicted: A Translation of Job 30." Teleioteti, 2017. Accessed January 8, 2018. https://teleioteti.ca/2017/12/15/the-lament-of-the-afflicted-a-translation-of-job-30/.

———. *Prevenient Grace: An Investigation into Arminianism.* 2nd Revised Ed. Teleioeti Technical Studies 2. Vancouver: Teleioteti, 2020.

———. *Revelation, Retribution, and Reminder: A Biblical Exposition of the Doctrine of Hell.* Airdrie, AB: Teleioteti, 2021.

———. "Review of Contemplating God with the Great Tradition." *Teleioteti*, March 22, 2021. Accessed August 23, 2021. https://www.teleioteti.ca/2021/03/23/review-of-contemplating-god-with-the-great-tradition/.

———. *The Book of Habakkuk: An Exegetical-Theological Commentary on the Hebrew Text.* A Teleioteti Old Testament Commentary 1. Vancouver, BC: Teleioteti, 2019.

———. *The Gift of Knowing: A Biblical Perspective on Knowing and Truth.* God's Gifts for the Christian Life - Part 1 1. Vancouver: Teleioteti, 2019.

———. *The Gift of Reading - Part 2: A Biblical Perspective on Hermeneutics.* God's Gifts for the Christian Life - Part 1 2b. Vancouver: Teleioteti, 2019.

———. "Towards an Evangelical Hermeneutic: A Critique of the Chicago Statement on Hermeneutics (1982)." Teleioteti, December 2016. Accessed January 23, 2018. https://teleioteti.ca/resources/papers/.

Ryken, Leland. *The Word of God in English: Criteria for Excellence in Bible Translation.* Wheaton: Crossway, 2002.

Sagan, Carl. *The Demon-Haunted World: Science as a Candle in the Dark.* 1st Ed. New York: Ballantine Books, 1997.

Sailhamer, John H. *Introduction to Old Testament Theology: A Canonical Approach.* Grand Rapids: Zondervan, 1995.

———. *The Pentateuch as Narrative.* Grand Rapids: Zondervan, 1992.

Schaeffer, Francis A. *He Is There and He Is Not Silent.* Carol Stream: Tyndale House Publishers, 2013.

———. *The God Who Is There.* 30th Anniversary Ed. Downers Grove: IVP, 1998.

———. *The Great Evangelical Disaster.* Westchester: Crossway Books, 1984.

Schaff, Philip. *A Select Library of the Nicene and Post-Nicene Fathers of the Christian Church: St Augustin's City of God and Christian Doctrine*. Vol. 2. A Select Library of the Nicene and Post-Nicene Fathers of the Christian Church. Buffalo: The Christian Literature Company, 1887.

Schreiner, Thomas R. *Commentary on Hebrews*. Edited by Andreas J. Köstenberger, T. Desmond Alexander, and Thomas R. Schreiner. Biblical Theology for Christian Proclamation. Nashville: B&H, 2015.

———. "Galatians." edited by Clinton E. Arnold. Zondervan Exegetical Commentary on the New Testament 9. Grand Rapids, MI: Zondervan, 2010.

———. *Interpreting the Pauline Epistles*. 2nd ed. Grand Rapids: Baker Academic, 2011.

———. *Romans*. Baker Exegetical Commentary on the New Testament 6. Grand Rapids: Baker Books, 1998.

Schreiner, Thomas R., and Ardel B. Caneday. *The Race Set before Us: A Biblical Theology of Perseverance & Assurance*. Downers Grove: InterVarsity, 2001.

Seow, Choon Leong. "Orthography, Textual Criticism, and the Poetry of Job." *Journal of Biblical Literature* 130, no. 1 (2011): 63–85.

Sickler, Bradley L. *God on the Brain: What Cognitive Science Does (and Does Not) Tell Us about Faith, Human Nature, and the Divine*. Wheaton, Illinois: Crossway, 2020.

Silva, Moisés. *Biblical Words and Their Meaning: An Introduction to Lexical Semantics*. Rev. and Expanded ed. Grand Rapids: Zondervan, 1994.

———, ed. *Foundations of Contemporary Interpretation*. Grand Rapids: Zondervan, 1996.

———, ed. *New International Dictionary of New Testament Theology and Exegesis*. 2nd Ed. Grand Rapids: Zondervan, 2014.

Singer, C. Gregg. "A Philosophy of History." In *Jerusalem and Athens: Critical Discussions on the Theology and Apologetics of Cornelius Van Til*, edited by E. R. Geehan. Phillipsburg: Presbyterian and Reformed Publishing Co., 1971.

Ska, Jean Louis. *"Our Fathers Have Told Us": Introduction to the Analysis of Hebrew Narratives*. Subsidia Biblica 13. Roma: Editrice Pontificio Instituto Biblico, 1990.

Skinner, Quentin. "A Reply to My Critics." In *Meaning and Context: Quentin Skinner and His Critics*, edited by James Tully, 231–288. Princeton

University Press, 1988.

———. "Meaning and Understanding in the History of Ideas." *History and Theory* 8, no. 1 (1969): 3.

Soulen, Richard N., and R. Kendall Soulen. *Handbook of Biblical Criticism: Now Includes Precritical and Postcritical Interpretation*. 3rd Revised and Expanded. Louisville; London: Westminster John Knox, 2001.

Sproul, R. C. *The Character of God: Discovering the God Who Is*. Ventura, Calif: Regal, 2005.

Sproul, R. C. *The Holiness of God*. Carol Stream, Ill.: Tyndale House Publishers, 2006.

Steinmetz, David C. "The Superiority of Precritical Exegesis." In *A Guide to Contemporary Hermeneutics: Major Trends in Biblical Interpretation*, edited by Donald K. McKim. Grand Rapids: Eerdmans, 1986.

Thompson, J. A. *The Book of Jeremiah*. NICOT. Grand Rapids, Mich.: WM. B. Eerdmans Publishing Co., 1980.

Thompson, Mark D. *A Sure Ground on Which to Stand: The Relation of Authority and Interpretive Method in Luther's Approach to Scripture*. Carlisle; Waynesboro, GA: Paternoster, 2004.

Tigay, Jeffrey H. *Deuteronomy [Devarim]: The Traditional Hebrew Text with the New JPS Translation*. 1st ed. The JPS Torah commentary. Philadelphia, Penn.: Jewish Publication Society, 1996.

Van Pelt, Miles. *A Biblical-Theological Introduction to the Old Testament: The Gospel Promised*. Edited by Miles Van Pelt. Wheaton: Crossway, 2016.

Van Pelt, Miles V. *Basics of Biblical Aramaic: Complete Grammar, Lexicon, and Annotated Text*. Grand Rapids: Zondervan, 2011.

Van Til, Cornelius. *An Introduction to Systematic Theology*. In Defense of the Faith V. Presbyterian and Reformed Pub. Co., 1974.

———. *Christian Theistic Evidences*. Edited by K. Scott Oliphint. Second Edition, Including the complete text of the original 1978 edition. Phillipsburg: P&R Publishing, 2016.

———. "Has Karl Barth Become Orthodox." *The Westminster Theological Journal* 16, no. 2 (May 1954): 135–181.

———. *The Defense of the Faith*. Edited by K. Scott Oliphint. 4th ed. Phillipsburg: P & R Pub, 2008.

VanGemeren, Willem. *Interpreting the Prophetic Word: An Introduction to the Prophetic Literature of the Old Testament*. Grand Rapids: Zondervan, 1996.

Vanhoozer, Kevin J. *Biblical Authority after Babel: Retrieving the Solas in the Spirit of Mere Protestant Christianity*. Grand Rapids: Brazos, 2016.

———. *Is There a Meaning in This Text?: The Bible, the Reader, and the Morality of Literary Knowledge*. Grand Rapids: Zondervan, 1998.

———. *The Drama of Doctrine: A Canonical-Linguistic Approach to Christian Theology*. 1st ed. Louisville: Westminster John Knox, 2005.

Wallace, Daniel B. *Greek Grammar Beyond the Basics: An Exegetical Syntax of the New Testament with Scripture, Subject, and Greek Word Indexes*. Grand Rapids: Zondervan, 1996.

Waltke, Bruce K., and Michael Patrick O'Connor. *An Introduction to Hebrew Syntax*. Winona Lake, Ind.: Eisenbrauns, 1990.

Waltke, Bruce K., and Charles Yu. *An Old Testament Theology: An Exegetical, Canonical, and Thematic Approach*. 1st ed. Grand Rapids: Zondervan, 2007.

Watson, Francis. *Text and Truth: Redefining Biblical Theology*. Edinburgh: T&T Clark, 1997.

Watson, Wilfred G. E. "Poetry, Biblical Hebrew." Edited by Geoffrey Khan. *Encyclopedia of Hebrew Language and Linguistics*. Leiden; Boston: Brill, 2013.

Webster, John. "What Makes Theology Theological?" In *God Without Measure: Working Papers in Christian Theology*. Vol. I. T&T Clark Theology. London ; New York: Bloomsbury T&T Clark, 2016.

Wells, Kyle B. *Grace and Agency in Paul and Second Temple Judaism: Interpreting the Transformation of the Heart*. Supplements to Novum Testamentum 157. Leiden; Boston, Mass.: Brill, 2015.

Westcott, Brooke Foss, ed. *The Epistle to the Hebrews the Greek Text with Notes and Essays*. 3d ed. London: Macmillan, 1903.

Whitehead, Alfred North. *Process and Reality*. New York: Simon and Schuster, 2010.

Williams, Ronald J., and John C. Beckman. *Williams' Hebrew Syntax*. 3rd ed. Toronto: University of Toronto Press, 2007.

Wright, N.T. *The New Testament and the People of God*. Christian Origins and the Question of God 1. Minneapolis: Fortress, 1992.

Würthwein, Ernst, and Alexander A. Fischer. *The Text of the Old Testament: An Introduction to the Biblia Hebraica*. 3rd ed. Grand Rapids: Eerdmans, 2014.

Yandell, Keith E. "David Hume on Meaning, Verification and Natural Theology." In *In Defense of Natural Theology: A Post-Humean Assessment*, 58–81. Downers Grove, Ill: InterVarsity Pr, 2005.

Young, Ian. "Is the Prose Tale of Job in Late Biblical Hebrew?" *Vetus Testamentum* 59, no. 4 (2009): 606–629.

Younger, K. Lawson. *Ancient Conquest Accounts*. Journal for the Study of the Old Testament Supplement 98. Sheffield: Sheffield Academic Press, 1990.

Zachhuber, Johannes. *The Rise of Christian Theology and the End of Ancient Metaphysics: Patristic Philosophy from the Cappadocian Fathers to John of Damascus*. Oxford University Press, 2020.

Zentall, Thomas R., Edward A. Wasserman, Olga F. Lazareva, Roger K. R. Thompson, and Mary Jo Rattermann. "Concept Learning in Animals." *Comparative Cognition & Behavior Reviews* 3 (2008).

Greek New Testament: The Text of UBS 5, Reader's Edition, 2015.

New International Dictionary of Old Testament Theology & Exegesis. Grand Rapids, Michigan: Zondervan, 2007.

"Review of the So-Called Historical Jesus and the Historic Biblical Christ." *Teleioteti*, July 25, 2018. Accessed April 27, 2019. https://teleioteti.ca/2018/07/25/review-of-the-so-called-historical-jesus-and-the-historic-biblical-christ/.

The Greek New Testament, Produced at Tyndale House, Cambridge, Reader's Edition. Wheaton: Crossway Books, 2018.

GLOSSARY[1]

Abstraction

In this book, and in several other works of mine, I offer a different view of abstraction than the standard non-Christian view. There are, therefore, at least two different ways we may define abstraction. For the non-Christian, an abstraction is an idea or generalization (animal – mammal – humanity) of related particulars (Bill, Bob, Jane, Judy). It also refers to the process of moving from particular objects (a specific rock, person, tree, or dog) to generalized categories (humanity, dogs, inanimate objects, being) or properties (red, green; largeness, smallness). In other words, moving from sensible (concrete) objects or events to mental (abstract) ideas.

I contend above that a more biblical view of abstraction is a relationship identified between particular objects of our experience (e.g. a specific dog, tree, person) that allows us to understand other particular objects of our experience better. It also refers to "the process of identifying similarities among particular objects." In other words, abstraction is the identification of a relationship between objects of our experience. See pgs. 636-651, 681-683.

Apologetics

Apologetics can be considered as the attempt to present or defend the Christian faith in a persuasive and intellectual manner. That is, apologetics aims to be *persuasive*, to make an argument in order to convince another. It does not merely state the truth but argue for and defend it. Particularly,

---

[1] This glossary is based on Volume 1, The Gift of Knowing. I have not seen a need to expand it further for this volume.

apologetics is an intellectual endeavour because it attempts to reason with others and persuade them about truth. John Frame defines apologetics as *"the discipline that teaches Christians how to give a reason for their hope."* He identifies three aspects in this, proof "presenting a rational basis for faith" (John 14:11, 20:24-31; 1 Cor 15:1-11); defence, "answering the objections of unbelief (e.g. Phil 1:7); and offence, "attacking the foolishness of unbelieving thought (Ps 14:1; 1 Cor 1:18-2:16).[2]

A Priori

In philosophy, *a priori* is used in a particular way: something is *a priori* when it is believed apart from sense experience. It could then refer to innate knowledge—knowledge we have from birth—or logically deduced knowledge.[3]

A Posteriori

A posteriori is the opposite of *a priori*; knowledge is *a posteriori* when it is derived from sense experience. Neither innate ideas or knowledge deduced from rationally derived propositions is *a posteriori*, but the knowledge derived from the senses and logical deductions from sense data are *a posteriori* knowledge.

Context

"Context" is a key word that will appear throughout this book. Essentially, "context" refers to the setting in which something is found, to the environment to which it relates. Above—in this context—I am using "context" to refer to the setting in which Christians must engage with Scripture. Christians must read scripture in interaction with, for the sake of, and with the help of Christian community. In the study of literature, and so in reading the Bible, "context" refers to the words, sentences, paragraphs, chapters, books, and book in which a particular object of study (word, sentence, etc.) is embedded. It interacts with all these layers of the text, which form a literary context or setting. Context in this sense, the text in

---

[2] *Apologetics: A Justification of Christian Belief,* (P&R, 2015), 1-2.

[3] This definition, and several of those that follow, are based on the glossaries of my book *Prevenient Grace* (Teleioteti, 2020) and my thesis *God's Kingdom Through His Priest-King* (ThM, Regent College, 2018).

which words and sentences are embedded, is what gives parts of a text their meaning.

Covenant

A covenant, in the Bible, is a formalized relationship between two groups that involves mutual commitments—promises made to one another—and, often, serious consequences for breaking those commitments. God's relationship with humans is consistently covenantal.

Covenant Community:

The covenant community refers to a body of people represented together in covenant. Under the New Covenant, the covenant community consists of all those who truly have believed, believe, and will believe in Jesus Christ (past, present, and future). Under the Old Covenant, all ethnic Israel (or at least those who were circumcised or connected to a male who was circumcised) and the sojourners who attached themselves to Israel were part of the covenant community.

Empiricism

Empiricism is the philosophical position that knowledge is derived from the senses and not from reason alone. Empiricists are not necessarily concerned with particular objects of experience, for experience is often seen as the way to arrive at **abstract** truth (as in Aristotle, for example). Empiricists nevertheless value the senses and are interested in gaining and analysing experience.

Epistemology

Epistemology is a 50-dollar philosophical word used to describe the study of knowledge and knowing. Epistemology addresses what we think and how we think it, what truth means and how we can find it—if we can at all. It is one of the three traditional divisions of philosophy—metaphysics, epistemology, and ethics.

Foundationalism

Foundationalism is a modernist epistemology, a view of knowing that emerged after the enlightenment. Foundationalism claims to be able to prove certain self-evident truths, or axioms, and then tries to establish all human knowledge on the basis of this foundation. Narrow foundationalists based everything on one or two axioms, as was the case with Descartes, but broad foundationalists base everything on a larger body of evident truths, such as the Christian philosophers Alvin Platinga and Ronald Nash.

Postmodern philosophy has rightly rejected foundationalist theories of epistemology. Narrow foundationalism fails to move past the self as its starting point; broad foundationalism fails to be persuasive and worldviews based upon it do not provide a robust enough response to the pluralism of our day. They are ultimately not successful in showing how they are the truth over against competing worldviews. Furthermore, neither broad nor narrow foundationalism locates ultimate authority in God and His revelation.[4]

Immanence

"Immanence" is another keyword in philosophy and theology. Like transcendence, it is also a spatial term: it refers to something near at hand, close by. God's immanence is his presence with humanity. The radical immanence of modernity refers to the belief that all truth and standards of truth lay in human beings, not in a distant idea or a supreme God.

Innate Ideas

Innate ideas are ideas that we do not and cannot learn from experience, for experience requires them. They are, therefore, **a priori** not **a posteriori** ideas. They differ from other *a priori* knowledge in that they are the basic ideas with which reason works; they are not the products of reason. Innate ideas in Western philosophy are **abstract ideas**, generalizations that give meaning to the objects of our experience.

In this book, I have used innate ideas in a slightly different way. Instead of viewing innate ideas as abstract ideas in the traditional sense, true knowledge waiting to be discovered, I have defined innate ideas as the interpretative categories necessary to make knowledge out of our sense experience. We are hardwired by God, for example, to recognize a pattern of relationship between different events that we call in English "love" and associate this idea with the character of God. Innate ideas are essential to

---

[4] For more on foundationalism, see my review of J. P. Moreland's *Scientism and Secularism*, https://teleioteti.ca/2018/11/07/review-of-scientism-and-secularism/.

human knowing; this is most clearly seen in the case of the **law the non-contradiction**. However, because of the fall, humans have suppressed these innate ideas—this tacit worldview—and need the Bible to re-form the proper interpretative lens.

Barring disability, we are also born with the concepts necessary to interpret light as different colours and to interpret this light in order to produce a mental picture.

Law of Non-Contradiction

The law of non-contradiction, an **innate idea** that is the **presupposition** of all rational thought, is the principle that no object or idea can be itself and its opposite at the same time in the same way. For example, the letter A cannot be whatever is not-A at the same time, nor can 2+3 = 5 and 6 at the same time and in the same way. A computer cannot be fully black and fully white in the same way and at the same time, though it could have a fully black layer on top of a fully white one. A phone cannot be totally unbroken and totally broken simultaneously. Such examples could be multiplied endlessly. It often summarized like this: nothing can be A and not-A at the same time in the same way. "A" is a placeholder for any attribute or state given to an object (black and not-black) or idea (true and not-true).

Without this law, learning is impossible: though I burned my hand on the stove once, it is possible that I could not burn it in these exact circumstances. Furthermore, all thought is nonsense: I could be black and white, male and female, up and down, left and right, bee or bird, human or monkey, in space or on earth, this or that, at any time and in any way.[5]

Meaning Potential

Meaning potential refers to all the possible applications a text could have. This is natural extension from our discussion in Volume 2a, Chapter 5. If meaning refers to the different ways a text may apply, then any text has many meanings, as many as there are possible circumstances to which it could apply. Furthermore, these meanings are only potential, or latent, until they

---

[5] If the statements "J. Alexander Rutherford is floating in space, not on earth, at 10:30 am, Nov. 11, 2017" and "J. Alexander Rutherford is on earth, not in space, at 10:30 am, Nov. 11, 2017" are both true, than any contradictory state can be true (e.g. it is only snowing and only not-snowing at the same time in the same place).

are met with a circumstance to which they apply. Thus, we may rightfully speak of a text's "meaning potential."

Metanarrative

A metanarrative can be described as the story of history, or an interpretation of all events that have happened and will happen. We discussed metanarratives in Volume 2a, Chapter 3.

Objectivism

Objectivism is the belief that truth is out there—beyond our minds—to be grasped. Because truth is external to minds, is objective, it would be the same no matter who thought about it. Objectivity is a key concept of modernity.

To be objective is to be neutral, to be free from bias: if truth is objective and is attained through objective thinking, it is the same no matter who is thinking it. No matter who runs the test, not only should the results be the same but their interpretation as well. Is, for example, a rock red if no one observes that it is red? If so, then "the rock is red" is objective truth, but if "the rock is red" is only true when someone observes that it is red, then it is **subjective** truth.

Objectivism is the belief that truth is outside of our minds and equally accessible to everyone. Because objectivism places truth *out there*, it implies a correspondence theory of truth. On this view, a belief is true if it corresponds to universally accessible, extra-mental reality. Modern objectivism places the "objective reality" in the **empirical** world of our senses. Pre-modern, Platonic objectivism places this objective reality in the world of the forms, a **transcendent** non-material realm.

Presupposition

A presupposition is one of our foundational beliefs by which we automatically—without deliberate thought—interpret all our experience and from which we do all our reasoning. They are someone's most base heart commitments, those beliefs that play a key role in all their reasoning and which are held with most certainty.

Referent:

A referent is the textual or, most often, extra-textual object to which a symbol such as a word may refer. Not all words have a "referent," but some do. Proper nouns, for example, refer to a person or place. The referent of a proper noun may not exist outside of the text in question (it may refer to a character earlier in the story) or it may be a person in a T.V. show, merely a product of human creative activity.

It may be helpful to observe that the *referent* is not the *meaning* of the word. For example, "Israel" has a specific function in the context—it means something specific. The nation of Israel does not *mean* anything. A word does not replace the thing it refers to but speaks about it to communicate something. In other words, words interpret reality, so a word interprets in one way or another its referent. It may speak to the referent, about the referent, or the referent may be a piece of scenery designed to evoke some response. When we consider referential words, we concern ourselves with meaning: why has the author referred to this here? What does he mean when uses this word and what does that—his use of the word—tell us about the referent?

Subjectivism

Subjectivism is the opposite of objectivism; it is the belief that truth is dependent on the interpreter. In some forms of subjectivism, the reality of an extra-mental world is denied (anti-realism). In others, an external world is affirmed but truth and knowledge are wholly dependent on the mind of the subject. In these strong forms, the inevitable implication of subjectivism is relativism; you and I can believe two mutually exclusive ideas and have mutually exclusive interpretations of the same reality—or you may not even exist.

The epistemology I present in this book is partly subjectivist but also partly objectivist. With the subjectivists, I claim that there is no knowledge or truth apart from the interpreting subject. However, with objectivist I argue that this interpretation is based on an extra-mental reality and can be right or wrong. The two views are mediated by truth that God is the first and absolute interpreter of all reality. He has granted us the ability to interpret the world correctly, as he has created and interpreted it, if we submit ourselves to him and look at the world through His lens. This means there are three interrelated aspects in human knowledge; a knowing subject, an object known, and God's interpretation to which truth will correspond and falsehood will deviate.[6]

Transcendence

Transcendence is a key idea in philosophy and theology, describing that which is other than man, that which is far off or different. It is basically a spatial concept, referring to something above us, "up there," but in philosophy or theology it refers to the quality of being greater than and so exercising control over. The universal ideas are greater than human thoughts, human ideas. They are the true content of human thinking and so exercise control over it.

Universal

Universals can be a difficult concept to wrap our minds around. A universal, for Plato, referred not to specific objects, such as a particular tree, but ideal or abstract conceptions of objects, such as the perfect "tree." By definition, such a tree could not physically exist—it could not exist in the sensible world—so it could only be an idea, a sort of template by which all other trees take their features.

In one illustration, Plato pictured the relationship of universal (treeness) and particular (a tree) with a jar and its shadow. As light shines on a jar and casts a rough copy of it on the wall behind, so the idea of something creates imperfect representations of itself in the material world. In morality, there is the idea of "goodness"; every good act is an imperfect example of ideal goodness.

If you are still struggling with the concept of universals, take comfort. I think these "universals" ultimately do not make sense and are false. You cannot imagine "goodness" apart from good acts because it does not exist apart from them; the same goes for humanness, being, etc. See Volume 1, chapter 10, and Volume 3, pg. 605.

Worldview

A worldview is essentially the interpretive framework, or the glasses, through which we view the world. That is, all of us look at the world with "rose-

---

[6] As should be evident from the recommended reading, this view is highly dependent on the work of John Frame, especially his book *The Doctrine of the Knowledge of God*.

coloured glasses": none of us see it without interpreting it. This interpretation comes from our worldview: I recognize a tree as a God's handiwork and praise him because he created it. An atheist thinks it is a testimony to evolution and wonders at the marvellous fact that something so intricate happens to exist. We have looked at worldviews throughout this book, especially in Volume 1, Chapter 2, and in Volume 3. We can define it as a comprehensive framework for interpreting and making decisions.

The term "worldview" often refers to that aspect of our interpretive framework that can be expressed in propositional statements. In this sense, a worldview is the sum-total of ones most basic beliefs, or presuppositions, about the nature of the world, knowledge, ethics, life's purpose, etc. James N. Anderson helpfully summarises the major beliefs of a worldview in this sense as TAKES, as in "what it TAKES to make a worldview." *Theology*, what is the absolute (God or alternate explanation of everything) in your worldview? *Anthropology*, what do you believe about man? *Knowledge*, what is truth and how do we get it? *Ethics*, what is right or wrong, good or bad? And *Salvation*, what is the problem with the world and how is it fixed? However, as we saw, this is merely the tip of the iceberg: worldviews also involve conceptual and person knowledge, which cannot be expressed in propositions and which function at a tacit level (see further, Volume 3).

God's Gifts for the Christian Life Part 1 – The Gift of Knowledge

ABOUT TELEIOTETI

Teleioteti (Τελειοτητι, te-ley-o-tey-tee)—meaning "unto maturity"—is dedicated to faithful, thoughtful ministry. We create resources for Christian discipleship, resources that address theological and pastoral concerns from a Biblical worldview. Our purpose is to see Christ's Church mature in its understanding of God and His Word. We do this through the production of Gospel-centred materials that connect the Bible with the heads, hearts, and minds of Christians. We hope to enable Christians from all walks of life to better understand and glorify God through service in His Church.

To achieve this purpose, Teleioteti publishes online materials and books researched with academic rigour yet based upon Biblical presuppositions. That is, we are neither academic nor lazy. We use methods, or epistemology, informed by the Bible along with the hard work usually associated with professional research and study. We produce resources directed towards all Christians, but most of our resources are directed towards students, pastors, and theologically inclined lay Christians.

To learn more about us and what we are doing, please visit us at https://teleioteti.ca or contact us at info@teleioteti.ca. If you have found this resource helpful, prayerfully consider supporting us by giving a review on the web (e.g. Amazon, Goodreads, etc.), praying with and for us, or giving financially so that we can produce more resources like this one. For more information on how you can support us, visit us at https://teleioteti.ca/about/partner/ or at our page on Patreon, https://www.patreon.com/teleioteti.

Other Books by J. Alexander Rutherford

God's Kingdom through his Priest-King: An Analysis of the Book of Samuel in Light of the Davidic Covenant (Teleioteti, 2019)

Though many studies have probed the significance of the Davidic Covenant (2 Sam 7:1-17) within the biblical canon, few have endeavoured to explore its significance within the narrative of Samuel. This thesis argues that by weaving references to God's promises made to David (collectively known as the Davidic Covenant) throughout his narrative, the author of Samuel reveals God's will to strip away all human pretension by bringing his promises to fulfilment through the lowly David, whose ascension to kingship and endurance therein is owing all to God. In this way, the author fulfils his purpose to demonstrate God's sovereign working in history to establish his kingdom on earth through his chosen priest-king, a descendant of David, in fulfilment of the promises he made beforehand. Engaging in a literary close-reading of the text of Samuel, the author shows how the narrative of Samuel is shaped towards this end.

Endorsements:

In the present environment of high interest in the Book of Samuel, this contribution by James Rutherford is most welcome. Rutherford is well versed in current scholarship on Samuel, but his work moves well beyond this scholarship to contribute fresh insights, not least in respect of the priestly character of King David. And concerning its structure, Rutherford argues that the Book of Samuel as a whole is arranged and narrated so as to draw attention to the centrality of the Davidic Covenant of 2 Samuel 7. Having myself studied 1 and 2 Samuel for decades now, I was nevertheless benefitted at numerous points from Rutherford's creative interpretive suggestions. His is a work well conceived, well written, and worthy of a serious read.

- V. Philips Long, PhD Cambridge
    Professor of Old Testament, Regent College

This thesis argues that by weaving references to God's promises made to King David throughout his narrative, the author of

Samuel reveals God's will to strip away all human pretension by bringing his promises to fulfilment through a lowly man whose ascension to kingship and endurance therein is entirely owing to God. In this way, the Samuel author fulfils his purpose of demonstrating God's sovereign working in history to establish his kingdom on earth through his chosen priest-king, a descendant of David. The thesis represents an excellent piece of work that does a great job of bringing together into one coherent argument, focused on the Davidic covenant, much of the best recent narrative-critical research on 1-2 Samuel, and from this point of view represents a distinctive contribution to the field of Samuel studies.

- Iain Provan, PhD Cambridge
  Marshall Sheppard Professor of Biblical Studies, Regent College

Prevenient Grace: An Investigation into Arminianism, 2nd Revised Edition (Teleioteti, 2020)

When a building is built on a poor foundation, the inevitable result is its collapse. But this isn't a book on architecture; foundations are found in thought structures as well as in material structures. In theology, a bad foundation will produce results as catastrophic as a bad foundation in architecture. How we think about God and His work in the world will profoundly affect how we live and work out our Christian faith; is your foundation strong? This book evolved from the conviction that a prominent theological system rests on a fragile foundation.

Endorsements:

This book is a fine piece of scholarship. Rutherford presents his arguments with admirable clarity. His intention is to offer guidance for pastors and teachers who may be faced with questions about whether human beings have the freedom to accept or reject God. The great strength of Rutherford's book is his knowledge of Biblical texts and an appropriate interpretation of them. He successfully shows that the claims of Arminianism with its view that prevenient grace allows an acceptance or rejection of God are not supported by Biblical texts. Nor are they justified by philosophical arguments. They layout of the book and its careful treatment of arguments both for and against prevenient grace is a model of excellent writing. His chapters are supplemented by a Glossary that explains all specific terms and Appendices where detailed theological discussions are given. Most helpful is his Index of Scripture passages discussed.

- Dr. Shirley Sullivan, FRSC (elected), Professor Emeritus of Classics, University of British Columbia

Believe the Unbelievable: A Study in the Book of Habakkuk (Teleioteti, 2018)

What would we do if our prayers for justice, our prayers that God's will be done in our nation, were answered with a vision of desolation, of utter destruction?

When Habakkuk prayed for salvation, a prayer for justice in the midst of chaos, violence, and suffering, that was God's answer. He revealed in a vision the invasion of the vicious armies of Babylon. God's answer contradicted everything Habakkuk thought he knew. Yet in the end, he praised God and trusted him for this horrid salvation.

What do we do when God's actions or words contradict our understanding, contradict what we have believed? The book of Habakkuk answers this question in the face of the Babylonian invasion of Judah. Habakkuk is a book of discipleship, a book written to bring its reader to a deeper faith in Yahweh in the presence of His unthinkable deeds.

Using study questions addressing the text, theology, and application of Habakkuk and explanatory comments on difficult themes, *Believe the Unbelievable* seeks to realize this purpose for the contemporary reader.

Endorsements:

James Rutherford is a capable and creative thinker, well equipped to tackle tough projects, such as the book of Habakkuk. In this study guide, Rutherford has produced a very useful resource for individual or group study. He combines theological acumen and well-honed linguistic and literary skills to discover and then to present, in highly understandable fashion, the riches of this not so "minor" Minor Prophet.

- V. Philips Long, PhD Cambridge
   Professor of Old Testament, Regent College

My good friend, James Rutherford, has given the church a gift. He has taken his love for God's Word and focused it on an Old Testament book that most Christians know very little about. The result is a study in Habakkuk that brings together deep insight and real relevance. Habakkuk is a voice among the Biblical chorus that believers need to hear today. Thank you, James, for helping us to hear it clearly and faithfully.

- Fredrick Eaton
   Pastor, Christ City Church, Kitsilano

J. Alexander Rutherford